VOLUME
TWO

INTERMEDIATE ACCOUNTING

FIFTH EDITION

Thomas H. Beechy
Schulich School of Business
York University

Joan E. D. Conrod
Faculty of Management
Dalhousie University

Elizabeth J. Farrell
Schulich School of Business
York University

McGraw-Hill Ryerson
Connect. Learn. Succeed.™

**McGraw-Hill
Ryerson**
Connect. Learn. Succeed.

Intermediate Accounting
Volume 2
Fifth Edition

ISBN-13: 978-0-07-000216-6
ISBN-10: 0-07-000216-9

1 2 3 4 5 6 7 8 9 10   TCP   1 9 8 7 6 5 4 3 2 1

Printed and bound in Canada.

Vice-President and Editor-in-Chief: Joanna Cotton
Executive Sponsoring Editor: Rhondda McNabb
Executive Marketing Manager: Joy Armitage Taylor
Developmental Editor: Rachel Horner
Senior Editorial Associate: Christine Lomas
Supervising Editor: Jessica Barnoski
Photo/Permissions Research: Lindsay MacDonald
Copy Editor: Karen Rolfe
Production Coordinator: Scott Morrison
Cover Design: Word & Image Design Studio Inc.
Cover Images: Jim Barber (flag); Getty (stock numbers); Shutterstock/Alex Saberi (buildings); Gualtiero Boffi (arrows); Getty (globe); Getty (money)
Interior Design: Word & Image Design Studio Inc.
Page Layout: Bookman Typesetting Co. Inc.
Printer: Transcontinental Printing Group

Library and Archives Canada Cataloguing in Publication

Beechy, Thomas H., 1937–
    Intermediate accounting / Thomas H. Beechy, Joan E.D. Conrod, Elizabeth J. Farrell.—5th ed.

Includes index.
ISBN 978-0-07-000150-3 (v. 1).—ISBN 978-0-07-000216-6 (v. 2)

    1. Accounting—Textbooks.   I. Conrod, Joan E. D. (Joan Elizabeth Davison), 1956–   II. Farrell, Elizabeth J.
III. Title.

HF5636.B44 2011   657'.044   C2010-905196-3

About the Authors

Thomas H. Beechy, York University

Thomas H. Beechy is a Professor Emeritus of Accounting at the Schulich School of Business, York University. He was also the Associate Dean of the Schulich School for many years. He currently holds the additional titles of Director of International Development (Academic) and Assistant Dean—Special Projects. Professor Beechy holds degrees from George Washington University (BA), Northwestern University (MBA), and Washington University (DBA). He has been active in research and publication for almost 40 years, having published six books, including *Advanced Financial Accounting*, and numerous articles in major accounting journals. Professor Beechy has been a leader in Canadian accounting education, emphasizing the importance of case analysis in developing students' professional judgement and accounting skills. He has been an active researcher and advocate in both business and non-profit financial reporting. He has been particularly active in international accounting circles.

Joan E. D. Conrod, Dalhousie University

Joan E. D. Conrod is a Professor of Accounting in the Faculty of Management at Dalhousie University. Her teaching excellence has been recognized through awards such as the PWC Leaders in Management Education Award, the Dalhousie University Alumni Award for Teaching Excellence, and the AAU Distinguished Teacher award. She was awarded her FCA from the Nova Scotia Institute of Chartered Accountants in 1999. Joan is an active member of the University community, and has served on the Dalhousie University Senate and the Board of Governors. She is a past president of the Canadian Academic Accounting Association. Joan has a lengthy history of involvement in professional accounting education. She has taught financial and managerial accounting courses to CA students across Canada, but particularly in Atlantic Canada, for 20 years. She has served on CA education committees at the local, regional, and national levels. Her publications include the text *Intermediate Accounting*, *Financial Accounting 3* for CGA-Canada, and a variety of case material and other publications.

Elizabeth J. Farrell, York University

Elizabeth J. Farrell is an adjunct professor and has taught at the Schulich School of Business for many years. In recognition of her excellence in teaching she was awarded the Seymour Schulich Award for Teaching Excellence in 1999, 2003, and 2009 and nominated for the award in 2004, 2005, and 2006. She has taught financial accounting courses for over 20 years. Liz is assistant coordinator of the Institute of Chartered Accountants of Ontario's School of Accountancy where she also has served as a seminar leader for many years. She has taught executive development courses for the Schulich Executive Education Centre (SEEC), as well as professional development courses for the ICAO and for CA firms. In addition to being a co-author of *Intermediate Accounting*, her publications include an accounting case analysis software package; study guides; an IFRS Property, Plant, and Equipment professional development course; and a variety of case material and other publications.

Brief Table of Contents—Volume 2

Table of Contents—Volume 2

LIABILITIES   683

SHAREHOLDERS' EQUITY   753

CHAPTER 14

COMPLEX DEBT AND EQUITY INSTRUMENTS   811

CHAPTER 15

ACCOUNTING FOR CORPORATE INCOME TAX   871

ACCOUNTING FOR TAX LOSSES

923

CHAPTER 16

LEASES

973

CHAPTER 17

POST-EMPLOYMENT BENEFITS 1041

CHAPTER 18

EARNINGS PER SHARE 1107

CHAPTER 19

ACCOUNTING CHANGES   1163

CHAPTER 20

FINANCIAL STATEMENT ANALYSIS   1215

CHAPTER 21

Preface

Welcome to the new Canadian GAAP environment. Public companies mostly comply with International Financial Reporting Standards (IFRS) set by the International Accounting Standards Board (IASB). Canadian private companies may choose to comply with either Canadian Accounting Standards for Private Enterprise (ASPE) or may choose instead to adopt IFRS. These two sets of GAAP are similar in many respects but quite different in other respects. The dual set of standards is new to the business community, and also new to the learning community. This duality represents a huge challenge as we all ramp up for the new reporting environment.

Clearly, policy choices are ever-expanding, and change is rapid; the expanding universe of accounting knowledge may be intimidating. Intermediate accounting is the essential course for developing both the technical skills and the judgement you need to succeed. We believe that neither technical knowledge nor judgement are sufficient on their own; it is the blend of the two that represents the value added by a professional accountant.

So that's what *Intermediate Accounting* will do for you: provide complete, appropriate technical knowledge, while also developing your professional judgement. Both these elements are clearly described in the broad range of topics that represent the challenges of corporate reporting. Many technical elements have changed under international standards, as compared to the old Canadian GAAP. This book clearly explains the standards, identifies patterns, and explores the impact of alternatives on users and uses of financial statements.

In selecting material to include in this book, we have assessed the realities of Canadian business practice and the choices that are currently available. We have a distinctly Canadian agenda, looking at the issues that matter in Canadian business. We are clear in our treatment of the body of knowledge. Our coverage does not get bogged down in the (sometimes twisted) past of a given issue, nor does it speculate needlessly on what might or might not happen in the future. Our emphasis is on preparing you to apply the standards now in place, providing an overview of some expected changes, and moving to develop the necessary judgemental skills to apply those standards wisely and effectively. These same judgemental skills will serve you equally well even as standards change in the future, as they undoubtedly will.

After you master the contents of *Intermediate Accounting*, you will be able to account for the wide range of events and transactions found in this unique and challenging business environment. The transition to an IFRS/ASPE world is an ongoing challenge that is engaging, interesting, and exhausting, all at the same time.

We're proud that this book is now in its fifth edition. Many thousands of students have started their substantive study of the corporate reporting environment with this text. Many people have supported the evolution of this book over the last fifteen years, and we are very grateful for their encouragement and continued goodwill. Tom and Joan are very pleased to welcome Liz Farrell to the author team for this edition; Liz is a great colleague who brings solid classroom experience and a history of expertise in professional accounting education.

IFRS AND ASPE

A Canadian agenda means that we all must master international standards. Every chapter is based first and foremost on IFRS. Differences between ASPE and IFRS are explained in a separate section, to provide clarity regarding one set of standards as compared to the other. Assignment material reflects both IFRS and ASPE, so that applications reflect the dual-GAAP environment.

TECHNICAL KNOWLEDGE

Accountants have to be able to account for things! There is a base level of expertise that must become part of every accountant's body of knowledge: how to record a receivable, capitalize a lease, account for a pension, or prepare a cash flow statement. Some of the transactions that we must account for are very complex, and the specific rules must be mastered. An affinity for numbers is important.

PROFESSIONAL JUDGEMENT

Judgement, it is often said, is the hallmark of a profession. There are often different ways to account for the same transaction. Professional accountants must become expert at sizing up the circumstances and exercising judgement to determine the appropriate accounting policy for those circumstances.

Once an accounting policy has been established, measurement estimates almost always must be made before the numbers can be recorded. Accounting estimates also require the exercise of professional judgement.

Professional judgement is not acquired overnight. It is nurtured and slowly grows over a lifetime. In this book, we begin the development process by explicitly examining the variables that companies consider when evaluating their options, and the criteria that accountants use to make choices. Many opportunities to develop and improve judgement are provided in the case material.

ACCURACY

The text has been extensively reviewed and proofread prior to publication. Chapter material has been reviewed by professional accountants. All assignment materials have been solved independently by multiple individual "assignment checkers" in addition to the authors. Nevertheless, errors may remain, for which we accept full responsibility. If you find errors, please e-mail the authors at **j.conrod@dal.ca**, **tbeechy@schulich.yorku.ca**, or **efarrell@schulich.yorku.ca**. Your help will be greatly appreciated.

Pedagogical Walkthrough

Introduction

Each chapter has an introduction that explains the objectives of the chapter in narrative form.

Concept Review

Throughout each chapter, there are periodic questions. Students can stop and think through the answers to these basic questions, covering the previously explained material. This helps comprehension and focus! Answers to these questions can be found online on *Connect*.

CONCEPT REVIEW

1. What is the difference between a public corporation and a private corporation? Which type is dominant in the Canadian economy?

2. How can private corporations obtain capital from outside investors without becoming public companies?

3. What is a control block?

4. Why would a Canadian private enterprise choose to use IFRS instead of ASPE?

Figures and Tables

Where appropriate, chapter material is summarized in figures and tables to establish the patterns and help reinforce material.

EXHIBIT 3-7

MARSUPIALS LIMITED

Statement of Comprehensive Income

For the year ended December 31, 20X1	Without Intraperiod Tax Allocation	With Intraperiod Tax Allocation
Sales	$1,000,000	$1,000,000
Expenses	700,000	700,000
Income from operations	300,000	300,000
Income tax expense:		
On operations ($300,000 × 40%)	—	120,000
On taxable income ($100,000 × 40%)	40,000	—
Income before discontinued operation	260,000	180,000
Loss from discontinued operation:		
Loss disposal of Australian division	(200,000)	(200,000)
Income tax expense	—	80,000
	(200,000)	(120,000)
Net income and comprehensive income	$ 60,000	$ 60,000

Ethical Issues

Many chapters discuss accounting issues that raise ethical concerns. These concerns are highlighted in the chapter. Where ethics is particularly problematic, we have included a separate "ethical issues" section to help students focus on the ethical aspects of policy choice.

Ethics assignment material has also been incorporated into the case material. Essentially, when an accountant makes a recommendation on a contentious choice of accounting policy, ethics are tested. Students exercise true-to-life ethical judgement when they have to make a tough judgement call and recommend an accounting policy that is "good" for one group but "bad" for another. These ethical overtones are highlighted in the case solutions to help instructors draw them out in discussion and evaluation.

ETHICAL ISSUES

The ability to make appropriate choices in accounting is **ethical professional judgement**. Professional judgement permeates the work of a professional accountant, and it involves an ability to build accounting measurements that take into account:

- The objectives of financial reporting in each particular situation;
- The facts of the business environment and operations; and
- The organization's reporting constraints (if any).

The result of properly applied ethical professional judgement is fair financial information. Failure of ethical professional judgement may result in false or misleading information. Think about the steps required to apply professional judgement in an ethical fashion. The building blocks for accounting choice were illustrated in Exhibit 2-1.

1. The first judgement, upon which all else is built, is to determine the objectives of financial reporting for the specific reporting entity. There are usually multiple objectives, and the objectives must be ethically and appropriately prioritized in order to be able to resolve conflicts between them when decisions about specific accounting policies or estimates

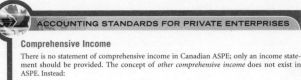

ACCOUNTING STANDARDS FOR PRIVATE ENTERPRISES

Comprehensive Income

There is no statement of comprehensive income in Canadian ASPE; only an income state-ment should be provided. The concept of *other comprehensive income* does not exist in ASPE. Instead:

- Net income after taxes is transferred directly from the income statement to retained earnings;
- Unrealized foreign exchange translation gains or losses (a component of other compre-hensive income under IFRS) are reported as a separate component of shareholders' equity; and
- Any other non-earnings items that affect shareholders' equity are reported in share-holders' equity, as appropriate.

Under ASPE, *consolidated* financial statements are not required. The statements of a pri-vate enterprise are not issued to the public, and users are presumed to be knowledgeable. If a user wants consolidated statements, he or she can request them (or insist on them, in the case of a major provider of capital such as an institutional investor).

Format

- ASPE does not specify a format based on either "functional" versus "nature of expense" approach.
- ASPE requires just one subtotal in the statement, and that is for "income or loss before

Accounting Standards for Private Enterprises

At the end of each chapter, there is a section that expands on essential items to understand for account-ing standards for private enterprise (ASPE) in Canada. These provide students and instructors with a detailed, but easy-to-use guide to these important standards.

RELEVANT STANDARDS

IASB:
- *Framework for the Preparation and Presentation of Financial Statements*

CICA Handbook, Part II
- *Section 1000*, Financial Statement Concepts

Relevant Standards

At the end of each chapter is a comprehensive list of IASB and Canadian standards that are relevant to the material in the chapter. We have not quoted the stan-dards directly in chapter material and we have not provided paragraph references to either the IASB pub-lications or *CICA Handbook*. This omission is inten-tional—the two sources are harmonized but may use different words. The focus is on the application of standards, not the technicalities.

SUMMARY OF KEY POINTS

1. Accounting principles consist of three different sets of concepts: (1) underlying assumptions, (2) qualitative criteria, and (3) measurement methods.

2. *Underlying assumptions* include the basic postulates that make accounting measure-ments possible (such as *time period, separate entity,* and *unit of measure*), as well as underlying measurement assumptions that usually, but not always, are true in a given reporting situation. These measurement assumptions include *proprietary approach, continuity,* and *nominal dollar financial capital maintenance.*

3. There are two feasible alternatives to nominal dollar financial capital maintenance. One is constant dollar financial capital maintenance, in which the purchasing power of the capital investment is maintained rather than simply the nominal number of dol-lars invested. The other alternative is physical (or productive) capital maintenance, in which sufficient capital is maintained to achieve the same level of physical production.

4. *Qualitative criteria* are the criteria used in conjunction with an enterprise's financial reporting objectives to determine the most appropriate measurement methods to use in that particular reporting situation.

Summary of Key Points

A summary of key points concludes each chapter. This provides a list of the key ideas and reinforces the chap-ter material.

KEY TERMS

Key Terms

Each chapter concludes with a list of key terms used and explained in the chapter.

REVIEW PROBLEM

The following information is taken from the adjusted trial balance of Killian Corporation at 31 December 20X5, the end of Killian's fiscal year:

Account	Amount
Sales revenue	$1,000,000
Service revenue	200,000
Interest revenue	30,000
Gain on sale of capital asset	100,000
Cost of goods sold[1]	630,000
Selling, general, and administrative expense[2]	170,000
Interest expense	20,000
Loss on sale of long-term investment	10,000
Loss from earthquake damage	200,000
Loss on sale of assets of discontinued business segment	60,000
Loss on operations of discontinued business segment	10,000

[1]Consists of depreciation of $30,000, employee wages and benefits of $40,000, and $580,000 of merchandise purchases less $20,000 increase in inventory.
[2]Includes depreciation of $35,000 and employee wages and benefits of $90,000.

Review Problem

There is a review problem with a solution in each chapter beginning in Chapter 3. This provides additional reinforcement of chapter content.

CASE 3-2

CASHGO LIMITED

CashGo Ltd. is a food distributor and retailer in eastern Canada. The company also owns both a bakery and a dairy, each of which has significant sales through other market channels in addition to CashGo's stores. CashGo is a public company whose restricted common shares are traded on the Toronto Stock Exchange. All of CashGo's unrestricted common shares are owned by the founder's family—the family has 10% of the total outstanding shares but holds 90% of the votes.

The company has not needed other external capital except for an operating line of credit from the company's banks.

The CashGo CFO currently is overseeing the preparation of the company's consolidated financial statements for 20X7. The change to international accounting standards has required several changes in CashGo's accounting policies, not all of which the CFO is sure that she understands. She has come to you for advice on how to report the results of some of the company's 20X7 transactions and events. She also would appreciate receiving a draft statement of comprehensive income. CashGo does not wish to provide any more detail in the statements than is necessary to comply with current reporting requirements.

Specific concerns:

1. In the final quarter of 20X7, the Halifax region suffered a major hurricane, which knocked out the electricity in the Halifax region for several days. Hurricanes are extremely uncommon in Nova Scotia. A great quantity of frozen and other perishable foods was spoiled and had to be discarded. The loss amounted to $11 million. The inventory was not insured against this type of loss.
2. Early in 20X7, the company invested $24 million of excess cash in a portfolio of marketable securities that are being held for training. The company sold some of these securities in November for $14 million; the original cost was $9 million. The remaining

Cases

More than 60 cases are included in *Intermediate Accounting,* and there is at least one new case in every chapter in the fifth edition. The cases are meant to portray circumstances reflective of real life. Students have to put themselves into the situation and grapple with the facts to arrive at appropriate accounting policies for the circumstances. A blend of professional judgement and technical skills is needed to respond to a case. Case coverage is not limited to "one chapter" bites, but often integrates material learned to date. For those trying to build a base of professionalism, the use of cases consistently over the term is highly recommended. Cases can be assigned for class debriefing, class presentations, or written assignments.

Assignment Material

There is an extensive range of assignment material at the end of each chapter. The assignments give students the opportunity to learn by doing.

★ ★ ★   Stars accompany each assignment to indicate length, with one star being the shortest assignment and three stars being the longest assignment.

 To help students practise on their own, we have selected a few assignments from each chapter and put their solutions online. These selected assignments are highlighted by the icon in the margin.

 Excel® templates for selected assignments provide an introduction to basic spreadsheet applications. These assignments are identified with the icon in the margin and are available online.

Integrative Problems

From time to time, we include integrative problems that formally deal with accounting topics covered in five or six chapters. These problems are a great pre-test review!

TOPICAL REVIEW IDENTIFYING KEY CHANGES

Chapter 1

The book starts by summarizing the reasons that Canada moved to IFRS and explaining the structure and operations of the International Accounting Standards Board. From there, we explain the multiple accounting frameworks in use in Canada for public companies and private companies—IFRS or US standards for public companies, IFRS or ASPE or DBA for private companies. The nature and rationale for IFRS for SMEs also is explained, so that readers will not be surprised to encounter this additional GAAP framework that can used by non-Canadian private enterprises.

After establishing the multiple GAAP frameworks, our attention turns to the basis of application of any framework. Before we can make judgements on choosing accounting policies and making accounting estimates, we must understand the many possible (and often conflicting) objectives underlying a company's financial reporting. The second major theme of the first chapter is how the many different factors and influences shape a company's financial reporting. This is fundamental material that supports professional judgement.

Chapter 1 has been extensively revised and rewritten for this edition, with new exhibits to further clarify the material.

Chapter 2

Having set the basic reporting framework in Chapter 1, Chapter 2 further develops the theme of professional judgement. This chapter explains the basic assumptions underlying financial reporting, and then moves on to develop the qualitative characteristics that must be considered when developing professional approaches to accounting issues. This material is extensively revised to follow the IASB's latest set of qualitative characteristics as set out in the IASB's Framework for Financial Reporting.

An important new section deals with issues of fair value reporting and the three levels of estimating fair value. Ethical issues are raised in this section, as they are throughout the textbook. After discussing the broad recognition issues for revenue and expense, the chapter then sets out the elements of financial reporting. The increased incidence of fair value measurement within IFRS requires that the traditional distinction between "revenue" and "gains" be modified, which is clarified both by discussion and by a revised Exhibit 2-4.

By the end of Chapter 2, all of the factors and elements underlying the exercise of professional judgement have been laid out and clarified. These factors and elements underlie the professional judgements that students must make as they move through the text, particularly in the case material at the end of each chapter.

Chapter 3

Chapter 3 discusses the nature of income and the difference between the economic and accounting concepts of income. The statement of comprehensive income is explained, including the important distinction between operating income and comprehensive income. The general presentation approach is explained, along with format variations that are accepted in practice.

The discussion of the statement of retained earnings that formerly was in this chapter has been moved to Chapter 4; under IFRS, changes in retained earnings are a part of a broader reporting obligation for shareholders' equity.

One component of a statement of comprehensive income is the separate after-tax reporting of discontinued operations. Discontinued operations is just one part of a broader issue of asset disposals. Therefore, we have introduced asset disposals in this chapter to provide a clearer context for understanding discontinued operations. We discuss and provide examples of all forms of asset disposals, including abandonment, sales of individual assets, sale of asset groups, and discontinued operations. Because asset disposals are often connected with restructurings, we also present the criteria and reporting requirements for restructuring plans as well as the requirements for reporting constructive obligations that frequently accompany restructurings.

The chapter ends with a discussion of ASPE and the ways in which the reporting requirements for private companies differ from those under IFRS.

Chapter 4

There are four major sections to this chapter. The first section discusses the IFRS requirements for the statement of financial position, which also may be called the balance sheet. IFRS requires certain items to be reported on the face of the statement, but does not prescribe a specific format. Therefore, we present real-company examples of various reporting formats so that students will not be surprised when they encounter the very different formats that are in use around the world.

The second section discusses and illustrates the statement of changes in equity, also known as the statement of changes in shareholders' equity. The chapter illustrates that the statement includes not only the "normal" shareholder accounts (e.g., share equity and retained earnings) but also each of the various components of other comprehensive income.

The third section gives a fairly brief overview of accounting changes, including changes in estimate, changes in accounting policy, and error correction. Accounting changes are pervasive, and this section prepares students to understand accounting changes as they move through the specific topics that comprise the rest of the book. A fuller discussion of accounting changes is reserved for the end of the book, Chapter 20.

The fourth and final section is a discussion and illustration of disclosure notes. This section has been fully revised to reflect the current disclosure requirements of IFRS, including related party transactions, segment reporting, contingencies, and guarantees.

Chapter 5

The statement of cash flow (SCF) is dealt with in sequence, as a primary financial statement. Coverage is linked to the reporting example of RoyalDutchShell, to emphasize IFRS presentation issues and judgemental presentation choices. In particular, presentation of investment revenue cash flow, interest, and dividends paid is discussed and illustrated. The chapter deals with the mechanics of statement preparation, using both a format-free approach and the T-account method. The journal-entry based worksheet approach is included in an appendix. SCF issues are reviewed in every subsequent chapter of the text and include SCF assignment material.

Chapter 6

Revenue and expense recognition are surely the most judgemental areas of accounting policy choice in the GAAP world. For the fifth edition of the book, we have introduced the important issue of remeasurements as a source of revenue, gains, and losses that must be recognized as operating revenue/expense. In particular, we have significantly expanded our illustration of fair-value accounting for biological assets and agricultural produce.

In accounting for long-term contacts, we illustrate only the percentage-of-completion method, as this is the only method normally acceptable under IFRS. The completed contract method is illustrated in the ASPE section at the end of the chapter. This separation helps students to better understand the difference between IFRS and ASPE as applied to long-term contracts. Barter transactions and exchanges of similar and dissimilar goods or services are important but challenging aspects of accounting. The chapter puts these transactions into a broader context and illustrates, based on IFRS, just how each of the various types of non-monetary exchanges should be measured and reported.

Throughout the chapter, there is extensive discussion of the criteria to be applied to determine appropriate revenue recognition policy and the numeric implications. Expense recognition is critically reviewed, both from a theoretical and practical perspective.

Chapter 7

Issues related to current financial instruments—cash, receivables, and payment—are gathered and reviewed together. Classification and valuation decisions are central to this coverage. Important topics such as foreign currency translation (a must, in this age of globalization) and the IFRS rules governing the transfer of receivables are incorporated. Material on bank reconciliations is in an appendix, and coverage of present and future value calculations is available online on Connect, as is a more extensive set of compound interest tables.

Chapter 8

We've revised this chapter to conform with the IFRS approach applying lower of cost or market valuation methods and the IFRS definition of "market," which is net realizable value. Also, we explain the process for writing inventory back up if NRV recovers before the inventory is sold. The allowance method of accounting for inventory writedowns is well illustrated, as it is the only feasible method when the LCM test is applied on a group basis.

Inventory valuation always raises the possibility of unethical behaviour. Therefore, the chapter includes discussion of the ethical issues surrounding inventory valuation and accounting.

Introductory accounting texts always deal with inventory systems and the cost flow assumptions and so we present that more basic material in the appendix, available for student review if needed.

Chapters 9 and 10

Accounting for capital assets and intangible assets is challenging in the IFRS context. There are three possible models to consider depending on the type of asset: the fair value model, the revaluation model, and the cost model. Also, component accounting and depreciation adds complexities to the accounting for capital assets. Impairment testing and reversals will create more volatility on the income statement using IFRS. These chapters systematically look at acquisition, amortization, impairment, and disposal considering both the IFRS standards and ASPE. The appendices cover the complexities related to investment property, government assistance, capital cost allowance, and the revaluation model.

Chapter 11

This chapter reflects coverage of IFRS 9, effective in 2013 but available for early adoption as a response from standard-setters to the upheaval in financial markets. Accounting for amortized cost, fair value through profit and loss, fair value through other comprehensive income, cost, significant influence, and control investments is covered. Both policy and numeric issues are thoroughly explored. The chapter includes a number of helpful diagrams and figures to help clarify the roadmap through this territory. ASPE alternatives are very different in this area, and the choices are documented and described.

Chapter 12

The IFRS measurement framework and terminology for provisions is new in Canada, and the chapter sections in this area have been completely rewritten from an IFRS perspective. ASPE rules are included in the final section. Measurement is under consideration by the IASB, and alternatives are covered in chapter and assignment material. The chapter reviews use of discounted cash flow models for liabilities, accompanied by the effective interest method of amortization, using bonds as the primary example. Various valuation and measurement complexities are covered, including the effect of upfront fees. A section on interest capitalization, new in the Canadian reporting environment, is included. Coverage of financing sources is necessary background for professionals, and is now located in an appendix.

Chapter 13

This chapter deals with straightforward shareholders' equity issues. Multi-column presentation of the shareholders' equity statement, consistent with *IAS* 1, is completely incorporated, and classification and presentation of unrealized amounts in other comprehensive income, (e.g., from FVTOCI investments, and certain unrealized foreign currency gains/losses) is included, and is supported by assignment material. Summary charts have been incorporated where appropriate.

Chapter 14

One major topic in this chapter is classification of debt versus equity and appropriate treatment of hybrid financial instruments. Classification is based on the substance of a financial instrument, rather than its legal form. A major new section covers the IFRS approach to share-based payments, emphasizing the estimates needed for measurement and forfeitures. Basic patterns for option accounting are established. Finally, the material on derivative instruments has been gathered in this chapter. While many of the complexities are appropriately left to advanced accounting courses, this introduction is vital. We think that the revised material is clear and understandable.

Chapters 15 and 16

Accounting for income tax remains two separate chapters, to acknowledge that many instructors prefer to spend two blocks of time on this most challenging area. The Chapter 15 material establishes a three-step process for typical situations. The focus of Chapter 16 remains accounting for the tax effect of losses—carrybacks and carryforwards. This is difficult material for students, but the Chapter 16 problems incorporate the prior chapter material and allow solid reinforcement of the steps associated with tax accounting. The ASPE section explains the flow-through method that is available for private enterprises.

Chapter 17

This chapter, focusing on lease accounting, has been revised extensively. While the primary focus remains on lessee accounting, lessor accounting is incorporated into the main body of the chapter. A side-by-side comparison of lease accounting for lessee and lessor has been added to the chapter. Changes to comply with IFRS have been introduced, particularly in the sections relating to lessor accounting where the distinction between direct-financing leases and sales-type leases has been eliminated. The ethical issues of financial statement "window dressing" related to leases are presented and discussed.

Chapter 18

Pensions and other post-retirement benefits are highly complex arrangements, with correspondingly complex accounting treatment. IFRS treatment includes significant new accounting policy alternatives for defined benefit plans, and these alternatives are clearly and succinctly illustrated in this chapter. The worksheet structure used is helpful to organize the material, and is tied in to disclosure requirements. This chapter also includes an example of accounting for other post-retirement benefits and enhanced coverage of defined contribution plans, including an example, since the latter are gaining in popularity. As always, ASPE standards are completely described.

Chapter 19

Earnings per share material includes an explanation of basic and diluted EPS. IFRS terminology is used throughout. The procedural steps associated with organizing a complex EPS question are emphasized to provide more comfort and support in this complicated area. There are a variety of useful summary figures and tables.

Chapter 20

Accounting policy changes and error corrections require restatement of one or more prior years' financial statements. Restatement is surely an important topic, given the number of fraud-based restatements reported in the public press in recent years. Also, the ongoing changes in accounting standards means that companies must often restate their accounts. This chapter deals with the theory and mechanics related to such restatement, reflecting current IFRS standards.

Chapter 21

The text concludes with a review of financial statement analysis and emphasizes the importance of accounting policy choice and disclosure in the analysis of published financial statements. There is an extensive case illustration, based on a real Canadian company, which demonstrates the importance of accounting policy choice.

ACKNOWLEDGEMENTS

Our initial draft of this text was reviewed by several colleagues with expertise in IFRS. Our manuscript benefitted significantly from the comments and suggestions from Judy Cumby, FCA, and Ingrid McLeod-Dick, CA. Many other reviewers had contributed valuable comments on the previous edition, which informed our decisions about coverage and approach for the fifth edition.

We're grateful to the team that exhaustively checked the assignment material and the solutions, including Matthew Ryan; Nola Lamoureux; Kimberly Morse, CA; Morgan Houston, CA; Alex Kogan, CA; Winnie Siu; Alex Fisher, CA; Shikha Gandhi, CA; Susan Cohlmeyer, FCA; and Cara Chesney, CA. The residual errors are our responsibility, but these expert individuals have significantly improved our accuracy. A special thanks to Laura Cumming and Tammy Crowell.

We appreciate the permissions granted by the following organizations to use their problem and case material:

- The Canadian Institute of Chartered Accountants
- The Certified General Accountants' Association of Canada
- The Ontario Institute of Chartered Accountants
- The Atlantic School of Chartered Accountancy
- The American Institute of Certified Public Accountants.

We are grateful to the people at McGraw-Hill Ryerson who guided this manuscript through the development process. We appreciate the strong support of Rhondda McNabb, our Executive Sponsoring Editor; Rachel Horner, our Developmental Editor; and the production team, led by Margaret Henderson and including Jessica Barnoski and Jennifer Hall, who have all contributed in significant ways to this final product. And, of course, Karen Rolfe has been a welcome and active partner in this enterprise, as our copy editor.

On a personal level, we would like to thank our friends and family members for their support and encouragement throughout the lengthy process of bringing this book to fruition, especially, in Toronto—Brian McBurney; in Halifax—Peter Conrod and Warren and Carmita Fetterly; and in Richmond Hill—Ed Farrell, Catherine, Michael, and Megan Farrell.

ENRICHED LEARNING WITH TECHNOLOGY

Connect

Connect is a web-based assignment and assessment platform that gives students the means to better connect with their coursework, with their instructors, and with the important concepts that they will need to know for success now and in the future. *Connect* embraces diverse study behaviours and preferences with breakthrough features that help students master course content and achieve better results. The powerful course management tool in *Connect* also offers a wide range of exclusive features that help instructors spend less time managing and more time teaching.

With *Connect*, you can deliver assignments, quizzes, and tests online. A robust set of questions and problems are presented and tied to the textbook's key concepts.

As an instructor, you can edit existing questions and author entirely new problems. Track individual student performance—by question, assignment, or in relation to the class overall—with detailed grade reports. Integrate grade reports easily with Learning Management Systems (LMS) such as WebCT and Blackboard. And much more.

Connect helps you teach for today's needs:

- **Unlimited Practice, Instant Feedback**
  Provide instant feedback to unlimited textbook practice problems, acknowledging correct answers and pointing to areas that need more work.

- **Automatic Grading**
  Focus on teaching instead of administrating with electronic access to the class roster and gradebook, which easily sync with your school's course management system.

- **Direct Textbook and Test Bank Questions**
  Assign students online homework and test and quiz questions with multiple problem types, algorithmic variation, and randomized question order.

- **Integrated eBooks**
  Connect directly integrates the McGraw-Hill textbooks you already use into the engaging, easy-to-use interface.

- **Dedicated Canadian Support and Training**
  The *Connect* development team and customer service groups are located in our Canadian offices and work closely together to provide expert technical support and training for both instructors and students.

INSTRUCTOR SUPPLEMENTS

Instructor resources for *Intermediate Accounting* are available online and include:

Solutions Manual This manual provides answers to the end-of-chapter and review and assignment material. Technically reviewed by Canadian accounting professionals to ensure accuracy, the solutions manual is a key component of the instructor resource package for *Intermediate Accounting*.

Instructor's Manual To provide assistance with lesson planning and lectures, the Instructor's Manual to accompany the fifth edition of *Intermediate Accounting* has been developed to specifically pinpoint changes to IFRS and accounting standards for private enterprises. This comprehensive, chapter-by-chapter manual comes in a format that is easily customizable, so instructors can add their own notes.

Computerized Test Bank There are over 2,000 questions to which instructors have access to assist with creating assignments, quizzes, and exams.. The computerized test bank is available through EZ Test Online—a flexible and easy-to-use electronic testing program—that allows instructors to create tests from book-specific items. EZ Test accommodates a wide range of question types and allows instructors to add their own questions. Test items are also available in Word format (Rich Text Format). For secure online testing, exams created in EZ Test can be exported to WebCT and Blackboard. EZ Test Online is supported at www.mhhe.com/eztest where users can download a Quick Start Guide, access FAQs, or log a ticket for help with specific issues.

Microsoft® PowerPoint™ Slides Make preparing for class a snap by providing an outline of the main points in each chapter and reproducing in-text exhibits.

OTHER SERVICES AND SUPPORT

Service takes on a whole new meaning with McGraw-Hill Ryerson (MHR). More than just bringing you the textbook, MHR has consistently raised the bar in terms of innovation and educational research.

*i*Services

McGraw-Hill Ryerson takes pride in developing the tools necessary to ensure a rich teaching and learning experience. MHR can assist in integrating technology, events, conferences, training, and more, into the services surrounding the textbook. MHR calls it *i*Services; for additional information, visit http://www.mcgrawhill.ca/higher education/iservices.

McGraw-Hill Ryerson National Teaching and Learning Conference Series

The educational environment has changed tremendously in recent years, and McGraw-Hill Ryerson continues to be committed to helping you acquire the skills you need to succeed in this new milieu. Our innovative Teaching & Learning Conference Series brings faculty

together from across Canada with 3M Teaching Excellence award winners to share teaching and learning best practices in a collaborative and stimulating environment.

Course Management

In addition, content cartridges are available for the course management systems **WebCT** and **Blackboard**. These platforms provide instructors with user-friendly, flexible teaching tools. Please contact your local McGraw-Hill Ryerson *i*Learning Sales Specialist.

Create

McGraw-Hill's **Create Online** gives you access to the most abundant resource at your fingertips—literally. With a few mouse clicks, you can create customized learning tools simply and affordably. McGraw-Hill Ryerson has included many of our market-leading textbooks within Create Online for e-book and print customization as well as many licensed readings and cases. For more information, go to www.mcgrawhillcreate.com.

CourseSmart

CourseSmart brings together thousands of textbooks across hundreds of courses in an e-textbook format providing unique benefits to students and faculty. By purchasing an e-textbook, students can save up to 50 percent off the cost of a print textbook, reduce their impact on the environment, and gain access to powerful Web tools for learning, including full-text search, notes and highlighting, and e-mail tools for sharing notes between classmates. For faculty, CourseSmart provides instant access to review and compare textbooks and course materials in their discipline area without the time, cost, and environmental impact of mailing print copies. For further details, contact your *i*Learning Sales Specialist or go to www.coursesmart.com.

CHAPTER 12

Liabilities

What is a liability? The answer might seem rather obvious: an amount owed from one entity to another. If the liability bears interest, how is interest expense measured? The simple answer is that interest expense is equal to interest paid. However, life can get a lot more complicated:

- Does a liability exist if there is no legal liability, but the company has announced a particular commitment or plan of action?
- How is a liability measured if the obligation is for services, not a set amount of money?
- How can a liability be measured if the amount of cash to be paid is uncertain?
- How should a liability be valued if the stated interest rate does not reflect the market interest rate?
- How is interest expense measured if the stated interest rate does not reflect the market interest rate?
- When is interest part of the cost of an asset instead of an expense?

Liability financing is an integral part, perhaps even a dominant part, of the capital structure of many companies. For example, Shaw Communications Inc. reported total assets of $8.9 billion in 2009. Of this amount, only $2.5 billion is financed through shareholders' equity, with the balance, $6.4 billion, provided by debt in various forms. A sizeable portion of the debt is unearned revenue and deposits ($0.8 billion, or 9% of total assets) and long-term debt is 35% of total assets. Interest expense is reported at $237 million, eating up a significant portion of the reported $956 million in operating earnings. Appropriate measurement of these amounts is critical.

This chapter reviews common liabilities, including both financial and non-financial liabilities. Technical measurement issues are reviewed in the context of bond liabilities. Chapter 13 will discuss accounting for share equity. Then, in Chapter 14, coverage returns to debt arrangements, those that have some attributes of debt and some attributes of equity. Innovative financial markets have introduced significant complexities into the accounting world!

LIABILITY DEFINITION

According to the conceptual framework, a liability is defined as a *present obligation* of the entity *arising from past events*, the settlement of which is expected to result in an *outflow* of economic benefits. Settlement could be through *future transfer or use of assets, provision of services, or other yielding of economic benefits*. These characteristics can be simplified for practical purposes by remembering that a liability:

- Is an expected *future* sacrifice of assets or services;
- Constitutes a *present* obligation; and
- Is the result of a *past* transaction or event.

Notice that there are three time elements in the definition: a *future* sacrifice, a *present* obligation, and a *past* event. All three elements are necessary for a liability to be recognized. It is not possible to have a liability from an anticipated future event, such as expected future operating losses. There must be some past transaction that is identifiable as an **obligating event**, which is an event that creates an obligation where there is no other realistic alternative but to settle the obligation.

Definition—Proposed Change As part of a review of the conceptual framework, the IASB is reconsidering the definition of financial elements, including the definition of a liability. One suggestion under consideration is that a liability is "a present obligation for which the entity is the obligor." This definition removes the requirement that the liability relates to a past event, but it does retain the requirement that there be a *present obligation*. If such a change is made, there would be a ripple effect through reporting standards.

Constructive Obligations Some liabilities are **legal obligations**, which are liabilities that arise from contract or legislation; this includes most liabilities, including trade payables and borrowings. Other liabilities are **constructive obligations**, where a liability exists because there is a pattern of past practice or established policy. A company can create a constructive obligation if it makes a public statement that the company will accept certain responsibilities, *because the statement creates a valid expectation that the company will honour those responsibilities.* Others rely on this representation. Thus, a liability can be created when a company reacts to moral or ethical factors.

ETHICAL ISSUES

A company has announced a voluntary product recall that will take several months to complete. Customers have been offered a replacement product or repair on the original unit. The recall was prompted by the company's code of ethics to support its product integrity and customer base. The recall is voluntary in that the defect is not covered by warranty, and no legislation exists to force the company to act. Clear communication to another party establishes the obligation. A constructive liability exists and the *costs of the program must be accrued.*

Categories of Liabilities

Accounting for liabilities depends on whether the liability fits into one of two categories:

- Financial liabilities; or
- Non-financial liabilities.

A **financial liability** is a *financial instrument*. A financial liability is a contract that gives rise to a financial liability of one party and a financial asset of another party. That is, one party has an account payable and the other party has an account receivable. Another example is a loan payable and a loan receivable. The two elements are mirror images of each other.

A **non-financial liability** can be defined by what it is *not*—any liability that is not a financial liability is a non-financial liability. A non-financial liability has no offsetting financial asset on the books of another party. Examples of non-financial liabilities include:

- Revenue received in the current period but not yet earned (that is, unearned revenue); or
- Cash outflows that are expected to arise in the future but that are related to transactions, decisions, or events that took place in the current period (e.g., a warranty liability).

NON-FINANCIAL LIABILITIES: PROVISIONS

Provisions are the major category of non-financial liability. A **provision** is defined as *a liability of uncertain timing or amount*. Provisions can be caused by both legal and constructive obligations. Since liabilities are "expected" outflows, some degree of uncertainty can exist. Most liabilities have a high degree of certainty, such as payables and accruals. A liability that has *some uncertainty about the amount or the timing*, but is judged to be "more likely than not" (probable), is recognized as a liability called a provision. A liability that is judged to have a lower degree of certainty, and falls below the "likely" threshold (that is, is *not probable*), is called a **contingency** and is not recognized; information about contingencies[1] is included in the disclosure notes. That is:

Degree of Certainty	Classification
Certain (completely certain)	Financial liabilities: Payables, accruals (recorded)
Certain (probable)	Provision (recorded)
Not certain (not probable)	Contingency (disclosed)

Measurement—Current Practice

If a liability is completely certain, then measurement is typically not a problem; there is a stated amount to pay at a certain point. However, when an obligation is characterized by a degree of uncertainty, there is often uncertainty about the amount involved. A reasonable estimate must be obtained.

First, to be recorded, there must be a *probable payout*. That is, the probability of payout must be more than 50%. Provisions are then recorded at the *best estimate*. This is the amount that would be rationally paid to settle the obligation at the reporting date, if such a payment were possible. The **most likely outcome** (highest probability alternative) should be considered. If there is a range of outcomes, the **expected value** (the sum of outcomes multiplied by their probability distribution) is also a factor.

For example, assume that there is a large population of items, each with a probability attached. *Expected value* should be used for valuation. A company might have 50 warranty claims outstanding, each with a $10,000 potential claim. If 30% are judged to be likely to end with no cost to the company, and 70% end with a $10,000 payout, payout is certain (>50%). The amount to be recorded is the *expected value* of $350,000 [(50 × 30% × $0) + (50 × 70% × $10,000)]. *Expected value is the best estimate for a large population scenario.*

If there is a small population, then the most likely outcome may be the best estimate. For example, assume that there are three lawsuits outstanding against a company, each for $100,000. There is a 30% chance that the company will have to make a payment on one lawsuit, a 50% chance for two payouts, and a 20% chance for three payouts. Some payout

---

[1] Under ASPE, the term *contingency* has a different meaning: *contingent liabilities* are those that will arise only if another event occurs; a contingent liability *may be recorded or disclosed* depending on the likelihood of payment and the ability to estimate amounts. Under IFRS, a "contingency" is a provision that is not probable and therefore fails the recognition test. It is disclosed.

is certain. The *most likely outcome* is two lawsuits because the probability of that outcome is highest, at 50%. This means that the company should accrue $200,000. The *expected value* is $190,000, which is close, and provides support for the $200,000 accrual [(30% × $100,000) + (50% × $200,000) + (20% × $300,000)]. For a small population, the most likely outcome is often recorded as the best estimate.

However, the *most likely outcome* is not always close to the *expected value*, especially in a small population. Assume now that there is a 40 percent chance that the company will have to make a payment on one lawsuit, a 30% chance for two payouts, and a 30% chance for three payouts. The most likely (40%) outcome is a $100,000 payment, but the expected value is $190,000 [(40% × $100,000) + (30% × $200,000) + (30% × $300,000)]. In this case, there are considerable odds (the cumulative probability is 60%) that either two or three lawsuits will have to be paid, and a $100,000 accrual is not enough. Therefore, $200,000 should be accrued; there is only a 40% chance that the payout would be less than this amount. For a small population, the expected value can provide evidence to support an accrual of a particular outcome, even if it *alone* is not the most likely.

To summarize, the best estimate is:

Population	Best Estimate	Adjusted for
Large population	Expected value	Discounted for time value of money
Small population	Most likely outcome, with judgement, considering: 1. Expected value, and 2. Cumulative probabilities	Discounted for time value of money

Re-estimate Annually If a provision is estimated, then the amounts are re-estimated at each reporting date. The change in any recorded amount is expensed in the year. For example, if the estimate of a payout is originally $35,000, then this amount is recorded. If the estimate increases from $35,000 to $50,000 in a later year, an additional $15,000 of expense is recorded *in the year that the estimate changed*. On the other hand, if the estimated payment were to decline to $5,000, a *recovery* (negative expense) would be recorded.

Discounting Liabilities, including provisions, must be discounted where the time value of money is material. The discount rate chosen must reflect current market interest rates, and the risk level specific to the liability. Interest expense on a discounted liability is recorded as time passes.

Exception If the amount and timing of cash flows is highly uncertain, *discounting cannot be accomplished in a meaningful fashion* and amounts are recorded on an undiscounted basis.

Example Assume that a provision of $200,000 is recorded for a lawsuit, on the expectation that the amount will be paid in two years' time. Timing can be estimated with certainty. The company can borrow for general operating purposes over this term at an interest rate of 8%. The discounted amount is $171,468 [$200,000 × (P/F, 8%, 2)] and is recorded as follows:

Loss on litigation	171,468	
Provision for litigation		171,468

In subsequent periods, interest expense is recorded, and then the liability is paid:

Year 1 interest:

Interest expense ($171,468 × 8%)	13,717	
Provision for litigation		13,717

Year 2 interest and payment:

Interest expense (($171,468 + $13,717) × 8%)	14,815	
Provision for litigation		14,815

Provision for litigation		
($171,468 + $13,717 + $14,815)	200,000	
Cash		200,000

The discount rate used must be evaluated annually; if market interest rates change, calculations are revisited and adjusted.

Contingency In *rare* circumstances, it may not be possible to obtain a dollar estimate for a provision at all; in this case, the provision is *reclassified as a contingency* and disclosed only. In general, contingencies exist when:

- The obligation is possible but not probable;
- There is a present obligation but no economic resources are attached; or
- There is a present obligation but rare circumstances dictate that an estimate cannot be established.

Measurement—Proposal for Change

Standard-setters are considering an alternate approach to the measurement of liabilities. Under this alternate approach, a liability would be measured at the least of:

a. The present value of the resources required to fulfil the obligation; or

b. The amount that would have to be paid to cancel the obligation; or

c. The amount that would have to be paid to transfer the obligation to a third party.

If the obligation cannot be cancelled or transferred, then (a) would be used. For example, consider a warranty obligation with the following estimates:

a. The expected present value of anticipated claims is $125,000;

b. The warranty could be cancelled by buying out warranty holders for $142,000; and

c. A third party could be paid $120,000 to take over the warranty and do all the work associated with the claims.

The company would record the liability at $120,000, the lowest of these amounts. In many cases, however, the obligation cannot be cancelled, and other companies are not willing to take on the risks that are inherent in the transfer of a liability. Thus, the expected present value of resources required to fulfill the obligation, alternative a, will be the common valuation metric.

Measurement of Expected Present Value—Proposal Measurement of the expected present value under the proposed standard would be as follows:

1. First, is the definition of a liability met? That is, is there an *obligating event* that creates a present obligation?

2. Second, what is the range of outcomes? Probabilities and present values are assigned to each outcome, and the *expected present value* is recorded.

Although this sounds similar to existing standards just described, it may result in radically different amounts recorded as compared to current practice, particularly when there is a small population.

For a large population, discounted expected value will prevail under both existing and proposed standards. Small populations require different analysis.

For example, assume that a company is being sued for $1,000,000 and the company's legal team advises that an *obligating event has occurred*, but that the probability of making a payout is quite low, say 20%. Under existing standards, *the payout is deemed not certain (unlikely) and no accrual is made.* Under the proposal, the expected value of $200,000 (20% × $1,000,000) would be recorded. This amount would be discounted if time periods were long. The amount recorded would be zero *only if the probability of payout were zero.* Estimates and probabilities would be revisited at each reporting date and amounts revised accordingly.

Interpreting the $200,000 accrual might be difficult for financial statement readers. When there is a large population, the odds can be expected to play out. However, there is no such workout when the population is small. Assuming that the estimates are correct, and the lawsuit is completed in the following year, the company has an 80% chance of winning the lawsuit, and would pay out nothing. In the books, this will result in a $200,000 recovery because the accrual would be reversed. Alternatively, there is a 20% chance that the company will lose the lawsuit and be required to pay out $1,000,000. On the books, this will result in $800,000 of additional expense. In either case, the $200,000 originally recorded is not correct.

If the odds are that the company *will make* a payout, then differences between current and proposed standards are less extreme. Recall a prior example, where there are three lawsuits outstanding against a company. Each is for $100,000, and there is a 30% chance that the company will have to make a payment on one lawsuit, a 50% chance for two payouts, and a 20% chance for three payouts. Under existing standards, an accrual of the $200,000 *most likely outcome* was made. Under the proposed rules, the *expected value* is recorded; this is $190,000 [(30% × $100,000) + (50% × $200,000) + (20% × $300,000)].

Different from Existing Practice *Under existing standards, the payout has to be above the certainty threshold to register in the financial statements.* Under the proposed approach, many more obligations will have to be recorded because "low certainty obligations" with *any* positive expected present value must be recorded.

The remaining material in this chapter is based on existing standards.

CONCEPT REVIEW

1. What is the definition of a financial liability? Non-financial liability?
2. What is a provision versus a contingency?
3. How is an expected value obtained for a provision?
4. When are provisions discounted?

EXAMPLES OF PROVISIONS

Lawsuits

If a company is being sued by another party, the company may be found guilty, and ordered to pay money or otherwise make restitution to the plaintiff. Alternatively, the courts may find the company not guilty. Court decisions are subject to appeals, and the process may last for years. The defendant and the plaintiff may agree in the meantime to an out-of-court settlement.

Based on the certainty of payout, an unsettled court case may result in a provision (probable payout) or a contingency (not probable). Probability is assessed by the legal team, and the accountant and auditor may rely on the opinion of these experts. Note, though, that a constructive liability may be present if a company has announced that a settlement is being sought. A contingency may be present if there is a probable payout but the amount cannot be estimated; this inability to measure the payout should be rare. That is:

First:	Then, either/or:	
Ability to Measure Degree of Certainty	**Measurable**	**Not Measurable**
Certain (Probable)	Provision (recorded)	Contingency (disclosed) (rare)
Not certain (Not probable)	Contingency (disclosed)	Contingency (disclosed)

Company lawyers are often willing to admit that their clients are *likely to lose* a lawsuit, although obviously there is a loser and a winner in every case. Therefore, disclosure of contingencies relating to lawsuits (and, for similar reasons, to other claims and tax assessments) is common, despite accounting standards regarding probability and measurability.

Measurement—Proposal As previously explained above, a proposal to change existing standards would mean that *certainty* would no longer be a factor in establishing the recognition threshold for lawsuits. Instead, if this proposal is adopted, any positive *expected value* would be recorded *as long as an obligating event has occurred.*

ETHICAL ISSUES

Assume that a company is being sued by an ex-employee for $500,000 for wrongful dismissal. The company is defending itself actively, but has privately admitted that a settlement of $200,000 would be acceptable. Should the $200,000 be recorded? Making it known would provide information to the plaintiff and possibly hurt the company's bargaining position in discussions to end the lawsuit. On the other hand, leaving the $200,000 out of the financial statements understates probable liabilities and overstates profits.

The company is ethically required to follow appropriate reporting, but is equally ethically bound to serve its shareholders' best interests. Recording the $200,000 is appropriate. If disclosure is expected to seriously prejudice the position of the company in a dispute with another company, clear disclosure of the accounting treatment may be avoided. The expense and the liability may be grouped with other items to avoid granting additional information to the plaintiff. The omission of disclosure must be explained.

Reporting Example The Nestlé Group has a recorded provision for outstanding lawsuits, but also has contingencies. Information from the disclosure notes is as follows (in millions of Swiss francs (CHF)); notice that disclosure of litigation is restricted in the best interests of the company, and measurement is problematic:

Provision for Litigation	
At 31 December 2007	1,999
Currency retranslations	(175)
Provisions made in the period	994
Amounts used	(51)
Unused amounts reversed	(283)
At 31 December 2008	2,484

continued on next page

Litigation

Litigation provisions have been set up to cover tax, legal and administrative proceedings that arise in the ordinary course of business. These provisions concern numerous cases whose detailed disclosure could seriously prejudice the interest of the Group. Reversal of such provisions refer to cases resolved in favour of the Group. The timing of cash outflows of litigation provisions is uncertain as it depends of the outcome of the proceedings. These provisions are therefore not discounted because their present value would not represent meaningful information. Group management does not believe it is possible to make assumptions on the evolution of the cases beyond the reporting date.

Contingencies

The Group is exposed to contingent liabilities amounting to a maximum potential payment of CHF 644 million (2007: CHF 1,016 million) representing potential litigations of CHF 590 million (2007: CHF 956 million) and other items for CHF 54 million (2007: CHF 60 million).

Executory Contracts and Onerous Contracts

Companies often have contracts outstanding that require them to pay another party in the future, after the other party has performed some service or act. These contracts are known as **executory contracts**, because they do not become liabilities until they have been *executed* by one party or the other. The contracts commit the enterprise to a future expenditure, but they are not *liabilities* until the other party has performed the service or act specified in the contract. Examples are employee contracts for future employment, contracts for future delivery of goods and services, and most unfilled purchase orders.

If the unavoidable costs of meeting the contract exceed the economic benefits under the contract, then the contract is classified an **onerous contract**. A *provision* must be recorded with respect to the onerous contract, for the net loss associated with the contract terms.

For example, assume that a company has agreed to purchase 10,000 kg of ore at a price of $1.00 per kg. The price in today's market is $0.80 per kg. A provision must be recorded for the expected loss of $2,000 (10,000 kg × ($1.00 − $0.80)):

Loss on purchase commitment	2,000	
Provision for loss on purchase commitment		2,000

If the ore is then purchased when the selling price is $0.95 per kg, there is a partial loss recovery, and the inventory is recorded at its fair value:

Ore inventory	9,500	
Provision for loss on purchase commitment	2,000	
Loss recovery on purchase commitment		1,500
Accounts payable		10,000

Restructuring

A *provision for restructuring* is an estimate of the money that will be paid out in connection with a future restructuring program. A restructuring program is a plan of action that is planned and controlled by management, which materially changes the scope of the business undertaken by the entity, or the manner in which the business is conducted. Examples include the sale or termination of a line of the business, closure or relocation of operations in a country or region, change in management structure, and the like.

A liability will be recorded if the entity has a detailed formal plan for the restructuring, *and* has started to implement the plan, or otherwise announced the specifics of the plan to those who will be affected. An announcement that creates a provision must include major specific facts and details that raise valid expectations that the restructuring will take place.

Common elements of restructuring provisions are employee termination costs and costs to end contracts. A more detailed review of impairment implications, including any impairment of assets triggered by such a decision, is found in Chapters 3 and 10.

Warranty

A warranty is often a *legal liability*, specifically awarded under the terms of a contract for sale. Warranties may also be in force as a *constructive obligation* based on a company's announced intentions. The amount to record must be estimated.

To illustrate accounting for warranties, assume that Rollex Limited sells merchandise for $200,000 during 20X2. Rollex's merchandise carries a two-year unconditional warranty for parts and labour. Rollex's past experience has indicated that warranty costs will approximate 0.6% of sales. Payout is certain and the amount estimated is an expected value. The entry to record sales and the warranty obligation in 20X2 will be as follows:

Accounts receivable	200,000	
Sales revenue		200,000
Warranty expense	1,200	
Warranty liability		1,200

If, in 20X3, Rollex incurs costs of $350 to repair or replace defective merchandise, the cash outflow is charged to the liability account:

Warranty liability	350	
Cash (and other resources used)		350

The expense for the year *is not the amount paid*; the expense is the *total of all expected future claims*. The balance in the warranty liability account will be $850, credit. The warranty liability will be carried forward from year to year, adjusted each year for management's estimate of the future warranty costs. As is the case for all accounting estimates, the estimate of annual warranty cost may be changed in the light of new experience or as the result of changed product design.

In 20X3, Rollex sells another $240,000 worth of merchandise. Rollex now plans to use an estimate of 0.4% of sales for warranties, and believes that it should have used this estimate in the prior year, as well. The current year expense is $560, which is $960 for this year ($240,000 × 0.4%), less a $400 adjustment to decrease last year's accrual ($200,000 × (0.6% − 0.4%)). The $400 correction is made this year, and *changes the current year expense.* Correction is not done retrospectively. An amount of $500 is spent on claims in 20X3, some for product sold in 20X2 and some related to goods sold in 20X3. After these entries, the warranty liability will have a credit balance of $910.

Accounts receivable	240,000	
Sales revenue		240,000
Warranty expense ($960 − $400)	560	
Warranty liability		560

Warranty liability	500	
Cash (and other resources used)		500

If, in any year, the charges to the warranty liability for warranty work done are higher than the balance in the liability account, the liability account will *temporarily* go into a debit balance until the year-end adjustment is made. The temporary existence of a debit balance simply indicates that the expense has not yet been accrued. The ending warranty liability has to be reviewed for reasonableness, though. If costs are creeping up, the liability will have a low balance and the estimate that is accrued each year may need upward revision. On the other hand, if the warranty credit balance builds up over time, the rate should be revised downward. Sometimes, the "excess" in a particular year may not call for an increase in the regular estimate if it is a one-time occurrence.

The warranty liability is current if the warranty is for one year or less. If the warranty is for a longer period, the liability should be split between current and long-term portions and the need for discounting should be considered.

Restoration and Environmental Obligations

Provisions are often created with respect to environmental obligations, as discussed in Chapter 9. If there are legislative remediation requirements, then the cost of the required activities must be estimated and accrued. If legislative requirements are *pending,* the provision is accrued only if there is **virtual certainty** that the legislation will be enacted. On the other hand, the liability may be a constructive liability, and be accrued absent legislative requirements. For example, if a company has a published policy concerning environmental cleanup activities, or otherwise accepts responsibility for remediation in a public forum, then a provision for expected costs must be recorded. Lengthy time periods are common in this area, and discounting is usually required.

Coupons, Refunds, and Gift Cards

Coupons are often used as sales incentives. A provision for outstanding coupons may be recorded, but only in limited circumstances. The key to a coupon offer is whether economic benefits are transferred. If the product is still sold at a profit, even after the coupon, then no economic benefits are deemed to transfer and the provision has no accounting value. If, on the other hand, retailers or customers are reimbursed in cash for coupons, or if products are sold at a loss, then a provision is appropriate. Note also that if the company reserves the right to cancel the coupons at any time, then there is no enforceable obligation. A reliable measurement for the provision includes estimating the take-up rate for the coupons; the **breakage** (unused) rate can be estimated based on past history or other valid evidence.

For example, assume 1,000 customers buying an appliance are given a coupon for a $10 cash rebate if proof of purchase is submitted. A liability exists because of the promise to pay cash, and the liability is a provision because the amount must be estimated. Based on past experience, 40% of the coupons will be submitted. The amount recorded is an expected value of $4,000 ($10 refund × 40% take-up rate × 1,000 coupons). The following entry would be made when the sale of 1,000 units is recorded:

Sales discounts	4,000	
Provision for coupon refund		4,000

If 370 coupons are honoured, and the remainder expire:

Provision for coupon refund	4,000	
Cash (370 coupons × $10 refund)		3,700
(Recovery of) sales discounts (remainder)		300

Many companies sell gift cards or service passes to customers. Issuance of these cards creates an unearned revenue liability. The cards usually have an unlimited life due to provincial legislation and thus represent an indefinite legal liability. However, if the entity believes that some cards will be unused, and can gather evidence to estimate *breakage,* then the liability becomes an estimate and thus is a provision. Discounting might be appropriate if the time period is long.

A company may allow merchandise to be returned for cash refund, creating a constructive liability because of a published policy of providing refunds even in the absence of legal obligation. An obligation exists, based on the cash to be returned. The company must estimate the extent of refunds based on experience and the presence of variables that cause refunds to arise.

Loyalty Programs

Another common sales incentive is a customer loyalty program, where the customer is awarded loyalty points, which can then be used to obtain free (or discounted) goods or services. There are many ways that these programs can be structured.

No separate expense is recognized—*the loyalty program is an allocation of original revenue.* That is, the sale transaction with the customer has multiple parts, and the value of the award credits is one such part. An *unearned revenue* account, or *provision for rewards,* is created. This provision is measured according to the value of the awards to the customer, not the cost of the goods to the company.

For example, assume that a sale of $65,000 to customers carries with it loyalty points that allow acquisition of product with a fair value of $5,000. This $5,000 estimate assumes some breakage of points awarded. The following entry would be made when the sale is recorded:

Cash	65,000	
Sales revenue		60,000
Provision for loyalty program rewards		5,000

The provision is reduced when the loyalty points are redeemed.

Repairs and Maintenance

Repairs and maintenance are expenses of the year in which the repair or maintenance activity occurs. Such costs are not accrued to smooth out earnings, even when they are "lumpy." For example, assume that a cargo vessel must be painted every five years. The cost of painting is simply an expense (or a capital item) of year five. The company may *not* accrue one-fifth of the cost each year, and establish a provision for maintenance. Essentially, no obligating event has taken place after one year or even four years; the decision to paint is still in the future.

As another example, assume that a company has a legislative obligation to overhaul an aircraft every five years. Again, no provision is set up prior to the overhaul, because there has been no obligating event. After all, the company could avoid the overhaul by selling the aircraft. When the overhaul is done, the cost is capitalized and then depreciated over the next five years. Similarly, if a lease requires maintenance activity after 1,000 hours of use, no obligating event occurs until the 1,000th hour is clocked. Up to that point in time, management could decide to leave the asset idle to avoid the maintenance activity.

Self-Insurance

Companies may choose to self-insure for known risks. Many large companies self-insure for fire and theft losses, meaning that they carry no external insurance. The cost of claims is assumed to be lower, over time, than the cost of insurance and so the choice is a rational business decision. Self-insurance does, however, retain certain risks for the company.

A provision for estimated losses must be established for *events (fire and theft) taking place prior to the reporting date,* but also for *loss events that have happened during the year but are not yet known,* such as undiscovered damage. Such damage might be discovered after the year-end and it must be accrued. This allows for a reasonable delay based on known events. The amount is a provision because it is estimated.

However, companies may not record a provision in excess of the cost of estimated incidents in the year. A company may wish to do this to smooth the expense between years with low losses and years with high losses. *A provision must be justified based on a loss event.* If there is no such event, no accrual can be made, even if the odds suggest that a future year will have heavier incidence of loss events.

Contingent Assets

While on the subject of contingencies, note that an asset is not recorded until a company is *virtually certain* of the related benefits to be obtained. *Virtual certainty i*s a much higher degree of certainty than just *certainty. Contingent assets* are assets that arise from past events, but whose existence must be confirmed by a future event that is not wholly in the control of management. If a company is suing a supplier, for instance, no amount is recorded for the claimed amount, even if it is likely that the company will win and the amount can be estimated. In fact, a winning court judgement would not be recorded until it seems virtually certain that the *amount will be paid.* Disclosure is the appropriate route.

Prohibited Practices

In the past, some companies have attempted to smooth earnings through the creation and reversal of provisions. For example, an expense and a liability might be recorded in years when earnings was high (e.g., "provision for future losses") just to lower earnings, and then reversed in a year when earnings was low to raise earnings. This practice is not permitted by accounting standards.

If a reversal of any provision takes place, there must be clear disclosure. That is, if some of the earnings for a given year is caused by an expense recovery, this needs to be clear to the readers of the financial statements. This can be achieved through disclosure of the changes to the provision accounts, as seen the Nestlé example, above.

Finally, it is not permitted to use a provision set up for one purpose to offset expenditures for another purpose. For example, only warranty expenditures can be used to reduce the warranty provision.

Summary

Refer to the following chart as a summary:

Possible Financial Statement Element—Provision	Record?
Lawsuits	Yes—if certain and measurable No—if not certain; classified as a contingency if not certain or if certain but not measurable (rare)
Executory contracts	No—wait and record only on delivery
Onerous contracts	Yes—record estimated loss
Restructuring	Yes—if formal plan that has been implemented or communicated
Warranty	Yes—estimate and record based on expected value
Restoration and environmental	Yes—record if constructive or legislative; estimate must be made
Coupons, refunds and gift cards	Yes—if distribution economic benefits involved (cash or products issued at a loss); breakage rate to be estimated No—if cancellable or non-cash and represent a small discount so that products still sold at a profit
Loyalty programs	Yes—assign fair value and allocate unearned revenue on initial sale; breakage rate to be estimated

continued on next page

Possible Financial Statement Element—Provision	Record?
Repairs and maintenance	No—normally accounted for in the year of the repair or maintenance activity Yes—if an obligating event (under contract) takes place
Self-insurance	Yes—for losses experienced and for expected losses where the incident has happened No—no general provision designed for smoothing permitted
Loan guarantees (see section below)	Yes—fair value is recorded

CONCEPT REVIEW

1. What is an onerous contract?
2. Why might a warranty expense be negative (a recovery) during a given year?
3. When is a provision for coupons recorded?
4. When is a provision for self-insurance recorded?

FINANCIAL LIABILITIES

As previously stated, a financial liability is a financial instrument, and is a contract that gives rise to a financial liability of one party and a financial asset of another party. Typically, financial liabilities are accompanied by an account receivable or an investment account on the "other side."

Classification

Accounting standards require that companies classify each financial liability. *Classification determines the subsequent measurement of the financial liability.* Specifically, the classification and measurement alternatives can be summarized as follows:

Classification	Summarized Classification Criteria	Initial Valuation	Subsequent Valuation
1. "Other" financial liabilities	Most financial liabilities; all those except those in category 2, below	Fair value, which is the transaction value and establishes the cost of the financial instrument ADD Transaction costs, if any	Cost (Amortized cost)
2. Fair value through profit or loss (FVTPL)	May be FVTPL if: a. The liability will be sold in the short term; and b. If management wishes to avoid an accounting mismatch (related/hedged financial instruments are FVTPL)	Fair value, which is the transaction value and establishes the cost of the financial instrument	Fair value; gains and losses in earnings

Most liabilities fall in the *other financial liabilities* category. The other category is a *FVTPL liability*, which is a liability held primarily for the purpose of selling in the short term. In some circumstances, management may designate liabilities as FVTPL. This might be appropriate, for example, if various hedging strategies were in place, and management wished to have both hedged asset and liability in the same category for valuation purposes.

Measurement of Other Financial Liabilities

Other financial liabilities are initially measured as the fair value of the consideration received, plus transaction costs, and then carried at this value (which is cost), or amortized cost, over their lives. That is, the initial fair value is the stated amount of the transaction, or the transaction price. For example, a company receives an invoice for the fair value of goods shipped by a supplier; the goods are the consideration, and their invoice price is the fair value of the liability.

If payments are to be paid over a period of time, fair value might be estimated as the present value of all future cash payments discounted using the market interest rate. The discount rate is *the borrower's interest rate for additional debt of similar term and risk,* also called the **incremental borrowing rate (IBR)**. However, current liabilities normally are not discounted because the short time span means that the difference between the nominal amount and the discounted amount will be immaterial.

Assume that Radial Information Limited bought a capital asset. The company paid no money upfront, but agreed to pay $18,000 in three years' time, with no additional interest. Radial could borrow a similar amount over three years from the bank at 9%. Assuming annual compounding, the present value of the liability is $13,900 ($18,000 × ((P/F, 9%, 3)). This is the value at which the capital asset and the liability will be recorded. As illustrated later in the chapter, the liability will increase by 9% interest on the balance each year, and be equal to $18,000 at maturity. If, on the other hand, Radial bought a capital asset and agreed to pay $18,000 for it in six months' time, again with no additional interest, the liability and the capital asset would be recorded at $18,000, with no interest, because the interest-free period is short.

Loan Guarantees A loan guarantee requires the guarantor to pay loan principal and interest if the borrower defaults. This is a financial liability of the guarantor. The financial instruments rules require that loan guarantees be recorded at their *fair value.* Assume that a loan guarantee for $500,000 is issued for a related company, and there is only a 10% chance that it will have to be honoured. The 10% probability means that the guarantee has a positive fair value of $50,000 ($500,000 × 10%) and must be recorded at this amount, with an expense recognized. Timing must be considered to evaluate the need for discounting. *Loan guarantees would not be recorded if there was a zero percent chance of payout.* Extensive disclosure of guarantees is also required, including the maximum potential future payment, the identity of the other party, and collateral, if any.

CONCEPT REVIEW

1. What are the two possible classifications for financial liabilities?
2. How is the fair value of a financial liability determined?
3. How is a loan guarantee valued in the financial statements?

LONG-TERM DEBT

Measurement of long-term debt and the related interest expense can be complex, and important because the variables will determine the company's *cost of debt*, which is a measure of risk and an input into various decision models.

Effective versus Nominal Interest Rates

The nominal interest rate is the interest rate stated in the loan agreement. The **effective interest rate**, or **yield**, is the true cost of borrowing. *The effective interest rate is the market* *interest rate, for debt of similar term, security, and risk.* Using the effective interest rate as the discount rate, the proceeds on issuing a liability can be calculated as:

$P = [I \times (P/A, i, n)] + [F \times (P/F, i, n)]$, where

P = current market price of the loan; issuance proceeds
I = dollar amount of each period's interest payment, or
  = nominal rate times the loan face value
F = maturity value of the loan
n = the number of periods to maturity
i = the market interest rate

When a liability pays the effective market interest rate, the liability will be issued for its par value, or maturity amount. When the nominal and market interest rates are different, price of the loan (issue proceeds) will be greater or less than the maturity amount.

Example Suppose that a company issues a five-year bond with a face value of $100,000, at a nominal interest rate of 7%, to be paid annually. The company is required to pay $7,000 interest at the end of each year. If the market rate of interest is 6%, then the bond will raise $104,213 on issuance ($[\$7,000 \times (P/A, 6\%, 5)] + [\$100,000 \times (P/F, 6\%, 5)]$). Alternatively, if one knew the issuance price, maturity amount, nominal interest and term, one could solve for the effective interest rate using the above equation.

Annual versus Semi-Annual Effective Rates Assume that interest payments are semi-annual instead of annual. Now, the bond has a face value of $100,000, and the nominal rate is 3.5% per six-month period, or $3,500 per period. Is the rate of return still 7%? No; because of compounding, the effective return is slightly higher, at 7.12%. Despite the difference between the stated rate of 7% and the real return of 7.12% for semi-annual compounding, financial markets still refer to the rate as 7%. *Financial markets express interest rates in annual rates.*

That is, the lender will quote the nominal interest rate and the compounding period, and expect the borrower to understand that the real return is higher. In this case, the rate would be described as 7% per annum, compounded semi-annually.

We will also, in this text, quote per annum rates and compounding periods. Just remember that if compounding is more than once per year, *the per annum interest rate understates the real return.*

Measurement of Interest Expense

Accounting for long-term debt is simple if the effective interest rate and the nominal interest rate are the same. If these two rates are the same, the liability is issued at its maturity value. Interest is accrued as time passes, and interest payments are accounted for as cash is disbursed. Cash amounts correctly state the liability amount and interest expense.

Premium or Discount Recognition If the nominal interest rate is different from the market interest rate at the time the note is issued, the loan is issued above or below par, or at a premium or a discount. Present value techniques are used to initially value the loan. The initial discount or premium has to be reduced to zero, or amortized, over the life of the liability. The net liability is carried on the SFP at amortized cost. *Amortized cost* simply means that the net liability is valued at its par value plus or minus the premium or discount still on the books.

There are two methods used to recognize, or amortize, the premium or discount over the life of the bond: (1) the straight-line method and (2) the effective-interest method. *Accounting standards clearly require the effective-interest rate method.* This is the preferable method because it measures the interest cost more accurately; that is, interest expense will be a contract percentage of the liability carrying value and the cost of debt is correctly stated. Accordingly, the examples in this text will emphasize the effective-interest method. Remember, however, that when the difference between the required method and a simpler alternative method is immaterial, either can be used, and thus the straight-line method will be encountered in practice. ASPE also allows use of the straight-line method.

Example Assume that Fema Company purchased equipment on 1 January 20X5, and issued a two-year, $10,000 note with a 3% stated or nominal interest rate at a time when the market rate of interest for debt of similar term and risk is about 8%. Interest is payable each 31 December and the entire principal is payable 31 December 20X6. The $10,000 principal amount is called the *face value, maturity value,* or *par value.* The 8% market rate is known as the borrower's incremental borrowing rate (IBR) and is the rate for a loan with similar term, similar risk, and similar security.

Since the nominal interest rate is less than the market rate, the principal amount of the note will not be used to value the transaction. Recording the asset and the liability at the face value of $10,000 will not only overstate both the asset and the liability, but also understate the interest expense in each year because interest would be recorded at 3% instead of the "true" rate of 8%. Instead, the transaction is valued at the loan's present value. At 8%, the present value of the note is computed as follows:

Present value of maturity amount: $10,000 × (P/F, 8%, 2)	$8,573
Present value of the nominal interest payments: ($10,000 × 3%) × (P/A, 8%, 2)	535
Present value of the note at 8%	$9,108

Initially, the note and the capital asset should be recorded on the books at present value. The difference between face value and present value ($10,000 − $9,108 = $892) represents the *discount* on the note, or implicit interest in addition to the 3% cash payments. This is amortized to interest expense over the life of the liability.

Effective-Interest Method Under the effective-interest method, the interest expense for each period is calculated as the outstanding net liability balance times the effective interest rate. The outstanding liability balance is calculated as the face value less any discount or plus any premium. The amount of cash outflow is governed by the nominal rate. The annual change to the premium or discount is the difference between the effective-interest expense calculation and the cash outflow. In the example for Fema Company, the entries are:

1 January 20X5—issue note		
Equipment	9,108	
Discount on long-term notes payable (contra notes payable)	892	
Long-term notes payable		10,000
The outstanding liability is $9,108 ($10,000 − $892)		
31 December 20X5—interest, effective-interest method		
Interest expense ($9,108 × 8%)	729	
Discount on long-term notes payable ($729 − $300)		429
Cash		300
The outstanding liability is $9,537: [$10,000 − ($892 − $429)]		
31 December 20X6—interest		
Interest expense ($9,537 × 8%)	763	
Discount on long-term notes payable ($763 − $300)		463
Cash		300
The outstanding liability is $10,000: [($10,000 − ($463 − $463)]		
31 December 20X6—note maturity		
Long-term notes payable	10,000	
Cash		10,000

In this example, there is a significant difference between the nominal interest rate of 3% and the market rate of 8%. The effect of simply accepting the 3% nominal rate as the basis for accounting is that the cost of the equipment would be overstated, at $10,000 instead of $9,108, and the interest expense would be understated, as $600 over the two years instead of $1,492 (that is, $600 cash plus the discount of $892). Note that a financial statement reader can easily determine the effective cost of borrowing by dividing interest expense by the carrying value of the loan (e.g., in 20X5, $729 ÷ (carrying value during the year, $9,108) = 8%).

Straight-line Method The straight-line method of discount amortization is acceptable *only* if it yields results not materially different from the effective-interest method. Under the straight-line method, Fema amortizes $446 ($892 ÷ 2) of the discount and recognizes $746 of interest expense ($300 + $446) each period. Interest expense for any period is the amount of cash paid out plus discount amortization or minus premium amortization. While simple, this method may inaccurately portray the cost of debt. For example, in 20X5, interest expense would be $746; divide this by the carrying value during the year of $9,108, and the cost of capital appears to be 8.2%. While that doesn't look like much of a difference, cost of capital is highly sensitive and a difference of 0.2% is material.

Subsequent Changes in Fair Value After issuance, the fair value of a liability will change due to changes in the market rate of interest. The price may also change in response to changes in the creditworthiness of the issuing company, for which the market will demand a higher (or lower) rate of interest. Changes in fair market value of a liability subsequent to the liability's initial issuance *are not recorded* by the issuing company. Fair market values are disclosed, however.

Price Quotations Liabilities are traded in financial markets, priced at fair value. Fair value is determined through present value models. Prices are stated as a percentage of face, or par, value. A $100,000 bond with a price of 92 would sell for $92,000. If the price were 103, it would sell for $103,000.

SFP Classification On a classified statement of financial position, long-term loans are obviously classified as long-term liabilities. However, the portion of *principal* that is due within the next year (or operating cycle) is classified as a current liability. Any accrued interest at the reporting date is also classified as a current liability.

Refinancing arrangements Sometimes a company will make an arrangement to *refinance* a maturing long-term liability. For example, say that a long-term loan will come due in 20X8. By the end of 20X7, plans are underway to replace this long-term loan with a new long-term loan. Does the maturing loan have to be classified as a current liability at the end of 20X7? The answer to that is *if* the plans are far enough along that there is a contractual commitment for the replacement financing by the reporting date, the amount may be left as long term. If the plans have *not been firmed up* through a legally enforceable arrangement, then the maturing loan is a current liability at the end of 20X7.

Bonds Payable

A bond (or *debenture*) is a debt security issued to secure large amounts of capital on a long-term basis. A bond represents a formal promise by the issuing organization to pay principal and interest in return for the capital invested.

Example To illustrate accounting for bonds payable, assume that on 1 January 20X5, Gresham Limited, a calendar-year firm, issues $100,000 of 7% debentures dated 1 January 20X5, which pay interest each 31 December. The bonds mature on 31 December 20X9. Notice the simplifying assumptions: this bond is for only a five-year term, and pays interest annually at the end of Gresham's fiscal year.

1. The **face value** or *par value* (also called *maturity*, or *principal value*) of a bond is the amount payable when the bond is due ($100,000 for Gresham).

2. The **maturity date** is the end of the bond term and the due date for the face value (31 December 20X9, for Gresham).

3. The **nominal interest rate** (also called *the coupon, stated,* or *contractual rate*) is the rate that determines periodic interest payments. For Gresham, the nominal rate is 7%, paid annually.

4. The **interest payment dates** are the dates the periodic interest payments are due (31 December for Gresham). Gresham pays $7,000 interest on the $100,000 bond on each 31 December regardless of the issue price or market rate of interest at date of issue.

5. The **bond date** (authorization date) is the earliest date the bond can be issued and represents the planned issuance date of the bond issue (1 January 20X5 for Gresham).

Three situations will illustrate accounting for bonds, under different effective interest rate assumptions. (Always assume that the effective interest rate is quoted for compounding periods identical to those offered by the bond unless told otherwise.)

Situation A: Effective interest rate = 7%

Situation B: Effective interest rate = 6%

Situation C: Effective interest rate = 8%

Situation A The bond will sell at face value because the market and stated interest rates are both 7%. The price of the bonds will be equal to the present value of the future cash flows at the market rate of 7%:

Issue price = [$100,000 × (P/F, 7%, 5)] + [($100,000 × 7%) × (P/A, 7%, 5)]
            = $100,000

When the bonds are issued, the issuer records a long-term liability, and interest is recorded as time passes. The bond is repaid at maturity.

1 January 20X5—issue bonds		
Cash	100,000	
Bonds payable		100,000
31 December each year, 20X5 through 20X9—		
interest payment		
Interest expense	7,000	
Cash ($100,000 × 7%)		7,000
31 December 20X9—bond maturity		
Bonds payable	100,000	
Cash		100,000

Interest expense for bonds issued at face value equals the amount of the interest payment. The book value of the bonds remains $100,000 to maturity. Changes in the fair market value of the bond, caused by changes in the market rate of interest subsequent to the issuance date, are not recognized in the financial statements but are disclosed.

Situation B The market rate of interest is 6%; the bonds sell at a premium.

Issue price = [$100,000 × (P/F, 6%, 5)] + [($100,000 × 7%) × (P/A, 6%, 5)]
            = $104,213

The bonds sell at a *premium* because they pay a stated rate that exceeds the market rate on similar bonds. The initial $4,213 premium is recorded in an account titled *premium on bonds payable*, which is shown with the bonds payable account on the statement of financial position. The following entry is made to record the issue:

1 January 20X5—issue bonds		
Cash	104,213	
Bonds payable		100,000
Premium on bonds payable		4,213

Total interest expense over the term of a bond is *not* equal to total cash interest when a bond is sold at a premium or discount. Instead, interest expense must equal the total cash payments required by the bond (face value and interest) less the aggregate issue price. Total interest expense is shown by this calculation:

Face value	$100,000
Total cash interest: 7% × $100,000 × 5 years	35,000
Total cash payments required by bond	135,000
Issue price	104,213
Total interest expense over bond term ($35,000 − $4,213)	$ 30,787

Gresham received $4,213 more than face value at issuance but will pay only face value at maturity. Therefore, the effective rate is less than the stated rate, and total interest expense for Gresham over the bond term is *less* than total interest paid.

Premium or Discount Recognition The premium or discount must be completely recognized, or amortized, over the bond term using the effective-interest method, so that net book value equals face value at maturity. Amortized premium reduces periodic interest expense relative to interest paid, and amortized discount increases interest expense. The net bond liability equals face value plus the remaining unamortized bond premium or less the remaining unamortized bond discount. The following entries illustrate this amortization:

31 December 20X5		
Interest expense ($104,213 × 6%)	6,253	
Premium on bonds payable	747	
Cash ($100,000 × 7%)		7,000
The carrying value of the bond is now $103,466		
($104,213 − $747)		
31 December 20X6		
Interest expense ($103,466 × 6%)	6,208	
Premium on bonds payable	792	
Cash		7,000
The carrying value of the bond is now $102,674		
($103,466 − $792)		

The bonds are disclosed in the long-term liability section of Gresham's 31 December 20X6, statement of financial position as follows:

Bonds payable	$100,000
Premium on bonds payable ($4,213 − $747 − $792)	2,674
Net book value of bonds payable	$102,674

Interest expense under the effective-interest method is the product of the effective interest rate (6%) and net liability balance at the beginning of the period. In effect, the company returns part of the original "excess" proceeds with each interest payment. In 20X5, this amount is $747, which reduces the net bond liability at the beginning of 20X6. Consequently, 20X6 interest expense is less than that for 20X5.

Proof of Book Value The book value of the bonds at 31 December 20X6 is the present value of remaining cash flows *using the effective interest rate at the date of issuance:*

$$PV_{31/12/20X6} = [\$100,000 \times (P/F, 6\%, 3)] + [(\$100,000 \times 7\%) \times (P/A, 6\%, 3)]$$
$$= \$102,674$$

An amortization table is often prepared to support bond journal entries. The table gives all the data necessary for journal entries over the term of the bond and each year's ending net liability balance. An amortization table is shown in Exhibit 12-1.

EXHIBIT 12-1

AMORTIZATION TABLE FOR GRESHAM LIMITED BONDS

Situation B—Bonds Sold at Premium; Effective Interest Amortization

Date	Interest Payment @ 7%	Interest Expense @ 6%	Premium Amortization[1]	Unamortized Premium[2]	Net Bond Liability[3]
1 Jan. 20X5				$4,213	$104,213
31 Dec. 20X5	$ 7,000	$ 6,253	$ 747	3,466	103,466
31 Dec. 20X6	7,000	6,208	792	2,674	102,674
31 Dec. 20X7	7,000	6,160	840	1,834	101,834
31 Dec. 20X8	7,000	6,110	890	944	100,944
31 Dec. 20X9	7,000	6,056	944	0	100,000
	$35,000	$30,787	$4,213		

[1] Interest payment − Interest expense
[2] Previous unamortized premium − Current period's amortization
[3] $100,000 face value + Current unamortized premium

Straight-line Amortization If straight-line amortization were to be used, then the $4,213 premium would be amortized over the five-year term of the bond, at the rate of $843 ($4,213 ÷ 5) per year. This produces interest expense of $6,157 ($7,000 − $843) annually. The premium is reduced to zero at the maturity date of the bond, and interest expense is less than interest paid. As compared to the effective-interest method, interest expense is not as accurately measured.

Situation C The market rate of interest is 8%; the bonds sell at a discount.

$$Issue\ price = [\$100,000 \times (P/F, 8\%, 5)] + [(\$100,000 \times 7\%) \times (P/A, 8\%, 5)]$$
$$= \$96,007$$

The Gresham bonds sell at a discount in this case because the stated rate is less than the yield rate on similar bonds. The discount is recorded in the discount on bonds payable account, a contra-liability valuation account, which is subtracted from bonds payable to yield the net liability. The entries for the first two years after the bond issuance follow, along with an amortization table (Exhibit 12-2) and the relevant portion of the statement of financial position after two years.

Journal Entries

1 January 20X5—issue bonds		
Cash	96,007	
Discount on bonds payable	3,993	
Bonds payable		100,000
31 December 20X5—interest expense		
Interest expense ($96,007 × 8%)	7,681	
Discount on bonds payable		681
Cash ($100,000 × 7%)		7,000
31 December 20X6—interest expense		
Interest expense (($96,007 + $681) × 8%)	7,735	
Discount on bonds payable		735
Cash ($100,000 × 7%)		7,000

Portion of Long-Term Liability Section of Statement of Financial Position

31 December 20X6

Bonds payable	$100,000
Discount on bonds payable	(2,577)
Net book value of bonds payable	$ 97,423

EXHIBIT 12-2

AMORTIZATION TABLE FOR GRESHAM LIMITED BONDS

Situation C—Bonds Sold at Discount: Effective Interest Amortization

Date	Interest Payment @ 7%	Interest Expense @ 8%	Discount Amortization[1]	Unamortized Discount[2]	Net Bond Liability[3]
1 Jan. 20X5				$3,993	$ 96,007
31 Dec. 20X5	$ 7,000	$ 7,681	$ 681	3,312	96,688
31 Dec. 20X6	7,000	7,735	735	2,577	97,423
31 Dec. 20X7	7,000	7,794	794	1,783	98,217
31 Dec. 20X8	7,000	7,857	857	926	99,074
31 Dec. 20X9	7,000	7,926	926	0	100,000
	$35,000	$38,993	$3,993		

[1] Interest expense − Interest payment
[2] Previous unamortized discount − Current period's amortization
[3] $100,000 face value − Current unamortized discount

Exhibit 12-3 summarizes several aspects of bond accounting. The exhibit relates to bonds with semi-annual interest payments, which is the usual situation.

EXHIBIT 12-3

SUMMARY TABLE: ACCOUNTING FOR BONDS ASSUMING SEMI-ANNUAL INTEREST PAYMENTS

Price of bond issue = Present value of the cash flow to the investor
= Discounted principal payments + Discounted interest payment annuity
= [(Face value) $\times$ (P/F, i, n)] + [(Face value $\times$ s) $\times$ (P/A, i, n)]

Where: i = effective interest rate *per six-month period*
n = number of semi-annual periods in bond term
s = stated (nominal) interest rate per six-month period

Discount or premium =
When effective rate (i) exceeds stated rate (s):
Initial discount = Face value − Price of bond issue

When stated rate (s) exceeds effective rate (i):
Initial premium = Price of bond issue − Face value

Net book value of bonds = Face value *plus* unamortized premium or *minus* unamortized discount

As Maturity Approaches:	Premium	Discount
The unamortized amount	Declines	Declines
The net book value	Declines	Increases
Annual interest expense	Declines*	Increases*

*Under effective-interest method; constant under straight-line method.

Two Methods of Amortizing Premium and Discount:

	Effective Interest	Straight-Line
Calculations:		
Calculation of interest expense	Effective rate $\times$ Net carrying value of bond	Cash paid + Discount amortization or − Premium amortization
Calculation of discount or premium amortization	Difference between cash paid and expense	Discount or premium ÷ Period that bond is outstanding
Patterns:		
Annual interest expense	Changes each year	Constant over term
Annual interest expense as a percentage of beginning book value (interest rate)	Constant over term	Changes each year

Interest Payment Dates Different from Statement Dates

In the preceding situations, all specified interest payment dates coincided with the fiscal year-end. However, this coincidence is not frequent in practice. When the end of a fiscal period falls between interest payment dates, it is necessary to accrue interest from the last (previous) interest payment date, and to bring the bond discount/premium amortization up to date.

For example, assume the facts for Situation C for Gresham Limited bonds, except that the fiscal year-end is 30 September. The bonds are issued on the bond date, 1 January 20X5, and interest is payable annually on 31 December. On 30 September 20X5, interest must be accrued and discount amortized:

30 September 20X5—interest accrued		
Interest expense[1]	5,761	
Accrued interest payable[2]		5,250
Discount on bonds payable[3]		511

[1] $7,681 (first full year's expense) × 9/12
[2] $100,000 × 7% × 9/12
[3] $681 (first full year's amortization) × 9/12

The amortization is derived from the amortization table in Exhibit 12-2 and is allocated evenly over the period between interest dates. The loan balance is not recalculated and included in the table (i.e., not recompounded), because *compounding is tied to interest dates and not to reporting periods*. That is, an amortization table is always based on the *bond's* dates and terms. Then it is possible to adjust calculations to fit the fiscal year.

When the interest is paid on 31 December, the following entry is made, assuming that the interest accrual has not been reversed:

31 December 20X5—interest payment		
Interest expense[1]	1,920	
Accrued interest payable	5,250	
Discount on bonds payable[2]		170
Cash		7,000

[1] $7,681 × 3/12
[2] $681 × 3/12

Bonds Issued between Interest Payment Dates

In the previous examples, bonds were issued on their original issue date, an assumption chosen in order to emphasize the accounting principles regarding effective interest rates and bond amortization. However, bonds may not necessarily be issued on their initial issue date. Bonds that are sold at some time later than their initial issue date are sold at a price that reflects the future cash flows discounted to the actual date of sale.

For example, suppose that the Gresham Limited bonds are sold on 1 January 20X6 instead of on their bond date of 1 January 20X5. This *is* an interest payment date, although one year late. The price of the bonds will be the present value of the future cash flows from interest ($7,000 per year for *four* years) and principal ($100,000 received *four* years hence). If the market rate of interest is 8% (Situation C), the price of the bonds will be:

$$\text{Issue price} = [\$100,000 \times (P/F, 8\%, 4)] + [(\$100,000 \times 7\%) \times (P/A, 8\%, 4)]$$
$$= \$96,688$$

This price can be verified by referring to the net bond liability shown in Exhibit 12-2 for 31 December 20X5. The discount will be amortized over the four years remaining until maturity.

More often, the delayed issuance of the bonds does not coincide with an interest date but is *between interest dates.* In this case, the bond issue price cannot be directly calculated as a present value figure, since the present value figure must be at a particular interest date. Instead, the present value of the bond must be calculated as of the two interest dates *around* the issuance date (one before, one after). The difference between these two values is then prorated to the issuance date. Alternatively, some calculators and spreadsheet models allow numbers other than whole numbers to be entered as n (e.g., $n = 14.75$; 14 years and 9 months.)

For example, if the Gresham bonds in Exhibit 12-2 were issued on 1 March 20X5 when the effective interest rate was 8%, the proceeds would be $96,121. This is the $96,007 present value on 1 January 20X5 ($n = 5$) plus 2/12 of the $681 difference between the present value of the bond on 1 January 20X5 and the $96,688 present value on 31 December 20X5 ($n = 4$). *The present value has to be calculated twice and the difference prorated.*

Accrued Interest When bonds are sold between interest dates, interest accrued since the last interest date is also collected in cash. Accrued interest is added to the price because the holder of the bonds on any interest date *receives the full amount of interest* since the last interest date, even if the investor held the bonds for a shorter period.

Example Assume that the Gresham Limited bonds are sold on 1 June 20X5, five months after the bond date but seven months before the next interest date. The holders of the bonds on 31 December 20X5 will receive the full 12-month interest payment of $7,000, despite the fact that they held the bonds for only 7 months. To compensate for the fact that they have earned only 7 months' interest but will receive 12 months' interest, they *pay the issuing company for interest during the period that they did not hold the bonds.*

On 1 June 20X5, Gresham would receive net proceeds of $96,291 for the bond, plus accrued interest of $2,917. Note that:

- The $96,291 proceeds is $96,007 plus 5/12 of the $681 difference between the two surrounding present values.
- Interest of $2,917 is five months' accrued interest ($100,000 × 7% × 5/12).

The bond issuance will be recorded by Gresham Limited as follows:

1 June 20X5—initial issuance of bonds		
Cash ($96,291 + $2,917)	99,208	
Discount on bonds payable[1]	3,709	
Interest expense[2]		2,917
Bonds payable		100,000

[1] $100,000 − $96,291
[2] $100,000 × 7% × 5/12

Initial Discount Amortization After a bond is issued between interest dates, the initial discount amortization recognized will be the amount needed to get the bond to the "end point" in the amortization schedule at the end of the relevant period. For this bond, the issuance proceeds were $96,291 and the 20X5 period ends with an amortized value of $96,688 in the table. Therefore, amortization of $397 is needed ($96,688 − $96,291).

When the company pays the $7,000 interest on 31 December 20X5, the entry to record the interest payment and the discount amortization will be as follows:

31 December 20X5—payment of interest and amortization of discount		
Interest expense	7,397	
Cash		7,000
Discount on bonds payable ($96,291 − $96,688)		397

The initial credit of $2,917 to interest expense when the bonds were issued offsets the actual interest payment of $7,000 plus discount amortization of $397 on 31 December 20X5, leaving a debit balance of $4,480 to flow through to earnings. This represents seven months' expense.

Interest Payable Treatment When the bonds were issued, the accrued interest portion of the proceeds could have been credited to *interest payable* instead of interest expense; the debit for the payment of interest on 31 December would then have to be split between interest expense and interest payable. The entries would appear as follows. They are identical to those shown above, except where highlighted. The end result is identical.

1 June 20X5		
Cash	99,208	
Discount on bonds payable	3,709	
Interest payable		2,917
Bonds payable		100,000
31 December 20X5		
Interest expense	4,480	
Interest payable ($7,000 × 5/12)	2,917	
Cash		7,000
Discount on bonds payable		397

Observations on Bond Amortization

Bond discount or premium is amortized over the life of the bond in order to measure the "true" cost of debt. Remember that the cost of debt is a sensitive issue for many companies. However, bond amortization is a form of interperiod allocation, departing (as all interperiod allocations do) from the underlying cash flow as the basis of financial reporting. The effective-interest method of amortization achieves a constant *rate* of interest expense over the life of the bond, while the straight-line method achieves a constant *amount* of interest expense each year.

This chapter has emphasized the use of the effective-interest method of amortization. The effective-interest method is the method required by accounting standards, because it best reflects the underlying basis of valuation for long-term debt. It also is the method used in other major areas of long-term liability accounting, such as lease accounting (Chapter 17) and pension accounting (Chapter 18).

Accounting measurement is based on the *historical* interest rate and fair value as of the date of issuance. Amortization does not reflect *current* market interest rates or fair values. Therefore, the only inherent advantage of the effective-interest method is that it provides a measure of interest expense (and liability valuation) that reflects the present value process by which the liability was originally valued and recorded.

Debt Issue Costs

Debt issue costs include legal, accounting, underwriting, commission, engraving, printing, registration, and promotion costs. These costs are paid by the issuer and reduce the *net proceeds* from the debt issue. This increases the overall cost, or the effective interest rate, for the issuer.

Accounting standards require that debt issue cost be recorded and amortized on an effective-interest basis, as is the debt discount or premium.[2] Often, the straight-line method is used in practice, due to the relatively small amounts involved. When debt issue costs are amortized, the additional expense is usually added to interest expense. Alternatively, it may be included in "other financing expense." On the SFP, companies must deduct unamortized debt issue cost from total long-term liabilities. The amount acts as an additional discount.

---

[2] The discussion relates to liabilities carried at amortized cost. If liabilities are classified as FVTPL, these costs are expensed immediately.

Upfront Fees

Banks often charge upfront administrative fees to process a loan application. If the bank decides *not* to extend the loan, the bank will report the fee as revenue immediately, and the prospective borrower will charge the fee to expense. If the loan *is* extended, the borrower will treat the fee as part of the loan. In effect, the fee increases the loan's effective interest rate. For example, assume that a firm borrows $100,000 for two years, and agrees to pay 7% interest annually. In addition, the bank charges the firm an administrative fee of $3,520 on the day the loan is granted. The lender will advance the borrower the net proceeds, or $96,480 ($100,000 − $3,520), at the inception of the loan.

The effective interest rate inherent in the cash flow pattern, including the fee, has to be calculated, in order to determine the effective interest rate charged. The payments to the lender are $3,520 at the beginning of the loan, $7,000 at the end of years 1 and 2, and then the principal after two years. That is,

$$\$100,000 = \$3,520 + [\$7,000 \times (P/A, i, 2)] + [\$100,000 \times (P/F, i, 2)], \text{ or}$$
$$\$96,480 = [\$7,000 \times (P/A, i, 2)] + [\$100,000 \times (P/F, i, 2)]$$

Since the cash flow streams are uneven, this calculation must be done with a financial calculator or computer spreadsheet with the IRR function. The discount rate that will equate the cash flow streams to the principal amount of $100,000 is 9%.

Accounting for the transaction is as follows:

At the inception of the loan		
Cash	96,480	
Deferred financing cost	3,520	
Bank loan payable		100,000
At the end of the first year, to record interest expense		
Interest expense[1]	8,683	
Deferred financing cost		1,683
Cash[2]		7,000
[1] $96,480 × 9%		
[2] $100,000 × 7%		
At the end of the second year, to record interest expense		
Interest expense[1]	8,837	
Deferred financing cost (balance)		1,837
Cash		7,000
[1] ($96,480 + $1,683) × 9%, rounded by $2		

Note that interest expense is measured using the effective-interest method. After the second entry, the balance in the deferred financing cost account is zero.

CONCEPT REVIEW

1. For a bond to sell at par, what must be the relationship between the nominal rate and the effective rate of interest? At a discount? At a premium?
2. What are the two methods of amortizing a premium or discount? Which method is required by accounting standards?
3. How should unamortized debt issue costs be reported in the financial statements?

CAPITALIZATION OF BORROWING COSTS

Borrowing costs are normally expensed. However, any such cost that is *directly attributable to the acquisition, construction, or production of a qualifying asset* forms part of the cost of that asset and is capitalized. This is consistent with the general principal that all acquisition costs, including all costs of getting the asset ready to use, are appropriately part of its capital cost. Capitalization is limited, though, by the fair value cap imposed through impairment tests. That is, the maximum asset value is fair value regardless of the component costs.

Qualifying Assets Borrowing costs can be capitalized for non-financial assets such as inventories, intangible assets, machinery, and office or manufacturing facilities. Borrowing costs cannot be capitalized on financial assets, such as investments.

Borrowing costs are to be capitalized if the assets take a substantial time to get ready for intended use or sale. There must be a time delay for acquisition, construction, or production. For example, inventory that is manufactured over a short period of time is not eligible for borrowing cost capitalization. Also, if an asset is ready for its intended use (or resale) when it is acquired, no borrowing costs can be capitalized. However, if an asset is purchased and the shipping time is lengthy, then borrowing costs may be capitalized for the shipping period.

Borrowing costs need not be capitalized on inventory if the inventory is carried at fair value (biological inventories, for example), or if borrowing costs relate to inventories that are *manufactured in large quantities on a regular basis*. For these two cases, companies may choose whether to capitalize or not, depending on their reporting objectives and circumstances.

Borrowing Costs Defined Borrowing costs that can be capitalized are interest, measured using the effective interest method, and any other cost that an entity incurs in connection with the borrowing of funds. This includes expensed debt issuance costs, upfront fees, and foreign currency adjustments to interest expense. **Imputed interest** on equity is not eligible for capitalization.

Generally, the borrowing costs that can be capitalized are those that are specific to the acquisition transaction. In other words, the borrowing cost is capitalizable if it would have been *avoided if the acquisition was not made*. If there is a specific loan in place to finance the acquisition, this decision is straightforward. If a qualifying asset is purchased from *general borrowings* rather than with a specific loan, then the calculations are more complex because it is harder to associate the borrowing with the acquisition. If this is the case, *the average borrowing rate is calculated on the total of general borrowings*, and this rate is applied to the specific expenditures made, for the time period involved.

Funds may be borrowed for an acquisition before they are needed, because of unavoidable timing issues in capital markets. Borrowed money is usually invested until payment for the asset is due. The borrowing costs for this period are capitalizable, but any investment revenue earned during this period is netted with the borrowing cost.

Capitalization begins, therefore, in various circumstances. Any of these events will trigger the commencement of capitalization:

- When money is borrowed;
- A payment is made on an asset; or
- Activities begin that will make the asset ready to use.

Capitalization ends when the asset is put into use, or is ready for its intended purpose. If *substantially all* the activities to get the asset into use are completed, then capitalization should cease. Finally, capitalization stops if the work is not progressing—if work is stopped because of a strike or other delay, capitalization is not permitted for the idle period.

Capitalization Calculations Hercules Limited has purchased a custom piece of machinery overseas, with the following payments made:

1 February deposit	$ 50,000	Manufacturing commences by supplier.
31 March payment	340,000	Equipment is shipped.
31 August final payment		Equipment arrives, is tested and accepted;
	40,000	the equipment is placed in use on this date.
Total cost	$430,000	

The company had no specific loan for this acquisition, but paid for the equipment out of general borrowed money. The company's capital structure and borrowing costs for the year:

	Average Balance	Borrowing Cost
Operating line of credit	$ 500,000	$ 31,000
Term bank loan	2,300,000	119,000
Long-term loan	5,200,000	210,000
Mortgage loan for manufacturing facility	4,800,000	185,000
Equity financing	8,500,000	—

The capitalization rate is based on the general loans, *excluding the mortgage loan specific to the manufacturing facility* and excluding any (imputed) cost of capital for equity financing. The mortgage loan is excluded because it is not *general borrowing*, and its specific purpose is not related to the machinery.

This produces a rate of 4.5% ($31,000 + $119,000 + $210,000)/ ($500,000 + $2,300,000 + $5,200,000). This rate is then used to calculate the borrowing cost that can be capitalized for the months between ordering and putting the asset into use:

Payment	Calculation	Capitalizable Borrowing Costs
1 February deposit	$50,000 × 7/12 × 4.5% (1 February–31 August)	$1,313
31 March payment	$340,000 × 5/12 × 4.5% (31 March–31 August)	6,375
31 August final payment	$40,000 × 0/12 × 4.5% (31 August–31 August)	—
		$7,688

The capitalization period ends when the machinery is put in service, but includes the shipping period. If the interest had previously been expensed, the following adjusting entry would now be made:

Machinery	7,688	
Interest expense		7,688

Depreciation for the machine is based on its total cost, which now includes interest and accordingly is higher than if the interest had not been capitalized. In the end, interest is expensed either way—*all upfront* if no capitalization were appropriate, or *over time*, through depreciation after capitalization. With capitalization, though, the cost of the asset is more completely captured, and the cost of acquisition is better reflected.

DEBT RETIREMENT

Derecognition

When debt is recorded in the accounts, it is *recognized*. When it is removed from the accounts, it is **derecognized** or *extinguished*. The vast majority of financial liabilities, both current and long term, are derecognized because the company *pays the amount of the liability* to the creditor or bond holder at maturity. Sometimes, debt is repaid and derecognized before its maturity, either by arrangement with the debt holder or through open-market transactions.

Derecognition at Maturity

Debt retirement at maturity is straightforward. By the time the debt reaches full maturity, all of the related discount or premium is fully amortized, thereby making the carrying value of the debt equal to its face value. As well, any debt issue cost will be fully amortized.

For example, assume that a company pays the full amount of an outstanding $1,000,000 bond at maturity. The entry to record extinguishment of the debt is:

Bonds payable	1,000,000	
Cash		1,000,000

There are no gains or losses to be recorded. Any costs incurred to retire the bond (such as trustee management fees, clerical costs, or payment fees) will be charged immediately to expense.

Early Extinguishment

Borrowers will sometimes retire debt before maturity. Retirement of debt improves the debt-to-equity ratio, facilitate future debt issuances, or eliminate debt covenants. *Bonds may be purchased on the open market* at any time. In an open-market purchase of bonds, the issuer pays the market price (which is the present value using current market interest rates), as would any investor buying the bonds.

Alternatively, the terms for early retirement might be set out in the original bond indenture. Bonds may be **redeemable**, which means that the *borrower* may pay back the loan using a **call option** that sets a specific price at a specific time prior to maturity. *Investors can force repayment* of a bond if the bond is **retractable**.

If bonds carry a call privilege, the issuer may retire the debt by paying the call price, or redemption price, during a specified period. Typically, the **call price** exceeds face value by a certain percentage (e.g., 5%), which may decline each year of the bond term. If the call premium were 5%, a $100,000 bond would be redeemed for a payment of $105,000, plus accrued interest, if any.

Fair Value and the Gain or Loss A major factor in retiring bonds before maturity is the change in fair market value that is caused when interest rates change. Open market retirement prices reflect this fair value. When interest rates increase, the fair value of an existing liability will decline, because the yield rate has increased. The fair value will then rest below book value. However, the only way to *record* this change in value is to repay the bond.

Examine the following cases, relating to a $500,000, 5% bond, originally sold to yield 6%, that pays interest semi-annually and has 18 periods left to maturity:

	Case 1 (yield rate now 7%)	Case 2 (yield rate now 4.5%)
Bond carrying value—amortized cost	$465,616	$465,616
Bond fair value—present value based on market interest rates	$434,052 (7% yield)	$518,335 (4.5% yield)
Retirement price	Fair value	Fair value
Gain or loss recorded	Gain of $31,564	Loss of $52,719

If market interest rates *increase* (causing bond prices to *fall*), firms could retire existing bonds by buying them on the open market, triggering a gain and immediate higher earnings. For example, in case 1, market interest rates are now 7%, and this bond, with a book value of $465,616, can be retired on the open market for $434,052. A gain of $31,564 is recorded. Since a replacement bond will have the same fair value as the old bond, this *economic decision* is value-neutral. However, it has distinct *accounting implications*.

If interest rates *drop* (causing bond prices to *rise*), firms could retire existing bonds at a loss, and earnings will fall in the retirement period. For example, in case 2, market interest rates are now 4.5%, and a bond with a book value of $465,616 can be retired on the open market for $518,335. A loss of $52,719 is recorded.

In both cases, the retirement decision results in recording a gain or loss that *reflects the changed fair value of the bond*. Of course, *whether the retirement happens or not, the fair value of the bond has still changed*, which has a natural impact on the value of the firm as a whole.

Some companies will enter into retirement transactions to trigger the earnings effect. Some might wish a boost to earnings in the current year (case 1) while others will accept a loss in one year (case 2). These companies may have various incentive contracts that provide motives for such activities. In other cases, bonds are redeemed simply to avoid *restrictive covenants*.

Now, consider the impact of a call provision. A call provision at the company's option protects the company from a change in fair value caused by a decline in interest rates. If the $500,000 bond above specified that the company could call the bond for 102% of par, the highest value to be paid out would be $510,000. This fair value has an implicit yield rate of approximately 4.7% when $n = 18$, and caps the fair value of the liability at this level. If market rates fell below 4.7%, the company would have an economic, if not an accounting, incentive to retire. The real frustration is that retirement at $510,000 would still trigger an accounting loss; this is the result when the accounting system records amortized cost rather than fair value.

Recording Early Debt Retirement Accounting for debt retirement prior to maturity involves:

- Updating interest expense to the retirement date, through recording interest payable, discount or premium amortization, and related debt issue costs;
- Removing the liability accounts, including the appropriate portion of the unamortized premium or discount and bond issue costs;
- Recording the transfer of cash, other resources, or the issuance of new debt securities; and
- Recording a gain or loss.

Gains or losses on bond retirements may be classified either as *ordinary* gains and losses or as *unusual* items, depending on their frequency and the circumstances surrounding the transaction. Gains and losses are *not deferred and amortized* over the term of any "replacement" debt.

As a basis for an example, Exhibit 12-4 repeats a portion of the amortization table for the Gresham bonds from Exhibit 12-1. Assume that interest rates have increased since the bonds were issued, and assume that on 1 March 20X6, Gresham purchases 20% ($20,000 face value) of the bonds on the open market at 90. The price decline reflects increased market interest rates. Gresham has undertaken this transaction because the company has idle funds and wishes to reduce its debt-to-equity ratio.

The $2,667 gain on bond retirement is the difference between the net book value of the bond and the cash paid on retirement. Brokerage fees and other costs of retiring the bonds also decrease the gain or increase the loss.

Extinguishment does not affect the accounting for the remaining 80% of the bond issue; 80% of the values in the amortization table would be used for the remaining bond term.

EXHIBIT 12-4

OPEN-MARKET EXTINGUISHMENT
Gresham Limited Bonds

Data:

Issue date: 1 January 20X5
Stated (nominal) interest rate: 7% per annum
Interest payment date: 31 December

Maturity date: 31 December 20X9
Bond repurchase date: 1 March 20X6
Bond face value extinguished: $20,000

Total face value: $100,000
Bond date: 1 January 20X5
Yield rate at issuance: 6% per annum

Bond repurchase price: 90

Partial Amortization Table

Date	Interest Payment @ 7%	Interest Expense @ 6%	Premium Amortization	Unamortized Premium	Net Bond Liability
1 Jan. 20X5				$4,213	$104,213
31 Dec. 20X5	$7,000	$6,253	$747	3,466	103,466
31 Dec. 20X6	7,000	6,208	792	2,674	102,674

Entries:

1 March 20X6—update interest and premium amortization on portion retired

Interest expense	207[1]	
Premium on bonds payable	26	
Interest payable		233[2]

1 March 20X6—record purchase of bonds; eliminate relevant accounts and recognize gain

Bonds payable	20,000	
Premium on bonds payable	667[3]	
Interest payable	233	
Cash		18,233[4]
Gain on bond redemption		2,667

Calculations

Jan-Feb 20X6

[1] 6% × $103,466 × 2/12 × 20% of the bond issue being redeemed
[2] $20,000 bonds being redeemed × 7% × 2/12
[3] ($3,466 unamortized bond premium × 20% being redeemed)
   − $26 amortized in previous entry
[4] ($20,000 being redeemed × 90% purchase price) + $233 interest payable

---

Defeasance

A transaction called a **defeasance** may be used to engineer derecognition of a bond liability without formally repaying it; repayment is often not appealing to the investor. To set the stage for a defeasance, the bond indenture will contain a provision that permits the corporation that issued the bonds to transfer investments into an irrevocable, trusteed fund. The trustee is then responsible for interest and principal payments on the debt, using money generated by the investments. If and when such a trust is set up and fully funded, accounting standards allow the liability to be derecognized. The bonds still exist, but the trust assumes all responsibility for them, and the issuer has no further liability. Furthermore, the *investor has consented* to the transaction as part of the original bond indenture. The entry to record a defeasance is a debit to the liability account and credit to cash or investments, with a gain or loss recorded for any difference in amounts.

Example   Assume that a bond with a par value of $100,000 and remaining unamortized premium of $6,000 is *defeased* according to the terms of the bond indenture for $92,600. The $92,600 is the present value of the bond payments, discounted at market rates, or the investment required in interest-bearing securities that will yield interest and principal amounts to cover the required future cash flows for the bond.

Note that market yields must have increased to the extent that investments of $92,600 generate sufficient cash to service the bond interest and principal over time. The following entry would be made:

Bonds payable (par value)	100,000	
Premium on bonds payable (remaining balance)	6,000	
Cash		92,600
Gain on bond defeasance		13,400

Taking the liability off the books in essence nets the liability with the investments segregated for liability repayment. Netting is not allowed unless very stringent criteria are met, and an important criterion for netting is that the *borrower has a legal release from the creditor.* The agreement in the bond indenture establishes this release.

In-substance Defeasance   In-substance defeasance establishes a trust for bond interest and principal repayment *even though the original bond indenture is silent on the possibility.* In essence, it establishes the trust without creditor permission or perhaps even creditor knowledge of the arrangement. In the past, an in-substance extinguishment might be recorded, derecognizing the bonds and setting up a gain or loss, if certain criteria were met. Under current accounting standards, this is no longer allowed because there is no legal release provided by the creditor. Accordingly, the company would record a separate investment account if funds were transferred to the trustee, and then would continue to report the liability and the separate investment.

The Concern with In-substance Defeasance   Standard-setters had many reasons to be concerned about in-substance defeasance transactions recorded as extinguishments.

Companies have a tendency to set up an in-substance defeasance if interest rates increase. The increase in interest rates reduces the amount of investment needed to fully service the related debts, (i.e., reduce the fair value of the debt). This defeasance transaction results in a gain for the company. The transaction might be used primarily to manipulate earnings.

Another concern of standard-setters is that the borrowing company would have debt legally outstanding that is not reported on the SFP. This situation does not appeal to the basic *representational faithfulness* of financial reporting. Finally, standard-setters were concerned that something might go awry with the trust or the debt to make the in-substance defeasance economically or legally unsuccessful. For example, if the debt were subject to financial statement covenants, and the covenants were breached, then the debt might become due immediately. Alternatively, assets in the fund may lose value unexpectedly. If this happened, the investments in the trusteed fund would not be sufficient to make all required payments. For all these reasons, *debt may not be recorded as extinguished through an in-substance defeasance.*

Substitution or Modification of Debt

A company may go to an existing lender, and essentially *repay a loan and reborrow in one transaction,* replacing an existing loan prior to its due date. As for an early retirement, the motive may be a desire to borrow at a different interest rate, record movement in fair value of the existing obligation, or to release a restrictive covenant.

If the exchange results in significantly different terms, the company must record an extinguishment (loan retired at a gain or loss), and a new loan, with the two transactions accounted for independently. This will be the case as long as the present value of the new loan arrangement is at least 10% different than the present value of the old loan arrangement, including fees and transaction costs. The presence of a 10% difference implies that there has been a change in the *substance* of the agreement.

On the other hand, if there is less than a 10% difference in present value, no gain or loss on retirement is recorded. Any additional fees from such a substitution or modification may be amortized over the remaining term of the modified liability.

CONCEPT REVIEW

1. Under what circumstances is the change in the fair value of a bond liability recorded in the financial statements?

2. What is a retractable bond?

3. How is a gain or loss on retirement of bonds calculated?

4. What are the accounting implications of a defeasance transaction? An in-substance defeasance?

FOREIGN EXCHANGE ISSUES

Many Canadian companies borrow from foreign lenders. The most common foreign lender to Canadian companies is the United States, both through U.S. banks and other financial institutions and, for a few large public companies, through the bond markets. Corporations also borrow in other currencies, such as euros, Japanese yen, etc.

The most obvious point about these loans is that the borrowing company has exchange risk, caused by exchange fluctuations. For example, if a company borrows US$100,000 when the exchange rate for US$1.00 is Cdn$1.05, the company will receive Cdn$105,000. If the exchange rate changes to US$1.00 = Cdn$1.12 by the time that the debt must be repaid, the company will have to pay Cdn$112,000 to buy US$100,000 dollars for debt principal repayment, and thus have to repay more than it borrowed. This $7,000 difference ($105,000 less $112,000) is called an *exchange loss*, and it is equal to the change in the exchange rates multiplied by the principal: ($1.05 − $1.12) × US$100,000.

Note that exchange rates can be expressed in U.S. dollar equivalencies, as shown above, where US$1.00 = Cdn$1.05, or can be described as Canadian dollar equivalencies, Cdn$1.00 = US$0.9524 (that is, $1.00 ÷ $1.05). There are also differences between buying and selling exchange rates, as quoted by exchange brokers or banks; the brokers make an element of profit on the spread between the buying and selling rates.

Hedging   Companies may take a number of actions to reduce their risk of losses (and gains) from changes in exchange rates. **Hedges** reduce risk and typically involve arranging equal and offsetting cash flows in the desired currency. Hedges are a protective measure. Hedging will be explored in Chapter 14.

ACCOUNTING FOR FOREIGN CURRENCY–DENOMINATED DEBT

The basic principle underlying valuation of foreign currency monetary liabilities is that they should be reported on the SFP in the equivalent amount of reporting currency (normally, Canadian dollars for Canadian companies) at the **spot rate** on the *reporting date*. The loan principal is originally translated into Canadian dollars on the day it is borrowed at the current, or spot, exchange rate. At every subsequent reporting date, the loan is *remeasured* at the spot rate. If exchange rates have changed, an exchange gain or loss will result. This gain or loss is *unrealized. The exchange gain or loss is included in earnings in the year in which it arises.*

Exhibit 12-5 illustrates accounting for a long-term loan, whose Canadian dollar equivalent is $545,000 when borrowed and $565,000 when retired. When the Canadian dollar equivalent goes up during the life of the bond, a loss is recorded. When the Canadian dollar equivalent goes down, a gain is recorded.

The effect of an exchange fluctuation appears in earnings in the year of the change in rates. This makes it easier for financial statement users to determine the impact of an exchange rate fluctuation on the company's financial position. Of course, it also makes earnings fluctuate if exchange rates are volatile. Note the volatility year-by-year in Exhibit 12-5 for the exchange gain or loss. Sizeable gains are followed by sizeable losses.

Interest Expense Annual interest, also denominated in the foreign currency, is accrued using the exchange rate in effect during the period—the *average exchange rate.* When it is paid, cash outflows are measured at the exchange rate in effect on that day. The difference between the expense and the cash paid is also an exchange gain or loss.

For example, if the US$500,000 loan had an interest rate of 7%, and exchange rates were US$1.00 = Cdn$1.08 on average over the first year, the interest expense accrual would be recorded as follows:

Interest expense ($500,000 × 7% × $1.08)	37,800	
Interest payable		37,800

At year-end, the exchange rate is $1.10, and the interest is paid:

Interest payable ($500,000 × 7% × $1.10)	37,800	
Exchange loss	700	
Cash		38,500

If the interest is not due at year-end, the interest payable account is adjusted to the year-end spot rate, and again an exchange gain or loss is recognized.

CONCEPT REVIEW

1. What is the purpose of hedging?

2. A Canadian company borrows US$1,000,000 when the exchange rate is Cdn$1.10. The exchange rate is $1.08 at the end of the fiscal year. How much long-term debt is reported on the statement of financial position? How much is the exchange gain or loss?

3. A loan requires that US$10,000 be paid in interest annually, at the end of each fiscal year. The average exchange rate is US$1 = Cdn$1.15, and the year end rate is US$1 = Cdn$1.10. How much interest expense and exchange gain is recorded?

EXHIBIT 12-5

EXCHANGE GAINS AND LOSSES ON LONG-TERM DEBT

Data:

Four-year term loan, US$500,000
Funds borrowed 1 January 20X6; due 31 December 20X9
Exchange rates:

1 January 20X6	US$1 = Cdn$1.09
31 December 20X6	US$1 = Cdn$1.10
31 December 20X7	US$1 = Cdn$1.12
31 December 20X8	US$1 = Cdn$1.08
31 December 20X9	US$1 = Cdn$1.13

Entries:

Note: entries are for principal only

1 January 20X6—to record receipt of loan proceeds		
Cash ($500,000 × $1.09)	545,000	
Long-term debt		545,000
31 December 20X6—to record adjustment to spot rate		
Exchange loss	5,000	
Long-term debt [$500,000 × ($1.09 − $1.10)]		5,000
31 December 20X7—to record adjustment to spot rate		
Exchange loss	10,000	
Long-term debt [$500,000 × ($1.10 − $1.12)]		10,000
31 December 20X8—to record adjustment to spot rate		
Long-term debt [$500,000 × ($1.12 − $1.08)]	20,000	
Exchange gain		20,000
31 December 20X9—to record adjustment to spot rate		
Exchange loss	25,000	
Long-term debt [$500,000 × ($1.08 − $1.13)]		25,000
31 December 20X9—to repay loan		
Long-term debt ($500,000 × $1.13)	565,000	
Cash		565,000

Summary:

Canadian dollar cash borrowed	$545,000
Canadian dollar cash repaid	565,000
Exchange loss over the life of the loan	$ 20,000

Accounting recognition of loss:

20X6	$ 5,000 dr.
20X7	10,000 dr.
20X8	20,000 cr.
20X9	25,000 dr.
Total	$20,000 dr.

STATEMENT OF CASH FLOW

The statement of cash flow will reflect cash paid and cash received. The presence of multiple accounts related to a particular liability can complicate analysis in the area. For example, consider the accounts of Hilmon Limited:

	20X5	20X4
Bonds payable, 8%	$5,000,000	0
Discount on bonds payable	246,000	0
Interest payable	125,000	$ 25,000
Bonds payable, 7 1/2%	0	2,000,000
Discount on bonds payable	0	18,000

During the year, the 8% bonds were issued for $4,750,000. The 7 1/2% bonds were retired for 102. Interest expense was $252,000, and a loss was reported on retiring the 7 1/2% bond. Discount amortization was recorded during the period—$4,000 on the discount for the 8% bond and $2,000 on the discount for the 7 1/2% bond before retirement.

These transactions would appear in the statement of cash flow as follows:

1. In the financing section, an inflow of cash from issuing the 8% bond, $4,750,000, is reported. The proceeds are reported at their actual cash amount, and par value is not separately reported.

2. In the financing section, an outflow of cash from retiring the 7 1/2% bond, $2,040,000 ($2,000,000 × 102%), is reported. Again, the par value of the bond is irrelevant, as is the carrying value. It is the cash flow that is important. It is *not acceptable* to net an issuance with a disposal, or lump several issuances and disposals together. Transactions are to be shown separately.

3. In the operating activities section, reported using the indirect method, the loss on the bond retirement must be added back to earnings. This loss is $56,000. (The carrying value of the bond on the day of retirement was $1,984,000, including the discount but after this year's $2,000 discount amortization. The cost of bond retirement was $2,040,000; the difference is the $56,000 loss.)

4. In the operating activities section, interest expense of $252,000 is added back.

5. In the SCF, interest paid can be classified as an operating activity or a financing activity. The cash paid for interest is $146,000 (the expense, $252,000 less $6,000 of discount amortization and also reduced for the increase in interest payable of $100,000).

REPORTING LIABILITIES

Most companies segregate their liabilities between current and long-term. A **current liability** is one that is due or payable *within the next operating cycle or the next fiscal year, whichever period is longer.* For many companies, the effective guiding time period is one year. A **long-term liability** has a due date past this time window. In North America, current liabilities normally are listed in descending order based on the strength of the creditors' claims. In other countries, this may be reversed. Either approach is acceptable. Remember as well that not all companies segregate their liabilities between current and long-term. For example, financial institutions normally do not segregate on the basis of maturity date.

Disclosures for Provisions and Contingencies

Provisions must be shown in a separate category from payables and accruals, and the nature of each recorded liability explained. In fact, extensive disclosure for each class of obligations is required in order to improve transparency in an area that is dominated by judgement. In particular, companies must disclose a reconciliation, or *a continuity schedule* (opening balance to closing balance), that explains the movement in each *class* of provisions. Unrecorded amounts, that is, contingencies, must be described completely, along with a discussion of their nature, and an estimate of their financial effect, if practicable.

Disclosures for Long-Term Liabilities

Most liabilities are financial instruments, and accordingly information must be included to describe *credit risk, liquidity risk,* and *market risk,* as appropriate. Objectives, policies, and processes for managing risk and managing capital must be disclosed. Information must be disclosed to allow assessment of the significance of liabilities for the company's financial position and performance. Such disclosure is extensive, and includes both qualitative and quantitative elements. In addition, companies must disclose accounting policies used for liabilities, the *fair value* of each class of financial liability, and the method used (discounted cash flow, most likely) to establish fair value.

Required disclosure for long-term debt also includes information primarily related to the terms of the debt contract, security, and future cash flows. Some of the highlights:

- The title of the issue, interest rate, interest expense on long-term debt in total, maturity date, amount outstanding, assets pledged as collateral, sinking fund, if any, and redemption or conversion privileges;
- The aggregate amount of payments required in the next five years to meet sinking fund or retirement provisions;
- If the debt is denominated in a foreign currency, then the currency in which the debt is to be repaid;
- Secured liabilities must be shown separately, and the fact that they are secured must be disclosed; and
- Details of any defaults of the company in principal, interest, sinking fund, or redemption provisions, carrying value of loans payable in default, and any remedy of the default that was undertaken by the financial statement completion date.

Reporting Example Exhibit 12-6 includes *selected* disclosures related to liabilities for ThyssenKrupp AG. The company reports accounting policy information relating to areas such as capitalization of borrowing costs, accounting for provisions, and financial liabilities.

The company has approximately €1.5 billion in long-term bonds outstanding, down from approximately €2 billion the year before. Information regarding interest rates, due dates, nominal (par) value, and fair value is provided for each bond issue. Most bonds were issued close to par, since the carrying values are close to the nominal values. The company has substantial unused credit facilities, which are also disclosed.

ThyssenKrupp AG also includes extensive information regarding its capital management strategy and its risk profile in relation to financial instruments. This information is not repeated here but can be accessed in the financial statements on the company web site.

EXHIBIT 12-6

SELECTED NOTE DISCLOSURE, 30 SEPTEMBER 2008

ThyssenKrupp AG

Summary of Significant Accounting Policies

Property, Plant and Equipment

Borrowing costs directly attributable to the production of assets that necessarily take a substantial period of time to get ready for their intended use, are added to the cost of those assets, until such time as the assets are substantially ready for their intended use.

Financial Liabilities

Financial liabilities are liabilities that must be settled in cash or other financial assets. These especially include trade accounts payable, derivative financial liabilities and components of financial debt, mainly bonds and other securitized liabilities, liabilities to financial institutions and finance lease liabilities. Financial liabilities are initially carried at fair value. This includes any transaction costs directly attributable to the acquisition of financial liabilities, which are not carried at fair value through profit or loss in future periods.

Provisions

Provisions are recognized when the Group has a present obligation as a result of a past event which will result in a probable outflow of economic benefits that can be reasonably estimated. The amount recognized represents best estimate of the settlement amount of the present obligation as of the reporting date. Expected reimbursements of third parties are not offset but recorded as a separate asset if it is virtually certain that the reimbursements will be received. Where the effect of the time value of money is material, provisions are discounted using a risk adjusted market rate.

A provision for warranties is recognized when the underlying products or services are sold. The provision is based on historical warranty data and a weighting of all possible outcomes against their associated probabilities.

Provisions for restructuring costs are recognized when the Group has a detailed formal plan for the restructuring and has notified the affected parties.

A provision for onerous contracts is recognized when the expected benefits to be derived by the Group from a contract are lower than the unavoidable cost of meeting its obligations under the contract.

Financial Debt

CARRYING AMOUNTS in million €	Sept. 30, 2007	Sept. 30, 2008
Bonds	€1,996	€1,497
Notes payable	50	479
Liabilities to financial institutions	604	968
Acceptance payables	2	0
Finance lease liabilities	136	98
Other loans	25	26
Non-current financial debt	**€2,813**	**€3,068**

Current financial debt includes financial debt with a remaining term up to one year, while the non-current financial debt has a remaining term of more than one year.

continued on next page

EXHIBIT 12-6 *(cont'd)*

BONDS, NOTES PAYABLE

	Carrying Amount in Million € Sept. 30, 2007	Carrying Amount in Million € Sept. 30, 2008	Notional Amount in Million € Sept. 30, 2008	Interest Rate in %	Fair Value in Million € Sept. 30, 2008	Maturity Date
ThyssenKrupp Finance Nederland B.V. Bond (€500 million) 2002/2009	€ 499	€ 500	€ 500	7.000	€ 502	03/19/2009
ThyssenKrupp AG Bond (€750 million) 2004/2011	748	748	750	5.000	743	03/29/2011
ThyssenKrupp AG Bond (€750 million) 2005/2015	749	749	750	4.375	678	03/18/2015
ThyssenKrupp AG note loan (€100 million) 2001/2007	100	—	—	5.450	—	10/25/2007
ThyssenKrupp AG note loan (€50 million) 2004/2009	50	50	50	4.500	51	01/19/2009
ThyssenKrupp AG note loan (€100 million) 2008/2013	—	100	100	5.150	98	04/15/2013
ThyssenKrupp AG note loan (€150 million) 2008/2013	—	149	150	5.300	148	04/25/2013
ThyssenKrupp AG note loan (€150 million) 2008/2014	—	150	150	5.375	147	05/21/2014
ThyssenKrupp AG note loan (€80 million) 2008/2016	—	80	80	5.710	78	09/15/2016
Total	**€2,146**	**€2,526**	**€2,530**		**€2,445**	

ThyssenKrupp AG has assumed the unconditional and irrevocable guarantee for the payments pursuant to the terms and conditions of the bond of ThyssenKrupp Finance Nederland B.V. In April 2008, ThyssenKrupp AG issued two note loans with a 5-year-maturity each and a volume of €250 million in total. Furthermore in May 2008, a €150 million note loan with a 6-year-maturity and in September 2008, an additional €80 million note loan with an 8-year-maturity were issued.

All bonds and note loans are interest only with principle due at maturity.

Current financial debt includes financial debt with a remaining term up to one year, while the non-current financial debt has a remaining term of more than one year.

As of September 30, 2008, ThyssenKrupp has available a €2.5 billion syndicated joint credit multi-currency-facility agreement. The agreement was fixed in July 2005 and has a term until July 10, 2014. The facility agreement was not utilized as of the reporting date.

Another component of financial liabilities are revolving credit agreements with banking institutions whereby ThyssenKrupp AG, ThyssenKrupp Finance USA, Inc. or ThyssenKrupp Finance Nederland B.V. can borrow in Euros, U.S. dollars, or in British Pounds Sterling up to approximately €2.2 million. Of these facilities, 76% have a remaining term of more than 5 years and 24% a remaining term of up to 5 years. As of September 30, 2008, there were no cash loans outstanding.

In total the Group has available unused, committed credit lines amounting to €4.6 billion.

Maturity of financial debt is as follows:

million € (for fiscal year)	Total Financial Debt	Thereof: Liabilities to Financial Institutions
2008/2009	€1,348	€ 711
2009/2010	168	112
2010/2011	823	52
2011/2012	96	81
2012/2013	581	325
thereafter	1,400	398
Total	**€4,416**	**€1,679**

Source: Reproduced with permission of ThyssenKrupp AG.

Canadian standards for private enterprise contain no comprehensive standards governing accounting policy for non-financial liabilities. Such liabilities are recognized if they meet the liability definition, are measurable, and if future sacrifices are probable. The outcome of applying this approach is largely consistent with IFRS; for example, warranty liabilities are recorded, expected losses on contracts are recorded when fair values decline, etc. There are some differences where IFRS have specific guidance, for example, with respect to measuring the amount to record (expected value versus most likely outcome) and choice of discount rate, if needed.

The term "provision" is not used under ASPE; IFRS use this term for liabilities that are uncertain as to timing or amount. Furthermore, constructive liabilities are not recorded under ASPE. Accordingly, in areas such as asset retirement obligations, only legal liabilities are recognized.

Under ASPE, *contingent liabilities* are defined as those that will result in the outflow of resources only *if* another event happens. Accounting treatment for contingencies follows the following grid:

Measurability: Probability:	Measurable	Not Measurable
Likely	Record (plus disclose if amount recorded is uncertain)	Disclose in the notes
Undeterminable	Disclose in the notes	Disclose in the notes
Not Likely	Do not record or disclose unless material	Do not record or disclose unless material

Under ASPE, a *contingent liability is either recorded or disclosed*; under IFRS, the liability is termed a contingency only if it is *disclosed and not recorded*. It is a *provision* if it is recorded. This is a different use of the word *contingency*.

Under both sets of standards, the general framework is the same—some situations result in only a disclosure note, and other situations in a recorded liability, depending on the likelihood and measurability of the outflow of economic resources. In addition, though, the specifics of the criteria established under IFRS and ASPE may dictate somewhat different results.

There are no standards for customer loyalty points under ASPE. The IFRS approach explained in this chapter may be adopted.

ASPE and IFRS for long-term liabilities are similar. There are some differences in terminology and approach, but the impact of these differences is not significant in the bigger picture. Much of the similarity stems from the common financial instruments rules, which were developed as a joint project between the IASB, Canada, and the United States. Since these standards govern the accounting model for a significant section of the financial statements, the similarity of standards between these major jurisdictions provides a fair bit of common ground.

Under ASPE, use of the effective interest method is not required. Straight-line amortization may be used.

If a long-term loan is coming due but is being renegotiated, IFRS requires that a legally-enforceable agreement be in place *by the end of the fiscal year (the reporting date)* if the loan is to be classified as long-term. Under ASPE, classification of such a loan as long-term would be permitted if renegotiation resulted in agreement by the *date the financial statements are released.*

Capitalization of borrowing costs *is not required* for private enterprises as it is under IFRS. Companies may choose to capitalize or not, although imputed interest may *not* be capitalized. If companies follow a policy of capitalization, ASPE includes no guidelines governing the kinds of borrowing costs to be capitalized, commencement and completion dates, or determining the costs of general borrowing pools. Companies must disclose policy in the area and the extent of interest capitalized.

Finally, disclosure is less onerous in all areas under ASPE as compared to IFRS. For example, no reconciliations or continuity schedules are required.

RELEVANT STANDARDS

IASB:
- *IAS* 1, Presentation of Financial Statements
- *IAS* 21, The Effects of Changes in Foreign Exchange Rates
- *IAS* 23, Borrowing Costs
- *IAS* 37, Provisions, Contingent Liabilities and Contingent Assets
- *IAS* 32, Financial Instruments: Disclosure and Presentation
- *IAS* 39, Financial Instruments: Recognition and Measurement

CICA Handbook, Part II:
- Section 1651, Foreign Currency Translation
- Section 3210, Long-Term Debt
- Section 3280, Contractual Obligations
- Section 3290, Contingencies
- Section 3856, Financial Instruments
- Acg-14, Disclosure of Guarantees

SUMMARY OF KEY POINTS

1. Liabilities are present obligations of a company resulting from past events, the settlement of which is expected to result in the outflow of economic benefits. Liabilities may be non-financial or financial, and may result from legal obligations or constructive obligations.

2. Non-financial liabilities include provisions, which are liabilities of uncertain timing or amount. Provisions are recorded if there is a present obligation as a result of a past event, the outflow of resources is probable, and an estimate can be made. If the liability is not probable or is not measurable, then it is not recorded and is only disclosed.

3. Provisions are recorded at the best estimate, discounted if needed, and are re-estimated each reporting period. Examples include lawsuits, onerous contracts, restructuring, warranties, restoration and environmental obligations, coupons, loyalty programs, repairs and maintenance, and self-insurance. Best estimate may be the expected value (large populations) or the most likely outcome informed by expected value and cumulative probability (small populations).

4. Financial liabilities are usually classified as other financial liabilities, and carried at amortized cost. Other financial liabilities are classified as FVTPL and carried at fair value.

5. The recorded value at date of issuance for long-term debt is the present value of all future cash flows discounted at the current market rate for debt securities of equivalent risk. The net book value of long-term debt at a reporting date is the present value of all remaining cash payments required, discounted at the market rate at issuance.

6. Using the effective-interest method, interest expense is the product of the market rate at issuance and the balance in the liability at the beginning of the period. Interest is accrued with the passage of time.

7. Bonds are long-term debt instruments that specify the face value paid at maturity and the stated interest rate payable according to a fixed schedule.

8. The price of a bond at issuance is the present value of all future cash flows discounted at the current market rate of interest for bonds of similar risk. Bonds are sold at a premium if the stated rate exceeds the market rate and at a discount if the stated rate is less than the market rate. The price of a bond issued between interest dates is based on a pro-rata calculation of present values at interest dates.

9. Accrued interest is paid by the investor when a bond is issued between interest dates; the investor is then entitled to a full interest payment on the next interest payment date. The issuer records accrued interest received as a credit to interest expense or payable; the choice affects appropriate recognition on the interest payment date.

10. Debt issue costs and upfront fees are sometimes involved in the issuance of debt. Such fees are a cost of borrowing, and are charged to interest expense over the life of the loan. This increases the effective interest cost of the loan.

11. Borrowing costs can be capitalized on eligible non-financial assets if there are costs relating to loans for the period of time to acquire, construct, or produce such an asset. Costs of specific loans or general borrowing can be capitalized, subject to a fair value cap.

12. Bonds retired at maturity are recorded by reducing the liability and the asset given in repayment. No gain or loss arises. Bonds retired before maturity, through call, redemption, or open market purchase, typically involve recognition of a gain or loss as the difference between the book value of the debt (including all related accounts, such as unamortized premium or discount, and upfront fees) and the consideration paid.

13. A defeasance is an arrangement whereby the debtor irrevocably places investments in a trust fund for the sole purpose of using those resources to pay interest and principal on specified debt. The creditor agrees to this and legal release is given.

14. If a bond is subject to a substitution or modification of terms, an extinguishment (with a gain or loss) must be recognized and a new loan recorded if the present value of the new arrangement is 10% different from the old arrangement.

15. Many long-term loans are denominated in a foreign currency, which causes exchange gains or losses when exchange rates fluctuate. Exchange gains and losses are reported in earnings.

16. Disclosures for long-term debt includes significant disclosure related to accounting policy, nature and extent of risks, as well as fair value. Other disclosure relates to the terms of debt contracts, including the major conditions and cash flows agreed to in the loan contract.

KEY TERMS

bond date, 700
bond indenture, 731
breakage, 692
call option, 711
call price, 711
constructive obligation, 684
contingency, 685
current liability, 718
defeasance, 713
derecognition, 711
effective interest rate, 696
executory contracts, 690
expected value, 685
face value, 699
financial liability, 684
hedges, 715
incremental borrowing rate (IBR), 696

imputed interest, 709
interest payment dates, 700
legal obligation, 684
long-term liability, 718
long-term loans, 729
maturity date, 700
most likely outcome, 685
nominal interest rate, 700
non-financial liability, 685
obligating event, 684
onerous contract, 690
provision, 685
redeemable, 711
retractable, 711
spot rate, 715
virtual certainty, 692
yield, 696

REVIEW PROBLEM

On 1 August 20X6, Pismo Corporation, a calendar-year corporation that records adjusting entries only once per year, issued bonds with the following characteristics:

a. $50,000 total face value

b. 12% nominal rate

c. 16% yield rate

d. Interest dates are 1 February, 1 May, 1 August, and 1 November

e. Bond date is 31 October 20X5

f. Maturity date is 1 November 20X10

Required:

1. Provide all entries required for the bond issue through 1 February 20X7 using the effective-interest method.

2. On 1 June 20X8, Pismo retired $20,000 of bonds at 98 through an open market purchase. Provide the entries to update the bond accounts in 20X8 (entries have been completed through 1 May 20X8) for this portion of the bond and to retire the bonds.

3. Provide the entries required on 1 August 20X8.

REVIEW PROBLEM—SOLUTION

1. *1 August 20X6—issue bonds*

Cash	43,917[1]	
Discount on bonds payable ($50,000 − $43,917)	6,083	
Bonds payable		50,000

[1] Four and one-quarter years, or 17 quarters, remain in the bond term: $43,917 = [\$50,000 \times (P/F, 4\%, 17)] + [(\$50,000 \times 3\%) \times (P/A, 4\%, 17)]$

1 November 20X6—interest payment date

Interest expense	1,757[1]	
Discount on bonds payable		257
Cash		1,500[2]

[1] $\$1,757 = \$43,917 \times 4\%$
[2] $\$1,500 = \$50,000 \times 3\%$

31 December 20X6—adjusting entry

Interest expense	1,178[1]	
Discount on bonds payable		178
Interest payable		1,000[2]

[1] $\$1,178 = (\$43,917 + \$257) \times 4\% \times (2/3 \text{ of quarter})$
[2] $\$1,000 = \$1,500 \times 2/3$

1 February 20X7—interest payment date

Interest expense	589[1]	
Interest payable	1,000	
Discount on bonds payable		89
Cash		1,500

[1] $\$589 = (\$43,917 + \$257) \times 4\% \times (1/3 \text{ of quarter})$

2. On 1 May 20X8, the remaining term of the bonds is 2 1/2 years, or 10 quarters, and the $20,000 of bonds to be retired have the following book value:

$$\$18,378 = [\$20,000 \times (P/F, 4\%, 10)] + [(\$20,000 \times 3\%) \times (P/A, 4\%, 10)]$$

On 1 May 20X8, the remaining discount on the portion of bonds to be retired is therefore $1,622 ($20,000 − $18,378).

1 June 20X8—update relevant bond accounts before retirement

Interest expense	245[1]	
Discount on bonds payable		45
~~Cash~~ *Interest payable*		200[2]

Interest payable 200

1 June 20X8—remove relevant bond accounts

→ | | | |
|---|---|---|
| Bonds payable | 20,000 | |
| Loss, bond extinguishment | 1,177 | |
| Discount on bonds payable | | 1,577[3] |
| Cash (.98 × $20,000) *+200* | | 19,600 |

[1] $\$245 = \$18,378 \times 4\% \times 1/3$ (one month of the three-month period) (or $16\% \times 1/12$)
[2] $\$200 = \$20,000 \times 3\% \times 1/3$ (or $12\% \times 1/12$)
[3] $\$1,577 = \$1,622 - \$45$

3. On 1 May 20X8, the remaining term of the bonds is 2 1/2 years, or 10 quarters, and the remaining $30,000 of bonds have the following book value:

$27,567 = $30,000 (P/F, 4%, 10) + [($30,000 × 3%) × (P/A, 4%,10)]

On 1 May 20X8, the remaining discount is therefore $2,433 (i.e., $30,000 − $27,567).

1 August 20X8—interest payment date

Interest expense	1,103[1]	
Discount on bonds payable		203
Cash		900[2]

[1] $1,103 = $27,567 × 4%
[2] $900 = $30,000 × 3%

APPENDIX

SOURCES OF FINANCING

The discussion that follows is a review of the common forms of financing, which are summarized in Exhibit 12-A1.

Short-term Financing

Trade Credit The most obvious source of short-term financing is through the trade credit extended by suppliers. Some corporations use trade creditor financing to its fullest extent as a source of "interest-free" financing, sometimes stretching the ethical boundaries of business practice. For example, large corporations may rely on their purchasing power and their "clout" as big customers of smaller suppliers to put off paying their trade accounts payable.

Some purchases are made by signing promissory notes that obligate the company to pay a supplier (or an intermediary, such as a bank) at or before a given date. Promissory notes are legally enforceable negotiable instruments. The notes may bear interest, or they may be non–interest bearing. The use of notes for trade purchases is particularly common in international trade, since the banks that act as intermediaries are better placed to enforce payment.

Short-term Bank Loans Like individuals, Canadian business entities borrow from chartered banks. Lending arrangements can be classified according to term and security.

Short-term bank loans to business entities usually take the form of operating lines of credit. These loans are granted to help finance working capital, and typically are secured by a lien or charge on accounts receivable and/or inventory. There normally is a gap between the time that cash is paid to suppliers for inventory and the time that money is received from customers who, in the end, buy the inventory. Businesses can use equity funds to finance this cash flow, but receivables and inventories are reasonable collateral for loans, and it is cheaper to borrow for this purpose. The interest rate on bank lines of credit is usually flexible and is based on the bank's cost of funds.

There is typically a limit on working capital loans, expressed as a percentage of the collateral base. For example, a business may have a line of credit (also called a *credit facility*) that

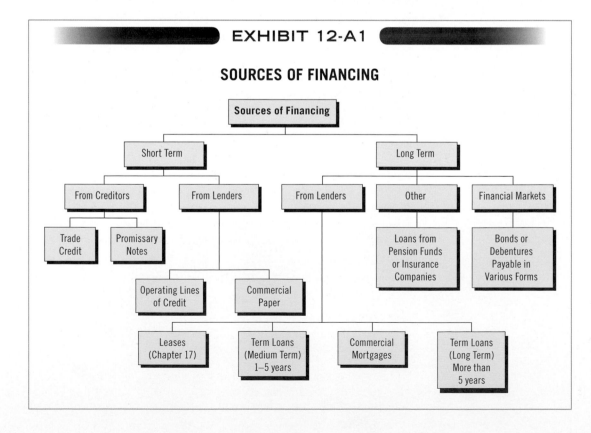

EXHIBIT 12-A1

SOURCES OF FINANCING

allows the company to borrow up to 75% of the net realizable value of accounts receivable and 50% of the book value of inventory. These loans often increase and decrease in seasonal businesses, following the ebb and flow of cash.

Operating lines of credit are due on *demand*, which means that if the bank gives the customer appropriate notice, usually a few business days, the loans have to be repaid immediately. In practice, repayment is not normally demanded unless the amount of collateral declines or the company otherwise violates some aspect of the loan agreement.

Despite their "due on demand" status, lines of credit often are a permanent fixture in a company's financial structure. The credit facility may be attached to the business's current account (i.e., the business chequing account) and drawn on as an overdraft. This is why the definition of *cash* on the statement of cash flow includes overdrafts. Companies use such loans as part of their cash management strategies.

Large corporations that have good credit ratings can issue *commercial paper*, which is a type of short-term promissory note that is sold (through a financial intermediary, again usually a bank) in open markets. The issuer of commercial paper does not know who the purchaser is, and settlement at the due date is through the financial intermediary.

Commercial paper is meant to be issued by only very stable companies. In the liquidity crunch that spiked in 2007, some asset-backed commercial paper (ABCP) turned out to be highly risky because the issuers lacked liquid resources to repay the loans. Under a court-supervised restructuring program, ABCP obligations were replaced with notes payable of varying maturities, some reasonably long-term.

A final type of short-term financing that merits mention is the sale or assignment of a company's receivables to a finance company. This represents another way current assets can be used as a source of short-term financing.

Long-term Financing

Long-term loans are often an attractive means of financing for the debtor, as compared to either short-term debt or equity. Short-term financing may not be available from period to period, and the cost may be higher than for long-term debt. Long-term creditors are not shareholders, and do not acquire voting privileges over the borrower, so issuance of debt causes no ownership dilution. Debt capital is obtained more easily than equity capital for many companies, especially private companies. Interest expense, unlike dividends, is tax deductible. Furthermore, a firm that earns a return on borrowed funds that exceeds the rate it must pay in interest is using debt to its advantage and is said to be successfully levered (or leveraged).

Leverage is risky. If sales or earnings decline, interest expense becomes an increasing percentage of earnings. Business failures frequently are caused by carrying too much debt in expectation of high sales and profits. If sales and profits (and operating cash flows) do not materialize, over-levered companies soon find themselves in financial difficulty. Firms often attempt to restructure their debt by extending maturity dates or requesting a reduction in principal or interest.

Debt is an attractive investment for *investors (lenders)* because it provides legally enforceable debt payments, eventual return of principal, and a priority claim to assets if the corporation restructures its debt or if it goes into receivership or bankruptcy. Creditors can further reduce their risk by extending secured debt, where the obligation is contractually tied to specific assets that the creditor can seize in the event of the debtor's default.

Long-term debt can take a wide variety of forms, including:

- Bank loans;
- Notes payable;
- Mortgages;
- Other asset-based loans;
- Publicly-issued bonds, secured or unsecured; and
- Long-term leases.

Long-term leases are the subject of Chapter 17. The other forms of financing are discussed in this chapter. More inventive forms of financing that have at least some of the characteristics of long-term debt are discussed in Chapter 14.

Long-term Bank Financing

Long-term loans can be identified as term loans and commercial mortgages. *Term loans* might better be characterized as *medium-term* loans because they are usually for periods of 1.5 to 5 years. Banks will lend on this term if there is appropriate collateral, such as tangible capital assets including equipment, land, or buildings. Land and buildings would also qualify for longer-term loans. Security is lodged in the form of a claim on the capital asset. At the end of the loan term, after all the payments have been made, the security is released. The repayment terms of medium-term loans can be structured in either of two ways:

1. *Blended payments.* The interest rate is fixed at the beginning of the loan term, and regular equal annuity payments are made, which include both principal and interest. For example, a $1,000,000, five-year loan at an interest rate of 7% could be repaid in five annual installments of $243,891 ($1,000,000 / (P/A, 7%, 5)). Each payment includes some interest and some principal.

2. *Designated monthly principal payments, plus accrued interest on the outstanding balance.* The interest rate may be *fixed* at the beginning of the loan term, or may *float* with prime interest rates. The borrower makes an interest payment at the end of every month, based on the loan balance for that month and the interest rate in effect. In addition, the borrower and lender work out a repayment scheme for the principal that will fully repay the loan by the end of its term. The payment terms may require equal monthly, quarterly, or semi-annual principal payments (plus interest), or lump-sum payments following a busy season. Sometimes there is a large final lump-sum payment required; this is known as a *balloon payment*.

For accounting purposes, interest is accrued as time passes, and is paid when due. If principal and interest payments are *blended*, the portion of each payment that represents principal is recorded as a reduction of the loan. Alternatively, if designated lump-sum principal payments are made, these are recorded as a direct reduction of the loan. Medium-term loans are classified as long term on the borrower's statement of financial position, although the principal portion due within one year or operating cycle is classified as a current liability.

Long-term Loans Long-term loans, *in the eyes of the lenders*, are loans with repayment terms extending beyond five years. Banks typically grant such loans as asset-based financing or as commercial mortgages. Commercial mortgages are secured against land and buildings, and involve regular blended payments (e.g., monthly or bimonthly). The amortization period of such loans could be for as long as 25 years, but the term, or the lender's commitment to extending the loan, is usually a shorter period. The term normally will not exceed five years, and may be shorter. The lender is under no obligation to renew the loan at the end of the term if it is not satisfied with the creditworthiness of the borrower.

When a long-term loan is extended at a fixed interest rate, the interest rate is fixed only for the term of the loan, not for the entire amortization period. The interest rate is reset at the beginning of each term. For example, a business could arrange a 25-year (amortization period) mortgage with a five-year term. Blended payments would be devised to repay all principal after 25 years, but the interest rate would be reset after every five years. The blended payments would be recalculated, and could go up, if interest rates increased, or down, if rates decreased.

For example, assume that Medical Arts Building Limited reported a mortgage in its 30 September 20X9 disclosure notes as follows:

6.75% mortgage loan, repayable at $18,880 per month
including principal and interest, due 1 April, 20X11 $2,213,335

Security for the mortgage consists of land and buildings, an assignment of insurance proceeds, and a general assignment of rents and leases.

1 April 20X11 is the end of the *term*, but the mortgage would not be fully repaid at that time, since the $18,880 blended monthly payments are not high enough to achieve this. Instead, repayment amounts and interest rates would be renegotiated at that time.

Long-term loans with a floating interest rate can also be arranged. Floating-rate loans normally provide for an adjustment of the interest rate (and the monthly payment) at six-month intervals. The blended payments for the next six months are recalculated at that time. Like fixed-rate loans, the term of a floating-rate loan is limited so that the lender can periodically reassess the risk of the loan.

Other Sources of Long-Term Debt

For small and most medium-sized private companies, chartered banks are the major source of financing. However, large companies (both public and private) have other sources of financing available. Larger corporations can arrange loans with life insurance companies or pension funds, which have money to invest for long periods of time. Leasing companies are another source of asset-backed lending.

Bonds or Debentures Payable

A bond (or *debenture*) is a debt security issued by corporations and governments to secure large amounts of capital on a long-term basis. A bond represents a formal promise by the issuing organization to pay principal and interest in return for the capital invested.

A formal bond agreement, known as a **bond indenture**, specifies the terms of the bonds and the rights and duties of both the issuer and the bondholder. The indenture specifies any restrictions on the issuing company, the dollar amount authorized for issuance, the interest rate and payment dates, the maturity date, and any conversion and call privileges. An independent trustee is appointed to protect the interests of both the issuer and the investors. The trustee (usually a financial institution) maintains the necessary records and disburses interest and principal. The investors receive bond certificates, which represent the contractual obligations of the issuer to the investors.

Debt Covenants

Debt agreements often restrict the operations and financial structure of the borrower to reduce the risk of default. Covenants are restrictions placed on a corporation's activities as a condition of maintaining the loan. If the covenants are broken, the lender has the right to call the loan: the lender can demand immediate repayment of the principal. Bankers also refer to covenants as *maintenance tests*. Restrictions can be either accounting-based or behavioural (restricted actions). Examples of each type are as follows:[3]

Accounting-based Covenants

- Maximum debt-to-equity ratio;
- Minimum interest coverage ratio;
- Minimum inventory turnover (i.e., the relationship between cost of goods sold and inventory); and
- Restrictions on dividend payout.

Restricted Actions

- Limitations on the issuance of additional debt without the permission of the lender;
- Restrictions on dividend payments;
- Prohibition or restriction on the redemption or retirement of shares;
- Limitations on the ability of the company to pledge assets as security for other purposes;
- Requirement that current management or key employees remain in place; and
- Limitations on transfer of control.

---

[3] These examples are the most common ones cited by Bilodeau and Lanfranconi, "The Contractual Use of Accounting Numbers," *CGA Magazine*, August 1993, pp. 36–40.

Sinking Funds

A debt agreement may require that the company establish a sinking fund. A sinking fund is a cash fund restricted so that the cash can only be used to retire the related debt. Each year, the company pays into the sinking fund. The sinking fund may be *trusteed,* in which case the fund is handled by the trustee and the company has no access to the funds. The trustee is responsible for investing the fund in appropriate investments, which often includes the purchase of the company's bonds in the open market. Repurchase of the bonds to which the sinking fund is linked has the effect of reducing the outstanding debt.

If a fund is not trusteed, the company must maintain the cash as a separate amount and not co-mingle the sinking fund with other cash reserves. However, the investments in the fund may be invested as a part of a larger investment pool, as long as the fiduciary requirements of the debt agreement are followed.

Whether trusteed or not, the balance of the cash and investments in the sinking fund is reported as an investment on the statement of financial position, usually under *investments and other assets.* The investments are accounted for as are other investments, as described in Chapter 11. The amount in the sinking fund is not offset against the company's liability unless the company is relieved of the risk of investment losses in the sinking fund once it makes the required payments into the fund.

CONCEPT REVIEW

1. How can leverage increase risk and return for common shareholders?

2. What is a blended payment?

3. What is a debt covenant?

4. If a company has a sinking fund for its long-term debt, can the company subtract the sinking fund from the debt (i.e., show the debt net) on the statement of financial position? Explain.

SUMMARY OF KEY POINTS

1. Debt financing introduces financial leverage in a company's capital structure, and increases financial risk.

2. Short-term financing is available through trade credit, trade notes payable, and short-term bank loans of various kinds.

3. Long-term financing can be sourced through financial institutions or capital markets. Common loan vehicles are term loans, commercial mortgages, and bonds.

4. Long-term debt often involves debt covenants to provide reassurance and recourse to lenders. Covenants include accounting-based covenants and restricted actions.

QUESTIONS

Q12-1 What three time elements are embedded in the definition of a liability?

Q12-2 What is a non-financial liability? Provide three examples, and explain how such liabilities are measured.

Q12-3 A firm is being sued for $550,000 by an unhappy customer; the lawsuit is in its early stages, and the firm feels that it has a good case and is willing to defend itself.

However, legal costs will be high, and the company, in all likelihood, will be prepared to settle with the ex-customer for $150,000. Why is liability recognition for this lawsuit complicated at this stage?

Q12-4 A company signs a purchase order for 5,000 cases of a product at $10 per case. The product will be delivered next year. Is a liability for $50,000 recorded? Under what conditions will some liability be recognized? Explain.

Q12-5 A company issues 10,000 coupons that allow a discount of $1 off the retail price of a $14 product. Will some liability be recorded? Explain.

Q12-6 The statement of financial position includes an obligation for insurance for a company that self-insures. How is this obligation measured? What is not included in this obligation?

Q12-7 A company borrows $10,000 for two years, interest free, when the market interest rate is 10%, compounded annually. At what amount should the liability be valued? How would your answer change if the liability were a current liability, with a term of six months?

Q12-8 Distinguish between the par value and the issue price of a bond. When are they the same? When are they different? Explain. If a $5,000 bond is sold for 101, how much cash is paid/received?

Q12-9 What is the primary conceptual difference between the straight-line and effective-interest methods of amortizing a discount or premium on a bond or note payable? Why is the effective-interest method required?

Q12-10 Explain why and how a bond discount and bond premium affect (a) the statement of financial position and (b) earnings of the issuer of the bond.

Q12-11 When the end of the accounting period of the issuer is not on a bond interest date, adjusting entries must be made for (a) accrued interest and (b) discount or premium amortization. Explain in general terms what each adjustment amount represents.

Q12-12 When bonds are sold (or purchased) between interest dates, accrued interest must be recognized. Explain why.

Q12-13 How would the payment of a $5,000 upfront administration fee on a $50,000, 6%, five-year loan affect subsequent recognition of interest expense?

Q12-14 When does capitalization of borrowing costs begin, if a company borrows money to finance the acquisition of capital assets that have a lengthy delivery period?

Q12-15 A company has a $2 million operating line of credit at an interest rate of 4% and (general use) long-term loans of $8 million at an interest rate of 7%. If general borrowings are used to finance inventory with a lengthy acquisition period, what average rate is used as the borrowing cost?

Q12-16 Under what circumstances will a gain or loss occur on the repayment of a bond payable?

Q12-17 When will a bond discount or premium be included in an entry to retire bonds? How is the amount calculated?

Q12-18 What is meant by defeasance? Can debt that is subject to a defeasance arrangement be derecognized? Contrast this with an in-substance defeasance.

Q12-19 Assume that a Canadian company borrowed US$325,000, for five years, when US$1 = Cdn$1.10. If the exchange rate at the end of the first year is US$1 = Cdn$1.08, and at the end of the second year is US$1 = Cdn$1.16, how much exchange gain or loss would be shown in earnings in the second year?

Q12-20 Interest expense of $45,500 is recorded, after discount amortization of $4,500. Interest payable has increased by $2,000 during the year. How much cash was paid for interest?

CASE 12-1

DRY CLEAN DEPOT LIMITED

"Kevin, it's such a relief to get this $2,000,000 of financing in place at a reasonable cost. We finally have the go-ahead for that new equipment! If we order now, we'll have it in place and operating next year this time, what with production, shipping, installation, and testing. We'll have to use some of our own money for this, but we'll now be able to pay for it." Max Benstead was excited as he called you, Kevin Mohammed, into his office.

Max is the CFO of Dry Clean Depot Limited (DCDL), a company with a chain of 40 dry cleaning stores in Southern Ontario. DCDL's retail stores are leased, under three- to five-year leases, in various malls and store-front locations. Each pod of retail outlets is served by one larger hub location where the dry cleaning operation is performed; clothes are transported to and from the hub locations daily.

The new loan has the following terms:

Principal:	$2,000,000
Term:	Ten years; money to be advanced in one payment, immediately, net of upfront fees
Security:	First charge on machinery, inventory, and accounts receivable
Upfront fees:	$377,000
Interest:	$90,000 paid at the end of each year
Covenants:	No dividends in excess of $100,000 per annum; Maximum 2-to-1 debt-to-equity ratio; Minimum cash balance of $500,000 on deposit required at all times

You are a professional accountant, reporting to Max, and he has asked you to analyze any accounting implications of the new loan, along with some other issues in relation to accounting policies for the areas that Max has listed (Exhibit 1). He has requested a brief report on his desk tomorrow.

DCDL has revenues of approximately $7,000,000, and an average gross profit rate of 60%. Operating costs, including occupancy and labour, are high. The company complies with IFRS, despite being a private company. Max influenced this decision, knowing that the company might be part of a public offering in the future, but also because Max wished to develop expertise in IFRS applications to enhance his own personal skills profile.

Required:
Write the report.

EXHIBIT 1

DCDL

Additional information

1. DCDL is a tenant at a retail location in Sudbury, one of its drop-off locations. Two years of the five-year lease will have expired as of the end of this fiscal period. DCDL has been disappointed with the sales volume at this location, and has decided to vacate the premises at the end of this year, even though it will still be responsible for the $27,500 annual rent payments for a further three years. The landlord has been informed of this decision. After considerable effort, DCDL has located an acceptable alternate tenant for the premises, but rent terms reflect the downturn in rental markets. This subtenant has signed a contract with DCDL, agreeing to pay $5,000 for the first year of the remaining lease period, with second and third year rent equal to $5,000 plus 10% of sales reported by the subtenant in excess of $150,000.

2. Dry-cleaning involves a cleaning process that uses an organic solvent, typically per-chloroethylene (called "perc"), rather than water. Perc is classified as a hazardous air

contaminant and it must be handled as a hazardous waste. In particular, special precautions for storage, use, and disposal are required to prevent perc from getting into any underground drinking water supply system. The landlords housing dry cleaning operations, rather than drop-off depots, require premise inspections and core soil samples on surrounding property to be completed regularly. DCDL is responsible for site remediation in the event of contamination under the terms of all such leases. One of the eight operating sites under lease appears to have some contamination, and may have to have remediation work performed. Additional tests are underway to determine the nature and extent of the issue. If there are indeed contamination issues, DCDL has agreed with the landlord that remediation will take place when the lease ends in two years' time, and DCDL will move its cleaning operation at that time. DCDL will not move if there is no contamination issue. The cost of remediation might be in the $250,000 to $500,000 range.

3. Starting in March of the current year, DCDL began offering customers the option of buying a prepaid card for dry cleaning services. The plastic cards can be loaded with "dry cleaning dollars" and offer a discount to encourage use. It costs $100 for a card that can be used for $120 of dry cleaning services. During the year, when a card is sold, a liability for $120 is recognized, and the $20 discount is entered in an account called promotion expense. The cards have no expiration date, in accordance with provincial legislation. To date, cards with a face value of $468,000 have been issued, and an expense of $78,000 has been recorded. Services with a retail value of $342,000 have been paid for through the cards. When the card is used, the retail value of the sale is transferred to revenue. Max is expecting that somewhere between 5 and 10 percent of the value on the cards will never be used, between cards that are lost or neglected, or with customers relocating.

4. DCDL is planning to order replacement dry cleaning equipment, with enhanced efficiency and perc recycling abilities. This equipment resembles large front-load washing machines, and acts as both washers and dryers. New technology is capable of extracting 99.99% of perc for re-use, in half the time that the existing models use. This will increase efficiency, allowing either more volume or fewer operating locations. The invoice price of equipment on order is $2,450,000, all of which is due when the order is placed. After a six-month lead time for production, it will be shipped from the manufacturer in the Pacific Rim. Shipping will cost approximately $34,000. Shipping will take three months. Import duties will likely amount to 20% of invoice price. DCDL expects to pay $17,000 to have the equipment installed and another $21,000 for labour and supplies during the one-month testing phase.

CASE 12-2

DARCY LIMITED

You are a professional accountant in public practice. You have just left a meeting with Michel Lessard, a local entrepreneur, who is considering a potential acquisition. Mr. Lessard, with four others, is considering buying Darcy Ltd (DL), a company that is now the subsidiary of Micah Holdings Limited (MHL), a private investment holding company.

The group of potential investors is scheduled to meet later in the week to finalize an offer for DL. You have the financial statements prepared by the company (Exhibit 1) and a page of notes from your discussion with Mr. Lessard (Exhibit 2). While the group has hired a lawyer to investigate various issues and appropriate conditions for the purchase, they would like advice on the price to be offered in the first round of negotiations.

You generally understand that the potential investors would be willing to pay six times earnings, a common valuation rule of thumb in this industry. Another valuation norm in this industry is 1.2 times net tangible assets less liabilities. Mr. Lessard has asked that both valuation rules be applied, and he is hoping the two results will be in the same ballpark.

When earnings are used for valuation purposes, earnings must be "sustainable" or "continuing" earnings, excluding unusual and infrequent items, and, in valuation, elements must be measured at fair values, neither high nor low. Appropriate accounting polices must be used for this measurement of earnings and net assets, recognizing the purpose of the accounting measurements.

Required:

Evaluate the investment based on the information given, and provide a report that provides a range of valuation for the potential investors to discuss next week and any other issues you think are important. Your report must include an explanation of adjustments made.

EXHIBIT 1

DARCY LIMITED
Statement of Financial Position

As of 31 December
(in thousands)

Assets	20X7	20X6
Current assets		
Cash	$ —	$ 1,400
Accounts receivable (less allowance of $270 in 20X7 and $420 in 20X6)	18,720	8,583
Inventory	2,680	3,200
Prepaid expenses and deposits	45	100
	21,445	13,283
Property, plant, and equipment (net)	19,800	16,600
Goodwill	400	350
	$41,645	$30,233
Liabilities		
Current liabilities		
Operating loan	$ 8,045	$ —
Accounts payable and accrued liabilities	3,750	3,188
Deferred revenue	850	790
Warranty	75	545
	12,720	4,523
Long-term liabilities		
Note payable, 2%, due 1 October 20X12	2,600	—
Deferred tax	1,835	2,210
Shareholders' equity		
Share capital	20,700	20,700
Retained earnings	3,790	2,800
	24,490	23,500
	$41,645	$30,233

DARCY LIMITED
Statement of Comprehensive Income

For the year ended 31 December
(in thousands)

	20X7	20X6
Revenue	$32,670	$44,960
Operating costs	24,180	32,970
	8,490	11,990
Other operating costs		
Selling general and administrative	3,580	3,980
Amortization	2,130	1,650
Research	120	350
Bad debts	60	120
Warranty	650	900
Gain on disposal of property	(80)	—
Gain on appreciation of goodwill	(50)	(50)
	6,410	6,950
Operating earnings	2,080	5,040
Financing		
Interest expense	430	410
Income before tax	1,650	4,630
Income tax	660	1,850
Net earnings and comprehensive income	990	2,780
Retained earnings, opening	2,800	20
Dividends	—	—
Retained earnings. closing	$ 3,790	$ 2,800

EXHIBIT 2

NOTES FROM MEETING WITH MICHEL LESSARD

(amounts in thousands)

1. The principal business activity of DL is the manufacturing of equipment for the oil and gas industry.
2. The note payable is a 2% loan offered as 100% financing by the equipment manufacturer, issued for new equipment bought on 1 October 20X7. The equipment has an eight-year life. Annual interest is paid on the anniversary date, and 2% interest for three months has been accrued in the financial statements as presented.
3. Goodwill has been written up by $50 each year based on management estimates of improved operations.
4. The pre-20X7 base of property, plant, and equipment includes land that is likely worth approximately 150% of its $7,000 cost. Other pre-20X7 property, plant, and equipment would likely have a replacement cost of 120% of net book value at the beginning of 20X7. Values have risen only slightly through 20X6 and 20X7.
5. For capital assets, straight-line amortization over periods ranging from four to eight years has been used. Amortization periods seem reasonable.

continued on next page

EXHIBIT 2 *(cont'd)*

6. DL provides a three-year limited warranty on equipment sold. The warranty expense has been recorded based on 2% of sales revenue. Warranty claims history is as follows:

Year	Sales	Claims Paid re: Current-Year Sales	Claims Paid re: Sales of One Year Prior	Claims Paid re: Sales of Two Years Prior
20X4	$31,020	$260	$160	$500
20X5	37,810	190	320	420
20X6	44,960	230	325	460
20X7	32,670	190	300	630

7. Revenue is recognized on delivery. Unearned revenue arises because of pre-paid orders.

8. During 20X7, DL provided inventory, with a cost of $23 and list price of $31, to a customer. In return, the customer will do machining work for DL during 20X8. This machining work is for a second customer's special order, which DL does not have the expertise to complete. DL expensed the cost of inventory provided, $23, as part of operating costs and made no other entries. The machining work would be worth something in the range of $28–$30 if DL had to have it done by another party.

9. The allowance for doubtful accounts has historically been approximately 5% of outstanding accounts receivable. The year-end balance of accounts receivable is extremely high this year because of a single, $7,620 account receivable ($7,000 U.S. dollars) with a foreign government. DL has stated, and Mr. Lessard agrees, that collection risk is minimal for this account.

10. The tax rate is 40% and market interest rates are in the range of 6%. The year-end exchange rate is US$1 = Cdn$1.12.

CASE 12-3

HOMEBAKE INCORPORATED

Homebake Inc. is a growing company in the consumer small appliance industry. After months of research and testing, Homebake introduced its new home breadmaker in retail stores in September 20X5, just in time for the Christmas season. The breadmaker had many more features than other similar models on the market, but it sold for the same price as the unit offered by the company's main competitor. Consumers were demanding products that would allow them to make preservative-free, fresh bread in their homes, and Homebake was anticipating that sales of its breadmaker would be high. The breadmaker came with a two-year warranty on all parts and labour and an unconditional guarantee that allowed consumers to return the product for a full refund if not completely satisfied.

In October 20X5, the company began to receive returns and complaints from some of the consumers who had purchased the product. Although the breadmaker had been tested thoroughly and all mechanical parts were performing satisfactorily, some consumers were having trouble removing the freshly baked bread from the breadpan. It seemed that the non-stick coating would allow for easy removal of the bread for a week or two, depending on the frequency of use, and then would suddenly stop working. Consumers were having to use spatulas and knives to remove the fresh, soft bread from the pan, often scarring the coating and making it even less effective, and ruining the bread in the process.

Research into the problem showed that although the breadpans themselves were manufactured by Homebake, the non-stick coating was applied by three independent suppliers. One of the suppliers had used a substandard coating mixture on the breadpans that it finished for Homebake. Homebake knew it would have to immediately remedy the problem and provide those consumers who complained with a new breadpan made by one of the other suppliers; otherwise, the consumers would return their breadmaker for a full refund.

Unfortunately, the breadpans could not be identified by supplier, and Homebake had no way of knowing how many of the substandard pans had been sold or were sitting on shelves in retailers' stores waiting for the Christmas rush.

The company set up a toll-free line that consumers or retailers could call for a replacement pan. When consumers or retailers called, highly trained customer service representatives explained the problem and reassured the callers that a replacement pan would be sent out immediately by courier. They reminded callers of the Homebake breadmaker's unique features and urged them not to return the product. They also told consumers about how much good feedback the company had received from other Homebake breadmaker owners who were using the good breadpans. Finally, they promised to send out free bread mixes and coupons with the breadpans and reminded callers that the pan would be delivered in less than three days. The company felt that there would be few breadmakers returned when consumers and retailers were treated with this kind of respect and courtesy.

It is now 6 January 20X6. You are employed as controller for Homebake. You are in the process of preparing year-end financial statements when the president of the company calls you into her office. You are glad for the meeting, for you were just considering what should be done about the potential warranty liability from the sale of breadmakers. A reasonable estimate and accrual of normal returns and warranty costs has been made from past experience with other similar products and from the experience of other manufacturers with this product. However, the breadpan failure is unique, and you have not yet determined how to account for the expenses relating to it.

From your data, you have learned that the breadmakers, which sell for $199.99 in retail stores, cost Homebake $75 to manufacture and are sold to retailers for $125. The cost of sending out a second breadpan, including shipping and the free mixes and coupons, is $20. Over 3,600,000 original breadpans have been shipped, and approximately one-third are estimated to be faulty. By 31 December 20X5, only 100,000 replacement breadpans had been shipped, since many of the breadmakers were purchased as Christmas gifts and had not yet been used.

When you arrive at the president's office, you learn that the breadpan liability is the focus of the meeting. The president is wondering how the returns will be accounted for in the year-end statements. Her comments to you are:

"I was thinking about the problem with the breadpans. I think the best way to deal with this is to expense all the costs of shipping new pans as we incur them. I know this is not our normal accounting procedure, but this is not a normal situation. We will be suing the supplier of the faulty pans, and more than likely we will recover all of the costs we have incurred. But there is no way this case will make it through the courts until sometime next year. If we recognize only the costs incurred to the year-end, then next year when we have the settlement from the lawsuit, we can put the settlement against the costs of shipping the new breadpans and there will be no impact on our profitability picture. You know that we are a small company, and this project is going to allow us to grow and expand to be a much bigger company. But we can't do that if we don't have the confidence of our banker and the general public. We need to show a good bottom line this year, so we can survive next year."

You leave the president's office feeling as if she used the meeting more to convince you of her ideas than to listen to your expertise. You are not convinced that the cash basis will provide the proper valuation of the liability for product replacement. However, the president did not seem very open to any other way of accounting for the costs of the faulty breadpans.

The president has asked you to jot down some rough figures for the next meeting, which is in two days. Your plan is to present both her approach and what you think would be more acceptable under GAAP, since Homebake requires audited statements for shareholders and bankers.

Required:
Respond to the president's request.

Source: Reproduced with permission from CGA-Canada.

ASSIGNMENTS

★★ **A12-1 Liability Issues:** For each of the following items, indicate whether the appropriate accounting treatment is to record a liability in the statement of financial position and report a loss in earnings, or whether there is no liability (and loss) to be recognized.

a. The ABC Mining Company has announced that it will restructure its Atlantic Canada operations, and lay off 80% of workers in the area. The employees affected are informed and given six months' notice and promised generous severance packages at the end of six months.

b. The Circle M Company has guaranteed the $8 million loan of another company. This amount is material. There is no real possibility of any payment ever having to be made.

c. The Board of Directors for the Dillon Timber Company has decided to lay off 10% of its Canadian workforce. The plan is still in the proposal stage, and it is not clear which workers will be affected. The cost is likely to be in excess of $5 million.

d. The Sweet Mining Company has a legislative requirement for site environmental remediation in its northern Manitoba operations. This remediation must be performed when the mineral resources are depleted and the site is closed to active mining, likely in four years.

e. Ming Metals Limited has announced that it plans to perform site environmental remediation at its active Quebec mine site. This remediation is in excess of provincial legislative requirements and will be performed when the mineral resources are depleted and the site is closed to active mining, likely in four years.

f. Jackson Limited has signed a lease with another company to rent a facility for three years at a cost of $27,000 per year.

g. On the leased premises per part f, Jackson will erect a transmission tower, at its own expense, on the building roof. At the end of the lease term, Jackson must remove the tower under the terms of the lease, and removal is expected to cost $50,000.

h. A customer has sued the Kerman Company for $2 million. The company may lose but may well offer to settle the suit for $400,000 in the next six months. The customer may or may not accept the settlement. The amount would have a significant impact on the company's financial position.

i. A prior employee has sued Luong Limited for $500,000 for health-related issues that the employee claims were caused by working conditions. The company will likely successfully defend itself. However, the amount is material and if the lawsuit is successful, other employees will likely also sue.

j. The Y34 Company has guaranteed the $10 million loan of another company. This amount is material. The other company has a poor credit rating and there is a 40% chance of having to make a $10 million payment under the guarantee.

k. The Week Company has been audited by CRA, resulting in a tax assessment for $1.5 million, an amount that would have a significant impact on the company's financial position. The company has appealed the decision, and feels it has a good case.

l. Siam Services Limited has 500 coupons outstanding that allow customers a $10 cash rebate from a $120 purchase price for a computer monitor. Customers must submit documentation to prove cash purchase. Approximately 65% of the coupons will be submitted by customers for payment.

★★ **A12-2 Liability Recognition:** The following items pertain to the 20X9 operations of Fillet Information Services Limited:

Solution ▶

a. The company issued a purchase order for manufacturing equipment with an invoice price of $850,000, to be installed next year.
b. The company issued a purchase order for $200,000 of computer equipment to be delivered next year. The price of this equipment subsequently declines to $160,000 but Fillet is committed to pay $200,000.
c. Fillet borrows $100,000 in US dollars when the exchange rate is $1 US = $1.10 Cdn. At year-end, the exchange rate is $1 US = $1.05Cdn.
d. A lawsuit for $2 million was brought against Fillet by a customer for lost profits after an information system failure. Lawyers estimate that there is only a 5% chance that the lawsuit will result in a $2,000,000 payment, but there is a 65% chance that there will be a $500,000 payment, and a 30% chance that the lawsuit will be dismissed with no payment.
e. Fillet has guaranteed a $550,000 bank loan taken out by another company; there is only a 10% chance that Fillet would have to make a payment under this guarantee. If any payment were made, it would not be the full amount; it would be only $300,000 because of other security held for the loan.
f. Fillet has issued 1,000 coupons allowing customers to get a $100 cash rebate from Fillet when they purchase a $1,000 technology hardware and software bundle from a retailer. Based on past history, only 10% of these coupons will be used. The technology bundle will still sell at a profit.
g. Fillet participates in a "loyalty points" program, where customers with certain loyalty point levels may receive free merchandise from Fillet's regular product and service line.

Required:
Explain how each of these items will affect the financial statements of Fillet at year-end 20X9.

★ **A12-3 Warranty:** Helpi Auto Parts Ltd. offers a six-month warranty that covers the cost of parts and labour for repairs. Warranty costs are estimated to be 1.5% of sales for parts plus 3% of sales for labour. On 1 April, the warranty liability had a $16,400 credit balance. Warranty work in April consumed $8,700 of parts and $14,000 of labour. Sales amounted to $550,000 in April.

Required:
1. What amount of warranty expense should be recorded in April?
2. What is the balance in the warranty liability at the end of April?

★★ **A12-4 Estimated Obligations:** In each of the following cases, indicate whether a liability is recorded or not. If recording is required, give the amount or explain how it will be estimated.

a. The company has guaranteed the $200,000 bank loan of another company. There is only a 10% chance that a payment will have to be made under the guarantee.
b. The company self-insures for fire hazards. That is, it pays no insurance but is liable to replace assets lost through fire or theft. No losses have been incurred this year, but there have been $100,000 of losses in most other years and the company is concerned that there might well be $200,000 of losses next year, evening out the pattern.

c. The company offers a two-year guarantee over parts and labour for products sold. There were no payments this year, and only 10% of products sold this year are expected to need repairs in the next year. The cost of this work would be in the range of $50,000.

d. The company has been sued by a supplier. The company returned raw materials that the company found to be of poor quality. The lawsuit is for $500,000. The company's lawyer has indicated that there is a 20% chance that the company will lose the lawsuit.

e. The company is required by legislation to undertake environmental remediation for a mining site that is currently active. The site will not be cleaned up until the mine closes, which is now scheduled for 2032. It isn't certain how much the cleanup will cost at that time, or how long it will take.

f. The company uses milk powder imported from China in one of its products. Milk products in China have been involved in significant health concerns because of an alleged toxic additive. No product safety issues have been identified with the milk powder used, but further testing is underway. Meanwhile, the product has been removed from stores in Canada as part of a voluntary recall. The recall is 40% complete and has cost $520,000 to date. No health concerns have yet been reported in Canada linked to the company's product.

★★ **A12-5 Liability Measurement:** Delivery Company Limited is gathering evidence to support an accrual for legal claims. Three lawsuits are outstanding:

Claim #1 is a lawsuit from an employee for $500,000. According to the legal team, there is a 10% chance that it will have to be paid in full, and a 90% chance that it will be dismissed.

Claim #2 is a lawsuit from a supplier for $10,000,000 for breach of contract. According to the legal team, there is a 70% chance that it will have to be paid out in full, and a 30% chance that it will be dismissed.

Claim #3 is a lawsuit from a customer for $800,000. According to the legal team, there is only a 30% chance that it will be dismissed in court. Accordingly, the company has made a settlement offer of $500,000 to the plaintiff but the plaintiff has not yet responded to the settlement offer. The legal team believes there is a 40% chance the settlement will be accepted. If it is not accepted, the action will go to court, with a 30% chance of dismissal and a 70% chance of an $800,000 payout.

Required:

1. For each case, indicate the amount that should be recorded as a liability for each lawsuit using existing standards. Assume that the payment period is relatively short so that discounting is not needed.

2. Repeat requirement 1 assuming that the accounting standards proposals for liability measurement are adopted. Assume in each case that an obligating event has occurred.

★ **A12-6 Measurement of Estimated Liabilities:** Fresh Products Limited is gathering evidence to support an accrual for warranty claims. Three products are under warranty:

For Product 1, there are 75 warranty claims outstanding. One-third have a potential value of $1,000 each (90% of these will be paid, based on past history), one-third have a potential value of $5,000 each (70% of these will be paid), and one-third have a potential payout of $12,000 each (60% will be paid). The claims that are not paid are likely to be dismissed because of an expired warranty, or incorrect statement of damages.

For Product 2, there are only nine claims outstanding, however, all are large, at $50,000 each. The experienced claims adjustor reviewing the files is completely confident that eight will be dismissed without any payment. For the remaining claim, there is a 60% chance that it will have to be paid in full, and a 40% chance that it will be dismissed.

Product 3 has only one potential claim outstanding. The claim is for $1,000,000, and the adjustor believes that there is a 60% chance it will be dismissed, a 10% chance it will result in a payout of $1,000,000, and a 30% chance that there will be a payout of $200,000.

Required:

1. Indicate the amount that should be recorded as a warranty obligation for each product using existing accounting standards.
2. Repeat requirement 1 assuming that the accounting standard proposals for liability measurement are adopted. Assume that an obligating event has occurred.

★★ **A12-7 Long-Term Note—Borrower and Lender:** On 1 January 20X9, a borrower signed a long-term note, face amount, $800,000; time to maturity, four years; stated rate of interest, 4%. The effective rate of interest of 6% determined the cash received by the borrower. The principal of the note will be paid at maturity; stated interest is due at the end of each year.

Required:

1. Compute the cash received by the borrower.
2. Give the required entries for the borrower for each of the four years. Use the effective-interest method.

★★ **A12-8 Note with Below-market Interest Rate:** Sable Company purchased merchandise for resale on 1 January 20X5, for $5,000 cash plus a $20,000, two-year note payable. The principal is due on 31 December 20X6; the note specified 3% interest payable each 31 December. Assume that Sable's going rate of interest for this type of debt was 8%. The accounting period ends 31 December.

Required:

1. Give the entry to record the purchase on 1 January 20X5. Show computations (round to the nearest dollar).
2. Complete the following tabulation:

Amount of cash interest payable each 31 December	$_____
Total interest expense for the two-year period	$_____
Amount of interest expense for 20X5	$_____
Amount of net liability reported on the statement of financial position at 31 December 20X5	$_____

3. Give the entries at each year-end for Sable.

★★ **A12-9 Debt Issuance, Fair Value:** Pinnacle Limited issued $5,000,000 in secured notes payable on 30 April 20X0. The notes mature on 30 April 20X6, and bear interest at 5% per annum, payable every 30 October and 30 April. The notes were issued to yield 6% per annum. Pinnacle's fiscal year ends on 31 December. Pinnacle uses the effective-interest method of amortization.

Required:

1. Calculate the proceeds from issuance.
2. Calculate the proceeds from issuance if the yield rate is 4% and the note is issued on 30 April 20X1, still with a maturity date of 30 April 20X6.
3. Calculate the proceeds from issuance if the yield rate is 8%, and the note is issued on 30 October 20X2, still with a maturity date of 30 April 20X6.
4. Assume that on 30 October 20X3 the market rate of interest is 10% for notes of similar risk and maturity. Determine:
   a. The book value (including unamortized discount/premium) that will be shown on the statement of financial position at that date assuming the note was issued as in requirement 1; and
   b. The fair value that will be disclosed in the notes.

★★★   **A12-10 Bonds—Compare Effective Interest, Straight-Line:** ABC Company issues a

$5,000,000, 8 1/2% bond on 1 October 20X4. At this time, market interest rates are in the range of 8%. The bond had a 20-year life from 1 October 20X4, and paid interest semi-annually on 31 March and 30 September.

Required:

1. Calculate the proceeds that would be raised on bond issuance.
2. Prepare an amortization table using the effective-interest method of amortization. Complete the first four payments *only*.
3. Prepare journal entries for 20X4 and 20X5, using the effective-interest method. ABC has a 31 December fiscal year-end
4. Repeat requirements 2 and 3 using straight-line amortization
5. Which method of amortization is required under IFRS? Why?

★★★   **A12-11 Bonds—Effective Interest, Straight-Line:** On 30 September 20X1, Golf Mania

Solution

Company issued $3 million face-value debentures. The bonds have a nominal interest rate of 10% per annum, payable semi-annually on 31 March and 30 September, and mature in 10 years, on 30 September 20X11. The bonds were issued at a price to yield 8%. Golf Mania Company's fiscal year ends on 30 September.

Required:

1. Determine the price at which the bonds were issued.
2. Prepare journal entries to record the issuance of the bonds, payment of interest, and all necessary adjustments for the first two years (that is, through 30 September 20X3), using the effective-interest method of amortization.
3. Prepare the journal entries relating to the bonds through 30 September 20X3, as above, but using the straight-line amortization method.
4. Compute the amount of unamortized bond premium remaining on 1 October 20X7 under the effective-interest method, without preparing an amortization schedule. (Note: At any point in time, the book value of the bonds is equal to the present value of the remaining cash flows.)
5. Calculate the amount of premium amortization, using the effective-interest method, for the six months ending 31 March 20X8.

★★   **A12-12 Bond Interest:** Ayaz MacDonald Ltd. (AML) issued $3,000,000 of 5% bonds payable on 1 September 20X9 to yield 6%. Interest on the bonds is paid semi-annually, and is payable each 28 February and 31 August. The bonds were dated 1 March 20X8, and had an original term of five years. The accounting period ends on 31 December. The effective-interest method is used.

Required:

1. Determine the price at which the bonds were issued.
2. Prepare a bond amortization table for the life of the bond.
3. Prepare journal entries to record the issuance of the bonds, payment of interest, and all necessary adjustments through to the end of 20X10, using the effective-interest method of amortization.
4. Calculate the interest expense that would be recorded in each of 20X9 and 20X10.
5. Show how the bond would be presented on the statement of financial position as of 31 December 20X9 and 20X10.

★★ A12-13 Bond Interest: The following partial amortization table was developed for a 5.4%, $800,000 5-year bond that pays interest each 30 September and 31 March. The table uses an effective interest rate of 5%. The bond was dated 1 April 20X1.

Amortization Schedule, Effective Interest Method:

Interest Period	Cash Interest	Interest Expense	Premium Amortization	Balance Unamortized Premium	Carrying Amount of Bonds
Opening				$14,003	$814,003
1 (30 Sept, 20X1)	$21,600	$20,350	$1,250	12,753	812,753
2	21,600	20,319	1,281	11,472	811,472
3	21,600	20,287	1,313	10,159	810,159
4	21,600	20,254	1,346	8,813	808,813
5	21,600	20,220	1,380	7,433	807,433
6	21,600	20,186	1,414	6,019	806,019
7	21,600	20,150	1,450	4,569	804,569

Required:

1. Assume that the bond was issued on 1 April 20X1. Prepare all entries for 20X1 and 20X2. The fiscal year ends on 31 December

2. Assume that the bond was issued in 20X2 on 1 June. Prepare all entries for 20X2 and 20X3.

3. Show how the bond would be reported on the statement of financial position as of 31 December 20X3 consistent with the entries in requirement 2.

★★★ A12-14 Bonds Issued between Interest Dates: Randy Corporation issued $200,000 of 7.6% (payable each 28 February and 31 August), four-year bonds. The bonds were dated 1 March 20X4, and mature on 28 February 20X8. The bonds were issued (to yield 8%) on 30 September 20X4, for appropriate proceeds plus accrued interest. The accounting period ends on 31 December.

Required:

1. Calculate the present value of the bond assuming that it was issued on 1 March 20X4.

2. Prepare an amortization schedule using the effective-interest method of amortization.

3. Calculate the proceeds of the bond reflecting the fact that it was issued on 30 September 20X4. Also calculate the accrued interest.

4. Give entries from date of sale through 28 February 20X5. Base amortization on (2) above. Credit the accrued interest collected on 30 September 20X4 to accrued interest payable in the initial journal entry.

★★ A12-15 Bonds—between Interest Dates; Effective Interest: On 1 January 20X1, Omega Additives Limited issued $500,000 of eight-year, 7.5% debentures at a net price of $485,635. Interest is payable annually, on the anniversary date of the bond. The company's fiscal year ends on 31 December.

Required:

1. Determine the effective interest rate or effective yield on the bonds.

2. What proceeds would the bond have raised if it were issued to yield 6%?

3. Prepare an amortization schedule for the life of the bond, reflecting the original issuance price of $485,635.

4. Assume instead that the bond was issued on 1 March 20X1 and the yield was as in requirement 1. Calculate the proceeds on issuance of the bond and accrued interest.

5. Assuming that the bonds were issued as in requirement 4, calculate interest expense for 20X1 and determine the net balance of bonds payable as of 31 December 20X1.

★★ **A12-16 Bonds Issued between Interest Dates:** Radian Company issued to Seivers Company $30,000 of three-year, 6% bonds dated 1 December 20X5. Interest is payable semi-annually on 31 May and 30 November. The bonds were issued on 28 February 20X6. The effective interest rate was 8%.

Required:

1. Calculate the present value of the bond assuming that it had been issued on 1 December 20X5.
2. Prepare a bond amortization schedule. Use the effective-interest method of amortization.
3. Calculate the proceeds of the bond reflecting the fact that it was issued on 28 February 20X6. Also calculate the accrued interest.
4. How much amortization is included in interest expense for the period ended 31 May 20X6?

★★ **A12-17 Upfront Fees:** A 2% loan was granted to Pegasus Technology Limited. The principal amount was $750,000 and the term was three years. Interest is paid at the end of each year. In addition, the lender charged an upfront fee of $61,273 for processing the loan application and filing necessary paperwork. Pegasus plans to expense this as a miscellaneous bank charge. Management was delighted to get a 2% loan, because other financial institutions had bid a much higher interest rate for the same terms and security.

Required:

1. Did Pegasus get a 2% loan? Explain, and calculate the effective interest rate associated with the loan.
2. What is the appropriate accounting treatment of the upfront fee? When is it expensed?
3. Give the required entries for Pegasus over the life of the loan.

★★ **A12-18 Upfront Fees and Notes Payable:** On 1 January 20X8, a borrower arranged a $500,000 three-year 2% note payable, with interest paid at the end of each loan year. There was an upfront fee of $53,460, which was deducted from the cash proceeds of the note on 1 January 20X8.

Required:

1. Calculate the effective interest rate associated with the loan. What net amount is received on 1 January 20X8?
2. Calculate the interest expense reported by the borrower for each year of the loan.

★★ **A12-19 Borrowing Costs:** Jerrow Corporation has recorded $520,000 of total interest expense from $9,500,000 of general borrowing, which consists of short-term bank debt of $1,500,000 and an $8,000,000 bond payable. Other financing for the company's $14 million operation was sourced through equity financing, which has an approximate cost of 18%.

In March 20X2, Jerrow acquired inventory for resale at an invoice cost of $730,000. The goods were paid for when they were shipped in early March. Due to delays in shipping, the goods arrived in late November, and were then available for sale, although they were still unsold at 31 December, the year-end.

In June 20X2, the company contracted for construction of a storage facility, which was nearing completion by the end of 20X2. Payments on the facility were $500,000 in late July, $400,000 in late October, and $1,200,000 in early December. One final payment of $200,000 is expected sometime in January after final inspection is completed. The company borrowed $1,000,000 in early December for this project, at an annual interest rate of 7%. No interest on this loan had been paid or recorded at 31 December, the year-end. This project is financed through the specific loan and general cash balances.

Required:

1. What accounting policy must Jerrow adopt for borrowing costs related to inventory and the storage facility under construction?

2. Prepare the adjusting journal entry to capitalize borrowing costs on inventory and the storage facility at year-end.

★★ **A12-20 Borrowing Costs:** Early in 20X1, Nitro Demolition Limited borrowed money to partially finance the acquisition of a bulldozer. The loan was a five-year, $90,000 loan, secured by a first charge on the bulldozer and the guarantee of the company president. The interest rate was 2%, with interest paid annually at the end of each year. An up-front fee of $15,165 was charged on the loan.

The loan was extended on 15 January, and the bulldozer was ordered and paid for on this date. It was delivered on 30 June 20X1. The invoice price of the equipment was $180,000. It was then customized at a cost of $15,000 in July. Staff training and testing on the equipment was completed in August at a cost of $10,000, and the machine was operational in early September 20X1.

In addition to the loan for this equipment, the company had the following capital structure and borrowing costs for the year:

	Average Balance	Borrowing Cost
Operating line of credit	$3,000,000	$160,000
Term bank loan	1,500,000	95,000
Mortgage loan for manufacturing facility	5,000,000	305,000
Equity financing	3,500,000	—

Required:

1. Provide journal entries to record the $90,000 loan on 15 January. What is the effective cost of this financing? How much cash is received?

2. Calculate the total cost of the equipment, including capitalized borrowing costs.

★★ **A12-21 Retirement—Open Market Purchase:** On 1 July 20X2, Copp Corporation issued $600,000 of 5% (payable each 30 June and 31 December), 10-year bonds payable. The bonds were issued to yield 6%. The company uses effective interest amortization for the discount.

Due to an increase in interest rates, these bonds were selling in the market at the end of June 20X5 at an effective rate of 8%. Because the company had available cash, $200,000 (face amount) of the bonds were purchased in the market and retired on 1 July 20X5.

Required:

1. Give the entry by Copp Corporation to record issuance of the bonds on 1 July 20X2.

2. Give the entry by Copp Corporation to record the retirement of $200,000 of the debt on 1 July 20X5. How should the gain or loss be reported on the 20X5 financial statements of Copp Corporation?

3. Was the retirement economically favourable to the issuer, investor, or neither?

★★★ **A12-22 Bond Retirement:** The following cases are independent:

Solution

Case A   On 1 January 20X5, Radar Company issued $200,000 of bonds payable with a stated interest rate of 12%, payable annually each 31 December. The bonds matured in 20 years and had a call price of 103, exercisable by Radar Company at any time after the fifth year. The bonds originally sold to yield 10%.

On 31 December 20X16, after interest was paid, the company called the bonds. Radar Company uses effective interest amortization; its accounting period ends 31 December.

Required:
Give the entry for retirement of the debt.

Case B On 1 January 20X2, Nue Corporation issued $200,000 of 10%, 10-year bonds to yield 11%. Interest is paid each 31 December, which also is the end of the accounting period. The company uses effective interest amortization. On 1 July 20X5, the company purchased all of the bonds at 101 plus accrued interest.

Required:
1. Give the issuance entry.
2. Give all entries on 1 July 20X5.

★★★ **A12-23 Bond Retirement:** The following three cases are independent.

Case A On 31 December 20X7, a company has the following bond on the statement of financial position:

Bond payable, 7%, interest due semi-annually on	
31 Dec. and 30 June; maturity date, 30 June 20X11	$10,000,000
Premium on bonds payable	84,000
	$10,084,000

On 28 February 20X8, 20% of the bond was retired for $2,200,000 plus accrued interest to 28 February. Interest was paid on this date only for the portion of the bonds that were retired. Premium amortization was recorded on this date in the amount of $800, representing amortization on the retired debt only.

Required:
Provide the entries to record the bond interest on 28 February and the bond retirement.

Case B On 31 December 20X7, Devon Company has the following bond on the statement of financial position:

Bond payable, 8%, interest due semi-annually on	
31 March and 30 September; maturity date,	
30 September 20X10	$18,000,000
Discount on bonds payable	132,000
	$17,868,000

Accrued interest payable of $360,000 was recorded on 31 December 20X7 ($18 million × 8% × 3/12) and the bond discount was correctly amortized to 31 December 20X7. On 31 March 20X8, semi-annual interest was paid and the bond discount was amortized by a further $12,000. Then, 40% of the bond was retired at a cost of $7,030,000 (exclusive of interest).

Required:
Provide the entries to record the bond interest and retirement on 31 March 20X8.

Case C At 31 December 20X3, Happy Ltd reports the following on its statement of financial position:

Bonds payable, due 30 June 20X16, 6%, interest	
payable annually on 30 June	$10,000,000
Discount on bonds payable	124,500
Upfront fees	35,700

Accrued interest payable of $300,000 was recorded on 31 December 20X3 ($10 million $\times$ 6% $\times$ 6/12) and the bond discount was correctly amortized to 31 December 20X3. On 1 March 20X4, 80% of the bond issue was bought back in the open market and retired at 99 plus accrued interest.

Required:

Provide the entries to record the interest and the retirement. Record interest and amortization only on the portion of the bond that is retired on 1 March 20X4; amortization of $381 must be recorded for the upfront costs and $1,328 on the discount.

★ **A12-24 Bond Retirement:** At 31 December 20X8, Hulu Ltd. reports the following on its statement of financial position:

Bonds payable, due 30 June 20X12, 6%, interest payable
   semi-annually on 30 June and 30 December
   The effective interest rate, or market interest rate,
   was 7% on issuance $8,000,000
Discount on bonds payable   245,000
                                            $7,755,000

On 1 March 20X9, 40% of the bond issue was bought back in the open market and retired at 99 plus accrued interest. The following table relates to 20X9 (numbers have been rounded):

Amortization Schedule, Effective Interest Method:

Interest Period	Cash Interest	Interest Expense	Discount Amortization	Balance Unamortized Discount	Carrying Amount of Bonds
reporting date (above)				$245,000	$7,755,000
1	$240,000	$271,425	$31,425	213,575	7,786,425
2	240,000	272,525	32,525	181,050	7,818,950

Required:

Provide the entries to record:

1. Interest to the date of retirement on the 40% of bond retired.

2. Bond retirement.

3. Interest on 30 June 20X9 for the portion of the bond still outstanding.

★★★ **A12-25 Bond Issuance and Retirement, Accrued Interest:** On 1 June 20X5, Bridle Corp. issued $40,000,000 of 7.5% bonds, with interest paid semi-annually on 30 April and 31 October. The bonds were originally dated 1 November 20X4, and were 15-year bonds. The bonds were issued to yield 8%; accrued interest was received on issuance. The company uses the effective-interest method to amortize the discount. On 31 December 20X5, 10% of the bond issue was retired for 99 plus accrued interest.

Required:

1. Calculate the issue proceeds and the accrued interest. Note: Begin by calculating the present value of the bond at 30 May and 31 October 20X5.

2. Provide the journal entry for 1 June 20X5.

3. Provide the journal entry at 31 October 20X5.

4. Provide the journal entry(ies) at 31 December 20X5.

★★★ **A12-26 Bond Issuance, Defeasance:** Computer Medic Limited issues $800,000 of 9.5% bonds on 1 July 20X1. Additional information on the bond issue is as follows:

Bond date	1 January 20X1
Maturity date	1 January 20X11
Yield rate	12%
Interest payment dates	30 June, 31 December

Required:

1. Record the bond issue and the first interest payment under the effective-interest method.

2. On 1 August 20X6, the company defeased 30% of the bonds for the market price of 103 plus accrued interest. Record the entries necessary to update the portion of the bond issue defeased (interest from 30 June 20X6) and to record the defeasance.

3. What critical element of a defeasance allows it to be recorded with derecognition of the bond? Contrast this to in-substance defeasance.

4. Have interest rates risen or fallen between the issuance of the bonds and the defeasance? (Assume no significant change in the company's risk.)

5. Discuss the nature of the gain or loss recorded in (2).

6. Record the entry to accrue interest expense on 31 December 20X6, on the remaining bonds.

★★★ **A12-27 Bonds, Comprehensive:** Batra Company sold $1,500,000 of five-year, 12% bonds on 1 August 20X2. Additional information on the bond issue is as follows:

Bond date	1 February 20X2
Maturity date	31 January 20X7
Yield rate	10%
Interest payment dates	31 July and 31 January
Bond discount/premium amortization	Effective-interest method
Proceeds on issuance	$1,606,617

Required:

1. Record the bond issuance on 1 August 20X2.

2. Prepare the adjusting journal entry on 31 December 20X2.

3. Give the entry to record the interest payment on 31 January 20X3.

4. On 31 July 20X5, after interest is paid, Batra purchases and retires 40% of the bond issue at 98. Record the bond retirement.

5. What item(s) will appear on the statement of cash flow with respect to the retirement? Indicate the amount and the section.

6. How will the remaining bond appear on the statement of financial position directly after the retirement?

7. Assume that bonds of similar risk and maturity are yielding 14%. What fair value disclosure will the company make?

8. If the market interest rate for low-risk investments was 8% on 31 July immediately after the retirement in requirement 5, how much money would have to be invested in securities to defease the remaining bond?

★ **A12-28 Foreign Exchange:** On 1 May 20X9, Nahal Imports Limited (NIL) obtained a five-year loan from a major New York bank. The loan is for US$13,000,000, bears interest at 5% per annum (paid annually on the loan anniversary date), and matures on 31 December 20X14. NIL reports in Canadian dollars. At the date the note was issued, the exchange rate was US$1.00 = Cdn$1.04. On 31 December 20X9, the exchange rate was US$1.00 = Cdn$1.01, and the average exchange rate for the last 8 months of the year was $1.03.

Required:

1. Prepare the journal entry to record the loan on 1 May 20X9.
2. What amounts relating to the loan will appear on NIL's statement of financial position on 31 December 20X9? What amount is included in earnings for 20X9?

★ **A12-29 Foreign Exchange:** In order to take advantage of lower U.S. interest rates, Zhang Limited borrowed $8 million from a U.S. bank on 1 May 20X2. Annual interest, at 7 1/4%, was due each subsequent 1 May, with lump-sum principal due on 1 May 20X5. Zhang Limited has a 31 December year-end. Exchange rates were as follows:

	US$1 =
1 May 20X2	Cdn$1.09
31 December 20X2	1.12
1 May 20X3	1.14
31 December 20X3	1.10
Average, 1 May 20X2–31 December 20X2	1.11
Average, 1 January 20X3–31 December 20X3	1.09

Required:

1. Calculate the loan principal that would appear on the 31 December 20X2 and 20X3 statement of financial position and the related exchange gain or loss in 20X2 and 20X3.
2. Calculate interest expense for the years ended 31 December 20X2 and 20X3. Why would there be an exchange gain or loss related to interest expense? Calculate this gain or loss for the year ended 31 December 20X2.

★★ **A12-30 Partial Statement of Cash Flow:** The following balances are from the statement of financial position of Merit Ltd.

Account	20X9	20X8
Bonds payable, 7%	$17,000,000	$20,000,000
Discount on bonds payable	116,800	152,500
Bonds payable, 6.5%	4,000,000	10,000,000
Discount on bonds payable	21,300	61,500
Bonds payable, 7.25%	5,000,000	0
Discount on bonds payable	132,000	0

OTHER INFORMATION:

a. A portion of the 7% bond payable was retired at 101. Discount amortization of $14,700 was recorded during the year.
b. A portion of the 6.5% bond payable was retired at 97.5. Discount amortization of $5,200 was recorded during the year.
c. The 7.25% bond was issued in 20X9 in exchange for land. Discount amortization of $17,200 has been recorded during the year.

Required:

1. Prepare statement of cash flow disclosures in financing activities related to the bond issuance and retirement. Interest paid is shown in operating activities.
2. Calculate the gain or loss on bond retirements in 20X9.

CHAPTER 13

Shareholders' Equity

Shareholders' equity represents the difference between the assets and liabilities of an entity. Equity is the *residual interest* in net assets because it is what is left when liabilities are subtracted from assets—the residual. Equity is therefore sometimes referred to as **net assets**. Equity has various components, or sources. Generally, shareholders' equity includes the *net contribution to the firm by the owners*, called contributed capital, plus the firm's *cumulative earnings retained* in the business.

Inmet Mining Company is a Canadian-based mining company that produces copper, zinc, and gold. The company owns and operates mining operations in Canada, but also in Turkey, Finland, Spain, Panama, and Papua, New Guinea. The company reports total assets of $2.9 billion in 2009, financed through approximately $0.7 billion in debt (24% of assets) and $2.2 in equity (76% of assets.) Equity includes $0.7 billion of share capital, contributed surplus from stock-based compensation totalling $68 million; ($42) million in reserves that are unrealized losses from investments, derivatives, and foreign exchange; and $1.5 billion of retained earnings. The notes disclose that the share capital relates entirely to common shares, although the company is authorized to issue preferred shares and subordinate voting participating shares if it wishes. Retained earnings represents cumulative earnings less dividends.

This chapter examines accounting issues related to contributed capital, particularly issuance and retirement of share capital. Accounting and disclosure for retained earnings is also covered, including accounting for dividends. Other components of shareholders' equity are also discussed, with special attention given to unrealized reserves.

THE CORPORATE FORM OF ORGANIZATION

The whole topic of accounting for shareholders' equity applies specifically to corporations; only corporations can have shareholders and shareholders' equity. Partnerships and sole proprietorships have ownership interests, but not share capital. A corporation may be formed either provincially or federally, and there is legislation governing the rights and responsibilities associated with incorporation. The discussion in this text is based on the federal *Canada Business Corporations Act (CBCA)*, with occasional references to provincial legislation.

Private versus Public Corporations

Private Companies Corporate entities may be either private or public. The vast majority of corporations in Canada are private, many of which are quite small. However, approximately half of the corporations on the *Financial Post*'s list of the 500 largest Canadian corporations are private. **Private companies** have a limited number of shareholders (generally limited to a maximum of 50 by the provincial securities acts.) Shares cannot be publicly-traded. Private companies generally have a **shareholders' agreement** that describes the ways in which shareholders can transfer their shares, as well as other rights and responsibilities of the shareholders.

Private companies in Canada may choose to adopt accounting standards for private enterprise (ASPE), avoiding the more complex IFRS standards. Such a choice is based on the users of financial information and their needs.

Public Companies **Public companies** are those whose securities, either debt or equity, are traded on stock exchanges. Public companies must, in addition to the reporting requirements required by IFRS, comply with the extensive reporting requirements that govern the particular stock exchange or exchanges on which the companies' securities trade.

Share Capital

Share capital, represented by share certificates, represents ownership in a corporation. Shares may be bought, sold, or otherwise transferred by the shareholders without the consent of the corporation unless there is an enforceable agreement to the contrary.

Common Shares A corporation may be authorized to issue several different **classes of shares**, each with distinctive rights. That is, different types of shares may be created, each with differing rights and privileges. Dividend entitlements and voting rights are characteristics that might be altered among classes. At least one class of shares must be **common shares**, which have the right to vote and the right to receive the residual interest in the net assets of the company on dissolution. Voting rights include the power to vote for the members of the Board of Directors. Common shareholders are entitled to dividends *only as declared*, and they are at risk if the Board of Directors chooses to reduce or eliminate a dividend.

Preferred Shares **Preferred shares** are so designated because they confer certain preferences over common shares. Preferred shares are not always titled "preferred," and may have a variety of names (for example, Class A shares). The most common feature of preferred shares is a priority claim on dividends declared, usually at a stated rate or amount. Characteristics of preferred shares often involve the following:

- *Limited or non-existent voting rights.* Typically, preferred shares are non-voting. They may be given voting rights in certain circumstances, such as when preferred dividends have not been paid or during a vote on a takeover bid.
- *Dividend priority.* A corporation generally has no obligation to declare any type of dividend. When the Board of Directors does declare a dividend, preferred shareholders have preference, which means that they get their preferred dividend before any common dividend. The dividend rate on preferred shares must be specified, usually as a dollar amount per share, such as $1.20 per share. Alternatively, the dividend may be described as a percentage or rate, such as 8¼%, 6%, or floating rate (i.e., tied to prime interest rates). When the dividend rate is a percentage, it must refer to some sort of

stated principal value for the share, which is a reference price, such as $25. This reference value has no special economic significance.

- *Cumulative dividends.* Preferred shares may have the right to receive cumulative unpaid past dividends (called **dividends in arrears**) in the current year before any common dividends can be paid.
- *Participating dividends.* Preferred shares may have the right to share additional dividends with common shares, once the annual dividend has been paid to the preferred shareholders and the common shareholders receive some kind of base return.
- *Assets upon liquidation.* In case of corporate dissolution, preferred shares may have a priority over the common shareholders on the assets of the corporation up to a stated amount per share.
- *Conversion.* Preferred shareholders may have the right to convert to common shares, or to another class of preferred shares with different entitlements.
- *Guarantee.* Preferred shareholders may have a guaranteed return of their invested principal at some point in time through redemption or retraction provisions.

The accounting implications of these terms will be explored in later sections of this chapter and the next.

Special Terms and Conditions While "classic" common and preferred shares abound, so do more exotic examples. In Canada, preferred issues may be structured to look a lot like debt—they pay a dividend related to interest rates, and provide for repayment at a specific point in time. These preferred shares are designed to be sold to investors who want the (preferential) tax treatment given to dividend (versus interest) payments, but also want some of the security provided by debt. The result is not permanent equity investment. We'll take a closer look at these types of preferred shares in the next chapter.

Some companies issue common shares that have *multiple* votes, or, at the opposite end of the spectrum, *limited or no voting* rights. These shares are called **special shares** or **restricted shares**. For example, Danier Leather Inc. has two types of common shares:

> The Multiple Voting Shares and Subordinate Voting Shares have identical attributes except that the Multiple Voting Shares entitle the holder to ten votes per share and the Subordinate Voting Shares entitle the holder to one vote per share. Each Multiple Voting Share is convertible at any time, at the holder's option, into one fully paid and non-assessable Subordinate Voting Share. The Multiple Voting Shares are subject to provisions whereby, if a triggering event occurs, that each Multiple Voting Share is converted into one fully paid and non-assessable Subordinate Voting Share. A triggering event may occur if Mr. Jeffrey Wortsman, President and Chief Executive Officer, (i) dies, (ii) ceases to be a Senior Officer of the Company; (iii) ceases to own 5% or more of the aggregate number of Multiple Voting and Subordinate Voting Shares outstanding or (iv) owns less than 918,247 Multiple Voting Shares and Subordinate Voting Shares combined.

The multiple voting shares are designed to allow the holders to *exercise voting control* but not to *pass control on* to another party.

Par Value versus No-par Value Shares

Par value shares have a designated dollar amount per share, as stated in the articles of incorporation and as printed on the face of the share certificates. Par value shares may be either common or preferred. The CBCA and most provincial business corporation acts *prohibit the use* of par value shares, but several provincial jurisdictions permit their issuance (e.g., Quebec, N.S., B.C.).

Par value shares sold initially at less than par are said to have been issued at a **discount**. Par value shares sold initially above par are said to have been issued at a **premium**. When par value shares are issued at a premium, only the par value is assigned to the share account. Any excess is allocated to the premium on share capital account, which is a separate component of contributed capital. Par values are usually set very low, and thus a major portion of the proceeds on issuance is classified as the premium. The classification of issuance proceeds in two separate accounts within the equity section, instead of one, has no economic significance.

No-par shares do not carry a designated or assigned value per share. This allows for all consideration received on sale of the securities to be classified in the share capital account, and it avoids the need to divide the consideration into two essentially artificial components, par value and the premium or excess over par.

TERMS RELATED TO SHARE CAPITAL

The following terms are used to describe important aspects of share capital:

- *Authorized share capital.* The maximum number of shares that can be legally issued. Under the CBCA, a corporation is entitled to issue an unlimited number of shares, so there is no legal maximum. However, the corporation may choose to place a limit on authorized shares. Such a limit must be stated in the articles of incorporation and can be changed at a later date by application to the appropriate ministry for an amendment to the corporation's articles of incorporation. Some provincial legislation establishes a maximum.

- *Issued share capital.* The number of shares that have been issued to shareholders to date.

- *Outstanding share capital.* The number of shares that have been issued and are currently owned by shareholders. Issued shares will be higher than outstanding shares if there are treasury shares outstanding. Shares that have been repurchased from shareholders and retired are considered to be neither issued nor outstanding.

- *Treasury shares.* Shares that are reacquired by the corporation, and held pending resale. Treasury shares are *issued* but not *outstanding*.

- *Subscribed shares.* Unissued shares set aside to meet subscription contracts (i.e., shares "sold" on credit and not yet paid for). Subscribed shares are usually not issued until the subscription price is paid in full in accordance with legislative requirements.

CONCEPT REVIEW

1. What is the essential difference between a public and a private corporation?
2. What is the most common preference right of preferred shares over common shares?
3. What are restricted shares?
4. What are treasury shares?

ACCOUNTING FOR SHARE CAPITAL AT ISSUANCE

Accounting for shareholders' equity emphasizes source; therefore, if a corporation has more than one share class, separate accounts must be maintained for each. If there is only one share class, an account entitled *share capital* may be used. In cases where there are two or more classes, account titles associated with the shares are used, such as *common shares; class A shares; preferred shares, $5;* or *preferred shares, $1.25.* The dollar amounts listed with no-par preferred shares indicate the dividend entitlement.

Authorization The articles of incorporation will authorize an unlimited (or, less frequently, a limited) number of shares. This authorization may be recorded as a memo entry in the general journal and in the ledger account by the following notation:

Common shares—No-par value (authorized: unlimited shares)		

Shares Issued for Cash

When shares are issued, a share certificate, specifying the number of shares represented, is prepared for each shareholder. This may be done in electronic form, with a brokerage house acting as an intermediary/custodian for the investor. Companies keep track of the number of shares held by each shareholder in a shareholder ledger, a subsidiary ledger to the share capital account.

In most cases, shares are sold and issued for cash rather than on a subscription (i.e., credit) basis. The issuance of 10,000 common shares, no-par, for cash of $10.20 per share would be recorded as follows:

Cash	102,000	
Common shares, no-par (10,000 shares)		102,000

Notice that the common share account is credited for the total proceeds received. Had the shares been assigned a $1 per share par value, the proceeds are divided between par value and premium:

Cash	102,000	
Common shares, $1 par (10,000 shares)		10,000
Contributed capital: premium on common shares		92,000

Both the $10,000 common share amount and the premium on common shares are separate equity accounts.

Shares Issued on a Subscription Basis

Prospective shareholders may sign a contract to purchase a specified number of shares on credit, with payment due at one or more specified future dates. Such contractual agreements are known as **stock subscriptions**, and the shares involved are called *subscribed share capital*. Shares are not issued until fully paid, according to the terms of incorporation legislation. Because financial statement elements have been created by a legal contract, accounting recognition is necessary. The purchase price is debited to stock subscriptions receivable, and share capital subscribed is credited.

To illustrate, assume that 120 no-par common shares of BT Corporation are subscribed for at $12 by J. Doe. The entry by BT Corporation would be as follows:

Stock subscriptions receivable—common shares (Doe)	1,440	
Common shares subscribed, no-par (120 shares)		1,440

The receivable will be paid in three $480 instalments. Assume the third and last collection on the above subscription is received. The entries would be as follows:

To record the collection		
Cash	480	
Stock subscriptions receivable—common shares (Doe)		480
To record issuance of shares		
Common shares subscribed, no-par (120 shares)	1,440	
Common shares, no-par (120 shares)		1,440

A credit balance in common shares subscribed reflects the corporation's obligation to issue the 120 shares on fulfilment of the terms of the agreement by the subscriber. This account is reported in shareholders' equity on the statement of financial position along with the related share capital account.

There are two alternative ways to present stock subscriptions receivable. Some argue it should be classified as an asset: a current asset if the corporation expects current collection; otherwise, a non-current asset under the category *other assets*. Others argue it should be offset against the common shares subscribed account in the shareholders' equity section of the statement of financial position. That is, the amount receivable is shown as a contra account in equity. This presentation ensures that the *net* equity balances reflect only paid-in amounts as capital; promises of future payment are recorded but netted out. *Presentation as a contra account is the preferred approach,* as it maintains the integrity of the equity elements of financial statements.

Default on Subscriptions   When a subscriber defaults after partial fulfillment of the subscription contract, certain complexities arise. In case of default, the corporation may decide to (1) return all payments received to the subscriber; (2) issue shares equivalent to the number paid for in full, rather than the total number subscribed; or (3) keep the money received with no shares issued. The first two options involve no disadvantage to the subscriber, although the corporation may incur an economic loss if share prices have dropped. The third option is not common, although legislation generally does not prevent it.

Non-cash Issuance of Share Capital   Corporations sometimes issue share capital for non-cash consideration. These transactions are also called *share-based payments*. Companies may pay for goods or services with shares, or acquire long-term assets. For example, the 2008 annual report of Pele Mountain Resources Inc. includes the following disclosures of issued shares:

From the disclosure notes:
Note 7

...

f) Issued 115,000 common shares for the total fair value of $41,950 to acquire certain mining claims for the Eco Ridge Mine project.

g) Issued 80,000 common shares for the total fair value of $31,600 to acquire certain mining leases for the Highland Gold Project.

Source: Reproduced with permission from Pele Mountain Resources.

When shares are issued for non-cash assets or services or to settle debt, the transaction should be recorded at the *fair value of the assets received*, assuming that this value can be reliably determined. The fair value of the equity shares issued cannot be used to value the transaction unless the fair value of the assets *cannot be determined*. This should be a rare occurrence.

To illustrate, assume that Bronex Corporation issued 136,000 Class A no-par shares in exchange for land. The land was appraised at $420,000, while the shares, based on several prior transactions in the shares, were valued at $450,000. The transaction would be valued at $420,000:

Land	420,000	
Share capital, Class A no-par (136,000 shares)		420,000

In the past, Canadian valuation rules have required that both fair values be assessed to see which is the more reliable, with preference given to the more reliable valuation. IFRS valuation of share-based payments instead rests on the fair value of assets received.

Basket Sale of Share Capital   A corporation usually sells each class of its share capital separately. However, a corporation may sell two or more classes for one lump-sum amount (often referred to as a *basket sale*).

When two or more classes of securities are sold and issued for a single lump sum, the total proceeds must be allocated logically among the several classes of securities. Two methods used in such situations are (1) the *proportional method*, in which the lump sum received is allocated proportionately among the classes of shares on the basis of the relative fair value of each security, and (2) the *incremental method*, in which the fair value of one security is used as a basis for that security and the remainder of the lump sum is allocated to the other class of security. When there is no fair value for any of the issued securities, proceeds may be allocated arbitrarily.

To illustrate, assume Vax Corporation issued 1,000 no-par common shares, and 500 no-par preferred shares, in three different situations:

Situation 1—Proportional method The common shares were selling at $40 per share and the preferred at $20. Assume the total cash received is $48,000, which has been approved by the Board of Directors. Because reliable fair values are available for both share classes, the proportional method is preferable as a basis for allocating the lump-sum amount, as follows:

Proportional allocation	
Fair value of common (1,000 shares × $40)	$40,000 = 4/5 of total
Fair value of preferred (500 shares × $20)	10,000 = 1/5
Total fair value	$50,000 = 5/5

Allocation of the lump-sum sale price of $48,000	
Common ($48,000 × 4/5)	$38,400
Preferred ($48,000 × 1/5)	9,600
Total	$48,000

The journal entry to record the issuance:

Cash	48,000	
Common shares, no-par (1,000 shares)		38,400
Preferred shares, no-par (500 shares)		9,600

Situation 2—Incremental method The common shares were selling at $40; a market for the preferred has not been established. Because there is no market for the preferred shares, the fair value of the common ($40,000) must be used as a basis for the entry:

Cash	48,000	
Common shares, no-par (1,000 shares)		40,000
Preferred shares, no-par (500 shares)		8,000

Management discretion

Situation 3—Arbitrary allocation When there is no established market for either class of shares, an arbitrary allocation is used. In the absence of any other logical basis, a temporary allocation may be made by the Board of Directors. If a fair value is established for one of the securities in the near future, a correcting entry based on such value would be made.

Share Issue Costs Corporations often incur substantial expenditures when they issue shares in a public offering. These expenditures include registration fees, underwriter commissions, legal and accounting fees, printing costs, clerical costs, and promotional costs. These expenditures are called **share issue costs**. If the share issuance is planned but then abandoned, the costs are expensed. The costs of a successful share issuance are included "in equity"; they are not expensed. Two methods of accounting for share issue costs are found in practice:

1. *Offset method.* Under this method, share issue costs are treated as a reduction of the amount received from the sale of the related share capital. The rationale to support this method is that these are one-time costs that cannot be reasonably assigned to future periodic revenues and that the net cash received is the actual appropriate measure of capital raised. Therefore, under this method, share issue costs are debited to the share capital account.

2. *Retained earnings method.* Companies will charge share issue costs directly to retained earnings. Retained earnings are reduced as a result. This reduces common equity, but records the gross proceeds received from the sale of shares to the share capital account.

Both methods are found in practice, although the offset method is more common.

RETIREMENT OF SHARES

A company can buy back any of its shares, preferred or common, at any time, if they are offered for sale. Such a sale can be a private transaction, or a public (stock market) transaction. Legislation provides conditions (typically solvency tests that must be met subsequent to the purchase) for the purchase and cancellation of outstanding shares. Corporations that intend to buy back their own shares must file their plans with the relevant securities commissions; the plan is known as a **normal course issuer bid**.

Shares may also be bought back according to the terms of the shares themselves. Some preferred shares are *retractable*, which means that, at the option of the shareholder, and at a contractually arranged price, a company is required to buy back its shares. Other preferred shares are **callable**, or *redeemable*, which means that there are specific buy-back provisions, at the option of the company. In either of these transactions, the company deals directly with the shareholder.

Reasons for Share Retirement Why is repurchase of shares a good strategy for the company? The company may want to:

- *Increase earnings per share* (EPS). EPS is the ratio obtained by dividing earnings by outstanding shares. EPS is considered a critical indication of a company's earning performance and future prospects, and is closely watched by financial markets. Idle cash, earning minimal interest income, can be spent to retire shares that will reduce the denominator (number of shares outstanding) of the EPS ratio. Because of the negligible return given up, this will not hurt the numerator (earnings) in a proportional fashion. Accordingly, EPS will rise, and the market price per share should rise as well.

- *Provide cash flow to shareholders in lieu of dividends.* A repurchase offer enables those shareholders who want to receive cash to do so through offering all or part of their holdings for redemption. There may be tax advantages of this form of payout, because the recipient will pay taxes on capital gains on the shares rather than tax on ordinary dividend income. Those shareholders who do not wish to receive cash at the time can continue to hold their shares.

- *Acquire shares when they appear to be undervalued.* A corporation with excess cash may feel that buying undervalued shares for cancellation will benefit the remaining shareholders. These transactions also help make a market (i.e., provide a buyer) for the shares.

- *Buy out one or more particular shareholders, and thwart takeover bids.*

- *Reduce future dividend payments by reducing the shares outstanding.*

Accounting for Retirement There are no standards issued by the IASB that describe appropriate policy to follow when a company purchases and retires its own shares. Accordingly, existing Canadian practice is described, on the basis that it is an acceptable, or perhaps preferable, approach. Legislation dictates accounting treatment.

When shares are purchased and immediately retired, contributed capital allocated to the shares is removed from the accounts. Where the reacquisition cost of the acquired shares is different from the average original issuance price, (i.e., the *paid-in* capital) accounting standards require that the cost be allocated as follows for no-par shares:

Condition	First, DEBIT	Then, Either/Or	
		CREDIT	DEBIT
When the reacquisition cost is *lower* than the average price per share issued to date	Share capital, at the *average paid-in value* per issued share	Other contributed capital from share retirement	n/a
When the reacquisition cost is *higher* than the average price per share issued to date	Share capital, at the *average paid-in value* per issued share	n/a	1. Other contributed capital that was created by earlier cancellation or resale transactions *in the same class of shares,* if any, then 2. Retained earnings

The effect of this approach is to ensure that a corporation records no income effect (i.e., no gain or loss in earnings) from buying back its own shares. If a company could record gains and losses from transactions in its own shares, the potential for income manipulation is obvious.

Illustration: Case 1 Assume that Sicon Corporation has 200,000 no-par common shares outstanding. There is $1 million in the common share account, the result of an average issuance price per share of $5. The contributed capital account from previous retirement transactions of common shares has a $7,200 credit balance. The corporation acquired and retired 10,000 shares at a price of $6.25 per share. The specific shareholder who sold these shares back to Sicon Corporation had originally paid $4 per share. The transaction would be recorded as follows:

Common shares (10,000 shares)		
[($1,000,000 ÷ 200,000) × 10,000]	50,000	
Contributed capital, common share retirement	7,200	
Retained earnings ($62,500 − $50,000 − $7,200)	5,300	
Cash (10,000 × $6.25)		62,500

The first step in constructing this journal entry is to compare the cash paid to retire the shares ($62,500) with the *average* initial issuance price to date ($50,000). The specific issue price of these shares ($4) is irrelevant. The corporation paid $12,500 more to retire these shares than the average original proceeds. The $12,500 is debited first to contributed capital from prior common share retirements until that account is exhausted. *This contributed capital account may never have a debit balance.* Retained earnings is debited for the remainder. The effect of this transaction is to reduce paid-in capital by $57,200, retained earnings by $5,300, and total shareholders' equity by $62,500. No loss is recorded in earnings. Assets are reduced by $62,500.

Illustration: Case 2 If the shares were reacquired for $4.25 per share, the entry to record the transaction would be:

Common shares (10,000 shares)		
[($1,000,000 ÷ 200,000) × 10,000]	50,000	
Contributed capital, common share retirement		
($50,000 − $42,500)		7,500
Cash (10,000 × $4.25)		42,500

Total shareholders' equity and paid-in capital go down by $42,500 ($50,000 less $7,500), reflecting the fact that the corporation paid less to repurchase the shares than the average issuance price to date. No gain is recorded. Assets are reduced by $42,500.

The price paid for the shares may be the current market price, or a price agreed on when the shares were originally issued, as is the case for redeemable or retractable shares. In all cases, the entries follow the same pattern: retirement price is compared to the average issuance price to date, and the difference is a capital amount.

Note that the contributed capital account involved in the above example was identified as contributed capital, common share retirement. Subsequent common share retirements will increase or decrease this account. However, if there are retirements of any other class of shares (e.g., preferred shares) then a *separate contributed capital account* would have to be set up. These contributed capital accounts are used only for transactions involving the *same class of shares.*

Reporting Example Compton Petroleum Corporation provides an example of the repurchase and cancellation of shares in its 2008 financial statements:

From the consolidated statement of retained earnings:

Premium on redemption of shares	($2,892)

From the disclosure notes:

8. Capital stock

   A) Authorized

   The Company is authorized to issue an unlimited number of common shares and an unlimited number of preferred shares, issuable in series

   B) Issued and outstanding

continued on next page

	2008	
	Number of shares (000s)	**Amount**
Common shares outstanding, beginning of the year	129,098	$235,871
Shares issued for services	50	490
Shares issued under stock option plan	1,388	10,363
Share repurchased	(4,776)	(9,021)
Common shares outstanding, end of the year	125,760	$237,703

The Company maintains a normal course issuer bid program that will expire on March 24, 2009. Under the current program, the Company may purchase for cancellation up to 6 million of its common shares, representing approximately 5% of the issued and outstanding common shares at the time the bid received regulatory approval. During the year, the Company purchased for cancellation 4,775,900 common shares at an average price of $1.85 per share pursuant to the normal course issuer bid. Any excess of the purchase price over book value has been charged to retained earnings ...

[Comparative data has been omitted.]

Source: http://www.sedar.com; Compton Petroleum Corporation, annual financial statements, posted March 23, 2009.

Conversion of Shares

Shares of any class may include the provision that they may be converted, at particular times and/or in particular quantities, into shares of another class. For example, preferred shares may be convertible into common shares. Conversions are accounted for at *book value,* with an equal decrease to one share class and increase to another. For example, if 20,000 no-par preferred shares, issued for an average of $36.70 per share, were to convert according to pre-established terms to 60,000 no-par common shares (that is, 3-for-1):

Preferred shares (no-par, 20,000 shares)		
(20,000 × $36.70)	734,000	
Common shares (no-par, 60,000 shares)		734,000

TREASURY STOCK

A firm may buy its own shares and hold them for eventual resale. This is called **treasury stock.** *Such shares may not vote at shareholder meetings or receive dividends.* The CBCA (and provincial legislation modelled after the act) provides that corporations that reacquire their own shares must immediately retire those shares. Thus, corporations may not engage in treasury stock transactions in most Canadian jurisdictions. However, some provincial legislation does allow treasury stock transactions (e.g., British Columbia), and there are some circumstances where shares may be purchased and held in trust before they are distributed to an employee under a share compensation arrangement. Treasury shares are far more common in other countries, where corporations regularly engage in treasury stock transactions, subject to the insider trading rules of the various stock exchanges.

The key to a treasury stock acquisition is that reacquired shares may be reissued. The company may eventually reissue the shares to raise additional capital—a process far faster through the issuance of treasury stock than a new share issue. The shares may also be used for stock dividends, employee stock option plans, and so on. A corporation that is permitted to engage in treasury stock transactions may have additional flexibility over one not so permitted. However, the importance of this aspect of treasury shares has decreased in recent years due to the prevalence of **shelf registration**, which is a standing approval from the securities commissions to issue more shares as needed.

Accounting for Treasury Stock Again, existing Canadian practice regarding policy for the acquisition and resale of treasury stock is presented in this discussion because there are no standards issued by the IASB in this area.

When a company buys treasury stock, the cost of the shares acquired is debited to a treasury stock account, which appears as a *deduction* at the end of the shareholders' equity section. When the shares are resold, the treasury stock account is credited for the average cost, and the difference, which is the "gain or loss," affects various equity accounts. The "gain or loss" is not reported in earnings; a firm cannot improve reported earnings by engaging in capital transactions with its own shareholders.

When treasury stock is resold at a price in excess of its cost, the excess should be recorded as contributed capital in a separate contributed capital account. Where the shares are sold at less than their cost, the deficiency should be charged to contributed capital, if any, then retained earnings. The rules are as follows:

Condition	First, CREDIT	Then, Either/Or	
		CREDIT	**DEBIT**
When the resale price is *higher* than the average price per share	Treasury stock, at the average price per share	Other contributed capital from treasury stock transactions	n/a
When the resale price is *lower* than the average price per share	Treasury stock, at the average price per share	n/a	1. Other contributed capital from treasury stock transactions, if any, then 2. Retained earnings.

This method of accounting for treasury stock is called the **single-transaction method**. The treatment is the same as that used for share retirement. An example will illustrate the sequence of entries.

1. To record the initial sale and issuance of 10,000 common shares at $26 per share

Cash (10,000 shares × $26)	260,000	
Common shares (10,000 shares)		260,000

2. To record the acquisition of 2,000 common treasury shares at $28 per share

Treasury stock, common (2,000 shares × $28)	56,000	
Cash		56,000

Note: The cash price paid is always the amount debited to the treasury stock account.

3. To record sale of 500 treasury shares at $30 per share (above cost)

Cash (500 shares × $30)	15,000	
Treasury stock, common (500 shares at cost, $28)		14,000
Contributed capital from treasury stock transactions		1,000

Note: Had this sale been at cost ($28 per share), no amount would have been entered in the contributed capital account. If treasury shares are bought in a series of acquisitions at different prices, weighted average cost is used on disposition.

4. To record the sale of another 500 treasury shares at $19 per share (below cost)

Cash (500 shares × $19)	9,500	
Contributed capital from treasury stock transactions*	1,000	
Retained earnings	3,500	
Treasury stock, common (500 shares at cost, $28)		14,000

*The debit is limited to the current balance in this account (see entry (3)); any remainder is allocated to retained earnings.

Assuming entries (1) through (4), and a beginning balance in retained earnings of $40,000, the statement of financial position will reflect the following:

Shareholders' Equity

    Contributed capital

Common shares, 10,000 shares issued, and 9,000 shares outstanding; 1,000 shares are held as treasury stock	$260,000
Retained earnings ($40,000 − $3,500)	36,500
Total contributed capital and retained earnings	$296,500
Less: Treasury stock, 1,000 shares at cost	28,000
Total shareholders' equity	$268,500

Reporting Example Calfrac Well Services Ltd. included the following accounts in its 2007 financial statements:

Shareholders' Equity	2007	2006
Capital stock	$155,254	$139,841
Shares held in trust (note 7)	(2,199)	(3,869)
Contributed surplus	6,025	4,393
Retained earnings	198,039	163,145
Other comprehensive income (loss) [Reserves]	(6,204)	—
	$350,915	$303,510

From the Disclosure Notes:
Note 7

The Company has established a trust to purchase and hold Company stock on behalf of certain employees who have elected to receive a portion of their annual bonus entitlement in the form of Company shares. These shares are not considered outstanding.

[References to other disclosure notes have been omitted.]

Source: http://www.sedar.com; Calfrac Well Services Limited, annual financial statements, posted March 27, 2008.

1. What value is given to shares when they are issued in exchange for non-cash assets?

2. How can the separate classes of shares be valued when shares are issued as a basket?

3. When shares are redeemed and retired, how should the cost of the redemption be charged to the shareholders' equity accounts?

RETAINED EARNINGS

Retained earnings represents accumulated net earnings or net loss, error corrections, and retrospective changes in accounting policy, if any, less accumulated cash dividends, property dividends, stock dividends, and other amounts transferred to contributed capital accounts. If the accumulated losses and distributions of retained earnings exceed the accumulated gains, a **deficit** will exist (i.e., a debit balance in retained earnings). The following items directly affect retained earnings:

Decreases (debits)

- Cash and other dividends;
- Spinoff of investment to shareholders;
- Stock dividends;
- Share retirement and treasury stock transactions;
- Share issue costs;
- Adjustments related to complex financial instruments, such as hybrid financial instruments (see Chapter 14);
- Error correction (may also be a credit) (see Chapter 20); and
- Effect of a change in accounting policy applied retrospectively (may also be a credit) (see Chapter 20).

Increases (credits)

- Earnings (including discontinued operations) (will be a debit if a net loss); and
- Removal of deficit in a financial reorganization.

Appropriations and Restrictions of Retained Earnings

Appropriated retained earnings and restricted retained earnings constrain a specified portion of accumulated earnings for a specified reason. Retained earnings are appropriated and restricted primarily to reduce the amount of retained earnings that financial statement readers might otherwise consider available to support a dividend declaration. Constrained retained earnings are sometimes called a *reserve*. **Appropriated retained earnings** are the result of discretionary management action. **Restricted retained earnings** are the result of a legal contract or corporate law.

The following are examples of some of the ways in which appropriations and restrictions of retained earnings may arise:

- To fulfill a contractual agreement, as in the case of a debt covenant restricting the use of retained earnings for dividends that would result in the disbursement of assets;
- To report a discretionary appropriation of a specified portion of retained earnings in anticipation of possible future losses; or
- To fulfill a legal requirement, as in the case of a provincial corporate law requiring a restriction on retained earnings equivalent to the cost of treasury stock held.

An appropriation of retained earnings *does not involve any segregation of assets.* Retained earnings appropriations are just accounting entries that divide existing retained earnings into multiple accounts. If management actually sets aside funds for a specific purpose, restricted cash investments will be reported as an asset.

Appropriation or restriction of retained earnings is formally made by transferring (debiting) an amount from retained earnings to (crediting) an appropriated retained earnings account. The entry has no effect on assets, liabilities, or total shareholders' equity. When the need for an appropriation or restriction no longer exists, the appropriated balance is returned to the unappropriated retained earnings account. Both appropriations and restrictions are rarely seen in practice.

DIVIDENDS

Nature of Dividends

A dividend is a distribution of earnings to shareholders in the form of assets or shares. A dividend typically results in a credit to the account that represents the item distributed (cash, non-cash asset, or share capital) and a debit to retained earnings.

Some corporate legislation and bond covenants place restrictions on the amount of assets and/or retained earnings that may be used for dividends. These constraints recognize the effects of dividends; that is, dividends require (1) a disbursement of assets and (2) a reduction in retained earnings, by the same amount. The company must have both assets and retained earnings to be eligible to declare/distribute dividends. Dividends may not be paid from legal capital (share capital) without specific creditor approval. Under the CBCA, a liquidity test must also be met: Dividends may not be declared or paid if the result would be that the corporation became unable to meet its liabilities as they came due, or if the dividend resulted in the realizable value of assets being less than liabilities plus stated capital.

Relevant Dividend Dates

Four dates have legal significance for dividends:

Declaration Date On the **declaration date**, the corporation's Board of Directors formally announces the dividend declaration. The courts have held that formal declaration of a cash or property dividend constitutes an enforceable contract between the corporation and its shareholders. Therefore, on the dividend declaration date, such dividends are recorded and a liability (i.e., dividends payable) is recognized.

Record Date The **record date** is the date on which the list of *shareholders of record,* who will receive the dividend, is prepared. Usually, the record date follows the declaration date by two to three weeks, to allow for changes in share ownership to be recorded. No entry is made in the accounts on the record date, but the shareholder list will determine the names on the eventual dividend cheques.

Ex-dividend Date An investor who holds (buys) shares on or after the **ex-dividend date** *does not* receive the dividend. Technically, the ex-dividend date is the day following the record date, but, to provide time to record the transfer of shares, the effective ex-dividend date is usually three or four days prior to the date of record. Thus, the investor who holds shares on the day prior to the stipulated ex-dividend date receives the dividend.

Payment Date This date is also determined by the Board of Directors and is usually stated in the declaration. It is the date on which dividends are paid or distributed to the shareholders of record. The **payment date** typically follows the declaration date by four to six weeks. At the date of payment, the liability recorded at date of declaration is debited and the appropriate asset account is credited.

Note that, of these four dates, the only ones that affect the accounting records of the company that declares the dividend are (1) the declaration date and (2) the payment date. The other two dates are significant for investors, but not for accounting.

Cash Dividends

Assume the Board of Directors of Bass Company, at its meeting on 20 January 20X2, declares a dividend of $0.50 per common share, payable 20 March 20X2, to shareholders of record on 1 March 20X2. Assume that 10,000 no-par common shares are outstanding.

At declaration date—20 January 20X2		
Common dividends declared* (10,000 shares × $0.50)	5,000	
Cash dividends payable		5,000
*Later closed to retained earnings; alternatively, retained earnings may be debited directly		
At payment date—20 March 20X2		
Cash dividends payable	5,000	
Cash		5,000

Cash dividends payable is reported as a current liability.

Preferred shares typically have first preference on amounts declared as dividends. Assume that Bass Company, in addition to the 10,000 common shares mentioned above, also has 5,000 $1.20 preferred shares outstanding. The Board of Directors declared dividends totalling $10,000, with the same declaration and payment dates as in the previous example. The first $6,000 will go to the preferred shareholders (5,000 shares × $1.20 per share); the remaining $4,000 will be distributed to the common shareholders at the rate of $0.40 per share ($4,000 ÷ 10,000 shares). Entries will be as follows:

At declaration date—20 January 20X2		
Preferred dividends declared*	6,000	
Common dividends declared*	4,000	
Cash dividends payable, preferred (5,000 × $1.20)		6,000
Cash dividends payable, common (10,000 × $0.40)		4,000
*Later closed to retained earnings; alternatively, retained earnings may be debited directly		
At payment date—20 March 20X2		
Cash dividends payable, preferred	6,000	
Cash dividends payable, common	4,000	
Cash		10,000

If Bass Company were to have declared $5,000 of dividends, the preferred shareholders would have received it all. They have preference for the first $6,000 each year.

In corporate reporting, it is important to distinguish the portion of the dividend attributable to the preferred shares versus the common. Accordingly, these are recorded separately in the accounts.

Cumulative Dividends on Preferred Shares

Cumulative preferred shares provide that dividends not declared in a given year accumulate at the specified rate on such shares. This accumulated amount must be paid in full if and when dividends are declared in a later year *before any dividends can be paid on the common shares*. If cumulative preference dividends are not declared in a given year, they are said to have been *passed* and are called *dividends in arrears* on the cumulative preferred shares.

If only a part of the preferred dividend is met for any year, the remainder of the cumulative dividend is in arrears. Cumulative preferred shares carry the right, on dissolution of the corporation, to dividends in arrears to the extent that the corporation has retained earnings. However, different provisions for dividends in arrears may be stipulated in the articles of incorporation and bylaws.

Dividends in arrears are not liabilities. Since preferred shareholders cannot force the Board of Directors to declare dividends, dividends in arrears do not meet the definition of a liability. Dividends in arrears for cumulative preference shares must be disclosed in the notes to the financial statements.

Participating Dividends on Preferred Shares

Participating preferred shares provide that the preferred shareholders participate above the stated preferential rate on a pro rata basis in dividend declarations with the common shareholders. This works as follows:

- First, the preferred shareholders receive their preference rate.
- Second, the common shareholders receive a specified matching dividend if the amount declared is high enough.
- If the total declared dividend is larger than these two amounts, the excess is divided on a pro rata basis between the two share classes.

The pro rata distribution may be based simply on the respective number of shares outstanding, the two classes' *total* base level dividends, or the respective *total* capital balances. Participation terms often reflect relative capital invested, and must be specified in the articles of incorporation and stated on the share certificates.

Reporting Example An example of a company that has participating shares is the Power Corporation of Canada, a diversified international management and holding company active in financial services, communications, and a variety of other business sectors. Total assets are $144 billion. In its capital structure, the Power Corporation reports subordinated voting shares, which are common shares, and participating preferred shares with the following terms:

> Entitled to ten votes per share, entitled to a non-cumulative dividend of 0.9375¢ per share before dividends on the subordinated voting shares and having the right to participate, share and share alike, with the holders of the subordinated voting shares in any year after payment of a dividend of 0.9375¢ per share on the subordinate voting shares.

The preferred shares are non-cumulative, but participate in dividends after both classes receive a base dividend.

Partially versus Fully Participating Shares may be *partially participating* or *fully participating*. If partially participating, preferred shares may participate in dividend declarations in excess of their preference rate, but the participation is capped at a certain level. Dividends above this level accrue solely to the common shareholders. Fully participating shares, on the other hand, share in the full extent of dividend declarations.

For example, a corporation may issue preferred shares entitled to a dividend of $0.50, with participation up to $0.70 after common shareholders receive $0.25 per share. In this case, participation with the common shareholders would be limited to the additional $0.20 above the regular $0.50 rate. The $0.25 dividend to the common shareholder is the matching dividend, and it is specified in the articles of incorporation. It is meant to provide the same rate of return on the common shares in the initial allocation and acknowledges that the share classes are of different relative size and value.

Example The following three cases, A, B, and C, illustrate various combinations of cumulative versus non-cumulative rights and of participating versus non-participating rights. Assume that Mann Corporation has the following share capital outstanding:

Preferred shares, no-par, dividend entitlement, $0.50 per share; 10,000 shares outstanding	$100,000	
Common shares, no-par, 40,000 shares outstanding	200,000	

Case A Preferred shares are non-cumulative and non-participating; dividends have not been paid for two years; dividends declared, $28,000.

	Preferred	Common	Total
Step 1—Preferred, current ($0.50 × 10,000)	$5,000		$ 5,000
Step 2—Common (balance)		$23,000	23,000
Total	$5,000	$23,000	$28,000

Because the preferred shares are non-cumulative, preferred shares may receive dividends only for the current year regardless of the fact that dividends were missed in two previous years.

Case B Preferred shares are *cumulative* and *non-participating*; dividends are two years in arrears; total dividends declared, $28,000.

	Preferred	Common	Total
Step 1—Preferred in arrears ($0.50 × 10,000 × 2)	$10,000		$10,000
Step 2—Preferred, current ($0.50 × 10,000)	5,000		5,000
Step 3—Common (balance)		$13,000	13,000
Total	$15,000	$13,000	$28,000

Preferred shares receive their dividends in arrears and the current dividend before the common shares receive any dividend.

Case C Preferred shares are cumulative, two years in arrears and fully participating after common shares have received $0.25 per share. *Participation is based on the respective total base dividend for one year.* Total dividends declared in this case are $37,000. Participation is based on one year's dividends: preferred are entitled to $0.50 per share ($5,000 total), and common will receive $0.25 per share ($10,000 total). The base dividend is $15,000 (that is, $5,000 + $10,000). Payment of dividends in arrears does not affect this calculation, which is based on *one* year's base dividend. Participation is 1/3 ($5,000/$15,000) for the preferred and 2/3 ($10,000/$15,000) for the common.

	Preferred	Common	Total
Step 1—Preferred, in arrears ($5,000 × 2)	$10,000		$10,000
Step 2a—Preferred, current (10,000 × $0.50)	5,000		5,000
b—Common, matching (40,000 × $0.25)		$10,000	10,000
c—Extra dividend, participating 1/3 : 2/3	4,000	8,000	12,000*
Totals	$19,000	$18,000	$37,000

*Extra dividend available: $37,000 − $10,000 − $5,000 − $10,000 = $12,000.

Had the preferred shares been *partially* participating, say, to a *total* of $0.75 per share, then the current year (excluding arrears) preferred dividend would have been limited to $7,500, and participation would have been a maximum of $2,500 ($7,500 − $5,000). The common shares would then have received more of the final $12,000 layer of dividends ($9,500, or $12,000 − $2,500).

In the absence of an explicit stipulation in the articles of incorporation or bylaws, preferred shareholders have no right to participate in dividends with common shares beyond their stated dividend rate.

Property Dividends

Corporations occasionally pay dividends with non-cash assets. Such dividends are called **property dividends** or *dividends in kind*. The property may be investments in the securities of other companies held by the corporation, real estate, merchandise, or any other non-cash asset designated by the Board of Directors. The dividend is recorded at the fair value of the assets distributed, and a gain (or loss) is recorded for the difference between book value and fair value of the asset.

Liquidating Dividends

Liquidating dividends are distributions that are a return of the amount received when shares were issued, rather than assets acquired through earnings. Owners' equity accounts *other than retained earnings* are debited. Since such dividends reduce contributed capital, they typically require creditor approval.

Liquidating dividends are appropriate when there is no intention or opportunity to conserve resources for asset replacement. A mining company might pay such a liquidating dividend when it is exploiting a non-replaceable asset. Mining companies sometimes pay dividends on the basis of "earnings plus the amount of the deduction for depletion." Shareholders must be informed of the portion of any dividend that represents a return of capital, since the liquidation portion of the dividend is not income to the investor and is usually not taxable as income; it reduces the cost basis of the shares.

When accounting for a liquidating dividend, the debit would not go to retained earnings. For example, share capital might be debited. However, any other contributed capital accounts would be debited and eliminated before share capital would be reduced.

Scrip Dividends

A corporation that has a temporary cash shortage might declare a dividend to maintain a continuing dividend policy by issuing a **scrip dividend**. The dividend takes the form of a certificate issued. This certificate may take the form of a promissory note, which will be repaid in cash on its due date. This form of dividend is also called a *liability dividend*.

Stock Dividends

A stock dividend is a proportional distribution to shareholders of additional shares of the corporation. A stock dividend does not change the assets, liabilities, or total shareholders' equity of the issuing corporation. It does not change the proportionate ownership of any shareholder. It simply increases the number of shares outstanding.

For instance, assume Early Broadcasting Limited has 120,000 common shares outstanding. One shareholder, J.S. Brown, owns 12,000 shares, or one-tenth of the shares. The corporation declares and issues a 10% stock dividend. This has the following effect on share capital:

	Before Dividend		After Dividend*	
Total shares outstanding	120,000	*100%*	132,000	*100%*
Brown's shareholding	12,000	*10%*	13,200	*10%*

*Previous outstanding total × 110%.

Brown's relative ownership percentage has not changed. If the shares sold for $20 per share before the dividend, what will happen to that market value after the split? Logically, it should decline.

	Before	After	
A. Total market value of the company (120,000 × $20)	$2,400,000	$2,400,000	(i.e., no change)
B. Shares outstanding	120,000	132,000	
Price per share (A ÷ B)	$20	$18.18	
Brown's total market value			
12,000 × $20.00	$ 240,000		
13,200 × $18.18		$ 240,000	

What will really happen to the market price of the shares in this situation? The answer is unclear. Often, there is a smaller decrease in market price than the size of the stock dividend would seem to dictate. That is, market value might fall to $18.50 rather than $18.18. Some believe that this is a market reaction to other factors (e.g., an anticipated increase in cash dividends that historically follows a stock dividend). Because of the complexity and sophistication of the stock markets, it is very difficult to determine why a share price does or does not change on a given day. However, it is generally recognized that if a company doubles its outstanding shares through a stock dividend, the market price will reduce by approximately one-half.

A stock dividend can cause the transfer of an amount from retained earnings to the contributed, or paid-in, capital accounts (i.e., share capital). Therefore, it changes only the internal account balances of shareholders' equity and not the total shareholders' equity.

Reasons for a Stock Dividend Numerous reasons exist for a company to issue a stock dividend:

- To reveal that the firm plans to permanently retain a portion of earnings in the business. The effect of a stock dividend, through a debit to retained earnings and offsetting credits to permanent capital accounts, is to raise contributed capital and reduce retained earnings. This will shelter this amount from future declaration of cash or property dividends.

- To increase the number of shares outstanding, which reduces the market price per share and, in turn, tends to increase trading of shares in the market. Theoretically, a broader range of investors can afford investments in equity securities if the unit cost is low.

- To continue dividend distributions without disbursing assets (usually cash) that may be needed for operations. The effect of a stock dividend may be purely psychological: management hopes that shareholders will feel they have received something of value.

- To allow shareholders to acquire additional shares without incurring transaction costs such as commissions.

Some companies allow shareholders to choose between a cash dividend and a stock dividend. The terms of this might appear as follows:

Common shareholders may elect to have their cash dividends reinvested in common shares of the Company in accordance with the Company's Shareholder Dividend Reinvestment and Share Purchase Plan. Under the Plan, the Board of Directors determines whether the common shares will be purchased on the stock market or issued by the Company from treasury shares.

Accounting Issues Related to Stock Dividends

One major issue in accounting for stock dividends is the value that should be recognized. The shares issued for the dividend could be recorded at fair value, at stated (or par) value, or at some other value.

There are no specific accounting standards on these issues, but the CBCA requires shares to be issued at fair market value. In Ontario, on the other hand, legislation specifically permits the Board of Directors to capitalize any amount it desires. In the United States, small stock dividends (i.e., less than 20 to 25% of the outstanding shares) *must* be recorded at fair value, while large stock dividends are recorded only as a memo entry (i.e., no value). When the shareholder has the choice between cash and shares, it seems most logical to record the full fair value of the dividend. We will examine three alternatives: fair value, stated value, and memo entry.

Fair Value Method The Board of Directors would require capitalization of the current fair value of the additional shares issued. The fair value of the stock dividend should be measured on the basis of the market price per share on the declaration date.

Assume that Markholme Corporation has 464,000 common shares outstanding, originally issued for $2,784,000. The company declares and distributes a 5% common stock dividend on 1 July 20X2, and determines that an appropriate fair value is $7.25 per share. The following entry will be recorded:

Stock dividend (or, retained earnings)		
(464,000 × 5% = 23,200 × $7.25)	168,200	
Common shares, no-par (23,200 shares)		168,200

Stated Value Method The Board of Directors in certain jurisdictions may decide to capitalize a stated amount per share—average paid in per share to date, or par value, if applicable. Strong arguments can be made for some sort of stated value because (1) the corporation's assets, liabilities, and total shareholders' equity are not changed and (2) the shareholders' proportionate ownership is not changed. If the market price per share is proportionately reduced by the stock dividend, then it is clear that the shareholders have received nothing of value and should not be encouraged to believe that they have. In these circumstances, capitalization should be limited to legal requirements.

If Markholme Corporation, explained above, declares the same 5% stock dividend, but the Board of Directors determines that the average amount paid in to date for the outstanding common shares is to be used, then $6 ($2,784,000 ÷ 464,000) will be used to determine the capitalization amount. The entry will be identical, except the amount recognized will be $139,200 (464,000 × 5% × $6).

Memo Entry Since a large stock dividend may be issued for the primary purpose of reducing market price per share, it is obvious at least in this case that the shareholder has received nothing of value. A memo entry may be recorded to identify the number of shares issued, outstanding, and subscribed. No change is made in any capital account. This parallels the treatment of a stock split, to be discussed later in this chapter. Large stock dividends are often called *stock splits effected as a stock dividend*. For example, in March 2006, the Royal Bank of Canada announced a 100% stock dividend. If a shareholder owned 100 shares before the dividend, the shareholder had 200 shares afterward. The stock dividend was accounted for with a memo entry. However, this treatment may also be used for small stock dividends. Markholme Corporation, above, could record a memo entry documenting the distribution of 23,200 (464,000 × 5%) shares.

Timing of Recognition

Fundamentally, a stock dividend is recorded as a debit to retained earnings and a credit to the share capital account. However, unlike a cash dividend, a stock dividend *can be revoked prior to the issuance date*. As a result, many companies do not record the dividend on the declaration date, but instead record it on the issuance date. Either recording approach can be used.

Example Marvel Corporation, which has 100,000 common shares outstanding, declares a 10% common stock dividend. The Board of Directors directs that the dividend be recorded at fair value. A total of 10,000 no-par common shares are issued. The fair value is $5 per share. The entries are as follows:

Alternative 1: Originating Entry at Declaration		
Declaration date		
Stock dividends (or, retained earnings)	50,000	
Stock dividends distributable*		50,000
*Reported as a credit in shareholders' equity until issuance.		
Issuance date		
Stock dividends distributable	50,000	
Common shares, no-par (5,000 shares)		50,000

Alternative 2: Originating Entry at Issuance		
Declaration date		
No entry		
Issuance date		
Stock dividends (or, retained earnings)	50,000	
Common shares, no-par (5,000 shares)		50,000

The differences between these two approaches are trivial. The stock dividends distributable account is not a liability, for it does not involve settlement by the future transfer of assets (cash, etc.) It is an obligation to issue equity and is properly classified in shareholders' equity. Note disclosure would accompany both alternatives.

Special Stock Dividends

When a stock dividend is of the same class as that held by the recipients, it is called an *ordinary stock dividend* (e.g., common shares issued to the owners of common). When a class of share capital other than the one already held by the recipients is issued, such a dividend is called a *special stock dividend* (e.g., preferred shares issued to the owners of common). In this case, the fair value of the preferred shares issued as a dividend should be recorded.

Fractional Share Rights

When a stock dividend is issued, many shareholders will own an "odd" number of shares and be entitled to a fraction of a share. For example, when a firm issues a 5% stock dividend and a shareholder owns 30 shares, the shareholder is entitled to 1.5 shares (30 × 5%). When this happens, the firm may issue *fractional share rights* for portions of shares to which individual shareholders are entitled. It is also quite common for the company to write a cheque for the fair value of the fractional entitlement.

To demonstrate, suppose Moon Company has 1,000,000 outstanding no-par common shares. Moon issues a 5% stock dividend. The fair value of the common shares is $80 per share, and this value will be used to record the stock dividend. The number of shares to be issued is 5% of the number of shares outstanding (1,000,000 × 5%), or 50,000 shares.

Assume the distribution of existing shares is such that 42,000 whole or complete shares can be issued. The firm will issue fractional share rights for the remaining 8,000 shares. Each fractional share right will entitle the holder to acquire 5%, or 1/20, of a share. Since there are 8,000 shares yet to be issued, there will be 8,000 × 20, or 160,000 fractional share rights issued. A market will develop for the fractional share rights, with each having a fair value of approximately 1/20 of a whole share ($80 ÷ 20), or $4. Shareholders can buy or sell fractional share rights to the point where whole shares can be acquired. A holder will have to turn in 20 fractional share rights to receive one common share.

The entry for recording the issuance of the stock dividend and fractional share rights is as follows:

Stock dividends (or, retained earnings)		
(50,000 × $80)	4,000,000	
Common shares, no-par (42,000 shares × $80)		3,360,000
Common share fractional share rights		
(8,000 shares; 160,000 rights) (8,000 × $80)		640,000

When rights are turned in for redemption in common shares, the common share fractional share rights account is debited and common shares are credited. Suppose, for example, that 150,000 fractional share rights are turned in for 7,500 common shares (150,000 ÷ 20). The entry to record the transaction would be:

Common share fractional share rights	600,000	
Common shares, no-par (7,500 shares × $80)		600,000

If the remaining rights are allowed to lapse, the corporation would record contributed capital:

Common share fractional share rights	40,000	
Contributed capital, lapse of share rights (500 × $80)		40,000

Cash Alternative An alternative to the issuance of fractional share rights is to make a cash payment to shareholders for any fractional shares to which they are entitled. The shareholder above who owns 30 shares and is entitled to 1.5 shares will receive one share from the firm and a cash payment of $40 ($80 per share × .5 shares), representing the value of the one-half share at current fair value. The entry to record the cash payment is a debit to retained earnings and a credit to cash. This procedure is simpler for the shareholder, because there is no need to buy or sell fractional shares.

If cash were offered for fractional shares, the stock dividend would be recorded, in summary form, as follows:

Stock dividends (or, retained earnings)		
(50,000 × $80)	4,000,000	
Common shares, no-par (42,000 shares)		3,360,000
Cash (8,000 shares × $80)		640,000

This alternative clearly has cash flow implications for the company, but it avoids the complications of dealing with fractional shares for all concerned.

Summary Dividends and distributions are summarized as follows:

Type	Shareholder Receives	Recorded At	Watch Out For
Cash	Cash	Exchange amount; cash	Amount allocated to common versus preferred shares
Property	Some company asset as designated by the Board of Directors: inventory, investments, etc.	Fair value; gain or loss recorded on declaration	
Scrip	Promissory note or occasionally common shares	Exchange amount; as stated	Shareholders get a receivable; company sets up a liability, Or, occasionally: Shareholders get common shares; company increases share capital
Stock	Shares	May be recorded at fair value, book value, or an arbitrary value May also be recorded as a memo entry only	May issue fractional shares for part shares or cash for part shares
Stock split (next section)	Shares	n/a	Memo entry only; not recorded

CONCEPT REVIEW

1. Of the four dates pertaining to cash dividends, which dates require accounting entries? What are the entries?
2. What effect does a cash dividend have on shareholders' equity? How does the effect of a stock dividend differ from that of a cash dividend?
3. What is a participating preferred dividend?

STOCK SPLITS

A **stock split** is a change in the number of shares outstanding with no change in the recorded capital accounts. A stock split usually increases the number of shares outstanding by a significant amount, such as doubling or tripling the number of outstanding shares. Shares that sell at high market values are perceived to be less marketable, especially to smaller investors. Therefore, the primary purpose of a stock split is to increase the number of shares outstanding and decrease the market price per share. In turn, this may increase the market activity of the shares. By increasing the number of shares outstanding, a stock split also reduces earnings per share.

In contrast, a **reverse split** decreases the number of shares. It results in a proportional reduction in the number of shares issued and outstanding, and an increase in the average book value per share. Reverse splits may be used to increase the market price of shares with a low market value per share. For example, consider Domtar Paper (Canada) Inc, which implemented a 1-for-12 reverse split in 2009, with fractional shares distributed in cash:

As a result of the reverse stock split, every 12 shares of the Company's issued and outstanding exchangeable shares at the Effective Time have been automatically combined into 1 issued and outstanding exchangeable share, without any change in the par value of such shares, subject to the elimination of fractional shares resulting from the reverse stock split which have been aggregated and sold into whole shares on the open market by the Company's transfer agent with proceeds of such sales allocated to the record holders' respective accounts pro rata in lieu of fractional shares.

Accounting for Stock Splits

In a stock split, *a memo entry is recorded*. No consideration has been received by the corporation for the issued shares. Shares issued, outstanding, and subscribed are changed, as is par value, if any. The following dollar amounts are *not* changed:

1. Share capital account;

2. Additional contributed capital accounts;

3. Retained earnings; and

4. Total shareholders' equity.

Consider a 200%, or 2-for-1, stock split (two new shares for each old share) and compare it with a 100% stock dividend (one additional share for each share already outstanding). For example, assume Technology Corporation has 40,000 shares outstanding, which were issued initially at $10 per share. The current balance of retained earnings is $450,000. A 100% stock dividend and a 200% stock split accomplish the same things in economic terms, in that they double the outstanding shares but halve the market value per share. However, the two transactions can appear differently on the books if the dividend is capitalized and the split is recorded in memo form. The difference is shown in Exhibit 13-1, where the stock dividend is recorded at $10 per share, and the split is accorded memo treatment.

EXHIBIT 13-1

TECHNOLOGY CORPORATION

Stock Dividend and Stock Split Compared

	Total Prior to Share Issue	Total After 100% Stock Dividend	Total After 2-for-1 Stock Split
Initial issue 40,000 × $10 =	$400,000		
100% stock dividend: (40,000 + 40,000) × $10 =		$800,000*	
Two-for-one stock split: 80,000 × $5			$400,000
Share capital	$400,000	$800,000*	$400,000
Retained earnings	450,000	50,000*	450,000
Total shareholders' equity	$850,000	$850,000*	$850,000

*Retained earnings capitalized: 40,000 shares × $10 = $400,000 (entry: debit retained earnings, $400,000; credit share capital accounts, $400,000.) After the stock dividend, share capital equals $800,000, which is $400,000 + $400,000. Retained earnings is $450,000 − $400,000, or $50,000.

In Exhibit 13-1, notice that the stock dividend changes both share capital and retained earnings. The stock split, however, changes neither of these amounts. *Total* shareholders' equity is unchanged by both the stock dividend and the stock split.

Commentary Remember that the shareholder is left in the same position whether there is a 200% stock split or a 100% stock dividend—two shares will be owned for every one share previously held. Similarly, the market price of the shares should be the same whether the transaction is described as a split or a dividend.

This similarity of results makes the different accounting methods suspect, since there are alternatives available for transactions that are basically the same. This hardly seems to promote the idea of *substance over form*. Accordingly, *memo treatment* of a large stock dividend is the preferable approach because it produces the same result as the memo treatment for a stock split.

Adjustments Required for Stock Splits When a stock is split, the per-share values all change. For example, in a 2-for-1 split, the paid-in value per share is halved. If Sincon Corporation has 40,000 outstanding shares and total contributed capital of $800,000, the average issue price is $20. After a 2-for-1 split, the company will have 80,000 shares, and the average issue price drops to $10 per share.

Similarly, other per-share amounts such as earnings per share (EPS) will change. Suppose that Sincon had EPS of $3.00 before the split and paid dividends of $2.00 per share. The equivalent EPS after the split will be $1.50. To pay dividends after the split that are equivalent to the dividend rate before the split, Sincon needs to pay only $1.00—but on twice as many shares.

Because of the change in number of shares in a stock split (or a reverse split), the company must recalculate all prior years' per-share amounts so that they will be comparable to post-split per-share amounts. Earnings per share and dividends per share must be restated.

Conversion rights for senior securities must also be adjusted. If preferred shares are convertible into three common shares prior to a 2-for-1 common share split, the preferred share will be convertible into six common shares after the split.

Implementation A stock split is implemented by either:

1. Calling in all of the old shares and concurrently issuing the split shares, or, more commonly,

2. Issuing the additional split shares with notification to shareholders of the change in outstanding shares.

It is more common simply to issue additional shares. If the shares have an assigned par value, share certificates must be replaced to reflect revised par value.

ADDITIONAL CONTRIBUTED CAPITAL

Contributed capital is created by a number of events that involve the corporation and its shareholders. Several accounts for additional contributed (paid-in) capital were introduced in this chapter, such as contributed capital on share repurchase.

Donated Capital Sometimes a corporation will receive a donation of assets, which creates **donated capital**. An example would be a donation of land from a shareholder. In this case, the corporation records the donated asset at its fair market value, with a corresponding credit to donated capital. The donation is viewed by the accounting profession as a capital contribution rather than as an earnings item (i.e., it is not a gain.) Donated capital appears in shareholders' equity as additional contributed capital. It must be described as to source.

Other Shares may also be donated back to a company. Corporate legislation typically requires that such shares be retired, and the retirement entry is similar to the examples given earlier, except that there is no cash consideration given—the entire paid-in value of the shares (at average cost) is transferred to an additional contributed capital account. If the shares can be legally held and reissued, the shares may be accounted for as treasury shares.

Exhibit 13-2 summarizes some of the transactions that may cause increases or decreases in additional contributed capital.

EXHIBIT 13-2

TRANSACTIONS THAT MAY CHANGE ADDITIONAL CONTRIBUTED CAPITAL

Increase

1. Receipt of donated assets
2. Retirement of shares at a price less than average issue price to date
3. Issue of par-value shares at a price or assigned value higher than par
4. Treasury stock transactions, shares reissued above cost
5. Stock option transactions (see Chapter 14)

Decrease

1. Retirement of shares at a price greater than average issue price to date, when previous contributed capital has been recorded
2. Treasury stock transactions, shares issued below cost, when previous contributed capital has been recorded
3. Financial restructuring

RESERVES

Reserves are caused by unrealized gains and losses that are part of *other comprehensive income* but not part of *earnings*. Such amounts are a component of shareholders' equity, usually presented below retained earnings. The reserve reflects the *cumulative amounts* of the items that are added to or subtracted from earnings to arrive at comprehensive income. The reserves are also called *accumulated other comprehensive income*.

Example Assume the following fact for AgriCorp Limited, a company with investments carried at fair value, with unrealized gains and losses recorded in other comprehensive income. That is, the company holds investments classified as fair value through other comprehensive income (FVTOCI) investments:

	20X2	20X3	20X4
FVTOCI investments			
Cost; purchased in January 20X2	$100,000		
Fair value, end of year	$130,000	$110,000	$160,000
Earnings	$345,000	$287,000	$371,000

Based on this information, comprehensive income is as follows:

	20X2	20X3	20X4
Earnings	$345,000	$287,000	$371,000
Other Comprehensive Income:			
Change in fair value			
($130,000 − $100,000)	30,000		
($110,000 − $130,000)		(20,000)	
($160,000 − $110,000)			50,000
Comprehensive income	$375,000	$267,000	$421,000

The cumulative reserve (also called *accumulated other comprehensive income*) would be:

	20X2	20X3	20X4
Shareholders' equity			
Reserve caused by FVTOCI investments			
($130,000 − $100,000)	$30,000		
($110,000 − $100,000), or ($30,000 − $20,000)		$10,000	
($160,000 − $100,000), or ($10,000 + $50,000)			$60,000

This example has ignored income tax implications. Elements that are taxable, either in the current period or in the future, have tax assigned to them when recognized, and are reported net of tax in other comprehensive income and in the reserve. Reporting issues related to income tax are explored in chapters 15 and 16.

Sources of Reserves   There are a limited number of unrealized amounts that are part of comprehensive income and thus cause reserves, as follows:

- Gains and losses on FVTOCI financial instruments (Chapter 11);
- Revaluation reserves caused by revaluing property, plant, and equipment to fair value (Chapter 10);
- Gains and losses on certain hedging instruments (Chapters 12 and 14); and
- Translation gains and losses on foreign operations whose functional currency is a foreign currency rather than the presentation currency.

Standards require these unrealized amounts to be shown separately in equity.

Translation Gains and Losses on Foreign Operations   One equity reserve listed above is the **cumulative foreign currency translation account**. This item represents unrealized gains and losses that arise from a certain type of foreign currency exposure.

In Chapter 12, accounting for a liability denominated in a foreign currency was reviewed; gains and losses caused by changes in foreign exchange rates are included in earnings as they arise, and no reserve is involved. However, many corporations have subsidiaries in one or more foreign countries. The basic operations of these foreign subsidiaries are carried out in a currency other than the Canadian dollar, and their separate entity financial statements are reported in the host country foreign currency. In order for the parent company to prepare consolidated financial statements, the foreign operation's *foreign currency* financial statements must be translated into the parent's *presentation currency*. The process of translation is a topic for advanced accounting courses and is not discussed here.

However, translation of foreign operations gives rise to an overall exchange gain or loss. If the foreign operation is essentially autonomous and transactions are primarily in the foreign currency, the subsidiary has a **functional currency** that is the foreign currency. The exchange gains and losses that arise from translating the financial statements of such foreign operations do not flow through earnings, but instead the annual amounts are included in other comprehensive income. The cumulative amount is a reserve. If the foreign subsidiary's cash flows are *interdependent* with the parent, its functional currency is the Canadian dollar, and exchange gains and losses are part of earnings.

SHAREHOLDERS' EQUITY DISCLOSURE

The details of the components of equity can be shown on the face of the statement of financial position, in a statement of changes in equity, or in the disclosure notes. That is, it is possible to show only a single line for equity in the SFP, with the break-down shown in the notes or on a statement of changes in equity.

Statement of Changes in Equity

The general format of a statement of changes in equity is illustrated below. Each company will tailor this statement to its own shareholders' equity accounts and transactions. There are columns for each account within equity. The statement starts with opening dollar balances, and has a line item for each source of change to an account, resulting in the end-of-year balance.

Note that *comprehensive income* affects retained earnings (for the amount of earnings) and a reserve (for the unrealized amounts that are part of other comprehensive income but not earnings, here assumed to be caused by FVTOCI investments). Some companies will include extra columns to include the *number of shares* for common and preferred shares, in addition to the dollar amount.

	Preferred Shares	Common Shares	Retained Earnings	Reserve Caused by FVTOCI Investments	Total Equity
Balance at 1 January 20X1	$xx	$xx	$xx	$xx	$xx
Comprehensive income	—	—	xx	xx	xx
Shares issued	xx	xx	—	—	xx
Share buy-back	—	(xx)	(xx)	—	(xx)
Dividends to shareholders	—	—	(xx)	—	(xx)
Balance at 31 December 20X1	$xx	$xx	$xx	$xx	$xx

Other Disclosure

For each class of share capital, the legal rights, preferences, and restrictions must be described in the disclosure notes. This includes all authorized share classes, whether shares are issued or not. The number of shares issued and fully paid at year-end must be disclosed, as well as shares issued and not fully paid (shares subscribed). The *number of shares* issued, repurchased, and retired during the year must be disclosed, if this information is not in the statement of changes in equity.

Companies must disclose their objectives, policies, and processes for *managing capital*. This includes their definition of capital, which obviously includes equity but also may include some forms of debt. If there are externally imposed capital requirements, these requirements and compliance with the requirements must be disclosed.

Reporting Example Exhibit 13-3 shows the statement of changes in shareholders' equity for Santos Ltd., an Australian company active in petroleum exploration, production, treatment, and marketing of natural gas, liquefied natural gas, crude oil, condensate, naphtha, and liquid petroleum gas, as well as pipeline operations. The statement has a separate reconciliation column for each of the *four* shareholders' equity elements.

Comprehensive income is $1,717.0 million, which is distributed to retained earnings and two reserve accounts. That is, $1,632.9 represents net earnings, which increases retained earnings. Another $93.5 is a foreign exchange gain on subsidiaries whose functional currency is not the Australian dollar. Gains from this source are allocated to the translation reserve. This reserve is in a cumulative loss position so the gain reduces the loss to date. A further $9.4 million of comprehensive income represents losses on investments recorded at fair value; the $9.4 is allocated to the fair value reserve, taking it to a cumulative loss position. The statement also shows, in the share capital account, that shares were issued during the period, and shares were repurchased. In the repurchase, share capital declined by $56.4, and retained earnings declined by $245, indicating that the shares were repurchased for a price higher than their original issuance price. Finally, dividends to shareholders reduced retained earnings.

Exhibit 13-4 shows excerpts from the Shaw Communications share capital note, which includes the terms of the Class A voting participating shares, and Class B non-voting shares. Share transactions during the year are documented, both with dollar values and with the number of shares.

EXHIBIT 13-3

RECONCILIATION OF MOVEMENT OF CAPITAL AND RESERVES ATTRIBUTABLE TO EQUITY HOLDERS OF SANTOS LIMITED

in Australian $

	Share Capital $ million	Translation Reserve $ million	Fair Value Reserve $ million	Retained Earnings $ million	Total Equity $ million
Balance at 1 January 2008	2,331.6	(280.3)	7.4	1,034.4	3,093.1
Movement per recognized income and expense statement	—	93.5	(9.4)	1,632.9	1,717.0
Share options exercised by employees	2.5				2.5
Shares issued	253.1				253.1
Share buy-back	(56.4)			(245.0)	(301.4)
Dividends to shareholders				(286.3)	(286.3)
Equity attributable to equity holders of Santos	2,530.8	(186.8)	(2.0)	2,136.0	4,478.0
Equity attributable to minority interests	0.5			(0.2)	0.3
Balance at 31 December 2008	2,531.3	(186.8)	(2.0)	2,135.8	4,478.3

Comparative numbers have been omitted.

Source: Reproduced with permission from Santos Ltd.

EXHIBIT 13-4

SHAW COMMUNICATIONS INC. EQUITY DISCLOSURES (EXCERPTS)

Note 11 Share Capital

Authorized

The Company is authorized to issue a limited number of Class A voting participating shares ("Class A Shares") of no par value, as described below, an unlimited number of Class B non-voting participating shares ("Class B Non-Voting Shares") of no par value, Class 1 preferred shares, Class 2 preferred shares, Class A preferred shares and Class B preferred shares.

The authorized number of Class A Shares is limited, subject to certain exceptions, to the lesser of that number of shares (i) currently issued and outstanding and (ii) that may be outstanding after any conversion of Class A Shares into Class B Non-Voting Shares.

2008 Number of securities	2007 Number of securities		2008 $ thousands	2007 $ thousands
22,550,064	22,563,064	Class A shares	2,471	2,473
405,882,652	408,770,759	Class B Non-Voting shares	2,060,960	2,050,687
428,432,716	431,333,823		2,063,431	2,053,160

Class A Shares and Class B Non-Voting Shares

Class A Shares are convertible at any time into an equivalent number of Class B Non-Voting Shares. In the event that a take-over bid is made for Class A Shares, in certain circumstances, the Class B Non-Voting Shares are convertible into an equivalent number of Class A Shares.

Changes in Class A Share capital and Class B Non-Voting Share capital in 2008 are as follows: [comparative figures are omitted]

	Class A Shares		Class B Shares	
	Number	$	Number	$
August 31, 2007	22,563,064	2,473	408,770,759	2,050,687
Class A Share conversions	(13,000)	(2)	13,000	2
Purchase of shares for cancellation	—	—	(4,898,300)	(24,794)
Stock options exercises	—	—	1,997,193	35,065
August 31, 2008	22,550,064	2,471	405,882,652	2,060,960

During 2008 the Company purchased for cancellation 4,898,300 Class B Non-Voting Shares, pursuant to its outstanding normal course issuer bid or otherwise, for $99,757. Share capital has been reduced by the stated value of the shares amounting to $24,794 with the excess of the amount paid over the stated value of the shares amounting to $74,963 charged to the deficit.

Source: Shaw Communications Inc., © 2010.

CONCEPT REVIEW

1. How do a stock split and a stock dividend differ in their impact on the shareholders' equity accounts?
2. Identify at least two ways in which a corporation can obtain contributed capital other than by the issuance of new shares.
3. What items create unrealized gains and losses that give rise to reserves reported in equity?

ACCOUNTING STANDARDS FOR PRIVATE ENTERPRISES

There are very few differences between public and private companies in the area of accounting for equity interests. However, private companies are *required* to follow the standards governing share retirement and treasury stock transactions as described. The IASB has no standards in this area; the chapter material is presented as a logical approach, but not the required approach, for public companies.

Shares with special terms and conditions are frequently encountered in private companies. This is caused by opportunities for tax planning, the need to balance competing shareholder interests, and various succession and incentive plans. Disclosure of the terms and conditions of shares is just as important for private companies as for public companies.

When shares are issued for non-cash consideration, a private company will value the transaction at the fair value of the shares given up, unless the valuation of the shares is problematic. If the fair value of the assets is more clearly determinable, then this value should be used. The IASB standards *require that the fair value of the assets received* be used to value the transaction.

For private companies, net income is reported, but there is no reporting of comprehensive income. There are no unrealized amounts that must be included in such a measure. For example, the investment category FVTOCI does not exist for private companies. If there are specific unrealized amounts that are excluded from net income, such as unrealized gains and losses from a foreign subsidiary, they are allocated directly to a separate equity account and are not channelled first through comprehensive income.

The approach to classifying foreign subsidiaries is different under ASPE. While IFRS relies on identification of a functional currency, ASPE requires foreign subsidiaries to be classified as self-sustaining or integrated, based on the nature and extent of parent company relations and transactions. Self-sustaining subsidiaries cause unrealized exchange gains and losses in equity, while integrated operations cause exchange gains and losses recorded in earnings.

Finally, a private company has no requirement to prepare a comprehensive statement of changes in equity. Only a retained earnings statement must be included with the financial statements. The changes in other equity accounts may be included in the disclosure notes.

RELEVANT STANDARDS

IASB:
- *IAS* 1, Presentation of Financial Statements
- *IAS* 32, Financial Instruments; Presentation
- *IFRS* 2, Share-Based Payments
- *IFRIC* 17, Distributions of Non-cash Assets to Owners

CICA Handbook Part II:
- Section 1535, Capital Disclosures
- Section 3240, Share Capital
- Section 3251, Equity
- Section 3260, Reserves
- Section 3831, Non-monetary Transactions

SUMMARY OF KEY POINTS

1. Equity is a residual amount on the statement of financial position but has various component elements. The major sources are contributed capital from shareholders and earnings.

2. Ownership claims are represented by shares. Different share classes have different contractual rights; the two basic types of shares are common and preferred. Preferred shares have one or more contractually specified preferences over common shares, while common shares generally are voting, and have a residual claim to the firm's assets.

3. In conformity with legislative requirements, most shares issued are no-par shares. The entire amount of consideration received on the issuance of no-par shares is recorded in the share capital account.

4. Authorized capital represents the total number of shares that legally can be issued. Issued shares are the number of shares that have been issued to shareholders to date. Treasury stock exists when outstanding shares are reacquired by the corporation and are held pending resale. Outstanding shares are those currently held by shareholders. Subscribed shares are unissued shares that must be used to meet subscription contracts.

5. When a corporation issues shares for assets or for services, the fair value of the goods or services received is used to value the transaction. If shares are issued as a basket, the proportional or incremental method could be used to value the transaction, based on information available.

6. Share issue costs are either offset against the proceeds received, resulting in the net proceeds being recorded in share capital, or deducted from retained earnings.

7. When shares are retired, an amount of share capital relating to the shares is first removed at average cost. If the remaining balance is a credit, it is used to increase a contributed capital account on share retirement. If the remaining balance is a debit, it is debited to existing contributed capital account from prior retirements in this class of shares, if any, and any remaining balance is debited to retained earnings.

8. Treasury stock is debited to a contra shareholders' equity account titled "treasury stock," at cost. When the stock is resold, the difference between the acquisition price and the resale price is accounted for using the same rules as retirements.

9. Retained earnings represents the accumulated profit or loss, less dividends declared since the inception of the corporation, and certain adjustments arising from share retirement, error correction, and changes in accounting policy.

10. Dividends are distributions to shareholders and may be in the form of cash, non-cash assets, debt, or the corporation's own shares.

11. Dividends are allocated to the various share classes based on their respective contractual claims. If preferred shares are cumulative, and dividends are not paid in full in a given year, dividends declared in a later year are first paid to the preferred shares for the amount in arrears plus their current dividend before any amount is allocated to common shares. If preferred shares are participating, they receive a base dividend, then the common shares receive a base dividend; any dividend declared over the base is allocated between the two share classes.

12. Stock dividends are proportional issuances of additional shares. Stock dividends may be recorded at fair value, at a stated amount, or in a memo entry. In general, small stock dividends are recorded at fair value, while large dividends are recorded in a memo entry.

13. Fractional shares are issued when a shareholder would receive a portion of a share as a result of a stock dividend. Fractional shares are recorded in a shareholders' equity account that may lapse and create contributed capital, or may be turned in for whole shares, creating share capital. Alternatively, the company may pay out money in lieu of fractional shares.

14. A stock split is a change in the number of shares outstanding accompanied by an offsetting change in value per share. A memo entry reflects the changed number of outstanding shares.

15. Reserves within equity are caused by cumulative unrealized gains and losses. These amounts are part of comprehensive income but not earnings. Examples are unrealized fair value changes in FVTOCI investments, exchange gains and losses from certain foreign subsidiaries, and hedging transactions.

16. Companies are required to disclose the components of shareholders' equity, along with details of the changes in each account within shareholders' equity during the year. Complete disclosure of the terms of shares is also required.

KEY TERMS

appropriated retained earnings, 766
callable, 760
classes of shares, 754
common shares, 754
cumulative foreign currency translation account, 780
declaration date, 767
deficit, 766
discount, 755
dividends in arrears, 755
donated capital, 778
ex-dividend date, 767
functional currency, 780
net assets, 753
no-par shares, 756
normal course issuer bid, 760
par value shares, 755
payment date, 767
preferred shares, 754

premium, 755
private companies, 754
property dividends, 771
public companies, 754
record date, 767
reserve, 779
restricted retained earnings, 766
restricted shares, 755
reverse split, 776
scrip dividend, 771
share issue costs, 760
shareholders' agreement, 754
shelf registration, 764
single-transaction method, 764
special shares, 755
stock split, 776
stock subscriptions, 757
treasury stock, 763

REVIEW PROBLEM

On 2 January 20X1, Greene Corporation was incorporated in the province of Ontario. It was authorized to issue an unlimited number of no-par value common shares, and 10,000 shares of no-par, $8, cumulative and non-participating preferred shares. During 20X1, the firm completed the following transactions:

8 Jan.   Accepted subscriptions for 40,000 common shares at $12 per share. Down payment on the subscribed shares totalled $150,000.

30 Jan.   Issued 4,000 preferred shares in exchange for the following assets: machinery with a fair market value of $35,000, a factory with a fair market value of $110,000, and land with an appraised value of $295,000.

15 Mar.	Machinery with a fair market value of $55,000 was donated to the company.
25 Apr.	Collected the balance of the subscriptions receivable and issued common shares.
30 June	Purchased 2,200 common shares at $18 per share. The shares were retired.
31 Dec.	Closed the income summary to retained earnings. The income for the period was $198,000.
31 Dec.	Declared sufficient cash dividends to allow a $1 per share dividend for outstanding common shares. The dividend is payable on 10 January 20X2, to shareholders of record on 5 January 20X2.

Required:

1. Prepare the journal entries to record the above transactions.
2. Prepare a multi-column statement of changes in equity that explains the change in each equity account.
3. Prepare the shareholders' equity section of the SFP for Greene Corporation at 31 December 20X1.

REVIEW PROBLEM—SOLUTION

Account for subscription of common shares		
Cash	150,000	
Stock subscription receivable	330,000	
Common shares subscribed (40,000 shares)		480,000
Issue preferred shares in exchange for assets;		
recorded at fair market value of the assets		
Machinery	35,000	
Factory	110,000	
Land	295,000	
Preferred shares (4,000 shares)		440,000
Record receipt of donated assets		
Machinery	55,000	
Contributed capital—donations		55,000
Record receipt of cash for subscribed shares and		
issuance of shares		
Cash	330,000	
Stock subscription receivable		330,000
Common shares subscribed (40,000 shares)	480,000	
Common shares (40,000 shares)		480,000
Record acquisition and retirement of common shares		
Common shares ($480,000 ÷ 40,000) × 2,200	26,400	
Retained earnings	13,200	
Cash ($18 × 2,200)		39,600
Close the income summary		
Income summary	198,000	
Retained earnings		198,000

continued on next page

Record dividends declared		
Preferred dividends declared (or, retained earnings)	32,000	
Common dividends declared (or, retained earnings)	37,800	
Dividends payable, preferred shares		32,000
Dividends payable, common shares		37,800
Preferred dividend: 4,000 shares × $8		
Common dividend: 37,800 shares × $1		

GREENE CORPORATION

Changes in Shareholders' Equity for the Year Ended 31 December 20X1

	Preferred Shares	Common Shares	Common Shares Subscribed	Donated Capital	Retained Earnings	Total Equity
Balance at 1 January 20X1	$ —	$ —	$ —	$ —	$ —	$ —
Earnings and comprehensive income					198,000	198,000
Shares subscribed			480,000			480,000
Shares issued	440,000	480,000	(480,000)			440,000
Share buy-back		(26,400)			(13,200)	(39,600)
Donation of assets				55,000		55,000
Dividends to shareholders					(69,800)	(69,800)
Balance at 31 December 20X1	$440,000	$453,600	—	$55,000	$115,000	$1,063,600

GREENE CORPORATION

Shareholders' Equity at 31 December 20X1

Contributed capital	
Share capital	
Preferred shares, no-par, $8, cumulative and non-participating (10,000 shares authorized, 4,000 shares issued)	$ 440,000
Common shares, no-par (unlimited shares authorized, 37,800 shares issued and outstanding)	453,600
Other contributed capital	
Donation of machinery	55,000
Total contributed capital	$ 948,600
Retained earnings	115,000
Total shareholders' equity	$1,063,600

QUESTIONS

Q13-1 Describe the main categories of shareholders' equity.

Q13-2 If common shares are issued for capital assets, how is a value determined for the transaction?

Q13-3 What is the difference, from an accounting perspective, between par and no-par shares?

Q13-4 Briefly explain the alternatives for accounting for share issue costs.

Q13-5 When a company has 100,000 shares issued, and 10,000 shares held as treasury shares, how many shares are outstanding? If a cash dividend of $2 per share were declared, how much total dividend would be paid?

Q13-6 How can shares that are not callable be reacquired by a company? Why must corporations exercise caution in these transactions?

Q13-7 Why will EPS increase when shares are retired?

Q13-8 Identify and explain a transaction that causes *other contributed capital* to increase but does not result in any increase in assets or decrease in the liabilities of a corporation.

Q13-9 Explain how the purchase price is allocated when shares are reacquired and retired at a cost lower than average issuance price to date. What changes if average issuance price is lower?

Q13-10 When shares are retired, is the original issue price of those individual shares relevant? Why or why not?

Q13-11 Is treasury stock an asset? Explain.

Q13-12 What is the effect on assets, liabilities, and shareholders' equity of the (a) purchase of treasury stock and (b) sale of treasury stock?

Q13-13 Explain the difference between cumulative and non-cumulative preferred shares, and the difference between non-participating, partially participating, and fully participating preferred shares.

Q13-14 Contrast the effects of a stock dividend (declared and issued) versus a cash dividend (declared and paid) on assets, liabilities, and total shareholders' equity.

Q13-15 What are fractional share rights and why are they sometimes issued in connection with a stock dividend?

Q13-16 How is the entry to record a (cash) liquidating dividend different from the entry to record a normal cash dividend?

Q13-17 What do shareholders receive when a scrip dividend is declared?

Q13-18 Compare a stock split, both its substance and accounting recognition, to a large stock dividend. In what ways are the two the same or different?

Q13-19 If a shareholder donates a valuable piece of art to a company, to be displayed in the company boardroom, does the company record a gain on the transaction?

Q13-20 What are the common sources of reserves in equity?

CASE 13-1

TOPSAIL LTD.

Topsail Ltd. was founded ten years ago by Dave Jetson, a carpenter and entrepreneur. Topsail Ltd. is a growing construction company, building houses and doing major renovations for residential customers throughout the greater Moncton area. Dave is the president and sole common shareholder of the company.

Topsail approached its credit union in early 20X1 to increase its long-term debt in order to finance the purchase of equipment. A great deal of Topsail's equipment had been showing the strain of increased use and its efficiency was slipping. The credit union agreed to finance this purchase using the new equipment as collateral, but has imposed a reasonably stringent debt-to-equity covenant. They also require audited financial statements. In the fall of 20X1, Dave met Carlie Smith, a partner with Morash and Bruce, Professional Accountants LLP (MB), at a mutual friend's dinner party. He phoned her a week later because he decided to hire MB to help him out on various matters. You work as a staff accountant at MB.

Topsail has a fiscal year-end of 31 December 20X1. The credit union will require an audit. Prior statements have not been audited and have been prepared solely for preparation of Topsail's tax return. Earnings in recent years has averaged $300,000. Dave has already appointed another public accounting firm as Topsail's auditor; he wants advice from MB on identifying and setting accounting policy issues. Carlie took notes on the call and has turned the notes over to you for analysis (Exhibit 1).

Required:

Prepare a report for Carlie to use as the basis for advice to Dave on financial reporting issues.

EXHIBIT 1

Notes from Phone Conversation with Dave Jetson

Topsail received an order from a recurring customer, Skyline, for custom-built cabinets for its new large retail store in Dieppe. Topsail completed the cabinets on 30 November, well ahead of the contract delivery date of 9 December. Topsail had received a $100,000 deposit for the cabinets in early October, with the balance of the contract of $150,000 to be paid upon delivery and acceptance of the cabinets by Skyline. In early December, Skyline notified Topsail that it could not take delivery of the cabinets until 15 January 20X2 due to the unexpected delay in opening of the company's new store. Dave has heard a rumour that the reason for the delay in opening was because of Skyline's inability to arrange financing for inventory.

Over the years, Topsail has acquired an extensive range of machinery and equipment, ranging from small hand-held pieces to its most costly piece of equipment, a top-of-the-line insulation blowing machine, purchased five years ago for $45,000. It now has a net book value of $30,000. A similar but more efficient machine will become available in February 20X2. Topsail plans to replace this aging equipment when this new product comes out on the market. Dave anticipates being able to sell the existing piece of equipment for $10,000.

In March 20X1, Dave spent $20,000 on an extensive advertising and marketing campaign to generate additional business for Topsail. This expenditure was set up as an intangible asset.

Dave mentioned that a former Topsail client, Bob Swaine, is suing the company for failure to finish the basement in his new home, which was purchased from Topsail. Despite there being no mention of completion of a basement in the sale contract, Bob thought all new homes came totally finished. Topsail's lawyer is quite certain the case will be thrown out of court.

Dave recently issued Topsail preferred shares in the amount of $25,000 to one of his key employees, Doug Smith. The shares have a cumulative rate of return of 7% per annum and are redeemable and retractable in two years' time at face value plus dividends in arrears, if any.

Dave used this money to help finance a $120,000 acquisition of common shares in Abel Electricity Ltd., owned by a group of electricians providing electrical services to Topsail and a number of other contractors in the Moncton area. Abel is the sole provider of electrical services to Topsail. Dave explained "Thank goodness I have pull with Abel since I use their services all the time, especially now that my business is growing! I would have paid about $10,000 more for the work the company did this year if I had dealt with any other electrical company. Plus we did that swap, which is a big help with cash flow."

Dave reported that he swapped a used van that still worked but was no longer being used by Topsail, in exchange for 100 hours of electrician time from Abel. Abel was all too happy to offer this service since its cash flow has been sporadic and the bank had been threatening to cut its line of credit. Abel's income has continued to grow but the company seems to have trouble collecting receivables from customers on a timely basis. Dave said "I sure hope this investment pans out. I figure the initial $120,000 I paid for the shares will be worthwhile in the future. After all, Abel had income of over $200,000 last year and it's only Abel's fourth year of operation!" Dave owns 25% of the shares of Abel.

Dave has not declared any dividends this year, but usually takes out a mix of salary and common share dividends as recommended by his tax advisor. He will declare the common dividend soon, but plans to wait for all the dividends on the preferred shares when they come due in two years' time. He has cleared this with Doug Smith, who agreed, because Doug figures that he can avoid paying income tax on the dividends for a couple of years under this scheme.

(Tammy Crowell, used with permission)

CASE 13-2

BIRCH CORPORATION

Birch Corporation is a small, owner-managed company that manufactures and distributes wood mouldings. At 30 June 20X6, Reg Muise owned 70% of the shares of Birch while Fran Cote owned the remaining 30%. There had been a third shareholder, Harry Ma, but his shares were repurchased and retired in March 20X6. The company was established in 20X0 and has a 30 June year-end.

Reg is a talented craftsman and a natural salesman. He has taken care of production and marketing (originally assisted by Harry) while Fran has dealt with company administration, including accounting records.

It is now August 20X6. Fran has decided that she would like to become more active in the company and has approached Reg with the proposition of purchasing his 70% share of the company. After brief negotiations, Reg agreed to sell his interest in Birch to Fran at the greater of:

a. Five times 20X6 earnings according to GAAP; or
b. 1.2 times the sum of present value of 20X7 through 20X9 projected cash flows from operations.

However, given that Birch Corporation has not used the services of a professional accountant in recent years, Reg has approached Smith and Toll, Chartered Accountants, LLP to provide him with recommendations as to the proposed sale of his shares. You, CA, are a staff accountant with Smith and Toll. Fran has provided the most recent internal financial statements (Exhibit I) miscellaneous information (Exhibit II), and accounting policy information (Exhibit III).

The engagement partner asked you, CA, to provide her with a detailed memo that specifically discusses the company's accounting practices. In addition, the engagement partner would be interested in any comments you may have concerning the proposed purchase price formula.

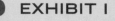

EXHIBIT I

BIRCH CORPORATION

Excerpts from the Financial Statements
Statement of Financial Position

As at 30 June
(unaudited, in thousands of dollars)

	20X6	20X5
CURRENT		
Cash	$ 110	$ 87
Accounts receivable	883	664
Inventory	1,208	988
Prepaids	83	57
	2,284	1,796
Capital assets	761	1,087
Investment in Feine Corporation	101	189
Investment in Spencer Incorporated	—	1,000
	$3,146	$4,072
CURRENT		
Accounts payable and accrued liabilities	$1,141	$1,416
Warranty payable—Rubberwood	61	10
Current portion of long-term debt	78	78
	1,280	1,504
Deferred gross profit	605	390
Long-term debt	539	583
	2,424	2,477
SHAREHOLDERS' EQUITY		
Common shares	169	179
Retained earnings	553	1,416
	722	1,595
	$3,146	$4,072

BIRCH CORPORATION

Excerpts from the Financial Statements
Statement of Comprehensive Income

For the year ended 30 June
(unaudited, in thousands of dollars)

	20X6	2005
REVENUE	$1,874	$1,723
COST OF GOODS SOLD		
Beginning inventory	988	889
Purchases	976	1,003
	1,964	1,892
Ending Inventory	1,208	988
	756	904
GROSS PROFIT	1,118	819
OPERATING EXPENSES		
Amortization	326	362
Bad debts	11	9
Insurance	27	21
Interest and bank charges	23	19
Interest on long-term debt	53	66
Repairs and maintenance	25	22
Utilities	59	56
Wages and benefits	137	114
Warranty expense	55	10
	716	679
Loss from investment in Feine	(88)	(22)
Loss from share repurchase	(240)	—
Net earnings before income tax	74	118
Income tax	27	36
NET EARNINGS AND COMPREHENSIVE INCOME	$ 47	$ 82

EXHIBIT II

MISCELLANEOUS INFORMATION

1. Birch owns 40% of the common shares of Feine Corporation (Feine), located in Fredericton, New Brunswick. Birch also holds four of ten seats on Feine's Board of Directors. Feine's year-end is 30 June. Feine has suffered losses of $88,000 in the current year and $22,000 in the previous year. To date, Feine has not paid any dividends.

2. Birch directly repurchased and retired the shares of Harry Ma, who had owned a minor stake in the company from its inception. Harry was involved in the marketing end of the business, but was going through a divorce and decided to leave the company, liquidate his investment, and pursue other interests. His shares were repurchased for $250 in cash.

continued on next page

EXHIBIT II (cont'd)

3. During fiscal 20X3, Birch introduced "RubberWood®"—a rubber-like moulding that can be shaped into virtually any crevice, corner, or archway possible. Birch's new product was initially slow to be accepted in the marketplace due to the perception that such a product would not provide a wood-like appearance. Birch was so confident that its new product would look like wood and would last longer than its traditional wood mouldings that it offered its customers a life-time guarantee that if they found any manufacturer defect, or became dissatisfied with the product in any way. Birch offered to refund the purchase price 100%— no questions asked. To date, Reg has indicated that virtually everyone has been satisfied with the new product, and sales are growing. He expects growth of at least 10% a year.
4. Gross profit is expected to increase by approximately 5% over the next two years and by 6% in the third year following.
5. Operating expenses, given recent increases in oil, insurance, and wage costs, are expected to increase approximately 5% over the next two years and by 4% in the third year.
6. For purposes of calculating the present value of projected cash flows from operations, Fran feels that a 10% discount factor is appropriate. All receivables, payables, and inventory levels are expected to be stable over the projection period.

EXHIBIT III (cont'd)

ACCOUNTING POLICY INFORMATION

The engagement partner indicated, from her discussions with Fran, the following accounting policies have been consistently adhered to since the inception of Birch. Fran also indicated that all accounting policies have been reviewed with Reg.

1. Moulding revenue is recorded upon delivery of mouldings to customers.
2. RubberWood® sales have been deferred as Fran is concerned that not enough time has elapsed since the new product was introduced. She believes taking a more conservative approach to reporting RubberWood® sales has portrayed a much more realistic look at the economic substance of those transactions when reporting to Reg. She points out she also set up a warranty expense and warranty liability of roughly 10% of sales because of the generous warranty offered to RubberWood® customers.
3. Birch's investment in Feine Corporation has been accounted for using the equity method.
4. When Birch was first established in 20X0, Reg contributed cash and equipment, along with his expertise, in exchange for his common shares. Reg acquired this equipment in a previous venture, which he was rolling into Birch. The capital assets included machinery and equipment, with an expected 15-year life. Because the operation was just starting up, and valuation was tricky, the shareholders agreed that the capital assets would be valued at $1, but Reg would receive common shares that gave him a substantial interest in the company. Reg estimated that the equipment was worth somewhere between $500,000 and $1,000,000, although the market for this equipment on a used basis was almost non-existent.

Source: Atlantic School of Chartered Accountancy, © 2010.

CASE 13-3

LORENZONI WINERY

In September 20X4, Giovanni Lorenzoni purchased a 40 hectare grape vineyard in southern Ontario. Giovanni is a successful restaurateur who owns and operates a family-oriented restaurant that offers fine cuisine at reasonable prices. As a restaurateur, Giovanni had always been interested in wines and had developed a discerning palate. He had become increasingly fascinated by the prospect of developing his own wines, and when a vineyard became available, he quickly purchased it before the land became yet another suburban housing tract.

Giovanni had two sources of financing for the purchase. First, he borrowed money from the bank, using his ownership of the restaurant as collateral. Second, he convinced a retired wine master to lend him money for the land. The wine master also agreed to contribute his expertise for developing the vineyard and the wine that would be produced from the hybrid grapes.

It now is early 20X5. Giovanni wishes to establish a corporation to own and manage the vineyard and the winery. He must incorporate in order to obtain a licence to produce wine; otherwise, he is considered simply a farmer. Before he establishes the corporation, he must decide on the share structure that is most appropriate for his purposes. The main factors that he must consider are as follows:

- The wine master's loan will be converted to shares. However, the wine master is not a young man any more, and he does need regular income in addition to his retirement pension from the large winery for which he used to work.

- The wine master will be responsible for developing the wine, with Giovanni's assistance and participation as a restaurateur and as a knowledgeable consumer. There is no immediate prospect of a positive cash flow, however, as it will take at least two years before any drinkable wine is produced and much longer before quality wine can be produced and sold in any reasonable volume.

- The manager of the venture capital arm of a large pension fund is interested in investing some of the fund's money in Giovanni's venture. The fund investment would repay Giovanni's bank loan for buying the vineyard, pay for wine-producing equipment, and possibly pay to acquire adjacent land for extending the vineyard. The pension fund wants to have high priority for a reasonable return on its investment, while also being able to maintain a long-term equity interest that enables the fund to participate in future success of the venture.

- Giovanni has a wife, two sons, and a daughter. He wants all members of his family to have an equity interest in the corporation, with hopes that perhaps his children will become interested in the wine business and in building it further after Giovanni retires from active participation.

- Giovanni has hopes of eventually establishing a restaurant at the vineyard, as some other wineries in the region have done. The region's summer "wine tour" has become a popular tourist attraction for visitors from both Canada and the United States, as well as from abroad. A well-known and highly reputed sous chef from another restaurant has already expressed interest in participating in such a venture. The menu for the restaurant would be based around wines of the region, but not on Giovanni's wines until they are well developed.

- An opportunity must be available for investment from other equity participants in the future, as the company's need for capital increases.

- Giovanni's income from the restaurant has placed him in a high tax bracket. He will not need dividends from the winery in the foreseeable future.

- Giovanni wishes to retain voting control of the venture.

Giovanni will consult with a lawyer who specializes in corporate start-ups. Before going to the lawyer, he would like to obtain some informal advice. For this purpose, he has asked his younger son, Paolo, to give his views on the appropriate capital structure to use. Paolo is well on his way to becoming a chartered accountant and has some experience with small business corporate structures. At the minimum Paolo should be able to advise his father on the types of shares that are appropriate for satisfying the above factors and laying the groundwork for the company's future growth and development.

Required:

Assume that you are Paolo Lorenzoni. Prepare a report for your father in which you outline and explain a corporate share structure that will satisfy Giovanni's needs.

ASSIGNMENTS

★★ **A13-1 Components of Shareholders' Equity:** The following accounts are taken from the general ledger of GRL Trading Limited on 31 December 20X1:

Preferred shares, no-par value, $2, unlimited number authorized, cumulative and fully participating; 27,000 shares issued and outstanding	$ 168,000
Bonds payable, 7%	500,000
Stock subscriptions receivable, common shares	3,000
Common shares, no-par, unlimited number authorized; 45,000 shares issued and 44,900 outstanding	1,350,000
Discount on bonds payable	6,000
Retained earnings	653,000
Treasury shares, 100 common shares	8,600
Unrealized exchange gain on translation of foreign subsidiary's financial statements	150,500
Fractional common share rights	9,200
Contributed capital on common share retirement	18,900
Common shares subscribed, 100 shares	9,000

Required:

1. Prepare the shareholders' equity section of the SFP at year-end.
2. Explain the meaning of each account in equity.

★★ **A13-2 Effect of Transactions:** The following transactions will change the SFP in some way:

a. Declare a cash dividend, to be paid in three weeks' time.
b. Declare and issue a stock dividend, recorded at fair value.
c. Pay a cash dividend already declared and recorded.
d. Issue common shares for land.
e. Declare and issue a stock dividend, recorded as a memo entry.
f. Record comprehensive income for the period, comprising both earnings and unrealized foreign exchange gains on a foreign subsidiary whose functional currency is the foreign currency.
g. Retire preferred shares for cash at a price higher than average issuance price to date. This is the first time preferred shares have been retired.

Required:

In the table below, indicate the effect of each transaction on the accounts listed. Use I = increase, D = Decrease, and NE = No effect. The first one is done as an example.

Item	Assets	Liabilities	Share Capital (Preferred and Common)	Retained Earnings	Reserve for Foreign Exchange Gains and Losses	Total Shareholders' Equity (Combined Effect of Prior Three Columns)
a.	NE	I	NE	D	NE	D
b.						
c.						
d.						
e.						
f.						
g.						

★★ **A13-3 Effect of Transactions:** The following statement of changes in shareholders' equity summarizes various equity transactions that occurred during 20X2:

HEISLER CORPORATION

**Changes in Shareholders' Equity
for the year ended 31 December 20X2
(in thousands)**

	Preferred Shares	Common Shares	Contributed Capital from Common Share Retirement	Retained Earnings	Total Equity
Balance at 1 January 20X2	$140	$500	$50	$650	$1,340
Net earnings and comprehensive income				210	210
Shares issued	120	200			320
Share issue costs				(11)	(11)
Share buy-back	(54)			(18)	(72)
Share buy-back		(26)	4		(22)
Stock dividend to shareholders		98		(98)	—
Cash dividends to shareholders				(42)	(42)
Balance at 31 December 20X2	$206	$772	$54	$691	$1,723

Required:
Journalize the transactions in the statement of shareholders' equity. For earnings, close the income summary to retained earnings.

★★ **A13-4 Share Issuance:** Lake Simcoe Limited (LSL) has unlimited no-par common shares authorized. The following transactions took place in the first year:

a. To record authorization (memorandum).
b. Issued 120,000 shares at $32; collected cash in full and issued the shares. Share issue costs amounted to $71,100. Treat this amount as a reduction of the common share account.
c. Received subscriptions for 45,000 shares at $34 per share; collected 70% of the subscription price. The shares will not be issued until collection of cash in full.
d. Issued 500 shares to a lawyer in payment for legal fees related to trademark registration. The lawyer estimates that the legal services provided would have been worth $15,000.

e. Issued 10,000 shares and assumed an $80,000 mortgage in total payment for a building with a fair value of $310,000.

f. Collected balance on subscriptions receivable in (c).

Required:

Journalize the above transactions.

★★ **A13-5 Entries and Reporting:** Donroy Corporation was authorized to issue unlimited preferred shares, $0.30, no-par value, and unlimited common shares, no-par value. During the first year, the following transactions occurred:

a. 80,000 common shares were sold for cash at $12 per share.

b. Share issue costs of $18,200 were paid; this amount was treated as a reduction to retained earnings.

c. 4,000 preferred shares were sold for cash at $25 per share.

d. 8,000 common shares were reacquired and retired for $12.50 per share.

e. Cash dividends of $10,000 were declared and paid. Indicate the split between common and preferred dividends.

f. 5,000 common shares and 500 preferred shares were given as payment for a small manufacturing facility that the company needed. This facility originally cost $90,000 and had a depreciated value on the books of the selling company of $45,000. The fair value of the facility was estimated to be $80,000.

Required:

1. Give journal entries to record the above transactions. State and justify any assumptions you made.

2. Prepare the shareholders' equity section of the SFP at year-end. Net earnings and comprehensive income was $216,400.

★★ **A13-6 Share Retirement—Entries and Account Balances:** The accounting records of Farhad Corporation showed that the company acquired and retired shares as following during the year:

5 January	2,000 common shares at $10 per share
6 January	1,500 preferred shares at $25 per share
20 February	2,000 common shares at $13 per share
20 February	300 preferred shares at $10 per share
15 March	3,000 common shares at $14 per share

Before these transactions, the following balances were reported:

Preferred shares, 3,000 shares outstanding, no-par	$ 72,000
Common shares, 20,000 shares outstanding, no-par	235,000
Retained earnings	75,000

Required:

1. Give journal entries to record each share retirement transaction.

2. Calculate the closing balance in each account in shareholders' equity.

★ **A13-7 Share Retirement—Analysis:** During 20X5, Veech Corporation had several changes in shareholders' equity. The comparative equity accounts for 20X4 and 20X5:

Balances 31 December	20X5	20X4
Common shares	$600,000	$700,000
Preferred shares	180,000	230,000
Contributed capital, retirement of preferred shares	27,000	0
Retained earnings	135,000	120,000

In 20X5, the only transactions affecting common and preferred share accounts were the retirement of 2,000 common shares and 1,000 preferred shares, respectively. Earnings was $50,000 in 20X5, and dividends declared, $20,000.

Required:

1. What was the original issue price of the common shares? The preferred?
2. What amount was paid for the common shares retired? The preferred? (*Hint:* Reconstruct the journal entries to record the retirement.)

★ **A13-8 Equity, Interpretation:** The following is the share capital note to the financial statements of Capital Corporation for the year ended 31 December 20X4:

Note 17 Share capital
Authorized share capital consists of an unlimited number of common shares and 100,000 non-voting, cumulative preference shares with a $4 dividend.

Transactions during the period:

	Number of Shares	Share Capital
Preferred shares		
Balance as of 1 January 20X4	46,800	$ 4,567,300
Issued for cash during the period	2,450	269,500
Balance as of 31 December 20X4	49,250	$ 4,836,800
Common shares		
Balance as of 1 January 20X4	965,350	$16,584,700
Issued for cash during the period	4,200	151,200
Issued to employees under option contracts	2,000	39,000
Balance as of 31 December 20X4	971,550	$16,774,900

The company also reported $6,234,900 in retained earnings.

Required:

1. In what way are the preferred shares likely different than the common shares?
2. What does the term "cumulative" mean?
3. If the company declared a total of $350,000 of dividends on 31 December 20X4, how much would the common shareholders receive? No other dividends had yet been declared in 20X4 but dividends had been declared in all prior years.
4. What was the average issuance price for all common shares outstanding at 31 December 20X4? How does this compare to the price received for shares issued during the period?
5. Give the journal entry that would be recorded if 2,500 common shares were retired for $23 per share on 31 December 20X4.
6. Give the journal entries that would be recorded if 8,200 common treasury shares were purchased for $21 per share and then resold for $28 per share.

★★★ **A13-9 Retired Shares—Entries and Reporting:** On 1 January 20X5, BC Ventures Corporation reported the following in shareholders' equity:

Preferred shares, no-par value, $0.70, cumulative; authorized, unlimited shares; issued, 80,000 shares	$ 386,000
Common shares, no-par value; authorized, unlimited shares; issued, 80,000 shares	642,000
Contributed capital on retirement of common shares	14,000
Retained earnings	1,250,000
Reserve for foreign exchange gains on foreign subsidiary	38,000

During 20X5, certain shares were reacquired. In accordance with the regulations in BC Ventures' incorporating legislation, all reacquired shares were retired. Transactions were as follows:

15 January	Bought 7,000 preferred shares for $5.20 per share
12 February	Bought 2,000 common shares for $11 per share
25 February	Bought 4,000 preferred shares for $4.00 per share
26 April	Bought 5,000 preferred shares for $6.00 per share
16 July	Bought 8,000 common shares for $7.50 per share

Other transactions during the year:

| 30 July | Stock dividend on common shares, 5%, declared and distributed. The Board of Directors agreed to capitalize the dividend at the market value of $7.75. |
| 30 November | The Board of Directors declared a dividend adequate to pay $1 per share to all common shareholders. This meant that they also had to declare the preferred dividend. |

Required:

1. Prepare journal entries to reflect the above transactions. Show the split between common and preferred dividends in the dividend entries, as appropriate.

2. Prepare the shareholders' equity section of the SFP after reflecting the above transactions. Earnings were $308,200, and total comprehensive income was $351,000, reflecting earnings plus an additional gain of $42,800 on foreign exchange caused by a foreign subsidiary.

★ **A13-10 Treasury Stock—Entries and Reporting:** On 1 January 20X1, Winnipeg Corporation issued 10,000 no-par common shares at $50 per share. On 15 January 20X5, Winnipeg purchased 100 of its own common shares at $55 per share to be held as treasury stock. On 1 March 20X5, 20 of the treasury shares were resold at $62. On 31 March 20X5, 10 of the treasury shares were sold for $59. The remaining shares were sold for $48 on 1 June 20X5. The balance in retained earnings was $25,000 prior to these transactions.

Required:

1. Provide all 20X5 entries.
2. Calculate the resulting balance in each of the shareholders' equity accounts.

★★ **A13-11 Treasury Stock—Entries and Account Balances:** At the end of 20X2 Provoe Products Limited had 222,000 common shares outstanding, with a recorded value in the common share account of $875,000. Retained earnings was $673,500.

During 20X3, the following transactions affecting shareholders' equity were recorded:

a. Split common shares 3-for-1.
b. Purchased 8,000 shares of treasury stock at $4.25 per share.
c. Purchased 6,000 shares of treasury stock at $5.00 per share.
d. Sold 5,000 shares of treasury stock at $9.25.
e. Sold 6,000 shares of treasury stock at $3.00.
f. Retired 500 shares of treasury stock.
g. Declared and paid a dividend of $0.25 per common share.

Required:

1. Give entries for each of the above transactions.
2. Give the resulting balances in each capital account. Earnings for 20X3 was $472,000.

★★ **A13-12 Compute Dividends, Preferred Shares—Four Cases:** Western Horizons Limited has the following shares outstanding:

| Common, no-par | 54,000 shares |
| Preferred, no-par, $0.75 | 18,000 shares |

The matching dividend, if applicable, is $1.00 per share.

Required:

Compute the amount of dividends payable in total and per share on the common and preferred shares for each separate case:

Case A Preferred is cumulative and non-participating; dividends declared, $64,800. Dividends have not been paid for the last three years prior to this year.

Case B Preferred is non-cumulative and non-participating; no dividends have been paid for the last three years prior to this year; dividends declared, $40,500.

Case C Preferred is cumulative and fully participating after the common shares receive a matching dividend; no dividends have been paid in the last two years prior to this year; dividends declared, $120,000. Participation is based on relative annual total base dividends.

Case D Preferred is cumulative and partially participating up to an additional $0.90 after the common shares receive a matching dividend. Dividends have been paid in all prior years; dividends declared, $160,000. Participation is based on relative annual total base dividends.

★★★ **A13-13 Compute Dividends, Comprehensive—Four Cases:** Mountain Construction
eXcel Corporation is authorized to issue unlimited $0.40 no-par preferred shares and unlimited no-par common shares. There are 15,000 preferred and 45,000 common shares outstanding. In a five-year period, annual dividends paid were $1,000, $4,000, $32,000, $5,000, and $90,000, respectively.

Required:

Calculate the amount of dividends that would be paid to each share class for each year under the following separate cases. Where applicable, the matching dividend per common share is $0.50.

Case A Preferred shares are cumulative and non-participating.

Case B Preferred shares are non-cumulative and non-participating.

Case C Preferred shares are non-cumulative and fully participating. Participation is based on the relative number of shares outstanding.

Case D Preferred shares are non-cumulative and partially participating up to an additional $0.40 per share. Participation is based on relative annual total base dividends.

★★ **A13-14 Compute Dividends, Retire Shares:** Australia Ltd. reported the following items in shareholders' equity at 31 December 20X3:

Preferred shares, $4, 120,000 shares outstanding, cumulative, participating in dividends with common shares after the common shares have received $2.40 per share; participation is based on relative annual total base dividends	$13,500,000
Common shares, 640,000 shares issued and 600,000 shares outstanding	28,800,000
Contributed capital on retirement of $4 preferred shares	37,200
Retained earnings	26,679,500
Treasury stock, 40,000 common shares	2,400,000

Required:

1. No dividends were declared in 20X1 or 20X2. In 20X3, $6,500,000 in cash dividends was declared but has not been recorded. How much would be distributed to each class of shares, as described above?

2. Prepare journal entries for the following transactions, which took place after the dividend in requirement 1. The transactions occurred in chronological order:

   a. Repurchase and retirement of 30,000 common shares for $76.25 per share.

   b. Repurchase and retirement of 5,000 $4 preferred shares for $120 per share.

   c. Sale of 10,000 treasury shares at $80 per share.

   d. Declaration and distribution of a 10% stock dividend on common shares valued at $77 per share; there were fractional rights issued for 2,000 shares. The Board of Directors agreed that treasury shares would not receive the stock dividend.

★★ **A13-15 Stock Dividend and Stock Split:** At the end of the 20X4 fiscal year, the shareholders' equity section of the statement of financial position of Chomney Corporation was as follows:

Shareholders' Equity	
Contributed Capital:	
Share capital:	
Preferred shares, no-par value, $1.25, cumulative and	
non-participating, unlimited shares authorized,	
40,000 shares issued and outstanding	$ 1,000,000
Common shares, no-par value, unlimited shares authorized,	
366,000 shares issued and outstanding	2,675,000
Other contributed capital: common share retirement	45,900
Total contributed capital	3,720,900
Retained earnings	12,001,000
Reserve for unrealized exchange gain on translation of	
foreign subsidiary	90,500
Total Shareholders' Equity	$15,812,400

The Board of Directors was considering three alternatives:

1. A 200% stock dividend for common shares, to be recorded as a memo entry.
2. A 200% stock dividend to be recorded at the fair value of the common shares, or $11 per share.
3. A three-for-one common stock split.

Required:

1. Prepare the shareholders' equity section, in three columns, each column reflecting one of the alternatives above.
2. Evaluate the alternatives, and indicate what course of action you would recommend to the Board of Directors.

★★ **A13-16 Stock Dividend Recorded—Dates Cross Two Periods:** The records of Victoria Corporation showed the following balances on 1 November 20X5:

Share capital, no-par, 40,000 shares	$344,300
Retained earnings	592,100

On 5 November 20X5, the Board of Directors declared a stock dividend to the shareholders of record as of 20 December 20X5. The dividend was one additional share for each five shares already outstanding; issue date, 10 January 20X6. The appropriate market value of the shares was $12.50 per share. The annual accounting period ends 31 December. The stock dividend was recorded on the declaration date with a memo entry only.

Required:

1. Give entries in parallel columns for the stock dividend assuming:

   Case A   Fair value is capitalized.
   Case B $10 per share is capitalized.
   Case C   Average paid in is capitalized.

2. Explain when each value is most likely to be used.
3. In respect to the stock dividend, what should be reported on the statement of financial position at 31 December 20X5?
4. Explain how the financial statements as of 31 December 20X5 would be different if the stock dividend were recognized on the declaration date.

★★ **A13-17 Stock Split—Adjustments:** NovaCor Limited had the following shareholders' equity on 31 December 20X8:

$2 Preferred shares (50,000 shares issued and outstanding; cumulative, non-participating, and convertible into three common shares for each preferred share)	$ 700,000
Common shares (160,000 shares issued and outstanding)	320,000
Retained earnings	1,345,000
Reserve: unrealized gains from investments	82,000
Total shareholders' equity	$2,447,000

Earnings for 20X8 had been $307,000 and comprehensive income, which also included a $12,000 unrealized gain on an investment, was $319,000. Basic earnings per share was calculated as $1.29:

Net earnings and comprehensive income	$307,000
Preferred dividend entitlement (50,000 shares × $2)	100,000
Earnings available for common dividends	$207,000
Earnings per share ($207,000 ÷ 160,000 shares)	$ 1.29

During 20X8, the company paid the $2 per share preferred dividends and also paid $1.00 per share dividend to common shareholders. Dividends are reported in total and per share in the financial statements.

On 1 April 20X9, NovaCor executed a 4-for-1 split of its common shares. On 15 July 20X9, the company repurchased 22,000 common shares from one of the company's founders at $12.00 per share.

Required:

1. Prepare the journal entry to record the 20X9 share repurchase.

2. Post-split, how many common shares would the holder of 5,000 preferred shares receive on conversion?

3. When the company prepares its comparative financial statements for 20X9, what amount will be reported for 20X8 earnings per share? What amount would be reported for 20X8 cash dividends per common share?

4. Explain any other ways, in addition to the recalculation of earnings per share, that the 20X8 comparative amounts and disclosures would be changed, when presented in the 20X9 financial statements.

★★ **A13-18 Stock Dividend with Fractional Shares:** Gupta Corporation was authorized to issue unlimited common shares, and had 452,000 common shares outstanding on 8 March 20X2, with a recorded value of $1,367,000. On this date, the Board of Directors declared a 5% stock dividend, valued at the fair value of shares, $4.50 per share.

Required:

Prepare journal entry(ies) for each of the following independent circumstances:

1. The stock dividend is declared and issued on 8 March, and all shares are distributed on this date.

2. The stock dividend is declared and issued on 8 March, resulting in the issuance of a number of whole shares but also entitlement to the sum of 1,600 shares as fractional shares. These shares were outstanding until 30 April, at which time 70% were redeemed for whole shares and 30% expired.

3. The stock dividend is declared and issued on 8 March, resulting in the issuance of a number of whole shares but also involved entitlement to the sum of 1,600 shares as fractional shares. Cash was distributed to shareholders in lieu of fractional shares.

4. The stock dividend is declared on 8 March, and distributed on 8 April. The dividend is recorded on 8 March. On distribution on 8 April, a number of whole shares are issued as

well as entitlement to the sum of 1,600 shares as fractional shares. These fractional shares were outstanding until 30 April, at which time 70% were redeemed for whole shares and 30% expired.

5. Comment on the differences between requirements 2 and 3. What might be the advantages and disadvantages of issuing cash instead of fractional shares?

★★ **A13-19 Stock Dividends and Splits; Fractional Share Rights:** UMG Corporation reported balances in shareholder's equity:

Common shares (unlimited shares authorized; 500,000 shares issued)	$14,000,000
Retained earnings	26,533,100

Each of the following cases is independent:

Case A   The Board of Directors declared and distributed a 14% stock dividend, to be recorded at the fair value of the common shares, $37 per share.

Case B   The Board of Directors approved and distributed a 3-for-1 stock split.

Case C   The Board of Directors declared and distributed a 6% stock dividend. The dividend resulted in the distribution of 28,000 whole shares and 12,000 fractional share rights, allowing the acquisition of 2,000 whole shares. The dividend was valued at the average price paid for common shares to date. The fractional share rights were 75% exercised, but 25% were allowed to lapse.

Required:

1. For each case, prepare entries, or memo entries, to reflect the transactions.
2. For each case, calculate the closing balances in shareholders' equity accounts.
3. Comment on the differences and/or similarities between the results in requirement (2).

★★ **A13-20 Equity; Retirement and Stock Dividend:** Davison Enterprises reported the following description of shareholders' equity on 31 December 20X6:

Contributed Capital	
Preferred shares, $1, no-par, 100,000 shares authorized, cumulative, redeemable at company's option at $107 plus dividends in arrears. Each preferred share is convertible into 10 common shares. Issued and outstanding, 20,000 shares	$2,040,000
Common shares, no-par, unlimited shares authorized and 80,000 issued and outstanding	640,000
Contributed capital on retirement of common shares	120,000
	2,800,000
Retained earnings	1,600,000
	$4,400,000

There were no dividends in arrears. The following transactions took place in 20X7:

20 Feb.   Redeemed 1,000 preferred shares at the call price.

28 Feb.   Declared $100,000 in dividends. Specify the distribution of the dividend between common and preferred shares.

31 Mar.   Retired 8,000 common shares for $12 per share.

2 Apr.   Declared and distributed a 3% stock dividend on the common shares, valued at $11.50 per share. Fractional share rights were issued for 200 of the shares.

30 Apr.   40% of the fractional share rights were exercised, and the remainder lapsed.

Required:

1. Journalize the listed transactions.
2. Prepare the revised contributed capital section of the statement of financial position, reflecting the entries in requirement (1). Earnings were $820,000 for the year.

★★ **A13-21 Retained Earnings Calculation and Equity:** Below are selected accounts from Serious Sound Corp. at 31 December 20X1. The accounts have not been closed for the year but transactions have been correctly recorded.

Stock dividend distributable, common shares	220,100
20X1 earnings before discontinued operations	655,400
Common shares	$2,631,700
Class A preferred shares	3,750,000
Cash dividends, common shares	140,000
Error correction, net of tax (increases prior earnings)	104,200
Reserve re: unrealized gain on FVTOCI investments, 1 January 20X1	100,600
Cash dividends, preferred shares	150,000
Retained earnings, 1 January 20X1	7,800,300
Stock dividend, common shares	533,000
Treasury stock, common	72,000
Contributed capital on preferred share retirement	6,500
Fractional common share rights outstanding	31,500
Excess on common share retirement (shares retired for $321,000 while average cost was $301,000)	20,000
Discontinued operations, loss, net of tax	9,400
Increase in unrealized FVTOCI investment fair value in 20X1	15,000

Required:

1. Calculate the closing balance in retained earnings.
2. Prepare the shareholders' equity section of the SFP as of 31 December 20X1.

★ **A13-22 Statement of Changes in Equity:** Below is a partially completed statement of changes in equity for Torino Capital Limited (in thousands of $).

	Preferred Shares	Common Shares	Fractional Shares Outstanding	Retained Earnings	Reserve for Foreign Exchange Gains of Foreign Subsidiary	Total Equity
Balance at 1 January 20X1	3,000	7,400	240	6,780	451	17,871
Comprehensive income, including earnings of $871 and foreign exchange on subsidiary, a gain of $39						
Common shares issued for cash of $788						
Preferred shares bought back; 10% of opening balance bought back for cash; paid $85 more than average issue price						
Cash dividends to shareholders; $170 to preferred and $367 to common						
Fractional shares turned in for common (80% of fractional rights); remainder are still outstanding						
Balance at 31 December 20X1						

Required:

Complete the statement of changes in equity to reflect the transactions and events described.

★ **A13-23 Statement of Changes in Equity:** Robinson Industries reported the following statement of shareholders' equity for the year ended December 31, 20X7:

	Common Share Capital	Preferred Share Capital	Other Contributed Capital (All Sources)	Retained Earnings	Reserve Re: Unrealized Gains, Investments
Balance, January 1, 20X7	$ 5,992	$3,500	$1,202	$ 775	$48
Issuance of common shares for cash	7,650				
Retirement of common shares	(1,005)		(356)		
Costs associated with equity issue				(124)	
Stock dividend	247			(247)	
Comprehensive income				1,980	13
Retirement of preferred shares		(630)	(116)	(35)	
Balance, December 31, 20X7	$12,884	$2,870	$ 730	$2,349	$61

Required:
Answer the questions below.

1. What is the nature of the reserve? Where does it appear in the financial statements?
2. Earnings were $1,980. How much is comprehensive income?
3. What amount was paid to retire common shares during the year?
4. What amount was paid to retire preferred shares during the period? Why is there a deduction from contributed capital and also from retained earnings?
5. Costs associated with share issuance have been deducted from retained earnings. What other alternative could the company have considered?
6. What is the nature of the stock dividend? What are the alternatives for recording such a dividend?

★★ **A13-24 Statement of Changes in Equity:** Green Energy Limited began 20X2 with shareholders' equity as follows:

eXcel

Preferred shares; $1,240,000 shares issued and outstanding	$ 6,000,000
Common shares; 1,200,000 issued and 1,000,000 shares outstanding	7,500,000
Contributed capital on retirement of preferred shares	40,000
Retained earnings	2,165,000
Reserve for foreign exchange on foreign subsidiary	(320,000)
	$15,385,000
Treasury stock; 200,000 common shares	(2,200,000)
	$13,185,000

The company's tax rate is 40%. In 20X2, the company reported transactions that affected equity accounts:

1. Common shares, 2-for-1 stock split.
2. Common shares, 182,000 shares post-split, were repurchased and retired for $879,050.
3. All of the treasury shares were reissued for $2,175,400.
4. Green reported earnings of $421,800, including an after-tax discontinued operation loss amount of $34,600. There was an after-tax foreign exchange gain of $131,000 related to the foreign subsidiary.
5. Cash dividends of $326,500 were paid. This represented the required dividend on the preferred shares plus some common share dividend.
6. After the dividend was paid, 60,000 preferred shares were repurchased and retired for $23.50 per share.

7. Share retirement costs, legal fees relating to both preferred and common shares, amounted to $133,000 for the year.

8. The company recorded an error correction during the year, resulting in a $90,000 pre-tax increase to prior year's earnings.

Required:

Complete a columnar statement of changes in equity that reflects the transactions and events described. Use one column for each individual equity account, and show preferred dividends separately from common dividends.

★★★ **A13-25 Entries and Shareholders' Equity:** On 31 December 20X1, Kingdom Corporation had the following shareholders' equity:

Series A preferred shares, no-par, $0.75, cumulative; 480,000 shares issued and outstanding	$12,100,000
Series B preferred shares, no-par, $0.25, cumulative, participating in dividends with common shares to an additional $0.50 after the common shares have received a $0.25 matching dividend; 100,000 shares issued and outstanding. Participation is based on relative annual total base dividends.	10,500,000
Common shares; 1,200,000 issued and outstanding	18,600,000
Contributed capital on retirement of Series B preferred shares	101,000
Retained earnings	14,600,000
	$55,901,000

Dividends are two years in arrears on the Series B preferred shares.
The following events and transactions took place during 20X2:

15 January	25,000 Series A preferred shares were retired for $31 per share.
1 February	Issued 80,000 common shares for machinery with an appraised value of $1,600,000; the shares were estimated to be worth $21 per share.
11 March	15,000 Series B preferred shares were retired for $116 per share.
30 April	60,000 common shares were retired for $22 per share.
30 December	Dividends of $810,000 were declared and paid (indicate the amount of dividend for each share class).
31 December	A stock dividend of 10% was declared and issued on the common shares. The Board of Directors agreed that the dividend would be recorded at the fair value of the common shares, $22. The dividend involved issuing fractional share rights that, if entirely exercised, would result in the issuance of 500 common shares.

Required:

1. Record all transactions in general journal form.

2. Prepare the shareholders' equity section of the SFP at 31 December 20X2. Assume earnings for the year was $1,609,000.

★★★ **A13-26 Shareholders' Equity:** Howard Corporation is a publicly-owned company whose shares are traded on the TSX. At 31 December 20X4, Howard had unlimited shares of no-par value common shares authorized, of which 15,000,000 shares were issued. The shareholders' equity accounts at 31 December 20X4 had the following balances:

Common shares (15,000,000 shares)	$230,000,000
Retained earnings	50,000,000

During 20X5, Howard had the following transactions:

a. On 1 February, a distribution of 2,000,000 common shares was completed. The shares were sold for $18 per share.

b. On 15 February, Howard issued, at $110 per share, 100,000 of no-par value, $8, cumulative preferred shares.

c. On 1 March, Howard reacquired and retired 20,000 common shares for $14.50 per share.
d. On 15 March, Howard reacquired and retired 10,000 common shares for $20 per share.
e. On 31 March, Howard declared a semi-annual cash dividend on common shares of $0.10 per share, payable on 30 April 20X5, to shareholders of record on 10 April 20X5. (Record the dividend declaration *and* payment.) The preferred share dividend will be paid on schedule in October.
f. On 15 April, 18,000 common shares were acquired for $17.50 per share and held as treasury stock.
g. On 30 April, 12,500 of the treasury shares were resold for $19.25 per share.
h. On 31 May, when the market price of the common was $23 per share, Howard declared a 5% stock dividend distributable on 1 July 20X5, to common shareholders of record on 1 June 20X5. Treasury shares were not given the stock dividend. The stock dividend was recorded at market value only on distribution. The dividend resulted in fractional share rights issued, that, when exercised, would result in the issuance of 2,300 common shares.
i. On 6 July, Howard issued 300,000 common shares. The selling price was $25 per share.
j. On 30 September, Howard declared a semi-annual cash dividend on common shares of $0.10 per share and the yearly dividend on preferred shares, both payable on 30 October 20X5, to shareholders of record on 10 October 20X5. (Record the dividend declaration and payment.)
k. On 31 December, holders of fractional rights exercised those rights, resulting in the issuance of 1,850 shares. The remaining rights expired.
l. Earnings for 20X5 was $25 million.

Required:
Prepare journal entries to record the listed transactions. Round per-share amounts to two decimal places.

★★★ **A13-27 Compute Dividends, Record Share Transactions:** Zu Corp. has the following items in shareholders' equity at 31 December 20X8:

Preferred shares, $0.60 cumulative dividend, participating with common shares after the common shares have received $0.30 per share, 15,000 shares authorized and 4,000 shares issued and outstanding. Participation is based on the relative annual total base dividends.	$ 360,000
Common shares, unlimited shares issued, 93,000 shares issued and 92,000 shares outstanding	1,080,000
Contributed capital on preferred share retirement	17,000
Retained earnings	4,356,900
Treasury stock, common, 1,000 shares	18,000

The following transactions and events happened in 20X9, in chronological order:

a. A cash dividend of $38,000 was declared and paid.
b. 4,000 additional common shares were issued for land. The land was valued at $50,000, while recent transactions in common shares indicated a share value of $75,000.
c. Treasury shares (common), 500 shares were bought at $12,500.
d. Preferred shares, 500 shares, were purchased and retired for $130 per share.
e. Treasury shares, 600 shares were reissued at $15 per share.
f. A common stock dividend of 10% was issued. Treasury shares were considered ineligible for the stock dividend, by order of the Board of Directors. The stock dividend resulted in a number of whole shares issued, but 350 shares had to be issued in the form of fractional share rights, still outstanding at year-end. The dividend was valued at $40 per share.
g. Earnings for the year were $1,450,000.

Required:

1. From item (a), specify the amount of cash dividend to the preferred shareholders, and the dividend to the common shareholders.
2. Calculate the final balance in each shareholders' equity account.
3. From item (b), justify the value used to record the common shares issued.

★★ **A13-28 Effect of Transactions:** The following transactions may change an account in shareholders' equity in some way:

a. Declare and issue a 3-for-1 stock split.
b. Record donated land.
c. Acquire treasury shares.
d. Record an increase in the value (an unrealized gain) of FVTOCI investments carried at fair market value.
e. Declare dividends on preferred shares.
f. Declare a stock dividend, to be issued in four weeks' time.
g. Issue the stock dividend in (f), resulting in the issuance of common shares and fractional share rights.
h. Fractional shares issued in (g) are exchanged for common shares (75%) and the rest lapse (25%).
i. Retire common shares for cash at a price higher than the average issuance price to date. This is the first time common shares have been retired.
j. Reissue treasury shares for cash at a price higher than average acquisition cost. This is the first time treasury shares have been reissued.
k. After the transaction in (j), reissue treasury shares for cash at a price lower than average acquisition cost.
l. Record earnings for the year.

Required:

In the table below, indicate the effect of each transaction on the accounts listed. Use I = Increase, D = Decrease, and NE = No effect. The first one is done as an example.

Item	Share Capital	Fractional Share Rights	Other Contributed Capital	Retained Earnings	Reserve: Unrealized Gains on Investments	Treasury Stock
a.	NE	NE	NE	NE	NE	NE
b.						
c.						
d.						
e.						
f.						
g.						
h.						
i.						
j.						
k.						
l.						

★★ **A13-29 Transactions, Statement of Cash Flow:** The following data is related to Cold Brook Resources Ltd.:

	20X9	20X8
Preferred shares, no-par	$ 2,000,000	$ 3,000,000
Common shares, no-par	45,000,000	36,000,000
Preferred shares subscribed	4,000,000	0
Common share fractional rights	0	574,000
Contributed capital on lapse of rights	114,800	0
Contributed capital on preferred share retirement	122,000	0
Retained earnings	8,005,000	5,940,000
Subscriptions receivable, preferred shares	(700,000)	0

During the year, the following transactions took place:

a. Earnings were $2,600,000.
b. Cash dividends were paid.
c. The common share fractional rights converted into common shares (80%) and the remainder (20%) lapsed.
d. Common shares plus $2 million cash were issued to acquire a patent that was valued at $6,500,000.
e. Contracts were signed to issue preferred shares with a total consideration of $4,000,000. The prospective shareholders paid $3,300,000 and will pay the balance within 12 months.
f. Preferred shares were retired for cash.
g. Additional common shares were issued for cash.
h. Retained earnings was reduced by $200,300 as the result of share issue costs.

Required:
1. Show the retained earnings T-account, beginning with the opening balance and going to the closing balance. Label all items that caused the change in the account.
2. Prepare the investing and financing sections of the SCF, in as much detail as possible with the information given. Dividends paid are included in financing activities.

★★ **A13-30 Statement of Cash Flow:** The following data relates to Ottawa Limited:

31 December	20X5	20X4
Preferred shares, no-par	$ 520,000	$ 460,000
Common shares, no-par	8,438,350	6,840,000
Common share fractional rights	8,750	—
Contributed capital on preferred share retirement	29,000	22,000
Contributed capital on common share retirement	—	96,000
Retained earnings	3,867,000	3,911,500

TRANSACTIONS DURING THE YEAR:
1. Preferred shares were issued for $100,000 during the year. Share issue costs of $2,000 were charged directly to retained earnings. Other preferred shares were retired.
2. On 31 December 20X4, there were 570,000 common shares outstanding.
3. A total of 20,000 common shares were retired on 2 January 20X5 for $18 per share.
4. There was a 10% stock dividend on 1 April 20X5. This dividend was capitalized at $17.50, the fair value of common shares. The stock dividend resulted in the issuance of fractional rights for 3,200 whole shares. Of these, 2,700 whole shares were subsequently issued and fractional rights for a remaining 500 shares are still outstanding at the end of the year.
5. Cash dividends were declared during the year.
6. Common shares were issued in June 20X5 for land. The transaction involved issuing 3,000 common shares for land valued at $52,000.
7. Common shares (46,000 shares) were issued for cash on 30 December 20X5.
8. Earnings were $1,200,000 in 20X5.

Required:
Prepare the financing activities section of the SCF, including dividends paid, based on the above information.

CHAPTER 14

Complex Debt and Equity Instruments

INTRODUCTION

When accountants prepare financial statements, a major task is to classify and organize the accounts into categories. Unfortunately, some things are hard to classify. For example, RONA Inc. has $4 million in Class D *preferred share capital*, entitled to a 4% cumulative dividend. The company is required to buy back $1 million in shares, at book value, every year. These shares don't seem to be a permanent, residual equity interest: the company is required to repay the investment, and RONA classifies these preferred shares as debt. Criteria will be reviewed in this chapter that help determine whether a security is debt or equity *in substance*.

Financial instruments that have elements of *both* debt *and* equity are called *compound financial instruments*. In this chapter, recognition and measurement of convertible debt will be used to illustrate accounting for compound financial instruments.

Another topic in this chapter is accounting for share-based payments, whether the contract is equity-settled, or cash-settled with the cash payment based on the value of shares. Share-based payments may be made to employees, or provided to suppliers, or to existing shareholders. The cost of share-based payments to employees (employee stock options) can be considerable. RONA has options for approximately 3 million shares outstanding, mostly to employees, that allow the purchase of shares at an average price in the range of $11.50 per share. Since market value is over $15 per share, it's obvious that the option holders are receiving something of value. Representational faithfulness dictates that this cost has to be reflected in the financial statements.

This chapter also examines the use of derivative financial instruments to mitigate financial risk, specifically the use of hedges and swaps. The use of derivatives significantly alters the risk profile of a company, and they are recognized at fair value to ensure that the SFP reflects the complete financial position of the company.

In the Appendix to this chapter, posted on the OLC, the various forms of *financial restructuring* are reviewed. When a company is in financial distress, debt may be settled for less than the amount owing, in cash or other assets, or lenders may accept share capital instead of their existing claims and become the residual risk takers.

FINANCIAL INSTRUMENTS—GENERAL PRINCIPLES

The Debt-to-Equity Continuum

Throughout most of the 20th century, the distinction between debt financing and shareholders' equity was clear. Debt financing was an amount borrowed, at some specific interest rate, payable at a fixed time in the future or at the option of the lender. Shareholders' equity was any investment in shares, plus residual interests accruing through retained earnings or capital transactions. The legal form of debt versus equity was unmistakable, and substance generally followed legal form.

Accountants traditionally relied on the legal nature of capital instruments for classification. If there was a stock certificate, the instrument was accounted for as equity; if there was a debt contract or agreement, the instrument was accounted for as a liability.

However, there came to be many forms of financing where the legal description did not seem to correspond with the parties' rights and obligations. The financial markets support a continuum of investments, with features that range from pure debt to pure equity, with a lot of grey in the middle. These financial instruments do not comfortably fit into two simple categories.

For example, perpetual debt is a liability that pays annual interest, but the principal *never* has to be repaid. An **income bond** pays interest and principal, but interest is paid *only when the corporation has reported a certain level of earnings or operating cash flow* in the year. Then there are preferred **redeemable shares,** as reported by RONA, that have to be retired for cash at a certain time.

Some **hybrid financial instruments** have elements of both debt and equity. They are also called **compound financial instruments. Convertible debt**, convertible into a fixed number of shares at the investor's option, is an example. The issuing company allows the investor to convert the principal portion of the bond into a specific number of common shares on a certain date. The issuing company usually hopes that the bond will be converted to avoid paying out cash. Investors will convert only if the shares are worth more money. Perhaps the company will avoid having to repay principal, if share prices increase, but perhaps the company will have to repay the debt, if share prices are soft. This is an uncertain outcome, and obviously hard to place into debt-or-equity slots.

Classification by Substance

Financial instruments must be classified as liability or equity in accordance with the *substance* of the contractual arrangement. If the financial instrument is part debt and part equity, it is a *compound financial instrument,* and *the component parts are classified separately.*

These requirements are an important application of the qualitative characteristic of *substance over form*: if it looks like a duck and it quacks like a duck, then it should be classified as a duck, even when it has a sign around its neck that says it's a moose! That is, classification depends on the nature of the instrument as debt or equity, and not on its name or label.

Furthermore, payments to investors for the use of capital should be presented in accordance with the nature of the financial instrument as a liability or as equity. Payments that are associated with financial liabilities are an expense and should be presented in earnings, and payments associated with equity instruments should be presented in the statement of changes in equity. Gains and losses associated with debt retirement are reported in earnings. Gains and losses associated with equity are capital transactions and are *not* reported in earnings, but rather affect equity accounts.

Tax Status Unaffected It is important to remember that the accounting classification will not change the tax classification of an investment vehicle, because the tax classification is established by Canada Revenue Agency rulings. Thus, "interest" payments on instruments that legally are debt but in substance are equity will be tax deductible as "interest" *even if the interest is reported as a deduction from retained earnings.*[1]

---

[1] An exception is that the interest paid on income bonds generally is not tax deductible. This is a specific provision of the *Income Tax Act*, and the tax treatment is not affected by the accounting treatment.

Similarly, if an "equity" item is classified as debt in the financial statements, and the "dividend" payment is reported as an expense in earnings, the "dividend" *will not be a tax-deductible expense*. The "dividend" in earnings will be adjusted in order to reconcile from accounting income to taxable income. This process is discussed in Chapter 15.

Debt versus Equity Classification Implications

Assume that a company raises $100,000 by issuing a financial instrument that will pay $6,000 per year to the investor. At the end of the fifth year, the company retires the financial instrument in a transaction in the open market, buying it back at market value of $109,500. The financial statements are affected by whether the instrument is classified as debt or equity. The impact of each classification can be summarized as follows:

Event	Liability Classification	Equity Classification
Issuance	Increases long-term liabilities	Increases shareholders' equity
Annual $6,000 payment	Increases interest expense; decreases earnings and thus decreases retained earnings	Reduces retained earnings as a dividend distribution; no impact on earnings
Annual $6,000 payment on SCF	In operating or financing section; company's choice of classification	In operating or financing section; company's choice of classification
Classification of $9,500 amount higher than book value at retirement	Recorded as a loss in earnings	Reduces shareholders' equity directly; no impact on earnings
$100,000 "repayment" of initial investment	Decreases long-term liabilities	Decreases shareholders' equity

There are two major differences between these alternative classifications:

1. Reported earnings is affected by interest expense and gains and losses on retirement when the classification is a liability. In contrast, these items bypass earnings if the classification is equity. For firms that jealously guard reported earnings and related trends, this distinction is important.

2. The classification of the element (i.e., as debt or equity) may be crucial to some corporations. The debt-to-equity ratio is often used in loan covenants to help control a major risk to lenders: the amount of debt outstanding. If debt-to-equity ratios are close to their contractually-agreed maximums, then a new financial instrument issued and classified as equity is good news indeed; one classified as a liability is not. The classification rules attempt to ensure that classification follows substance, not form, to limit the potential for manipulation.

CLASSIFICATION FACTORS

To classify a financial instrument, it is essential to look at the payment arrangements. A basic characteristic of debt is that the *creditors have an enforceable legal right to receive payment*. In most ordinary debt arrangements, the debtor is obligated both to pay regular interest amounts and to repay the principal amount at a fixed and known time. Some debt has no fixed maturity, such as demand loans or lines of credit from a financial institution, but the lenders have the option of demanding their money back. The crucial aspect of debt is that *the creditors can demand payment*. Equity investors, on the other hand, cannot demand payment; any payment of dividends and the redemption or repayment of the amount invested is a voluntary action of the company.

Therefore, to determine whether a financial instrument is debt or equity *in substance*, the following questions must be considered:

1. *Is cash payment of the periodic return on capital (i.e., cash interest or dividend payment) mandatory?*

   Any cash payment that is mandatory or at the investor's option is a liability.

2. *Is the debtor legally required to repay the principal in cash, either at a fixed, predetermined date (or dates), or at the option of the investor/creditor?*

   Any cash payment that is mandatory or at the investor's option is a liability.

3. *Does the issuer have the unconditional right to defer payments indefinitely?*

   If payments can be deferred *forever*, then the element is equity. Classic dividends are only payable if the company declares them and thus can be deferred indefinitely by simply not having any declaration; they represent equity. *If deferral is only for a period of time, then the element is a liability.*

4. *If cash payment is dependent on the outcome of an uncertain future event beyond the control of both the investor and the issuer, is the future event extremely rare/very unlikely to occur?*

   If the event is *abnormal* or *highly unlikely and uncontrollable*, then the element does not have to be repaid and the element is equity. If a financial instrument only has to be repaid on the dissolution of the company, this is deemed to be abnormal and the element is equity. If the financial instrument must be repaid only if a covenant is violated, this is within the control of the company at some level, and the element is a liability.

5. *If the annual periodic return and/or the principal can be settled in the company's own shares, is the number of shares fixed by contract, or does it vary based on the market value of shares at the time of distribution?*

   If the share price is fixed, then the risk of share price fluctuation rests with the investor, and *the element is equity.* If shares to be issued are valued at the share price on the date of payment, then the company has to issue shares with a cash value equal to the amount owing, and the element is a liability.

SPECIFIC EXAMPLES OF FINANCIAL INSTRUMENTS CLASSIFICATION

Retractable Preferred Shares

Most preferred shares have a call provision, whereby the corporation can call in the shares and redeem them at a given price *if the company wishes*. The call price is specified in the corporate articles governing that class of share. Preferred share *call provisions* give management more flexibility in managing the corporation's capital structure than would be the case without a call provision. These shares *do not have to be repaid*; they are equity.

Some preferred shares include the provision that the shares *must* be redeemed on or before a specified date (**term preferred shares**), or an option to redeem that can be exercised *at the option of the shareholder* (**retractable shares**). When redemption is required or is at the option of the holder, then the mandatory final cash payout effectively makes the preferred shares a liability. The key is that cash repayment must either be contractually required, or is at the option of the *investor*.

Effect of Escalation Clause   Sometimes, a preferred share issue will not have a direct or explicit requirement for the company to repay. Instead, the repayment obligation may be established indirectly through its terms and conditions. For example, suppose that a redeemable preferred share issue requires the company to triple the dividend rate after five years, or double the redemption price after five years. No prudent Board of Directors would leave the shares outstanding past year five at their significantly higher cost. The escalation clause clearly indicates that the shares will be redeemed before escalation. These shares will be classified as debt.

Classification of Dividends When preferred shares are classified as debt, *their dividends are reported as a financing expense*, a deduction from earnings, and are not reported on the statement of changes in equity as a reduction of retained earnings.

Recording Dividends Normally, dividends are a legal liability *only when declared*, and the classification of preferred shares as a liability does not alter this. Dividends on preferred shares are normally recorded as declared. However, if dividends are *mandatory*, then their status changes. Mandatory dividends are a liability. The present value of the dividend stream must be estimated when the shares are first issued, and recorded as a liability at that point. Dividends are then recorded annually whether declared or not. For example, if dividends are mandatory *and must be paid in cash at redemption*, then dividends are accrued as time passes.

Required Redemption at a Premium If preferred shares *must be redeemed at a value higher than book value*, the redemption premium should be accrued over the life of the shares using the effective interest method. For instance, assume that redeemable preferred shares were issued at $100 but have to be bought back for $110 at the end of five years. Each year, the company must accrue a portion of the premium, and expense it as a cost of financing.

Reporting Example BAM Investments Corp. is an investment holding company with total assets of just over $1,212 million. The company reports approximately $370 million of retractable preferred shares as a liability, presumably because shareholders can trigger cash repayment at any time. Terms are described in the disclosure notes as follows (emphasis added):

---

8. RETRACTABLE PREFERRED SHARES

. . .

Holders of Class A Preferred Shares and Class AA Preferred Shares, Series I and Class AA Preferred Shares, Series III are entitled to receive cumulative quarterly dividends of $0.390625, $0.309375 and $0.271875 per share respectively, payable on the 7th day of March, June, September and December in each year.

Class A and Class AA Series I Preferred Shares may be surrendered for retraction at any time. The Class A and Class AA Series I Preferred Share Retraction Price will be paid in cash equal to the lesser of (i) 95% of Net Asset Value per Unit of BAM Split; and (ii) $25.00 less 5% of the Net Asset Value per Unit of BAM Split, in either case, less $1.00.

. . . The "Net Asset Value per Unit" is defined as the fair value of the Portfolio shares held by BAM Split plus (minus) the amount by which the value of the other assets of BAM Split exceed (are less than) the liabilities (including any extraordinary liabilities) of BAM Split and the redemption value of the preferred shares, divided by the total number of Units outstanding.

Other Redeemable Shares

"Redeemable" does not automatically mean that shares are liabilities. Shares that are redeemable *at the company's option* are not a liability. The company cannot be forced to pay cash, since redemption is voluntary; redemptions that can be avoided do not create a liability. Also, any senior shares that are *convertible into common shares* are clearly equity.

Mutual Funds

In some open-ended mutual funds, all shares are redeemable in cash at the option of the investor, who also has the legal right to cash payouts for accumulated earnings. These entities accordingly have no equity at all, since all ownership interests have the characteristics of debt and are classified as liabilities.

Perpetual Debt

Perpetual debt provides the holder with a contractual right to receive cash interest, but the principal either (1) never has to be repaid, (2) has to be repaid only in the indefinite future, or (3) has to be repaid only in highly unlikely situations, such as upon liquidation of the company. For example, ING Group has outstanding perpetual debt of over €10 billion, at interest rates from 4.2% to 9%.

Reporting *Perpetual debt is reported entirely as a liability.* This is a compound instrument, with the equity portion valued at zero. The principal amount of perpetual debt is equity, in that it is an obligation due only on liquidation. What is the value of a payment that has a due date in the infinite future? *The present value of such an indefinite payment is zero.* However, the interest payments are a liability because they represent an obligation at fixed dates. The lender will be willing to pay for the interest stream, and it is the interest stream that generates loan proceeds. Only a liability is recorded, which is valued at the present value of the stream of future interest payments.

For example, assume that a $1,000,000, 10% perpetual debt instrument is sold to yield 10%. The present value of the principal, which never has to be repaid, is zero. The present value of the interest, $100,000 a year in perpetuity, is $1,000,000 (that is, $100,000 ÷ 0.10). Thus, the bond sells for the value of the interest stream only. The interest stream is clearly a liability, because it must be paid. Therefore, the $1,000,000 is classified as a liability. The principal portion, with its equity overtones, exists, but is valued at zero.

✓ Convertible Debt

Convertible debt is a common example of a *compound instrument*, classified in the financial statements as part debt, part equity. These bonds often are issued by a corporation with the provision that they may be converted by the holder into shares (usually, common shares) at a specified price or ratio of exchange.

The conversion date might be the bond's maturity date, or at various points prior to maturity (e.g., for the last four years of the bonds' life). There are often different conversion rights during different conversion windows. For example, an investor might be entitled to 10 common shares for every $1,000 bond if converted within the first five years of a 15-year bond, 7.5 shares for conversion in the sixth through tenth year, but only five common shares during years 11 through 15.

The conversion ratio is expressed either in the number of shares per bond, or in a price per share. For example, a bond that is convertible into 20 common shares per $1,000 bond is the same as one that is convertible at a price of $50 ($1,000 ÷ $20).

For example, Alcatel-Lucent has Series B convertible bonds outstanding with a principal amount of US $880.5 million. These bonds are convertible at the investor's option from June 20, 2009 through June 19, 2013, and continue on with a conversion option during an optional redemption period after that date. The bonds mature in 2025. Alcatel-Lucent has the option to redeem the bonds in 2013 through 2019. The conversion share price is fixed at $15.35, also described as a 'conversion ratio of 65.1465,' or $100/$15.35.

Characteristics of Convertible Debt A key element of convertible bonds is that, in issuing the bonds, management fully expects (or hopes) that the conversion privilege will be attractive to the investors: the investors will convert at or before the maturity date, and therefore the company will never have to repay the principal amount of the bonds in cash.

Conversion of a bond becomes attractive when the market price of the share entitlement rises above the conversion price. For example, suppose that an investor has a $1,000 bond (purchased at par) that is convertible into 25 common shares (i.e., the conversion price is $40). If the market price of the common shares is $46, the investor can make a profit of $6 per share, less any transaction costs, by converting the bonds and then selling the shares on the open market:

Market value of shares obtained on conversion ($46 × 25)	$1,150
Less: cost of bond	1,000
Profit from conversion	$ 150

The market recognizes this reality, and therefore the market price of the bonds will increase to follow the conversion value of the shares. Therefore, once the market price of the shares rises above the conversion price, the bonds will sell at a price that is related to the value of the conversion privilege rather than at a price related to the merits of the debt instrument. In the eyes of the market, the bond ceases to trade as debt, and effectively is traded as equity.

Forced Conversion A convertible debenture can often be called for cash redemption by the company prior to maturity; Alcatel had this right in the example cited earlier. The point of the cash redemption option is that management can **force conversion** before maturity if the market price is higher than the conversion price of the shares. The company calls the bond for *cash redemption,* knowing that the shares are worth more, and the investor opts for the higher value of shares. By forcing early conversion, the company makes sure that the share conversion takes place and cash repayment will not be necessary.

Convertible Debt with a Floating Conversion Price per Share Convertible debt may be issued where the *number of shares to be issued on conversion is not fixed by contract,* but rather is based on the market value of the shares on the conversion date. If this is the case, the conversion option has *no intrinsic value to the investor,* because the investor has no upside benefit. For example, if a $1,000,000 bond were convertible into shares at the market value of shares on the conversion date and this value was $80, then 12,500 shares would be issued. If the market value were $82, then 12,195 shares would be issued. *This type of bond has no equity component and is all debt.*

The reason for this conclusion is that if the conversion price is not fixed, the risks and rewards of changing share prices stays with the company. The investor has no upside potential or downside risk. The bond will always trade in financial markets as a pure liability, with no option attached. Essentially, when the price is based on the fair value of the day of conversion, the investor could just as well take cash, and use this cash to purchase shares in the market. The conversion option simply allows transaction costs to be minimized.

Accounting Treatment of Convertible Debt A convertible bond with a fixed conversion price per share has elements of both debt and equity. The liability and the equity component are recognized separately when the bond is first recorded, and then are accounted for separately to maturity. This treatment will be demonstrated in the next section.

CONCEPT REVIEW

1. What is a compound financial instrument?

2. What questions must be answered to aid in classifying a financial instrument as debt or equity?

3. What is the distinguishing characteristic that causes retractable preferred shares to be reported as debt rather than as shareholders' equity?

4. Under what circumstances will the fair value of a convertible bond reflect the fair value of the shares that would be obtained on conversion?

CONVERTIBLE DEBT, CONVERSION AT THE INVESTOR'S OPTION

Convertible debt that is convertible at the option of the investor at a fixed conversion price is initially recognized as a compound instrument, where *proceeds from issuance are divided between the liability and the equity element. The equity element represents the value of the option on common shares.*

PV given

Initial Recognition Assume that Tollen Corporation sells $100,000 of 8% convertible bonds for $106,000. The market interest rate on the day of issuance is 10%. Each $10,000 bond is convertible into 100 common shares on any interest date after the end of the second year from the date of issuance. Conversion is at the option of the investor. Also assume that it is appropriate to assign a value of $92,418 to the bond and $13,582 to the conversion privilege. (Measurement of these amounts will be analyzed in the next section.) The issuance will be recorded as follows:

Shortcut entry DO NOT USE

Cash	106,000	
Bonds payable		92,418
Contributed capital: common share conversion rights		13,582

In order to simplify subsequent accounting for interest expense on the liability portion of the convertible bond, it is helpful to separately record the discount on initial recognition. A discount of $7,582 is recorded: the difference between the $92,418 net proceeds attributable to the bond and its $100,000 face value. The entry is now:

(Highlighted section is the only difference.)

1st entry →

hybrid. { debt / Sh's equity

Cash	106,000	
Discount on bonds payable ($100,000 − $92,418)	7,582	
Bonds payable		100,000
Contributed capital: common share conversion rights		13,582

The account, *common share conversion rights,* is an equity account that will be reported as contributed capital. In later years, *the amount in that account will be transferred to share equity if and when the conversion rights are exercised, or transferred to other contributed capital if the conversion rights lapse.*

Using this approach, *the substance of the transaction* is recognized. Both a bond *and* an option were issued, and both are now reflected in the financial statements. Accounting for the debt will reflect an effective interest rate that approaches the true interest rate on the debt alone. Finally, the proceeds received for the equity portion of the instrument are reflected in equity.

Conversion When convertible bonds are submitted for conversion, the first task is to update any accounts relating to bond premium or discount, accrued interest, and foreign exchange gains and losses on foreign currency–denominated debt. Following these routine adjustments, the balance of the liability account (and related unamortized premium or discount) that pertains to the converted bonds must be transferred to the share account. *As well, the proportionate balance of the stock option account must also be transferred to the share equity account.*

The conversion is recorded using the **book value method,** and the book value, or carrying value, of the debt is simply transferred to equity. For example, assume that all of the $100,000 Tollen bonds payable are converted to 1,000 common shares on an interest date. Assume that on this date, the stock price is $140 per share, and calculations show that $4,550 of discount remains unamortized after updating the discount account. The entry to record the conversion is:

during life of bond.

Bonds payable	100,000	
Contributed capital: common share conversion rights	13,582	
Discount on bonds payable		4,550
Common shares		109,032

The market value of the common shares is not recorded. The value assigned to common shares ($109,032) is the carrying value of the bond ($100,000 − $4,550) plus the option value ($13,582).

Settlement or

Repayment at Maturity If the market value of underlying shares is less than face value at maturity, investors will request repayment and the conversion rights will expire. Since this happens *at maturity*, all discount or premium accounts will be zero. The option value remains in equity, but its description should be changed to indicate that the option is no longer outstanding. This is done in a reclassification entry The entries on cash repayment of the Tollen bonds would be:

Loss of conversion rights

Bonds payable	100,000	
Cash		100,000
Contributed capital: common share conversion rights	13,582	
Contributed capital: lapse of conversion rights		13,582

Repayment Prior to Maturity If the bond is repaid prior to maturity, the amount paid for early retirement is allocated between the debt and equity components, using the incremental method as explained in the next section. Any gain or loss on the liability retirement is recorded in earnings, while the retirement of equity results in adjustments to equity accounts, as illustrated in Chapter 13.

For example, return to the prior example of the Tollen bonds. Assume that the $100,000 Tollen bond is retired for $104,000 on an interest date prior to maturity. On this date, $4,550 of discount remains unamortized. Valuation models indicate that $97,000 of the $104,000 price paid represents the present value of the bond at current interest rates and the remaining $7,000 relates to the equity portion. The entry to record the retirement is:

Bonds payable	100,000 *(given)*	
Contributed capital: common share conversion rights	13,582 *(given)*	
Loss on retirement of bonds ($100,000 $4,550)		
− $97,000	1,550	
Discount on bonds payable		4,550
Contributed capital: retirement of common share		
conversion rights ($13,582 − $7,000)		6,582
Cash		104,000 *(given)*

Measurement

When fair values must be estimated, the **fair value hierarchy** is consulted.

In Level 1, there are quoted market prices for *this exact financial instrument* in active markets, and the result is objectively verifiable.

If the financial instrument is not actively traded, a Level 2 estimate might be made. In Level 2, observable values from similar financial instruments are used to imply value. Adjustments must be made for differences such as credit risk, term, or conditions. For example, if the company's bonds do not trade in active markets, there are no separate objective prices provided by arm's-length market transactions. However, the fair value of another fairly similar bond might be verified. The second bond fair value could be used as a reference point, adjusted for interest rate differentials, or credit rating, and so on. The resulting fair value is less reliable than a Level 1 directly observable value.

Finally, at Level 3 in the fair value hierarchy, there are observable fair values, but multiple or significant adjustments have to be made to infer a fair value, including a company's own data or estimation of unobservable factors. The resulting fair value can be used for reporting, but is correspondingly less reliable.

Measurement of the fair value of debt versus equity components of convertible debt can be problematic because the component elements *do not separately trade* in financial markets. In the fair value hierarchy, this moves the valuation to at least a Level 2 estimate.

Valuation rests on the *liability portion of the compound instrument*: the fair value of a comparable, non-convertible bond must be established through reference pricing to a non-convertible liability. This valuation is based on the bond's present value. The conversion option is valued at the residual; issuance price less the present value of a comparable *non-convertible* bond. This is called the **incremental method of valuation.**

For example, for the Tollen Corporation bond above, assume that the market interest rate for a similar, non-convertible was established to be 10%. The present value of the cash flows of an 8%, five-year, $100,000 bond (assuming annual interest payments) at an effective interest rate of 10%, can be calculated as $92,418. This is a Level 2 estimation. Subtracting $92,418 from the net proceeds of $106,000 leaves $13,582 attributable to the conversion option.

The key to this method is *to establish an appropriate discount rate*, with reference to financial markets and established, observable prices. Ten percent should represent the market interest rate for a bond of similar term, security, and credit risk; this may be straightforward to establish, or not, depending on the activity in the bond market and the presence of similar companies.

Example Assume that Easy Company issues $1,000,000 of $1,000 bonds dated 1 January 20X2, due 31 December 20X4 (i.e., three years later), for $1,002,000. Interest at 6% is payable annually and each bond is convertible at any time up to maturity into 250 common shares. When the bonds are issued, the prevailing interest rate for similar debt without a conversion option is 9%.

Using the incremental method, the amount of the proceeds that is attributable to the liability is measured as the present value of the cash flow, using the market rate of interest of 9%:

Face value [$1,000,000 × (P/F, 9%, 3)]	$772,180
Interest [($1,000,000 × 6%) × (P/A, 9%, 3)]	151,877
Total liability component	$924,057

The issuance of the convertible bonds will be recorded as follows:

Cash	1,002,000	
Discount on convertible bonds		
($1,000,000 − $924,057)	75,943	
Bonds payable		1,000,000
Contributed capital: common share conversion		
rights ($1,002,000 − $924,057)		77,943

Impact on Earnings Interest expense is affected by the allocation of bond proceeds between debt and equity. In the entries above, a discount is recorded. The discount is amortized over the life of the bond, using the effective interest method, as illustrated in Chapter 12. Interest expense will decrease earnings.

Remember that the higher the value that is allocated to the option, the higher the discount. The higher the discount, the more interest expense is recognized, and the lower earnings will be. This effect may influence the valuation adopted by management when the bond proceeds are initially recorded. For example, if there is a corporate bias to maximize earnings, a valuation that minimizes the amount allocated to the common share conversion rights and the discount will likely be chosen.

Note also that the amount allocated to the common share conversion rights stays in the contributed capital section of shareholders' equity permanently and never has an impact on earnings. The conversion rights account is *either folded into the common share account, if the option is exercised, or is part of other contributed capital, if the option is not exercised.*

Convertible Debt with a Floating Conversion Price per Share The previous example involved a bond with a fixed conversion price per share. If the conversion option was based on the market value of the common shares on the conversion date, then the option has no value to the investor. Such a convertible bond is classified entirely as debt.

Reporting Example

Refer to the sample financial statements excerpts in Exhibit 14-1. The statement of financial position shows a convertible bond at €607 million, and an equity account of €22.5 million related to the share option. The disclosure notes indicate that the bonds are convertible into common shares, and that the option was valued at a residual amount on initial recognition.

EXHIBIT 14-1

SAMPLE COMPANY LIMITED

Selected Financial Statement Disclosures

From Disclosure Note 1

The fair value of the liability component of a convertible bond is determined using a market interest rate for an equivalent non-convertible bond. This amount is recorded as a liability on an amortized cost basis until extinguished on conversion or maturity of bonds. The remainder of the proceeds is allocated to the conversion option. This is recognized in equity.

From Disclosure Note 18

Convertible Bond

On 15 November 2008, the Company issued convertible bonds valid from 15 November 2008 to 15 November 2015 and with a coupon of 2.625%, for a total of €617 400 000. During the conversion period, these bonds with a nominal value of €5000 may be converted into registered shares of the Company at €26.00 each.

The bond issue has been split into an equity component and a liability component. The fair value of the liability component, recognized as long-term debt, was determined by reference to the market rate (3.248% per year) of an equivalent non-convertible bond. The residual value (the conversion option) was recognized as equity. Until conversion or redemption of the bond issue, the liability component and all related adjustments will be accounted for using the effective interest rate method. The equity portion was determined at the time of issue and will not be modified at a later date.

The convertible bond issue is recognized, net of discount, as follows:

	2011	2010
Liability component at 1 January	€603	€599
Coupon interest at market rate	21	21
Coupon interest at 2.625%	−17	−17
Liability component at 31 December	€607	€603

In 2011 and 2010, no bonds had been converted. The closing fair value of the convertible bond on public financial markets at end-2011 was 101% (142.0% at end-2010).

From Disclosure Note 25

	2011	2010
Equity component of convertible bond	€22.5	€22.5

CONVERTIBLE DEBT, CONVERSION MANDATORY

The preceding discussion dealt exclusively with debt that is convertible at the investor's option. Corporations may also issue convertible debt that pays interest in cash, but principal *must be settled by issuance of a specific number of shares on maturity.* This is a compound financial instrument, where the obligation to pay cash interest is a liability and the *entire* principal portion is equity. As long as shares can be forced on an investor at a price set in advance, a bond falls in this category. *If the company has the right to repay principal in cash or shares, the bond is still classified as "conversion mandatory."* This is because, again, the company cannot be forced to pay cash.

Measurement Using the *incremental method,* the liability portion of the compound instrument is valued based on present value using an appropriate market yield rate, which reflects similar term, security, and credit risk. This is a Level 2 approximation of fair value. The equity portion of the bond is then the residual amount, the difference between issuance proceeds and liability present value. Over the life of the bond, interest expense is recorded on the interest portion *only*, and cash payments are applied against the interest liability *only*, reducing it to zero by maturity. At maturity, the equity portion of the bond is transferred to share capital.

Example Suppose that Gagnon Ltd. issues a $100,000, 6%, four-year debenture for $103,500, repayable at maturity through the issuance of a fixed number of common shares (fixed conversion price). Interest is payable annually, in cash. A similar bond that was not convertible would have carried an interest rate of 8%. Since conversion is mandatory, and the number of shares to be issued is fixed, principal is equity. The interest must be paid in cash, so it is a liability. The issuance price is disaggregated as follows:

Issuance proceeds	$103,500
Interest present value [$6,000 × (P/A, 8%, 4)]	19,873
Equity portion	$ 83,627

When the bond is issued, the entry will be:

Cash	103,500	
Interest liability on debenture		19,873
Share equity—debenture		83,627

As time passes, interest will be accounted for by the effective interest method, calculated only on the *outstanding balance of the interest liability.* The carrying amount of the interest liability will be increased by 8% each year, and the $6,000 annual payment of interest will reduce the liability. At the end of the first year, Gagnon will make the following entries to record the interest expense and the annual payment:

Interest expense ($19,873 × 8%)	1,590	
Interest liability on debenture		1,590
Interest liability on debenture	6,000	
Cash		6,000

Note that the amount that is paid as "interest," $6,000, is treated as the reduction of the liability and interest expense is a far different number, based only on the recognized liability. The amortization of the interest liability over the four-year period is shown in Exhibit 14-2. At maturity, the interest liability will be zero by virtue of the payments made over the four years. The balance in the debenture equity account will be transferred to common share equity:

Share equity—debenture	83,627	
Common shares		83,627

Share Equity Alternatives Some companies have chosen to increase the recorded value of the share equity account from the initial assigned value, *up to par value*, through a **capital charge** to retained earnings. This can be accomplished in one lump sum entry at maturity, or gradually over the life of the bond. At maturity, *par value* would then be transferred to the common share account.

In the example above, this would involve increasing the $83,627 share equity-debenture account to $100,000, an increase of $16,373. This might be done over the four years to maturity by decreasing retained earnings for a capital charge, and increasing the share equity-debenture account annually. Alternatively, the $16,373 amount could be recorded in one year, at maturity. For example:

Capital charge (retained earnings)	16,373	
Share equity—debenture		16,373

Share equity—debenture	100,000	
Common shares		100,000

The capital charge would be reported as a line item in retained earnings, and reduce the earnings available to common shareholders. There is variation in practice in this area.

EXHIBIT 14-2

CONVERTIBLE DEBT—CONVERSION MANDATORY

Amortization of Interest Liability

Year	Beginning Balance of Interest Liability	Interest Expense at 8%	Payment	Ending Balance of Interest Liability
1	$19,873	$1,590	$6,000	$15,463
2	15,463	1,237	6,000	10,700
3	10,700	856	6,000	5,556
4	5,556	444	6,000	0

Interest Obligation Payment Variations   If the company *must* pay interest in cash, the interest portion of the issue proceeds is a liability. If the company is permitted, at the company's option, to issue shares at their current fair value in full payment of interest, the interest is still a liability and is recorded as such. However, if the bond agreement allows the company to issue shares at a *fixed price* in payment of interest, then this interest portion of the debt *is equity*. Risk falls on the debenture holder when the price per share is set, because the holder's ultimate benefit from interest payments will depend on the market value of the shares, and is not on a fixed monetary amount. To summarize:

Bond Terms—Interest arrangement	Classification
Interest that must be paid in cash	Debt
Interest that the company has the option of paying in a fixed number of shares, or by using a fixed price per share	Equity
Interest that the company has the option of paying in a variable number of shares, using current market prices to establish value	Debt

Debt with a Floating Conversion Price per Share   Standard-setters have determined that when the number of shares (price per share) required to settle the obligation is fixed, then the principal is equity, as illustrated above. If the number of shares is not fixed, but rather is based on the current fair value of shares, the principal is a *financial liability* of the entity and the bond is accounted for as a straightforward bond liability, as illustrated in Chapter 12. Remember that if the conversion price is the current share price, there is no transfer of risk and the price risk stays with company.

CONCEPT REVIEW

1. If a bond must be converted to a fixed number of shares at maturity, how is the equity portion of the compound instrument measured?

2. If a bond must be converted to a fixed number of shares at maturity, will reported annual interest expense be higher or lower than the contractual interest paid?

STOCK OPTIONS

Stock options or **stock rights** are financial instruments that give the holder the right, but not the obligation, to buy shares at a fixed price at a certain point in time, called the **exercise date**. When an option is first issued, it usually has an exercise price that is equal to or higher than the current market price of the shares. The option has an **intrinsic value** when the current share price rises above the exercise price. An option term can be lengthy and share prices can be volatile, so an option has a **fair value** depending on market expectations about the *eventual share price on the exercise date*, combined with the time value of money.

Stock options are a form of **derivative instrument**. They are derivative because their value arises or is *derived* solely from the value of the primary equity shares that they can be used to buy. Derivative instruments are designed to transfer risk by setting the conditions of an exchange of financial instruments at a particular time at fixed terms. Derivative instruments derive their values from the underlying equity or debt instruments.

Suppose that Mercurial Limited issues 10,000 stock options to its employees. Each option permits the employee to buy one Mercurial common share for $5 in four years' time. When the options are issued, the market price of Mercurial's shares is $4. These options are said to be **under water** when they are first issued, because the exercise price is higher than the fair value of the shares. If the current market price of the shares rises to $8, the option then has an *intrinsic value* of $3. The option is also described as being **in-the-money** when it has an intrinsic value. However, the fair value of the option may still be zero, if the market price is expected to decline below $5 by the exercise date. If the market price of the common shares is below $5 on the expiration date, the rights will expire unexercised.

The fair value of the option is *the risk-adjusted present value of any positive difference between the market value and the option price on the day the rights are exercised.* For the Mercurial Limited options, the "perfect" valuation would be to predict the market price—accurately—in four years' time, and discount the gain to today's dollars at an appropriate discount rate. Assume that the market price were to be $18 in the future. The option would be worth $130,000 at exercise (that is, 10,000 shares × ($18 − $5)). If the appropriate discount rate were 8%, the present value of this option would be $95,554 (that is, $130,000 × (P/F, 8%, 4)). Unfortunately, there is no crystal ball available to predict the future stock market price or the risk-adjusted four-year discount rate.

The fair value of options can be established by use of an option pricing model, such as the Black-Scholes, Monte Carlo, or binomial pricing models. Option pricing models price an option based on factors including the share price of the option contract, length of the option, current market value of the stock, volatility of stock price, expected dividends, and the risk-free interest rate. Use of option pricing models to account for some options is contentious, though, because option pricing models were not developed to price long-term options. Furthermore, the results are a Level 2 (or perhaps Level 3) measurement in the fair value hierarchy, and have no Level 1 measurement validity. That is, these options are never separately traded and any suggested fair value is an educated guess. Standard-setters feel, though, that it is better to be imprecise than to give up, and valuation based on these models is becoming increasingly entrenched in the financial reporting model.

Recording Assume that a corporation issues rights allowing the holder(s) to acquire common shares in four years' time at an acquisition price of $20 per share, which is the now-current market price of the common shares. The corporation issues 100,000 rights, and specifies that it takes five rights to acquire a share, so 20,000 shares could be issued if all rights are exercised. The corporation receives $18,000 for the rights. Valuation is straightforward because there is a market transaction.

The relevant dates are the (1) announcement date, (2) issuance date, or grant date, (3) exercise date, and (4) expiration date. Consider the following entries:

Announcement date:		
Memorandum: 100,000 stock rights approved, allowing purchase of 20,000 shares at $20 in four years' time.		
Issuance date; rights sold for a total of $18,000:		
Cash	18,000	
Contributed capital: stock rights outstanding		18,000

At exercise, assuming that the current market price of the common shares was $28 and all rights were exercised:

Exercise date:		
Cash (20,000 shares × $20)	400,000	
Contributed capital: stock rights outstanding	18,000	
Common shares		418,000

Alternatively, assuming that the current market price of common shares was $14 and all rights expired:

Expiry date:		
Contributed capital: stock rights outstanding	18,000	
Contributed capital, lapse of stock rights		18,000

Notice that the stock rights outstanding account ends up in one of two places: *either folded into the common share account, if the rights are exercised, or as part of other contributed capital, if the rights are not exercised.* Both of these accounts are equity accounts and both are elements of contributed capital.

Notice also that the current fair value of the shares on the exercise date, $28, is not reflected in the entry that records exercise of the options. Financial statement users would often like to judge the terms of the rights offering, as approved by the Board of Directors. Details of all options are disclosed in the financial statements so anyone can make these calculations. But comparison of issuance price versus fair value requires some digging!

WARRANTS

Stock rights that are issued as a *detachable contract* with another security (usually bonds) are called **stock warrants**. Stock warrants will trade separately from the bond to which they were originally attached, and have a Level 1 fair value because of this separate market. Like rights, stock warrants may be exercised to acquire additional shares from the corporation, or allowed to lapse on the expiration date (if any).

Stock warrants issued in conjunction with debt have three important characteristics that differentiate the "package" from convertible debt:

1. The warrants usually are *detachable*, which means that they can be bought and sold separately from the debt to which they were originally attached;

2. The warrants can be exercised without having to trade in or redeem the debt; and

3. The exercise of warrants results in cash paid for shares, which is not the case for convertible bonds.

On issuance, a portion of the bond price is allocated to the warrants. The allocation is credited to a contributed capital (shareholders' equity) account, calculated based on the market values of the two securities on the date of issuance (a **proportional method**). The fair value of debt is based on present value at the market interest rate, and warrants are valued based on trading values as soon as they begin to trade.

14-13

Example Embassy Corporation issues $100,000 of 8%, 10-year, non-convertible bonds with detachable stock purchase warrants. Nuvolari Corporation purchases the entire issue for 105 exclusive of accrued interest. Each $1,000 bond carries 10 warrants. Each warrant entitles Nuvolari to purchase one common share for $15. The bond issue therefore includes 1,000 warrants (100 bonds × 10 warrants per bond). Shortly after issuance, the warrants trade for $4 each ($4,000 in total) and the bonds were trading at 103 ex-warrants (that is, without warrants attached) ($103,000 in total). *PV given*

These fair values total to $107,000, $2,000 higher than the $105,000 issuance price, implying market inefficiencies or changed market conditions in the short gap between issuance and active trading. An allocation of the $105,000 issuance proceeds is based proportionally on both values:

basket sale using proportional method

Market value of bonds ($100,000 × 1.03)	$103,000
Market value of warrants ($4 × 1,000)	4,000
Total market value of bonds and warrants	$107,000
Allocation of proceeds to bonds	
[$105,000 × ($103,000 ÷ $107,000)]	$101,075
Allocation of proceeds to warrants	
[$105,000 × ($4,000 ÷ $107,000)]	3,925
Total proceeds allocated	$105,000

Issuance entry		
Cash	105,000	
Bonds payable		100,000
Contributed capital: detachable stock warrants		3,925
Premium on bonds payable ($101,075 − $100,000)		1,075

If the warrants are exercised when the market value of shares is $22:

Contributed capital: detachable stock warrants	3,925	
Cash ($15 × 1,000)	15,000	
Common shares		18,925

If the warrants expire:

If shares less than 15$

Contributed capital: detachable stock warrants	3,925	
Contributed capital: lapse of warrants		3,925

The contributed capital account either rolls into the common share account on exercise, or remains in contributed capital with a different description on lapse. *This is the same pattern* as established for the contributed capital account created for the conversion option for bonds convertible at the investor's option and that used for options.

Options Not Recognized

It will occasionally be appropriate to simply disclose the presence of outstanding stock options. For example, corporations trying to make themselves less attractive as a takeover target will sometimes issue rights or options that would make it far more expensive for an outsider to gain control. These are known as **poison pill** options. They are issued to existing shareholders for no consideration and are recorded by memorandum only because they have no fair value. If the rights were allowed to expire, a further memorandum entry would be recorded.

Example Kinross Gold Corporation adopted a Rights Plan in 2006, described as follows:

Under the Plan, one right is issued for each common share of the Company. The rights will trade together with the common shares and will not be separable from the common shares or exercisable unless a take-over bid is made that does not comply with the Permitted Bid requirements. In such event, such rights will entitle shareholders, other than shareholders making the take-over bid, to purchase additional common shares of the Company at a substantial discount to the market price at the time.

That is, in the event of a hostile takeover bid, the current shareholders *not involved* in the takeover bid would be allowed to buy shares at significantly reduced prices. This would greatly increase the shares outstanding and severely dilute the value of the shares held by the parties backing the takeover bid.

Poison pill rights are recorded only as a memo in the books. Disclosure is prominent, to scare off the wolves!

CONCEPT REVIEW

1. When does an option have an intrinsic value? How is this different from fair value?

2. When options are exercised, is the value assigned to the common shares issued equal to the fair value of the shares? Explain.

3. Past Limited issues common stock warrants as part of an issue of debentures. The exercise price for common shares under the warrants is higher than the market price of the common shares when the bonds are issued. Should any part of the proceeds of the bond issue be credited to shareholders' equity? Explain.

4. What are poison pill options?

SHARE-BASED PAYMENTS

Share-based payments result from transactions in which an entity acquires or receives goods or services, where the consideration is in the form of shares or referenced to (based on) the price of shares. This includes transactions where share options are granted for goods and services. Long-term compensation to employees is a common example of a share-based transaction, but shares or options may also be used to compensate suppliers. These share-based arrangements may be **equity-settled plans** (the recipient receives shares) or **cash-settled plans** (the recipient receives cash based on the value of shares.) Alternatively, the arrangement may allow the recipient or the company to choose between cash or share consideration.

Share-based Payment to Non-Employees

Transactions involving equity-settled share-based payments with *non-employees* are recognized when the service is rendered or the goods are received. Such transactions are valued at the fair value of the goods or services acquired. In the rare circumstances that fair value *cannot be measured*, then the fair value of the share rights granted must be estimated and recorded.

Example Assume that Terry Technologies Ltd. issues 500 no-par common shares to Vilt Holdings Limited for October 20X2 rent, which has been set in the lease agreement at $1,000 per month. The shares are currently trading at $2.10 per share. The entry:

1 October 20X2		
Rent expense	1,000	
Common shares, no-par (500 shares)		1,000

The transaction is valued at the contractually set rent amount. The market value of the common shares is in the same range ($1,050; 500 shares × $2.10) but is not used to value the transaction. The Board of Directors, who must authorize this transaction, would consider this information, though, because they have a legislative duty to issue shares at fair value.

Example Assume that GT Ltd. issues 500 stock rights to Laura Brown as a director's fee. Two rights entitle Brown to purchase one common share for $30. The rights were issued on 1 March 20X2, expire on 31 December 20X2, and are exercised by Brown on 1 July 20X2 when the shares are trading for $36.50. Other directors were paid $800 cash. The entries to record issuance and exercise are:

1 March 20X2—issuance date		
Administrative expense (director's fees)	800	
Contributed capital: stock rights outstanding		800
1 July 20X2—exercise date		
Cash (250 shares × $30)	7,500	
Contributed capital: stock rights outstanding	800	
Common shares, no-par (250 shares)		8,300

The market value of the shares on the date the common shares were issued, $36.50, is not recognized. If the options were to expire, the entry would be:

Contributed capital: stock rights outstanding	800	
Contributed capital: lapse of stock rights		800

Notice the pattern established: the contributed capital account either is folded into the common share account on exercise, or remains in contributed capital with a different description on lapse.

Valuation Valuation may not be as simple as presented in these examples. For example, if all GT directors were compensated through options, no cash reference price would exist. Could the directors' fees of other companies be used as a reference price? There might be no comparable companies, or the companies might have different compensation practices. In the *fair value hierarchy,* adjustments would move the fair value to Level 2 or perhaps Level 3 equivalents. In the rare circumstances that no fair value is obtainable, the stock option would be valued using an option pricing model.

Cash-settled Plans Suppliers and other non-employees might also have entitlements under cash-settled plans, where they would be entitled to money rather than shares. In this case, a liability would be established and measurement would be important. Cash-settled plans are illustrated for employees in the following section.

Share-based Payment to Employees

Share-based payments are a common form of long-term compensation granted to employees, senior management in particular. *Plans may be equity-settled or cash-settled.* There are many alternative structures, including **stock option plans**, **stock appreciation rights** (SARs), **phantom stock plans,** and **restricted share units**. The range of these alternatives reflects certain tax strategies, and also the understanding that employees might prefer to have cash, rather than company shares. (It can be complicated, under insider trading rules, for managers to buy shares under an option plan and then sell them to raise cash.)

Also, volatility in stock price may make classic option programs unpopular. For instance, when stock prices go down, instead of up, employees may be disappointed and leave the company. When stock prices shoot up, stakeholders may be concerned with the generous returns granted to employees. For example, the CEO of Thomson Reuters Company earned total compensation of over $39 million in 2009, of which only $1.6 million was salary. This is an extremely high level of compensation.

Some of the more common long-term compensation arrangements are summarized in the table, below.

Share-based Arrangement	Employee Receives	Description
Stock option	Shares	Employee has right to buy shares at a set price during a particular period.
SARs— cash-settled	Cash	Employee receives positive difference between set reference price of shares and (later) fair value of shares; share price is hoped to increase over a period of time; value paid in cash.
SARs— equity-settled	Shares	As above, only value is distributed in shares.
SARs— employee option	Cash or perhaps shares (at the employee's option)	As above, only value may be taken in cash or shares at the employee's choice.
SARs— employer option	Cash or perhaps shares (at the company's option)	As above, only it is the company's choice as to whether cash or shares are distributed.
Phantom stock plan—cash	Cash	Employee receives cash award equal to the fair value of a certain number of shares at a certain point in time.
Phantom stock plan— employee option— cash or shares	Employee has choice of cash or shares; often higher value of shares is offered as incentive to take shares	Employee receives cash award equal to the fair value of a certain number of shares at a certain point in time. Payment is in cash or shares.
Restricted share units	Cash	Depending on terms, employee is awarded units and is paid cash after certain performance standards are met or time passes. Amount is based on the value of the *increase in underlying share value* or the *total value* of underlying shares.

Summary of Characteristics of Share-based Arrangements

The vesting period for share-based arrangements is significant for accounting purposes. **Vesting** is achieved when the employee is entitled to the compensation, regardless of other conditions. In other words, rights irrevocably pass to the recipient. For example, if an option vests after three years of employment, and is exerciseable after year five, an individual who leaves the company in year four would still be able to exercise the option, while one who left in year three would **forfeit**, or give up, the option.

Accounting Patterns Accounting for the share-based arrangements with employees can follow several patterns:

1. If the plan is *equity-settled,* then the fair value is estimated *once, and once only,* when the equity rights are granted: this value is accrued over the *vesting period.* Expected forfeiture rates are estimated annually and the amounts are adjusted to actual forfeiture rates each period and at maturity (that is, the plan is **trued up,** or brought to the correct final amount). If the plan vests immediately, the fair value is immediately recorded in full. Accrual increases an equity account, and results in an expense that decreases earnings. The expense and equity accounts are recorded/adjusted annually.

2. If the plan is *cash-settled,* then the *fair value* is *recalculated annually.* Fair value is based on a valuation model, which would include factors such as share price volatility, plan duration, and so on. The yearly accrual represents the current year amount plus a correction of the prior cumulative estimate, reflecting cumulative accrual over the vesting period. Expected forfeiture rates are estimated annually and the amounts are adjusted to actual forfeiture rates each period and at maturity. That is, a cash-settled plan is *trued up* for *both* fair value and forfeiture. The accrual increases a liability account, and results in an expense that decreases earnings.

3. If the plan allows employees to choose between cash and shares at maturity, then the plan is a compound instrument. The equity portion is recorded as in #1, above, while the liability portion reflects the treatment in #2.

In summary:

Classification	Amount	Re-measure for	Elements	Comment
Equity-settled plan	Fair value set by option pricing model on date of grant, adjusted for forfeitures	Forfeitures	Expense and Equity	Recorded over period to vesting; no adjustment of initial fair value estimate Remeasured annually for estimated forfeitures
Cash-settled plan	Cash to be paid estimated at fair value each year-end, adjusted for forfeitures	Fair Value and Forfeitures	Expense and Liability	Recorded over period to vesting; Remeasured annually for estimated fair value and forfeitures
Compound instrument	Initial recognition of both liability and equity component	Liability—fair value and forfeitures; Equity—forfeitures only	Expense and Liability and Equity	Liability element measured as above; Equity element measured as above

Equity-settled Plans

Equity-settled plans all follow the same accounting pattern, and will be demonstrated through employee stock option plans.

Employee Stock Options Suppose that 20 employees are granted options for 250 shares each, a total of 5,000 common shares, at an option price of $20 per share. The options *vest* immediately, meaning that the employees can exercise the options whether employment continues or not. The options are exercisable after five years and expire after eight years, which means that there is a three-year exercise window starting after five years. The company must determine the fair value of the option *on the date it is granted*, using an option pricing model. Assume that this total value is $48,000 for all 5,000 shares. Recognition of this amount is over the vesting period; it is recognized *all upfront* if the options vest immediately, or *over a period of years* if vesting spans more than one year. For this example, vesting is immediate, so the cost of the option is recognized as follows:

On the vesting date:		
Compensation expense	48,000	
Contributed capital: common share options outstanding		48,000

Now assume that the options do not vest until four years after they have been granted, and there is no risk of the employees forfeiting the options (that is, all will stay with the company through the vesting period). In that case, one-quarter of the expense is recorded in each year:

Annual entry:		
Compensation expense ($48,000 ÷ 4)	12,000	
Contributed capital: common share options outstanding		12,000

Note that this amortization period is the *vesting period*, not the period of time before the options may be exercised (five years) or the window during which the options can be exercised (three years). The vesting period often coincides with the period before the options can first be exercised (five years) but this is not always the case.

After this entry is made annually for four years, $48,000 of total compensation expense is recorded and there is a $48,000 balance in the contributed capital account. The $48,000 estimate is not revisited; this fair value is *not subsequently adjusted for changes in option pricing variables.*

When the options are exercised, the contributed capital amount is moved into the common share account along with cash paid:

At exercise:		
Cash (5,000 shares × $20)	100,000	
Contributed capital: common share options outstanding	48,000	
Common shares		148,000

Options may *lapse* because the exercise price is lower than the common share price. If the options lapse, the amount recorded as contributed capital remains, but its classification is changed to indicate that the options have expired:

If the options lapse:		
Contributed capital: common share options outstanding	48,000	
Contributed capital: share options expired		48,000

The ironic part of a "lapsed options" situation is that the company has recorded an expense for an option plan, which has turned out to be of no value to the employee. Expired options would have been *under water* on the maturity date. However, the accounting valuation is based on the initial assessment of fair value on the date the options are granted. *The intrinsic value of the option on the exercise date, or the lack thereof, is not recognized in any circumstances.*

Measurement with forfeiture estimated Forfeiture during the vesting period must be estimated annually, and the amounts *trued up* at the end of the vesting period. For example, assume that the company *initially* estimates that only 16 of the 20 employees covered by the option agreement illustrated above are expected to stay until vesting. Three leave the first year, one the second, two the third, and none in the fourth. By the end of the vesting period, 6 forfeit and 14 receive options. Estimates of forfeitures are updated at the end of each period, and actual turnover is instructive in this estimate. Data is as follows:

Year	1	2	3	4
Estimate made by management:				
Employees expected to remain until vesting	16 (80%)	14 (70%)	13 (65%)	n/a
Employees expected to forfeit	4 (20%)	6 (30%)	7 (35%)	n/a
Factual history:				
Employees actually forfeiting in the year (6 in total)	3	1	2	0
Employees actually receiving options (20 − 6)				14 (70%)

The expense for each period is as follows:

Time period	1	2	3	4
Fair value	$48,000	$48,000	$48,000	$48,000
× *Cumulative* vested fraction	1/4	2/4	3/4	4/4
× Estimate of retention (above)	80%	70%	65%	70%*
= Required balance in the equity account at year-end	$ 9,600	$16,800	$23,400	$33,600
Opening balance	0	9,600	16,800	23,400
Expense for the period (Debit expense, credit contributed capital)	$ 9,600	$ 7,200	$ 6,600	$10,200

*Actual; 14/20

The annual expense is no longer an equal $12,000 amount, even though it is still based on the initial measure of $48,000 of fair value. Each year, the accrual is adjusted to the appropriate level of expected take-up, *on a cumulative basis*. In the first year, the expense of $9,600 is simply the $12,000 one-quarter fair value allocation multiplied by the expected 80% retention rate.

The year 1 entry:

Compensation expense	9,600	
Contributed capital: common share options outstanding		9,600

In the second year, however, the expected retention rate has declined to 70%. There is an annual expense of $12,000 multiplied by the new retention rate of 70% ($8,400) *combined with* an adjustment to the first year expense to bring it down to the now-expected 70% retention rate (10% of $12,000, a recovery of $1,200.) The result is an expense of $7,200.

The year 2 entry:

Compensation expense	7,200	
Contributed capital: common share options outstanding		7,200

Fortunately, since the cumulative adjustments are tedious, all adjustments are subsumed on one line on the table shown above, and do not have to be separately calculated. By the end of the fourth year, the equity account reflects the balance for the employees who actually receive vested options, and the cumulative expense is *trued up* at $33,600, or $48,000 × 14/20 employees.

Entries in years 3 and 4:

Compensation expense	6,600	
Contributed capital: common share options outstanding		6,600

Compensation expense	10,200	
Contributed capital: common share options outstanding		10,200

ETHICAL ISSUES

Management must use *best estimates* in estimating compensation cost accruals. There are many estimates required by the option pricing models that are used to establish fair value. In addition, though, retention rates are critical. If retention rates decline, the expense is lower, not only because the annual portion of the expense is lower, but also because the cumulative correction reduces expense in the current year. The expense could even be a *recovery* if retention estimates are significantly lowered and the company is well into the vesting period. Evidence to support retention must be gathered, but trends may be difficult to predict, making this area high risk for manipulation and misstatement.

Reporting example An example of a stock option plan and accounting policies for Sample Company Limited:

From Disclosure Note 1

The Company has an equity-settled, share-based compensation plan. Under the terms of this plan, share options are granted to managers and employees who distinguished themselves by a particularly strong commitment to the company or an above-average performance. The fair value of the employee services received in exchange for the grant of the options is recognized as an expense. The total amount to be expensed over the vesting period is determined by reference to the fair value of the options granted, calculated using the Black-Scholes model, allowing for expected forfeitures. At each balance sheet date, the Company revises its estimates of expected forfeitures.

continued on next page

From Disclosure Note 32

	2011 Options	2010 Options
Options outstanding at 1 January	194,886	180,773
Granted	165,234	156,637
Forfeited or lapsed	−451	−144
Exercised	−132,744	−142,380
Options outstanding at 31 December	226,925	194,886

All options included in the table above have an exercise price of €6.00.

Cash-settled Plans

Cash-settled plans all follow the same accounting pattern, and will be demonstrated through a cash-settled SARs plan.

Cash-settled SARs Forty employees are awarded a total of 10,000 units of stock appreciation rights (SARs) at the beginning of 20X5. Each employee receives 250 units in a program that entitles him or her to a cash payment equal to the appreciation in stock price over the life of the SARs contract. The employees will receive cash at the end of the 20X7 year, if still with the employer at that time. The cash to be distributed is calculated as the fair value of company shares in 20X7, less a $10 *reference price*, which the company has chosen because it is the fair value of company shares when the SARs were granted in 20X5. These terms are set by contract, and are different for every SARs arrangement. Each of these SARs units has an *intrinsic value* at any point in time, which is the difference between $10 and the current market price of the shares. Each SARs unit also has a fair value, which is the *expected time-adjusted value of the SARs unit at maturity*. Fair value is not just intrinsic value.

Data is as follows:

End of year	20X5	20X6	20X7
Intrinsic value:			
Market value per share	$18	$12	$19
Reference price per share	10	10	10
Intrinsic value per share	$ 8	$ 2	$ 9
Fair value:			
Estimated fair value per share *(provided by a valuation model)*	$ 8.70	$ 3.00	n/a
Total fair value (for 10,000 units)	$87,000	$30,000	n/a
Cash payout:			
Total intrinsic value ($9 × 10,000 units)			$90,000

No forfeitures are expected. The entries make an annual accrual *with an adjustment for the cumulative balance, referenced to the new fair value.* Unlike the share-settled pattern, these entries are based on a new fair value each period, and are trued up to intrinsic value when the cash payout is made. These calculations can be done with or without the structure of the table that was illustrated for options.

20X5 entry:		
Compensation expense ($87,000) × (1 year ÷ 3 years))	29,000	
Long-term compensation liability		29,000

20X6 entry:		
Long-term compensation liability		
(($30,000) × (2 years ÷ 3 years)		
= $20,000 versus $29,000 recorded)	9,000	
Compensation expense (recovery)		9,000

20X7 entry; adjustment and employees paid cash:		
Compensation expense ($90,000 Intrinsic		
value × (3 years ÷ 3 years)) = $90,000		
versus $20,000 recorded	70,000	
Long-term compensation liability		70,000
Long-term compensation liability	90,000	
Cash		90,000

Compensation expense can be a recovery, as shown in 20X6. Cumulative compensation expense recorded cannot fall below zero. If the *fair value* of the SARs units falls to zero, the balance in the liability account is then zero, and compensation expense recorded to date is reversed.

Measurement with forfeiture estimated Once expected forfeiture is incorporated, the calculations get one step more complicated, as illustrated below. The approach is the same as for options, but cash-settled plans *refer to a new fair value each period*, and so the approach is conceptually much different. As for options, forfeiture during the vesting period must be estimated annually, and the amounts *trued up* at the end of the vesting period to the real retention level *and the real cash cost*.

The cumulative actual level of forfeiture during the vesting period should be the base level of forfeiture rates but is also predictive evidence. In this example, the company initially estimates that 10 employees will leave and 30 remain, for 75% retention. Seven actually leave and 33 are paid under the SARs contract in 20X7, a retention level of 82.5%.

End of Year	20X5	20X6	20X7
Estimate made by management:			
Employees expected to remain until vesting	30 (75%)	32 (80%)	n/a
Employees expected to forfeit	10 (25%)	8 (20%)	n/a
Factual history:			
Employees actually forfeiting in the year	6	1	0
Employees actually receiving SARs (40 − 7)			33 (82.5%)

The expense for the each period is as follows:

End of Year	20X5	20X6	20X7
Fair value	$87,000	$30,000	$90,000
× *Cumulative* vesting fraction	1/3	2/3	3/3
× Estimate of retention (above)	75%	80%	82.5%*
= Required balance in the liability account at year-end	$21,750	$16,000	$74,250
Opening balance	0	21,750	16,000
Expense for the period (recovery) (debit expense, credit liability, or the opposite for the recovery year)	$21,750	($ 5,750)	$58,250

*actual; 33/40

As for options, the annual expense is the combination of the new layer of expense and a correction of old estimates. This time, both the fair value and the retention rate are corrected, which makes compensation cost even more volatile. Annual entries:

20X5 entry:		
Compensation expense	21,750	
Long-term compensation liability		21,750

20X6 entry:		
Long-term compensation liability	5,750	
Compensation expense (recovery)		5,750

At the end of 20X7, the liability is trued up, and money is paid to the 33 employees who are still with the company:

20X7 entry; adjustment and employees paid cash:		
Compensation expense	58,250	
Long-term compensation liability		58,250
Long-term compensation liability	74,250	
Cash (33 employees × 250 units × $9 intrinsic value)		74,250

Compound Plans

If plans allow employees the choice of taking cash or shares at the exercise date, then the plan is a compound financial instrument and represents both a financial liability *and* an option on shares. The liability is valued on initial recognition, and a residual value is assigned to equity rights. Established patterns are then used to account for each element. Compound plans will be demonstrated through phantom stock plans.

Phantom Stock Plan with Employee Payment Option As an example, assume that an employee is awarded units in a phantom stock plan, where, after two years of employment, the employee is entitled to receive *either* 22,000 common shares *or* the right to a cash payment equal to the then-market value of 18,000 shares. The choice is up to the employee.

This employee is expected to remain with the company for this period so retention is not an issue. The shares are worth $8 each when the plan is established, at the beginning of year 1, and share price increases to $9 and then $12 at the end of years 1 and 2.

The equity portion is valued when the plan is established. At the beginning of year 1, *valuation models* indicate that the fair value of the share alternative is $7 per share, or $154,000 ($ 7 × 22,000) in total. Initially, the cash alternative appears to be worth $144,000 ($8 × 18,000). Therefore, the option is valued at the residual, or $10,000 ($154,000 − $144,000.

That is:

Equity alternative fair value, plan initiation, valuation model	$154,000
Cash alternative fair value, plan initiation	144,000
Equity portion	$ 10,000

The equity portion is accrued over the two-year vesting period, or $5,000 per year. *The fair value of the option is recognized over the vesting period but is not subject to new estimates of fair value.*

The liability is revalued each period, and is also recorded over the two-year vesting period. A valuation model is consulted, as for a cash-based SARs plan. In this example, the intrinsic value of the shares is used as the best estimate of the fair value of the liability. Note that the first time recognition is required is at *the end of the first year*, at which time the entry is based on a calculation that relies on the end-of-year $9 share value, or a total of $162,000 ($9 × 18,000). *The initial value of $144,000 is not used for this period.*

If there were forfeitures expected, these would be *re-estimated each year for both elements.*

Year 1 entry:		
Compensation expense	86,000	
Contributed capital: common share options		
outstanding [($10,000) × (1 year ÷ 2 years)]		5,000
Long-term compensation liability		
[($162,000) × (1 year ÷ 2 years)]		81,000

The liability is then *trued up* to the cumulative value with a calculation at the end of year 2, $216,000 ($12 × 18,000). If there were forfeitures expected, these would be re-established each year for both elements.

Year 2 entry:		
Compensation expense	140,000	
Contributed capital: common share options		
outstanding [($10,000) × (1 year ÷ 2 years)]		5,000
Long-term compensation liability		
[($216,000) × (2 year ÷ 2 years), less $81,000]		135,000

This second entry updates the accounts at the end of year 2. The employee may then elect to receive shares:

Year 2 entry; employee receives shares:		
Contributed capital: common share options outstanding	10,000	
Long-term compensation liability	216,000	
Common shares		226,000

Alternatively, the employee may take cash:

Year 2 entry; employee receives cash and the option expires:		
Contributed capital: common share options outstanding	10,000	
Contributed capital: share options expired		10,000
Long-term compensation liability	216,000	
Cash		216,000

These entries reflect the pattern for equity-settled plans, in that the value of the option is recorded over time, and then is either folded into common shares (issuance) or contributed capital (lapse). It also reflects the pattern for liability-settled plans, in that the liability fair value is remeasured annually, and trued up to annual estimates of fair value.

Additional Complications Compensation plans are complex, and the accounting standards that govern their measurement, recognition, and disclosure are equally complex. There are rules that deal with performance conditions, market conditions, award restrictions and changes after vesting, as well as rules that address indexed plans, combination plans, plan modifications, and so on. This section has looked at the overall patterns rather than the detailed rules for the many possible situations.

CONCEPT REVIEW

1. What do employees receive under a SARs compensation plan?

2. When there is a long-term compensation plan, under what circumstances is a liability recorded? A contributed capital account?

3. If a plan is equity-settled, what will change if the fair value of the compensation contract increases? How would your response change if the plan were cash-settled?

DERIVATIVES

General Nature of Derivatives

Corporations issue certain types of securities that are neither debt nor equity in themselves, but that set terms and conditions for future exchange of financial instruments. There are many types of such derivative instruments, which have value because of shifts in value of the underlying security or index. Stock options are one example. By themselves, stock options represent neither an obligation of the corporation nor a share interest in the corporation; their *value is derived* from the value of the underlying security (shares) that can be acquired by exercising the option.

Accounting standards define a derivative as a financial instrument that has three characteristics:

1. The value of the derivative changes in response to the change in the underlying primary instrument or index;

2. It requires no initial net investment, or a very small investment; and

3. It is settled at a future date.

There are three main types of derivatives:

1. Options;

2. Forward contracts; and

3. Futures contracts.

Options An option is the right to buy or sell something in the future. A **call option** is the right to buy something at a given price in the future, and a **put option** is the right to sell something at a given price in the future. Options may be for commodities or financial instruments. For example, a company may issue a call option to buy 20,000 tonnes of coal at a given price at a given time. Alternatively, the company may be party to a put option to sell 1,000 shares of another company, now held as an investment, at a given price at a given time, if the company wishes.

Forward Contracts A **forward contract** is an obligation to buy or sell something in the future. Both the price and the time period are specified, and there is no way to avoid the transaction. For example, if a company agrees to sell 12,000 shares (now held as an investment) at $60 per share in 60 days, with no ability to avoid the transaction, this is a forward contract. If the transaction would take place only if the company wanted, then it would be an option. *done privately thru' a bank*

Futures Contracts A **futures contract** is also an obligation to buy or sell something in the future. Both the price and the time period are specified, and there is no way to avoid the transaction. Futures contracts differ from forward contracts, though, in that they are traded on stock markets, brokers act as collection and delivery agents, and the company usually has to put some money upfront, which is collateral, in the form of a **margin**. For example, if a company agrees to buy US$1,000 for Cdn$1,200 in 60 days through a financial institution that requires an initial payment of $120, this would be a futures contract and $120 is the margin. *done in mkt & complicated.*

Embedded Derivatives Some financial instruments are compound financial instruments and include both a **host contract** and an **embedded derivative** contract. The embedded derivative is not related to the economic risks and characteristics of the host contract and changes the cash flows of the contract over the life of the contract in some fashion, consistent with the presence of the derivative. If the derivative could be detached and transferred separately, it would be a *stand-alone derivative* and accounted for as such. Embedded derivatives cannot be detached from the host contract but also must be *separated on initial recognition* to allow the host contract and the derivative to be accounted for separately.

For example, assume that Brava Limited enters into a lease with an inflation factor, which requires that rent is adjusted for changes in a consumer price index each year. The host contract is the lease, and the embedded derivative is the adjustment to the consumer price index. The lease and the embedded derivative are separately accounted for when the lease is signed. The derivative is valued at fair value and remeasured to fair value on each reporting date.

Accounting Recognition

Accounting standards require that companies:

- Recognize derivatives on the statement of financial position when the company becomes a party to the contract;
- Recognize the derivative instrument at fair value on initial recognition;
- At each reporting date, *remeasure* derivative assets or liabilities at their fair values; and
- Recognize gains and losses from the changed fair value, and gains and losses at settlement, in profit and loss in the period in which they arise, unless the derivative is a hedge.

Although a derivative should be recorded when it is acquired (i.e., the company becomes a party to the contract), it often has no cost and a zero fair value at that time. Therefore, no entry is made. Adjustments to fair value are made on reporting dates and when the contract matures. The *fair value* of the derivative changes as underlying values change, and is based on a valuation model that incorporates factors such as duration, volatility, and risk. This change in fair value is recognized in earnings.

Example Assume that Bent Limited agrees to a futures contract to buy 4,000 shares of Resto Limited for $30 per share in 60 days. The current fair value of the shares is $30, so the initial fair value of this derivative is zero. This contract is not a hedge; accounting for hedges is explained below. The broker requires a 10% payment, or $12,000, on margin, which has to be recorded:

Derivative investment	12,000	
Cash		12,000

The shares of Resto are trading at $34 after 30 days, and the company has a gain because it can buy shares that are worth $136,000 for $120,000. The gain on the contract is recorded to reflect fair value and an additional $1,600 (136,000 × 10% = $13,600 − $12,000) is required on margin.

Derivative investment (($34 − $30) × 4,000)	16,000	
Gain on derivative instrument		16,000
Derivative investment	1,600	
Cash		1,600

When the shares are purchased, they have a fair value of $31 per share. A loss of $3 ($34 − $31) per share on the derivative contract is recorded, and then the contract is closed out.

Loss on derivative instrument	12,000	
Derivative investment (($31 − $34) × 4,000)		12,000
Investment—Resto Ltd. shares ($31 × 4,000 shares)	124,000	
Cash [($30 × 4,000 shares) − $13,600]		106,400
Derivative investment (balance)		17,600

Hedges

If an investor speculates in derivatives, the risk is *high* because derivatives essentially bet on future price changes. However, the real purpose of derivatives in the corporate environment is usually to reduce risk. Derivatives often are used as **hedges**—as a way to offset a risk to which the company would otherwise be exposed. Hedged risks can include changes in exchange rates, interest rates, securities, and commodities (e.g., fuel, grain, nickel, gold). For an item to be a hedge, the company must first *have risk* in an area, and then put a hedge in place to *counter the risk*. That is, a loss on a primary instrument will offset a gain on a hedge instrument and vice versa. The related gains and losses must be recognized in earnings concurrently.

Hedge accounting is complex, and is a subject dealt with in advanced accounting courses. This discussion will focus on a brief look at the outcome in financial statements.

Hedge Example Suppose that Clix Incorporated sells goods to a U.S. customer. The selling price is stated in U.S. dollars. Assume that the amount of the sale is US$100,000, and that the U.S. dollar is worth Cdn$1.10 at the date of sale. Clix now has an account receivable (a primary financial asset) for US$100,000. On Clix's books, the receivable will be translated into Canadian dollars at the current exchange rate and reported at Cdn$110,000. Now, suppose that while Clix is waiting for the customer to pay, the exchange rate changes to US$1.00 = Cdn$1.02. The value of the receivable drops to Cdn$102,000; Clix has suffered a loss of $8,000 due to the exchange rate change.

Clix can protect itself by creating an offsetting financial liability for US$100,000. Any loss on the receivable will be exactly offset by a gain on the liability. It is possible that, in the normal course of business, the company will incur U.S. dollar–denominated liabilities. For example, assume that the company buys inventory from a U.S. supplier and agrees to pay in U.S. dollars. Even if the offset is not exactly $100,000, gains and losses will tend to cancel out.

That is:

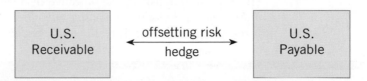

More commonly, however, a company will go to a financial institution and arrange a *forward contract.* The company will receive US$100,000 from the customer, and will turn it over to the bank. The bank agrees upfront to the value (the price the bank will pay) for the U.S. dollars. For example, assume the forward price is $1.04. Clix is willing to "firm up" its future cash flow at $104,000. At maturity, Clix receives $104,000 from the bank, and turns over US$100,000.

A forward contract is a common type of hedge. The bank will charge a small fee for this service, but the fee is like an insurance policy—a small expense will eliminate the risk of a large loss. Although Clix would realize a gain if the value of the U.S. dollar went the other way, most companies prefer to deal with known cash flows. Hedging is widely practised by companies with exchange risk.

Criteria for Hedge Accounting The substance of a hedge is that the company is protected from gains or losses on the risk being hedged. Since there are so many ways to hedge, the designation of a hedge is largely left to management. *Hedge accounting* is voluntary, and happens only after an element is designated as a hedge. Hedges may be identified as *cash flow hedges* or *fair value hedges,* and accounting treatment is dictated by the classification. A financial statement element such as a derivative is a hedge when a company has:

1. An established strategy for risk management that involves hedging; and

2. Formal designation and documentation of the specific hedging relationship; and

3. Expectation that the hedge will be highly effective, and the hedge is assessed each period. This includes the requirement that the fair value of the hedge can be reliably measured.

Accounting Implications of Hedge Accounting Once the element has been designated as a hedge, accounting standards require that the gain or loss on a hedge be recorded in earnings *at the same time* that the gain or loss on the item being hedged is recognized. This simultaneous recognition of gains and losses allows for *offset*, and therefore the substance of the hedge is reflected in the financial statements.

Accounting mismatch Sometimes it will happen that the primary financial statement element is hedged by an item that does not generate accounting gains or losses. The *offset accounting treatment* must then be *created.* For example, assume that Clix had the US$100,000 receivable, and also had a purchase order outstanding to buy inventory in U.S. dollars. Clix designates the purchase order as a hedge of the receivable, since Clix plans to use the US$100,000 receivable to pay for the inventory, and the timing of collection and payment coincide.

If there is an $8,000 loss on the account receivable, there will be *no offsetting gain on the purchase order payable because it is not recorded until the inventory is delivered.* The hedge is effective, but the accounting records do not reflect it. In this case, the $8,000 loss on the receivable is not recorded in earnings. Instead, it is recorded in *other comprehensive income* and flows to an equity account, *reserve for hedging.* This remains as an element in shareholders' equity until the transaction takes place.

In other circumstances, the hedge item may be on the books, but valued at amortized cost and thus no gains and losses would be recorded to offset those of the primary financial instrument. To avoid this, the company may reclassify the hedge as an element that will be carried at fair value, so that it will be measured at fair value, and generate recognized gains and losses for the purpose of offset.

However accomplished, the objective of hedge accounting is to *arrange valuation and recording so that the gains on one side will offset losses on the other side of the hedge relationship*, reflecting the economic reality of the hedge relationship.

CONCEPT REVIEW

1. Explain the difference between a derivative financial instrument and a primary financial instrument.

2. What is an embedded derivative?

3. How should an existing derivative financial liability be measured at each reporting date?

STATEMENT OF CASH FLOW

The cash flows relating to complex financial instruments must be reported in the statement of cash flow (SCF) in a manner that is consistent with their substance. The net proceeds from the issuance of any financial instrument will be reported as a financing activity, with the nature of the instrument disclosed in the notes to the financial statements. If an instrument is a compound that consists of both equity and liability components, then the individual components are reported together on the SCF—one line, not two, because one financial instrument was issued. Since conversions do not involve cash flow, they are not reported on the SCF. Cash flows for interest and dividends may be presented in operating or financing sections, as determined by company policy.

As an example, consider the following liability and equity accounts of YTR Limited:

	20X5	20X4
Term preferred shares	—	$ 3,000,000
Convertible bonds payable	$ 8,000,000	—
Discount on bonds payable	245,000	—
Common stock conversion rights	457,000	—
Stock rights outstanding	—	55,000
Common shares	13,800,000	13,645,000

Convertible bonds were issued in 20X5. Discount amortization in 20X5 was $15,000. The term preferred shares were redeemed during the year, at par. Stock rights were issued to a law firm for legal services performed in 20X4 and were exercised in 20X5. There were no other common share transactions. Interest expense is $525,000, and the company classifies interest paid in the operating activities section of the SCF.

As a result of these transactions, the SCF would report:

1. In financing, as a source of funds, proceeds on issuance of convertible bonds, $8,197,000. The bonds were originally allocated $7,740,000 of the original proceeds. (That is,

$8,000,000 less $260,000; the original discount before this year's amortization.) In addition, proceeds of $457,000 were allocated to the equity account, $7,740,000 + $457,000 = $8,197,000.

2. In financing, as a use of funds, redemption of preferred shares, $3,000,000.

3. In financing, as a source of funds, sale of common shares, $100,000. The common shares account has actually increased by $155,000 (or, $13,800,000 − $13,645,000). However, this represents not only the cash received on the sale of shares, but also the rights account, $55,000, that was transferred to common shares. Only the cash portion is shown on the SCF.

4. In operations, add-back of the non-cash interest expense caused by discount amortization, $15,000. Interest expense of $525,000 would be added back and replaced with an outflow of $510,000 ($525,000 − $15,000) for interest paid.

The key to preparing a SCF is to reconstruct the changes to the various accounts, looking for cash flow. This cash flow is reportable. In operating activities, one must examine sources of revenue and expense that *do not reflect the underlying cash flow.* Discount and premium amortization, and gains and losses from retirements must be adjusted.

DISCLOSURE

The financial instruments described in this chapter are subject to common disclosure requirements. That is, extensive information must be disclosed in the following general categories:

1. The accounting policy used for reporting each type of financial liability.

2. The fair value for each class of financial liability, presented in such a way that enables the user to compare the fair value with the reported carrying value. The methods and assumptions used to measure fair values must be disclosed.

3. Information to assess the significance of financial instruments for the entity's financial position and performance.

4. The nature and extent of risks arising from financial instruments. This includes objectives, policies, and processes for managing risk, and changes in risk profile or policies during the period. Risks are categorized as *credit risk, liquidity risk, and market risk,* with such disclosures made through the eyes of management to provide an insider perspective. Quantitative disclosures and sensitivity analysis is required.

With respect to risk, note the following interpretations:

• *Credit risk:* the risk that one party will fail to discharge the obligation.

• *Liquidity risk:* the risk that a company will encounter difficulty in meeting obligations associated with financial liabilities.

• *Market risk:* the risk that fair values or cash flows attached to a financial instrument will fluctuate because of changes in market prices. This may be caused by fluctuations in currency prices, interest rates, or other factors.

Critical to these general categories is the requirement that *financial instruments be completely described.* This would include the carrying amount, principal amount, amounts issued or retired, options issued and retired, maturity dates, share prices, early settlement options, futures contracts, forward contracts, scheduled future cash commitments, stated interest rate, effective interest rate, repricing dates, collateral, currency, payment dates, interest rates, security, conditions, changes in valuation allowances, and any breach of conditions or covenants.

To say that these disclosures are extensive is an understatement. The more complex the situation, the more extensive the disclosure. The emphasis is on terms and conditions, and also on analyzing the risk associated with recognized and unrecognized financial instruments.

Reporting Example A financial instruments risk assessment of the Sample Company Limited is shown in Exhibit 14-3. Many pages of notes would be needed to capture all the required disclosure; this is a small taste. Notice that:

1. The company identifies and evaluates various sources of financial risk, and its policy/process to manage this risk. In particular, the company identifies that it is vulnerable to exchange rate fluctuations, and specifies that contracts and options are used to mitigate this risk. Significant additional disclosure would have to be provided to document outstanding exchange risk and hedge positions at year-end.

2. Liquidity risk is defined, risk management processes are described, and available financial resources are quantified.

EXHIBIT 14-3

SAMPLE COMPANY LIMITED

Selected Financial Instrument Risk Assessment Statement Disclosures

3. Financial Risk Management

In view of the global and varied nature of its activities, the Company is exposed to financial market risk (including foreign currency risk, fair value and cash flow interest rate risk, and price risk), credit risk, and liquidity risk.

The Company's risk management is essentially focused on identifying and analyzing exchange rate risk, with the aim of minimizing its impact on Company earnings before taxes and net income. In order to hedge exchange rate risk, the Company uses derivative financial instruments such as forward currency contracts or currency options.

Risk management is conducted by the central treasury department (Company Treasury), which follows the directives issued by the Company's management bodies. Risks are assessed in collaboration with the operating units and the hedging methods are decided and implemented under the regular supervision of the Company's Top Management.

. . . .

[A description of specific risks:]

1. Market Risk

The Company is exposed to market risk, primarily related to foreign exchange, interest rates, and the market value investments of liquid funds. The Company actively monitors these exposures. To manage the volatility relating to these exposures, the Company uses a variety of derivative financial instruments, such as foreign exchange forward contracts or options. The Company's objective is to reduce, where it deems appropriate to do so, fluctuations in earnings and cash flows associated with changes in interest rates, foreign currency rates, and market rates of investments of liquid funds. It is the Company's policy and practice to use derivative financial instruments to manage exposures and to enhance the yield on the investment of liquid funds.

. . . .

3. Liquidity Risk

Liquidity risk is defined as the risk that the Company could not be able to meet its financial obligations on time. The close monitoring of liquidity at Company level and of the allocation of resources allow the Company's treasury department to maintain adequate levels of liquidity at all times. In order to meet any exceptional liquidity requirements, the Company maintains lines of credit with a number of financial institutions.

continued on next page

> ## EXHIBIT 14-3 (cont'd)

As at the balance sheet date, the available liquidity can be summarized as follows:

(CHF million)	31 Dec. 2008	31 Dec. 2007
Cash and cash equivalents	680	1,286
Marketable securities	530	653
Liquidity reserves	1,210	1,939
Committed credit facilities	613	589
Utilized credit facilities	−137	−114
Total liquidity reserves and non-utilized credit facilities	1,686	2,414

. . . .

ACCOUNTING STANDARDS FOR PRIVATE ENTERPRISES

One might expect that a private company would have significantly different (simpler) capital structure and that complex financial instruments, including options and hedges, would be rare. However, uniquely tailored debt and equity instruments flourish in private companies, and foreign exchange contracts are common risk management tools. The accounting standards governing these elements are reasonably similar under IFRS and ASPE, but there are several important differences:

1. Private companies sometimes issue preferred shares, redeemable in cash at the shareholder's option as part of tax-planning structures (so-called *high-low shares*). However, the clear intent is to retain an equity investment and not to redeem for cash. Under ASPE, these shares will be classified as equity, and can be recorded at par, stated, or assigned value. Conversely, *shareholder loans*, which many shareholders and lenders alike consider to be part of equity in a private company, are classified in the liability section regardless of intent.

2. Convertible debt must still be treated as a compound financial instrument, but the standard allows the company to record the equity element (the conversion option), at zero, which effectively makes the convertible debt entirely a liability.

3. The stock-based compensation structure is largely the same, in that expense and equity elements are recognized for an equity-settled plan over the vesting period. Volatility measures used as an input for option pricing models are estimated based on *sector values*, since they are not observable through company share price changes. This valuation may be difficult to substantiate. In addition, ASPE models account for forfeiture when it occurs; no *estimates are made of forfeiture when making accruals*.

4. Standards established for share-based payments have a narrower scope, which may affect reporting of any such distributions to suppliers or others. In addition, measurement is often based on the fair value of the consideration given up, or the fair value of what is received, *whichever is the more reliable measure*. IFRS measurements rest on the fair value of goods and services received, except in rare circumstances.

5. Hedge accounting follows a different approach, as does accounting for embedded derivatives. For example, since *other comprehensive income* does not exist under ASPE, standards cannot allow for recognition of cash flow hedge amounts in OCI with the cumulative amount set in an equity reserve. Hedge accounting is available, bypassing net income, only when the critical terms of the hedge match the hedged instrument.

6. Disclosures in all areas are less onerous under ASPE.

RELEVANT STANDARDS

IASB:

- *IAS* 32, Financial Instruments: Presentation
- *IAS* 39, Financial Instruments: Recognition and Measurement
- *IFRS* 2, Share-Based Payments
- *IFRS* 7, Financial Instruments: Disclosure

CICA Handbook Part II:

- Section 3856, Financial Instruments
- Section 3865, Hedges
- Section 3870, Stock-Based Compensation and Other Stock-Based Payments

SUMMARY OF KEY POINTS

1. Financial instruments must be classified as debt or equity in accordance with their substance, not necessarily their legal form. If there are two component parts to a financial instrument, the two components are separately recognized on issuance.

2. Annual payments associated with a financial instrument that is classified as debt are classified as an expense; annual payments associated with a financial instrument classified as an equity instrument are not an expense and are classified on the statement of changes in equity.

3. Classification factors include whether the company can be forced to pay cash for principal and/or interest, whether payments can be deferred indefinitely, whether payment is required only if a highly unlikely event outside management control occurs, and whether payments that can be made in shares have a fixed or variable value.

4. Bonds that are convertible into a fixed number of common shares at the *investor's* option embody two financial instruments: a liability and an option contract on common shares, each of which are recognized separately on issuance.

5. Bonds that are mandatorily redeemable in a fixed number of shares will be classified as a compound instrument: a liability as to their annual cash interest component, and the residual, which is assigned to equity.

6. Stock options of various kinds are recognized on issuance and recorded as an element of shareholders' equity. On issuance of the underlying shares, the options account is folded into the share account. If the options lapse, the options account becomes contributed capital.

7. Share-based payments to suppliers are recognized when goods and services are received, and measured at the fair value of those goods or services.

8. Share-based payments with employees that are equity-settled result in recognition of an expense and an equity element. The options are valued using an option pricing model. Compensation is recognized over the vesting period, with forfeiture estimated; forfeitures are *trued up* by maturity but fair value is not re-estimated.

9. Share-based payments with employees that are cash-settled result in recognition of an expense and a liability, accrued over the vesting period. Fair value and forfeiture are estimated over this period, and both estimates are *trued up by* maturity.

10. Share-based payments with employees where the employee has the choice between cash and equity settlement are compound instruments, with both an equity and liability element recognized.

11. Derivatives are contracts that specify an exchange of financial instruments at a specified price. Derivatives include options, forward contracts, and futures contracts. They can be used to hedge various types of risk, including exchange risk.

12. Derivative contracts are recorded at fair value. Gains and losses from changes in fair value are reported in earnings.

13. If a financial instrument is designated as a hedge, then gains and losses on the hedge will be recognized in earnings at the same time as gains and losses on the risk being hedged, so they offset. Under certain conditions, gains and losses on hedges are recorded in other comprehensive income and accumulated in equity reserve accounts.

14. The cash flows relating to financial instruments should be reported on the SCF in a manner that is consistent with the substance of the payments, both for payments *on* capital (i.e., interest and dividends) and repayments *of* capital (i.e., principal and share buybacks).

15. A company must disclose extensive information with respect to accounting policies used for financial instruments, fair values, significance of financial instruments, and nature and extent of risks. Financial instruments must be fully described in the disclosure notes.

KEY TERMS

book value method, 818
call option, 839
capital charge, 823
cash-settled plan, 828
compound financial instrument, 812
convertible debt, 812
derivative instruments, 824
embedded derivative, 839
equity-settled plans, 828
exercise date, 824
fair value, 824
fair value hierarchy, 819
forced conversion, 817
forfeiture, 830
forward contract, 839
futures contract, 839
hedges, 840
host contract, 839
hybrid financial instrument, 812
intrinsic value, 824
in-the-money, 824

income bond, 812
incremental method of valuation, 820
margin, 839
perpetual debt, 816
phantom stock plan, 829
poison pill, 827
proportional method, 826
put option, 839
redeemable shares, 812
restricted share units, 829
retractable shares, 814
share-based payment, 828
stock appreciation rights, 829
stock options, 824
stock option plan, 829
stock rights, 824
stock warrants, 826
term preferred shares, 814
trued up, 830
under water, 824
vest, 830

REVIEW PROBLEM

Each of the following cases is independent.

Case A

On 1 January 20X1, Amershi Limited issues $1,000,000 face amount of 8%, five-year, convertible debentures. Interest is payable semi-annually on 30 June and 31 December. The debentures are convertible at the investor's option at the rate of 20 common shares for each $1,000 bond. The market rate of interest for non-convertible bonds of similar risk and maturity is 6%. The net proceeds received by Amershi amounted to $1,250,000.

Required:

1. Record the issuance of the bonds on 1 January 20X1.

2. Prepare the journal entries for interest expense on 30 June 20X1 and 31 December 20X1. Amershi uses effective interest amortization for bond premium and discount.

3. Indicate how all amounts relating to the bonds will be shown on Amershi's statement of financial position and statement of comprehensive income for the year ending 31 December 20X1.

4. Assume that the holders of $300,000 face value bonds exercise their conversion privilege on 1 January 20X4, when the market value of the common shares is $65. Prepare the journal entry to record the conversion.

Case B

On 1 January 20X5, Bateau Incorporated issued $10,000,000 face amount of 4%, 10-year, subordinated convertible debentures for $10,500,000 in a private placement. The debentures pay interest annually, in cash, on 31 December. At maturity, the principal must be paid through the issuance of 50 common shares for each $1,000 of the bonds' face value. A market rate of interest for financial instruments with similar risk, security, and term is 8%.

Required:

1. Record the issuance of the bonds on 1 January 20X5.

2. Record the interest expense and payment on the first interest date of 31 December 20X5.

REVIEW PROBLEM—SOLUTION

Case A

1. The first step is to calculate the present value of the cash flows at the market rate of 6%, using semi-annual interest periods:

Principal [$1,000,000 × (P/A, 3%,10)]	$ 744,090
Interest [$40,000 × (P/F, 3%,10)]	341,208
	$1,085,298

$1,000,000 \times .04$

Journal entry to record issuance

Cash	1,250,000	
Bonds payable		1,000,000
Premium on bonds payable (1085298 − 1000000)		85,298
Common share conversion rights (1250,000 − 1085,298)		164,702

(164,702)

2. Entries for interest expense during 20X1:

30 June 20X1

Interest expense ($1,085,298 × 3%)	32,559	
Premium on bonds payable	7,441	
Cash		40,000

Liability balance: $1,085,298 − $7,441 = $1,077,857

31 December 20X1

Interest expense ($1,077,857 × 3%)	32,336	
Premium on bonds payable	7,664	
Cash		40,000

3. Bond-related items on 20X1 financial statements:

Statement of comprehensive income

Interest expense	$	64,895

Statement of financial position
Long-term debt

Bonds payable	$1,000,000
Premium on bonds payable	70,193
	$1,070,193

Shareholders' equity

Common share conversion rights	$	164,702

4. Conversion of $300,000 face value bonds into 6,000 common shares on 1 January 20X4:

The present value of the converted bond on 1 January 20X4:

Principal [$300,000 × (P/A, 3%,4)]	$266,547
Interest [$12,000 × (P/F, 3%,4)]	44,605
	$311,152

Bonds payable	300,000 (given)	
Premium on bonds payable	11,152	
Common share conversion rights ($164,702 × 3/10)	49,411	
Common shares		360,563

Case B

1. Interest:

These debentures pay interest annually, in cash; the present value of this cash flow is recorded by Bateau as a liability, using the market rate of interest:

$$\$400,000 \times (P/A, 8\%, 10) = \$2,684,032$$

Principal:

The bond must be settled though the issuance of common shares, so the remainder of the issuance price is equity.

Cash	10,500,000	
Interest liability—subordinated debentures		2,684,032
Share equity—subordinated debentures		7,815,968

2. *Entry to record interest expense on 31 December 20X5*

Interest expense ($2,684,032 × 8%)	214,723	
Interest liability on subordinated debentures		214,723

Entry to record interest payment on 31 December 20X5

Interest liability on subordinated debentures	400,000	
Cash ($10,000,000 × 4%)		400,000

QUESTIONS

Q14-1 Historically, what factors have dictated classification of a financial instrument as debt or equity? How is the classification made when based on the financial instruments rules?

Q14-2 What is a compound financial instrument? Give an example.

Q14-3 What is the distinguishing feature of debt?

Q14-4 Assume a company issues a financial instrument for $50,000 in 20X2 and retires it through an open market purchase for $56,000 in 20X5. In each of the intervening years, an annual payment of $2,500 was paid to the investor. How will the financial instrument affect earnings in each of the years if it is classified as debt? As equity?

Q14-5 Explain appropriate financial statement classification of retractable preferred shares, which have a required maturity date or are to be repaid at the option of the investor.

Q14-6 How is convertible debt classified if it is mandatorily convertible into a fixed number of shares? If it is convertible at the investor's option into a fixed number of shares?

Q14-7 Explain how to classify convertible debt if the conversion option specifies that the number of shares to be issued depends on the fair value of shares at the conversion date.

Q14-8 What happens to the common share conversion rights account, created when convertible debt is issued, when the bond is actually converted? What if the bond is repaid in cash instead?

Q14-9 If a $400,000, 8% mandatorily convertible bond is issued at par and $76,400 of the issuance price is attributable to the interest obligation, how much interest expense will be recorded in the first year? The effective yield is 8%. How much is paid to the investor each year?

Q14-10 What is the distinction between stock options and stock warrants?

Q14-11 How is a share-based payment to a supplier measured in the financial statements?

Q14-12 If share rights are recognized on issuance, what happens to the share rights account if the share rights are exercised? Allowed to lapse? Compare this to the treatment of the common share conversion option account associated with convertible bonds.

Q14-13 When would a share-based compensation contract, payable after three years, result in an equity account being recognized in the first year? A liability? Both equity and a liability?

Q14-14 Assume that a cash-settled share-based payment scheme is established for an employee group. It will vest over five years, and be paid at the end of the fifth year. The total fair value of the plan is estimated to be $400,000 at the end of year 1, $175,000 at the end of year 2, and $400,000 at the end of year 3. No forfeiture is expected. How much compensation expense is recognized in the third year?

Q14-15 Repeat question 14 assuming that retention rates are estimated to be 80% at the end of year 1, 75% at the end of year 2, and 60% at the end of year 3. How much compensation expense recognized in the third year?

Q14-16 Share-based payments to employees are trued up by the end of the vesting period. If the plan is cash-settled, for what factors is it trued up? If it is equity-settled?

Q14-17 Explain the terms of a SARs program for employees.

Q14-18 Define a derivative, and a hedge.

Q14-19 Assume that a Canadian company sells a product to a U.S. customer, and that the sale is denominated in U.S. dollars. What kind of a derivative instrument will eliminate the exchange risk? How will the transaction balance and the derivative instrument be reflected in the financial statements?

Q14-20 What areas of disclosure are required for financial instruments?

CASE 14-1

TECHNO WIZARD LTD.

Omni Services Ltd., a Canadian public company, is a conglomerate involved in publication of newspapers, media services, and information technology consulting. It recently entered into an agreement to purchase Techno Wizard Limited (TWL), which operates a printing business in Manitoba. Omni assumed control on 1 November 20X7.

It is now 14 November 20X7 and Omni has just received the 31 October 20X7 financial statements of TWL. Omni is now concerned that the price to be paid is excessive, and is looking for advice leading up to its pre-closing negotiations, scheduled for next week. Accordingly, you have been approached, as an outside accounting advisor, for your advice and expert opinion. The purchase agreement is described in Exhibit 1 and financial statement extracts are in Exhibit 2.

Required

Prepare a report that identifies potential issues. Include quantification of issues where possible.

EXHIBIT 1

PURCHASE AND SALE AGREEMENT EXTRACTS

Omni Services Ltd. (Purchaser) and Techno Wizard Ltd. (Vendor)

7.0 Purchase Price

7.1 The purchase price shall be $7.0 million Canadian dollars ($15 per share) subject to adjustment, if any, in 7.3, to be established two weeks after the reporting date in 7.4.

7.2 The purchase price shall be payable $2 million in cash plus $2 million in Omni shares on 1 November 20X7, with the balance paid in cash on 15 December 20X7. Issued shares are valued using quoted prices for Omni shares on the TSX on 1 November 20X7.

7.3 The purchase price will be increased dollar-for-dollar for any excess over $7 million obtained as the product of two times the assets less liabilities of Techno Wizard on the SFP dated 31 October 20X7. Assets and liabilities are to be calculated as defined under IFRS standards.

7.4 Techno Wizard will provide 31 October 20X7 financial statements before the reporting date of 21 November 20X7.

EXHIBIT 2

EXTRACTS FROM TECHNO WIZARD LTD. FINANCIAL STATEMENTS

31 October 20X7

Statement of financial position (in thousands)

Assets

Current Assets

Cash	$ 1,420
Receivables	2,690
Inventory	3,700
Prepaid expenses	290
	8,100

Non-current Assets

Capital assets, net	3,100
	$11,200

Liabilities

Current Liabilities

Bank indebtedness	$ 860
Accounts payable	2,100
Deferred revenue	1,740
	4,700

Non-current liabilities

Bonds payable	2,100
Future income tax	162
Other	230
	$ 7,192

Equity

Preferred shares	500
Print shop equity—bond	300
Contributed capital—share plan	320
Common shares	1,080
Retained earnings	1,808
	$ 4,008
	$11,200

Disclosure Notes Extracts

1. Foreign exchange losses are part of "prepaid expenses" in the amount of $160. All gains are included in earnings.

2. Bonds payable consists of $2.4 million face value of 10-year debentures issued on 1 December 20X6. The debentures were issued at par, and require annual interest of 3.5% payable each 31 May.

    Debentures of similar term and risk were issued by another company at par carrying an interest rate of 8% within a month of this transaction.

    The debenture holders are entitled to the use of 1,000 hours of print shop capacity at any time after 1 June 20X7. Print shop usage is to be negotiated with a 30-day lead time and TWL is responsible for all overhead and direct labour. Paper product used in printing is the responsibility of the debenture holder. No print shop capacity has been used to date under the agreement.

3. Included in accounts receivable is a $710 two-year delayed-payment arrangement set on 1 January 20X7. The customer will pay $710 on 31 December 20X8, plus 3% interest each 31 December. Interest rates for comparable term are in the range of 7%. No interest has been accrued to date.

4. Preferred shares are held by the founding family of TWL and carry a cumulative dividend of 4% annually. Omni did not acquire these shares, but has the right to redeem them for cash at book value.

5. Deferred revenue includes various advance payments made by customers under long-term contracts. Some contracts involve up-front fees that are recognized in revenue when received. Other contracts allow a final year of free service, or stipulate that a renewal contract will include a free year of average usage covered under the expiring contract. The average length of a contract is three years.

6. TWL has a SARs plan that allows eight managers a cash payment based on the value of 10,000 shares each. The plan was set up in 20X6, and payment will be made in 20X8 for any increase in share value above $10 per share to any manager still employed with TWL at that time. Share value was to be determined using a formula, since TWL is not a public company. The valuation model used placed a value at $6 per unit as the expected payout when the plan was established in 20X6. To date, $320,000 of cost has been recognized. Two of the eight managers have left the firm but all others are expected to continue through 20X8.

7. TWL has entered into a foreign currency exchange contract with respect to $200,000 of U.S.–dollar long-term debt at 31 October 20X7. The company has recorded an asset and a gain of $76 in relation to this arrangement, based on its expectations regarding currency movements over the period to maturity.

CASE 14-2

ON-THE-CREST LTD.

On-the-Crest Ltd. (OCL) is a company operating in the used-vehicle industry. OCL derives its revenue from selling, licensing, and servicing software products for car dealers, from the sale of products to car dealers, and from the sale of used vehicles. Both through internal growth and acquisitions, OCL revenue has grown at the rate of 25% per year for each of the last five years. An initial public offering is planned in the next fiscal year.

Ida Wong, the audit partner, is seeking a summary memo from the senior in charge of the audit (see Exhibit 1). Ida has a meeting scheduled with Bill Valarian, CFO of OCL, tomorrow and needs to be aware of major reporting issues.

Required:
Review the notes and prepare a memo outlining accounting and reporting issues and alternatives. This memo will be the basis for the meeting with Bill Valarian.

EXHIBIT 1

ON-THE-CREST LTD.

Notes

From: Audit Senior
To: File
Re: Potential accounting issues—On-the-Crest Ltd. (OCL)

The following issues have come to light during the audit and may impact on the financial statements of OCL:

continued on next page

EXHIBIT 1 *(cont'd)*

Convertible Debt

At the beginning of the current year, OCL issued $7 million of 7.25% debt with interest payable semi-annually on 30 June and 31 December. Bond issue costs were $300,000, which are being amortized over 10 years. The maturity date is 10 years from issuance unless either of the following options is exercised:

a. On the date of the IPO, the lender can submit the bond for cash repayment. OCL may, at that time, choose to repay the liability in cash or in OCL shares. The number of OCL shares to be issued is based on the chosen IPO price.

b. After the debt has been outstanding for 36 months, there is a 2-week period during which the lender can submit the bond for repayment in cash.

The $7 million proceeds on issuance of debt were recorded in a long-term liability account.

Options Granted to a Supplier

OCL issued options to Software Supply Limited for 40,000 OCL shares. The options were issued in order to ensure that SSL made OCL a priority customer for the coming period, as SSL's services are critical for modifications to software that OCL provides to car dealers. The options are non-revocable and are exercisable six months after any IPO. If there is no IPO, the options are to be repurchased and retired at a price based on a set formula. The presence of these options has been disclosed in the financial statements.

Fair Value Investment

To utilize idle cash, OCL made a $350,000 investment in the shares of Motors Company (MC), a public company also in the automotive industry. This acquisition took place in the prior fiscal year, and an unrealized loss of $100,000 was recognized in equity reserves at the end of last year because market value had declined to $250,000. Market price is unchanged at the end of the current fiscal year, and OCL is unwilling to sell the investment until market prices rebound. OCL is confident this will occur in the next two to five years.

Exchange Rate Hedge

OCL placed an order with a Japanese supplier during the year when the exchange rate was ¥1 = $0.0095. On the delivery date, the exchange rate was ¥1 = $0.0090. OCL paid for the merchandise 90 days later when the exchange rate was ¥1 = $0.0104. However, OCL had hedged the account payable at a rate of ¥1 = $0.0085 and accordingly paid $161,500 to the exchange broker for the required yen. The inventory was recorded at the cash cost of $161,500.

Convertible Preferred Shares

Late in the fourth quarter of the current fiscal year, OCL issued $1.7 million of convertible preferred shares in a private placement. Under the terms of the share agreement, the $1.7 million investment will automatically be converted into 600,000 common shares of OCL on the commencement of trading of OCL common shares on the TSX. Investors may choose a cash payout instead, and would receive $1.7 million. There are no provisions for alternate arrangements if common shares are not traded on the TSX; the preferred shares would remain as preferred shares if OCL did not go public. The preferred shares have no preference rights to assets on the dissolution of the company, but have a stated cash dividend of $100,000 per year. The dividend is paid quarterly, and on conversion, OCL must pay the dividend up to date in cash including arrears, if any, whether declared or not. All the $1.7 million proceeds are recorded in the equity account, preferred shares. No dividend was due; none was declared or recorded in the current fiscal year.

Pricing Agreement

For the first time, OCL provided certain price and payment incentives to customers in order to spur demand. OCL extended payment terms from the current 30 days to 60 days, and specified that if pre-agreed list prices to *end consumers* are not realized, OCL would provide rebates. For example, assume OCL sold a product to a customer for $100 and expected it to be resold to the final customer for $165. If the final sale were to be priced at $155, OCL has agreed to accept $90 ($100 − ($165 − $155)). OCL has accrued an allowance for all amounts expected to be lost under the guarantee, based on market research.

CASE 14-3

CREATIVE TRADERS LIMITED

Creative Traders Ltd. (CTL) is a Canadian company that conducts business in several countries, using a variety of currencies. The notes to the financial statements pertaining to fair values of financial instruments for the past year, the year ended 31 December 20X1, are shown in Exhibit 1. CTL is quite thorough in explaining its exposure to risk of foreign currency fluctuations, interest rate changes, and changes in the fair value of financial instruments. Some of these risks are managed through derivatives.

Fair values have been included in the disclosure notes but not recorded, up to the current year. This coming year, derivatives will be recognized on the statement of financial position at fair value. Changes in fair value are to be included in earnings.

You are a professional accountant in the financial reporting group at CTL. A report for the audit committee has been requested, as a basis for discussion at an upcoming meeting. Specifically, you've been asked to quantify the impact of recording derivatives. You also must explain why recording fair value is required. Finally, your report should explain any concerns about accurately measuring fair value.

Required:
Prepare a report addressing the issues raised.

Source: Reproduced with the permission of CGA-Canada.

EXHIBIT 1

CREATIVE TRADERS LIMITED
Notes to the Financial Statements 31 December 20X1

Note 8: Financial Instruments (all numbers are in millions)

Foreign Exchange Risk

The Company's global operations require active participation in foreign exchange markets. Currency exposures primarily relate to assets and liabilities denominated in foreign currencies, as well as economic exposure, which is derived from the risk that currency fluctuations could affect the dollar value of future cash flows related to operating activities. The company uses financial instruments, which are not reflected on the SFP, to regulate the cash flow variability of local currency costs or selling prices denominated in currencies other than the Canadian dollar.

continued on next page

EXHIBIT 1 *(cont'd)*

The Company had forward contracts and options to buy, sell, or exchange foreign currencies with a Canadian dollar equivalent of $11,017 at 31 December 20X1 and $6,866 at 31 December 20X0. These contracts and options had various expiration dates, primarily in the first quarter of the next year. The net unrealized loss based on the foreign exchange rates at 31 December 20X1 was $(146). The net unrealized gain based on the foreign exchange rates at 31 December 20X0 was $45.

Interest Rate Risk

Interest rate risk reflects the sensitivity of the Company's financial condition to movements in interest rates. To manage the Company's exposure to interest rate risks, the Company has entered into various interest rate contracts. Neither the notional principal amounts nor the current replacement value on these financial instruments are carried on the consolidated SFP. The notional principal amounts on all types of interest derivative contracts at 31 December 20X1 totalled $1,052 with a weighted-average remaining life of 6.8 years. At 31 December 20X0, the notional principal amounts totalled $1,299 with a weighted-average remaining life of 6.3 years.

Fair Value of Financial Instruments

The fair value of the foreign currency and interest rate derivatives at December 31 were:

	Carrying Value	Gain	Loss	Fair Value
20X1				
Derivatives relating to:				
Foreign currency	NIL	$441	$(587)	$(146)
Interest rates	NIL	32	(7)	25
20X0				
Derivatives relating to:				
Foreign currency	NIL	$173	$(128)	$45
Interest rates	NIL	2	(20)	(18)

The following table presents the carrying amounts and estimated fair values of the Company's other financial instruments as at 31 December 20X1 and 20X0 for which the carrying amounts are different from their fair values:

December 31	Carrying Value 20X1	Fair Value 20X1	Carrying Value 20X0	Fair Value 20X0
Financial Liabilities				
Long-term debt (including current portion)	$3,476	$3,800	$3,476	$2,905
Other				
Convertible preferred securities; reported as debt	$327	$315	$327	$281

ASSIGNMENTS

★★ **A14-1 Impact of Debt versus Equity:** Laffoley Corporation needs to raise $7,000,000 in order to finance a planned capital expansion. The company has investigated two alternatives:

1. Issue $7 million of preferred shares at par. The shares can be redeemed at the company's option at the end of 10 years for a price estimated to be in the region of $7,200,000. Annual (cumulative) dividends would amount to $420,000.
2. Issue bonds, which the company can buy back on the open market at the end of 10 years; analysts estimate that it would cost $7,200,000 to reacquire the $7,000,000 issue. Annual interest would amount to $600,000.

Required:

1. Assume Laffoley's tax rate is 30%. What is the *after-tax* annual cost of the two alternatives?
2. Provide journal entries to record issuance, annual dividends, or interest (for one year only) and retirement of both the shares and debt.
3. Assume that earnings, before interest and tax, in Year 10 was $2,000,000. The tax rate was 30%. Calculate earnings if equity were outstanding in Year 10, and retired at the end of the year. Calculate earnings if debt were outstanding in Year 10 and retired at the end of the year.

★ **A14-2 Classification:** A description of several financial instruments follows:

a. Series D shares, voting, annual $4 non-cumulative dividend, redeemable at the investor's option for $60 per share.
b. Subordinated notes payable, bearing an interest rate of 4%, interest reset every five years with reference to market rates; principal due to be repaid only on the dissolution of the company, if ever, although may be repaid at the company's option on interest repricing dates.
c. Series B preferred shares, annual $6 cumulative dividend, convertible into four common shares for every $100 preferred share at the investor's option, redeemable at $32 per share at the company's option in 20X10.
d. Subordinated 8% debentures payable, interest payable in cash semi-annually, due in 20X8. At maturity, the face value of the debentures must be converted into common shares at a price of $12.50 per share.
e. Subordinated 8% debentures payable, interest payable semi-annually, due in the year 20X8. At maturity, the face value of the debentures may be converted, at the company's option, into common shares at the market price at that time. Interest may also be paid in shares using the market value of shares at the interest payment date.

Required:
Classify each financial instrument as debt, equity, or compound (part debt and part equity). Explain your reasoning.

★★ **A14-3 Classification:** Description of several financial instruments follows:

Case 1   Class D Series 2 shares, carrying a dividend entitlement equal to $5 per share or an amount equal to common share dividends, whichever is higher, redeemable at the investor's option at $62 per share. The company may, at its option, redeem the shares with class A common shares instead of cash, valued at their current market value.

Case 2   Convertible subordinated bonds payable, entitled to annual cash interest at 3.2%. At maturity, the bonds will be settled through the issuance of shares using an exchange price of $14 per share. Interest may also be paid in shares valued at $14 per share at the company's option.

Case 3   Series F second preferred shares, carrying a fixed cumulative dividend of $1.00 per share. The shares must be redeemed by the company at a price of $21 per share, plus dividends in arrears, if any, in 20X4.

Case 4   Convertible subordinated debentures payable, entitled to annual interest at 3.2%. At maturity, the debentures may, at the company's option, be paid out in cash or converted into common shares using an exchange ratio governed by the market value of shares at the conversion date.

Case 5   Series C first preferred shares, carrying a fixed cumulative dividend of $1.25 per share per annum, redeemable at the company's option at $25 per share.

Case 6   Series II preferred shares, carrying a fixed cumulative dividend of $1.75 per share increasing to $6.10 in 20X8. The shares are redeemable at the company's option at a price of $28 per share until 31 December 20X7 and at a price of $62 thereafter.

Case 7   Convertible subordinated 6% notes payable. At maturity, the debentures may, at the company's option, be paid out in cash or converted into common shares at the set exchange price of $30 per share.

Required:

Classify each of the above items as a financial liability, equity instrument, or compound instrument (part debt and part equity).

★★ **A14-4 Classification:** Elkridge Corporation issued the following financial instruments in 20X4:

1. *Convertible debentures* issued at 103. The debentures require interest to be paid semi-annually at a nominal rate of 7% per annum. The debentures are convertible by the holder at any time up to final maturity at a ratio of 10 common shares for each $1,000 principal amount.

2. *Convertible debentures* issued at par. The company is required to pay interest in cash quarterly at a nominal rate of 8% per annum. At maturity, principal must be settled through issuance of common shares valued at $20 per share.

3. *Redeemable preferred shares* issued to Elkridge's founding family. The shares carry an annual cash dividend at the rate of $12 per share. On or after 1 July 20X8, the preferred shareholders may require the company to repurchase the shares at the original issue price plus any unpaid dividends.

Required:

Discuss the appropriate financial statement classification of each of these financial instruments.

★★ **A14-5 Convertible Debt:** Marjorie Manufacturing Limited issued a convertible bond on 2 July 20X5. The $5 million bond pays annual interest of 8% each 30 June. Each $1,000 bond is convertible into 50 shares of common stock, at the investor's option, on 1 July 20X10 until 1 July 20X15, after which time each $1,000 bond may be converted into 45.6 shares until bond maturity on 30 June 20X20. Market analysts have indicated that, had the bond not been convertible, it would have sold for $4,240,000, reflecting a market interest rate of 10% annually. In fact, it was issued for $5,325,000.

[Solution]

Required:

1. Provide the journal entry to record the initial issuance of the bond. Justify the amount allocated to the conversion privilege.

2. Verify the $4,240,000 price of the bond.

3. Calculate the interest expense that would be recorded in the first 12 months of the bond.

4. Would more or less interest expense have been recorded in requirement 3 if the conversion option were not recognized and the proceeds above par value ($325,000) were assigned to a premium account? Explain, do not calculate.

★★ **A14-6 Convertible Debt, Investor's Option:** Nero Solutions Company issued an $800,000, 6%, three-year bond for $806,000. The bond pays interest annually, at each year-end. At maturity, the bond can be repaid in cash or converted to 60,000 common shares at the investor's option. The market interest rate for bonds of similar term and risk, but that are not convertible, is in the range of 7%.

Required:

1. Calculate the portion of the bond to be recorded as a liability.
2. Provide the entry to record issuance of the bond.
3. Provide the entries to record interest expense and the annual cash payment each year over the bond's three-year life.
4. Provide the entry to record the maturity of the bond, assuming that shares were issued.
5. Provide the entry to record the maturity of the bond, assuming that cash is paid.
6. Provide the entry to record early repayment of the bond, assuming that it was repaid in cash in an open market transaction after two complete years. Cash of $810,000 was paid, of which $802,000 related to the liability and $8,000 related to the conversion option.

★★ **A14-7 Convertible Bond, Investor's Option:** Bixon Corp. Ltd. issued convertible bonds payable on 1 January 20X1, when the market interest rate was 10%. The bond indenture stated:

> $7,500,000 of 8% subordinated convertible debentures payable, interest payable semi-annually, convertible at the investor's option in 10 years' time into class A common shares of the company at the rate of 70 shares for each $1,000 bond issued.

The bonds were issued for net proceeds of $7,400,000.

Required:

1. At what price would the bonds be issued if they were not convertible?
2. How is the option valued?
3. Provide the entry to record issuance of the bond on 1 January 20X1.
4. Provide the journal entry to record interest payment and interest expense on 30 June 20X1. Use the effective interest method to record discount amortization.
5. Provide the entry to record bond conversion to common shares at maturity, on 31 December 20X10. Common shares had a fair value of $25 per share at this time.
6. Assume instead that the bond was repaid in cash at maturity. Provide all entries to record the repayment/bond maturity. If repayment is in cash, what fair value for common shares is implied?

★★ **A14-8 Convertible Debt, Comprehensive Scenarios:** NewTech Ltd. has a 31 December fiscal year-end. The company issued convertible bonds on 1 July 20X4. The $5,000,000 bonds pay annual interest of 8% each 30 June and mature on 30 June 20X19. At the investor's option, each $1,000 bond is convertible into 50 common shares on the bond's maturity date.

Bond market analysts indicated that if the bonds had not been convertible, they would likely have sold for $4,597,000. They were in fact issued for $5,350,000.

Required:

1. Provide the journal entry to record the initial issuance of the bond.
2. Provide the entry to accrue interest at 31 December 20X4, using the effective interest method. (Hint: you will need the IRR implicit in the bond price.)

3. Assume that the bond was convertible at the investor's option at the current market price of the common shares on the maturity date. Explain what difference this would make to your response to requirements 1 and 2. Would this bond likely be issued for $5,350,000? Explain.

4. Assume that, instead of being convertible at the investor's option, the bond was mandatorily convertible at the set price of $50 per share. Explain what difference this would make to your response to requirements (1) and (2).

★★★ **A14-9 Convertible Debt, Three Cases:** The following cases are independent:

Case A

On 1 November 20X1, Bertha Builders Limited issued a convertible bond that was convertible in 15 years' time into 78,000 common shares at the investor's option. The bond had a $5,000,000 par value, and 7% interest was paid semi-annually on 1 November and 1 May.

The bond sold for $5,200,000 when the market interest rate was 8%.

Required:
Provide entries on issuance and on 31 December 20X1, the fiscal year-end.

Case B

On 1 January 20X1, Pong Lake Resources Limited issued a bond when market interest rates were 8%.

Bonds payable, $10,000,000, 8%, due in 20 years' time. The bonds pay interest semi-annually each 30 June and 31 December. The bonds were issued at 104. The bonds are mandatorily convertible at the company's discretion into common shares at the rate of six shares for each $100 bond at maturity. The company may, at its discretion, repay the bond for cash in lieu of shares.

Required:
What would appear on the SFP in relation to the bond as of 1 January 20X1? What would be recorded as interest expense for the year ended 31 December 20X1? Provide accounts and amounts.

Case C

On the 31 October 20X1 SFP, Cherub Metalworks Limited reported the following:

Debt		
Convertible bond payable, 10%, due 31 October 20X4,		
convertible into 810,000 shares	$6,000,000	
Less: discount	(557,202)	
		$5,442,798
Equity		
Contributed capital: common share conversion rights		$ 107,000

Interest is paid *annually* on 31 October and the bonds were originally valued to yield 14%.

Required:

1. Provide entries on 31 October 20X2 to record interest and show the conversion of the bonds to common shares on this date. The market price of common shares was $11 per share on 31 October 20X2.

2. Assume instead that the bond is repurchased on the open market on 31 October 20X2 and retired. The price paid was $6,020,000, of which $25,000 related to the option. Journalize the transaction.

★★ **A14-10 Convertible Debt, Investor's Option:** Liu Lakes Ltd. issued a 10-year, $7,000,000 debenture with a nominal interest rate of 6.7%; cash interest is paid semi-annually. The market rate of interest for debt of similar size, risk, and term is 8%. The obligation can be satisfied at maturity either by cash or by issuing common shares valued at $25 per share, at the option of the investor. The debenture was issued for $6,950,000.

Required:

1. Classify this debenture as debt, equity, or a compound instrument. Explain your reasoning.
2. Provide the entry to record issuance of the debenture.
3. What amount(s) pertaining to this debenture will be shown on the SFP at the end of the second year (after adjustments)?
4. Give the entry to record conversion to common shares at maturity. The average market value of common shares at this time was $62.
5. Suppose instead that the $7,000,000 debenture was convertible into common shares using a value of 101% of the average market value of common shares in the five trading days prior to conversion. Explain how that difference would affect your treatment of the debenture. Calculations are not necessary.

★★ **A14-11 Convertible Debt, Mandatory Conversion:** Twixt Corporation issued $5,000,000 of convertible bonds on 1 January for $4,790,000 cash. The bond had the following terms:

- Bonds mature in five years' time.
- Annual interest, 5%, is paid each 31 December.
- Bonds are convertible to 400,000 common shares at maturity, or can be repaid in cash, if Twixt prefers.

Current market interest rates are 6%.

Required:

1. Assign a value to the liability and the equity portions of the bond.
2. Provide the journal entry to record issuance of the bond.
3. Provide a schedule to show interest expense and amortization of the liability over the life of the bond.
4. How much is charged to retained earnings over the life of the bond, in relation to the principal portion? Explain.
5. What financial statement elements would be changed if common shares are issued at maturity? Explain.

★★★ **A14-12 Convertible Debt, Investor Option versus Conversion Mandatory:** AMC Limited issued five-year, 8% bonds for their par value of $500,000 on 1 January 20X1. Interest is paid annually. The bonds are convertible to common shares at a rate of 50 common shares for every $1,000 bond.

Required:

1. Assume that the bonds were convertible at the investor's option and that the conversion option was valued at $37,908.
   a. Provide the journal entry on issuance.
   b. Calculate interest expense for each year of the bond's five-year life. Use an interest rate of 10% for this requirement.
   c. Provide the journal entry to record maturity of the bond assuming shareholders convert their bonds to common shares.
   d. Assume instead that the bonds were repaid for $540,000 after interest was paid in Year 3. Provide the journal entry for retirement, assuming $32,000 of the payment related to the option and the rest related to the bond.
2. Assume that the bonds were mandatorily convertible at maturity.
   a. Calculate the portion of the original proceeds relating to interest, and the equity portion. Use a discount rate of 8%.
   b. Provide the journal entry on issuance.

c. Calculate interest expense for each year of the bond's five-year life.

d. Explain the financial statement elements that change when the bond is converted at maturity.

★ **A14-13 Warrants:** Ferguson Memorials Limited issued a $1,000,000, 5% annual interest non-convertible bond with detachable stock warrants. One warrant is attached to each $1,000 bond and allows the holder to buy two common shares for $28 each at any time over the next 10 years. The existing market price of Ferguson shares is $18. The bond issue sells for 104.

Required:

1. Assume that, shortly after the bond is issued, bonds alone are selling for 102 and that warrants are selling for $32 each. Record the issuance of the bond.
2. What is the difference between a convertible bond and a bond with detachable warrants?
3. Assume that 60% of the warrants are exercised and the remaining 40% are allowed to lapse. Provide a journal entry(ies) to record the exercise and lapse.

★★ **A14-14 Share Rights and Warrants:** On 31 December 20X2, the shareholders' equity section of Sersa Corporation's statement of financial position was as follows:

Common shares, no-par, unlimited shares authorized, issued and outstanding, 4,543,400 shares	$16,876,400
Contributed capital: common share warrants outstanding, 12,300 warrants allowing purchase of three shares each at a price of $26 per share	110,000
Share options outstanding	161,000
Retained earnings	34,560,900
Total shareholders' equity	$51,708,300

There were 46,000 share options outstanding, issued for legal services, valued at $161,000. These allow purchase of one share each for $19 cash; the options are exercisable over several years.

TRANSACTIONS DURING THE YEAR:

a. Options were issued to existing shareholders as a poison pill in the case of a hostile take-over. These options allow purchase of two shares for each existing share held at a price of $1 each, to be exercisable only under certain limited conditions.

b. Warrants outstanding at the beginning of the year were exercised in full. The market value of the shares was $40.

c. Some outstanding $19 share options were exercised and 10,000 shares were issued. Remaining share options were not exercised in the current year. The market value of the shares was $40.

d. Options were issued that allow purchase of a total of 2,000 shares at a price of $32 per share, beginning in 20X4. The options were issued for four months of 20X3 rent, which was set by contract at $4,000 per month

e. Options were issued for proceeds of $45,000, allowing purchase of 40,000 shares at a price of $35 per share.

f. One-quarter of the options issued in (e), above, were exercised. The market value of the shares was $48.

Required:

1. Provide journal entries for each of the transactions listed above.
2. Prepare the shareholders' equity section of the statement of financial position, reflecting the transactions recorded in requirement (1).

3. What items would appear on the statement of cash flow in the financing activities section as a result of the changes in the equity accounts documented in requirement (2)?

★ **A14-15 Share Rights—Recognition:** Maritime Corp. is a junior mining company listed on the TSX. The common share price of Maritime fluctuates in value. Recent swings went from a high of $16 to a low of $0.30. Maritime issued stock rights on 1 September 20X5 to a consultant, in exchange for a project completed over the last year. The consultant estimated her time was worth $37,000, but the company estimated that it could have had the necessary work done for about $31,000 cash. The rights specified that 4,000 common shares could be bought for $0.20 per share at any time over the next 10 years. The market price of common shares was $1.50 on the day the rights were issued. At the same time options were issued to the consultant, identical rights were issued to the company lawyer for work done to date. An option pricing model valued each set of stock rights at $35,000.

Required:

1. Provide journal entries to record issuance of the two sets of rights. Justify values used.
2. Assume that, two years after issuance, when the market price of the shares was $14, the consultant exercised her rights. Provide the appropriate entry.
3. Assume that, 10 years after issuance, when the market price of the shares was $0.10, the lawyer's rights expired. Provide the entry, if any.

★ **A14-16 Share Rights—Recognition:** Acorn Growth Limited is a small technology company listed on the TSX. To conserve cash, the company frequently settles obligations through the issuance of rights and options. Shares are now trading for $8 per share, but have fluctuated between $5 and $22 in the last year. Selected transactions:

a. Sold 10,000 rights that allow purchase of 2,000 common shares at $4 per share. The options were sold for $71,200 cash.
b. Issued 10,000 rights to the company lawyer for legal work done to date. These options also allow purchase for 2,000 shares at $4 per share. The lawyer had billed $86,000, but the company felt it could have negotiated this down to $65,000 for cash payment.
c. Issued rights to a supplier allowing the supplier to receive 2,000 common shares in three years' time, for no cash cost. The rights have been granted based on the long service relationship between the two companies and are unconditional.
d. Options in (a) and (c) above were exercised when the shares were trading at $25 per share. Options in (b) later expired.

Required:
Provide journal entries to record the transactions listed above. Justify values used.

★★ **A14-17 Share-based Compensation, Cash-settled:** Just In Co. issues 500,000 SARs to its eight-member top management group. These SARs allow the managers to receive a cash payment, after holding the SARs for five years. The SARs vest on the payment date. The value of the SARs is calculated as the difference between the $34 per share fair market value of 500,000 common shares on the date the SARs were issued, and the fair market value on the date of payment. The company estimates that six of eight managers will remain with the company over the five-year period. This estimate remains unchanged over the first four years. One manager leaves after year 2, one after year 3, and one in year 5, so that only 5 managers were paid at the end of year 5.

eXcel

The fair value of one SARs unit was estimated using a valuation model and was, at the end of year 1, $4; year 2, $1; year 3, $2; year 4, $17; and in year 5, the actual market price of common shares was $53.

Required:

1. Why are SARs issued instead of common stock options?
2. How much compensation expense would be recorded in each of years 1 to 5?
3. What would appear on the SFP at the end of each of years 1 to 4?
4. What entry would be made on the maturity (payment) of the SARs?
5. Describe how the accounting for this compensation scheme would be different if the employees could choose between cash and shares at settlement.

★★ **A14-18 Share-based Compensation, Cash-settled:** Pacific Trading Company has a SARs program for managers. These individuals receive a cash payment after three years of service, calculated as the excess of share price over $10. In early 20X3, the 30-member management team in total are granted 25,000 units in the program. The payment is made at the end of 20X5. Data on estimated and actual retention:

End of year	20X3	20X4	20X5
Employees expected to remain until vesting	25 (83%)	24 (80%)	n/a
Employees expected to forfeit	5 (17%)	6 (20%)	n/a
Employees actually forfeiting in the year	1	4	2
Employees actually receiving SARs (30 − 8)			22 (73.3%)

The fair value of one SARs unit is estimated at $3 at the end of 20X3 and $12 at the end of 20X4. The actual share price is $19 at the end of 20X5.

Required:

1. Provide the entry to record compensation expense in each year of the SARs plan, including the entry for cash payment in 20X5.
2. What evidence suggests that the level of retention must be increased at the end of 20X4?
3. Describe how the accounting for this compensation scheme would be different if the employees could choose between cash and shares at settlement.

★★ **A14-19 Share-based Compensation, Cash-settled:** Sousa Minerals has a SARs program for managers. These individuals receive a cash payment after four years of service, calculated as the excess of share price over $2. In early 20X1, individuals in the 40-member management team are granted a total of 100,000 SARs units. The payment is made at the end of 20X4. Data on estimated and actual retention:

eXcel

End of year	20X1	20X2	20X3	20X4
Employees expected to remain until vesting	25 (63%)	28 (70%)	30 (75%)	n/a
Employees expected to forfeit	15 (37%)	12 (30%)	10 (25%)	n/a
Employees actually forfeiting in the year	5	2	2	0
Employees actually receiving SARs (40 − 9)				31 (77.5%)

The fair value of the entire 100,000 units was estimated to be $100,000 at the end of 20X1, $50,000 at the end of 20X2, and $110,000 at the end of 20X3. The actual share price was $2.90 at the end of 20X4.

Required:

1. Calculate compensation expense in each year of the SARs plan, and the balance of the SARs liability at the end of each year.
2. What evidence suggests that the level of retention must be revised at the end of 20X2?
3. Explain why compensation expense is volatile.

★ **A14-20 Stock Options:** Ming Limited has an executive stock option plan as follows: Each qualified manager will receive, on 1 January, an option for the computed number of common shares at a computed price. The number of option shares and the option price are determined by the Board of Directors, with advice from the compensation committee. The options are non-transferable. The vesting period is two years. Options can be exercised after they vest but expire six years after the date of issuance.

On 1 January 20X3, manager Ms. Smoke was given options for 1,200 shares at $60. She is expected to remain with the company indefinitely. Option pricing models produced a value for the option of $30,000 on 1 January 20X3. The market value of common shares was $12 at that time. Ms. Smoke exercised 1,000 of the options on 3 January 20X6 when the share price was $88. She did not exercise the remaining 200 options because the share price fell to $40 and remained there until the options expired.

Required:
Provide all entries relating to Ms. Smoke's options.

★★ **A14-21 Share-based Compensation, Equity-settled:** Ding Solutions Limited is authorized to issue unlimited numbers of common shares, of which 1,675,000 have been issued at an average price of $75 per share. On 1 January 20X3, the company granted stock options to each of its 24 senior executives. The stock options provide that each individual will be eligible to purchase, no earlier than 31 December 20X7, 2,000 common shares at a base option price of $110 per share. The options are non-transferable, vest on 31 December 20X7, and expire on 31 December 20X8. Option pricing models indicate that the options have a total value of $900,000. Estimates of retention:

Year	20X3	20X4	20X5	20X6	20X7
Employees expected to remain until vesting	22 (92%)	21 (87%)	20 (83%)	18 (75%)	n/a
Employees expected to forfeit	2 (8%)	3 (13%)	4 (17%)	6 (25%)	n/a
Employees actually forfeiting in the year	0	1	3	1	0
Employees actually receiving options (24 − 5)					19 (79%)

Sixteen individuals who received the options exercised on 31 December 20X7, when the share price was $168. The remaining individuals did not exercise the options. The share price fell to $105 in 20X8 and the options lapsed.

Required:

1. Prepare the entries to record the granting of the options, annual expense, exercise, and lapse.
2. Why is the compensation expense not an equal amount each year? Be specific.
3. What intrinsic value was received when the options were exercised? Is this reflected in the financial statements? Explain.

★★ **A14-22 Share-based Compensation, Compound Plan:** Five vice presidents of Spinner Entertainment Limited are awarded units in a phantom stock plan at the beginning of 20X2. At the end of 20X4, after three years of employment, each vice president is entitled to receive *either*

- 5,000 common shares; or
- Cash equal to the market value of 3,500 shares.

When the rights were granted, the shares had a market value of $20, and valuation models indicated that the share alternative was worth $21.20 per share. Based on this information, the equity portion of the plan was valued at $180,000 for accounting purposes. The share price was $19 at the end of 20X2, $23 at the end of 20X3, and $20 at the end of 20X4. The fair value of the cash alternative is to be based on the intrinsic value of the plan on each reporting date. All vice presidents were expected to stay with the company, and all did. Four of the five executives elected to take cash in 20X4, and the remaining vice president took shares.

Required:

1. Verify the $180,000 option value at the inception of the plan.

2. Prepare the entries to record the annual expense entries, and disbursement in 20X4.

★ **A14-23 Share-based Compensation:** Able Co. had compensation plans in effect for senior managers that included two long-term compensation elements. Retention levels were estimated to be 80% at the end of 20X4. SFP accounts at the end of 20X4:

Liability—SARs plan	$ 70,000
40,000 units are under SARs agreement, where the reference market price is $52 per common share, one share per SARs unit; valuation models indicate a fair value of $8.75 per SARs unit; the SARs have been outstanding for one year and must be held for a total of four years before vesting.	
Contributed capital—employee share options outstanding	$336,000
35,000 shares are under option at an exercise price of $42. The options were valued using a binomial valuation model and determined to be worth $700,000. The options have been outstanding for three years and must be held for a total of five years before they can be exercised.	

Required:

1. Describe the likely features of the two kinds of compensation plans above. Provide the calculation to support the balances recorded.

2. Assume no new compensation entitlements were offered in 20X5. At year-end, the common share price was $60 and the fair value of a SARs unit was estimated to be worth $9.25. Retention is now assumed to be 75%. Give the entries to record compensation expense related to the above plans.

★★ **A14-24 Share-based Compensation:** Mercury Limited issued long-term compensation contracts for its 10-member executive team as follows:

1. Mercury issued a total of 40,000 SARs units at the beginning of 20X3. These SARs units vest and are exerciseable after three years. The value of a SARs unit, to be paid in cash, is calculated as the difference between the market value of common shares on the date the SARs were issued ($16), and the market value on the date of exercise. All executives were paid their SARs entitlements at the end of 20X5.

2. Mercury issued 4,000 units in a phantom stock plan at the beginning of 20X3. These units allow the executives to receive either 4,000 shares or the cash value of 3,200 shares, at their choice, after holding the units for three years. The share alternative was valued at $14,000 at inception for accounting purposes. The fair value of the liability was estimated to be $56,000 at the end of 20X3, and $75,000 at the end of 20X4. The employees elected to receive shares at maturity in 20X5.

3. Mercury issued options at the beginning of 20X3, allowing 20,000 shares to be issued for $1 per share after four years. At the end of 20X3, each unit is estimated to be worth $8; and then $9 (20X4), $13 (20X5), and $16 (20X6). An option pricing model valued the options at a total of $260,000 in early 20X3.

Market values of common shares at the end of 20X3, $19; 20X4, $24; and 20X5, $22. The fair value of a SARs unit was estimated to be $7 at the end of 20X3 and $9 at the end of 20X4. Retention levels were expected to be 90% at the end of 20X3 and 80% at the end of 20X4.

Seven executives were still with the company at the end of 20X5 and this 70% retention rate was expected to be maintained through 20X6.

Required:

1. Provide the journal entries for 20X3, 20X4, and 20X5.
2. What would appear on the SFP at the end of 20X4?

★ **A14-25 Derivatives:** Treetoo Limited wishes to buy 10,000 shares of YCo, a publicly-traded company. Treetoo enters into a contract, through a broker, to buy the shares in 40 days' time, at a price of $3 per share, the current fair value. The broker requires a 10% margin to be maintained at all times. After 10 days, at the fiscal year-end, the price of the YCo shares is $4 per share, and is $4.50 per share at the end of 40 days. At that time, the shares are purchased and the contract is closed out.

Required:

1. Is this a forward contract or a futures contract? Explain.
2. What risk is the company hedging?
3. Prepare journal entries to record the inception of the contract, the change in its fair value at year-end and the additional margin payment, and its maturity.

★ **A14-26 Derivatives:** Starco Corp. wishes to purchase 5,000 shares of Gertrom Ltd., a publicly-traded company. Starco contracts to buy the shares from a related party, Unit Ltd., for $62 per share in 90 days' time. The fair value was $62 per share on this day. One month later, at year-end, the fair value of the Gertrom shares is $54 per share, and it is $55 per share at the end of 90 days. At that time, the shares are bought and the contract is closed out.

Required:

1. Is this a forward contract or a futures contract? Explain.
2. What risk is the company hedging?
3. Prepare journal entries to record the inception of the contract, the change in its fair value at year-end, and its maturity.

★ **A14-27 Derivatives:** Notting Hill Limited reported the following amounts on the 31 December 20X2 SFP:

Assets		Liabilities	
Derivative asset	$192	Derivative obligation	$733
		Equity	
		Reserve: hedge gain	$ 43

Notting Hill has material accounts receivable and purchase orders that are denominated in U.S. dollars. The company follows a policy of hedging all exchange exposure with futures contracts.

Required:

1. Explain how futures contracts can be used to hedge exchange exposure caused by U.S. dollar accounts receivable.
2. Explain the conditions that cause a derivative instrument to be an asset or a liability.
3. Are gains and losses from derivatives included in earnings? Explain.
4. What conditions must be met for hedge accounting to be invoked?
5. What is the most likely explanation for the presence of the $43 hedge reserve?

★★★ **A14-28 Statement of Cash Flow—Individual Transactions:** The following cases are independent:

Case A

Information from the 31 December 20X5 SFP of Holdco Limited:

	20X5	20X4
Bonds payable	$5,000,000	$ —
Discount on bonds payable	234,000	—
Common stock conversion rights	695,000	—

Convertible bonds were issued during the year. Discount amortization was $14,000 in 20X5.

Case B

Information from the 31 December 20X5 SFP of Sellco Limited:

	20X5	20X4
Bonds payable	$ 5,000,000	$10,000,000
Discount on bonds payable	160,000	346,000
Common stock conversion rights	695,000	1,390,000
Common shares	$17,000,000	7,100,000

One-half of the bonds converted to common shares during the period. Other common shares were issued for cash. Discount amortization during the year was $26,000.

Case C

Information from the 31 December 20X5 SFP of Buyco Limited:

	20X5	20X4
Stock rights outstanding	$ 240,000	$ 295,000
Common shares	9,000,000	6,550,000

During the year, 10,000 stock rights originally valued at a price of $5.50 were exercised, and 10,000 common shares were issued for the exercise price of $14. One million stock rights, allowing qualified shareholders to acquire common shares at one-tenth the then-current fair value in the event of hostile takeover, were also issued during the year. Other common shares were sold for cash.

Case D

Information from the 31 December 20X5 SFP of Bothco Limited:

	20X5	20X4
Bonds payable	$ —	$10,000,000
Discount on bonds payable	—	26,450
Common stock conversion rights	—	1,390,000
Contributed capital, lapse of conversion right	1,390,000	—

Bonds payable matured in the year, but were redeemed in cash at par and not converted.

Required:
For each case, list the appropriate items on the statement of cash flow caused by issuance, conversion, or derecognition of financial instruments. Do not include disclosure of interest.

★★★ **A14-29 Statement of Cash Flow—Comprehensive Equity:** The following data is related to Cole Resources Ltd.:

	20X9	20X8
Bonds payable, 7%	$4,000,000	0
Discount on bonds payable	(320,000)	0
6% Preferred share liability, due 20X11	400,000	400,000
5% Preferred shares, no-par	1,600,000	$1,600,000
Common shares, no-par	8,000,000	5,000,000
Common share fractional rights	34,000	0
Contributed capital: common stock conversion rights	255,000	0
Contributed capital: common share retirement	122,000	0
Contributed capital: employee stock options outstanding	387,500	160,000
Contributed capital on treasury stock transactions	65,000	0
Retained earnings	7,005,000	5,940,000
Treasury stock, 5% preferred shares	(700,000)	0

During the year, the following transactions took place and have been correctly recorded:

a. Reported earnings and comprehensive income was $2,600,000. This includes $267,500 of compensation expense recorded for options to employees and the 6% preferred share dividends.
b. Cash dividends were paid.
c. Convertible bonds were issued during the year. Discount amortization of $23,600 was recorded by the end of the year.
d. There was a common stock dividend during the year that resulted in a reduction to retained earnings of $544,000. Most of the shares were issued as whole shares, but some were issued in the form of fractional rights. All these rights are still outstanding at year-end.
e. Common shares with an average original issuance price of $655,000 were retired during the year.
f. 5% preferred shares with an original average book value of $600,000 were purchased as treasury shares early in the fiscal year. Half were resold almost immediately, and half were kept.
g. Additional common shares were issued for cash and others for the options in (i).
h. Retained earnings was reduced by $200,300 as the result of share issue costs.
i. Employee stock options, along with $50,000 of cash, were exchanged for common shares during the year.
j. Any remaining change in accounts should be assumed to flow from a logical transaction.

Required:

1. List the items and amounts that caused the retained earnings account to change from its opening to closing balance. For the dividend through retained earnings, specify the amount to each share class.
2. List the items and amounts that caused the common share account to change from its opening to closing balance.
3. List the items that would appear in the financing activities section of the SCF. The company classifies dividends in the operating activities section.

★★★

Solution

A14-30 Comprehensive Equity: Acer Corporation reported the following balances at 1 January 20X1:

Interest liability—8% bond ($10,000,000 par value). Conversion into 76,000 common shares at maturity is mandatory	$ 4,997,000
Share equity—8% bond	5,102,000
Convertible $8, no-par preferred shares, 60,000 shares outstanding; convertible into 8 common shares for every 3 preferred shares outstanding	6,060,000
Class A no-par common shares, unlimited shares authorized, 915,000 issued and 899,000 outstanding	32,940,000
Common share warrants, allowing purchase of 90,000 shares at $32.50	660,000
Contributed capital: employee share options outstanding*	160,000
Contributed capital on preferred share retirement	55,000
Retained earnings	116,300,000
Less: Treasury shares, 16,000 common shares	(512,000)

*Forty thousand common stock options are outstanding to certain employees allowing purchase of one share for every two options held at a price of $27.50 per share. These options are vested and expire in 20X4.

The following events took place in 20X1:

a. Common shares were issued to employees under the terms of existing outstanding share options. 16,000 options were exercised when the share market value was $45.

b. Options were issued in exchange for a piece of land, appraised at $75,000. The options allow purchase of 100,000 shares at $15 each in five years' time. The market value of the shares was $46 on this date. The option was valued at $81,000 using the Black-Scholes option pricing model.

c. 40,000 common shares were acquired and retired at a price of $47 each.

d. 10,000 common treasury shares were acquired at a price of $44 per share.

e. A cash dividend was declared and paid. The annual dividend for the preferred shares and $1 per share for the common shares were both declared and paid.

f. 24,000 preferred shares were converted to common shares.

g. The annual interest expense was accrued on the 8% bonds, using the effective rate of 7.8%. The annual payment was made.

h. Two-thirds of the common share warrants outstanding at the beginning of the year were exercised when the market value of the shares was $49.50; the remainder lapsed.

i. Options were granted to employees at the beginning of the year, allowing purchase of one share for every two options held at a price of $35. Fifty thousand options were issued. These options become vested at the beginning of 20X5. The fair value of the options was $720,000 and the retention rate for the employee groups covered was estimated at 90%.

j. 10,000 preferred shares were retired for $107 each.

k. 20,000 treasury shares were sold for $32 each.

l. A 10% stock dividend was declared and issued. Treasury shares were not eligible for the stock dividend. The Board of Directors decided that the stock dividend should be valued at $30 per share. Most of the dividend was issued in whole shares; however, 41,000 fractional shares allowing acquisition of 4,100 whole shares were issued.

Required:

1. Provide journal entries (or memo entries) for the events listed.

2. Calculate the closing balance in each of the listed accounts at 31 December 20X1, reflecting the entries in requirement (1). Earnings for the year were $6,200,000 including interest in (g) and stock option expense in (i).

CHAPTER 15

Accounting for Corporate Income Tax

INTRODUCTION

Suncor Energy Inc. reported 2008 pre-tax earnings of $3,132 million. The company paid $514 million to the government in income taxes. Yet the income statement showed income tax expense of $995 million. On the right side of Suncor's balance sheet, the second largest single item (other than retained earnings) was a long-term *deferred income tax* liability of $4,615 million, amounting to 14% of total assets or 32% of net assets. How did Suncor avoid paying so much income tax in 2008 and instead report $4.6 billion in long-term tax liabilities?

Accounting for corporate income tax might seem rather straightforward. After all, the exact amount of income tax for each year is computed on the corporation's income tax return. Why is income tax expense usually different (and sometimes vastly different) from the actual taxes paid in a year?

In fact, Suncor paid the income taxes that it owed to the government for 2008; the company didn't "avoid" paying income taxes at all. The difference arises from an accounting practice known as *interperiod income tax allocation*.

At any point in time, many individual assets (and liabilities) will have an *accounting carrying value* that differs from its *tax basis*. That difference will have an impact on the income taxes that will be due in a future period when the asset is used or disposed of. Accountants recognize that future tax liability in the accounts as deferred income tax. Deferred income tax liabilities are not amounts that are actually owed to the government. The subject of this chapter is the method of accounting for the future tax effects of differences between the tax basis and the accounting carrying value.

A second aspect of interperiod income tax allocation pertains to the recognition of future benefits of tax loss carryforwards. This aspect is explored in the following chapter.

One other aspect of accounting for income taxation is the *investment tax credit*, a special tax provision intended to encourage certain types of capital investment by businesses. This specialized topic is discussed in the Appendix to this chapter.

One important note about the chapter title: only corporations are subject to income tax because only corporations are recognized as legal entities. The profits of partnerships and proprietorships are taxed to the owners. Income tax expense does not appear on the financial statements of either partnerships or proprietorships.

INCOME TAX PROVISION VERSUS EXPENSE

It is common in practice for companies to label income tax expense in the income statement as the **provision for income tax.** This is a somewhat confusing label because we usually use "provision" to indicate an estimated liability, such as "Provision for Warranty Costs."

For example, Suncor's statement of comprehensive income shows income taxes as follows:

	2008	2007	2006
Earnings Before Income Taxes	$3,132	$3,549	$3,797
Provision for income taxes			
Current	514	382	20
Future	481	184	808
	995	566	828
Net earnings	$2,137	$2,983	$2,969

Companies use the term "provision" for income tax expense because when a company has a loss for tax purposes, the income statement entry for income tax may be a credit rather than a debit. Rather than switch the income statement label from "expense" to "benefit," companies use the vague term "provision" to fit all circumstances. This practice might be viewed as sloppy terminology, but it is not apt to cause confusion to readers and it is easier to use.

In this book, in order to avoid confusion between the income statement item and the tax liability, we henceforth will typically use the title "income tax expense," even when the expense is a credit (that is, a recovery of previously paid income taxes). IFRS does not apply the word "provision" to income tax expense or recovery, although use of the word is common in practice.

INTERPERIOD TAX ALLOCATION—INTRODUCTION

Interperiod tax allocation deals with allocating tax expense to an appropriate year, regardless of when it is actually paid. A company adopts those accounting policies that management perceives will best satisfy the objectives of financial statement users and preparers. One broad objective of accounting standards and accounting policies is to measure net income, which usually is the result of many accruals, interperiod allocations, and estimates. In contrast, the major objective of the *Income Tax Act* and Regulations is to generate revenue for the government.

Because it is easier and more objective to assess tax when cash is flowing, tax policy generally favours taxing revenues and expenses on the basis of cash flows rather than coping with the results of accounting allocations. Some important exceptions relate primarily to inventories, capital assets, and multiperiod earnings processes (e.g., revenue from long-term contracts), but cash flows are crucial. In addition, the *Income Tax Act* exempts certain types of income from taxation and prohibits the deduction of certain types of expenses.

Differences between Taxable and Accounting Income

Both accounting income and taxable income are the net result of matching revenues and expenses (and gains and losses) of a period. Most items of revenue and expense are recognized in the same period for both accounting and tax purposes. But there are some differences. These differences can be categorized as:

- Permanent differences; and
- Temporary differences.

Permanent Differences A **permanent difference** arises when an income statement element—a revenue, gain, expense, or loss—enters the computation of either taxable income or pre-tax accounting income but never enters into the computation of the other. For example, dividend income received from another tax-paying Canadian corporation is included in accounting income but is not included in taxable income. Such dividends are tax-exempt revenue. They are a *permanent* difference because they are not subject to taxation.

Similarly, a company may sell land that it has held for a long time. Since land is a capital asset, the gain from selling the land is known as a *capital gain* for tax purposes. The full amount of the gain will be recognized on the company's income statement, but only 50% of a capital gain is included in taxable income. Therefore, the 50% of a capital gain that is *not* taxed is a permanent difference.

Certain types of expense are not deductible for tax purposes. A common example is golf club dues paid by a corporation. The *Income Tax Act* specifically identifies golf club dues as non-deductible for tax purposes, but they are a legitimate expense if the corporation believes they should be part of, say, a sales or marketing effort. Therefore, the difference between pre-tax accounting income and taxable income that arises from golf club dues is a permanent difference.

There also may be deductions that are allowed in computing taxable income that have no equivalent for accounting income. In some years, for example, companies have been permitted to deduct tax depreciation, called capital cost allowance or CCA, based on an amount higher than the cost basis of the assets (e.g., the CCA rate could be based on 150% of the specified asset's cost). Since accounting depreciation expense can never exceed 100% of an asset's cost, the excess CCA was a permanent difference.

Accounting standards don't discuss permanent differences at all, because they are specific to each nation and have no counterpart in accounting.

Temporary Differences A **temporary difference** arises when the tax basis of an asset or liability differs from its accounting carrying value.

A temporary difference *originates* in the period in which it first enters the computation of either taxable income or accounting income, and *reverses* in the subsequent period when that item enters into the computation of the other measure. An item can either:

- Be included in accounting income first, and then included in taxable income in a subsequent period; or
- Enter into the calculation of taxable income first, and then be included in accounting income in a later period.

Origination and Reversal Revenue on a long-term contract should be recognized on a percentage of completion basis for accounting purposes. For income tax purposes, the recognition of revenue can be delayed until the contract is completed, provided that the contract lasts no more than two years. The revenue recognized in the first year will enter into the determination of net income, thereby giving rise to an originating temporary difference. In the following year, assuming that the contract has been completed, the revenue (and related expenses) will be included in taxable income; including the revenue in taxable income reverses the temporary difference:

- A temporary difference is said to *originate* when the difference between accounting recognition and tax treatment first arises, or when a recurring temporary difference *increases* the accumulated balance of temporary differences.
- A temporary difference is said to *reverse* when the accumulated temporary differences are *reduced* by the "catch up" recognition for tax and accounting.

Other Examples Another example is capitalized development costs. For income tax purposes, development costs can be deducted when incurred. For financial reporting, however, capitalized development costs are recognized in determining net income only as amortization in later periods. The temporary difference relating to development costs originates when the costs are deducted on the tax return and reverses over several future years as the capitalized costs are amortized for accounting purposes.

Similarly, temporary differences arise from the difference between accounting amortization and CCA deducted for tax purposes. This is the most complex example, because the temporary difference arises from the fact that the historical cost of the capital assets is being allocated simultaneously for accounting and tax purposes, but in different patterns. Straight-line amortization is commonly used for reporting purposes by Canadian corporations, but CCA usually follows a declining-balance pattern of allocation.

The CCA/depreciation temporary difference doesn't arise from the fact that amortization expense is deducted for tax purposes but not for accounting, but rather from the fact that the amortization expense usually is lower than CCA in the early years of an asset's life, giving rise to *originating* temporary differences. In later years, as CCA declines, the straight-line amortization becomes larger than CCA and the temporary difference *reverses*. The CCA/depreciation temporary difference is the most common type of temporary difference.

Exhibit 15-1 lists some of the more common types of permanent differences and temporary differences.

EXHIBIT 15-1

EXAMPLES OF PERMANENT AND TEMPORARY DIFFERENCES IN CANADA

Permanent Differences

- Dividends received by Canadian corporations from some other taxable Canadian corporations *deduction*
- Equity in earnings of significantly influenced associate companies
- 50% of capital gains *deduction*
- Golf club dues *deduction*
- 50% of meals and entertainment expenses *Addition*
- Interest and penalties on taxes *Addition*
- Political contributions *Addition*

*[handwritten margin notes: do not include X / Treatments in IT / * Addition in ITax / * deduction]*

Temporary Differences

[handwritten margin note: Add]

- Depreciation for accounting purposes; CCA for tax
- Amortization of capitalized development costs for accounting; immediate deduction for tax
- Amortization of capitalized interest for accounting; deducted when paid for tax
- Writedown of inventories, investments, or tangible capital assets for accounting; loss recognized only when realized for tax
- Gains and losses on inventories valued at net realizable value for accounting; taxed when realized
- Instalment sales income recognized for accounting at time of sale; taxed when cash received
- Bad debt expenses recognized in year of sale for accounting; tax deductible when uncollectible
- Capital assets written up under the revaluation method; no taxable gain until asset class closed
- Fair value increases for investment properties or biological assets; gain taxable only when property is sold
- Warranty costs accrued for accounting in period of sale; tax deductible when paid
- Bond discount or premium, amortized for accounting but taxable expense or revenue only when the principal is settled at maturity

[handwritten margin note: Reverse or add back in TR]

CONCEPT REVIEW

1. Explain why accounting income is different from taxable income.

2. What is a permanent difference? Give an example.

3. A company deducts warranty expense in 20X0 on the income statement but pays warranty claims in 20X1. In what year does this temporary difference originate? In what year does it reverse?

CONCEPTUAL ISSUES IN INTERPERIOD TAX ALLOCATION

Interperiod income tax allocation has long been very contentious. Conceptually, there are three basic underlying issues:

1. The extent of allocation;
2. The measurement method; and
3. Discounting.

Before illustrating the mechanics of tax allocation, we will briefly address each of these three issues. Every accountant should have a basic understanding of these issues because tax allocation accounting standards have changed several times over the years, and different countries have used different methods. The fact that a single approach is now widespread (due to IFRS) does not mean that the issue is settled. There still is much dissatisfaction with current standards within the accounting profession; both accountants and financial statement users should have a basic understanding of the dimensions of the issue.

Furthermore, private enterprises are not required to follow the IFRS techniques explained in this chapter. Private companies can choose whether or not to follow income tax allocation. Substantial numbers of bankers, financial analysts, and accountants believe that the non-allocation "taxes payable" method that is acceptable for private enterprises should be standard for publicly-accountable enterprises as well.

The IASB proposed changes in income tax allocation in 2009, but withdrew the proposals. At the time of writing, the IASB says simply that the Board, in conjunction with the FASB, "indicated that they would consider undertaking a fundamental review of accounting for income taxes at some time in the future." Change can be expected, so we had best understand the basic concepts.

Extent of Allocation

Extent of allocation refers to the range of temporary differences to which interperiod tax allocation is applied. The two basic options are:

1. No allocation—the taxes payable method; and
2. Full allocation—the comprehensive tax allocation method.

An intermediate approach known as *partial allocation* has been used in some countries in the past (notably, in the United Kingdom), but this method has largely been discarded.

Taxes Payable Method   The **taxes payable method** recognizes the amount of taxes assessed in each year as the income tax expense for that year: income tax expense = current income tax. This is also known as the **flow-through method** because the actual taxes paid "flow through" to the income statement.

Advocates of the taxes payable method argue that income tax is an aggregate measure, applied to the overall operations of the company as a whole, and that it is artificial to disaggregate the income tax amount as though each item of revenue and expense were taxed individually. As well, the taxes payable method corresponds with the actual cash outflow for income tax. If cash flow prediction is a primary objective of financial reporting, the taxes payable method may be superior to earnings measured by using full allocation.[1]

Viewed in the aggregate, temporary differences in a stable or growing company typically reverse and originate each year, with new originating temporary differences replacing those that are reversing. Taxes payable advocates argue that these aggregated temporary differences are "permanent" and will never result in a real cash flow. They also argue that the "future liability" that is created through tax allocation is not a genuine obligation—the

---

[1] On the other hand, one research study suggests that "deferred tax information leads to superior forecasts of future tax payments and that deferred tax data enhance prediction of future cash flows." Joseph K. Cheung, Gopal V. Krishnan, and Chung-ki Min, "Does Interperiod Income Tax Allocation Enhance Prediction of Cash Flows?" *Accounting Horizons* (December 1997), pp. 1–15.

government does not view the deferred tax "liability" as an amount owed to the government and there certainly is no legal or constructive obligation to pay that amount.

The taxes payable method is currently permitted for private enterprises, but not for publicly-accountable enterprises.

Comprehensive Tax Allocation Accountants who support **comprehensive tax allocation** are in the clear majority, at least among standard-setters. They argue that a future cash flow impact arises from all temporary differences, no matter how far in the future that impact occurs. Tax "saved" this year via an early tax deduction will have to be "paid" in a future year when the expense is recognized for accounting but cannot be deducted for tax. Furthermore, they argue that it is a serious violation of the matching concept to recognize a revenue or expense in net income without simultaneously recognizing its inevitable deferred income tax effect. And while aggregate temporary differences may not decline, the individual temporary differences that make up the aggregate do in fact reverse, even if they are replaced by new temporary differences.

Example The following example illustrates the two tax allocation bases: (1) the taxes payable method and (2) comprehensive tax allocation, both of which are used in Canada.

Suppose that Dominic Ltd. has pre-tax income in each of three years of $1,000,000. The first year's income includes a gain of $600,000 that won't be collected until 20X3. That is, there is a gain on the 20X1 income statement that will not be taxed until the money is collected in 20X3. Dominic's income tax rate is 25%.

In 20X1 and 20X2, Dominic's financial statements will show an account receivable of $600,000. So far as Canada Revenue Agency is concerned, there is no receivable because Dominic owes nothing until the company actually collects the cash. The accounting basis of the receivable is $600,000, while the tax basis is zero. Dominic has a $600,000 temporary difference relating to the receivable, which has a future (or *deferred*) income tax impact of $150,000 (that is, $150,000 × 25%).

If Dominic gives no recognition of the temporary difference, the company's taxable income will be $400,000 in 20X1, $1,000,000 in 20X2, and $1,600,000 in 20X3. Assuming an income tax rate of 25%, the taxes due for each period are $100,000 in 20X1, $250,000 in 20X2, and $400,000 in 20X3. This information is summarized as follows:

	20X1	20X2	20X3
Income before taxes (accounting basis)	$1,000,000	$1,000,000	$1,000,000
20X1 accounting gain that is taxable in 20X3	− 600,000		+ 600,000
Taxable income	$ 400,000	$1,000,000	$1,600,000
Tax rate	× 25%	× 25%	× 25%
Income tax assessed for the year	$ 100,000	$ 250,000	$ 400,000

Under the *taxes payable method*, each year's full tax assessment *flows through* to net income:

	20X1	20X2	20X3
Net income before income tax	$1,000,000	$1,000,000	$1,000,000
Income tax expense	100,000	250,000	400,000
Net income	$ 900,000	$ 750,000	$ 600,000

In the view of most accountants, reporting on a taxes payable basis "distorts" net income because the income tax relating to the $600,000 gain is reported in 20X3, while the gain itself is reported in 20X1. The corporation's apparent net income has declined significantly from 20X1 through 20X3, but the difference is due solely to the fact that income tax on part of 20X1's net income tax is included in income tax expense for 20X3.

When the *comprehensive tax allocation method* is used, the $150,000 income tax impact of the $600,000 gain is recognized in the same period (for accounting purposes) as the gain itself:

	20X1	20X2	20X3
Income before income tax	$1,000,000	$1,000,000	$1,000,000
Income tax expense:			
Current	100,000	250,000	400,000
Deferred	150,000	—	(150,000)
	250,000	250,000	250,000
Net income	$ 750,000	$ 750,000	$ 750,000

The entry to record the income tax expense in each year is:

20X1
Income tax expense (I/S)	250,000	
Income tax payable (B/S)		100,000
Deferred income tax liability (B/S)		150,000

20X2
Income tax expense (I/S)	250,000	
Income tax payable (B/S)		250,000

20X3
Income tax expense (I/S)	250,000	
Deferred income tax liability (B/S)	150,000	
Income tax payable (B/S)		400,000

The deferred income tax liability will be shown on the balance sheet at the end of 20X1 and 20X2, and then is *drawn down in* 20X3 when the temporary difference *reverses* and the tax actually becomes due. Notice the distinction in terminology:

- A temporary difference *reverses*, while
- The deferred income tax liability/asset that relates to the temporary differences is *drawn down*.

CONCEPT REVIEW

1. What is the flow-through method of accounting for income tax expense?
2. Why does comprehensive tax allocation result in better income reporting?

Measurement Method

When the effects of temporary differences are measured, should the tax rate be:

1. The rate in effect at the time that the temporary difference *first arises* (the deferral method), or

2. The rate that is *expected to be in effect* when the temporary difference reverses (the liability method)?

This is the *measurement method* issue.

Deferral Method　The **deferral method** records the future tax impact by using the corporation's effective average tax rate in the year that the temporary difference first arises, or *originates*. Advocates of the deferral method argue that interperiod income tax allocation is simply a method of moving expense from one period to another, and that the best measure of that expense is the effect that it had in the year that the temporary difference originated. The implication of the deferral method is that the balance sheet credit (or debit) for deferred income taxes is simply a deferred credit (or deferred debit), and should not be accorded the status of a liability (or asset). Deferred income tax credits and debits on the balance sheet are simply a necessary result of matching and improving income measurement. Conceptually, the focus is on the income statement.

Liability Method　In contrast, the **liability** (or **accrual**) **method** uses the tax rate that will be in effect in the year of *reversal*. Proponents of this view argue that ultimate realization of the amount of the temporary difference depends on the tax rates in effect when the temporary differences reverse, and thus the amounts to be realized bear no necessary relationship to the tax rates in effect when they originated. Conceptually, the emphasis is on measurement of the future cash flow impact, and the future amount to be paid (or received, if there is a net tax benefit) is viewed as a liability (or asset). The focus, therefore, is on the statement of financial position.

How can the tax rate in the year of reversal be projected? Prediction of future tax rates is a very tenuous proposition, and might also tempt a company's management to use a high or low prediction that has a desired impact of increasing or decreasing net income. Therefore, the practical solution is that only *enacted* rates of tax will be used. If this year's tax rate is 30%, and the tax rate for next year has already been enacted and is, say, 26%, then 26% is used to measure the balance in deferred income tax.

Effect of Tax Rates　In a world of stable tax rates, there would be no difference between the two methods. But tax rates are not always stable. Tax rates in Canada are subject to annual adjustment by the governments (federal and provincial), including the use of surtaxes (that is, an extra tax calculated as a percentage of the basic income tax at the statutory rate).

What happens when tax rates change? Under the deferral method, no consequence for tax allocation arises from a change in tax rates. In contrast, the liability method requires that the liability (or asset) be adjusted to reflect each year's *best estimate* of the future tax liability (asset) arising from temporary differences. Therefore, every time there is a change in the corporate tax rate, companies must increase or decrease the SFP amount for the deferred tax liability or asset. The offset to the adjustment is the income tax expense in the income statement.

Example　In the earlier example, the tax rate was assumed to be constant throughout the three years. The problem becomes more interesting, however, if tax rates change while a temporary difference exists. We will illustrate the impact of the liability and deferral methods using the same example but with a modification in the tax rates:

- Net income before income taxes is $1,000,000 in each of 20X1, 20X2, and 20X3.
- A gain of $600,000 is included in accounting income in 20X1 but is not subject to tax until 20X3.
- The income tax rate in 20X1 is 25%; during 20X2, the rate is reduced by act of Parliament to 22%, which remains in effect for both 20X2 and 20X3.

The calculation of income tax payable under this revised scenario is as follows:

	20X1	20X2	20X3
Income before taxes (accounting basis)	$1,000,000	$1,000,000	$1,000,000
20X1 accounting gain that is taxable in 20X3	− 600,000		+ 600,000
Taxable income	$ 400,000	$1,000,000	$1,600,000
Tax rate	× 25%	× 22%	× 22%
Income tax payable	$ 100,000	$ 220,000	$ 352,000

Entries for the liability method are shown below. The 20X1 entry is identical to the earlier illustration:

20X1		
Income tax expense	250,000	
Income tax payable		100,000
Deferred income tax liability (.25×600,000)		150,000

In 20X2, using the liability method, the deferred income tax account must be adjusted to reflect the tax rate change. The temporary difference of $600,000 now will result in taxation of only $132,000 (that is, the $600,000 temporary difference × 22%) instead of $150,000 ($600,000 × 25%). Therefore, we must reduce the balance of the deferred income tax liability by $18,000.

20X2		
Deferred income tax liability	18,000	
Income tax expense	202,000	
Income tax payable		220,000

The tax expense recorded is the net amount of the payable ($220,000) minus the reduction in deferred income tax ($18,000). The tax expense of $202,000 is an effective tax rate of 20.2%, which is neither the old rate nor the new rate. It is a residual.

In 20X3, the temporary difference is *reversed* and the deferred tax liability is *drawn down* because the gain enters taxable income.

20X3		
Income tax expense	220,000	
Deferred income tax liability	132,000	
Income tax payable		352,000

Discounting

A final conceptual issue is whether deferred income tax balances should be discounted to present values. If the future tax consequence of a temporary difference is a liability, then the time value of money can be taken into account. If a corporation delays paying large amounts of income tax by taking advantage of completely legal provisions of the *Income Tax Act* (such as large CCA deductions), then the balance sheet credit represents, in effect, an interest-free loan from the government.[2]

---

[2] Bear in mind, however, that the government does not view the amount as owing to it. The liability is an accounting construct, not a "real" liability; the government cannot demand payment in the event of the company's financial distress.

In general, accounting standards require that non-current monetary assets and liabilities be shown at their discounted present value. Non-interest-bearing loans normally are discounted at an imputed rate of interest. Therefore, many accountants argue that tax assets and liabilities also should be discounted in order to measure these monetary assets and liabilities in a manner that is consistent with the measurement of other monetary items.

Despite the strength of the theoretical arguments in favour of discounting, practical problems get in the way. There are difficulties in determining the interest rate to be used in discounting, and the timing of reversals is particularly problematic as they depend on accounting policy, management judgements, and prediction of future years' taxable income.

Largely as the result of the many estimates that must be made in order to apply discounting, discounting is not applied to interperiod tax allocation. *IAS* 12 contains a single nine-word paragraph on this issue: "Deferred tax assets and liabilities shall not be discounted" [¶53].

CONCEPT REVIEW

1. What is the essential difference between the deferral method and the liability method of tax allocation?

2. A company records a deferred income tax liability in 20X1. In 20X2, the income tax rate changes. In 20X4, the future tax liability is drawn down and disappears. In what year is the impact of the rate change recognized, using the liability method?

3. Why aren't deferred income tax amounts discounted, as are other long-term liabilities?

APPROACH TO INCOME TAX QUESTIONS

We will approach income tax questions in three steps:

Step 1—calculate taxable income and income tax payable.

Step 2—determine the change in deferred income tax.

Step 3—combine income tax payable with the change in deferred income tax to determine tax expense for the year.

After finishing these three steps, we can determine the current year disclosure and account balances. Note that this approach is often called the balance sheet approach, as it is driven by balance sheet accounts—income tax payable and deferred income tax. This three-step approach provides a robust calculation methodology that also provides proof of balance sheet accounts.

We'll look at a shortcut approach later in the chapter that can be used *only when tax rates have not changed*. However, in Canada, corporate tax rates (federal and provincial) tend to change rather frequently, usually downward, lately.

Step 1—Calculate Taxable Income and Income Tax Payable

To calculate taxable income, first adjust accounting income for temporary and permanent differences. Such differences are typically identified in the data, and have to be sorted into permanent and temporary differences, and those items that are added back versus subtracted. Start with accounting income, and identify the differences. If the item is:

- An expense now on the income statement, but is not tax deductible, it must be added back (e.g., amortization, fines).
- A revenue now on the income statement, but not taxable, it is subtracted (e.g., dividend revenue).
- An expense not on the income statement but allowable for tax purposes, it is subtracted (e.g., CCA).

- A revenue that is taxable but not on the income statement, it is added (e.g., collections of accounts receivable that are taxable this year but were income statement revenue in a prior year).

After calculating taxable income, multiply by the tax rate to obtain income tax payable.

Example The following facts pertain to accounting and taxable income for Mirage Limited in 20X1, Mirage's first year of operations: *very imp*

- Net income before taxes is $825,000; there are no discontinued operations.
- Net income includes dividends of $150,000 received from an investment in a taxable Canadian corporation that Mirage reports on the cost basis.
- In determining pre-tax accounting income, Mirage deducted the following expenses:
  - Golf club dues of $25,000;
  - Accrued estimated warranty expense of $150,000; and
  - Depreciation of $200,000 (Mirage owns capital assets of $1,600,000, which are being depreciated straight-line over eight years).
- For tax purposes, Mirage deducts the following expenses:
  - Actual warranty costs incurred of $100,000; and
  - Capital cost allowance (CCA) of $300,000.
- The 20X1 tax rate is 30%.

The intercorporate dividend is a permanent difference, because it is not taxable income. The golf club dues are also a permanent difference because this expense is not deductible for tax purposes. There are two types of temporary differences in this example: warranty costs and CCA/depreciation.

When accounting income is adjusted for permanent differences, the result is *accounting income subject to tax*. In this example, the result is $700,000. Temporary differences are then included, to yield taxable income. Multiplying by the tax rate gives tax payable, $195,000.

Pre-tax accounting income		$ 825,000
Permanent differences		
Intercorporate dividends		−150,000
Golf club dues		+ 25,000
Accounting income subject to tax		700,000
Temporary differences		
Warranty expenses accrued, not tax deductible	+150,000	
Warranty costs incurred, tax deductible	−100,000	+ 50,000
Depreciation, not tax deductible	+200,000	
Capital cost allowance (CCA), tax deductible	−300,000	−100,000
Taxable income		$ 650,000
Tax rate		× 30%
Income tax payable		$ 195,000

Exhibit 15-2 summarizes the calculation of taxable income for each of the three years of our example: 20X1, 20X2, and 20X3. Assume that in 20X1, Parliament legislated a reduction in tax rates for the following two years, to 28% for 20X2 and then to 27% for 20X3. The other data shown in the exhibit for 20X2 and 20X3 is assumed. Each column shows the adjustments for the two types of temporary differences: warranty costs and CCA/depreciation. Income tax payable is then calculated from taxable income.

EXHIBIT 15-2

MIRAGE LIMITED—CALCULATION OF TAXABLE INCOME

	20X1	20X2	20X3
Net income, before tax	$ 825,000	$ 900,000	$ 725,000
Permanent differences			
Intercorporate dividends	−150,000	−100,000	−125,000
Golf club dues	+ 25,000	0	0
Accounting income subject to tax	700,000	800,000	600,000
Timing differences			
Warranty expense	+150,000	+200,000	+160,000
Warranty claims paid	−100,000	−140,000	−230,000
Depreciation	+200,000	+200,000	+200,000
Capital cost allowance (CCA)	−300,000	−240,000	−180,000
Taxable income	$ 650,000	$ 820,000	$ 550,000
Enacted tax rate	30%	28%	27%
Income tax payable	$ 195,000	$ 229,600	$ 148,500

If the *taxes payable method* is used, analysis stops at this point. Tax expense is equal to tax payable, and no other financial statement elements are created.

Step 2—Determine the Change in Deferred Income Tax

The change in deferred income tax can be calculated in total for financial statement purposes. However, a total calculation is not quite adequate because individual types of temporary differences will reverse in different years. Thus, to determine the change in deferred income tax from year to year, we must calculate the required balance in deferred income tax for each source of temporary difference. We'll then compare this required closing balance to the existing balance, and get the adjustment needed.

To establish an appropriate format, we'll use a table for this calculation. The following example table has some data filled in for a hypothetical capital asset example, which we'll explain as we proceed. Assume that the enacted tax rates are 30% for Year 1 and 25% for Year 2:

	[1]	[2]	[3]	[4]	[5]	[6]
		− Accounting	= Year-end Temporary	× t = Deferred Tax Liability,	− Opening	
	Tax Basis	**Basis**	**Difference**	**Year-end Balance**	**Balance**	**= Adjustment**
Year 1 (30% tax rate)						
Capital asset	$172,000	$190,000	$(18,000)	$(5,400)	0	$(5,400)
Year 2 (25% tax rate)						
Capital asset	$136,000	$160,000	$(24,000)	$(6,000)	$(5,400)	$ (600)

Deferred income tax is caused when the carrying value (book value) of an asset or liability is different for tax versus accounting. This table records *tax carrying values* (column 1), *accounting carrying values* (column 2), takes the difference between them (column 3), multiplies this difference by the tax rate (column 4), compares that to the existing balance in the deferred income tax account (column 5), and calculates the difference as the needed adjustment (column 6). The year-end balance (column 7) is the opening balance (column 4) plus or minus the adjustment (column 6) for the year.

Looking at the table, column by column:

Column 1—If there were a set of books kept for tax purposes, this would be the balance in the capital assets account. In this example, a capital asset was bought for $200,000 at the beginning of Year 1, and $28,000 of CCA was charged for tax purposes in Year 1. CCA, of course, is the tax equivalent depreciation, so cost less accumulated CCA is $172,000. Looking vertically down this column, CCA was $36,000 in Year 2, bringing tax book value down to $136,000. These amounts are assets, so the numbers are not in brackets.

Column 2—This is the net book value of capital assets on the books of the company. This $200,000 asset had $10,000 of depreciation in Year 1 and $30,000 in Year 2. Net book value is therefore $190,000 in Year 1 and $160,000 in Year 2. Again, the amounts are assets, and are not in brackets.

Column 3—Column 3 is calculated by subtracting column 2 from column 1. Notice that the difference is negative, because column 2 is the larger number; the column 3 amount is in brackets because it is negative.

Column 4—Column 4 is calculated by multiplying column 3 by the enacted tax rate. This is $5,400 in Year 1 ($18,000 × 30%) and $6,000 in Year 2 ($24,000 × 25%). This is in brackets; it keeps its character as a negative number, which means it will be a credit on the balance sheet. Column 4 is important—it's the *closing balance sheet position* of deferred income tax, and thus reflects the correct balances for financial position.

Column 5—Column 5 is the opening balance in the deferred income tax account. In Year 1, it is zero, assuming that this is the first year of the temporary difference. In subsequent years, the opening balance is the closing balance of the prior year. That is, the $5,400 closing balance in Year 1 is the opening balance in Year 2. In our case, the Year 2 opening balance was a credit, and thus is in brackets.

Column 6—This is the adjustment column, and is the difference between the desired year-end balance (4) and the opening balance (5). It can be either a debit or a credit. In our example, the credit balance grows each time, so additional credits, in brackets, are needed. *These amounts are part of the journal entries prepared in step 3.*

Observe that the adjustment in Year 2 automatically captures the two factors that affect the year-end closing balance of the deferred tax amount—(1) the change in tax rate from 30% to 25%, applied to the beginning balance of the temporary difference, and (2) the $6,000 increase in the temporary difference times the current tax rate:

(1) $ (18,000) × −5% rate change	$ 900
(2) $ (6,000) × 25% tax rate for Year 2	(1,500)
	$ (600)

Separate calculation of the impact of these two factors is not necessary for each item, but IFRS does require disclosure of the impact of each year's two changes for deferred tax liability as a whole, as we will discuss later.

Naturally, this analysis can be done without the table format. However, the information is logically organized in the table, and we will use this presentation in this text. Most of the table columns are mechanical, with no great computational challenge. The problematic columns are the first two—determining the tax basis and accounting basis of temporary differences.

Determining the Accounting Basis Think about the common sources of temporary differences listed in the first column below, and identify the related SFP account that gives rise to each type of temporary difference:

Source of Temporary Difference	Related SFP Account
Depreciation and amortization	Net book value of capital assets, tangible and/or intangible
Inventory writedowns	Inventory
Fair value increases	Inventory
Revenue	Accounts receivable or deferred revenue
Warranty	Warranty liability
Bond discount and premium amortization	Net bond liability
Revaluation surplus	Capital assets

At this stage in your accounting studies, there should be little problem in establishing the accounting basis (or carrying value) of these types of accounts.

Determining the Tax Basis Determining the tax basis is not so obvious and needs some further analysis. We have already seen that for capital assets, the notional "tax balance sheet" would show cost less accumulated CCA charged. Cost less accumulated CCA is referred to as unclaimed capital cost, or UCC. As another example, assume that inventory is written down from cost of $400,000 to market value of $375,000 on the books. The accounting basis is $375,000, but the expense is not allowable for tax purposes and therefore the inventory has a tax basis of $400,000 until sold.

With respect to assets:

- For monetary assets (i.e., receivables), the tax basis of a taxable asset is its accounting carrying value less any amount *that will enter taxation in future periods.*
- For non-monetary assets, the tax basis is the tax-deductible amount less all amounts *already deducted* in determining taxable income of the current and prior periods.

With respect to liabilities:

- For monetary liabilities, the tax basis is the accounting carrying value less any amount *that will be deductible for income tax in future periods.*
- For non-monetary liabilities (e.g., unearned revenue), the tax basis is its carrying amounts less any amount that *will not be taxable in future periods.*

An important aspect of these definitions of tax basis is that they all relate to future impacts on taxable income. That is, the tax bases are determined with respect to both the past and future impacts on taxable income.

Application The following examples apply these rules:

- Company A has a non-strategic investment in the shares of Company Z. Company Z declares a dividend on 31 December 20X5, payable on 31 January 20X6 to shareholders of record on 15 January 20X6. Company A reports $15,000 dividend income in earnings for 20X5, but the dividend will be not be taxed until 20X6. The tax basis of the dividend receivable is zero: the carrying value of $15,000 less the amount that will be taxable in the future, which is the full $15,000.
- Company B has capital assets. The tax basis of this non-monetary asset is the tax-deductible amount, its full cost, less accumulated tax deductions to date, or accumulated CCA.
- Company C has a $45,000 warranty liability. The accounting liability is established because an expense is charged on the books, some of which is paid in the period, but $45,000 of which will be paid in the future. For tax purposes, warranty claims are deducted when paid—in the future. The tax basis is the accounting carrying value,

$45,000, less amounts that will be deducted in the future, the whole $45,000. Therefore, the tax basis is *zero*.

- Company D has a $75,000 unearned revenue account. The cash was received, and is taxable, in this period. It will be recognized on the income statement later, when earned. The tax basis is *zero*: the accounting carrying value of $75,000 less the amount already included in taxable income; it will therefore not be taxable again in the future.

You must carefully reason your way through these definitions, then do a reality check: *for balance sheet items other than capital assets, the tax basis is often zero.* If there is a non-zero tax basis for an account related to a temporary difference, check your logic carefully! A non-zero result is plausible but relatively rare other than for capital assets and asset writedowns.

Permanent Differences By definition, permanent differences do not create deferred income tax. However, there may be SFP accounts that relate to permanent differences (e.g., prepaid golf club dues). If this is the case, the tax basis is equal to the accounting basis.

For example, suppose that a company has been fined $2,000 for a building code infraction. The fine is not yet paid and the company carries it as a current liability. Fines are not deductible for income tax purposes. Therefore, the tax basis of the fine is $2,000.

Clearly, the fine is a permanent difference and will have no tax impact. The fine has already been included in accounting income, since it has been accrued. For a monetary liability, the rule is that the tax basis is the accounting value ($2,000) less the amount that will be deductible for tax purposes (zero) so the tax basis is $2,000.

Since the tax basis is equal to the accounting basis for permanent differences, deferred income taxes are always zero for these items, and we simply exclude them from the table.

The equation becomes more complicated when an asset is partially tax deductible. For example, certain intangible assets such as purchased goodwill and purchased subscription lists are classified as eligible capital property for tax purposes, and 75% of the cost is subject to CCA at a declining-balance rate of 7%. The other 25% of the cost is not tax-deductible and therefore is a permanent difference. The tax basis is determined separately for the two components that make up the accounting carrying value. The cost of these assets must be broken down, with 75% included in calculations of deferred income tax, and 25% excluded.

Example To illustrate the calculation of deferred income tax balances and adjustments, we will continue the Mirage Limited example.

At the end of 20X1, the tax bases and the accounting carrying values are as follows:

	Tax Basis dr. (cr.)	Carrying Value dr. (cr.)
Capital assets	$1,300,000	$1,400,000
Accrued warranty liability	0	(50,000)

The tax basis of the capital assets is the cost less accumulated CCA claimed: $1,600,000 − $300,000 = $1,300,000. Similarly, the carrying value of the capital assets is the cost less accumulated depreciation. Since 20X1 is the first year of operations and the year in which the assets were acquired, the carrying value is $1,600,000 − $200,000 = $1,400,000.

The carrying value of the warranty liability is the year-end balance in the accrual account: $150,000 − $100,000 = $50,000. The tax basis for a monetary liability is the accounting carrying value less the amounts that will be deducted for tax purposes in the future. Therefore, the tax basis of the warranty liability is $50,000 − $50,000 = $0.

These values are entered in the table in Exhibit 15-3, in columns 1 and 2. The difference between columns 1 and 2 is the temporary difference, shown in column 3. Columns 4 to 6 are completed by applying the 30% tax rate, entering the zero opening balances for this first year of operation, and then subtracting.

Return to Exhibit 15-2 and note the facts assumed for 20X2 and 20X3. In 20X2, Mirage Limited claims CCA of $240,000 and $140,000 in warranty costs on its tax return, while recognizing $200,000 in depreciation and $200,000 in accrued warranty expense on its income statement. Return to Exhibit 15-3 and note the tax and accounting bases. The carrying value of the capital assets declines to $1,200,000, while the tax basis declines by the amount of the 20X2 CCA, to $1,060,000. The difference is $140,000. At the 20X2 tax rate of 30%, the balance of the future tax liability relating to the CCA/depreciation temporary difference is $140,000 × 28% = $39,200 credit at 20X2 year-end.

For the warranty liability, the temporary difference is $110,000 at the end of 20X2. That is, the opening warranty liability on the books was $50,000. This is increased by 20X2 expense of $200,000, and decreased by payments of $140,000. The accounting liability is $110,000 at the end of 20X3. The tax basis is still zero. At 28%, the balance in the deferred income tax asset is $30,800. Opening balances are carried down from the closing balances of 20X1, totalled, and the required adjustment calculated.

We must calculate the ending deferred tax balance relating to *each type* of temporary difference because this information is needed for disclosure, as we will illustrate shortly. However, it is not necessary to calculate the *adjustment* for each type of temporary difference; only the total adjustment need be calculated.

The year 20X3 continues, with the data included in calculating taxable income from Exhibit 15-2. CCA was $180,000, reducing the tax basis to $880,000. Depreciation was $200,000, and the accounting basis is now $1,000,000. The warranty liability on the books began at $110,000. It was increased by warranty expense of $160,000, and reduced by claims paid of $230,000, to end the year at $40,000. The tax basis is zero, since claims will be deducted when paid. Arithmetically, the row is extended, noting the tax rate is now 27%.

It is important to remember at this point that the adjustment for each year is the result of two factors:

1. *The effect of the change in the tax rate on opening temporary differences.* For example, the 20X2 tax rate decreased by 2%. The total opening temporary difference was $50,000, and

EXHIBIT 15-3

MIRAGE LIMITED—DEFERRED INCOME TAX TABLE

	[1] Year-end Tax Basis dr. (cr.)	[2] Year-end Accounting Carrying Value dr. (cr.)	[3] = [1] − [2] Temporary Difference Deductible (Taxable)	[4] = [3] × t Deferred Tax Asset (Liability) at Year-end Rate	[5] = Previous Year Beginning Balance [4] dr. (cr.)	[6] = [4] − [5] Adjustment for Current Year dr. (cr.)
20X1—30%						
Capital assets	$1,300,000	$1,400,000	$(100,000)	$(30,000)	0	$(30,000)
Accrued warranty liability	0	(50,000)	50,000	15,000	0	15,000
Total	$1,300,000	$1,350,000	$ (50,000)	$(15,000)	0	$(15,000)
20X2—28%						
Capital assets	$1,060,000	$1,200,000	$(140,000)	$(39,200)	$(30,000)	$ (9,200)
Accrued warranty liability	0	(110,000)	110,000	30,800	15,000	15,800
Total	$1,060,000	$1,090,000	$ (30,000)	$ (8,400)	$(15,000)	$ 6,600
20X3—27%						
Capital assets	$ 880,000	$1,000,000	$(120,000)	$(32,400)	$(39,200)	$ 6,800
Accrued warranty liability	0	(40,000)	40,000	10,800	30,800	(20,000)
Total	$ 880,000	$ 960,000	$ (80,000)	$(21,600)	$ (8,400)	$(13,200)

cr to show liability

starts reversing

* Tip is cumulative & not individual year.

thus the decrease in the tax rate decreases deferred income tax liability by $1,000 (i.e., $50,000 × 2%).

2. *The effect of current-year temporary differences.* In 20X2, the total temporary difference was reduced from a liability of $50,000 to a liability of $30,000. The impact of this is to *reduce* deferred income tax liability by $5,600—that is, ($50,000 − $30,000) × 28%.

The $6,600 credit adjustment in the table is the result of both factors. Both amounts need to be disclosed in the notes, as we will demonstrate shortly.

What Tax Rate? In the table, the tax rate that must be used is the enacted tax rate for the expected year of reversal. In our example, all rates were enacted in the year to which they pertain, as is normal practice in Canada. Thus, the 20X1 rate is used to measure deferred income tax at the end of 20X1, and so on. However, if the 20X2 rate were enacted in 20X1, then the 20X2 enacted rate would be used to measure deferred income tax at the end of 20X1.

After all, deferred income tax is an asset or liability, and if the temporary differences will reverse and cause income tax when the rate is 28%, then this is the most reliable measure of the future cash flow. Our prior comments on tax rates still stand—a future tax rate must be enacted to be used. This is to enhance reliability.

Also note that in 20X1, even if the 20X2 tax rates were enacted, only the 20X1 rates can be used to determine income tax payable in Step 1. That's the whole meaning of the current-year tax rate—it dictates income tax payable!

Step 3—Combine Income Tax Payable with the Change in Deferred Income Tax to Determine Tax Expense for the Year

Our final step is to combine the calculation of tax payable with the change in the deferred income tax accounts to produce tax expense. This can be done in a schedule but is easily summarized in a journal entry, where there is:

1. A credit to tax payable, from step 1;

2. A debit or credit to deferred income tax asset/liability from step 2; and

3. A debit to tax expense, to balance.

Example Refer to the entries in Exhibit 15-4, based on the Mirage example. In each year, there is a credit to tax payable and a debit or credit to the deferred tax account, and tax expense is debited to balance the entry. The *balance* in the deferred income tax asset/liability account will be as follows in each year:

Year	Year-end Balance Asset/(Liability)
20X1	(15,000)
20X2	(8,400)
20X3	(21,600)

In this example, the balance is a credit in each year and thus a net liability will be shown as a long-term liability on the statement of financial position.

SFP ELEMENTS

Deferred Income Tax Liabilities

Deferred income tax liabilities are created when tax paid is less than accounting accrual-based income tax expense. This occurs when revenue is recognized on the books but is not taxable until a later period. An accounting asset, such as an account receivable, exists and its tax basis is zero. Deferred income tax liabilities are also created when tax expense deductions precede

---

EXHIBIT 15-4

MIRAGE LIMITED—INCOME TAX JOURNAL ENTRIES

Income tax journal entry, 20X1

Income tax expense	210,000	
Deferred income tax asset/liability		15,000
Income tax payable		195,000

Income tax journal entry, 20X2

Income tax expense	223,000	
Deferred income tax asset/liability	6,600	
Income tax payable		229,600

Income tax journal entry, 20X3

Income tax expense	161,700	
Deferred income tax asset/liability		13,200
Income tax payable		148,500

(handwritten margin notes: "refers to current tax", "refers to depreciation", "refers to warranty a/c")

---

accounting expense deductions. For example, a declining-balance CCA results in higher expense in early years than straight-line accounting depreciation expense. As a result, UCC (unclaimed capital cost) is less than net book value. Deferred income tax liabilities result.

Deferred Income Tax Assets

Deferred income tax assets are created when tax is effectively prepaid. That is, tax on revenue is paid before the revenue is reflected on the books. For example, unearned revenue might appear on the accounting books, but deposits may be taxable when received. Tax is therefore paid before revenue is recognized for accounting purposes. A future tax asset is also created when expenses are on the accounting income statement before they are tax deductible, as for accrued warranty liabilities and the related expenses.

Asset Recognition Limit There are special concerns when deferred income tax is a debit balance. As you know, assets must represent future economic benefits, and those benefits must be probable. Deferred income tax assets will be realized only when future years come to pass and those temporary differences reverse in taxable income. If the company is in financial distress, there may not be sufficient taxable income in future years to benefit from the deferred income tax assets—if there is no taxable income and thus no tax due, the company can't realize the benefit of lower taxes. Therefore, deferred income tax assets on the balance sheet can be recognized only to the extent that their realization is probable. *Probable* means a greater than 50% likelihood of the company generating enough taxable income to draw down the deferred tax asset. We will explore this issue in more depth in the next chapter.

Classification

On the face of the statement of financial position, income taxes currently receivable or payable must be shown separately. Current taxes cannot be combined with deferred income tax balances. Current income tax is a current item, while deferred income tax is always a long-term item under IFRS. The classification of deferred tax balances is not affected by the nature of the asset or liability that gave rise to the deferred tax (that is, current or non-current) and regardless of the time frame within which the temporary differences will reverse.

Netting The deferred income taxes relating to all assets and liabilities are lumped together and netted as a single amount *for the same taxable company and the same taxing government*.

Since consolidated financial statements include several taxable entities, consolidated statements often show both a deferred tax *asset* and a deferred tax *liability*. For example, the company might have a net deferred tax liability relating to the parent company, but a net deferred tax asset relating to a subsidiary.

Example Calgary-based energy company TransAlta Corporation operates through numerous subsidiaries and has revenues and assets in Canada, the United States, and Australia. The company reports in many different taxing jurisdictions. As a result of its multijurisdictional taxation, TransAlta shows two very substantial amounts for deferred income taxes in its 2009 SFP (in millions):

Deferred income tax assets	$221
Deferred income tax liabilities	$694

TransAlta's total assets at 31 December 2009 were $9,762 million; net assets were $2,929 million. The deferred tax liability equals 7% of total assets and 24% of net assets—not an insignificant amount!

CONCEPT REVIEW

1. What condition is necessary before a company can report a net deferred tax debit as an asset on its SFP?

2. A corporation has two types of temporary differences. One type of temporary difference gives rise to a deferred tax liability, while the other gives rise to a deferred tax asset. Under what circumstances would the asset and liability be shown separately on the balance sheet?

DISCLOSURE

General Recommendations

The general recommendations for disclosure of the components of the provision for income tax expense are as follows:

- The amount of income tax expense (or benefit) on earnings from continuing operations must be reported separately in the income statement; income tax expense should not be combined with other items of expense.
- The amount of income tax expense that is attributable to (1) current income taxes and (2) deferred income taxes should be disclosed, either on the face of the statement or in the notes.
- Discontinued operations and each component of OCI are reported net of income tax, but the amounts of income tax expense that relate to each item should be disclosed. Also, any income taxes relating to capital transactions should be disclosed.
- The change in deferred income taxes due to (1) changes in temporary differences and (2) tax rate changes (or imposition of new taxes) should be disclosed in the notes.

Example These disclosure standards, applied to the Mirage example, would result in the following disclosure on the income statement:

	20X1	20X2	20X3
Income before income tax	$825,000	$900,000	$725,000
Income tax expense:			
Current	195,000	229,600	148,500
Deferred	15,000	(6,600)	13,200
	210,000	223,000	161,700
Net income	$615,000	$677,000	$563,300

This disclosure breaks income tax expense down into the portion that is paid during the year, and the portion that relates to deferred income tax. This breakdown could also be shown in the disclosure notes.

In the notes, Mirage would break down the annual change in the deferred tax liability into the amounts caused by (1) tax rate changes and (2) changes in temporary differences:

	20X1	20X2	20X3
Increase (decrease) in deferred tax liability due to:			
Change in income tax rate applied to opening balance*	—	$(1,000)*	$ (300)**
Change in temporary differences	$15,000	(5,600)†	13,500††
Total change	$15,000	$(6,600)	$13,200

*$50,000 opening balance × 2% rate decrease = $(1,000)
**$30,000 opening balance × 1% rate decrease = $(300)
†$20,000 decrease in temporary differences × 28% = $(5,600)
††$50,000 increase in temporary differences × 27% = $13,500

Sources of Temporary Differences Publicly-accountable enterprises also are required to disclose the types of temporary differences. For *each type*, an entity should disclose the amount of deferred tax recognized in the deferred tax balance on the SFP. Obviously, materiality becomes an issue. Some companies have many different kinds of temporary differences. Some of these are substantial while others may be quite small. Usually, the smaller ones are combined into an "other" category rather than actually disclosing the detail for every single type.

Exhibit 15-5 presents the disclosure given by Canadian National Railway Company. CNR groups its temporary differences by asset versus liabilities. The company had four types that led collectively to deferred tax assets of $328 million in 2008, and two types that amounted

---

EXHIBIT 15-5

CANADIAN NATIONAL RAILWAY COMPANY— DISCLOSURE OF TEMPORARY DIFFERENCES

December 31 (in millions)	2008	2007
Deferred Income Tax Assets		
Workforce reduction provisions	$ 16	$ 22
Personal injury claims and other reserves	177	146
Post-retirement benefits	87	85
Losses and tax credit carryforwards	48	24
	328	277
Deferred Income Tax Liabilities		
Net pension asset	352	429
Properties and other	5,389	4,688
	5,741	5,117
Total net deferred income tax liability	$5,413	$4,840

Source: www.sedar.com, Canadian National Railway Company, ("CN"), Audited Financial Statements, February 5, 2009, reproduced by authorization of CN.

to a deferred tax liability of $5,741 million. Netting the assets against the liabilities yields a net liability position of $5,413 million. CNR can net the assets against the liabilities because they pertain to the same tax jurisdictions.

By far, the largest item is "properties and other." This is due to the CCA-depreciation difference, and is typical of companies that have a high level of tangible capital property, such as the Suncor example cited at the beginning of the chapter. In CNR's case, the accumulated deferred income tax due to the CCA-depreciation difference amounts to 23% of the "properties" reported on CNR's balance sheet. Near the end of this chapter, we will discuss a possible interpretation of this amount.

Reconciliation of Effective Tax Rates   The tax status of the corporation may not be obvious to the financial statement users. The reason is that the income tax expense (including both current and deferred taxes) reported by the company on its financial statements may appear to bear little resemblance to the expected level of taxes under the prevailing statutory tax rate. There is no way for an individual investor or creditor to know what factors caused the variation in the apparent tax rate for a public company.

Therefore, IFRS requires company to provide a reconciliation between the statutory tax rate and the company's effective tax. The reconciliation can be either in percentages or in dollar terms.

As we have already seen, there are two general categories of causes for variations in the rate of tax:

1. Permanent differences, which cause items of income and/or expense to be reported in accounting income that are not included in taxable income, and

2. Differences in tax rates, due to
   a. Different tax rates in different tax jurisdictions;
   b. Special taxes levied (and tax reductions permitted) by the taxation authorities; or
   c. Changes in tax rates relating to temporary differences that will reverse in future periods.

Temporary differences themselves are *not* a cause of effective tax *rate* variations. The "effective tax rate" is based on income tax expense, and not on the amount of taxes a company actually paid. Therefore, deferred income tax expense is included in the apparent effective tax rate.

Exhibit 15-6 shows an example of the tax rate reconciliation for Power Corporation of Canada. This company provides its reconciliation in percentages. The 2008 reconciliation begins by showing that the statutory rate that Power normally would be expected to pay is

---

EXHIBIT 15-6

POWER CORPORATION OF CANADA EFFECTIVE TAX RATE DISCLOSURE

The following table reconciles the statutory and effective tax rates·

	2008	2007
Combined basic federal and provincial tax rates	32.4%	34.8%
Increase (decrease) in the income tax rate resulting from:		
Non-taxable investment income	(10.7)	(4.1)
Lower effective tax rates on income not subject to tax in Canada	(16.1)	(3.9)
Earnings of investments at equity	4.7	(1.3)
Miscellaneous	(7.5)	(1.6)
Effective income tax rate	2.8%	23.9%

Source: http://www.sedar.com, Power Corporation of Canada, Audited Annual Financial Statements, March 11, 2009.

32.4%. However, the effective rate was sharply reduced by the fact that net income included non-taxable investment income and earnings not subject to tax in Canada—both are permanent differences. These permanent differences appear to reduce Power's effective tax rate to only 2.8%.

However, Power Corporation discloses that the effective tax rate of 2.8% would be 24.5%, excluding impairment charges relating to goodwill and intangible assets of $2,178 million. In other words, the impairment charges were recognized for accounting purposes but not yet deductible for income tax. This fact brings us to the next section—just what is meant by the "effective tax rate"?

Accountant's versus Analyst's Concepts of Effective Tax Rate   The definition of effective tax rate prescribed by accounting standards (e.g., 2.8% in Power Corporation's disclosure) includes deferred income tax. On the other hand, financial analysts usually view the effective tax rate as the amount of current taxes divided by pre-tax earnings, which is quite different from effective tax rate as defined by accounting standards.

For example, Power Corporation had 2008 pre-tax earnings from continuing operations of $1,347 million. Income tax expense was $38 million, composed of the following (in millions):

Current income taxes	$686
Deferred income taxes	(648)
Income tax expense	$ 38

Under accounting standards, the effective tax rate is 2.8%, calculated as $38 \div \$1,347 = 2.8\%$. In contrast, financial analysts would ignore the deferred income taxes and focus on the amount actually due to the government for the year, calculated as follows:

$$\$686 \div \$1,347 = 50.9\%$$

That's quite a difference! Financial analysts (and banks) are interested in what the company has to pay in cash, not what they might have to pay sometime in the future when the temporary differences all reverse (if ever). Comprehensive interperiod tax allocation is good at achieving matching, but not so good at measuring the effect of income taxes on liquidity. That is why accounting standards insist that the income tax expense be disaggregated and that both current and deferred taxes be disclosed.

SHORTCUT APPROACH IF RATES HAVE NOT CHANGED

In some cases, a shorter computational approach may be used to account for income tax. This approach should be used *only if the income tax rate has not changed from the prior year*—if there is a change in tax rates, this simplified approach may give you the wrong answer. However, if the facts support the shortcut, it will save time.

The steps are as follows:

Step 1—Calculate taxable income and income tax payable.

Step 2—Determine the change in deferred income tax through a direct calculation.

Step 3—Combine income tax payable with the change in deferred income tax to determine tax expense for the year.

Only Step 2 has changed. A table such as that shown in Exhibit 15-3 need not be prepared; all that is needed is a direct calculation of the change in deferred income tax balances. Remember that the adjustment that flows from the table has two components—a change to opening deferred income tax balances because of the tax rate change, and the current year increase. If the tax rate has not changed, there is no adjustment of opening deferred income tax balances, and the current-year increase is all that is needed. The balance in deferred income tax can be tracked with a simple T-account.

In Step 2, to determine the change in deferred income tax for the year, the calculation is:

> Change in deferred income tax = the temporary difference during the year (accounting revenue or expense less the tax revenue or expense) × tax rate.

To illustrate the shortcut method, we will calculate the tax amounts for KelCo. Facts are as follows:

	20X2	20X3	20X4
Income before income tax	$242,000	$934,000	$1,361,000
Depreciation	230,000	230,000	230,000
CCA	287,000	197,000	312,000
Tax-free dividend revenue	—	75,000	—
Non-tax-deductible expenses	32,000	—	—
Tax rate	25%	25%	25%

The first step in the solution is to calculate taxable income and income tax payable for each year:

	20X2	20X3	20X4
Accounting income	$242,000	$934,000	$1,361,000
Permanent differences			
Dividend revenue	—	(75,000)	—
Non-deductible expenses	32,000	—	—
Temporary differences			
Depreciation	230,000	230,000	230,000
CCA	(287,000)	(197,000)	(312,000)
Taxable income	217,000	892,000	1,279,000
Tax rate	25%	25%	25%
Income tax payable	$ 54,250	$223,000	$ 319,750

The second step is to determine the change in deferred income tax each year. There is only one source of deferred income tax, the depreciation/CCA on capital assets. In 20X2, CCA is $57,000 ($287,000 − $230,000) larger than depreciation. This translates into a $14,250 (i.e., $57,000 × 25%) increase (credit) in a deferred income tax liability. Since this is the first year, the balance in deferred income tax is also $14,250.

In 20X3, depreciation is larger than CCA by $33,000 (i.e., $230,000 − $197,000). This will reduce the credit balance in the liability by $13,200: ($33,000 × 25%). The balance in deferred income tax liability is now $6,000: ($14,250 − $8,250). This $6,000 balance can be verified as being the cumulative temporary differences multiplied by the tax rate. In this example, we have total depreciation over the two years of $460,000, versus $484,000 of CCA, for a $24,000 cumulative difference, multiplied by the tax rate of 25% to again give $6,000.

In 20X4, CCA is larger than depreciation, this time by $82,000: ($312,000 − $230,000). This will increase the deferred income tax liability by $20,500: ($82,000 × 25%). The balance in deferred income tax liability is now $26,500: ($6,000 + $20,500). This can also be verified as $796,000 of cumulative CCA minus $690,000 of cumulative depreciation = $106,000 × 25% = $42,400.

The last step is to prepare the tax entries, which determine the tax expense for the year:

20X2

Income tax expense	68,500	
Deferred income tax ($287,000 − $230,000) × 25%		14,250
Income tax payable		54,250

20X3

Income tax expense	214,750	
Deferred income tax ($230,000 − $197,000) × 25%		8,250
Income tax payable		223,000

20X4

Income tax expense	340,250	
Deferred income tax ($312,000 − $230,000) × 25%		20,500
Income tax payable		319,750

With this information, appropriate financial statement disclosure may be prepared.

Evaluation This method is far simpler. Remember, though, that it is to be used *only when the tax rate does not change*—and, in the Canadian business world, changing tax rates are a fact of life.

Actually, it is possible to use the shortcut method if the tax rate changes by also preparing a separate calculation of the effect of the tax rate change on opening deferred income tax. However, the possibility for error starts to become high, and the table approach is far more reliable. The other significant advantage of the table approach is that the deferred income tax account is proven each year, with the difference between tax and accounting basis backing up the integrity of this account. It is important to have such proof for all financial statement elements.

STATEMENT OF CASH FLOWS

The impact of income tax accounting on the statement of cash flows is clear: all tax allocation amounts must be reversed out of transactions reported on the statement of cash flows. The statement of cash flows must include only the actual taxes paid. When a company uses the direct method of presenting cash flow from operations, the amount of tax paid (recovered) during the year is a deduction (addition).

When the indirect method of presentation is used for operating cash flow, the deferred tax liability (and/or asset) that has been charged (or credited) to earnings must be added back to (or subtracted from) net income. That is, the change in deferred income tax is an add-back or deduction in operating activities. The change in income tax payable is another adjustment in operating activities.

IFRS requires a company to disclose the amount of income taxes paid on the face of the statement of cash flows. The indirect approach described above does not accomplish this result, because only the deferred tax add-back is displayed on the face of the statement. Therefore, companies that use the indirect approach take one of two approaches:

1. The reconciliation starts with earnings before taxes, so that the amount of taxes paid (recovered) is disclosed directly as a disbursement (receipt) of cash; or

2. The cash amount of taxes paid (received) is simply presented at the bottom of the statement, following the final reconciliation of the cash balance.

Either approach is satisfactory.

CONCEPT REVIEW

1. What breakdown of tax expense must be provided?
2. What is the purpose of the reconciliation of the effective tax rate?
3. What amounts relating to income tax should appear in the operating activities section of the statement of cash flows?

IS DEFERRED INCOME TAX A LIABILITY?

It is possible to raise many questions about the validity of the deferred income tax concept. Deferred income tax is an allocation of an amount that arises largely from other allocations. It seems firmly grounded on the income statement concepts of revenue-expense recognition and matching, even though the FASB and IASB have strained mightily to justify income tax allocation under the asset-liability definitional approach. Even the name of basic concept, income tax *allocation*, is derived from an income statement approach rather than a balance sheet approach.

The most important question, however, is the validity of viewing deferred income tax credits as a true liability when they arise as the result of major recurring temporary differences. We observed earlier in this chapter that the major single cause of temporary differences is the difference between two other allocations: depreciation for accounting versus CCA for tax. In aggregate, these temporary differences will not reverse as long as the company continues to invest in replacing its physical assets.

One important aspect of the liability definition is that *a liability represents an existing obligation*. But to whom is this obligation owed? Supporters of tax allocation argue that deferred income tax is similar to a warranty liability—the obligation is real even though the specific parties to whom the liability will be fulfilled cannot be specifically identified. It is true that a warranty requires a cash outflow to as-yet-unknown parties. However, any income tax liability must be owed to specific known government jurisdictions. The other party is known precisely, but there is no current obligation for future taxes. The government does not consider the amount that we show as deferred income tax liabilities to be owing.

The reality of having to pay out cash in the future as recurring temporary differences (e.g., depreciation-CCA differences) are reversed depends on the joint occurrence of two conditions:

1. The asset basis of the temporary differences (i.e., the capital assets being depreciated) must shrink before there can be a net reversal, precipitating an actual cash outflow; and

2. The company must be earning taxable income while the net reversals are occurring.

While it is *possible* for these two conditions to co-exist, co-existence is unlikely. Asset bases contract when old assets are not being replaced, and that usually happens when the company is in decline. If a company is in decline it is unlikely to be generating taxable income.

Accounting standards call for recognizing a contingent liability when a cash flow *probably* will be realized. It can be argued that, at best, deferred income tax liabilities relating to recurring temporary differences should be disclosed as a contingent liability because the conditions necessary to precipitate a cash flow are not likely to occur—the liability is neither likely to occur, nor is the amount of future cash flow measurable.

ACCOUNTING STANDARDS FOR PRIVATE ENTERPRISES

Accounting Method Private enterprises may elect to use either the *taxes payable method* of accounting for income taxes or *comprehensive allocation.*

Under the taxes payable method, income tax expense is simply the amount of current income tax paid (or payable) to the government. There is no interperiod allocation of income taxes, and there are no deferred income tax amounts reported on the balance sheet.

Intraperiod allocation is still applied, however. Income tax expense must be allocated to:

- Earnings from continuing operations;
- Discontinued operations;
- Gains and losses recorded directly in retained earnings; and
- Gains and losses recorded directly in share capital.

The choice of accounting for income taxes is an all-or-nothing affair. A company cannot decide to use deferred income tax accounting for some types of temporary differences while using the taxes payable basis for other types.

Terminology The *CICA Handbook*, Part II uses the term *future* income tax instead of *deferred* income tax. This is a carryover from the pre-2011 Canadian standard, which also is consistent with the terminology used by the FASB in the United States. However, there is no *requirement* to use that particular terminology—the two terms are used interchangeably. Many companies use "deferred" instead of "future."

Classification The Canadian standard requires companies to classify deferred/future income tax liabilities and assets as either current or long-term. This is in contrast to the IFRS (which prohibits a "current" classification for any deferred tax amounts), but is consistent with U.S. standards.

Deferred tax amounts are classified as current or non-current on the basis of the assets or liabilities that generated the temporary differences. For example, in the Mirage example used in this chapter, the deferred tax relating to the warranty temporary difference would be classified as current because the deferred tax relates to a current liability. Similarly, deferred taxes relating to inventory will be classified as current. The expected period of time before the temporary difference reverses is irrelevant for the current–non-current classification.

Disclosure There is less disclosure required for private enterprises. In the accounting policies note, a company should disclose the fact that it is using the taxes payable method. The *CICA Handbook*, Part II also recommends disclosure of the company's significant tax policies, such as revenue recognition methods, applicable CCA rates, deductibility of pension costs, and deduction policy for costs that may be capitalized for accounting purposes.

In addition, the company should reconcile its income tax expense to the average statutory income tax rate. This disclosure is similar to that described above for public companies, but with the important exception that the impact of temporary differences is not included in the reconciliation. The reconciliation would include items such as:

- Large corporations' tax;
- Non-deductible expenses;
- Non-taxable gains, including the non-taxable portion of capital gains; and
- The amount of deductible temporary differences for which a future tax asset has not been recorded.

RELEVANT STANDARDS

IASB:
- *IAS* 12, Income Taxes

CICA Handbook, Part II:
- Section 3465, Income Taxes

SUMMARY OF KEY POINTS

1. The amount of taxable income often differs from the amount of pre-tax net income reported for accounting purposes.

2. The difference between taxable income and accounting income arises from two types of sources: *permanent* differences and *temporary* differences.

3. Permanent differences are items of revenue, expense, gains, or losses that are reported for accounting purposes but never enter into the computation of taxable income. Permanent differences also include those rare items that enter into taxable income but are never included in accounting income.

4. Temporary differences arise when the tax basis of an asset or liability is different from its carrying value (i.e., its accounting basis) in the financial statements.

5. The objective of *comprehensive interperiod income tax allocation* is to recognize the income tax effect of every item when that item is recognized in accounting net income. The alternative to comprehensive allocation is the *taxes payable method*, which also is known as the *flow-through method* because the taxes paid "flow through" to the income statement.

6. When the item of revenue, expense, gain, or loss first enters the calculation of *either* taxable income or accounting income, it is an *originating* temporary difference.

7. A temporary difference *reverses* when it is recognized in the other measure of income. For example, if an item is recognized first for tax purposes and later for accounting purposes, the temporary difference originates when the item is included in the tax calculation and reverses when the item is recognized for accounting.

8. Under the liability method of tax allocation, the tax effect is recorded at the currently enacted rate that will apply in the period that the temporary difference is expected to reverse. The current rate is used if no future years' tax rates are enacted.

9. Under the liability method, the balance of deferred income tax assets and liabilities must be adjusted to reflect changes in the tax rate as they are enacted. Deferred income taxes are not discounted.

10. Accounting for income tax involves calculating tax payable, calculating the change in the deferred income tax accounts, and then combining all elements to determine tax expense. Deferred income tax is calculated as the difference between the tax basis and the accounting carrying value of related balance sheet accounts, multiplied by the enacted tax rate.

11. Deferred income tax assets and liabilities are classified as non-current assets or liabilities. Deferred income tax balances relating the same taxing jurisdiction and the same taxable entity are netted and reported as a single amount. Deferred taxes relating to different taxing jurisdictions cannot be offset against each other.

12. A reporting enterprise must explain in a note the difference between its effective tax rate and the statutory rate. In this context, the effective tax rate is the income tax expense (including deferred taxes) divided by the pre-tax net income. Entities must also disclose the sources of temporary differences.

13. The statement of cash flows must disclose the amounts of taxes actually paid or received for the year as part of cash flow from operations.

14. Private enterprises may choose to use the taxes payable method for income tax, in which case no deferred income tax is recorded, and tax expense equals tax paid.

KEY TERMS

accrual method, 878
comprehensive tax allocation, 876
deferral method, 878
flow-through method, 875
interperiod tax allocation, 872

liability method, 878
permanent difference, 872
provision for income tax, 872
taxes payable method, 875
temporary difference, 873

REVIEW PROBLEM

The following information pertains to Suda Corporation at the end of 20X1:

	Tax Basis	Accounting Basis
Equipment	$400,000 UCC	$500,000
Capitalized development costs	0	$200,000

At the end of 20X1, Suda had a balance in its deferred income tax liability account of $105,000, pertaining to both the amounts above. That is, there is $35,000 related to equipment and $70,000 to the capitalized development costs. The enacted income tax rate (combined federal and provincial) at the end of 20X1 was 35%.

The following information pertains to the next three years:

	20X2	20X3	20X4
Net income (including amortization)	$200,000	$160,000	$100,000
New equipment acquired	—	100,000	—
Depreciation expense on equipment	65,000	70,000	75,000
CCA claimed	80,000	74,000	69,000
Amortization of development costs	40,000	50,000	45,000
Development costs incurred (deductible for tax purposes)	50,000	30,000	70,000
Income tax rate (enacted in each year)	35%	38%	38%

Required:

For each of 20X2, 20X3 and 20X4, calculate:

1. The income tax expense that would appear on Suda's income statement.

2. The balance of the deferred income tax liability or asset account(s) that would appear on Suda's balance sheet.

REVIEW PROBLEM—SOLUTION

Calculation of taxable income and tax payable:

	20X2	20X3	20X4
Net income	$200,000	$160,000	$100,000
Plus depreciation on equipment	65,000	70,000	75,000
Less CCA	(80,000)	(74,000)	(69,000)
Plus amortization of development costs	40,000	50,000	45,000
Less development costs incurred	(50,000)	(30,000)	(70,000)
Taxable income	$175,000	$176,000	$ 81,000
Tax rate	35%	38%	38%
Tax payable	$ 61,250	$ 66,880	$ 30,780

Calculation of tax basis and carrying value:

	Equipment		Development Costs	
	Tax Basis	Carrying Value	Tax Basis	Carrying Value
20X1 ending balances	$400,000	$500,000	0	$200,000
Additions	—	—		+ 50,000
CCA & depreciation/ amortization	(80,000)	(65,000)		(40,000)
20X2 ending balances	320,000	435,000	0	210,000
Additions	100,000	+100,000		+ 30,000
Depreciation/amortization	(74,000)	(70,000)		(50,000)
20X3 ending balances	346,000	465,000	0	190,000
Additions				+ 70,000
Depreciation/amortization	(69,000)	(75,000)		(45,000)
20X4 ending balances	$277,000	$390,000	0	$215,000

Calculation of changes in deferred income tax liability:

	Year-end Tax Basis dr. (cr.)	Carrying Value dr. (cr.)	Temporary Difference Deductible (taxable)	Deferred Tax Asset (Liability) at Yr.-end Rate	Less Beginning Balance dr. (cr.)	Adjustment for Current Year dr. (cr.)
20X2—35%						
Equipment	320,000	435,000	(115,000)	(40,250)		
Development costs	0	210,000	(210,000)	(73,500)		
				(113,750)	(105,000)	(8,750)
20X3—38%						
Equipment	346,000	465,000	(119,000)	(45,220)		
Development costs	0	190,000	(190,000)	(72,200)		
				(117,420)	(113,750)	(3,670)
20X4—38%						
Equipment	277,000	390,000	(113,000)	(42,940)		
Development costs	0	215,000	(215,000)	(81,700)		
				(124,640)	(117,420)	(7,220)

Tax entries:

20X2

Tax expense	70,000	
Tax payable		61,250
Deferred income tax		8,750

20X3

Tax expense	70,550	
Deferred income tax—equipment		3,670
Tax payable		66,880

20X4

Tax expense	38,000	
Deferred income tax—development costs		7,220
Tax payable		30,780

1. *Income tax expense*

	20X2	20X3	20X4
Current	$61,250	$66,880	$30,780
Deferred	8,750	3,670	7,220
Income tax expense	$70,000	$70,550	$38,000

2. *Deferred income tax liability balance*
   Per table, column [4] above. Each year's balance will be reported as a single long-term credit amount, as follows:

20X2	$113,750
20X3	$117,420
20X4	$124,640

APPENDIX

THE INVESTMENT TAX CREDIT

General Nature

A **tax credit** is a direct, dollar-for-dollar offset against income taxes that otherwise are payable. The advantage of a tax *credit* (instead of a tax *deduction* for the expenditures) is that the amount of the tax credit is not affected by the tax rate being paid by the corporation. For example, if a $100,000 expenditure qualifies for a 7% tax credit, the tax reduction will be $7,000 regardless of whether the corporation is paying taxes at 20%, 30%, 40%, or any other rate.[3]

The Canadian *Income Tax Act* provides for **investment tax credits** (**ITC**) for (1) qualifying research and experimental development expenditures and (2) specified types of expenditures for capital investment. The expenditures that qualify for the investment tax credit are matters of government policy and change from time to time. By giving a tax credit, the government can influence companies to increase investments in certain types of facilities and in selected geographic areas by effectively reducing their cost. Qualifying expenditures can vary on three dimensions:

1. Type of expenditure;

2. Type of corporation; and

3. Geographic region.

To realize the benefit of a tax credit, it usually is necessary for the qualifying corporation to have taxable income and to generate income tax payable. If there is not sufficient tax payable in the year of the qualifying expenditures, the tax credit can be carried back three years and forward 20 years. Certain types of corporations may be eligible to receive the credit in cash, even if there is not enough tax due within the current and carryback periods to completely utilize the tax credit.

ACCOUNTING TREATMENT

In theory, there are two possible approaches to accounting for the investment tax credit (ITC):

1. The *flow-through approach*, whereby the ITC for which the corporation qualifies is reported as a direct reduction in the income tax expense for the year; or

2. The *cost-reduction approach*, in which the ITC is deducted from the expenditures that give rise to the ITC; the benefit of the ITC is thereby allocated to the years in which the expenditures are recognized as expenses.

International standards do not specifically discuss investment tax credits. However, *IAS* 20 does address the more general topic of government assistance, and tax credits clearly are a form of government assistance.

IAS 20 prescribes the **cost reduction approach**. The two categories of "cost" are:

• Costs recorded as expenses in the current period; and

• Costs that are recorded as assets.

The general approach for government grants, including ITCs, is to recognize them in profit or loss over the same periods in which the company recognizes the related costs as expenses. The following sections describe the accounting treatment for each type of cost.

COSTS REPORTED AS CURRENT EXPENSES

The government often grants ITC for research and development expenditures. Some of those expenditures will not qualify for capitalization as development costs and will be charged to expense in the period in which they are incurred.

Investment tax credits that relate to expenditures that are reported as expenses in the income statement are permitted to flow through to the income statement.

---

[3] Depending on the type of capital expenditure and the location of the enterprise, the investment tax credit may range from 7% to 35%.

The ITC on current expenses may be reported in either of two ways:

1. As an item of "other income" in the profit and loss section of the statement of comprehensive income; or

2. As a reduction of (or offset against) the expense that gave rise to the ITC.

The second method may seem more consistent with the cost-reduction approach, but it is contrary to the general principle that revenues and expenses should not be shown net of taxes. Both treatments are acceptable under international standards.

Since the ITC will reduce the effective tax rate being paid by the corporation, a publicly-accountable enterprise will treat the ITC as a tax rate reduction and will include it in its tax rate reconciliation.

COSTS CAPITALIZED

If the ITC qualifying expenditures are for a capital asset or are for development costs that can be capitalized and amortized, then the ITC itself is deferred and amortized on the same basis as the asset. This can be accomplished either by reducing the capitalized cost of the asset or by separately deferring and amortizing the ITC:

EXHIBIT 15A-1

RECORDING THE INVESTMENT TAX CREDIT

Illustrative Data

1 *May 20X5*
   Purchased eligible transportation equipment (30% CCA rate) costing $100,000, to be depreciated straight-line over 10 years, no residual value, with a half-year's depreciation in the year of acquisition for both accounting and tax purposes.

31 *December 20X5*
   Pre-tax income (after depreciation on new equipment), $150,000. Investment tax credit ($100,000 × 7%; not included in previous amounts), $7,000. The tax rate is 30%.

Entries for 20X5

a. *1 May—purchase qualified equipment*

Equipment	100,000	
Cash		100,000

b. *31 December—record ITC*

Income tax payable	7,000	
Deferred investment tax credit		7,000

c. *31 December—record depreciation expense*

Depreciation expense ($100,000 × 1/10 × 1/2)	5,000	
Accumulated depreciation		5,000

d. *31 December—record amortization of investment tax credit for 20X5*

Deferred investment tax credit ($7,000 × 1/10 × ½)	350	
Amortization expense		350

e. *31 December—record income tax on 20X5 earnings**

Income tax expense ($150,000 × 30%)	45,000	
Deferred income tax liability		
($13,950 − $4,650) × 30%		2,790
Income tax payable		42,210

*See Exhibit 15A-2 for the calculation of these amounts.

Investment tax credits related to the acquisition of assets would be either:

1. Deducted from the related assets with any amortization calculated on the net amount; or

2. Deferred and amortized to income on the same basis as the related assets.

The first option is to deduct the deferred ITC from the balance of the asset. The second approach is to recognize the ITC as *deferred income* on the balance sheet and then to amortize it along with the asset itself. The second approach seems more consistent with the cost-reduction theory than the first, but either may be used in practice.

EXHIBIT 15A-2

REPORTING THE INVESTMENT TAX CREDIT

Calculation of Income Tax Expense

Tax and accounting cost of asset:	
Capital cost of equipment	$100,000
Less: investment tax credit of 7%	7,000
Net capital cost	$ 93,000
Accounting income	$150,000
Depreciation	
[($100,000 × 1/10 × 1/2 year) − ($7,000 × 1/10 × 1/2)]	+ 4,650
CCA ($93,000 × 30% × 1/2 year*)	− 13,950
Taxable income	$140,700
Tax rate	× 30%
Current tax due before ITC	$ 42,210
Less investment tax credit ($100,000 × 7%)	7,000
Income tax payable	$ 35,210
Current income tax	$ 42,210
Deferred income tax liability [($13,950 − $4,650) × 30%]	2,790
Income tax expense	$ 45,000

*Assuming that only a half-year's deduction for CCA is claimable in the first year, as is usual.

Income Statement Reporting, Year ended 31 December 20X5

Depreciation expense ($5,000 − $350 amortization of ITC)		$ 4,650
Pre-tax income		$150,000
Income tax expense—current (from above)	$42,210	
—deferred (from above)	2,790	45,000
Net income		$ 90,000

Balance Sheet Reporting, 31 December 20X5

Equipment (at cost)		$100,000
Accumulated depreciation	$ 5,000	
Deferred investment tax credit ($7,000 − $350)	6,650	11,650
Reported carrying value		$ 88,350
Income tax payable (from above)		$ 35,210
Deferred income tax liability (from above)		$ 2,790

For income tax purposes, the ITC is deducted from the tax basis of the asset.[4] The effect is as follows:

- For expenditures that are capitalized for accounting purposes but are deducted immediately for tax purposes (e.g., development costs), a temporary difference is created because the cost (net of ITC) is being deducted immediately but is charged to income via amortization over several years; and

- For capital assets, the tax basis and the accounting basis start out the same (i.e., both reduced by the amount of the ITC benefit), but temporary differences arise from any differences between CCA and depreciation.

Exhibits 15A-1 and 15A-2 demonstrate the relevant accounting procedures. Exhibit 15A-1 contains the basic data and illustrates the journal entries used to record the qualifying expenditure and the ITC. Exhibit 15A-2 shows the impacts on the financial statements. The exhibits assume that the deferred ITC is deducted from the asset on the balance sheet.

DISCLOSURE OF ITC AND OTHER GOVERNMENT GRANTS

ITCs (and other types of government assistance) affect both the income/expense structure of the entity's operations and its cash flows. Therefore, the notes should disclose:

- The accounting policy and the method of presentation in the financial statements;
- The nature and extent of ITCs (and any government grants); and
- Any unfulfilled conditions or contingencies.

RELEVANT STANDARDS

IASB:
- IAS 20, *Accounting for Government Grants and Disclosure of Government Assistance*

CICA Handbook, Part II:
- Section 3805, *Investment Tax Credits*

SUMMARY OF KEY POINTS

1. The investment tax credit (ITC) is a direct reduction of income taxes that is granted to enterprises that invest in certain types of assets or in research and development costs.

2. There are two possible approaches to accounting for ITCs: (1) the flow-through approach and (2) the cost reduction approach.

3. IFRS recommends using the cost reduction approach, wherein the ITC is deducted (either directly or indirectly) from the asset or expense that gave rise to the ITC.

4. ITCs on expenditures that are reported as current expenses can be shown as an item of "other income" or deducted from the investment expense.

5. When qualifying expenditures are made to acquire an asset (including capitalized development costs), the ITC can either be (1) deducted from the asset's carrying value,

---

[4] Actually, it's a bit more complicated, because the accounting deduction is made in the year of purchase while the deduction from the tax base occurs only in the year(s) in which the ITC is *realized,* which is always at least one year later than the expenditure. We will ignore this additional temporary difference in this discussion.

with depreciation based on the net amount or (2) deferred separately as "deferred income" and amortized on the same basis as the asset itself.

6. The nature and amount of ITCs should be disclosed in the notes, as well as the company's accounting policy for ITCs, the method of presentation, and any unfulfilled conditions or contingencies.

QUESTIONS

Q15-1 Why is it common for companies to label income tax expense as a *provision* for income taxes?

Q15-2 How can differences between accounting and taxable income be classified? Define each classification.

Q15-3 XTE Corporation (a) uses straight-line depreciation for its financial accounting and accelerated depreciation on its income tax return and (b) expenses golf club dues for its top management. What kind of tax difference is caused by each of these items? Explain.

Q15-4 Temporary differences are said to "originate" and "reverse." What do these terms mean?

Q15-5 Give three examples of a permanent difference, and three examples of a temporary difference.

Q15-6 Explain the two acceptable alternative options for the extent of allocation possible in dealing with interperiod tax allocation.

Q15-7 Sometimes the taxes payable method is called the flow-through method. Why might this name seem appropriate? When is this method generally accepted in Canada?

Q15-8 Why is the balance in a deferred income tax liability account not discounted?

Q15-9 Thertot Limited reported $100,000 of income in 20X4, $300,000 of income in 20X5, and $500,000 of income in 20X6. Included in 20X4 income is an expense, $50,000, that cannot be deducted for tax purposes until 20X6. Assume a 40% tax rate. How much income tax is payable in each year? How much income tax expense will be reported? Why are the total three-year payable and total three-year expense equal?

Q15-10 ATW Corporation has completed an analysis of its accounting income, taxable income, and the temporary differences. Taxable income is $200,000, and there are two temporary differences, which result in (a) a deferred income tax asset of $15,000 and (b) a deferred income tax liability of $20,000. The income tax rate for the current period and all future periods is 40%. There were no deferred income tax assets or deferred income tax liabilities as of the beginning of the current year. Give the journal entry to record income tax.

Q15-11 A company has $200,000 in originating temporary differences in 20X6, its first year of operation. The temporary differences give rise to a deferred income tax liability. The tax rate is 34% in 20X6. In 20X7, there were no new temporary differences, but the tax rate increases to 40%. If the liability method is used, at what amount will deferred income taxes be shown on the 20X7 statement of financial position?

Q15-12 A company reports a $1,000,000 revenue (long-term receivable and associated revenue) in accounting income in year 1. It is taxable income when collected in year 4. What is the accounting carrying value of the receivable at the end of year 1? The tax basis? Assuming that the tax rate is 40% in years 1 and 2, and 35% in years 3 and 4, what will be the balance in the deferred income tax account at the end of each year?

Q15-13 A company bought $1,000,000 of capital assets at the beginning of year 1. Year 1 amortization was $200,000 and CCA was $100,000. What is the tax basis of the assets at the end of year 1? The accounting carrying value? If the tax rate is 20%, what is the balance in the deferred income tax account at the end of year 1?

Q15-14 When do items on the statement of financial position have a different accounting carrying value and tax basis?

Q15-15 Do permanent differences cause the accounting carrying value and tax basis of the related item on the statement of financial position to differ?

Q15-16 On the statement of financial position, are deferred income taxes debits or credits? Explain. Is a debit to a deferred income tax account always a decrease, and a credit always an increase? Explain.

Q15-17 Assume that a company reports a deferred income tax liability of $500,000. The enacted tax rate goes down. How will the account on the statement of financial position change if the liability method is used?

Q15-18 What kinds of differences cause a company to report taxes at a rate different than the statutory rate?

Q15-19 What is an investment tax credit?

Q15-20 Explain two different approaches to account for an investment tax credit for a capital asset.

Q15-21 How might an ITC received because of qualifying expenditures for capital assets be reported on the statement of financial position?

CASE 15-1

SOFTWARE INCORPORATED

Software Incorporated (SI) is a private corporation formed in the 1990s. SI develops and sells software for many purposes; theft recovery, geomapping, data and device security, and IT asset management. To help motivate management, SI has a stock option plan.

To help fund continued software development, SI has a bank loan with a major bank. The bank requires annual audited financial statements and has a financial covenant that stipulates a minimum current ratio.

SI has an expected taxable loss of $10,000,000 in 20X9. For the last three years the company has had taxable profits of $2,000,000 in 20X6; $5,000,000 in 20X7, and $1,000,000 in 20X8. SI taxable loss this year was due to intensive development of new software for security over personal data. SI anticipates sales of this product to be significant due to concerns over identity theft.

You have recently been hired to develop new accounting policies for SI's December 31 year-end. You have been asked by the owners to discuss alternatives and provide recommendations on the appropriate accounting policies for events below that have occurred during 20X9. Where possible, you have been asked to quantify the impact of the accounting policies. SI is seriously considering going public next year and would like to know how your recommendations would be different if it was a public company. The incremental borrowing rate for SI is 10%. The tax rates for the last few years were 20X6 (38%), 20X7 (39%), both 20X8 and 20X9 (40%).

1. SI offers computer theft recovery and secure asset-tracking services. These services are provided for a period of one to five years. The customer pays a fee that includes software, monitoring, and maintenance. The fee is due 30 days after installation of the software. Sales staff are paid a commission based on the number of service contracts they sell.

2. SI offers a warranty with its theft recovery software. If a computer equipped with the software is stolen and SI is unable to recover the stolen software using its software or delete data on the stolen computer then the customer is eligible for a warranty of up to $1,000. To qualify, customers must file a police report. The amount of the warranty depends on the value of the stolen computer. Estimated warranty liabilities on the balance sheet at the end of 20X8 were $8 million. During 20X9, the estimated warranty costs based on a percentage of sales will be an additional $5 million. Actual warranty costs during 20X9 were $1 million.

3. SI currently uses the taxes payable method of accounting for income taxes. In 20X8, SI changed its method of accounting for software development from expensing to capitalizing as an intangible asset.

4. SI entered into a forward contract for the purchase of new equipment that the company is purchasing from Germany in 20X9 to protect itself against changes in the value of the euro. SI often enters into forward contracts, interest rate swaps, and foreign currency swaps to protect the company from risks. SI also has shares in a number of companies for the purposes solely of earning money. It has an investment department that manages this portfolio of investments. These investments are traded on a frequent basis.

5. SI has installed a series of satellite towers as part of its software-tracking services. SI installed a series of satellite towers at a cost of $15 million. There is a regulatory obligation to dismantle these satellite towers in 20 years. The anticipated cost at that time is $2.5 million.

6. SI issued $15,000,000 convertible bonds, 8% semi-annual dividend on January 1, 20X9. The bonds were issued for net proceeds (cash) of $14,800,000. The bonds are convertible at the bondholders' option in 10 years into Class A common shares at the rate of 70 shares for each $1,000 bond.

7. SI uses the Black-Scholes method for estimating its stock option expense. During 20X9, SI estimated an expense of $15 million using the following assumptions:

	20X8	20X9
Expected life of options	4	3
Expected stock price volatility	71%	60%
Risk free interest rate	4%	3%

Required:

Prepare the requested report.

CASE 15-2

DEEP HARBOUR LIMITED

Deep Harbour Limited (DHL) is a private company owned by Daniel Lalande. Lalande started the company in 20X1, and DHL has reported reasonably consistent growth in profits from fiscal 20X1 to 20X7. The company is in the plastic moulding business, making everything from toys to dashboards.

The year ended 30 November 20X8 has been challenging for DHL. The company invested $8.2 million in new injection moulding machinery in February 20X8. This meant a two-week scheduled production shutdown to allow for installation and training. The two weeks stretched to five weeks when last-minute replacement parts were delayed at the U.S. border. The machinery was fully operational in late March 20X8; however, additional costs were incurred.

DHL has used the taxes payable method using accounting standards for private enterprises to account for corporate income taxes, but now has to adopt comprehensive tax allocation for its bank. The Chartered Bank of Canada (CBC) provided a $7 million 10-year term loan for the new equipment, but insisted that certain covenants be met with financial results measured using specific required policies. DHL has no differences from required accounting policies except for the tax accounting policy.

DHL must meet the following two balance sheet ratios under the terms of debt covenants:

1. The current ratio must exceed 1-to-1.
2. The total debt-to-equity ratio must be less than 4-to-1 (all non-equity credit accounts included in the numerator).

If covenants are breached, the loan may be called for repayment with 30 business days' notice. In practical terms, it is likely that a breach would result in higher financing costs, now prime plus 1/2%.

DHL has asked you, a public accountant, to review the financial statements and adjust the statement of financial position for the effects of the new income tax policy. DHL is aware that this policy will be applied retrospectively, and thus will affect comparative retained earnings statements.

For now, though, DHL would like the statement of financial implications quantified. Management understands that any change to deferred income tax changes the retained earnings balance.

The draft statement of financial position is shown in Exhibit 1, calculation of taxable income is in Exhibit 2, and other information is in Exhibit 3.

DHL has also asked you to evaluate (and make changes for) any other accounting policies that might concern you. DHL has no wish to fall afoul of CBC's judgements in any credit review process.

Required:
Prepare a report that responds to the concerns raised.

EXHIBIT 1

DEEP HARBOUR LIMITED STATEMENT OF FINANCIAL POSITION
As of 30 November 20X8
(in thousands)

Assets
Current

Accounts receivable	$ 2,690
Inventory, at lower-of-cost-or-market	513
Prepaid expenses	219
Investment tax credit receivable	1,200
	4,622
Capital assets, net of depreciation	12,850
	$17,472
Current Liabilities	
Bank operating line of credit	$ 295
Accounts payable and accrued liabilities	3,071
Deferred investment tax credit, net of amortization (written off straight-line over 4 years)	900
	4,266
Long-term debt	7,500
Shareholders' equity	5,706
	$17,472

EXHIBIT 2

DEEP HARBOUR LIMITED TAXABLE INCOME
Year ended 30 November 20X8

(in thousands)

Accounting income	$2,252
Depreciation (including $3.5 on capitalized interest)	1,306
Capital Cost Allowance[(1)]	(404)
Inventory writedown to LCM[(2)]	40
Interest capitalized	(35)
Non-deductible entertainment and marketing expenses	84
Amortization of deferred investment tax credit	(300)
Taxable income	2,943
Income tax payable (@ 42%)	1,236
Less: Investment tax credit	1,200
Net tax payable	$ 36

[(1)] UCC at the end of 20X8, correctly calculated, was $9,100. This includes the new machinery net of the investment tax credit.

[(2)] Tax deductible when inventory is sold.

EXHIBIT 3

DHL OTHER INFORMATION

1. DHL has paid $120,000 of tax instalments in 20X8, recorded as prepaid expenses on the 30 November 20X8 statement of financial position.

2. No tax expense or liability has been recorded for 20X8 as yet. Accounting income was closed to retained earnings on a pre-tax basis to prepare the statement of financial position in Exhibit 1.

3. DHL offers a six-month warranty on certain products. In past years, warranty expense had been expensed when claims were paid, since the warranty was new and not easily estimable. However, DHL has now had three years' experience with the warranty program and can safely estimate that the warranty liability at the end of 20X8 is in the $60,000 to $80,000 range.

4. DHL capitalized $35,000 of interest on the bank loan for the period that the new equipment was being installed. Capitalized interest is deductible for tax purposes when paid.

5. A full year's depreciation was charged on all assets, including the new machinery. This machinery is being depreciated straight-line over its expected life of 10 years. A full year's depreciation is charged in the first year.

CASE 15-3

CANADIAN PRODUCTS LIMITED

Canadian Products Limited (CPL) is a very large private Canadian company. CPL has been contemplating going public, which, according to business analysts, is just a matter of time. Recently, the president wrote a letter to you, the accounting advisor, complaining about Canadian tax standards and asking for your comments:

> We at CPL are very concerned that our current operating performance and debt-to-equity position are grossly misstated due to the standards for accounting for income tax. These standards do not reflect the economic reality of our tax position. In fact, I have heard that many financial analysts ignore deferred income tax accounts. Is that true?
>
> Our deferred income tax balances arise because we are allowed to depreciate our capital assets far more rapidly for tax purposes than they actually wear out. Thus, deductible expenses for tax purposes exceed our book expenses. Last year, our tax expense exceeded taxes payable by $17.2 million. When combined with prior amounts, we have a cumulative difference of $190.6 million, and this difference is expected to continue to increase. Isn't this increasing amount misleading to our investors if it is just going to continue to grow and never decrease?
>
> We estimate that this year's $17.2 million could not possibly be required to be repaid for at least 12 years—and perhaps never if we continue to expand. I understand that if we followed accounting standards for private enterprises instead of international accounting standards, using no allocation, we wouldn't have to expense this amount at all this year. What advantage is there of following these international standards. Should we not just use accounting standards for private enterprises?
>
> We are also disturbed that discounting is not allowed for future tax amounts. If we had any other non-interest-bearing, long-term liability on our books, discounting would be considered appropriate. This inconsistency in the way supposedly analogous liabilities are treated highlights the fact that the deferred income tax liability is, in fact, different.

Required:

Respond to the president's concerns and questions, looking at both sides of each issue raised.

Source: Reproduced with permission from CGA-Canada.

ASSIGNMENTS

★ **A15-1 Income Tax Allocation—Two-Year Period:** Graham Corporation provided the following data related to accounting and taxable income:

	20X4	20X5
Pre-tax accounting income (financial statements)	$400,000	$440,000
Taxable income (tax return)	240,000	600,000
Income tax rate	40%	40%

There are no existing temporary differences other than those reflected in this data. There are no permanent differences.

Required:

1. How much tax expense would be reported in each year if the taxes payable method was used? What is potentially misleading with this presentation of tax expense?

2. How much tax expense and deferred income tax would be reported using comprehensive tax allocation and the liability method? Why is the two-year total tax expense the same in requirements (1) and (2)?

★ **A15-2 Income Tax Allocation—Two-Year Period:** Maynes Limited reported the following information (in thousands) for 20X6 and 20X7:

	20X6	20X7
Income from continuing operations, before unusual item, discontinued operation, and income tax	$300,000	$250,000
Unusual item—gain on sale of capital assets (before income tax)	10,000	
Gain from discontinued operations, before income tax		22,000

Mayne's income tax rate is 35%. The 20X6 unusual gain is not taxable until 20X7. The 20X7 gain on discontinued operations is fully taxable in 20X7.

Required:

1. Prepare a partial statement of profit and loss in good form for 20X6 and 20X7, starting with "Income from continuing operations, before unusual item and discontinued operations, and income tax," using two different methods:
   a. Taxes payable method.
   b. Comprehensive tax allocation.

2. Explain the circumstances under which Maynes Limited could use the taxes payable method.

★ **A15-3 Temporary Differences:** Listed below are six independent sources of deferred income tax. For each item, indicate whether the deferred income tax account on the balance sheet would be a debit or a credit.

Item	Debit or Credit
a. Accelerated amortization (CCA) for income tax and straight-line amortization for accounting	
b. Estimated warranty costs: cash basis for income tax and accrual basis for accounting	
c. Sales revenue when payment is deferred: cash basis for tax purposes but recognize on delivery for accounting	
d. Construction contracts: completed-contract for income tax and percentage of completion for accounting	
e. Unrealized loss: loss recognized only on later disposal of the asset for income tax but market value (LCM) recognized for accounting	
f. Rent revenue collected in advance: cash basis for income tax, accrual basis for accounting	

★★ **A15-4 Income Tax Allocation, Alternatives:** The financial statements of Dakar Corporation for a four-year period reflected the following pre-tax amounts:

Solution

	20X4	20X5	20X6	20X7
Statement Profit and Loss (summarized)				
Revenues	$110,000	$124,000	$144,000	$164,000
Expenses other than depreciation	(80,000)	(92,000)	(95,000)	(128,000)
Depreciation expense (straight-line)	(10,000)	(10,000)	(10,000)	(10,000)
Pre-tax accounting income	$ 20,000	$ 22,000	$ 39,000	$ 26,000
Statement of Financial Position (partial)				
Machine (four-year life, no residual value), at cost	$ 40,000	$ 40,000	$ 40,000	$ 40,000
Less: Accumulated Depreciation	(10,000)	(20,000)	(30,000)	(40,000)
	$ 30,000	$ 20,000	$ 10,000	$ 0

Dakar has a tax rate of 40% each year and claimed CCA for income tax purposes as follows: 20X4, $16,000; 20X5, $12,000; 20X6, $8,000; and 20X7, $4,000. There were no deferred income tax balances at 1 January 20X4.

Required:

1. For each year, calculate net income using the taxes payable method.

2. For each year, calculate the deferred income tax balance on the statement of financial position at the end of the year using the liability method of tax allocation. Also calculate net income using the liability method of tax allocation.

3. Explain why the liability method is usually viewed as preferable to the taxes payable method.

★ **A15-5 CCA-Depreciation Differences:** Rundle Corporation acquired new equipment for $400,000 in 20X4. For accounting purposes, the equipment will be depreciated over four years, straight-line, with a full-year's depreciation in the first year. For income tax purposes, Olivetti can take CCA over the next three years of : $200,000 in 20X4, $125,000 in 20X5, and $75,000 in 20X6. Olivetti's income tax rate is 30%.

Required:
For each 31 December, 20X4 through 20X7, determine:

1. The tax basis for the equipment.
2. The accounting basis for the equipment.
3. The amount of the temporary difference relating to the equipment.
4. The amount of the deferred income tax expense.
5. The balance of deferred income tax asset or liability that would be shown on the statement of financial position.

★★ **A15-6 Cumulative CCA-Depreciation Differences:** Agnew Corporation started operations in 20X1. The company acquired equipment in the first year for a price of $90,000. The equipment will be depreciated for accounting purposes over three years on a straight-line basis (with a full year's depreciation in the year of acquisition). For determining income tax payable, the company can deduct one-half of the purchase cost as CCA in the first year, one-third in the second year, and one-sixth in the third year.

The company's 20X1 startup was successful, and in 20X2 the company bought identical equipment for $96,000. In 20X3, a third set of equipment was acquired for $99,000. The pattern of depreciation and CCA is proportionately the same for each acquisition. Agnew's tax rate is 30%.

The company's management plans to continue the same level of investment for the foreseeable future, as long as the company remains profitable.

Required:

1. Determine the temporary difference relating to the tax versus accounting bases of the equipment (that is, CCA versus accounting depreciation) for each of 20X1 through 20X3. What is the accumulated balance of the temporary difference at the end of each year?

2. What is the balance of the *deferred income tax* account at the end of each year?

3. What will happen to the accumulated temporary differences and deferred income tax if Agnew continues to maintain its current level of investment in equipment, replacing each asset as it comes to the end of its useful life?

4. What conditions will be necessary to cause the timing difference balance to decline in future years?

5. Under what conditions will reversal of the accumulated timing differences cause a cash outflow?

★★ **A15-7 Cumulative Temporary Differences:** At the end of 20X3, Foster Limited's statement of financial position showed equipment at total cost of $8,000,000. The equipment was being amortized at 10% per year, straight-line, and was 40% depreciated at the end of 20X3. The income tax files showed unclaimed capital cost (UCC) for the equipment of $2,200,000. Foster's statement of financial position also showed an asset of $1,200,000 for unamortized development costs. The development costs had been incurred in previous years and had been deducted for income tax purposes in those prior years.

In 20X4, Foster acquired an additional $1,200,000 in equipment while scrapping equipment that originally cost $500,000. The CCA rate for Foster's equipment is 20%. Total CCA claimed for 20X4 was $460,000. Foster amortized $200,000 of the development costs.

Foster pays income tax at a rate of 40%.

Required:

1. Determine the cumulative temporary differences relating to equipment and development costs at the end of each of 20X3 and 20X4.

2. What is the balance of the *deferred income tax* account at the end of each year?

3. What are the accounting basis and the tax basis of the equipment and of the development cost at the end of each of 20X3 and 20X4?

4. If Foster maintains its capital asset base by reinvestment and renewal in future years, when will the deferred income tax balance begin to decline? Explain.

★ **A15-8 Tax Calculations:** The following is selected information from the accounting records of Drummond Incorporated for 20X6, its first year of operations:

Net income before income taxes	$750,000

In determining pretax accounting income the following deductions were made:

a. Golf club dues	35,000
b. Accrued warranty costs	95,000
c. Depreciation	150,000

For tax purposes the following deductions were made:

a. Warranty costs incurred	75,000
b. CCA	250,000

The capital assets, originally costing $1,500,000, are depreciated on a straight-line basis over 10 years, zero salvage value with a full year amortization taken in year one. The tax rate is 40%.

Required:

1. Prepare the journal entry to record income tax at the end of 20X6.
2. Prepare the journal entry to record income tax at the end of 20X6 assuming Drummond Incorporated elects to use the taxes payable method in accounting standards for private enterprises.

★ **A15-9 Tax Calculations:** The records of Retter Corporation, at the end of 20X4, provided the following data related to income taxes:

a. Golf club dues expense in 20X4, $16,000, properly recorded for accounting purposes but not tax deductible at any time.
b. Investment income in 20X4, $700,000, properly recorded for accounting purposes but not taxable at any time.
c. Estimated expense for warranty costs, $260,000; accrued for accounting purposes at the end of 20X4; to be reported for income tax purposes when paid. There were no warranty costs incurred in 20X4.
d. Gain on disposal of land, $960,000; recorded for accounting purposes at the end of 20X4; to be reported as a capital gain for income tax purposes at the end of 20X6.

Accounting income (from the financial statements) for 20X4, $1,600,000; the income tax rate is 40%. There were no deferred tax amounts as of the beginning of 20X4.

Required:

1. Are the individual differences listed above permanent differences or temporary differences? Explain why.
2. Prepare the journal entry to record income tax at the end of 20X4.
3. Show the amounts that will be reported on (a) the statement of financial position and (b) the statement of profit and loss for 20X4.

★ **A15-10 Tax Calculations:** Scarlett Corporation reported accounting income before taxes as follows: 20X4, $150,000; 20X5, $92,000. Taxable income for each year would have been the same as pre-tax accounting income except for the tax effects, arising for the first time in 20X4, of $2,400 in rent revenue, representing $400 per month rent revenue collected in advance on 1 October 20X4, for the six months ending 31 March 20X5. Rent revenue is taxable in the year collected. The tax rate for 20X4 and 20X5 is 40%, and the year-end for both accounting and tax purposes is 31 December. The rent revenue collected in advance is the only difference, and it is not repeated in October 20X5.

Required:

1. Is this a temporary difference? Why or why not?
2. What is the accounting carrying value for the unearned rent at the end of 20X4? The tax basis? Explain.
3. Calculate taxable income, and income tax payable, and prepare journal entries for each year-end.
4. Prepare a partial statement of profit and loss for each year, starting with pre-tax accounting income.
5. What amount of deferred income tax would be reported on the 20X4 and 20X5 statements of financial position?

★ **A15-11 Tax Calculations:** The pre-tax income statements for VCR Corporation for two years (summarized) were as follows:

	20X5	20X6
Revenues	$740,000	$800,000
Expenses	640,000	685,000
Pre-tax income	$100,000	$115,000

For tax purposes, the following income tax differences existed:

a. Revenues on the 20X6 statement of profit and loss include $45,000 rent, which is taxable in 20X5 but was unearned at the end of 20X5 for accounting purposes.
b. Expenses on the 20X6 statement of profit and loss include membership fees of $40,000, which are not deductible for income tax purposes.
c. Expenses on the 20X5 statement of profit and loss include $32,000 of estimated warranty costs, which are not deductible for income tax purposes until 20X6.

Required:

1. What was the accounting carrying value and tax basis for unearned revenue and the warranty liability at the end of 20X5 and 20X6?
2. Compute (a) income tax payable, (b) deferred income tax and (c) income tax expense for each period. Assume an average tax rate of 30%.
3. Give the entry to record income taxes for each period.
4. Complete statements of profit and loss to include income taxes as allocated.
5. What amount of deferred income tax will be reported on the statement of financial position at each year-end?

★ **A15-12 Tax Calculations:** Hogarth Incorporated recorded instalment sales revenue of $60,000 in 20X1 and $200,000 in 20X2. The revenue is not taxable until collected. Of the year 20X1 revenue, $50,000 was collected in 20X2 and the remaining $10,000 collected in 20X3. Of the year 20X2 revenue, $90,000 was collected in 20X3 and the rest in 20X4. Hogarth's accounting earnings before income tax for the three years was as follows:

20X1	$500,000
20X2	600,000
20X3	540,000

On 1 January 20X1, the enacted rate for all years was 40%. During 20X3, the rate was revised to 38%.

Required:

Prepare the necessary journal entries to record income tax for the years 20X1, 20X2, and 20X3.

Source: Reproduced with permission from CGA-Canada.

★ **A15-13 Tax Calculations:** Thomas Incorporated started operations on 1 January 20X5 and purchased $400,000 of capital assets. Information on the first two years of operations is as follows:

	20X5	20X6
Accounting income before income tax	$145,000	$160,000
Depreciation expense on capital assets	40,000	40,000
Capital cost allowance	34,000	44,000
Equity in earnings of subsidiaries (not taxable)	22,000	40,000
Income tax rate	36%	38%

Required:

Prepare all income tax journal entries for 20X5 and 20X6.

Source: Reproduced with permission from CGA-Canada.

★

A15-14 Deferred Income Tax, Change in Tax Rates: DCM Metals Limited has a 31 December year-end. The tax rate is 30% in 20X4, 35% in 20X5, and 42% in 20X6. The company reports income as follows:

20X4	$550,000
20X5	123,000
20X6	310,000

Taxable income and accounting income are identical except for a $300,000 revenue reported for accounting purposes in 20X4, and reported one-half in 20X5 and one-half in 20X6 for tax purposes. The revenue is related to a long-term account receivable, taxable only when collected.

Required:

Compute tax expense and deferred income tax on the statement of financial position for 20X4, 20X5, and 20X6.

★★

A15-15 Deferred Income Tax, Change in Tax Rates: Stacy Corporation would have had identical income before tax on both its income tax returns and statements of profit and loss for the years 20X4 through 20X7, except for a capital asset that cost $120,000. The operational asset has a four-year estimated life and no residual value. The asset was depreciated for income tax purposes using the following amounts: 20X4, $48,000; 20X5, $36,000; 20X6, $24,000; and 20X7, $12,000. However, for accounting purposes, the straight-line method was used (that is, $30,000 per year). The accounting and tax periods both end on 31 December. Income amounts before depreciation expense and income tax for each of the four years were as follows:

	20X4	**20X5**	**20X6**	**20X7**
Accounting income before tax and depreciation	$60,000	$80,000	$70,000	$70,000
Tax rate	30%	30%	40%	40%

Required:

1. Explain why this is a temporary difference.
2. Calculate the accounting carrying value and tax basis of the asset at the end of each year.
3. Reconcile pre-tax accounting and taxable income, calculate income tax payable and tax expense, compute the balance in the deferred income tax account, and prepare journal entries for each year-end.

★★ **A15-16 Deferred Income Tax, Change in Tax Rates:** Solway Company has a deferred income tax liability in the amount of $200,000 at 31 December 20X4, relating to a $500,000 receivable. This sale was recorded for accounting purposes in 20X4 but is not taxable until the cash is collected. In 20X5, $300,000 is collected. Warranty expense in 20X5 included in the determination of pre-tax accounting income is $150,000, with the entire amount expected to be spent and deductible for tax purposes in 20X6. Pre-tax accounting income is $650,000 in 20X5. The tax rate is 35% in 20X5.

Required:

1. What is the accounting carrying value, the tax basis of the account receivable, and the warranty liability, at the end of 20X4 and 20X5? What was the enacted tax rate at 31 December 20X4?
2. Calculate taxable income and income tax payable, compute the balance in the deferred income tax accounts, and prepare journal entries for year-end 20X5.
3. Calculate the deferred income tax that would be reported on the statement of financial position at the end of 20X5.

★★ **A15-17 Tax Calculations; Change in Tax Rates:** On 1 January 20X3, Highmark Corporation reported the following amounts on the statement of financial position:

Deferred income tax asset related to warranty	$ 16,000
Deferred income tax liability related to capital assets	$120,000

On this date, the net book value of capital assets was $1,750,000 and undepreciated capital cost was $1,450,000. There was a warranty liability of $40,000. Taxable income of $500,000 (in total) in 20X1 and 20X2 had resulted in the payment of $195,000 of income tax.

In 20X3, accounting income was $170,000. This included non-tax-deductible expenses of $42,000, dividend revenue (non-taxable) of $12,000, depreciation of $75,000, and a warranty expense of $39,000. Warranty claims paid were $51,000 and CCA was $99,000.

Required:
Provide the journal entry to record tax expense in 20X3. The enacted tax rate was 41% in 20X3.

★★ **A15-18 Tax Calculations; Change in Tax Rates:** On December 31, 20X6, Silk Corporation reported the following amounts on the statement of financial position:

Deferred income tax asset related to warranty	$ 20,000
Deferred income tax liability related to capital assets	$182,000

On this date, the net book value of capital assets was $1,380,000 and undepreciated capital cost was $980,000. There was an estimated warranty liability of $10,000.

In 20X7, accounting income was $1,600,000. This included golf club dues of $22,000, depreciation of $200,000, and a warranty expense of $90,000. Warranty claims paid were $60,000 and CCA was $300,000.

Required:

1. Provide the journal entry to record tax expense in 20X7. The enacted tax rate was 40% in 20X7.

2. Identify the following balances for December 31, 20X7:
   a. Deferred income tax asset.
   b. Deferred income tax liability.
   c. Estimated warranty liability.
   d. Net book value of capital assets.
   e. Undepreciated capital cost.

★★ **A15-19 Tax Calculations—Tax Rate Change:** The statements of profit and loss for Gardner Corporation for two years (summarized) were as follows:

	20X4	20X5
Revenues	$400,000	$360,000
Expenses	362,000	304,000
Pre-tax accounting income	$ 38,000	$ 56,000
Taxable income (per tax return)	$ 94,000	$ 56,000

The income tax rate is 38% in 20X4 and 40% in 20X5. The 20X5 tax rate was enacted in 20X5. For tax purposes, the following differences existed:

a. Expenses (given above) on the 20X4 and 20X5 statements of profit and loss include golf club dues of $20,000 annually, which are not deductible for income tax purposes.
b. Revenues (given above) on the 20X5 statement of profit and loss include $20,000 rent revenue, which was taxable in 20X4 but was unearned for accounting purposes until 20X5.

c. Expenses (given above) on the 20X4 statement of profit and loss include $16,000 of estimated warranty costs, which are not deductible for income tax purposes until paid in 20X6.

Required:

1. Explain whether each difference is a permanent or temporary difference.
2. Calculate income tax payable for each year.
3. Calculate income tax expense for each of 20X4 and 20X5. Also calculate the balance in the deferred income tax account at the end of 20X4 and 20X5.

★★   **A15-20 Tax Calculations—Tax Rate Change:** The records of Morgan Corporation provided the following data at the end of years 1 through 4 relating to income tax allocation:

e**X**cel

	Year 1	Year 2	Year 3	Year 4
Pre-tax accounting income	$58,000	$70,000	$80,000	$88,000
Taxable income (tax return)	28,000	80,000	90,000	98,000
Tax rate	30%	35%	40%	40%

The above amounts include only one temporary difference; no other changes occurred. At the end of year 1, the company prepaid an expense of $30,000, which was then amortized for accounting purposes over the next three years (straight-line). The full amount was included as a deduction in year 1 for income tax purposes. Each year's tax rate was enacted in each specific year—that is, the year 2 tax rate was enacted in year 2, etc.

Required:

1. Calculate income tax payable for each year.
2. Calculate income tax expense.
3. Comment on the effect that use of the liability method has on income tax expense when the income tax rate changes.

★★   **A15-21 Tax Rate Change, Two-Stage:** At the end of 20X4, Varna Ltd. had accumulated temporary differences of $500,000 arising from CCA/depreciation on capital assets. The balance of the deferred income tax liability account was $200,000. Over the next three years, Varna experienced the following:

	20X5	20X6	20X7
Accounting income, before income taxes	$200,000	$220,000	$250,000
Expenses not deductible for computing income tax	8,000	10,000	6,000
Temporary differences*	44,000	50,000	52,000

*Excess of tax-deductible expenses over expenses recognized in accounting income

The tax rate was 40% for taxation years 20X4 and 20X5, 34% for 20X6, and 30% for 20X7.

Required:

1. Calculate income tax expense for each year, 20X5, 20X6, and 20X7. Assume that the rates for 20X6 and 20X7 were enacted year by year. Distinguish between current income tax expense and deferred income tax expense. State any additional assumptions that you make.
2. Assume instead that the rates for 20X6 and 20X7 were enacted in 20X5. How, if at all, would this affect income tax expense in each of the three years?

★★   **A15-22 Tax Calculations:** Timmis Limited, in the first year of its operations, reported the following information regarding its operations:

a. Income before tax for the year was $1,500,000 and the tax rate was 38%.

b. Depreciation was $120,000 and CCA was $67,000. Net book value at year-end was $840,000, while UCC was $893,000.

c. The warranty program generated an estimated cost (expense) on the statement of profit and loss of $257,000 but the cash paid out was $174,000. The $83,000 liability resulting from this was shown as a current liability. On the income tax return, the cash paid is the amount deductible.

d. Entertainment expenses of $55,000 were included in the statement of profit and loss but were not allowed to be deducted for tax purposes.

In the second year of its operations, Timmis Limited reported the following information:

a. Income before income tax for the year was $1,750,000 and the tax rate was 40%.

b. Depreciation was $120,000 and the CCA was $370,000. Net book value at year-end was $720,000, while UCC was $523,000.

c. The estimated costs of the warranty program were $287,000 and the cash paid out was $242,000. The liability had a balance of $128,000.

Required:

Prepare the journal entry to record income tax expense in the first and second year of operations. The second-year tax rate was not enacted until the second year.

Source: Reproduced with permission from CGA-Canada.

★★ **A15-23 Tax Calculations, Rate Change:** In its first year of operations, Lee Corporation reported the following information:

a. Income before income taxes was $2,000,000.

b. The company acquired capital assets costing $1,800,000; depreciation was $300,000 and CCA was $180,000.

c. The company recorded an expense of $400,000 for the one-year warranty on the company's products; cash disbursements amounted to $160,000.

d. The income tax rate was 36%.

In the second year, Lee reported the following:

a. Legislation was enacted that changed the tax rate to 38%.

b. Income before income tax was $2,400,000.

c. Depreciation was $300,000; CCA was $324,000.

d. The estimated warranty costs were $500,000 while the cash expenditure was $440,000.

e. Entertainment expenses of $50,000 included on the statement of profit and loss were not deductible for tax purposes.

Required:

Prepare the journal entries to record income tax expense for the first and second years of operation.

★★ **A15-24 Tax Calculations, Rate Change:** Golf Incorporated, which began operations in 20X3, uses the same policies for financial accounting and tax purposes with the exception of warranty costs and franchise fee revenue. Information about the $60,000 of warranty expenses and $90,000 franchise revenue accrued for book purposes is provided below:

	20X3	20X4	20X5
Warranty cost for book purposes	$60,000	—	—
Warranty cost for tax purposes (claims paid)	15,000	$20,000	$25,000
Franchise fee revenue, book, on account	90,000	—	—
Franchise fee revenue, tax, cash received	9,000	51,000	30,000
Effective tax rate	38%	40%	45%
Income before tax	$75,000	$90,000	$80,000

Required:

Prepare journal entries to record taxes for 20X3 to 20X5. The company uses the liability method. Separate deferred income tax accounts are used for each source of temporary differences. The tax rate for a given year is not enacted until that specific year.

Source: Reproduced with permission from CGA-Canada.

★★ **A15-25 Tax Calculations:** A. Grossery Limited is a wholesale grocery distributor formed in 20X4, with warehouses in several locations in southern Ontario. The company uses the liability method of tax allocation. In fiscal 20X4, the company had net income before tax of $90,000. The following items were included in the determination of net income:

a. Depreciation on buildings and equipment owned of $50,000. The assets' original cost was $650,000.
b. Pension expense of $44,747. Pension amounts paid were $48,395. There is a deferred pension asset on the balance sheet of $3,648 as a result.
c. Depreciation of capitalized leased assets and interest expense on the lease liability totalled $14,300; the assets' lease payments in 20X4 amounted to $21,000.

In calculating the amount of income tax owed to the government in 20X4, the following factors must be taken into account:

a. CCA amounts to $80,000 for 20X4.
b. Pension costs are tax deductible at the time of *funding*.
c. The capitalized leases are taxed as operating leases. That is, cash lease costs are tax deductible and depreciation, interest, etc., recognized for accounting purposes are not tax deductible. Over time, cash payments will equal the total of these expenses, but the timing of expense recognition is different. The net accounting carrying value for lease-related amounts at the end of 20X4 was a net debit of $6,700. The tax basis was zero.
d. The tax rate is 40%.
e. Golf club dues of $20,000 are included in the net income of $90,000.
f. Tax instalment payments during the year amounted to 75% of the payable amount.

Required:

Prepare the final sections of the statement of profit and loss for 20X4, starting with income before tax. Clearly support your calculations of income tax and other amounts. Also show what would appear on the statement of financial position and statement of cash flows in relation to tax for 20X4. Use the direct method in the operating activities section.

★★ **A15-26 Tax Expense; Comprehensive:** At the end of 20X8, Lambert Corporation reported the following items in the financial statements:

Deferred income tax liability related to accounts receivable	180,000
Deferred income tax liability related to capital assets	456,000

In 20X8, the company reported $214,500 of taxable income. It also reported a $450,000 long-term receivable, taxable when collected. Capital assets, with a net book value of $3,700,000, had a lower UCC and thus caused the second deferred income tax account above.

In 20X9, Lambert reported accounting income of $1,200,000. Collections on the long-term receivable amounted to $300,000. There were non-deductible golf club dues of $22,000. Depreciation was $240,000 and CCA was $300,000. The tax rate was 38%.

Required:

1. Prepare a journal entry to record tax expense in 20X9. Tax rates were enacted in the year to which they pertain.
2. What would appear on the statement of financial position at the end of 20X9 with respect to income tax? Give accounts and amounts.

★★   **A15-27 Tax Expense; Comprehensive:** Liquid Limited reported income before income tax of $175,900 in 20X9. The tax rate for 20X9 was 38% and was enacted during the year. The enacted tax rate at the end of the previous year was 35%.

At the end of 20X8, the balance sheet of Liquid included the net book value of depreciable capital assets of $795,000, long-term accounts receivable of $120,000, and a warranty liability of $49,000. Long-term receivables represent taxable income when collected.

In 20X9, dividends (tax free) received from taxable Canadian corporations were $16,000. Non-deductible entertainment expenses were $30,000. UCC was $480,000 at the beginning of the year. In 20X9, CCA was $50,000, and depreciation expense was $63,000.

During 20X9, long-term receivables of $42,000 were collected. There were no new long-term receivables. The warranty expense of $71,400 was equal to the warranty claims paid.

Required:

1. Calculate income tax expense for 20X9.
2. List the accounts on the statement of financial position as of the end of 20X9.

★★★   **A15-28 Tax Calculations, Comprehensive:** Crandall Corporation was formed in 20X1. Relevant information pertaining to 20X1, 20X2, and 20X3 is as follows:

eXcel

	20X1	20X2	20X3
Income before income tax	$100,000	$100,000	$100,000
Accounting income includes the following:			
Depreciation (assets have a cost of $120,000)	10,000	10,000	12,000
Pension expense*	5,000	7,000	10,000
Warranty expense	3,000	3,000	3,000
Dividend income (non-taxable)	2,000	2,000	3,000
Taxable income includes the following:			
Capital cost allowance	25,000	15,000	7,000
Pension funding (amount paid)	7,000	8,000	9,000
Warranty costs paid	1,000	4,000	3,000
Tax rate—enacted in each year	40%	44%	48%

*Pension amounts are tax deductible when paid, not when expensed. Over the long term, payments will equal total expense. The tax basis for the pension will always be zero. For accounting purposes, there will be a statement of financial position asset account asset called "deferred pension cost" for the difference between the amount paid and the expense, since the amount paid is higher.

Required:
Prepare the journal entry to record income tax expense for each year.

★★★   **A15-29 Tax Calculations, Comprehensive:** At the beginning of 20X1, Farcus Corporation had the following future tax accounts:

Deferred tax asset $19,600

Warranty expense to date has been $126,000; claims paid have been $70,000. There is a $56,000 warranty liability included in short-term liabilities on the statement of financial position.

Future tax liability $497,000

The net book value of capital assets was $2,276,000 at the beginning of 20X1; UCC was $856,000. Over time, CCA has been $1,420,000 higher than depreciation.

INFORMATION RELATING TO 20X1 AND 20X2:

	20X1	20X2
Net income	$625,000	$916,000
Items included in net income		
Golf dues	8,000	9,000
Tax penalties, not tax deductible	3,000	1,000
Depreciation	287,000	309,000
Warranty expense	22,000	41,000
Percentage of completion income		
(reported for the first time in 20X1) (Note 1)	17,000	10,000
Other information		
CCA	395,000	116,000
Warranty claims paid	16,000	50,000
Completed-contract income (used for tax purposes)	0	27,000
Tax rate—enacted in each year	40%	42%

Note 1—The construction-in-progress inventory is classified as a current asset.

Required:

1. Indicate the amount and classification of all items that would appear on the statement of financial position in relation to income tax at the end of 20X1 and 20X2. Assume no tax is paid until the subsequent year.

2. Draft the bottom section of the statement of profit and loss for 20X2, beginning with "Income before taxes." Show all required disclosures. Include comparative data for 20X1.

★★ **A15-30 Investment Tax Credit (Appendix):** Pegasus Printing began operations in 20X4, and has bought equipment for use in its printing operations in each of the last three years. This equipment qualifies for an investment tax credit of 14%. Information relating to the three years is shown below:

	20X4	20X5	20X6
Income before income tax	$165,000	$456,000	$468,000
Income tax rate	25%	25%	25%
Equipment eligible for ITC	$ 40,000	$689,000	$450,000
Estimated life of equipment	10 years	13 years	12 years

a. Income before tax includes non-deductible advertising expenditures of $20,000 each year.

b. Equipment is depreciated straight-line over its useful life for accounting purposes, assuming zero salvage value. A full year of depreciation is charged in the year of acquisition. CCA claims in 20X4 were $12,000; 20X5, $135,000; and 20X6, $216,000.

Required:

1. Calculate the depreciation expense in each of the three years, net of the investment tax credit amortization.

2. Calculate taxes payable in each of the three years. Note that depreciation added back is net depreciation, as calculated in requirement (1).

3. Calculate tax expense for each year, using Canadian standards (cost reduction) to account for the investment tax credit.

4. Calculate tax expense, using the flow-through approach for all tax amounts.

5. Why is the cost reduction approach preferable?

6. Show how capital assets, and the deferred investment tax credit, would be presented on the statement of financial position at the end of 20X4.

CHAPTER 16

Accounting for Tax Losses

INTRODUCTION

In 2008, Quebec-based ADF Group[1] recognized deferred income tax assets of almost $26 million. The deferred tax assets were created by recognizing the probable *future* tax benefit of *past* years' losses. By recognizing these deferred tax assets in 2008, the company almost tripled its net earnings, from $12 million earnings before income taxes to $34 million net earnings after taxes. There was no cash flow effect in 2008 from recognizing the future benefits of these past years' losses. Basic EPS was $1.02 in 2008, as compared with $0.32 in 2007 and $0.43 in 2009.

When a corporation's taxable "income" is actually a loss, the corporation can use that loss to reduce past and future income taxes. A loss will normally have tax benefits, but the benefits might not be *realized* in the period of the loss. Should future benefits be *recognized* in the year of the loss in order to achieve matching, or should their recognition be delayed in the interests of conservatism?

This chapter begins with an explanation of the income tax benefits that arise from a loss. Then we will discuss the issue of when and how to recognize those benefits.

---

[1] ADF Group Inc. designs, engineers, and fabricates complex steel structures.

RECOGNIZING THE TAX BENEFITS OF A LOSS

Accounting income is converted to taxable income by making appropriate adjustments for all temporary and permanent differences. This is true whether the accounting records report a net income or a net loss. Accounting income may become a taxable loss, and an accounting loss may become taxable income or a taxable loss, depending on the nature of the permanent and temporary differences. When a corporation prepares its tax return and finds it has a taxable loss, the corporation is entitled to offset the loss against past and future taxable income as follows:

- The loss can be *carried back* for three years for a refund of tax previously paid.
- Any remaining loss can be *carried forward* for 20 years to reduce taxes that would otherwise be payable.

If the sum of the previous three years' plus the next 20 years' taxable income turns out to be less than the loss, any remaining potential benefit is lost.

It is simple to account for the tax benefits of the loss *carrybacks*; the taxes recovered are recognized on the income statement as a tax recovery in the loss year, and the refund receivable is shown on the statement of financial position as a current asset. Recognition occurs in the period of the loss because there is no uncertainty about whether or not the company will actually receive the benefit. Accounting for loss carrybacks will be demonstrated in the next section.

However, if the carrybacks do not fully utilize the loss, a recognition problem arises. Income taxes can be reduced in *future* periods as a result of the tax **loss carryforward**. Should the benefit of reduced future taxes be recognized in the period of the loss, or only in the period in which the benefits are realized?

Since the future benefits arise from the current year's loss, the matching principle suggests that the benefits should be matched to the loss that created the benefits, and should be recognized in the loss year. However, the definitional approach to measuring financial statement elements says that assets should not be recognized unless they have probable future benefit. The general principle, therefore, is that the tax benefits of tax losses should be recognized in the period of the loss, *to the extent that they are probable.*

The actual amount of the benefit can be *measured* with reasonable assurance. If a company has a tax loss of $1 million and the tax rate is 35%, the potential benefit of the tax loss is that past and future income taxes will be reduced by $350,000 (that is, $1 million × 35%). Tax rate changes may cause some variation, but the potential benefit is readily estimable.

What is not certain is whether the benefits of any carryforwards will actually be *realized*. In order to realize the benefit, the company must have enough taxable income during the carryforward period to use up the loss carryforward. Basically, the carryforward benefit is a contingent gain—a benefit will be realized only *if* something happens in the future. The prudence principle (also known as conservatism) suggests that contingent gains should not be recognized prior to their realization. However, the IASB has chosen to favour earlier recognition over conservatism. Therefore, current accounting standards require recognition of the carryforward benefit whenever management decides that it is *probable* (i.e., greater than 50% probability) that the future tax benefits will be realized.

Tax Loss versus Tax Benefits

To avoid confusion, it is necessary to keep track separately of the amount of the tax *loss* and the amount of the tax *benefit*. The **tax loss** is the final amount of taxable loss on the tax return. The **tax benefit** is the total present and future benefit that the company will be able to realize from the tax loss through a reduction of income taxes paid to governments. Basically, the tax benefit is equal to the tax loss multiplied by the tax rate. Put another way, *the tax loss is the gross amount and the tax benefit is the tax savings.* Since tax rates can change, keeping track of the gross amount is essential for calculating the tax savings.

TAX LOSS CARRYBACKS

A tax **loss carryback** entitles the corporation to recover income tax actually paid in the previous three years. For example, assume that Fabian Corporation was established in 20X1.

For the first four years, the company was moderately successful, but in the fifth year it suffered a tax loss of $500,000. Fabian's taxable income for the first five years was as follows:

Year	Taxable Income	Tax Rate	Income Tax Paid
20X1	$100,000	40%	$ 40,000
20X2	240,000	40	96,000
20X3	160,000	35	56,000
20X4	300,000	37	111,000
20X5	(500,000)	38	—

The loss will be carried back to the preceding three years to recover tax previously paid. Normally, the loss is carried back to the earliest (oldest) year first, and then applied to succeeding years until the loss is used up. The year 20X1 is outside the three-year carryback period, and therefore the loss can be carried back only as far as 20X2. The tax recovery will be as follows:

Year	Carryback	Tax Rate	Tax Recovery
20X2	$240,000	40%	$ 96,000
20X3	160,000	35	56,000
20X4	100,000	37	37,000
Totals	**$500,000**		**$189,000**

In this example, the carryback completely utilizes the 20X5 tax loss of $500,000. Note that the tax is recovered at the rate at which it was originally paid. The tax rate in the year of the loss (i.e., 38% for 20X5) is irrelevant for determining the amount of tax recoverable via the carryback. Fabian will record the benefit of that carryback as follows:

Income tax receivable (SFP)	189,000	
Income tax expense (recovery) (I/S)		189,000

The *credit* to income tax expense reflects the fact that it is a recovery of taxes paid in earlier years. A company will usually label this amount as "provision for income tax" or "income tax recovery" in its income statement. If any part of the tax loss is attributable to discontinued operations, the recovery must be allocated to the relevant components of income, as we described in Chapter 3 for *intraperiod* allocation.

In 20X3, the tax rate was 35%; in 20X4 it had increased to 37%. The company could maximize its recovery by applying more of the carryback to 20X4 instead of 20X3; there is no requirement in the *Income Tax Act* to apply the carryback sequentially. If the company follows a recovery maximization strategy, the carryback would be applied as follows:

Year	Carryback	Tax Rate	Tax Recovery
20X2	$240,000	40%	$ 96,000
20X4	260,000	37	96,200
Totals	**$500,000**		**$192,200**

Maximizing the carryback tax recovery is a viable strategy, but it is a bit of a gamble because if the company has a loss in 20X7, the 20X4 carryback potential will have already been used up and the 20X3 tax is then out of reach because it is no longer within the allowable carryback period of three years. Therefore, companies usually apply the carry-back sequentially even if there may be a slight advantage to applying the carryback non-sequentially, to the years that had the highest tax rate.

TEMPORARY AND PERMANENT DIFFERENCES IN A LOSS YEAR

Step 1: Calculate Taxable Income

The first step in doing a tax question is always to calculate taxable income. This involves adjusting accounting income for permanent and temporary differences. Temporary differences continue to originate and/or reverse, regardless of whether the company is experiencing profits or losses. Permanent differences are likewise the same, whether accounting and/or taxable income are positive or negative. Indeed, it is quite possible for temporary differences and permanent differences to convert a pre-tax accounting profit to a tax loss. For example, assume the following facts for Michelle Limited for the fiscal year ending 31 December 20X8:

- Net income before taxes of $90,000, after deducting depreciation expense of $150,000;
- CCA totalling $280,000 deducted on the tax return;
- Net book value of capital assets of $1,700,000 and unclaimed capital cost (UCC) of $1,200,000 on 1 January 20X8, a temporary difference of $500,000 that is reflected in an accumulated deferred income tax liability balance of $200,000 at 1 January 20X8;
- Non-deductible golf club dues of $10,000;
- Taxable income in the three-year carryback period of $360,000; and
- Tax rate of 40% in the current and previous years.

Michelle Limited's taxable income for 20X8 will be computed as follows:

Accounting income	$ 90,000
Permanent difference:	
Golf club dues	+ 10,000
Temporary difference:	
Depreciation	+150,000
CCA	−280,000
Taxable income (loss)	$ (30,000)

Step 2: Determine Deferred Income Tax

The next step is to determine the change to deferred income tax caused by current-year temporary differences and/or any change in the tax rate. This is normally done with a table such as Exhibit 15-3 on page 886, but since the tax rate did not change this year, the shortcut approach can be used.

The difference between CCA and depreciation yields a temporary difference of ($130,000) (i.e., $150,000 − $280,000). This temporary difference increases the deferred income tax liability by $52,000 (i.e., $130,000 × 40%).

The $30,000 tax loss creates a potential tax benefit of $12,000 (at 40%).

Step 3: Journal Entries

The third step is to prepare the journal entries. These entries reflect temporary differences, income tax payable, if any, and the disposition of the tax loss.

The $52,000 of deferred income tax arising from temporary differences is recorded as follows:

Income tax expense (I/S)	52,000	
Deferred income tax liability—capital assets (SFP)		52,000

The $30,000 tax loss is carried back, which results in a tax recovery (@ 40%) of $12,000:

Income tax receivable—carryback benefit (SFP)	12,000	
Income tax expense (I/S)		12,000

If these two entries are combined, the summary entry to record the provision for income tax will be:

Income tax expense	40,000	
Income tax receivable—carryback benefit	12,000	
Deferred income tax liability—capital assets (SFP)		52,000

The bottom of the income statement will show:

Income before income tax		$90,000
Income tax expense (Note 1)		40,000
Net income		$50,000
Note 1:		
Deferred income tax	$52,000	
Recovery of amounts paid in prior years	(12,000)	
Income tax expense	$40,000	

Tax Planning—Adjusting Temporary Differences

In the Michelle Limited example above, the temporary difference created a tax loss of $30,000. Since the company had available taxable income in the carryback period against which the loss can be offset, good tax strategy calls for taking the maximum allowable CCA in 20X8 in order to obtain a refund of taxes previously paid.

Suppose instead that the company did not have taxable income in the preceding three years. A tax loss in 20X8 would not permit the company to realize any tax benefit in 20X8 because there would be no possibility of receiving a tax refund. In a sense, the tax loss would go to waste unless the company generates profits in the carryforward period, never a sure thing.

Instead of having a tax loss, the company can simply reduce the amount of CCA that it deducts on its tax return for 20X8 by $30,000, from $280,000 to $250,000. CCA is an *optional* deduction; in any year, a company can deduct anywhere from zero to the maximum percentage allowed by tax regulations. A company will have a higher amount of unclaimed capital cost (and CCA) in *future years* if it claims less CCA in the *current year*. Companies make these decisions based on advice from their tax-planning advisors.

CONCEPT REVIEW

1. How many years can a tax loss be carried back? How many years into the future can it be carried forward?

2. What is the difference between the tax loss in a particular year and the tax benefit of the loss?

3. Why do companies usually apply a loss carryback sequentially (i.e., to the earliest year first), even if the tax refund might be slightly larger if they applied it to the carryback year that had the highest tax rate?

TAX LOSS CARRYFORWARDS

In the Fabian Corporation example earlier in the chapter, the tax benefit of the $500,000 tax loss in 20X5 was fully realized through the carryback. But suppose instead that the loss in 20X5 was $1,000,000. Then the carryback could utilize only $700,000 of the loss:

Year	Carryback	Tax Rate	Tax Recovery
20X2	$240,000	40%	$ 96,000
20X3	160,000	35	56,000
20X4	300,000	37	111,000
Totals	**$700,000**		**$263,000**

The tax benefit ($263,000) relating to $700,000 of the $1 million tax loss is realized through the carryback; the tax benefit is both *recognized* and *realized* in 20X5. After the carryback, there is a carryforward of $300,000 remaining. The tax benefit of the loss carryforward cannot be realized until future years, when the carryforward is applied against otherwise taxable income.

The accounting question is whether the future tax benefit of the carryforward can be *recognized* in 20X5, the period of the loss. Companies often want to recognize the benefits of a loss carryforward because that recognition decreases the apparent accounting loss. The income tax recovery is a credit entry in the income statement, reducing the amount of the reported loss. Recognition will also either (1) reduce the deferred tax liability or (2) create an asset on the SFP if there is no future tax liability to offset it against.

Basic Probability Principle—"More Likely Than Not"

The criterion for recognizing the future benefits is simply a matter of probability. If it is probable that the carryforward will be realized, then the benefit is recognized. On the other hand, if realization is unlikely, then the potential benefit should not be recognized. The threshold under U.S. standards (and Canadian ASPE) is whether it is *more likely than not* that the benefit will be realized. IFRS uses "probable" rather than "more likely than not," but the meaning is the same.

Conceptually, it's simple: a 51% probability of realization requires recognition; 49% probability means no recognition. In practice, estimation is more difficult.

In deciding whether the probability is greater than 50%, management may consider possible tax-planning strategies, including actions such as:

- Reducing or eliminating CCA in the year of the loss and future years;
- Amending prior years' tax returns to reduce or eliminate CCA; or
- Recognizing taxable revenues in the carryforward period that might ordinarily be recognized in later periods.

Whether or not the over-50% criterion has been met is obviously a matter of judgement. In theory, there should be objective evidence as to the likelihood of realization.

Evidence of Probability

IAS 12 provides some guidelines to help managers (and auditors) decide whether the probability threshold has been met. Favourable evidence to support recognition includes the following:

- A strong earnings history, interrupted only by an unusual event that caused the loss;
- Enough accumulated temporary differences to absorb the unrealized loss as the temporary differences reverse; or
- The existence of tax planning opportunities that will create taxable profit in the carryforward period.

(leave)

Another factor that can contribute to a positive probability assessment is the existence of contracts or back orders that are likely to generate more than enough taxable income to absorb the loss carryforward.

On the other hand, the probability criterion will *not* be met if:

- The company has a history of tax losses expiring without being used;
- A change in the company's economic prospects indicates that losses may continue for the next few years; and
- There are pending circumstances that, if not resolved in the company's favour, will impair the company's ability to operate profitably (e.g., significant patent infringement lawsuits or potential major environmental impacts caused by the company's operations).

When a company's management decides that the probability criterion for recognition of any part of the benefit of a tax loss carryforward has been met, the "nature of evidence supporting its recognition" must be disclosed in the notes.

Reducing CCA

Two tax-planning strategies by which a company can increase the likelihood of realizing the benefits of a carryforward are (1) reducing or eliminating capital cost allowance deductions in the current and future years and (2) amending prior years' tax returns to reduce or eliminate CCA.

Earlier in this chapter, we pointed out that a company can reduce its tax loss by reducing or eliminating CCA in a loss year. The lower the loss, the more likely that its tax benefits can be realized. The key to this strategy is that CCA not claimed is not lost. CCA is an *optional deduction* for tax purposes. It is limited to a maximum, but there is no minimum. If a company chooses not to claim CCA in a year, the unclaimed capital cost (UCC) remains unchanged—except for additions to and retirements from the class—and CCA on the undiminished balance remains available as a deduction in future years.

One way of increasing the likelihood that a company will fully utilize a carryforward is to eliminate CCA in the carryforward years. In capital-intensive industries, CCA is very large, both in absolute amount and in relation to net income. Not claiming CCA has the effect of increasing taxable income, against which the carryforward can be used. After the carryforward benefits have all been realized, the company can resume deducting full CCA to reduce its taxable income in the following years.

A further strategy is to *amend prior years' returns* to reduce or eliminate CCA. The relevant time frame is the three previous years, those to which carrybacks apply. If CCA is reduced in those years, taxable income increases. If taxable income increases, more of the carryback can be used. Indeed, it may be possible to reduce prior years' CCA enough to completely use up the tax loss as a carryback. The CCA that is removed from prior-year tax returns is restored to the balance of UCC and available for deduction in future years.

The *Income Tax Act* imposes various restrictions on the amendment of prior years' returns, and these need not concern us here. But "playing around" with CCA is a fully legitimate way of either reducing a tax loss or using it up in prior and subsequent years.

Reassessment in Years Subsequent to the Loss Year

Once the future tax benefit of a tax loss carryforward has been recognized as an asset, the asset is subject to review at each reporting date. If the probability of realization drops to 50% or less, the deferred income tax asset should be reduced. There is nothing unusual about this requirement; assets are generally subject to review and to writedown if their value has been impaired. If an asset is unlikely to recover its carrying value, either through use or through sale, it should be written down.

The potential benefit of a tax loss carryforward may be recognized not only in the year of the loss, but also in years subsequent to the loss year. Management may decide that the 50% probability threshold is not attained in the year of the loss and therefore will not recognize the tax loss carryforward benefits. In any subsequent year (that is, prior to actually realizing the benefits), management may decide that the probability of realization has increased to over 50%. When the probability is judged to become greater than 50%, the future benefit of a prior year's tax loss carryforward should be recognized in that year. Previous years are not restated.

Examples of Recognition Scenarios—Direct Recognition

We can illustrate the various basic recognition points by means of a simple illustration. Suppose that Parravano Limited has been in business for five years, and incurs a loss of $500,000 in 20X5. The company has no temporary or permanent differences, and therefore the pretax accounting loss is the same as the loss for income tax purposes. The history of the company's earnings since the company began operations is as follows:

Year	Taxable Income (Loss)	Taxes Paid (Recovered)
20X1	$100,000	$40,000
20X2	(60,000)	(24,000)
20X3	140,000	56,000
20X4	30,000	12,000

The tax rate has been constant at 40% from 20X1 through 20X5.

In 20X5, Parravano incurs a loss of $500,000. A further loss of $100,000 occurs in 20X6.

In 20X5, Parravano can carry back $170,000 of the loss to recover taxes paid in 20X3 and 20X4, a total of $68,000. A carryforward of $330,000 remains, the potential tax benefit of which is $132,000 ($330,000 × 40%). Recognition of the future benefits of the carryforward depends on management's conclusions regarding the likelihood of realizing the benefits. The following scenarios illustrate recognition of the benefits of tax loss carryforwards under various possible assumptions concerning the likelihood of realization. The entries under each scenario are summarized in the "Direct Recognition" columns of Exhibit 16-1.

Scenario 1: Assuming future realization is judged to be probable in each year of the losses. If the probability of realizing the future tax benefit of the carryforward is judged to be more than 50%, the potential $132,000 benefit of the $330,000 20X5 carryforward is recognized in the year of the loss. The entry to record taxes for 20X5 will be as follows, assuming a 40% tax rate:

Entry in loss year 20X5		
Income tax receivable—carryback benefit (SFP)	68,000	
Deferred income tax asset—carryforward benefit (SFP)[1]	132,000	
Income tax expense (recovery) (I/S)		200,000
[1]$330,000 × 40% = $132,000		

EXHIBIT 16-1

COMPARISON OF METHODS FOR RECORDING TAX LOSS CARRYFORWARD BENEFITS

Scenario	Year	Direct Recognition			Using Valuation Account		

1a. C/B + full recognition of 20X5 C/F benefit	**20X5**	IT rec.—C/B
		DIT asset—C/F
		  IT exp. (recovery)
			68,000
			132,000
			
				200,000
					IT rec.—C/B
					DIT asset—C/F
					  IT exp. (recovery)
						68,000
						132,000
						
							200,000

1b. Full recognition of 20X6 C/F benefit	**20X6**	DIT asset—C/F
		  IT exp. (recovery)
			40,000
			
				40,000
					DIT asset—C/F
					  IT exp. (recovery)
						40,000
						
							40,000

2a. C/B, but no recognition of C/F benefit	**20X5**	IT rec.—C/B
		  IT exp. (recovery)
			68,000
			
				68,000
					IT rec.—C/B
					DIT asset—C/F
					  IT exp. (recovery)
					IT exp. (recovery)
					  Val. allow.—DIT asset
						68,000
						132,000
						
						132,000
						
							200,000
							
							132,000

2b. Recognize full 20X5 + 20X6 C/F benefit	**20X6**	DIT asset—C/F
		  IT exp. (recovery)
			172,000
			
				172,000
					DIT asset—C/F
					  IT exp. (recovery)
					Val. allow.—DIT asset
					  IT exp. (recovery)
						40,000
						
						132,000
						
							40,000
							
							132,000

3a. C/B but no recognition of C/F benefit	**20X5**	IT rec.—C/B
		  IT exp. (recovery)
			68,000
			
				68,000
					IT rec.—C/B
					DIT asset—C/F
					  IT exp. (recovery)
					IT exp. (recovery)
					  Val. allow.—DIT asset
						68,000
						132,000
						
						132,000
						
							200,000
							
							132,000

3b. Partial recognition of C/F benefit	**20X6**	DIT asset—C/F
		  IT exp. (recovery)
			80,000
			
				80,000
					DIT asset—C/F
					  IT exp. (recovery)
					Val. allow.—DIT asset
					  IT exp. (recovery)
						40,000
						
						40,000
						
							40,000
							
							40,000

4a. Same as scenario 1, above—full recognition	**20X5**	IT rec.—C/B
		DIT asset—C/F
		  IT exp. (recovery)
			68,000
			132,000
			
				200,000
					IT rec.—C/B
					DIT asset—C/F
					  IT exp. (recovery)
						68,000
						132,000
						
							200,000

4b. Only $200,000 of total C/F benefit is now deemed probable	**20X6**	IT expense
		  DIT asset—C/F
			52,000
			
				52,000
					DIT asset—C/F
					  IT exp. (recovery)
					IT expense
					  Val. allow.—DIT asset
						40,000
						
						92,000
						
							40,000
							
							92,000

Legend: IT = income tax; DIT = deferred income tax; C/B = carryback; C/F = carryforward

The total income tax expense (recovery) account on the 20X5 income statement (i.e., $68,000 + $132,000 = $200,000) is equal to 40% of the tax loss for 20X5 ($500,000 × 40%). The full potential tax benefit of the loss has been *recognized*, although only $68,000 will be *realized* in the current year.

In 20X6, the $40,000 potential tax benefit of the $100,000 loss will also be recognized, if management believes that the loss carryforwards from both years are likely to be realized within the carryforward period:

> *Entry in loss year 20X6*
> Deferred income tax asset—carryforward benefit (SFP)[1]   40,000
>   Income tax expense (recovery) (I/S)   40,000
>
> [1]$100,000 × 40% = $40,000

Scenario 2: Assuming future realization is judged to be improbable in 20X5, but becomes probable in 20X6. Now, suppose instead that, due to Parravano's erratic earnings history, realization of the benefit of the carryforward is judged to be unlikely. The entry to record the tax benefit in 20X5 would then be limited to the amount of tax recovered through the carryback:

Entry in loss year 20X5		
Income tax receivable—carryback benefit (SFP)	68,000	
Income tax expense (recovery) (I/S)		68,000

In the following year, 20X6, Parravano Limited has a loss for both accounting and tax purposes of $100,000. Since there is no available taxable income in the carryback period, the $100,000 tax loss will be carried forward. The company now has two carryforwards that have been neither realized nor recognized:

- $330,000 from 20X5, expiring in 20X25; and
- $100,000 from 20X6, expiring in 20X26.

The total carryforward is $430,000.

However, suppose that Parravano obtained a large contract late in 20X6. The 20X6 operating results do not yet reflect the profit that will be generated by the contract, but the contract is expected to boost earnings considerably in 20X7 and the next several years. Therefore, management decides when preparing the 20X6 financial statements that it is probable that the full benefit of tax loss carryforwards from both 20X5 and 20X6 will be realized within the carryforward period.

Assuming a continuing tax rate of 40%, the future tax benefit of the total $430,000 carryforward is $172,000. Since, in management's judgement, the probability criterion has now been satisfied, the future benefit is recorded as an asset:

Recognition in 20X6 of future benefits		
Deferred income tax asset—carryforward benefit (SFP)[1]	172,000	
Income tax expense (recovery) (I/S)		172,000
[1]$430,000 × 40% = $172,000		

When the future benefit of $172,000 is recognized in the income statement, the 20X6 pre-tax loss of $100,000 will be converted into a net *income* of $72,000 simply as the result of recognizing the still-unrealized tax loss carryforward benefit:

Net income (loss) before income tax	$(100,000)
Income tax expense (recovery)	(172,000)
Net income (loss)	$ 72,000

Scenario 3: Partial recognition. In Scenario 2, we assumed that Parravano recognized all of the accumulated tax benefits in 20X6. It is possible, however, that management may decide that realization of only part of the benefit is probable. Suppose, for example, that Parravano management decided in 20X6 that the benefits from only $200,000 of the accumulated tax loss carryforwards had a probability of greater than 50% of being realized. At a tax rate of 40%, the entry to record the recognition in 20X6 will be:

Recognition in 20X6 of future benefits		
Deferred income tax asset—carryforward benefit (SFP)[1]	80,000	
Income tax expense (recovery) (I/S)		80,000

[1]$200,000 × 40% = $80,000

The benefits from the remaining $230,000 tax loss carryforward can be recognized in a later period (within the carryforward period), if the probability of realization becomes greater than 50%.

Scenario 4: Reduction of previously recognized benefit. Like any other asset, the deferred income tax asset that arises from recognizing the future benefit of a tax loss carryforward must continue to have probable future benefit. If an asset no longer is likely to be recoverable or realizable, it must be written down to its probable future benefit. If the probable future benefit is zero, the asset must be completely written off. If the probable future benefit is greater than zero but less than the originally recorded amount, the balance should be reduced accordingly.

For example, return to the Scenario 1 entry for 20X5, when Parravano recorded a $132,000 deferred income tax asset because of a loss carryforward in 20X5:

Income tax receivable—carryback benefit (SFP)	68,000	
Deferred income tax asset—carryforward benefit (SFP)	132,000	
Income tax expense (recovery) (I/S)		200,000

But suppose that in 20X6, Parravano experiences an additional loss of $100,000. The total tax loss carryforward is now $430,000: $330,000 from 20X5 plus $100,000 from 20X6. When preparing the 20X6 financial statements, Parravano's management decides that realization of the future benefit of only $200,000 of the tax loss carryforward is probable within the carryforward period. The deferred income tax asset of $132,000 must be reduced to the lower amount of probable recovery: $200,000 × 40% = $80,000. The entry to reduce the balance of the deferred income tax asset is $52,000, the amount necessary to reduce the balance from $132,000 to $80,000:

Income tax expense (I/S)	52,000	
Deferred income tax asset—carryforward benefit (SFP)		52,000

There is nothing final about the estimate of future recovery. The probability of realizing the benefit is evaluated at each reporting date until the carryforward expires. In future years within the carryforward period, Parravano may decide that the probability of realization of the full carryforward benefit has become probable. If that happens, then the deferred income tax asset can be increased to reflect the higher probable amount.

Impact of Recognition Assumption on Net Income

The only difference between these four scenarios is the estimated probability of realizing the loss carryforward benefits. The earnings impacts of these different scenarios are summarized in Exhibit 16-2. Depending on management's realization estimates, the after-tax net loss in 20X5 varies from $(300,000) to $(432,000). In 20X6, the bottom line varies from a loss of $(152,000) to a net income of $72,000. Indeed, the potential net loss in 20X6 could be as high as $(192,000) if all of the previously recognized carryforward benefits were deemed improbable of realization.

These scenarios demonstrate two points: (1) the importance of management's estimates of the probability of recognition, and (2) the potential range of earnings management that is

---

EXHIBIT 16-2

COMPARISON OF NET INCOME UNDER DIFFERENT RECOGNITION SCENARIOS

Scenario		20X5	20X6
1	Income (loss) before income taxes	$(500,000)	$(100,000)
	Income tax expense (recovery)	(200,000)	(40,000)
	Net income (loss)	$(300,000)	$ (60,000)
2	Income (loss) before income taxes	$(500,000)	$(100,000)
	Income tax expense (recovery)	(68,000)	(172,000)
	Net income (loss)	$(432,000)	$ 72,000
3	Income (loss) before income taxes	$(500,000)	$(100,000)
	Income tax expense (recovery)	(68,000)	(80,000)
	Net income (loss)	$(432,000)	$ (20,000)
4	Income (loss) before income taxes	$(500,000)	$(100,000)
	Income tax expense (recovery)	(200,000)	52,000
	Net income (loss)	$(300,000)	$(152,000)

---

possible under the probability criterion for recognition. Financial statement readers should be wary of income tax "recoveries" that are recognized but not realized. These recoveries may well be reversed in future years, with resulting impacts on reported net earnings. They also are subject to manipulation if management is tempted to "manage" reported earnings—this is a potential ethical issue that professional accountants must be sensitive to.

USING A VALUATION ALLOWANCE

In the example above, we increased or decreased the balance of the deferred income tax asset directly. An alternative approach is to record the full amount of the potential future benefit and then use a **valuation allowance** to adjust for the probability of realization. The entries, using a valuation allowance, are summarized in the final columns of Exhibit 16-1.

As an analogy, think of accounts receivable. The full amount of accounts receivable is always recorded in the accounts, and then an allowance for doubtful accounts is used to reduce the balance to its estimated realizable value. The same principle can be applied to potential tax benefits of tax loss carryforwards. Return to the Parravano example. In every scenario, the full amount of the future tax benefit is recorded in 20X5, the loss year:

Deferred income tax asset—carryforward benefit[1]	132,000	
Income tax expense (recovery)		132,000
[1] $330,000 × 40%		

A valuation account is then considered, depending on the amount of recovery that is *probable*.

Scenario 1: Full recovery is probable. No valuation allowance is needed in this situation because management estimates that the company probably can realize the full benefit of the tax loss carryforward.

Scenario 2: Recovery is improbable at first, becoming probable in a later year. The full amount of the future benefit is recorded, as shown in the entry above. However, in 20X5, management believes that the probability of recovery is less than 50%. None of the future benefit should appear on the 20X5 SFP. An allowance for the full amount is required:

Income tax expense (recovery)	132,000	
Valuation allowance—deferred income tax (DIT) asset		132,000

When the company prepares a statement of financial position for 20X5, the valuation allowance will completely offset the DIT asset and none of the asset will appear on the statement of financial position.

In 20X6, none of the 20X5 loss carryforward is used, and the company has an additional loss carryforward of $100,000. The full future benefit of the 20X6 loss is recorded (at 40%):

Deferred income tax asset—carryforward benefit	40,000	
Income tax expense (recovery)		40,000

The deferred income tax asset and its related valuation account now appear as follows:

Deferred income tax benefit relating to 20X5	$132,000
Deferred income tax benefit relating to 20X6	40,000
Total potential future benefits	172,000
Less: valuation allowance	(132,000)
Balance prior to year-end 20X6 adjustment	$ 40,000

At the end of 20X6, management decides that full realization of the benefits now is more probable than not. Therefore, the valuation allowance is reduced to zero in order to permit the full future value of the asset (i.e., $172,000) to appear on the 20X6 statement of financial position:

Valuation allowance—DIT asset	132,000	
Income tax expense (recovery)		132,000

Scenario 3: Partial recognition. In 20X5, a potential future tax benefit of $132,000 is recorded, which then is completely offset by a valuation account for $132,000:

Income tax receivable—tax loss carryback	68,000	
Deferred income tax asset—carryforward benefit	132,000	
Income tax expense (recovery)		200,000

Income tax expense (recovery)	132,000	
Valuation allowance—deferred income tax (DIT) asset		132,000

In 20X6, an additional $40,000 tax benefit is recorded for the 20X6 loss carryforward of $100,000:

Deferred income tax asset—carryforward benefit	40,000	
Income tax expense (recovery)		40,000

After this additional entry, there is a debit of $172,000 in the DIT asset account and $132,000 in the valuation allowance—a *net* balance of $40,000. Management decides that $200,000 of the carryforward is likely to be utilized. Therefore, the valuation account must be *reduced* by $40,000 to show the probable recovery of $80,000 as the net balance. The adjustment is:

Valuation allowance—DIT asset	40,000	
Income tax expense (recovery)		40,000

Only the net amount of $80,000 will be reported on the 20X6 statement of financial position:

Deferred income tax asset—carryforward benefit	$172,000
Valuation allowance—DIT asset	(92,000)
Balance reported on 31 December 20X6 statement of financial position	$ 80,000

Scenario 4: Reduction of previously recognized benefit. In this scenario, the benefit is fully recognized (at $132,000) in the year of the loss, 20X5. No valuation allowance is created because management feels that realization of the benefits is likely.

In 20X6, the company has another loss of $100,000. The potential future benefit of this loss is recognized:

Deferred income tax asset—carryforward benefit	40,000	
Income tax expense (recovery)		40,000

The gross accumulated tax loss carryforward is now $430,000 (that is, $330,000 + $100,000) and the total recorded deferred income tax asset is $172,000 (i.e., $132,000 + $40,000).

At this point, management decides that the company probably will realize the benefits of only $200,000 of the total carryforward. The benefit is $200,000 × 40% = $80,000. Therefore, the valuation allowance is credited for $92,000 to bring the reported DIT asset balance down from $172,000 to the estimated probable realizable value of $80,000:

Income tax expense	92,000	
Valuation allowance—DIT asset		92,000

Write-off of Expired Carryforward Benefits When a company reaches the end of the carryforward period for any tax loss, any remaining DIT asset balance must be written off. When an allowance account is used, the expired portion of both the DIT asset and the valuation account must be written off.

For example, suppose that Parravano has not been able to utilize any of the tax loss carryforwards from 20X5 and 20X6. Assume that in recognition of this fact, the company had already credited the valuation account for the full amount of the benefits relating to those two years, $172,000. The carryforward period for the 20X5 loss ends 20 years later, in 20X25. At the end of 20X25, the 20X5 potential benefit of $132,000 must be eliminated:

Valuation allowance—DIT asset	132,000	
Deferred income tax asset—carryforward benefit		132,000

Both accounts will still contain the $40,000 balance relating to 20X6, but that amount will have to be eliminated in the following year (20X26) when the carryforward period for the 20X6 loss expires.

Use of the Valuation Allowance Method The valuation allowance method may seem more cumbersome than simply recognizing or not recognizing the deferred income tax asset represented by a tax loss carryforward. However, many companies prefer the valuation allowance method because it keeps track of the full tax loss carryforward benefits. They are comfortable with the valuation allowance method because it is consistent with the approach used for other financial statement elements such as accounts receivable and inventory LCM valuations.

Of course, one reason for its popularity is that U.S. standards *require* use of the valuation allowance method. Therefore, any Canadian companies that report into the United States necessarily will use a valuation allowance.

Bear in mind that a valuation allowance is simply a bookkeeping convenience. Using a valuation method is *not a choice of accounting policy* because it has no effect on the numbers reported in the financial statements. The amount of future tax benefit that is reported on the SFP and in profit or loss will not be affected by the bookkeeping method the company chooses.

WHICH TAX RATE?

IFRS requires deferred tax assets and liabilities to be recognized at the rate(s) that are expected to be in effect when the temporary differences reverse or the tax loss carryforward benefits are realized. In most instances, that will be the rate that is enacted at the reporting date. However, if Parliament has approved a rate change that will take effect in one or more future years, the future benefits of tax loss carryforwards should be measured at the substantially enacted rates for those future years in which the benefits are expected to be realized. Given the difficulty of estimating exactly which year the benefits will be realized, companies may need to make adjustments to the recorded DIT asset for the carryforwards.

Tax Rate Changes

Once a deferred income tax asset has been recorded for a tax loss carryforward, the balance of that account must be maintained at the tax rate that is expected to be in effect when the carryforward is utilized. As noted above, the usual presumption is that the **substantially enacted tax rate** will be used.

In Scenario 1, above, Parravano recorded the full amount of the tax benefit from its $330,000 accumulated tax loss carryforwards in 19X5. Parravano will have a deferred income tax asset of $132,000 on its statement of financial position, recorded at a 40% tax rate.

Suppose that the tax rate goes down to 38% before Parravano actually uses any of the carryforward. The asset will have to be revalued to $330,000 × 38%, or $125,400. This change will be included as part of the annual re-evaluation of the DIT asset or liability. If the carryforward benefit is the only component of Parravano's DIT asset, the writedown would be recorded as follows:

Income tax expense ($132,000 − $125,400) (I/S)	6,600	
Deferred income tax asset—carryforward benefit (SFP)		6,600

If, instead, the tax rate goes up, the increase in the asset account will be *credited* to income tax expense.

1. What is the basic criterion for recognizing the benefit of a tax loss carryforward prior to its realization?

2. What tax rate should be used to recognize the future benefits of a tax loss carryforward?

3. Is it possible to recognize the future benefits of tax loss carryforwards in years subsequent to the loss year? If so, explain the necessary circumstances. If not, explain why not.

4. Once the future benefit of a tax loss carryforward has been recognized, does the asset always remain on the statement of financial position until the benefit has been realized?

BASIC ILLUSTRATION

To illustrate the recognition of tax loss carryforward benefits over a series of years, we will start with a fairly simple example that has no other types of temporary differences. To keep things interesting, however, we will include tax rate changes.

Assume the following information for Dutoit Limited:

	20X1	20X2	20X3	20X4
Net income before tax	$100,000	$(300,000)	$150,000	$250,000
Taxable income*	100,000	(300,000)	150,000	250,000
Tax rate	45%	40%	42%	43%

*Prior to including any tax loss carrybacks or carryforwards.

The first year of operations for Dutoit was 20X1. Assume that the tax rate for each year is determined during that year. For example, we do not know in 20X2 that the tax rate for 20X3 will be 42%. Dutoit does not use a valuation allowance.

Assuming Realization Is Not Probable

We will first assume that at no point does management believe that there is greater than a 50% probability that the company will be able to realize the benefits of any unused tax loss carryforward. This is a pessimistic assumption, of course, but in an uncertain environment, management may really not know if the company will have a profitable year until it is well underway.

20X1   The income tax is simply the taxable income times the tax rate:

| Income tax expense ($100,000 × 45%) | 45,000 | |
| Income tax payable | | 45,000 |

20X2 $100,000 of the loss can be carried back to 20X1, to recover the prior year's taxes paid:

| Income tax receivable—carryback benefit | 45,000 | |
| Income tax expense (recovery) | | 45,000 |

There is an unrecognized tax loss carryforward of $200,000.

20X3 Taxable income prior to deducting the tax loss carryforward is $150,000. The tax loss carryforward of $200,000 more than offsets the otherwise-taxable income for 20X3. No taxes will be due, and no income tax expense will be recorded or reported. There is a tax loss of $50,000 still unused.

For the sake of clarity, two entries can be made in a year where a loss carryforward is used. The first entry records income tax as though there were no loss carryforward:

Income tax expense ($150,000 × 42%)	63,000	
Income tax payable		63,000

Of course, the income tax payable does not have to be paid, so the second entry eliminates it, recording the use of the loss carryforward:

Income tax payable	63,000	
Income tax expense (recovery)		63,000

The company should show the offsetting effects of the two opposite income tax expenses on 20X3 earnings. The disclosure could be either on the face of the income statement or in the notes. If income statement presentation is used:

Net income		$150,000
Income tax expense (recovery):		
Income tax on current year's earnings	$63,000	
Tax reduction from tax loss carryforward	(63,000)	—
Net income		$150,000

20X4 There is $250,000 of taxable income, on which $250,000 × 43%, or $107,500, of tax would be paid. The remaining $50,000 carryforward is used, reducing the taxes otherwise due by $50,000 × 43%, or $21,500. The net amount owing is $86,000:

Income tax expense	107,500	
Income tax payable		107,500
Income tax payable	21,500	
Income tax expense (recovery)		21,500

The breakdown of income tax expense may be included in the notes or in the income statement. The income statement will show:

Income before income tax		$250,000
Income tax expense (recovery)		
Tax on current earnings	$107,500	
Recovered through loss carryforward	(21,500)	86,000
Net income		$164,000

Notice that in each year, the carryforward is applied against taxable income in that year at the current rate. *The tax rate in the year of the loss is irrelevant.*

Assuming Realization Becomes Probable

Now, let's re-examine the situation assuming instead that, in 20X3, Dutoit's management judges that it is probable that the benefits of the remaining carryforward will be realized.

The entries in 20X1 and 20X2 will not change. In 20X3, however, $150,000 of the carry-forward is used to reduce 20X3 taxable income to zero. The remaining $50,000 carryforward is also recognized. The benefit of the full $200,000 carryforward is *recognized*, even though the benefit of only $150,000 is *realized* in that year by applying it against the taxable income in that year. The entries for 20X3 now are:

Income tax expense	63,000	
Income tax payable (unchanged)		63,000
Deferred income tax asset—carryforward benefit	21,000	
Income tax payable	63,000	
Income tax expense (recovery)		84,000

The full benefit of the $200,000 carryforward has been *recognized* in 20X3. Income tax expense is a net credit on the income statement of $21,000, the unrealized portion of the carryforward.

Income before income tax		$150,000
Income tax expense (recovery):		
Income tax on current earnings	$63,000	
Recovery from tax loss carryforward	(84,000)	(21,000)
Net income		$171,000

The income statement may simply show the $21,000 recovery, but the detail should be disclosed in the notes.

In 20X4, the remaining $50,000 of tax loss carryforward is used, but it has already been *recognized*. The result, therefore, is that the balance of the deferred income tax (DIT) asset goes from $21,000 at the beginning of 20X4 to zero at the end of the year. The entries are:

Income tax expense	107,500	
Income tax payable ($250,000 × 43%)		107,500
Income tax payable ($50,000 × 43%)	21,500	
Deferred income tax asset—carryforward benefit		21,000
Income tax expense (recovery)		500

In the entry above, the credit to the DIT asset is the amount recorded. The change in the tax rate has made the loss carryforward worth an extra $500 ($50,000 × 1% = $500) which is credited to income tax expense.

EXTENDED ILLUSTRATION

In this illustration of accounting for the tax benefits of tax losses, we will assume that (1) the company has one type of temporary difference relating to capital assets, (2) a loss arises in the second year, and (3) the income tax rate changes in the third and fourth years. The facts for Birchall Incorporated are as follows:

- In 20X1, Birchall begins operations and acquires equipment costing $1 million.
- The equipment is being amortized straight-line at 10% (i.e., at $100,000 per year), and the company's policy is to expense a full year's depreciation in the year of acquisition.

- Birchall claims CCA of $350,000 in 20X1, $200,000 in 20X2, $150,000 in 20X3, and $100,000 in 20X4.
- The tax rate is 40% in 20X1 and 20X2. During 20X3, Parliament increases the tax rate to 42%, applicable to 20X3 and following years, and, in 20X4, the rate is changed to 43%.
- Birchall's earnings before income tax for 20X1 through 20X4 are as follows:

20X1	$ 300,000
20X2	$(600,000) (loss)
20X3	$ 200,000
20X4	$ 600,000

The first step is to calculate taxable income, shown in Exhibit 16-3. In 20X1, taxable income is $50,000. At 40%, the current tax payable is $20,000.

Next, the change in deferred income tax is calculated. This is done in table format, as shown in Exhibit 16-4. The initial cost of the capital assets (i.e., equipment) was $1,000,000. In 20X1, Birchall deducts CCA of $350,000 on its tax return and depreciation of $100,000 on its income statement. As a result, the *tax basis* of the capital assets at the end of 20X1 is $650,000 (i.e., $1,000,000 − $350,000) while the accounting carrying value is $900,000; a temporary difference of $250,000 exists. At the 40% enacted tax rate, the deferred income tax (DIT) liability for the capital assets is $100,000. Combining these two elements gives Birchall's 20X1 income tax expense of $120,000:

Income tax expense	120,000	
Income tax payable		20,000
Deferred income tax liability—capital assets		100,000

In 20X2, Birchall has a loss. The accounting loss (pre-tax) is $600,000, but the loss for tax purposes is $700,000 after adding back depreciation and deducting CCA (Exhibit 16-3). Of the tax loss, $50,000 can be carried back to 20X1 to claim a refund of the $20,000 paid in that year. The remaining $650,000 of the tax loss will be carried forward.

The tax basis of the capital assets declines to $450,000 (after the 20X2 CCA of $200,000), while the carrying value declines to $800,000 (after deducting another $100,000 of

---

EXHIBIT 16-3

EXTENDED ILLUSTRATION—CALCULATION OF TAXABLE INCOME, INCOME TAX PAYABLE, AND DEFERRED INCOME TAX

	20X1	20X2	20X3	20X4
Tax Rate (t)	40%	40%	42%	43%
Accounting income (loss) subject to tax	$300,000	$(600,000)	$200,000	$600,000
Temporary difference:				
+ Depreciation	100,000	100,000	100,000	100,000
− CCA	(350,000)	(200,000)	(150,000)	(100,000)
Taxable income (loss) for current year	$ 50,000	$(700,000)	$150,000	$600,000
Income tax payable (before using the loss carryforward)	$ 20,000		$ 63,000	$258,000

EXHIBIT 16-4

EXTENDED ILLUSTRATION—DEFERRED INCOME TAX TABLE

	[1] Year-end Tax Basis dr. (cr.)	[2] Year-end Carrying Value dr. (cr.)	[3] = [1] − [2] Temporary Difference Deductible (Taxable)	[4] = [3] × t Deferred Tax Asset (Liability) at Yr.-end Rate	[5] = prev.[4] Less Beginning Balance dr. (cr.)	[6] = [4] − [5] Adjustment for Current Year dr. (cr.)
20X1 *[t = 40%]:* Capital assets	$650,000	$900,000	(250,000)	$(100,000)	0	$(100,000)
20X2 *[t = 40%]:* Capital assets	450,000	800,000	(350,000)	(140,000)	$(100,000)	(40,000)
20X3 *[t = 42%]:* Capital assets	300,000	700,000	(400,000)	(168,000)	(140,000)	(28,000)
20X4 *[t = 43%]:* Capital assets	200,000	600,000	(400,000)	(172,000)	(168,000)	(4,000)

depreciation) at the end of 20X2. The temporary difference relating to the capital assets therefore is $350,000, resulting in a DIT liability of $140,000 at the end of 20X2. The year-end DIT liability is an increase of $40,000 over the previous year. These components can be summarized as follows:

- Tax loss is $700,000, of which $50,000 is carried back and $650,000 is carried forward.
- DIT liability relating to capital assets increases by $40,000.
- Birchall has a receivable for tax recovery (carryback) of $20,000.

From this point on, we must make assumptions about the probability of realizing the benefits of the $650,000 carryforward.

Situation 1: Assuming Probability of Realization is ≤ 50%

20X2

If realization is *not* probable, the components already identified above are recorded as follows for 20X2:

Income tax expense	20,000	
Income tax receivable—carryback benefit	20,000	
Deferred income tax liability—capital assets		40,000

Exhibit 16-5 shows the journal entries to record income tax expense.

20X3

In 20X3, taxable income is $150,000, as is shown in the third numeric column of Exhibit 16-3. This permits Birchall to use some of the tax loss carryforward to offset the otherwise taxable income. The entries to record income tax expense can be condensed into a single entry, but it may be more helpful to present them as two separate entries so we can see what is going on:

1. Without the carryforward, the income tax expense for 20X3 would be the tax payable on taxable income of $150,000 plus the change in the DIT liability. The tax basis of the capital assets is $300,000, and the carrying value is $700,000, which yields a temporary

---

EXHIBIT 16-5

EXTENDED ILLUSTRATION—SITUATION 1 CARRYFORWARD

Realization Probability ≤ 50%
Income Tax Journal Entries

Income tax journal entry, 20X1

Income tax expense	120,000	
Deferred income tax liability—capital assets		100,000
Income tax payable		20,000

Income tax journal entry, 20X2

Income tax expense	20,000	
Income tax receivable—carryback benefit	20,000	
Deferred income tax liability—capital assets		40,000

Income tax journal entries, 20X3

Income tax expense	91,000	
Deferred income tax liability—capital assets		28,000
Income tax payable ($150,000 × .42)		63,000
Income tax payable	63,000	
Income tax expense—carryforward benefit		63,000

Income tax journal entries, 20X4

Income tax expense	262,000	
Deferred income tax liability—capital assets		4,000
Income tax payable ($600,000 × .43)		258,000
Income tax payable	215,000	
Income tax expense—carryforward benefit		215,000

---

difference of $400,000. The tax rate is changed to 42% in 20X3, which means that the ending balance of the FIT liability should be $168,000 (that is, $400,000 × 42%). The entry to record the income tax expense *without* the carryforward is:

Income tax expense	91,000	
Deferred income tax liability—capital assets		
($168,000 − $140,000)		28,000
Income tax payable ($150,000 × 42%)		63,000

2. Applying $150,000 of the carryforward against the taxable income eliminates the amount of tax payable and reduces income tax expense:

Income tax payable ($150,000 × 42%)	63,000	
Income tax expense—carryforward benefit		63,000

The result for 20X3 is that net income tax expense of only $28,000 is recognized. At the end of 20X3, Birchall has an unused gross tax loss carryforward of $500,000:

20X2 tax loss	$ 700,000
Carryback to 20X1	− 50,000
Carryforward used in 20X3	−150,000
Remaining carryforward at end of 20X3	$ 500,000

20X4

For 20X4, taxable income is $600,000. In this year, CCA is equal to depreciation, and therefore there is no change in the amount of temporary difference relating to the capital assets. However, there is a change in the tax rate, from 42% to 43%, and there is a change in the DIT liability. The DIT liability is $400,000 × 43% = $172,000, an increase of $4,000 over the 20X3 year-end DIT liability. The $500,000 loss carryforward is used to reduce income tax payable. The entries to record income tax expense are:

Income tax expense	262,000	
Income tax payable ($600,000 × 43%)		258,000
Deferred income tax liability—capital assets		4,000
Income tax payable	215,000	
Income tax expense—carryforward benefit		215,000

As the result of these three entries, the net income tax expense reported on the income statement is $47,000: ($262,000 − $215,000). The series of entries for this scenario is summarized in Exhibit 16-5.

Situation 2: Assuming Probability of Realization is >50%

20X1

No change from the prior example. See Exhibit 16-6 for a summary of the entries for this situation.

20X2

If realization is probable, then a tax asset will be recognized for the carryforward. In 20X2, the future benefit of the carryforward of $650,000 is recognized at the then-enacted rate of 40%. The income tax entry is:

Income tax receivable—carryback benefit	20,000	
Deferred income tax asset—carryforward benefit		
($650,000 × 40%)	260,000	
Deferred income tax liability—capital assets		40,000
Income tax expense (recovery)		240,000

This entry reflects that three things are going on:

1. Recognition of carryback benefits of $20,000 (debit);

2. Recognition of the future benefits of the carryforward of $260,000 (debit); and

3. Change in the temporary difference for equipment of $40,000 (credit).

The balancing amount is the income tax recovery for 20X2 that will be shown on the income statement.

The loss carryforward can be included in the deferred income tax table, as shown in Exhibit 16-6. Refer to 20X2. The loss carryforward is included as a positive number in column 3; the first two columns are left blank. Each year the *remaining* gross tax loss carryforward is entered in column 3 and the rest of the table is completed as usual. Capital asset data is included in Exhibit 16-6 for the sake of completeness. Note that column 4 shows the SFP position at year-end. The statement of financial position at the end of 20X2 will show a single amount, a non-current deferred income tax *asset* of $120,000:

DIT asset—carryforward benefit	$260,000
DIT liability—capital assets	(140,000)
DIT asset (non-current, net)	$120,000

EXHIBIT 16-6

EXTENDED ILLUSTRATION—SITUATION 2 CARRYFORWARD

Realization Probability > 50%

Deferred Income Tax Table:

	Year-end Tax Basis dr. (cr.)	Year-end Carrying Value dr. (cr.)	Temporary Difference Deductible (Taxable)	Deferred Tax Asset (Liability) at Yr.-end Rate	Less Beginning Balance dr. (cr.)	Adjustment for Current Year dr. (cr.)
20X1 [$t = 40\%$]:						
Capital assets	$650,000	$900,000	(250,000)	$(100,000)	0	$(100,000)
20X2 [$t = 40\%$]:						
Capital assets	450,000	800,000	(350,000)	(140,000)	$(100,000)	(40,000)
Carryforward benefit	n/a	n/a	650,000	260,000	0	260,000
				120,000		
20X3 [$t = 42\%$]:						
Capital assets	300,000	700,000	(400,000)	(168,000)	(140,000)	(28,000)
Carryforward benefit	n/a	n/a	500,000	210,000	260,000	(50,000)
				42,000		
20X4 [$t = 43\%$]:						
Capital assets	200,000	600,000	(400,000)	(172,000)	(168,000)	(4,000)
Carryforward benefit	n/a	n/a	0	0	210,000	(210,000)
				(172,000)		

Income Tax Entries:

20X1

Income tax expense	120,000	
Deferred income tax liability—capital assets		100,000
Income tax payable		20,000

20X2

Deferred income tax asset—carryforward benefit	260,000	
Income tax receivable—carryback benefit	20,000	
Deferred income tax liability—capital assets		40,000
Income tax expense (recovery)		240,000

20X3

Income tax expense	91,000	
Deferred income tax liability—capital assets		28,000
Income tax payable		63,000
Income tax payable ($150,000 × 42%)	63,000	
Deferred income tax asset—carryforward benefit		50,000
Income tax expense (recovery) [$650,000 × (42% − 40%)]		13,000

20X4

Income tax expense	262,000	
Deferred income tax liability—capital assets		4,000
Income tax payable ($600,000 × 43%)		258,000
Income tax payable ($500,000 × 43%)	215,000	
Deferred tax asset—carryforward benefit		210,000
Tax expense (recovery) [$500,000 × (43% − 42%)]		5,000

20X3

In 20X3, there is initial taxable income of $150,000, after adjusting accounting income for the additional $50,000 temporary difference relating to capital assets but before applying the tax loss carryforward. There is a net change in the DIT—capital assets of $28,000 (see Exhibit 16-6). Applying $150,000 of the tax loss carryforward against the $150,000 taxable income reduces the tax loss carryforward to $500,000 (column 3) and the recorded amount to $210,000 (column 4). This is an adjustment of $50,000 (column 6). Again, we will record the results as two separate entries—the first as though there were no loss carryforward, and the second recording loss usage.

20X3		
Income tax expense	91,000	
Income tax payable		63,000
Deferred income tax liability—capital assets		28,000
Income tax payable ($150,000 × 42%	63,000	
Income tax expense (recovery) [$650,000 ×		
(42% − 40%)]		13,000
Deferred income tax asset—carryforward benefit		50,000

The second entry reflects the impact of the change in tax rates on the opening loss carryforward. Use of $150,000 of the loss carryforward clearly eliminates $63,000 of tax payable. This is the debit. The table tells us to credit the loss carryforward DIT asset by $50,000, to arrive at the correct closing balance. To make the journal entry balance, a further $13,000 credit to tax expense is needed. This amount can be proven as the change in the tax rate (2%, or 42% − 40%) multiplied by the *opening* tax loss of $650,000. In other words, the tax loss carryforward is more valuable because the tax rate increased, and tax expense is credited to reflect this.

20X4

In 20X4, there is taxable income of $600,000, tax payable (before any loss carryforward is used) of $258,000, and an increase in the DIT—capital assets account of $4,000, as is shown in Exhibit 16-6. The entire remaining tax loss carryforward of $500,000 is used. Therefore, the entries to record income tax expense for 20X4 are:

Income tax expense	262,000	
Income tax payable ($600,000 × 43%)		258,000
Deferred income tax liability—capital assets		4,000
Income tax payable ($500,000 × 43%)	215,000	
Tax expense (recovery) [$500,000 × (43% − 42%)]		5,000
Deferred tax asset—carryforward benefit		210,000

The DIT table shows no remaining loss carryforward at the end of 20X4, and this account must be reduced by $210,000 to zero. Again, the increase in tax rate has caused an adjustment to tax expense because of the higher value of the opening tax less carryforward. This is the $5,000 remaining credit.

On the statement of financial position at the end of 20X4, only the DIT—capital assets remains, at a credit balance of $172,000: $400,000 accumulated temporary differences at a tax rate of 43%.

Comparison of Results The earnings impact of the above scenarios is summarized in the partial income statements shown in Exhibit 16-7. When the probability of realization is less than or equal to 50%, matching is not achieved. The income tax expense in each year has no relationship to the pre-tax earnings, except in the first year. Instead of matching, the adjustments are driven by the need to show an asset when the probability of realization is greater than 50%.

EXHIBIT 16-7

COMPARISON OF RESULTS
IMPROBABLE VERSUS PROBABLE REALIZATION OF TAX LOSS CARRYFORWARD BENEFITS

Probability ≤ 50% (Exhibit 16-5):	20X1	20X2	20X3	20X4
Earnings (loss) before income tax	$300,000	$(600,000)	$200,000	$600,000
Less: Income tax expense (recovery)	120,000	(20,000)	91,000	47,000
Net income (loss)	$180,000	$(580,000)	$109,000	$553,000
Probability > 50% (Exhibit 16-6):				
Earnings before income tax	$300,000	$(600,000)	$200,000	$600,000
Less: Income tax expense (recovery)	120,000	(240,000)	78,000	257,000
Net income (loss)	$180,000	$(360,000)	$122,000	$343,000

When the initial probability of realization is greater than 50%, however, the full benefits of the tax loss are recognized in the year of the loss, thereby matching the benefits in the year that the loss arose. Of course, it may seem a little odd to be talking about the "benefits" of a loss. A loss itself is not beneficial, but at least it can have some favourable consequences if the company is able to utilize the tax loss carryforward.

Reporting Objectives

We have already pointed out that the matching doctrine is well served if the benefit of a loss carryforward is reported in the loss year. For example, assume that a company had an accounting and taxable loss of $100,000 in 20X2, and then accounting and taxable income of $100,000 in 20X3. The tax rate is 40%. It seems appropriate reporting to show both years net of $40,000 tax, and report an after-tax net loss of $60,000 in 20X2 and an after-tax net income of $60,000 in 20X3. It is understood that the $40,000 benefit of the loss carryforward can be recorded in 20X2 before it is realized in 20X3 as long as realization is probable.

However, what if realization is not probable? In this case, the 20X2 net loss would be reported as $100,000, and the benefit of the loss carryforward would be recorded in 20X3. This would result in net tax expense of zero in 20X3, and reported net income would be $100,000. While the $100,000 loss is greater in 20X2 than the after-tax $60,000 alternative, the $100,000 20X3 reported results are greater, as well. Management may prefer the "bounce" and be prepared to take a "big bath" in 20X2.

The swing caused by recognition may be even more pronounced. For example, assume that the $100,000 loss in 20X2 is followed by two years of breakeven results. If the probability of loss carryforward use shifts to "probable" in one of these years, $40,000 of net income will be reported, reflecting recognition of the loss carryforward deferred income tax asset. In this case, a positive trend in earnings can be manufactured by reassessment of probability. Alternatively, two or three years of loss carryforward may be recognized in one particular year, increasing results materially.

The reporting decision is based on the probability of realization. Probability is assessed by management, with the decision reviewed by external auditors. Accounting standards provide some guidance for evaluating probability, but auditors must proceed with great caution, given the magnitude of tax expense.

DISCLOSURE

Income tax expense relating to continuing operations should be shown on the face of the income statement. The amount of income tax expense may include benefits from either carrybacks or carryforwards, but there is not a requirement that those benefits be disclosed on the face of the income statement. Information on tax losses is confined to the disclosure notes, and generally focussed on *unrecognized* tax loss carryforwards rather than on amounts *realized* during the period. Disclosure is recommended for:

- The amount of benefit arising from a *previously unrecognized* tax loss that is used to either:

  1. Reduce current income tax expense by using the carryforward in the current period *if* it had not been recognized as a deferred tax asset in prior periods; or

  2. Reduce current deferred tax expense, such as by reducing CCA in prior periods and thereby reducing the amount of temporary differences relating to capital assets (as well as the remaining tax loss carryforward).

- The amount of deferred tax expense arising from the writedown or reversal of a previous writedown of deferred tax assets.

- The amount and expiry date of *unused* tax losses for which no deferred tax asset has been recognized in the SFP.

Companies usually do disclose the amounts of tax loss carrybacks and carryforwards that were used during the year, whether or not they had been previously recognized as a deferred tax asset.

The problem with most disclosures is that it is very difficult, and often impossible, for a reader to figure out whether an income tax recovery has been *realized* or merely *recognized*. Recourse to the notes, to the effective tax rate disclosure, and to the statement of cash flows may provide clues, but often the information relating to income tax assets and liabilities is so summarized that it is impossible to figure out the details.

Disclosure Example

Thunderbird Resorts Inc. had a pre-tax loss of $31.3 million in 2008 and $1.3 million in 2007. The company's 2008 SFP shows a deferred tax asset of $2.8 million and DIT liabilities of $2.1.

Exhibit 16-8 shows Thunderbird's income tax disclosure. The company reports potential tax benefits of loss carryforwards of $30.5 million. This is largely offset by a valuation allowance of $27.7 million. The company doesn't actually report the amount of its unused operating tax loss carryforwards; instead, it reports the potential income tax benefit.

Thunderbird reports very little actual tax due to the fact that it is based for tax purposes in the British Virgin Islands (even though its executive offices are in Panama City). BVI has no income tax, and thus the "statutory rate" for the tax rate reconciliation is 0%, despite the fact that most of its properties are in other countries, such as the United States, that do have income taxes.

The unrecognized tax loss carryforward benefits relate to the company's U.S. operations. The small $2.7 million tax asset relates to its resort in Peru, where apparently Thunderbird managers believe that it is likely to realize the benefit of Peruvian tax loss carryforwards.

EVALUATION OF FUTURE BENEFIT ACCOUNTING

The international standard for accounting for the future benefit of a loss carryforward is consistent with U.S. practice. It is interesting to note, however, that the current U.S. position is the result of intense lobbying by the U.S. business community. When the United States first moved to the temporary differences approach, all future tax assets were prohibited, including those that arose from temporary differences as well as those that might arise from tax loss carryforwards. But the outcry was so intense that the FASB backed down and, in a sense, went to the opposite extreme by permitting *all* future tax assets to be recognized, as long as the probability of realization was *judged by management* to be greater than 50%. Both positions were rationalized within the FASB's conceptual framework, which indicates that the framework can be used rather flexibly as support for quite different positions.

The supporters of early recognition believe that, conceptually, future tax benefits should be matched to the loss that gave rise to those benefits. They argue that if benefits are recognized only when realized, net income in those future periods will be distorted.

EXHIBIT 16-8

TAX LOSS CARRYFORWARD DISCLOSURE EXAMPLE THUNDERBIRD RESORTS INC.

Years ended 31 December

(in thousands of U.S. dollars)

8. INCOME TAXES AND DEFERRED TAX LIABILITY
a) Tax charged in the income statement:

	2008	2007
Current income tax		
Foreign tax	$ 4,376	$ 1,910
Total current income tax	4,376	1,910
Deferred tax		
Origination and reversal of temporary differences	(2,159)	1,003
Total deferred tax	(2,159)	1,003
Tax charge in the income statement	$ 2,217	$ 2,913

b) Reconciliation of the total tax charge
The tax expense in the income statement for the year is higher than the standard rate of corporate tax in the British Virgin Islands of 0%. The differences are reconciled below:

	2008	2007
Accounting loss before income tax	$(31,288)	$ (1,313)
Accounting loss multiplied by the tax rate of 0%	—	—
Higher taxes on overseas earnings	2,217	2,913
Total tax expense in the income statement	$ 2,217	$ 2,913
Deferred income tax assets:		
Loss carryforwards	$ 30,500	$17,847
Total deferred tax assets	30,500	17,847
Valuation allowance	(27,718)	(17,554)
Deferred income tax assets, net of allowance	$ 2,782	$ 293
Deferred income tax liabilities:		
Property and equipment—net book value in excess of unamortized capital cost	$ 1,322	$ 546
Other assets—net book value in excess of unamortized tax	502	273
Withholding tax on repatriation of retained earnings from foreign subsidiaries	216	170
Other	85	17
Total deferred tax liabilities	$ 2,125	$ 1,006

Potential deferred tax benefits:

At 31 December 2008, the Group has United States tax trading losses of approximately $27,717,000. These operating losses expire at various dates prior to 2014 and 2024. The potential income tax benefits related to these loss carryforwards have not been reflected in the accounts. The Group has recorded a deferred tax asset for its Peruvian operation in the amount of $2,782,000 (2007—$293,000) attributable to losses. The losses will be offset against future net income.

Source: Reproduced with permission from Thunderbird Resorts Inc.

However, many observers are troubled by the recognition of tax loss carryforward benefits before their realization. The principal concern is that future tax assets do not satisfy the basic definition of an asset. There has been no transaction that establishes the corporation's right to receive the future benefit; realization of the benefits is contingent on generating sufficient taxable income in the future. And, clearly, the government does not consider that it owes any money to the company.

The recognition of unrealized tax assets for tax loss carryforwards has the effect of reducing the apparent accounting loss. The effect of an operating loss is softened by this practice and gives financial statement users the perception that the loss isn't as bad as it really is, since the benefit of a carryforward has not been realized and there may be no more than a marginal probability (i.e., 51%) that the benefit will ever be realized.

ETHICAL ISSUES

Management must estimate the probability of realizing future tax benefits. There is a lot of management discretion involved. Although auditors may challenge management's probability estimates, accounting standards give few effective levers to the auditor. If the likelihood of realization is arguable, management may prefer to delay recognition to one or more periods following the loss. This will enhance net income in those future periods.

Management has discretion over the probability estimates and thus the timing of recognition of tax assets. Management also has the ability to remeasure those benefits at any time within the 20-year carryforward period. Thus, the recognition of unrealized tax loss carryforwards can become an ethical morass.

INTERNATIONAL CONSISTENCY?

The primary purpose of international standards is to harmonize financial reporting across financial markets, so that all companies can report in financial markets other than that of their home country. Thus, it would appear that all international reporting would have to use the methods described in this chapter in order to conform to international standards.

While that may be true on the surface, the fact is that companies in some countries will be more conservative in their appraisal of realization probabilities, depending on the prevailing ethos in their home country. In a country that has very conservative accounting practices and a strong tradition of prudence in financial reporting (e.g., Germany and France), companies generally will view the probability of future recognition as being low. Thus, the future benefit of the carryforwards will not be recognized, even though they might have been recognized in similar circumstances if the reporting company were based in the United States or in Canada. The influence of the accounting and business environments of a company's home country can be very powerful.

ACCOUNTING STANDARDS FOR PRIVATE ENTERPRISES

Accounting Method As we said at the end of Chapter 15, private companies can choose between the taxes payable method and the comprehensive allocation method of accounting for income taxes. If the enterprise chooses to use comprehensive income tax allocation, everything in the preceding sections applies.

Tax Loss Carryforwards If an entity is using the taxes payable method, the company will not be able to recognize *future tax assets* arising from tax loss carryforwards. However, tax loss carryforwards will still be used to reduce income taxes in future years, but the benefit will be *recognized* only when *realized* via actual reductions in the company's tax bill when the carryforwards are used in future years. The company's accounting method doesn't affect the carryforwards themselves, or the way that a company can use them to reduce taxes.

Section 3465 uses the phrase "more likely than not" instead of "probable" for assessing recognition of tax loss carryforwards. There is no difference in meaning, however. *Likely*, *probable*, and *more likely than not* all have the same meaning—a greater than 50% probability.

The Canadian standard specifically refers to use of a valuation allowance in conjunction with tax loss carryforwards. In contrast, *IAS* 12 makes no specific reference to valuation allowances. However, any company can use a valuation allowance instead of direct write-down. A valuation allowance is simply a bookkeeping convenience that does not affect the net amount shown in the financial statements.

RELEVANT STANDARDS

IASB:

- *IAS* 12, Income Taxes

CICA Handbook, Part II:

- Section 3465, Income Taxes

SUMMARY OF KEY POINTS

1. In Canada, tax losses may be carried back and offset against taxable income in the three previous years. The company is entitled to recover tax paid in those years. The tax recovery is based on the tax actually paid and not on the tax rate in the year of the loss.

2. If the three-year carryback does not completely use up the tax loss, a company is permitted to carry the remaining loss forward and apply it against taxable income over the next 20 years.

3. The future benefits of tax loss carryforwards should be recognized in the year of the loss if there is a greater than 50% probability that the benefits will be realized.

4. The likelihood of realizing the tax benefits of a loss carryforward can be increased by reducing the corporation's claim for CCA on its tax return in the carryback and carryforward years.

5. Future benefits of unrecognized tax loss carryforwards may be recognized in years following the loss if the probability of realization becomes greater than 50%.

6. Management reporting objectives may bias the probability assessment to allow loss carryforward recognition in particular years to emphasize an earnings recovery or other favourable trends.

KEY TERMS

loss carryback, 924
loss carryforward, 924
substantially enacted tax rate, 937

tax benefit, 924
tax loss, 924
valuation allowance, 934

REVIEW PROBLEM

Dezso Development Limited is a Canadian-controlled public company. The company has a 31 December fiscal year-end. Data concerning the earnings of the company for 20X6 and 20X7 are as follows:

	20X6	20X7
Income (loss) before income taxes	$(90,000)	$30,000
Amounts included in income		
Investment income	$ 1,000	$ 2,000
Depreciation expense—capital assets	30,000	30,000
Depreciation expense—development costs	20,000	22,000
Amounts deducted for income tax		
Capital cost allowance	nil	35,000
Development expenditures	25,000	15,000
Income tax rate	38%	37%

Other information:

- Taxable income and the income tax rates for 20X2 through 20X5 are as follows:

Year	Taxable Income (loss)	Tax Rate
20X2	$ 7,000	40%
20X3	13,000	40
20X4	9,000	40
20X5	(12,000)	41

- At 31 December 20X5, capital assets had net book value of $570,000, and unclaimed capital cost of $310,000.
- At 31 December 20X5, the statement of financial position showed an unamortized balance of development costs of $200,000 under "Other Assets."
- The investment income consists of dividends from taxable Canadian corporations.

Required:

1. For each of 20X6 and 20X7, prepare the journal entry or entries to record income tax expense. Assume that management judges that it is more likely than not that the full benefit of any tax loss carryforward will be realized within the carryforward.

2. Show how the deferred income tax amounts would appear on the 20X6 year-end statement of financial position.

3. Suppose that early in 20X8, management decided that the company was more likely than not to use only $10,000 of the remaining gross tax loss carryforward.

   a. Show the entry that would be made to reduce the carryforward benefit. Use a valuation account.

   b. What impact would this entry have on the 20X8 financial statements for Dezso Development Limited?

REVIEW PROBLEM—SOLUTION

1. (a) 20X6 Tax Expense

The taxable income or loss can be calculated as follows:

	20X6	20X7
Accounting income (loss) before tax	$(90,000)	$30,000
Permanent difference: investment income	(1,000)	(2,000)
Accounting income (loss) subject to tax	(91,000)	28,000
Depreciation	30,000	30,000
CCA	nil	(35,000)
Depreciation of development costs	20,000	22,000
Development cost expenditures	(25,000)	(15,000)
Taxable income (loss)	$(66,000)	$30,000

The 20X5 tax loss will have been carried back to 20X2 ($7,000) and 20X3 ($5,000). After the 20X5 tax loss has been carried back, there remains $17,000 taxable income in the carry-forward period for the 20X6 loss:

Year	Taxable Income	Used in 20X5	Available in 20X6	Tax Receivable @ 40%
20X2	$ 7,000	$ (7,000)	—	—
20X3	13,000	(5,000)	$ 8,000	$3,200
20X4	9,000	—	9,000	3,600
20X5	(12,000)	12,000	—	—
			$17,000	$6,800

The gross carryforward that remains after the carryback is $66,000 − $17,000 − $49,000. Assuming that realization of these benefits is more likely than not and that the enacted tax rate remains at 38% when the 20X6 statements are being prepared, the carryforward benefit is $49,000 × 38% = $18,620.

The adjustments for the temporary differences for both years are summarized in the table below.

	Year-end Tax Basis dr. (cr.)	Year-end Carrying Value dr. (cr.)	Temporary Difference Deductible (Taxable)	Deferred Tax Asset (Liability) at Yr.-end Rate	Less Beginning Balance dr. (cr.)	Adjustment for Current Year dr. (cr.)
20X6 [t = 38%]:						
Capital assets	310,000	540,000	(230,000)	$(87,400)	$(106,600)[(1)]	$19,200
Development costs	0	205,000[(3)]	(205,000)	(77,900)	(82,000)[(2)]	4,100
Carryforward benefit	n/a	n/a	49,000	18,620	0	18,620

[(1)]($570,000 − $310,000) × .41
[(2)]($200,000) × .41
[(3)]$200,000 + $25,000 − $20,000

	Year-end Tax Basis dr. (cr.)	Year-end Carrying Value dr. (cr.)	Temporary Difference Deductible (Taxable)	Deferred Tax Asset (Liability) at Yr.-end Rate	Less Beginning Balance dr. (cr.)	Adjustment for Current Year dr. (cr.)
20X7 [t = 37%]:						
Capital assets	275,000	510,000	(235,000)	$(86,950)	$(87,400)	450
Development costs	0	198,000	(198,000)	(73,260)	(77,900)	4,640
Carryforward benefit	n/a	n/a	19,000	7,030	18,620	(11,590)

Putting all of these elements together gives us the following 20X6 summary of income tax expense:

Income tax receivable—carryback benefit	6,800	
Deferred income tax asset—carryforward benefit	18,620	
Deferred income tax liability—capital assets	19,200	
Deferred income tax liability—deferred development costs	4,100	
Income tax expense (recovery)		48,720

(b) 20X7 Tax Expense

The taxable income for 20X7 is $30,000, as calculated previously. No tax is due for 20X7 because there is an available tax loss carryforward of $49,000. After applying $30,000 of the carryforward against 20X7 taxable income, a carryforward of $19,000 remains. At the newly enacted tax rate of 37%, the DIT asset related to the carryforward is $7,030. In recording the income tax expense for 20X7, the balance of the DIT carryforward account must be reduced from its beginning balance of $18,620 (debit) to an ending balance of $7,030 (debit), a credit adjustment of $11,590.

The adjustments for all types of temporary differences are summarized in the preceding table. The entry to record income tax expense, exclusive of the loss carryforward, is:

Income tax expense	6,010	
Deferred income tax liability—capital assets	450	
Deferred income tax liability—deferred development costs	4,640	
Income tax payable ($30,000 × .37)		11,100

The entry to record loss carryforward use:

Income tax expense[1]	490	
Income tax payable ($30,000 × .37)	11,100	
Deferred income tax asset—carryforward benefit (per table)		11,590

[1] This is the reduction in value of the opening tax loss because of a 1% decline in the tax rate; ($49,000 × 1%)

2. 20X6 Statement of Financial Position Presentation

All three of the 20X6 temporary differences are non-current. Therefore, they will be combined into a single net amount when the SFP is prepared. The net amount is:

DIT asset—carryforward benefit	$ 18,620 dr.
DIT liability—capital assets	(87,400) cr.
DIT liability—deferred development costs	(77,900) cr.
DIT liability, non-current	$(146,680) cr.

3. (a) Adjustment to DIT-carryforward benefit

The remaining carryforward at the beginning of 20X8 is $19,000, as determined in the answer to part 1(b), above. At the enacted rate of 37%, the remaining carryforward benefit is $7,030 (that is, $19,000 × 37%). A valuation account must be created to reduce the *reported* balance of the benefit to $3,700 (i.e., $10,000 × 37%), an adjustment of $3,330:

Income tax expense ($7,030 − $3,700)	3,330	
Valuation allowance—DIT asset		3,330

Note that the amount of the gross *recorded* benefit (before the valuation allowance) will remain at $7,030.

(b) Financial Statement Impact

There will be two effects:

- Income tax expense will be increased by $3,330.
- The deferred income tax asset relating to the tax loss carryforward benefit will be reduced to $3,700 on the statement of financial position.

Deferred income tax asset—carryforward benefit	$7,030
Less valuation allowance	3,330
Net asset	$3,700

QUESTIONS

Q16-1 What is the benefit that arises as a result of a tax loss?

Q16-2 Over what period can a tax loss be used as an offset against taxable income?

Q16-3 Why do companies usually use tax losses as carrybacks before using them as carryforwards?

Q16-4 When do *recognition* and *realization* coincide for tax losses?

Q16-5 Why is it desirable to recognize the benefit of a tax loss carryforward in the period of the accounting loss? Under what circumstances would such a benefit be *realized*?

Q16-6 What criteria must be met to *recognize* the benefit of a tax loss carryforward in the period of the accounting loss?

Q16-7 ABC Company has a taxable loss of $100,000. The tax rate is 40%. What is the potential benefit of the tax loss?

Q16-8 A company reports an accounting loss of $75,000. Depreciation for the year was $216,000, and CCA was $321,000. The company wishes to maximize its tax loss. How much is the tax loss?

Q16-9 Refer again to the data in Question 16-8. Assume instead that the company wishes to minimize its taxable loss/maximize taxable income. How much is the taxable income (loss)? Explain.

Q16-10 Explain why a company might choose not to claim CCA when it reports (a) accounting income and (b) an accounting loss.

Q16-11 Define the term "more likely than not."

Q16-12 What strategies can be used to increase the likelihood that a tax loss carryforward will be used?

Q16-13 Provide three examples of favourable evidence in assessing the likelihood that a tax loss carryforward will be used in the carryforward period.

Q16-14 A company has a tax loss of $497,000 in 20X4, when the tax rate was 40%. The tax loss is expected to be used in 20X6. At present, there is an enacted tax rate of 42% for 20X5. The government intends to increase the tax rate to 45% in 20X6, but no legislation concerning tax rates has yet been drafted. At what amount should the tax loss carryforward be recorded, if it meets the appropriate criteria to be recorded?

Q16-15 A company recorded the benefit of a tax loss carryforward in the year of the loss. Two years later, the balance of probability shifts, and it appears that the loss will likely not be used in the carryforward period. What accounting entry is required if a direct adjustment is made (i.e., not to a valuation account)?

Q16-16 A company did not recognize the benefit of a tax loss carryforward in the year of the loss. Two years later, the balance of probability shifts, and it appears that the loss will likely be used in the carryforward period. What accounting entries are required in each year if a valuation account is used?

Q16-17 How will income change if a tax loss carryforward, previously recognized, is now considered to be unlikely?

Q16-18 A company has recorded a $40,000 benefit in relation to a $100,000 tax loss carryforward. The tax rate changes to 35%. What entry is appropriate?

Q16-19 Give three objections to the practice of recording a tax loss carryforward prior to realization.

Q16-20 What disclosure is required in relation to tax loss carryforwards?

CASE 16-1

DOWNHILL SKI COMPANY

Downhill Ski Company is experiencing financial difficulties. Earnings have been declining sharply over the past several years. The company has barely maintained profits over the last four years. In the current year, the company is expected to suffer a substantial loss for the first time in 10 years. A taxable loss will also be reported. The losses are expected to be significantly greater than the profits reported in the previous three years.

Downhill Ski Company is a manufacturer specializing in downhill racing skis and boots. The company supplies the Canadian National ski team but competition from larger manufacturers has forced Downhill Ski Company to keep its prices low when its expenses have been increasing. Also, the popularity of snowboarding has had a negative impact on sales. However, it has been found that many older adults who switch to snowboarding go back to skiing.

North Johnston, the sales and marketing manager, left the company last year to join Rossignol, a large multinational company. Cathy Thomas, former ski champion, was hired earlier this year as the new sales and marketing manager.

The owner of Downhill Ski Company, Wendy Hogarth, is not overly concerned with the loss for the current year and has the following comments to make:

"With the hiring of Cathy Thomas as sales and marketing manager we will develop relationships with the National Ski Team and work on improving sponsorship of events. This should increase our sales."

"Downhill Ski Company is developing a new type of ski that is not on the market yet. Some of the national ski team members tested the prototype of the ski and were thrilled with its performance. We are sure sales of the new ski will give us solid sales. We have already lined up buyers across Canada and the United States for this ski. Our financial forecast for next year is to make a profit."

"We have a new large piece of equipment acquired at the end of last year. This manufacturing equipment is more efficient and will save us money on maintenance and repairs."

You have been hired by Wendy to provide accounting advice. She wants to know if she can recognize the loss this year as an asset on the statement of financial position. She would also like to know the impact on the financial statements of recognizing versus not recognizing the loss and if there are any tax planning strategies the company should use in respect to recognition of the loss.

Required:
Write the report to Wendy.

CASE 16-2

SIGMA AUTO PARTS LTD.

Sigma Auto Parts Ltd. is an Ontario-based manufacturer of automobile parts. The Canadian operations supply automotive components and parts to three U.S. states and two Japanese auto manufacturers. Approximately 30% of Sigma's worldwide sales is generated by its Canadian operations.

The company has large operating subsidiaries in the United States, Mexico, Germany, and the Czech Republic. Sigma has recently established an operating subsidiary in the People's Republic of China to supply both international and domestic manufacturers in that country.

Sigma is a Canadian private company. However, the German subsidiary does have an outstanding public issue of non-voting common shares that are traded on the Frankfurt exchange. Generally, financing is obtained through a combination of retained earnings, debt, and private equity placements in each subsidiary's home country, with the exception of China (as explained below). The company reports using international accounting standards, using U.S. dollars as the reporting currency.

Angelo Zhang has recently been promoted to the position of chief accountant at the Sigma head office in Windsor, Ontario. The newly appointed chief financial officer, Jean Adams, has asked Mr. Zhang to review several reporting issues and advise her on appropriate treatments. The specific issues are as follows:

1. Earlier in the year, a Canadian supplier claimed the right to terminate its obligations to supply Sigma with certain stainless steel products at the prices stated in two standing supply contracts with Sigma. The supplier has continued to supply the products, but invoiced Sigma at market prices rather than at the contracted prices. Sigma has continued to pay the supplier, but only at the contract prices. The accumulated differential between the invoiced market prices and the contract prices has been accumulating for several months and now amounts to about $30 million. Sigma and the supplier have agreed to submit their disagreement to binding arbitration. The arbitration hearing is expected to be held late in the following fiscal year.

2. Sigma is building new manufacturing facilities in the Czech Republic to replace some older facilities that have become obsolete. The new facilities should be ready within two years, whereupon operations will be transferred to the new facilities and the old site will be abandoned. Recent legislation in the Czech Republic makes Sigma responsible for demolition and site restoration costs in the event that the old facilities cannot be sold to a buyer that is willing to bear the costs of demolition or rebuilding. The currently estimated costs are $25 million for demolition and $10 million for site restoration (at the current exchange rate).

3. The U.S. operations have experienced profitability problems over the past several years. The decline of some of the U.S. auto manufacturers has taken its toll on the auto parts industry. The auto companies have been forcing suppliers' prices down, a situation that has led to the bankruptcy of one major U.S.–based auto parts manufacturer. For a while, Sigma U.S. was just about breaking even on an accounting basis, but was in an operating loss position for tax purposes. However, for each of the most recent two years, Sigma's U.S. subsidiary has reported a significant loss for both accounting and tax purposes. In view of the basic strength of Sigma's cutting-edge operations and the strength of its worldwide operations, Jean Adams's predecessor felt confident in fully recognizing the income tax benefits that will be derived from any tax loss carryforwards. Now, however, the situation is not so clear-cut. It may be quite a while before the industry settles and Sigma is able to return the U.S. operations to profitability.

4. Generally speaking, the subsidiaries in each country are financed locally rather than through significant direct investment from Canada. An exception is the new subsidiary in China; substantial direct foreign investment was necessary in order to quickly establish the company and also to obtain certain government approvals and tax benefits.

Total direct investment in China currently is $103 million and is likely to increase over the next couple of years. The Chinese new yuan is tied to a basket of foreign currencies, of which the U.S. dollar represents the largest proportion. Due to the weakening of the U.S. dollar, the yuan has been gradually increasing in value.

5. During the current year, Sigma's German division issued €150 million of 7% unsecured subordinated debentures on a private placement basis. The debentures mature in five years and are not redeemable prior to maturity. Upon maturity, Sigma has the option of issuing non-voting common shares, the number of shares dependent on their market value at the time.

Required:

Assume that you are Angelo Zhang. Prepare the report to Ms Adams.

CASE 16-3

ELLIS INGRAM CORPORATION

Ellis Ingram Corporation (EIC) is a manufacturer of household appliances. The company is privately held with a broad shareholder group. The company has sizable loans outstanding, and audited financial statements are required to assess compliance with loan covenants, related to the current ratio and return on assets. A material component of management compensation is bonus payments, a fixed portion of net income.

After several years of positive earnings, EIC is reporting sizable losses in 20X5. These losses relate to a strike that shut down EIC's major manufacturing facility. While the operation was shut down, many customers found other suppliers. EIC is slowly regaining market share. Market projections are cautious for 20X6, as consumer demand is expected to be soft, and EIC's customer base is still impaired. No bonuses will be paid in 20X5. Lenders have agreed to a one-year exclusion on debt covenants related to return on assets for 20X5, but 20X6 profits will be carefully watched.

EIC has provided the following information with respect to operating results:

	(in thousands)	
	20X5	**20X4**
Accounting income (loss) before income tax	$(31,420)	$6,145
Income tax instalments paid during the year	nil	2,030
Income tax payable at year-end	?	177
Deferred income tax, a long-term liability, with respect to capital assets with a net book value of $6,950 at the end of 20X4 and $6,200 at the end of 20X5 (no additions in 20X5)	?	917
Impairment of goodwill, recorded on the income statement but not tax-deductible	8,410	nil
Other non-deductible expenses	540	357
Effective tax rate	41.6%	44.3%

EIC reported total taxable income of $2,680 in 20X3 and 20X2 combined, on which income tax of $1,187 was paid. No CCA will be claimed in 20X5.

A major issue for management and the Board of Directors of EIC is the probability assessment of loss carryforward use at the end of 20X5. In order to facilitate discussion, you, a public accountant, have been asked to prepare financial statement results for both alternatives—probable and not probable—and comment on the implications of the choice for 20X6. Your analysis must include all tax amounts and necessary calculations. You have also been asked to analyze the status of the gross profit on the late-20X5 sale of merchandise to Luciano Limited. If adjustment is needed, you are to revise the reported financial results (see Exhibit 1).

Required:
Prepare the requested analysis.

EXHIBIT 1

Data on Sale to Luciano Limited

EIC entered into two related transactions with Luciano Limited, a long-time supplier, at the instigation of Luciano, in December 20X5. EIC sold $2,050,000 of product to Luciano. Credit terms were 20 days, and Luciano paid on time, in late December. The cost of these goods was $1,685,000. EIC also purchased goods with a retail price of $2,100,000 from Luciano. Luciano likely booked a profit of 35% on the goods. EIC has paid for the merchandise, which is still in inventory. The goods are expected to be sold in February 20X6. EIC has recently been alerted that Luciano is under scrutiny by the SEC for transactions of this nature. (Luciano is the Canadian subsidiary of a U.S. public company)

The accounting policy for this sale has yet to be determined, but will be discussed at the next Board of Directors meeting. The profit will be taxable in 20X5 regardless of when it is recognized for accounting purposes.

From a recent article in the financial press:

> Recent SEC scrutiny has focused on barter and "round trip" transactions. In barter transactions, two companies swap products, with each company recognizing revenue on the transaction, at the fair value of the goods exchanged. GAAP states that revenue must be deferred on these transactions if the transaction does not represent the end of the earnings process. Another similar type of transaction is called "round tripping." One company sells a product to another company, for cash, which then turns around and sells equivalent product back to the company at a similar cash price. Both companies recognize revenue. The SEC is of the opinion that gross profit on these round-trip transactions must be deferred until the product is eventually sold to outside, final customers.

ASSIGNMENTS

★★ **A16-1 Income Tax Explanation:** Painter Corporation reported the following items with respect to income tax in the 20X4 financial statements:

Deferred income tax asset	$ 5,200
Deferred income tax liability	164,200

The 20X4 statement of comprehensive income shows the following income tax expense:

Income tax expense:	
Current	$37,500
Deferred	58,500
Impact of loss carryforward	(41,300)
	$54,700

The disclosure notes indicate that there is an unrecognized loss carryforward in the amount of $253,200. No tax loss carryforwards have been recorded as assets. The tax rate is 40%.

Required:

1. Explain the components of the 20X4 income tax expense. Why is there income tax expense if there is a loss carryforward?

2. Give an example of a statement of financial position account that could have caused a deferred income tax asset and a deferred income tax liability.

3. Why would the loss carryforward not have been recognized in its entirety in 20X4? What would change (amounts and accounts) if it could be recognized?

4. How much tax is currently payable? How much tax would have been payable if there had been no loss carryforward?

★★ **A16-2 Loss Carryback/Carryforward:** The statements of comprehensive income of Jackson Corporation for the first four years of operations reflected the following pre-tax amounts:

	20X4	20X5	20X6	20X7
Revenue	$480,000	$530,000	$340,000	$620,000
Expenses	460,000	620,000	310,000	510,000
Pre-tax income (loss)	$ 20,000	$ (90,000)	$ 30,000	$110,000

There are no temporary differences other than those created by income tax losses. Assume an income tax rate of 36% for all four years.

Required:

1. Give entries to record income tax expense for each year, assuming that Jackson's management believes in 20X5 that there is a 30% probability of realizing the benefits of the carryforward prior to their expiry. Show computations.

2. Repeat requirement (1) for 20X5 through 20X7, assuming that management believes in 20X5 that Jackson is almost certain to realize the benefits of the carryforward (and doesn't change their minds). Show computations.

★ **A16-3 Benefits of Carryback and Carryforward:** Daga Limited began operations in 20X3. For the first six years of operations, the company had the following pre-tax net income (loss):

Year	Taxable Income	Tax Rate
20X3	$ (60,000)	42%
20X4	360,000	43%
20X5	440,000	41%
20X6	(1,300,000)	38%
20X7	140,000	34%
20X8	300,000	36%

There have been no permanent or temporary differences between pre-tax accounting income and taxable income.

In 20X6, management was less than 50% certain that any tax carryforward would be realized. Management decided in 20X7 that full realization of carryforward benefits was probable, and did not change that opinion in 20X8.

Required:

For each year, determine:

1. Income tax currently payable (receivable).

2. Income tax expense (recovery).

3. Net income (loss).

★ **A16-4 Carrybacks and Carryforwards in Successive Years:** Zhang Enterprises Limited was founded at the beginning of 20X0. For the first 10 years, the company had the following record of taxable income and loss (before considering any tax loss carryforwards or carrybacks):

Year	Taxable Income (Loss)
20X0	$ 95,000
20X1	60,000
20X2	35,000
20X3	(140,000)
20X4	30,000
20X5	(265,000)
20X6	(45,000)
20X7	65,000
20X8	95,000
20X9	380,000

The company had no permanent or temporary differences in any of the 10 years. The income tax rate was 40% from 20X0 through 20X5. In 20X6, the government enacted new legislation that called for reducing the rate to 38% for 20X6 and to 35% for 20X7 and beyond. In each year, management believed that the company was more likely than not to realize the benefit of any tax loss carryforwards.

Required:
Calculate income tax expense for each year, 20X0 through 20X9.

★ **A16-5 Loss Carryback; Entries and Reporting:** Webb Corporation reported pre tax income from operations in 20X4 of $210,000 (the first year of operations). In 20X5, the corporation experienced a $90,000 pre-tax loss from operations. Future operations are highly uncertain. Assume an income tax rate of 40%. Webb has no temporary or permanent differences.

Required:

1. Assess Webb's income tax situation for 20X4 and 20X5. How should Webb elect to handle the loss in 20X5?

2. Based on your assessments in requirement (1), give the 20X4 and 20X5 income tax entries.

3. Show how all tax-related items would be reported on the 20X4 and 20X5 statement of comprehensive income and statement of financial position.

★ **A16-6 Loss Carryforward, Valuation Allowance:** The pre-tax earnings of Cranston Limited for the first three years were as follows:

	20X3	20X4	20X5
Revenues	$ 550,000	$600,000	$650,000
Expenses	665,000	575,000	615,000
Earnings (loss) before income taxes	$(115,000)	$ 25,000	$ 35,000

The company had no permanent or temporary differences in any of the three years. The income tax rate was constant at 30%.

In 20X3 and 20X4, the prospect for future earnings was highly uncertain. In 20X5, Cranston management decided that the future outlook for the company was quite good, and that significant earnings would be generated in the near future.

Required:

1. Restate the above statements of comprehensive income to reflect income tax effects for each year.
2. Show any amounts relating to income taxes that would be reported on Cranston's statement of financial position in each of the three years.
3. Prepare journal entries to record income taxes in each year. The company's accountant has recommended using the valuation allowance approach to recording tax loss carryforward benefits.

★★ **A16-7 Loss Carryforward, Valuation Allowance, Rate Change:** Fellows Corporation had the following taxable and pre-tax accounting income:

	20X1	20X2	20X3	20X4
Earnings (loss) before taxes	$(300,000)	$(60,000)	$40,000	$280,000
Tax rate	40%	40%	38%	38%

Assume that 20X1 is the first year of operations for the company. Tax rates are enacted in the year in which they become effective.

In 20X2, the company won some major contracts that management believed would bring the company into profitability. Therefore, management decided at the end of 20X2 that it was probable that 60% of the unused tax loss carryforward would be used within the carryforward period. In 20X4, management further decided it was probable that the full 100% of the unused carryforward would be realized.

Required:

1. Prepare the journal entries to record the provision for income tax for each year. Do not use a valuation allowance.
2. Prepare the journal entries to record the provision for income tax for each year. Use a valuation account.
3. Present the portion of the statement of comprehensive income, showing pre-tax earnings, income tax provision, and net earnings after tax.
4. Calculate the effective tax rate for each year.

★★ **A16-8 Recognition of Loss Carryforward:** Catalano Corporation experienced an accounting and tax loss in 20X5. The benefit of the tax loss was realized in part by carryback. The remainder was left as a tax loss carryforward but was not recognized as management felt that there was considerable doubt as to its eventual recognition. The gross tax loss carryforward amounted to $354,500. In 20X6, a further accounting and tax loss was recognized. This time, the tax loss was $43,000, and the benefit of the tax loss carryforwards was still not recorded. In 20X7, the company recorded accounting income. The taxable income prior to using the loss carryforward was $60,000. There were no permanent or temporary differences. The tax rate was 36% in 20X7. The enacted tax rate for 20X8 was 38%, enacted in 20X8.

Required:

1. Record 20X7 tax entries assuming that the likelihood of using the remaining tax loss carryforwards is still considered to be less than 50%.
2. Assume that in 20X8 accounting and taxable income was $520,000. Record income taxes.
3. Record 20X7 tax entries assuming that the probability of using the remaining tax loss carryforwards is considered to be greater than 50% for the first time.
4. Again, assume that accounting and taxable income in 20X8 was $520,000, but that the entries from requirement (3) were made. Record 20X8 income tax.

★ **A16-9 Calculate a Loss Carryback and Its Benefit, Temporary Differences:** Tyler Toys Limited uses the liability method of tax allocation. Tyler reported the following:

	20X3	20X4	20X5	20X6
Accounting income before tax	$10,000	$15,000	$(40,000)	$10,000
Depreciation expense (original cost of asset, $75,000)	6,000	6,000	6,000	6,000
Golf club dues	3,000	4,000	3,000	4,000
CCA (maximum available claim)	3,000	6,000	12,000	10,000
Tax rate—enacted in each year	20%	20%	30%	35%

Required:

1. Calculate taxable income each year, and the tax payable. Tyler claims the maximum CCA each year.

2. How much of the loss could Tyler use as a tax loss carryback? How much tax refund will it receive? How much is the tax loss carryforward? How much is the tax benefit?

★ **A16-10 Recording Temporary Differences, Loss, Rate Change:** Refer again to the data in A16-9.

Required:

Provide the journal entry to record the benefit of the tax loss in 20X5 assuming that the tax loss is first used as a tax loss carryback and the remainder is available as a tax loss carryforward. Be sure to adjust the deferred income tax account for the temporary difference between depreciation and CCA, and also the change in tax rates. What condition has to be met to record the loss in 20X5?

★ **A16-11 Calculate a Loss Carryback and Its Benefit, Temporary Differences:** Radvani Limited uses the liability method of tax allocation. Radvani reported the following:

	20X3	20X4	20X5	20X6
Accounting income before tax	$50,000	$90,000	$130,000	$(150,000)
Depreciation expense (original cost of asset, $200,000)	20,000	20,000	20,000	20,000
CCA claimed	25,000	43,750	32,813	
Tax rate—enacted in each year	30%	35%	40%	40%

Required:

1. Prepare the journal entries for income taxes for each of the four years. Assume that Radvani is worried that the company might have another significant loss in 20X7.

2. Prepare the journal entries for income taxes for each of the four years assuming that Radvani wants to maximize the amount it can recover from the tax carryback, and it sees the loss in 20X6 as an isolated incident, and anticipates large profits in the next few years.

★★ **A16-12 Loss Carryforward, Temporary Difference:** Haines Corporation began operations in 20X3. In its first year, the company had a net operating loss before tax for accounting purposes of $80,000. Depreciation was $94,000, and CCA was $106,000. The company claimed CCA in 20X3. Warranty costs expensed in the period were $90,000 and actual warranty costs incurred were $70,000. In 20X4, Bean had taxable income before the use of the tax loss carryforward of $250,000. This was after adding back $94,000 of depreciation and deducting $130,000 of CCA and adding back $100,000 of warranty costs accrued and deducting $85,000 of warranty costs incurred. The income tax rate is 40% in both years. Capital assets had an original cost of $1,000,000 in 20X3.

Required:

1. Prepare a journal entry or entries to record income tax in 20X3 and 20X4 assuming that the likelihood of using the tax loss carryforward is assessed as probable in 20X3. Also prepare the statement of profit and loss section showing income before tax and income tax effects for 20X3 and 20X4.

2. Repeat requirement (1) assuming that the likelihood of using the tax loss carryforward is assessed as improbable.

3. Which assessment—probable or improbable—seems more logical in 20X3? Discuss.

★★ **A16-13 Loss Carrybacks and Carryforwards, Rate Change:** Snowboards Limited has experienced the following accounting and taxable income:

	Accounting Income	Taxable Income*	Tax Rate
20X4	($86,000)	($62,000)	32%
20X5	80,000	50,000	34
20X6	90,000	82,000	32
20X7	50,000	(88,000)	30

*Before applying any available tax loss carryforwards

The differences between accounting and taxable income are caused by permanent differences between accounting and tax expenses. All tax rates are enacted in the year to which they relate. Snowboards Limited does not use a valuation account.

Required:

1. Record income tax for 20X4 through 20X7 assuming that the future use of tax loss carryforwards is considered to be improbable.

2. Repeat requirement (1) assuming that the use of tax loss carryforwards is considered to be probable in the loss year.

★ **A16-14 Deferred Tax Asset Revaluation; Rate Change:** Metallic Limited reports the following asset on the statement of financial position at 31 December 20X5:

Future tax asset, loss carryforward $334,400

This asset reflects the benefit of a tax loss carryforward recorded in 20X4. It was not used in 20X5. The enacted tax rate was 38%. In 20X6, the enacted tax rate changes to 40%.

Required:

1. Record 20X6 tax entries if Metallic reported accounting and taxable income of $50,000 in 20X6. The use of the tax loss carryforward is still considered to be probable.

2. Record 20X6 tax entries if Metallic reported accounting and tax losses of $220,000 in 20X6. The use of the tax loss carryforward is still considered to be probable.

★★ **A16-15 Loss Carryback/Carryforward; Temporary Difference:** Bogdan Limited shows the following on its 31 December 20X4 statement of financial position:

Deferred income tax liability $870,000

All this income tax liability relates to the difference between the NBV and UCC of capital assets. At 31 December 20X4, NBV is $9,630,000 and UCC is $7,455,000.

In 20X2, 20X3, and 20X4, the company had reported a total taxable income of $324,750 and paid taxes of $81,450.

In 20X5, Bogdan reported an accounting loss before tax of $480,000. Depreciation of $67,500 is included in this calculation. No CCA will be claimed in 20X5. The enacted tax rate was 40% in 20X5.

Required:

1. Calculate the tax loss in 20X5.
2. How much of the tax loss can be used as a loss carryback? What will be the benefit of this loss carryback?
3. How much of the loss is available as a tax loss carryforward? What is the benefit of this tax loss carryforward?
4. Under what circumstances can the benefit of the tax loss carryforward be recorded as an asset?
5. Record income tax for 20X5 assuming that the tax loss carryforward can be recorded.
6. Record income tax for 20X5 assuming that the tax loss carryforward cannot be recorded.
7. Assume that accounting and taxable income was $150,000 in 20X6, and the enacted tax rate was still 40%. Prepare the journal entry to record income tax in 20X6 assuming that the tax loss carryforward (a) was recorded in 20X5 as in requirement (5), and (b) was not recorded in 20X5 as in requirement (6).

 A16-16 Loss Carryback/Carryforward: Solway Limited had the following pre-tax income and losses:

Year	Pre-Tax Income (Loss)	Tax Rate
20X2	$ 360,000	34%
20X3	440,000	34
20X4	680,000	34
20X5	340,000	36
20X6	(2,680,000)	38
20X7	300,000	38
20X8	760,000	40

The tax rates are those effective for the year indicated. The rates were enacted the year in which they became effective. Taxable income (loss) equalled accounting income (loss) in each year. Solway does not use a valuation allowance.

Required:

1. Prepare the entry to record income tax expense for 20X6. At the end of 20X6, management estimates that there is greater than a 50% probability of realizing the benefits of only $300,000 of the loss carryforward.
2. Prepare the income tax expense entries for 20X7 and 20X8. In 20X7, management decides that the probability of realizing the benefits of the remaining loss carryforward is greater than 50%.

★ **A16-17 Loss Carryback/Carryforward, Valuation Allowance:** The following information pertains to Towers Corporation:

- From 20X1 through 20X3, Towers had pre-tax earnings totalling $150,000.
- In 20X4, Towers had a pre-tax loss of $550,000.
- The company has no permanent or temporary differences.
- The income tax rate was 40% from 20X1 through 20X4.
- In 20X4, a rate of 38% was enacted for 20X5 and a rate of 36% was enacted for 20X6 and following years.

- In 20X4, management predicted that the benefits of only $200,000 of the tax loss carryforward were probable of realization in the carryforward period. Management also estimated that pre-tax earnings for 20X5 would be no more than $60,000.
- Actual pre-tax earnings in 20X5 were $80,000. Management estimated that only $120,000 of the tax loss carryforward was probable of realization.
- Pre-tax 20X6 earnings were $100,000. Management decided that it was highly probable that the full benefit of the remaining tax loss carryforward would be realized.

Required:

Towers uses a valuation account for its deferred income tax assets. What are the balances in deferred income tax related accounts for each of 20X4, 20X5, and 20X6?

★ **A16-18 Loss Carryback/Carryforward; Entries:** Decker Limited began operations in 20X5 and reported the following information for the years 20X5 to 20X9:

	20X5	20X6	20X7	20X8	20X9
Pre-tax income	$10,000	$12,000	$15,000	$(106,000)	$13,000
Depreciation	10,000	10,000	10,000	10,000	10,000
Capital cost allowance	10,000	18,000	14,000	0	0

The income tax rate is 40% in all years. Assume that Decker's only depreciable assets were purchased in 20X5 and cost $200,000.

Required:

1. Prepare the journal entries for income taxes for 20X8 and 20X9. In 20X8, Decker's opinion was that realization of the loss carryforwards was probable.
2. What is the balance of deferred income tax at the end of 20X9? Show calculations.

★★ **A16-19 Loss Carryback/Carryforward; Rate Change:** In the years 20X2 through 20X4, Balne Corporation reported a total of $359,000 of taxable income. The enacted tax rate during those years was 38%. At the end of 20X4, Balne reported a deferred income tax liability related to capital assets. The net book value of these assets was $800,000, while the UCC was $630,000 at the end of 20X4.

During 20X5, Balne Corporation recorded an accounting loss of $536,000, after depreciation expense of $50,000. No CCA was claimed in 20X5. In 20X5, the enacted rate changed to 40% for both 20X5 and 20X6.

In 20X6, Balne reported income before tax of $450,000. Depreciation of $50,000 was equal to the CCA claim.

Required:

1. Determine after-tax net income for 20X5 and 20X6 assuming that the benefit of the tax loss carryforward can be recognized in 20X5.
2. Repeat requirement (1) assuming that the benefit of the tax loss carryforward cannot be recognized in 20X5.

★★ **A16-20 Loss Carryforward, Temporary Differences; Rate Change, Entries:** The Village Company manufactures and sells television sets. The company recorded warranty expense of 2% of sales for accounting purposes. The following information is taken from the company's books:

eXcel

(in thousands)	20X5	20X6	20X7	20X8	20X9
Sales	$3,000	$6,000	$8,000	$10,000	$15,000
Actual warranty claims paid	60	80	200	90	75
Accounting income (loss) before taxes	nil	(980)	nil	2,000	4,000
Depreciation	600	600	600	600	600
Capital cost allowance	600	nil	500	450	400
Dividend revenue (non-taxable)	nil	20	20	nil	nil

Net book value of depreciable assets at 31 December 20X5: $7,600,000. Undepreciated capital cost at 31 December 20X5: $5,600,000. There is a deferred tax liability of $800,000 with respect to this temporary difference. There is no taxable income remaining to absorb loss carrybacks prior to 20X5.

The tax rate is 40% in 20X5 through 20X7 and increases to 45% for 20X8 and 20X9. Tax rates are enacted in the year to which they pertain. There are no other sources of temporary differences.

Required:

Give journal entries to record income taxes for 20X6 to 20X9 inclusive. Realization of the loss carryforward is considered to be probable in 20X6.

★★ **A16-21 Loss Carryback/Carryforward; Temporary Differences; Rate Change:** On 1 January 20X6, Wilton Incorporated commenced business operations. At 31 December 20X8, the following information relates to Wilton: *started + no carry fwds*

	20X6	20X7 *(loss yr)*	20X8
Income (loss) before tax	$502,200	($754,000)	$1,200,000
Tax rate (enacted in each year)	36%	38%	40%
Depreciation expense (asset cost was $1,000,000)	50,000	50,000	50,000
Capital cost allowance	300,000	0	125,000
Dividends received (non-taxable)	10,000	75,000	10,000
Golf club dues	19,000	20,000	20,000

Required:

1. Prepare journal entries to record tax for 20X6, 20X7, and 20X8. Your entries should be in good form, and all calculations should be shown. Assume that the loss carryforward in 20X7 is considered probable for recognition.

2. How would your answer differ if the taxes payable method were used in accounting standards for private enterprises? Describe, do not calculate.

★★ **A16-22 Loss Carryback/Carryforward; Temporary Differences; Rate Change:** On 1 January 20X1, Morrison Incorporated commenced business operations. The following information is available to you:

	20X1	20X2	20X3	20X4
Income (loss) before tax	$220,000	($1,200,000)	$130,000	$200,000
Tax rate (enacted in each year)	36%	34%	32%	30%
Depreciation (historical cost of assets, $4,100,000)	200,000	200,000	200,000	200,000
Capital cost allowance	250,000	0	100,000	190,000
Rental revenue recognized*	65,000	—	—	—

*Rental revenue is recognized as earned for accounting purposes, in 20X1. It is recognized as collected for tax purposes in 20X3.

Required:

Prepare journal entries to record tax for 20X1, 20X2, 20X3, and 20X4. Your entries should be in good form, and all calculations should be shown. Assume that the tax loss carryforward in 20X2 is considered not probable of recognition but that in 20X3 the balance of probability shifts and, in 20X3, the loss is considered probable.

★★★ **A16-23 Loss Carryback/Carryforward, Rate Change; Comprehensive:** Dexter Limited began operations in 20X5 and reported the following information for the years 20X5 to 20X9:

e**X**cel

	20X5	20X6	20X7	20X8	20X9
Pre-tax income	$ 8,000	$15,000	$ 9,000	$(95,000)	$ 6,000
Depreciation	10,000	10,000	10,000	10,000	10,000
CCA	10,000	18,000	14,000	0	0
Net book value	90,000	80,000	70,000	60,000	50,000
UCC	90,000	72,000	58,000	58,000	58,000

Required:

1. Prepare journal entries to record income taxes in each year, 20X5 through 20X9. Assume that realization of the tax loss carryforward benefits is probable and the tax rate is 40% in all years.

2. Repeat requirement (1) assuming that the tax rate is now 40% in 20X5 and 20X6, 43% in 20X7, 45% in 20X8, and 47% in 20X9. Tax rates are enacted in the year to which they pertain.

3. Return to the facts of requirement (1) (the tax rate is 40%). Repeat your journal entries for 20X8 and 20X9 assuming that use of the tax loss carryforward is deemed to be not probable in 20X8, but probable in 20X9.

★★ **A16-24 Loss Carryback/Carryforward, Temporary and Permanent Differences, Use in Subsequent Year:** Dynamic Limited reported the following 20X5 income statement:

DYNAMIC LIMITED

Statement of Profit and Loss

For the year ended 31 December 20X5

Revenue	$2,715,000
Cost of goods sold	1,396,000
Depreciation	160,000
General and administrative expenses	75,000
Other	60,000
	1,691,000
Income before tax	$1,024,000

OTHER INFORMATION:

a. There is an $160,000 accrued rent receivable on the statement of financial position. This amount was included in rental income (revenue) this year, but will not be taxed until next year. This is the first time such an accrual has been made.

b. The CCA claim for 20X5 is $301,000. At the beginning of 20X5, UCC was $2,165,000 while net book value was $2,916,000. The balance in the related deferred income tax liability was $300,400 (cr.)

c. Revenue includes dividends received of $60,000, which are not taxable at any time.

d. Other expenses include non-deductible entertainment expenses of $80,000.

e. The statement of financial position shows an asset account called "deferred income tax asset $30,000," which is the benefit of a $75,000 loss carryforward, recorded in 20X3.

Required:

Prepare the journal entry or entries to record tax in 20X5. Show all calculations. The tax rate is 40%.

Source: Reprinted with permission from CGA-Canada.

★★★ **A16-25 Loss Carryback/Carryforward, Comprehensive, Rate Change:** Loo Corporation was incorporated in 20X5. Details of the company's results are presented below:

	20X5	**20X6**	**20X7**
Income (loss) before tax	$ 60,000	($200,000)	$100,000
Depreciation expense	40,000	40,000	40,000
Capital cost allowance claimed	50,000	0	50,000
Dividend income (non-taxable)	10,000	10,000	10,000
Tax rate	40%	40%	40%
Net book value, end of year	360,000	320,000	280,000
UCC, end of year	350,000	350,000	300,000

Required:

1. Prepare journal entries for tax for 20X5, 20X6, and 20X7. Assume that realization of the benefit of the loss carryforward is probable in 20X6. The company does not use a valuation allowance.

2. Repeat requirement (1), assuming that the tax rate is 40% in 20X5, but is changed to 42% in 20X6 and to 44% in 20X7. All tax rates are enacted in the year in which they are effective.

3. Revert to the facts of requirement (1) (i.e., 40% tax rate in each year). Assume that the use of the unused tax loss carryforward is considered not probable in 20X6, and is still not probable in 20X7, other than the loss carryforward actually utilized in 20X7. Provide journal entries for 20X5, 20X6, and 20X7.

★★★ **A16-26 Tax Losses: Subsequent Recognition and Revaluation; Valuation Allowance:** Partinni Limited reports the following items on the Statement of Financial Position at 31 December 20X4:

Deferred income tax, loss carryforward	$784,000 dr.
Deferred income tax, capital assets	340,000 cr.
Net future tax asset	$444,000 dr.

The loss carryforward had been recorded in 20X4. The enacted tax rate was 35% at the end of 20X4, and the net book value of capital assets was $2,650,000, while the UCC was $1,587,500.

In 20X5, Partinni reported accounting income of $27,000. Depreciation, the only temporary difference, was $80,000, while CCA of $90,000 was claimed. In 20X5, the enacted tax rate changed to 30%. Probability assessment regarding the loss carryforward did not change.

In 20X6, the enacted tax rate changed to 32%. Partinni reported accounting income of $17,000. Depreciation of $20,000 was expensed, and no CCA was claimed. Because of continued low profitability, the company reluctantly decided in 20X6 that the probability of using the remaining tax loss carryforward in the carryforward period now had to be considered low.

Required:

1. Record income tax entries for 20X5 and 20X6. Assume that a valuation account is not used.

2. Repeat the entries for 20X6 assuming that a valuation account is used.

★★ **A16-27 Tax Losses; Intraperiod Allocation, Income Statement:** At the beginning of 20X4, Caprioli Tracking Corporation (CTC) had a deferred income tax liability on its statement of financial position of $60,000. The deferred income tax balance reflects the tax impact of gross accumulated temporary differences of $95,000 relating to CCA/Depreciation and $55,000 relating to pension costs. The tax expense has been higher (that is, CCA and pension funding have been higher) than the accounting expense (that is, depreciation and pension expense). Over the past three years, taxes have been due and paid as follows:

Year	Taxable Income	Taxes Due
20X1	$60,000	$22,000
20X2	20,000	7,600
20X3	40,000	16,000
		$45,600

In 20X4, CTC suffered the first loss in its history due to a general economic turndown. The accounting loss amounted to $200,000 before taxes. In computing accounting income, CTC deducted depreciation of $10,000 per year. On its 20X4 tax return, CTC elected to take no CCA, and therefore the 20X4 loss for tax purposes was as follows:

Accounting income (loss)	$(200,000)
Depreciation	10,000
Pension expense (not deductible)	30,000
Pension funding (deductible)	(60,000)
Taxable income (loss)	$(220,000)

The income tax rate, which had gradually increased over several years to 40% in 20X3, remained at 40% for 20X4 taxable income. In 20X4, Parliament enacted legislation to reduce the income tax rate to 36% for 20X5 and following years.

In management's judgement, it is probable that any tax loss carryforward will be fully utilized in the carryforward period.

Required:

Show the journal entry to record income taxes. Prepare the lower part of the CTC statement of profit and loss for 20X4, starting with "earnings before income tax."

★★ **A16-28 Explain Impact of Temporary Differences, Tax Losses:** You are the new accountant for Evanoff Limited (EL). You have been asked to explain the impact of income tax on the financial statements for the year ended 31 December 20X5. You discover the following:

- EL's product development expenses of $2 million have been deferred, to be amortized over the anticipated product life of four years starting two years from now.

- EL had depreciation expense of $780,000 in 20X5 but claimed no CCA. In the past, CCA charges have been significantly higher than depreciation, resulting in a $460,000 deferred income tax liability on the statement of financial position.

- In 20X5, EL had a loss for tax purposes of $3 million. The company's tax rate is 40%, constant since incorporation 10 years ago.

- In the past several years, accounting and taxable income have been steady but unimpressive in the range of $250,000 to $450,000. EL is aware that management has to make significant strategic changes to combat disastrous operating results this year. In particular, EL is faced with the need to upgrade capital assets to remain competitive. However, raising money for this venture will be very difficult.

Required:
Explain the income tax impacts of the above and describe how results would be reported on the company's financial statements.

(ICAO, adapted)

★★ **A16-29 Tax Losses, Temporary Differences:** The 20X6 records of Laredo Incorporated show the following reconciliation of accounting and taxable income:

Net income per the financial statements	$124,000
Plus (minus)	
Dividend revenue	(2,900)
CCA in excess of depreciation	(42,300)
Warranty payments in excess of expense	(500)
Non-tax-deductible expenses	2,900
Taxable income	$ 81,200

In 20X5, Laredo Inc. had reported an operating loss, the tax benefit of which was fully recognized in 20X5 through loss carryback and recognition of a future tax asset.
Selected SFP accounts at the end of 20X5

Deferred income taxes (regarding warranty amounts)	$ 320
Income tax receivable	16,400
Deferred income tax (asset: loss carryforward)	20,000
Deferred income tax (liability)	48,000
Warranty liability	1,000
Net book value of capital assets, after depreciation of $41,000	618,000

UCC at the end of 20X5 was $468,000. Depreciation expense in 20X6 was $41,000. The enacted tax rate in 20X5 was 32%. The enacted tax rate in 20X6 was 38%.

Required:
Present the lower portion of the 20X6 statement of profit and loss. Also include the tax entries for 20X6.

Source: Atlantic School of Chartered Accountancy, © 2010.

★★ **A16-30 Tax Losses, Temporary Differences:** Boom Corporation was incorporated in 20X4. Its records show the following:

	20X4	20X5	20X6
Pre-tax income (loss)	—	$(1,700,000)	$ 900,000
Non-deductible expenses	—	40,000	50,000
Depreciation of capital assets	$ 25,000	150,000	250,000
Capital cost allowance	25,000	—	500,000
Net book value of depreciable capital assets*	225,000	3,070,000	2,870,000
Undepreciated capital cost (UCC)*	225,000	3,220,000	2,770,000
Tax-free revenue	4,000	10,000	12,000
Enacted income tax rate (at year-end)	38%	40%	45%

*As calculated at the end of the year, after appropriate recognition of acquisitions and the yearly charge for depreciation or CCA.

Required:

1. Present the lower portion of the 20X4 through 20X6 statements of profit and loss. Assume that the likelihood of tax loss carryforward realization is considered to be more probable than not in all years.
2. Repeat requirement (1) assuming that the likelihood of tax loss carryforward realization is considered to be indeterminable in all years.

Source: Atlantic School of Chartered Accountancy, © 2010.

CHAPTER 17

Leases

The 2009 SFP of the Canadian National Railway (CNR) shows total long-term debt of $6,391 million. Of this total, $1,054 million relates to finance lease obligations, which is about one-sixth of total long-term debt. In the financial statement notes, CNR explains that "During 2009, the Company recorded $75 million in assets it acquired through equipment leases, for which an equivalent amount was recorded in debt."

The concept of long-term equipment leasing originated in the railroad industry in the 1930s, when New York banker J. P. Morgan conceived a way of enabling bankrupt railroads to acquire new rolling stock (i.e., cars and locomotives) without having the new rolling stock become part of the general assets of the bankrupt railroad. Legal title remained with the bank, but the railroads got full use of the rolling stock, which they paid for through a long period of lease payments.

In another part of the transportation industry, Air Canada (AC) operated 200 aircraft in its mainline fleet at the end of 2008. AC's 2008 annual report disclosed that 41 were under finance leases, 70 were under operating leases, and the remainder were owned. Future contractual obligations amounted to $1.1 billion for finance leases and $2.7 billion for operating leases.

What is the difference between a finance lease and an operating lease? Why does CNR use finance leases while AC favours operating leases?

Accounting for a lease may not appear at first to be a big problem. After all, the lessee is paying rent to the lessor, so on the surface it would appear that the lessee simply recognizes rent expense on the income statement, while the lessor reports rent revenue. However, things are not always what they seem.

In accounting, a basic principle is that we should attempt to report transactions in accordance with their economic substance rather than their legal form. Often, the economic substance of a lease is that the lessor is really granting use of the asset over most of the asset's useful life in return for a full repayment of the cost of the asset, plus interest. When that happens, the lessor is really acting as a financial intermediary that is financing the asset for the lessee. The principle of reporting *substance over form* therefore leads us to account for the asset as though it were a purchase financed fully by debt. Therein lies the complication.

The purpose of this chapter is to explain the circumstances under which a lease is treated as a form of financing instead of a simple rental agreement, and how financing and operating leases should be reported by both lessees and lessors.

DEFINITION OF A LEASE

A **lease** is a contract that gives the rights to use an asset in return for the payment of rent. In the commonly-used sense of the term, a lease is a fee-for-usage contract between an owner of property and a renter. The asset's owner is the **lessor**, and the renter is the **lessee**. The lease specifies the terms under which the lessee has the right to use the owner's property and the compensation to be paid to the lessor in exchange.

Leased assets can include both real property and personal property. *Real property* means real estate: land and buildings. *Personal property* includes much more than the property that belongs to a person; it is any property that is not real property, and includes both tangible assets (such as machinery, equipment, or transportation vehicles) and certain intangibles (such as patents).

THE LEASING CONTINUUM

Every lease contract is individual. Some types of leases are more or less standard, such as long-term automobile leases. Nevertheless, every lease requires separate negotiation, and the lease contract must be signed by both the lessor and lessee.

Each lease is negotiated to satisfy the needs of both the lessor and the lessee. In the process of negotiation, the parties reach agreement on many contractual facets, such as the length of the lease (the *lease term*); the amount and timing of lease payments; each party's responsibility for maintenance, insurance, and property taxes (for real property leases); cancellation terms; upgrading responsibilities; etc.

As the lease term lengthens—in relationship to an asset's economic life—more and more of the risks and rewards pass from the lessor to the lessee. Suppose you want to rent a car. If you rent a car for one hour, you will pay a very high rate. If you rent for one day, you will pay a high rate, but the rate will be considerably less than the hourly rate times 24. If you rent for a month, the rate per day will be much lower than the rate to rent for one day. And if you rent for three years, a very low rental rate per day can be obtained. As the rental term lengthens, the daily rent goes down because more and more of the risk of ownership is transferred to the lessee.

At some point in this sliding scale of automobile rental payments, the lessee essentially agrees to pay for the car via the rent payments. As the lease term grows longer, you bear a greater risk of obsolescence and of declining usefulness, but you also get the rewards of using the car at minimal cost per day.

Thus, lease contracts cannot easily be categorized into neat slots; each one is different. The leasing continuum is from very short-term leases to very long-term leases, with many leases in the middle.

To cope with this continuum, the accounting profession has, for more than 40 years, used two classifications for leases:

- Finance leases, wherein the lessor transfers substantially all of the risks and rewards of ownership to the lessee; and
- Operating leases, wherein the lessor does *not* transfer substantially all of the risks and rewards of ownership to the lessee.

Notice the relationship between these two classifications. An operating lease is not defined directly. Essentially, an operating lease is defined as a lease that does not fit the definition of a finance lease.

Lessors and lessees can be very ingenious when drafting a lease agreement. Often, the motivation for the lessee's management is to negotiate a lease that has the appearance of an operating lease while still transferring most of the risks and rewards of ownership to the lessee. We will explain the reasons for this motivation later in the chapter.

Thus, the challenge for accountants is to decide which classification is appropriate for any particular lease. Accountants must be able to exercise their professional judgement and discern *substance over form*.

Operating Leases

A lessee enters into an **operating lease** to obtain temporary use of an asset without having to buy it. This is appropriate when there is no long-term need for an asset, or when the lessee's business is volatile and there is not a continuous need for the asset. The key to designating a lease as *operating* is not the actual length of the lease in time—it is the length of the lease in relation to the asset's economic life. An operating lease term covers a *relatively small proportion of the asset's economic life.*

Because an operating lease provides only a relatively short-term return to the lessor, the lessor bears the risk of ownership. If the lessee returns the asset after the rental period and the lessor cannot find another lessee, then the lessor incurs the costs not only of maintaining the asset but also of watching it sink slowly into obsolescence. Consequently, the longer the lease term, the lower the per-period rental cost.

Finance Leases

At the other end of the leasing continuum, a finance lease gives the lessee substantially all of the benefits of ownership. The lessee also has to bear most of the risks of ownership. For example, the lessee is committed to the lease contract even if the lessee has no further use for the asset.

When a lease transfers substantially all of the benefits and risks of ownership to the lessee, the lessee might as well have purchased the asset outright. Indeed, purchasing the asset would give more flexibility—there are no restrictions on what the owner does with an owned asset.

A little later in this chapter, we will explain the criteria for deciding whether a lease is a finance lease. First, however, we will look at operating lease accounting.

OPERATING LEASES

An operating lease is one that gives the lessee the right to use the asset for only a relatively short period of its useful life, such as renting a car or truck for a day, a month, or a year. Accounting for operating leases is not complicated. It is important to remember that the length of "term" is a relative phrase when it comes to asset leasing—10 years is short-term when applied to a building that may be useful for 60 years.

Overview of Operating Lease Accounting

Lessee Accounting   The lessee makes periodic lease payments that are accounted for as normal expense items by the lessee. If a lessee rents a piece of construction equipment (e.g., a crane) for $20,000 a month, the lessee's entry will be as follows:

Rent expense—crane	20,000	
Cash		20,000

The crane itself does not appear on the lessee's books.

Lessor Accounting   On the other side of the transaction, the lessor receives the periodic rent payment and credits rental income or lease income. The lessor credits the cash receipts to an income account such as *rent revenue* (or *other income* if leasing is not one of the company's mainstream business activities):

Cash	20,000	
Rent revenue—crane		20,000

However, the lessor must acquire a piece of equipment before it can be leased out. Suppose that the crane cost $1,500,000 to purchase and is expected to be useful for 10 years. The crane will appear on the lessor's balance sheet as "equipment available for lease," and will be depreciated over its estimated useful life.

Example Exhibit 17-1 illustrates the operating lease accounting for both the lessee and the lessor. In this example, assume the following:

- Empire Equipment Ltd. (EEL) buys a crane on 6 January for $1,580,000. The crane has an estimated useful life of 10 years and an estimated residual value of $260,000.
- On 25 January, EEL enters into 10-month lease contract with Builders Inc. The monthly rent is $20,000. The crane will be delivered to Builders Inc. on 1 February.
- After Builders Inc. returns the crane at the end of November, the crane is idle for the remainder of the year.
- EEL is charging a standard fee of $15,000 for the cost of the crane's assembly, disassembly, and transport cost.
- EEL uses straight-line depreciation, taking a full year's depreciation in the year of acquisition.
- EEL's fiscal year ends on 31 December.

Note that there are two dates for each lease:

- The *inception of the lease*, which is the date at which the lessor and lessee commit to the principle provisions of the lease; this usually coincides with the signing of the lease agreement, but could be earlier, such as in a *memorandum of agreement*; and
- The *commencement of the lease term*, which is the date upon which the lessee is entitled to use the asset.

EXHIBIT 17-1

OPERATING LEASES
COMPARISON OF LESSEE AND LESSOR ACCOUNTING

Lessee Accounting—Builders Inc.			Lessor Accounting—Empire Equipment Ltd.		
			6 January—purchase of crane:		
			Equipment for available for lease	1,580,000	
			Cash		1,580,000
1 February—payment of installation fee:			*1 February—receipt of installation fee:*		
Rental expense—crane	15,000		Cash	15,000	
Cash		15,000	Crane delivery expenses		15,000
Summary entry—payment of monthly rent			*Summary entry—receipt of rent:*		
Rent expense ($20,000 × 10 months)	200,000		Cash	200,000	
Cash		200,000	Lease income ($20,000 × 10 months)		200,000
			31 December—depreciation of crane		
			Depreciation expense*	132,000	
			Accum. Depreciation—crane		132,000

*$1,580,000 − $260,000 ÷ 10 years = $132,000

For the lease with Builders Inc., the *inception* of the lease is 16 January, while the *commencement* of the lease term is 1 February.

The *date of inception* is the date when the accounting treatment of the lease as either an operating lease or a finance lease is determined. A substantial period of time can elapse between inception and commencement, such as when the asset must be constructed before the lease can commence (e.g., aircraft ordered under lease agreement that won't be delivered for several years). However, no formal entries are made in the accounting records until the lease commences.

Executory Costs Many operating leases require the lessee to pay specified costs relating to the leased asset during the lease term. These are known as *executory costs*. In this example, the lessee is required to pay $15,000 for the lessor's delivery and construction of the crane. For the lessee, this is just part of the cost of renting the crane and is charged to rent expense. For the lessor, the payment is reimbursement for labour and transportation costs that the lessor incurs to make sure that the crane is handled and assembled safely. Therefore, the lessor will not normally treat this cost as additional income; instead, the cash received is credited to a contra account to offset the costs incurred.

Uneven Payments Sometimes the operating lease payments are uneven. For example, when office rental space is very scarce, the lessee may be required to make an initial lump-sum payment to the landlord in order to obtain space.[1] If there is an unusually large payment at the beginning (or inception) of the lease, the special payment is amortized over the period of time that the lessee is required to make lease payments. This period of time is called the **initial lease term**. The lease may be renewable, but since there is no obligation on the part of the lessee to renew the lease, the amortization must end with the initial term.

An alternative arrangement that also occurs, particularly for real estate rentals, is that the lessor will "forgive" lease payments (or operating cost payments) for a limited period of time at the beginning of the lease. For example, in a market that has excess supply, a lessor may attract a lessee by agreeing that lease payments will not begin until six months after the lease starts. These forgiven payments also are amortized over the initial term of the lease by charging the contractual monthly lease payments to income and then amortizing the forgiven amounts over the full initial lease term.

For example, assume that F212 Limited leases space in an office building for five years for an annual rental of $100,000. Because the office rental market is "soft," the lessor agrees that F212 need not begin paying rent until the second year; the first year's rent is forgiven. The substance of this deal is that F212 agrees to pay a total of $400,000 for five years; this averages out to an effective rental rate of $80,000 per year. For the first year, there is no cash flow for rent, but F212 will record an expense of $80,000, which is offset by a deferred credit:

Rent expense	80,000	
Deferred rent liability		80,000

For each of the next four years, the $80,000 will be amortized to rent expense, thereby reducing rent expense from the cash outflow of $100,000 to the average annual expense of $80,000. The annual entry on F212's books will be:

Rent expense	80,000	
Deferred rent liability	20,000	
Cash		100,000

The deferred rent will be reported as a current liability on the balance sheet, usually combined with other deferred credits and accrued liabilities.

---

[1] Such payments sometimes are known as *key money* and may be prohibited in some jurisdictions, particularly in those with rent controls on residential properties.

Example: Air Canada provides an example of the treatment of uneven rent. In its 2008 annual report, AC states that "Total aircraft operating lease rentals over the lease term are amortized to operating expense on a straight-line basis." If lease payments precede expense recognition, the difference between the straight-line aircraft rent expense and the lease payments are reported as "deposits and other assets." If expense recognition precedes lease payments, the difference is reported under "other long-term liabilities."

Definition of an Operating Lease

The preceding sections explained, in general terms, the accounting for an operating lease. However, a fundamental question remains: *when is a lease an operating lease?* Accounting standards answer this question only indirectly—an operating lease is *a lease that is not a finance lease.* Therefore, in order to understand the rather fuzzy distinction between an operating lease and a finance lease, we must examine the guidelines for designating a lease as a finance lease.

FINANCE LEASES

The more challenging type of lease (for accountants) is one in which the lessor agrees to purchase an asset (of any type) and lease it immediately to the lessee for substantially all of the economic life of the asset. When that happens, the lessor is not interested in using the asset, even though the lessor will have legal title. Instead, the objective is to provide financing to the lessee to permit the lessee to acquire the asset without actually buying it.

This type of lease is called a *finance lease* in accounting because, in substance, the lessor is providing an asset to the lessee in return for a cash flow stream that enables the lessor to recover its investment in the asset as well as earn a reasonable rate of return on the investment. A finance lease is a form of financing because the lessee acquires essentially full benefits of the leased asset without actually having to buy it.[2]

Thus, in accounting, a **finance lease** is defined as *any lease that transfers substantially all of the risks and rewards of ownership from the lessor to the lessee.*

A finance lease is reported in accordance with its substance as a financing instrument rather than as a simple rental. Most of the rest of this chapter will deal with accounting and financial statement reporting for finance leases.

Classification as a Finance Lease

A fundamental point is that classification of a lease as *finance* or *operating* depends on the substance of the lease rather than its legal form. This is a clear application of the qualitative characteristic of *substance over form.*

Thus, *IAS* 17, *Leases*, avoids using any quantitative guidelines. The basis for designating a lease as a finance lease is judgemental: *do the terms of the lease transfer substantially all of the benefits and risks of ownership from the lessor to the lessee?* The exercise of professional judgement requires criteria or guidelines. To fill this obvious need, IFRS 17 identifies circumstances that individually or in combination would indicate that substantially all of the risks and rewards of ownership are being passed to the lessee. If any of the following guidelines is satisfied, the lease should be classified as a finance lease:

1. *Is there reasonable certainty that the lessee will obtain ownership of the leased property at the end of the lease term?* This occurs (1) if the lease provides for automatic transfer of title to the lessee at the end of the lease, or (2) if the lessee is entitled to buy the asset at the end of the lease term at a price significantly lower than the expected fair value (often called a *bargain purchase option*).[3]

---

[2] Finance leases may also be called "capital leases," which is the term used by the FASB in the United States, as well as in the *CICA Handbook,* Part II, for private enterprises. The term "financial leases" is used in the finance industry.

[3] *IAS* 17 splits this into two separate situations—automatic transfer of title versus a bargain purchase. The outcome is the same either way.

criteria

2. *Will the lessee receive substantially all of the economic benefits expected to be derived through use of the leased property?* This normally is indicated by a lease term that covers most of the asset's useful life. Since the economic benefit of assets goes down over time (through deterioration and obsolescence), substantially all of the economic benefit can be derived during a lease term that falls significantly short of the full physical life of the asset.

measurement is upto mgmt

First 3 are questions to be answered in Yes or No?

3. *Will the lessor be assured of recovering substantially all of the investment in the leased property, plus a return on the investment, over the lease term?* This is determined on the basis of the present value of the lease payments.

4. *Is the leased asset so highly specialized that only the lessee can obtain the benefit without substantial modification?* This is particularly true of assets that are fixed in place and cannot be moved without significant cost, cost that probably would exceed the benefits remaining in the asset.

answer is Y or NO

Definitions To exercise our professional judgement in applying these guidelines, we need to define the measurement rules. The following definitions apply to both lessees and lessors:

- A **bargain purchase option** exists when there is a stated or determinable price given in the lease that is sufficiently lower than the expected fair value of the leased asset at the option's exercise date to make it likely that the lessee will exercise the option. Even if the lessee does not really want the asset after the end of the lease term, it would be advantageous to exercise the option and then resell the asset at its higher fair value. *Bargain purchase option* is not an explicit term in *IAS* 17, but it is a useful shorthand expression that is well used in practice.

- A **bargain renewal term** is one or more periods for which the *lessee* has the option of extending the lease at lease payments that are substantially less than would normally be expected for an asset of that age and type. *Bargain renewal term* also is a term not explicitly used in *IAS* 17 but used in practice because it captures the essence of renewal terms that would strongly entice a lessee to renew.

- The **lease term** includes:
  - All terms prior to the exercise date of a bargain purchase option;
  - All bargain renewal terms; and
  - All renewal terms at the *lessor's* option.

- A **guaranteed residual value** is an amount that the lessee promises the lessor can receive for the asset by selling it to a third party at the end of the lease term. If there is any deficiency in the sales proceeds when the lessor sells the asset, the lessee must make up the difference. The guaranteed residual value is decided when the lease contract is negotiated. A high guaranteed residual value will effectively reduce the periodic lease payments, while a low guarantee will increase the lease payments that a lessor will require to recover the lessor's investment in the asset.

- In contrast, the lessor may not guarantee the residual value, in which instance there is an **unguaranteed residual value**. The lessee has no liability for such an amount, but the size of the lessor's expected residual value will have a direct impact on the size of the lease payments.

- The lessee's **minimum net lease payments** are all payments that the lessee is required to make over the *lease term*, as described above (that is, including bargain renewal terms), *net* of any operating or executory costs that are implicitly included in the lease payment, *plus* any guaranteed residual value. A bargain purchase price (if any) also is included.

  It is important to deduct operating costs from the lease payments to find the **net lease payments**. For example, if the lessor pays insurance on the asset, the lessor includes an estimate of the cost of insurance premiums when setting the lease payments. The insurance is not a cost of *acquiring* the asset; however, it is a cost of *using* the asset. Therefore, any operating costs that are implicitly included in the lease payments must be estimated and subtracted in order to find the present value of the payments that represent, in substance, the cost of acquiring the asset.

  The lessee's minimum net lease payments also do not include any amounts for **contingent lease payments**, which are additional lease payments that are based on subsequent events, such as payments calculated on a percentage of a lessee's gross sales revenue.

- **Initial direct costs** are the costs incurred when negotiating and arranging a lease. For a lessor, these costs may include not only negotiations with the lessee, but also negotiations with the vendor or manufacturer from whom the lessor will obtain the asset to be leased.
- The **implicit lease interest rate** is the interest rate that equates (1) the minimum net lease payments, the initial direct costs, and the residual value (whether guaranteed or not) to (2) the fair value of the leased property at the beginning of the lease. This rate is calculated from the *lessor's* point of view—the lessor's estimated cash flows over the minimum lease term (as defined above).   *is Yield rate, bond rate*
- The lessee's **incremental borrowing rate (IBR)** is the interest rate that the lessee would have to pay to obtain financing through the bank (or other credit sources) to buy the asset, and is determinable with reasonable assurance.[4]

The interest rate used for discounting the net lease payments is the *lessor's* interest rate implicit in the lease, *if known by the lessee*. The lessor's implicit rate usually is *not* known by the lessee, because:

- The lessee will not know the lessor's direct costs of the lease;
- The lessee does not know the lessor's estimated unguaranteed residual value;
- The lessor undoubtedly takes into account the expected value of any contingent rent when negotiating the lease terms, but those expected amounts are not included in any calculation from the lessee's point of view; and
- The lessor normally calculates the lease with an eye to obtaining an *after-tax rate of return*, which is not at all relevant to the lessee's accounting (which must be without the effect of income taxes).

When the lessee does not know the lessor's interest rate implicit in the lease, the lessee's incremental borrowing rate is used. In practice, the lessee's IBR is almost always the rate used for the lessee's accounting.

Economic versus Useful Life The *economic* life of an asset is the maximum number of years that it can be economically productive. The *useful* life to a particular company may be shorter. For example, desktop computers may be useful for six years, but a company may choose to keep its desktop computers no more than four years in order to stay up to date. The economic life is six years, while the useful life is four years. Useful life can never be longer than economic life.

Fair Value Ceiling In no case should the asset be recorded at higher than its fair value. Consider a simple example. Suppose that a lessee agrees to pay the lessor $100,000 at the end of each year for four years. The fair value of the asset being leased is $300,000, and the asset has a four-year useful life. The lessor's implicit rate of return is unknown, and therefore the lessee's IBR of 10% is used. At 10%, the present value of the lease payments is $316,987:

$$PV = \$100,000 \times (P/A,\ 10\%,\ 4) = \$316,987$$

---

[4] In finance literature, the incremental borrowing rate is sometimes called the *borrowing opportunity rate*, or *BOR*.

If the lessee uses its IBR, the book value of the asset will be higher than the fair value of the asset. In such a case, the lessee must use a rate that discounts the lease payments to the $300,000 fair value of the asset. The equation is:

$$\$300,000 = \$100,000 \times (P/A, i, 4)$$

and must be solved for the value of i. The interest rate that solves this equation is 12.6%.[5]

An Informal Guideline While *IAS* 17 provides criteria for lease classification that are based on the nature of the lease contract itself, professional judgement still is required. The basic issue is whether, in substance, the risks and benefits have been transferred from the lessor to the lessee.

One criterion that is not explicitly cited by the standard-setters but that is very useful in practice is to look at the *nature of the lessor*. The nature of the lessor may be key to determining whether the lease is finance or operating.

For example, if the lessor is the leasing subsidiary of a bank, it should be clear that the lease is not an operating lease. Financial institutions have financial assets, not operating assets (except for their own tangible operating assets, of course) on their SFPs. A bank's leasing division will not assume the risks of owning an asset, even though it has title to many thousands of them through lease contracts. One can be assured that, from the point of view of the bank, the lease is a finance lease no matter how ingenious the drafting may have been to try to avoid the accounting finance lease criteria.

In order to fully realize the tax advantages that often are the driving force behind finance leases, a lessor must qualify as a lessor under the income tax regulations. That means that a lessor must derive at least 90% of its revenues from lease transactions. Any company that meets this criterion is a financial intermediary. Any lease that such a financial institution enters into can be assumed to be a finance lease, even if financial lease classification is not clear when the four finance lease guidelines have been applied.

CONCEPT REVIEW

1. What is the basic criterion that determines whether a lease is a finance lease?

2. When are operating lease rental payments allocated (as expense) to periods other than those in which the payments are made?

3. List the four guidelines that help financial statement preparers decide whether a lease is a finance lease.

4. Define the following terms:
   - Bargain renewal options;
   - Incremental borrowing rate; and
   - Lease term.

5. How can the nature of the lessor influence the lessee's accounting for a lease?

---

[5] The implicit rate can quickly be calculated with a financial calculator or with an Excel spreadsheet. An explanation for using Excel for present value and implicit interest calculations can be found online on Connect.

ACCOUNTING FOR FINANCE LEASES—LESSEE

If a long-term lease qualifies as a finance lease for accounting purposes, the asset is recorded on the lessee's books as though it had been purchased and financed by instalment debt. An outline of the accounting is described briefly below:

- The present value of the lease payments is determined by using:
  - The lessor's implicit rate, if known, and otherwise the lessee's IBR.
  - *Net* lease payments for the initial term, plus net lease payments for any bargain renewal terms, plus any renewal terms at the *lessor's* option, plus any *guaranteed* residual value or any bargain purchase price.
- The present value is recorded as the cost of the asset and is classified as a tangible or intangible capital asset. *The recorded cost cannot be higher than the asset's fair value.*
- The offsetting credit is to a *lease liability* account.
- Interest is accrued for each period, charged to interest expense and credited to the lease liability account.
- Lease payments are debited to the lease liability account.
- The asset is depreciated or amortized by following the company's normal depreciation or amortization policy for that type of asset. However, the depreciation or amortization period cannot exceed the lease term unless the lease contains a bargain purchase option or automatic transfer of title at the end of the lease. Otherwise, the asset will be depreciated or amortized over the lease term (including bargain renewal terms).

The leased asset is accounted for as though it was owned, and the payments are treated as payments on an instalment loan. Once the present value is recorded as an asset and a liability, *there is no connection between the asset and the lease liability in the subsequent accounting.*

FINANCE LEASE ILLUSTRATION—BASIC EXAMPLE

We will begin our illustration of accounting for finance leases with a fairly simple example that focuses on the most significant aspects of lease accounting.

Assume that Lessee Limited wishes to acquire equipment that has an expected economic life of eight years and a fair value of $66,000. Instead of buying the asset outright, the company enters into a lease with Borat Corp., a Canadian finance company that specializes in asset-based financing. The facts are shown in Exhibit 17-2.

▶ EXHIBIT 17-2 ◀

LEASE TERMS—BASIC EXAMPLE

- The fair value of the asset is $66,000.
- The lease begins on 1 January 20X2.
- The initial lease term is three years.
- Payments over the initial lease term are $20,000 per year, payable at the beginning of each lease year (that is, on 1 January 20X2, 20X3, and 20X4).
- At the end of the initial lease term, the lease is renewable for another two years *at Lessee Limited's option* for $5,000 per year. The normal rental cost of three-year-old equipment of this type is almost $10,000 per year.
- Lessee Limited is responsible for insuring and maintaining the equipment.
- The asset reverts to the lessor at the end of the lease; the lease agreement contains no obligation for Lessee Limited to *guarantee* the residual value. However, the lessor estimates that the asset will have an *unguaranteed* residual value of $15,000 at the end of five years.
- Lessee Limited does not know the lessor's implicit rate of interest in the lease. Lessee's incremental borrowing rate is 8%.

In this example, the important elements for analysis are as follows:

- The *lease term* is five years: the initial lease term of three years plus the bargain renewal term of two years. Five years is 63% of the asset's estimated economic life of eight years.
- The *minimum net lease payments* are $20,000 for each of the first three years and $5,000 per year for the fourth and fifth years, for a total of $70,000. The present value of the minimum lease payments is $63,310:

[handwritten annotations: "Bargain renewal @ 3", "Table 3", "Table 3", "Table 1 lumpsum for beginning of lease period.", "This is abbreviated shortcut. Do follow Prof's notes"]

PV = $20,000 (P/AD, 8%, 3) + $5,000 (P/AD, 8%, 2) (P/F, 8%, 3)

PV = $55,666 + $7,644

PV = $63,310

Note: P/AD means "present value of an annuity due," which has payments at the beginning of each period rather than at the end (which is P/A).

Applying the Lease Guidelines

Does this lease qualify for classification as a finance lease? Exhibit 17-3 applies the four finance lease guidelines to this example. The first and fourth guidelines clearly do not apply. Looking at the lease term relative to the asset's economic life, we can see that the lease covers *most* of the asset's economic life, but clearly not the full life. However, the lease clearly meets the third guideline and thus Lessee Limited should classify the lease as a finance lease.

LESSEE ACCOUNTING—BASIC EXAMPLE

The general approach is, first, to find the discounted present value of the lessee's cash flows over the lease term, as defined above. Then, that present value is recorded as:

- A capital asset (debit), and
- The principal amount of a long-term liability (credit) (with a current component).

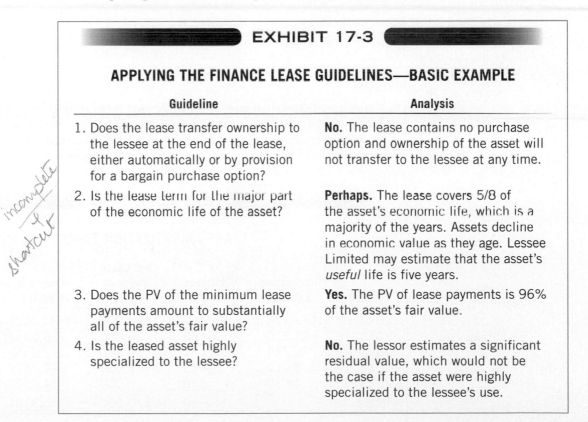

[handwritten annotation: "incomplete of shortcut"]

EXHIBIT 17-3

APPLYING THE FINANCE LEASE GUIDELINES—BASIC EXAMPLE

Guideline	Analysis
1. Does the lease transfer ownership to the lessee at the end of the lease, either automatically or by provision for a bargain purchase option?	**No.** The lease contains no purchase option and ownership of the asset will not transfer to the lessee at any time.
2. Is the lease term for the major part of the economic life of the asset?	**Perhaps.** The lease covers 5/8 of the asset's economic life, which is a majority of the years. Assets decline in economic value as they age. Lessee Limited may estimate that the asset's *useful* life is five years.
3. Does the PV of the minimum lease payments amount to substantially all of the asset's fair value?	**Yes.** The PV of lease payments is 96% of the asset's fair value.
4. Is the leased asset highly specialized to the lessee?	**No.** The lessor estimates a significant residual value, which would not be the case if the asset were highly specialized to the lessee's use.

The asset and liability are identical only when first recorded at the commencement of the lease. Subsequently, there is no parallel between accounting for the asset and the liability. In each year of the lease, the asset and the liability are remeasured individually:

- The leased asset is accounted for exactly as though it had been *purchased* by the lessee, except for some limitation on the depreciable life, if the asset is depreciable (which we will explain shortly).
- The liability is accounted for by the effective interest method, with each payment recorded (1) first as interest on the outstanding balance for the preceding accounting period. The residual of the payment is recorded as a reduction of the principal amount.

The principal amount at the inception of the lease, 2 January 20X2, is the full present value of $63,310. In general journal form, the lease will be recorded as follows:

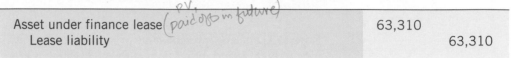

Asset under finance lease (PV, paid off in future)	63,310	
Lease liability		63,310

Amortization Table

Before accounting for the annual cash lease payments, we need to construct an *amortization table*. A lease amortization table is similar to the amortization tables illustrated in Chapter 12 for amortizing discount or premium on long-term debt. For leases, the purpose of a *lease amortization table* (or *amortization schedule*) is to determine how much of each year's cash lease payment goes to (1) interest expense and (2) reduction of principal.

An amortization table for our basic lease example is shown in Exhibit 17-4. The end-of-year cash flows are placed in the fourth column, and the net lease present value (at 8%) is placed at the beginning of the second column ("outstanding balance").

The first payment is made at the commencement of the lease, 1 January 20X2. Since this is the first day of the lease, there has been no elapsed time and therefore no accrued interest. The full amount of the net lease payment reduces the outstanding balance:

1 January 20X2:		
Lease liability	20,000	
Cash		20,000

Interest

On 1 January 20X3, the payment must be divided between interest and principal payment. Exhibit 17-4 shows that interest is $3,465 (that is, $43,310 × 8%), which means that of the second $20,000 lease payment (1 January 20X3), $3,465 is charged to interest expense and the remaining $16,535 of the lease payment will go to reducing the outstanding principal balance.

EXHIBIT 17-4

LEASE AMORTIZATION TABLE

1st pmt on day 1 can have no interest

1 January	Outstanding Balance	Interest @ 8%	Net Lease Payment 1 January	Decrease in Balance	31 December Balance
20X2	$63,310	$ —	$20,000	$(20,000)	**$43,310**
20X3	43,310	3,465	20,000	(16,535)	**26,775**
20X4	26,775	2,142	20,000	(17,858)	**8,917**
20X5	8,917	713	5,000	(4,287)	**4,630**
20X6	4,630	370	5,000	(4,630)	**0**
Totals		$6,690	$70,000	$(63,310)	

The interest that has accrued through 20X2 must be recorded at year-end:

31 December 20X2:		
Interest expense	3,465	
Lease liability		3,465

On 1 January 20X3, Lessee Limited makes the second lease payment:

or discount [handwritten]

1 January 20X3:		
Lease liability *(based on PV, increases by int factor + decreases by pmt)* [handwritten]	20,000	
Cash		20,000

Notice that the 31 December 20X2 interest accrual is credited directly to the lease liability account. Alternatively, the accrued interest could have been credited to *accrued interest payable*, in which case the credit for the cash payment would need to be broken down between interest and principal. In practice, it is much simpler just to credit accrued interest directly to the lease liability account—then the cash payments can be credited to the lease liability without having to figure out how much of the payment gets credited to which account.

Exhibit 7-5 shows all of Lessee Limited's entries for the liability. The final column of the exhibit shows the accumulated balance of the total lease liability account. The year-end interest accruals increase the balance, while the lease payments reduce the balance. The final lease payment, on 1 January 20X6, reduces the balance to zero.

Observe that the lease liability balance after each lease payment is exactly the same amount as shown in the final column (year-end balance) of Exhibit 7-4. These amounts are highlighted in both Exhibits.

Depreciating Leased Assets

Exhibit 7-5 illustrates only the entries for the liability. In addition, Lessee Limited must depreciate the asset. Depreciation is based on the discounted present value of the asset, as recorded, minus any guaranteed residual value.

IAS 17 identifies the depreciation period as being the shorter of (1) the asset's useful life or (2) the lease term (including bargain renewal terms). In practice, it is extremely unlikely that asset's useful life will be less than the lease term *when the lease is being negotiated*. After all, why agree to pay for an asset after it has stopped being useful? However, things happen. Perhaps an asset becomes obsolete during its lease term, or the lessee changes the nature of its business and no longer needs that asset. In any case, the lessee needs to change the useful-life estimate for depreciation and shorten the depreciation period.

The economic life of an asset usually exceeds the lease term. The really important point is that the depreciation period can never be *longer* than the lease term unless the lessor will obtain title to the asset at the end of the lease, either automatically or by exercising a bargain purchase option.

If we assume that Lessee Limited's accounting policy for this type of asset is to amortize it on the straight-line basis with a full year's depreciation taken in the first year, then the depreciation of the leased equipment on 31 December 20X2 will be $12,662 (i.e., $63,310 ÷ 5). The entry at the end of each year, 20X2 through 20X6, will be:

Depreciation expense	12,662	
Accumulated depreciation – asset under lease		12,662

At the end of the lease term, when the asset is returned to the lessor, Lessee Limited must write off the fully depreciated asset:

Accumulated depreciation – asset under lease	63,310	
Asset under finance lease		63,310

EXHIBIT 17-5

LESSEE'S RECORDING OF FINANCE LEASE LIABILITY—BASIC EXAMPLE

[Handwritten margin notes: "Each yr there should be a depriciating entry"; "Dep. expense 12662 / Acc. dep 12662"]

	Dr.	Cr.	Lease Liability Balance
1 January 20X2			
Asset under finance lease	63,310		
Lease liability		63,310	63,310
Lease liability	20,000		**43,310**
Cash		20,000	
31 December 20X2 *(accr. of int)*			
Interest expense	3,465		
Lease liability		3,465	46,775
1 January 20X3			
Lease liability	20,000		**26,775**
Cash		20,000	
31 December 20X3 *(accrual of interest)*			
Interest expense	2,142		
Lease liability		2,142	28,917
1 January 20X4			
Lease liability	20,000		**8,917**
Cash		20,000	
31 December 20X4			
Interest expense	713		
Lease liability		713	9,630
1 January 20X5			
Lease liability	5,000		**4,630**
Cash		5,000	
31 December 20X5			
Interest expense	370		
Lease liability		370	5,000
1 January 20X6 *(last pmt) (reducing lease liability to zero)*			
Lease liability	5,000		0
Cash		5,000	

Financial Statement Impacts—Lessee

Statement of Financial Position At the end of 20X2, the outstanding principal balance in the lease liability account is $43,310, as shown in both Exhibit 17-4 and 17-5. This liability must be shown as a long-term liability on Lessee Limited's SFP, except for the portion that will be paid within the next year. In our example, the next payment is at the start of the next fiscal year and therefore the entire payment will be classified as a current liability. The total balance of $46,775 will be classified on the SFP as follows:

Current liability	$20,000
Long-term liability	26,775
Total	$46,775

Although the full amount of the next payment is classified as current in this simple example, that situation will arise only when the payment is due immediately after the reporting date. The current liability is not normally the amount of the next payment due. The current liability is not the amount of cash that will be paid in the next year, but rather *how much of the year-end liability balance* will be paid in the next year. We will illustrate this point a little later in the chapter.

On the asset side, the leased equipment will be shown either separately or as a part of the general equipment account. Similarly, the accumulated depreciation will be shown either separately or combined with the accumulated depreciation of similar assets. If the leased asset and its accumulated depreciation are shown on the face of the balance sheet as part of the general equipment account, the company should disclose the amounts pertaining to leased assets in a disclosure note.

As usual, of course, the equipment can be shown net of accumulated depreciation on the face of the balance sheet with the gross amount and accumulated depreciation shown in a note.

Statement of Comprehensive Income The net earnings section of the SCI will include depreciation expense and interest expense. For 20X2, the amounts relating to the lease are:

Depreciation expense	$12,662
Interest expense	3,465

Each of these expenses can be combined with similar costs; the expenses relating to leased assets need not be reported separately. The interest expense for the lease will, however, be included with other long-term interest, which is reported separately from interest on short-term obligations.

Statement of Cash Flows If the indirect approach to operating cash flow is used, depreciation expense ($12,662) will be added back as an adjustment to net income for determining the cash flow from operations. As well, the principal component of the lease payment (for 20X2: $20,000 − $3,465 interest − $16,535 principal) is shown in the financing activities section as an outflow. Similarly, net income includes $3,465 in interest expense that was not a cash outflow in 20X2.

The only cash flow relating to the lease was the $20,000 payment at the beginning of the lease term. This amount will be shown as a financial outflow. The total amount of the finance liability will not enter the statement of cash flows because the offset to the lease liability was the leased asset, not cash.

Notes to Financial Statements The notes should disclose the commitment for future finance lease payments, both in total and individually for each of the next five years. The payments due under all of the reporting enterprise's finance leases can be added together and reported in the aggregate, of course.

CONCEPT REVIEW

1. Why must operating and executory costs be subtracted from finance lease payments before the lease payments are capitalized?
2. What impact does lease capitalization have on a company's total assets and on its debt-to-equity ratio?
3. Over what period should the lessee depreciate a leased asset?

Accounting by Lessees—Modified Example

The basic example was fairly simple because (1) the lease year coincided with the lessee's reporting year, (2) there was no guaranteed residual value, and (3) the lease included no

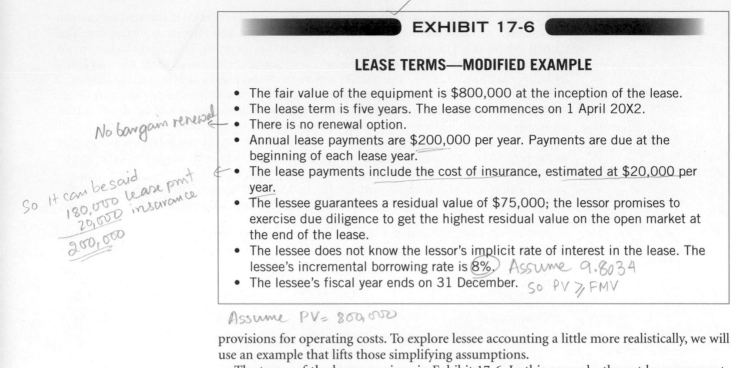

No bargain renewal

So it can be said
180,000 lease pmt
20,000 insurance
200,000

EXHIBIT 17-6

LEASE TERMS—MODIFIED EXAMPLE

- The fair value of the equipment is $800,000 at the inception of the lease.
- The lease term is five years. The lease commences on 1 April 20X2.
- There is no renewal option.
- Annual lease payments are $200,000 per year. Payments are due at the beginning of each lease year.
- The lease payments include the cost of insurance, estimated at $20,000 per year.
- The lessee guarantees a residual value of $75,000; the lessor promises to exercise due diligence to get the highest residual value on the open market at the end of the lease.
- The lessee does not know the lessor's implicit rate of interest in the lease. The lessee's incremental borrowing rate is 8%.   *Assume 9.8034*
- The lessee's fiscal year ends on 31 December.   *So PV ⩾ FMV*

Assume PV = 800,000

provisions for operating costs. To explore lessee accounting a little more realistically, we will use an example that lifts those simplifying assumptions.

The terms of the lease are given in Exhibit 17-6. In this example, the net lease payments are $180,000 per year—the $200,000 annual lease payment minus the annual insurance cost included therein. The present value of the lease includes both the net lease payments and the guaranteed residual value, even though the likelihood of having to pay that full guaranteed residual value is unlikely. The present value calculation is:

meets 3rd
criteria
so financial
lease

Table 3   *Table 1*

PV = $180,000(P/AD, 8%, 5) + $75,000(P/F, 8%, 5)

PV = $776,183 + $51,044 = $827,227

Observe that the guaranteed residual value increases the PV by about 7%, even though the lessee may not have to pay all or any of this amount. This additional amount will affect the implicit interest cost implicit in the annual payments. This causes the lessee's PV to be higher than the asset's fair value.

Fair Value Cap and Implicit Interest Rate   The fair value of the asset is the upper limit. In this example, the lessee's IBR yields a PV higher than the fair value. Therefore, the lessee must calculate the implicit interest rate that equates the lease payments (plus residual value) to the $800,000 fair value[6]:

$800,000 = $180,000(P/AD, *i*, 5) + $75,000(P/F, *i*, 5)

i = 9.8034%

Implicit interest rates seldom work out to nice round numbers.

---

[6] The implicit interest rate was determined by entering the cash flows in an Excel worksheet and letting the computer find the implicit rate. This approach is highly recommended and is explained online on Connect.

Amortization Table Exhibit 17-7 shows the amortization table for this lease, using the rate implicit in the lease. The entry at the commencement of the lease will be:

Asset under finance lease	800,000	
Lease liability		800,000

Executory Costs This lease includes a provision for insurance costs. Leases often include such cost estimates, including property tax estimates and operating costs, especially for real property leases. The costs are known as **executory costs**. As we have seen in the amortization table, executory costs are excluded from the discounted cash flows. Estimated executory costs included in the lease payments must be charged to the relevant expense accounts (e.g., insurance; taxes) when the lease payment is made.

In this example, the annual lease payment includes an amount for insurance. When the lessee makes the lease payment, the insurance cost is debited to an expense account. For the initial payment on 1 April 20X2:

Insurance expense	20,000	
Lease liability	180,000	
Cash		200,000

Note that the insurance expense debit is for the originally *estimated* amount and not for the actual amount, even if the lessor actually pays a different amount for insurance. The reason is that the estimate was used to determine the net lease payments, which then were discounted to find the present value. The only way that the liability accounting will work out is to stick to the predetermined *net lease* payments, even though the actual cost to the lessor may be different.

If the actual cost of the insurance is different from the estimate, and if the lease agreement requires (or permits) the lessor to refund any difference between the estimate and the actual cost, the lessee will credit the refund to the insurance expense account. Similarly, if the lessee is responsible for paying any additional amount, that extra payment will be charged to insurance expense. The basic PV and interest calculations will not be affected.

Interest Expense In the basic example, interest was easy to deal with because the lease year coincided with the lessee's fiscal year. In the modified example, however, the lease year starts in April while the fiscal year starts in January. This is normal, of course—leases aren't arranged for accountants' convenience.

EXHIBIT 17-7

LESSEE AMORTIZATION TABLE—MODIFIED EXAMPLE

Lease Year Ending 31 March	Outstanding Balance	Interest @ 9.8034%	Net Lease Payment 31 March	Change (Decrease) in Balance	Ending Balance
20X2	$800,000	$ —	$180,000	$(180,000)	$620,000
20X3	620,000	60,781	180,000	(119,219)	500,781
20X4	500,781	49,094	180,000	(130,906)	369,875
20X5	369,875	36,260	180,000	(143,740)	226,135
20X6	226,135	22,169	180,000	(157,831)	68,304
20X7	68,304	6,696	75,000	(68,304)	0
Totals		$175,000	$975,000	$(800,000)	

[Handwritten marginal notes:] Pretend PV of asset = fair value of asset. PV will be lower than Fair mkt Value. Not such a situation in exam.

At the end of 20X2, the lessee must accrue interest. The outstanding balance from 1 April to 31 December is $620,000. Interest at 9.8034% for 9 months is $45,586. The entry on 31 December 20X2 is:

Interest expense ($620,000 × 9.8034% × 9/12)	45,586	
Lease liability		45,586

After this interest accrual, the balance of the lease liability is $620,000 + $45,586 = $665,586. On 1 April 20X3, the interest expense must be updated:

Interest expense ($620,000 × 9.8034% × 3/12)	15,195	
Lease liability		15,195

Observe that the 1 April 20X3 accrual is based on the outstanding amount of $620,000 as shown in the amortization table. The 31 December balance is *not* the basis for the final lease quarter's accrual because the PV calculation was based on annual payments, not quarterly. The interest period must coincide with the lease period used for calculating the implicit interest rate. Exhibit 17-8 shows the interest allocation that will occur over the five-year lease term, which affects six fiscal periods because of the overlap between lease year and fiscal year.

When the 1 April 20X3 payment is made, the entry is as follows:

Insurance expense	20,000	
Lease liability	180,000	
Cash		200,000

The inter-period interest allocation has no impact on the lease payment entry.

Cost Allocation Interest is not the only cost that must be allocated to fiscal years. Any operating costs that are included in the gross lease payment would be allocated, if they are material. In this example, those costs consist of the insurance cost and the asset depreciation. Each cost must be allocated at 31 December of each year.

Residual Value The guaranteed residual value was $75,000. Suppose that at the end of the lease, the lessor is able to sell the asset to a third party for $50,000. The lessee will have to make up the difference between the guarantee and the actual—$25,000.

Remember that the present value calculations treated the $75,000 guaranteed residual value as part of the lessee's cash flow. Now, at the end, the cash flow turns out to be quite different. The anticipated final entry at the end of the lease term, 31 March 20X7, was:

Lease liability	75,000	
Cash		75,000

Now, however, the actual cash outflow will be only $25,000. What to do with the difference? The answer is quite simple—a reduction in the necessary cash flow is recognized as a gain in the earnings portion of the statement of comprehensive income. The actual entry will be as follows:

Lease liability	75,000	
Cash		25,000
Gain on lease termination		50,000

EXHIBIT 17-8

ALLOCATION OF INTEREST EXPENSE TO FISCAL YEARS

Lease Payment	Implicit Interest*			Allocation for Accounting	
				Fiscal Year	
				Interest Expense	Year-End
1 April 20X2	$ 0	=	0		
				= $ 45,586	31 Dec. 20X2
1 April 20X3	60,781	=	45,586		
			15,195		
				= 52,016	31 Dec. 20X3
1 April 20X4	49,094	=	36,821		
			12,273		
				= 39,468	31 Dec. 20X4
1 April 20X5	36,260	=	27,195		
			9,065		
				= 25,692	31 Dec. 20X5
1 April 20X6	22,169	=	16,627		
			5,542		
				– 10,564	31 Dec. 20X6
1 April 20X7	6,696	=	5,022		
			1,674	= 1,674	31 Dec. 20X7
Total interest	175,000		175,000	175,000	

*From Exhibit 17-7

Full Set of Entries All of the journal entries to record both the leased asset and the lease liability over the entire five-year lease term are shown in Exhibit 17-9. The last column shows the lease liability balance at each date. The amounts highlighted in **blue** show the balance after each payment; these amounts match the ending lease-year balances shown on the amortization table, Exhibit 17-7. The amounts highlighted in **green** show the liability balance at the end of each fiscal year.

The liability balance at the end of each fiscal year is the *total* liability; on the balance sheet, the total will be divided into current and long-term portions, as described above.

Calculating the Lease Liability Balance—Short-cut Method

Suppose that your business colleague (or your instructor) asks for the balance of a lease liability at a specific point in time, mid-lease. One way to calculate the information is to prepare an amortization table. That's simple enough if the lease is straightforward and has a short term, but it is time-consuming (especially in an examination) to make those calculations for a long and complex lease.

EXHIBIT 17-9

LESSEE'S RECORDING OF FINANCE LEASE—MODIFIED EXAMPLE

	Dr.	Cr.	Lease Liability Balance
1 April 20X2			
Asset under finance lease	800,000		
Lease liability		800,000	
Insurance expense	20,000		
Lease liability	180,000		**620,000**
Cash		200,000	
31 December 20X2			
Interest expense	45,586		
Lease liability		45,586	**665,586**
Depreciation expense (9 months)	120,000		
Accumulated depreciation		120,000	
Prepaid insurance	5,000		
Insurance expense		5,000	
1 April 20X3			
Interest expense	15,195		
Lease liability		15,195	
Insurance expense	20,000		
Lease liability	180,000		**500,781**
Cash		200,000	
31 December 20X3			
Interest expense	36,821		
Lease liability		36,821	**537,602**
Depreciation expense	160,000		
Accumulated depreciation		160,000	
1 April 20X4			
Interest expense	12,273		
Lease liability		12,273	
Insurance expense	20,000		
Lease liability	180,000		**369,875**
Cash		200,000	
31 December 20X4			
Interest expense	27,195		
Lease liability		27,195	**397,070**
Depreciation expense	160,000		
Accumulated depreciation		160,000	
1 April 20X5			
Interest expense	9,065		
Lease liability		9,065	
Insurance expense	20,000		
Lease liability	180,000		**226,135**
Cash		200,000	

Handwritten margin notes:
- any operating cost viz admin cost, etc if must be taken ent. Lease pmt must be pure.
- Ins exp 15,000 / cash 15,000 / can also be done.
- Depreciation expense (9 months) 120,000 $\left(800,000 \times \frac{9}{12}\right)$ = 120,000
- Interest expense $\left(60781 \times \frac{3}{12}\right)$ 15,195
- Insurance expense 20,000 db. / Lease liability 180,000 db
- 31 December 20X3 (accrue)
- Insurance entry missing

EXHIBIT 17-9 *(cont'd)*

LESSEE'S RECORDING OF FINANCE LEASE—MODIFIED EXAMPLE

	Dr.	Cr.	Lease Liability Balance
31 December 20X5			
Interest expense	16,627		
Lease liability		16,627	242,762
Depreciation expense	160,000		
Accumulated depreciation		160,000	
1 April 20X6			
Interest expense	5,542		
Lease liability		5,542	
Insurance expense	20,000		
Lease liability	180,000		68,304
Cash		200,000	
31 December 20X6			
Interest expense	5,022		
Lease liability		5,022	73,326
Depreciation expense	160,000		
Accumulated depreciation		160,000	
1 April 20X7			
Interest expense $\left(6\,696 \times \frac{3}{12}\right)$	1,674		
Lease liability		1,674	
Depreciation expense (3 months)	40,000		
Accumulated depreciation $160,000 \times \frac{3}{12}$		40,000	
Insurance expense	5,000		
Prepaid expenses		5,000	
Lease liability *(guaranteed residual)*	75,000		
Gain on lease termination		50,000	0
Cash		25,000	
Accumulated depreciation	800,000		
Asset under finance lease		800,000	
(return of asset)			

There is a quicker way of doing it. The trick is to remember that at any point during the lease term, *the balance of the lease liability account is the present value of the remaining cash flows, plus accrued interest, if any.*

For example, what is the lease liability of the previous example at 31 December 20X4? We can see from Exhibit 17-9 that the balance at that date, including accrued interest, is $397,070. That amount consists of two components:

PV of the remaining lease payments at 31 March 20X4 (see Exhibit 17-7)	$369,875
Accrued interest from 1 April through 31 December 20X4 (Exhibit 17-8)	27,195
Lease liability, 31 December 20X4 (Exhibit 17-9)	$397,070

To calculate this balance directly, we need to know only the remaining cash flows and the interest rate:

$$PV = [\$180,000(P/F, 9.8034\%, 1) + \$180,000(P/F, 9.8034\%, 2)$$
$$+ \$75,000(P/F, 9.8034\%, 3)] \times [1 + (.098034 \times 9/12)]$$
$$PV = [\$163,929 + \$149,294 + \$56,652] \times 1.0735255$$
$$PV = \$369,875 \times 1.0735255 = \$397,070$$

This is the same as the balance shown in Exhibit 17-9, obtained without calculating an amortization table. If you're asked to determine the liability balance at the end of year 34 of a 40-year lease, this method is definitely a time-saver!

CONCEPT REVIEW

1. How should the current portion of the lease liability be determined?
2. When lease payment dates do not coincide with the company's reporting periods, how is interest expense calculated?

SALE AND LEASEBACK

A **sale and leaseback** is a linked arrangement wherein a company sells an asset and simultaneously leases it back. Sale and leasebacks are most common for buildings. The transaction changes the asset from an *owned* asset to a *leased* asset.

A sale and leaseback gives an immediate cash inflow to the seller. The cash can be used to retire debt (particularly any outstanding debt on the asset, such as a mortgage or a collateral loan), used for operating purposes, or used for any other purpose that management wishes (e.g., paying a dividend).

The seller must evaluate the lease and identify it as either a finance lease or an operating lease. The criteria for this judgement are exactly as described in earlier sections of this chapter.

The sale portion of the deal is initially recorded just like any other sale, with a gain or loss recorded for the difference between the net proceeds from the sale and the asset's net book value. The gain or loss might not be recognized in income in the year of the sale, however.

If the lease part of the sale-and-leaseback arrangement is a finance lease, *any gain or loss is deferred and amortized over the lease term.*

If the lease is an *operating lease*, the treatment of the gain or loss depends on the relationship between the selling price of the asset and its fair value at the date of sale:

- If the sale price is *equal* to the fair value, gain or loss is recognized immediately.
- If the sale price is *greater* than fair value, the gain/loss is deferred and amortized over the lease term.
- If the sale price is *less* than the asset's fair value, any gain or loss is recognized in earnings immediately *unless* the lease payments are less than market lease terms, in which case the gain/loss is deferred and amortized over the lease term.

Bear in mind that the gain or loss is determined by the relationship between the selling price and the asset's carrying value. It is quite possible for the sales price to be below fair value and still trigger a gain.

The objective of gain deferral is to prevent income manipulation. Without this restriction, a company could sell property at an inflated amount and then lease it back under a finance lease, thereby recognizing a gain in the period of the sale. In fact, what the company really would be doing is using the property as collateral for a loan that is hidden as a lease. Therefore, any gain (except as noted above for an operating lease) must be deferred and amortized in proportion to the lease payments over the lease term.

Interestingly, the requirement for deferring a gain can still result in the enhancement of reporting income over a period of years. This opportunity arises when a company enters into a sale and leaseback arrangement for a building that it owns but only partially occupies. Suppose, for example, that a company occupies only 10% of a building. If the company sells the building at a profit and then leases back just the portion that it occupies under a finance lease, the full gain can be deferred and amortized. The amortized gain may more than offset the lease payments, thereby enhancing reported net income over the lease period.

Recording a Sale and Leaseback

Assume that Vendeur Limited owns a building in central Montreal. Vendeur enters into an agreement with Bailleur Incorporation, whereby Vendeur sells the building to Bailleur and simultaneously leases it back. The details are as follows:

- The original cost of the building was $10,000,000; it is 60% depreciated on Vendeur's books.
- Bailleur agrees to pay Vendeur $8,500,000 for the building.
- Bailleur agrees to lease the building to Vendeur for 20 years. The annual lease payment is $850,000, payable at the *end* of each lease year.
- There is no guaranteed residual value.
- Vendeur will pay all of the building's operating and maintenance costs, including property taxes and insurance.
- The effective date of the agreement is 1 January 20X1.
- Vendeur's incremental borrowing rate is 9%.
- Bailleur's interest rate implicit in the lease is computed after tax, and is not disclosed to Vendeur.

The building has a net book value, after accumulated depreciation, of $4,000,000. Since the selling price is $8,500,000, Vendeur realizes a gain of $4,500,000 on the transaction. However, this gain is not recognized in income but instead is deferred. The journal entry to record this sale on 1 January 20X1 is:

Cash	8,500,000	
Accumulated depreciation, building	6,000,000	
Building		10,000,000
Deferred gain on sale and leaseback of building		4,500,000

The gain on the sale will be amortized over the 20-year lease term, *regardless of whether the lease qualifies as a finance lease or as an operating lease.* It is necessary, however, to determine whether the lease is a finance lease for financial reporting purposes. Applying the three tests:

1. Is it likely that the lessee will obtain ownership of the leased property at the end of the lease? *No.*

2. Will the lessee receive substantially all of the economic benefits of the building? Uncertain. The building was 60% depreciated at the time of the sale, indicating that it is not a new building. The 20-year lease term could well be a major part of the remaining economic life of the building.

3. Is the lessor assured of recovering the investment in the leased property, plus a return on the investment, over the lease term? *Probably, because the present value of the lease payments is $7,759,264 at 9%, which is at least 90% of the sales price of the building.*

Since at least one of the guidelines for classifying the lease as a finance lease is satisfied, the leaseback should be recorded as a finance lease. Using Vendeur's IBR of 9% yields a present value of the 20-year stream of end-of-year payments equal to $7,759,264. The lease is recorded as follows:

Building under finance lease	7,759,264	
Lease liability		7,759,264

At the end of 20X1, Vendeur will:

- Record the interest expense (at 9%);
- Pay the $850,000 annual lease payment to Bailleur;
- Amortize the asset; and
- Amortize the deferred gain.

The interest expense and the lease payment will be recorded as follows:

Interest expense	698,334	
Lease liability		698,334
Lease liability	850,000	
Cash		850,000

Assume that Vendeur uses declining-balance depreciation for its buildings, at a rate that is double the straight-line rate. Since the lease term is 20 years, the straight-line rate would be 5%. Therefore, the declining-balance rate is 10% per annum. The entry to record depreciation of the leased building will be as follows:

Depreciation expense, leased building	775,926	
Accumulated depreciation, leased building		775,926

Finally, the deferred gain on the sale must be amortized. The gain should be amortized in proportion to the depreciation of the leased asset, and not in proportion to the lease payments. Since the asset depreciation is at 10% declining balance, the gain must similarly be amortized:

Deferred gain on sale and leaseback of building	225,000	
Depreciation expense, leased building		225,000

The depreciation of the gain is *credited* to the depreciation expense charged for the asset. The reason is that the sale and leaseback transaction had the effect of taking a building with a $4,000,000 book value and rerecording it on Vendeur's books at $7,759,264, close to its fair value. By offsetting the gain against the asset depreciation, the depreciation expense is reduced to $325,926, which is closer to the amount the building depreciation would have been if it had not been sold.

If the stream of lease payments had been discounted at a lower rate (7.75%, to be exact), the capitalized value of the asset would have been $8,500,000, the same as its selling price. Ten percent depreciation applied to $8,500,000 yields $850,000, which when reduced by the $450,000 amortization of the gain results in net depreciation of $400,000, exactly the amount that would have been recognized had the building not been sold.

Example

In its 2008 financial statements, Air Canada explains its acquisition of some large Boeing 777 aircraft:

> Five of the aircraft were financed under sales and leaseback transactions with proceeds of $708 [million]. The resulting gain on sale of $81 [million] was deferred and

is being recognized as a reduction to Aircraft rent expense over the term of the leases. The leases are accounted for as operating leases with 12 year terms, paid monthly.

Air Canada had originally purchased the planes; their net book value at the time of the sale and leaseback must have been $627 million. By selling the planes, AC received cash of $708, which the company could then put to use for other purposes. The $81 million gain is being amortized as a reduction of rent expense over the 12-year term of the lease.

CONCEPT REVIEW

1. Why may a company attempt to structure a lease in order to avoid having it classified as a finance lease for financial reporting purposes?

2. If a company sells an asset at a gain and then leases the asset back, how should the gain be recognized for financial reporting purposes?

OTHER ISSUES

Leases for Land and Buildings

A single long-term lease may cover the lease of a building as well as the land it's sitting on. In accounting for such a lease, *IAS* 17 requires the minimum lease payments be allocated between the land and building on the basis of "relative fair values of the leasehold interests in the land element and buildings element of the lease." This statement is easily misunderstood. It does *not* mean that the fair values of the land and building are the basis for the allocation. Instead, it means the fair value of each asset's benefits that are being transferred to the lessee.

Perhaps the simplest way of grasping this concept is look at the land first. Land does not normally lose its economic value over time, in the sense of its usefulness. Land will be as useful after the lease expires as it was before. There is no need for the lessor to be compensated for land deterioration, provided that the land is not being polluted and thus made less valuable during the lease term. The lessor just needs to earn a return on the lessor's investment in the land.

Buildings are different. Over the course of a long lease term, there is bound to be significant deterioration in a building, as well as obsolescence. For example, old multi-floor industrial buildings are largely obsolete now. Modern production generally requires vast floor spaces on a single level. Thus, those old buildings end up either getting torn down, or (if they are in good locations) they are converted for residential use, which has far less value. A long-term lease for a building, therefore, must compensate the lessor for significant loss of economic value.

Once the lease cash flows have been allocated to land and buildings, each component is accounted for separately. Usually, the land lease is reported as an operating lease, since the lease doesn't cover the major part of the land's life (being infinite) nor do the land-related portion of the lease payments cover most of the land's value.

The building, however, may be reported as either an operating lease or a finance lease. The guidelines for that reporting decision are the same as we've discussed above.

IAS 17 recognizes that the land portion of the lease may be immaterial. In that case, or if there is no basis on which to allocate the land and building portions, the lease can be accounted for as a whole.

Estimation Methods for Interest Expense

In the preceding discussion, we have emphasized the effective-interest method of accounting for finance leases. However, *IAS* 17 does permit the lessee to use "some form of approximation" for allocating the interest expense. There are two possible forms of approximation:

- Straight-line; and
- Sum-of-digits.

You already are familiar with these methods for amortization and depreciation.

Straight-Line Straight-line allocation simple divides the total lease expense by the number of reporting periods and allocates a proportionate part of the interest to each period. In our basic example, the total interest expense is $6,690. The lease is for five years; straight-line would allocate $1,338 to each year.

This method obviously doesn't achieve results that are anywhere near the "correct" interest charge in each year. A lessee should report all of its finance leases on the same basis. Therefore, this method would be appropriate only when the aggregate amount of finance leases is relatively immaterial to the reporting entity as a whole.

Sum-of-Digits This method sums the digits of the reporting periods (in our examples, the years) and then allocates the $6,690 on the basis of the declining fraction:

		Fraction	Sum-of-Digits Method	Effective Interest Method
20X2	5	5/15	$2,230	$3,465
20X3	4	4/15	1,784	2,142
20X4	3	3/15	1,338	713
20X5	2	2/15	892	370
20X6	1	1/15	446	0
	15	15/15	$6,690	$6,690

The sum-of-digits method comes somewhat closer to the true interest cost (shown in the last column), but still is quite a way off. There really seems little reason to use an approximation method if the total value of a lessee's finance leases is significant, since the present value must be calculated in the first place and an amortization table can easily be generated at the inception of the lease. It's not necessary to make a new calculation each year; it's all done in advance and can be stored in the computer for quick inclusion into each year's financial statements.

Contingent Rent

Contingent rent is rent that depends on specified future events. Leases for retail space offer a common example of contingent rent—in addition to basic rent, the lessee (i.e., a retailer) usually agrees to pay a percentage of the store's gross sales to the lessor. Contingent rent may also be based on an asset's volume of use, on variations in the lessor's operating expenses (including property taxes) in connection with the lease, on price indices, or on market interest rates, to name a few.

Contingent rent is excluded from accounting lease calculations for both lessor and lessee. However, they are a very important part of decision analysis for both the lessor and the lessee. Indeed, some lease agreements, especially for retail space, may well depend on achieving a certain volume of activity; if that volume is not achieved, the lessor may have the right to terminate the lease.

Contingent rents are reported as operating expenses in the year that they are incurred. Sometimes this will require the lessee to accrue estimated contingent rent payments, even if the exact amount will not be known until the end of the lease year.

Deferred Income Taxes

Leases normally are taxed in accordance with their legal form. The tax deduction is the amount of lease payments made during the tax year. The fact that a lease may be accounted for as a finance lease is of no interest to Canada Revenue Agency.

Therefore, many leases that are reported by the lessee as a finance lease may be taxed by CRA as an operating lease. This difference in treatment will give rise to a *temporary difference*. Accounting for deferred income taxes and temporary differences is explained in Chapter 15.

LESSEE DISCLOSURE

Operating Leases

In the notes to the financial statements, lessees should give a general description of their significant leasing arrangements, including the basis on which contingent rent (if any) is determined and whether there are any renewal and/or purchase options. If any lessor has imposed financial restrictions on the lessee, such as limitations on additional debt or on dividend distributions, those should be disclosed.

Quantitatively, lessees should disclose lease payments recognized as expense in the current period, separated into (1) minimum lease payments and (2) contingent rents. Lessees should also disclose the company's obligation for operating lease payments (1) for next year, (2) in total for the next four years, and (3) in total for all later years.

Operating leases that are on a year-by-year basis, with no obligation beyond the forthcoming year, are usually not included in the disclosure because there is no obligation beyond the current year.

Finance Leases

A company's rights to leased assets are different from its rights to owned assets. A company can sell, modify, or otherwise dispose of owned assets without restriction. Owned assets can also be used as collateral for a loan. Leased assets, on the other hand, belong to the lessor. The lessee does not have the same rights of ownership, even though the lessee bears substantially all of the risks and benefits of ownership.

In order to make it clear that some assets shown on the balance sheet have been obtained through finance leases, both the leased assets and the related lease obligations should be reported separately, either on the face of the balance sheet or in a note.

Of course, the current portion of the lease liability should be shown separately, as has been described earlier in this chapter, *if* the lessee's reporting practice is to use a current–non-current classification in the SFP.

Accounting standards also recommend other disclosures:

- A general description of the lessee's significant finance lease arrangements, including:
  - The basis for contingent rent, if any;
  - Any renewal terms, purchase options, or escalation clauses; and
  - Any financial restrictions imposed by the lessor, such as limits on dividend payments, additional debt, or additional leasing.
- The amount of any contingent rents recognized as expense during the period
- For each class of leased asset, the net carrying value at the reporting date
- The total of future minimum lease payments *and their present value* for:
  - The coming year;
  - Future years 2 through 5; and
  - All years after year 5.
- A reconciliation between total future minimum lease payments and their present value

Leases are financial instruments. Therefore, leases must conform to the general disclosure requirements for financial instruments, as discussed in Chapter 12.

Disclosure Example

An example of a finance lease disclosure note is shown in Exhibit 17-10. British Airways (BA) has both operating and finance leases. The company also has *hire purchase contracts*. A hire purchase contract is contract for renting an asset that contains a clause giving the renter an option to acquire title to the asset upon fulfillment of certain agreed-upon conditions. This type of contract qualifies as a finance lease.

EXHIBIT 17-10

BRITISH AIRWAYS LEASE DISCLOSURE

Obligations under Finance Leases and Hire Purchase Contracts

	Group	
Million euros	**2009**	**2008**
Future minimum payments due		
Within one year	687	389
After more than one years but within five years	1,163	1,218
In five years or more	1,672	1,268
	3,522	2,875
Less finance charges	607	578
Present value of minimum lease payments	2,915	2,297
The present value of minimum lease payments is analysed as follows:		
Within one year	620	310
After more than one years but within five years	926	989
In five years or more	1,369	998
At March 31	2,915	2,297

Operating Lease Commitments

The Group has entered into commercial leases on certain properties, equipment and aircraft. These leases have durations ranging from five years for aircraft to 150 years for ground leases. Certain leases contain options for renewal.

a. Fleet

The aggregate payments, for which there are commitments under operating leases as at March 31, fall due as follows:

	Group	
Million euros	**2009**	**2008**
Within one year	84	77
Between one and five years	334	169
Over five years	444	17
At March 31	862	263

b. Property and equipment

Within one year	84	86
Between one and five years	249	244
Over five years, ranging up to the year 2145	1,562	1,612
At March 31	1,895	1,942

Source: Used with permission from British Airways.

BA uses a simple approach to disclosing the amounts relating to finance leases. The company shows the required disclosures by years, totals them, and then subtracts the unearned finance revenue to derive the present value of the leases. The total present value is then broken down by year grouping, as required.

The company also has two other lease disclosures that we have not reproduced here, in the interests of space: (1) a section that shows lease amounts receivable from subleases, and (2) the carrying value of each class of assets, (a) fleet assets and (b) property and equipment.

LONG-TERM LEASES: PROS AND CONS

Some people argue that long-term leasing has several advantages over buying an asset. However, the perceived advantages to the lessee also have offsetting disadvantages. For each purported advantage we will look at the apparent benefits first (Pro), and then at the related disadvantages (Con).

Off-balance-sheet Financing

Pro If a company enters a long-term lease and that lease does not qualify as a finance lease for accounting purposes, the company effectively has obtained financing for an asset without having to show the asset (and any related liability) on its balance sheet. For example, airlines often use leasing in this manner by entering into operating leases that last for several years but don't last long enough for the lease to qualify as a finance lease. Lessees may view off-balance-sheet financing as an advantage because they effectively incur debt that doesn't appear on the balance sheet.

Con The shorter the lease, the greater the cost to the lessee. In shorter leases, more of the risk remains with the lessor. The lessor does not accept this risk out of generosity. The cost is passed back to the lessee in the form of higher annual lease payments and/or heavy cancellation penalties if the lessee does not renew. Therefore, a lessee may obtain "off-balance-sheet" financing but at a real economic cost in higher expenses and operating cash flow expenditures.

100% Financing

Pro A financial institution will not lend the full amount of the purchase price to a buyer. Normally, financing can be obtained for no more than 75% or 80% of the cost of the asset. In contrast, a lease can effectively provide full financing, since there is no substantial down payment to be made at the inception of the lease.

Con This advantage exists only for assets that are readily transferable if the lessee defaults (e.g., automobiles, airplanes), and only to lessees that have high credit ratings. For other assets and less creditworthy lessees, the lessor covers the risk by forward-weighting the lease payments, meaning that most of the cash flow for lease payments is in the early years of the lease. Also, since lease payments are payable at the beginning of each period, the first payment is, in effect, a down payment.

Protection against Obsolescence

Pro The shorter the lease term, the easier it is for the lessee to stay up to date with the latest technology. If a new product or process becomes available, the lessee can refuse to renew the existing lease and move to the newer product instead. An alternative is for the lessor to provide upgrade privileges in the lease. For example, an existing leased photocopier may be replaced by a newer model, or a leased automobile may be "rolled over" to a new model every second or third year. Such lease arrangements do help the lessee guard against obsolescence.

Con Flexibility comes at a price. The risk of obsolescence falls on the lessor, and the lessor will compensate for the added risk by charging higher lease payments. Lessor-provided upgrades can help provide flexibility, but they do lock the lessee into the lessor's product. As well, automatic upgrades are expensive. Many companies find it much less costly to skip a product generation unless it is crucial to be on the cutting edge of technology (e.g., many companies running Windows XP skipped Windows Vista and later installed Windows 7, thereby saving on both software costs and training costs with little or no loss of productivity).

Protection against Interest Rate Changes

Pro Lease payments are always determined on the basis of fixed interest rates, even when the lease contains escalation clauses or contingent payments. Therefore, a long-term or finance lease can protect the lessee from interest rate fluctuations.

Con If the lessee's business fluctuates in response to economic conditions, it may be better to use variable-rate loans from financial institutions to finance the assets. When the economy is down, interest rates are down, thereby not locking the company into a high implicit interest rate.

Transfer of Income Tax Benefits

The transfer of income tax benefits from the lessee to the lessor is perhaps the driving force behind the bulk of finance leases. The legal owner of an asset can deduct CCA on the tax return. But the owner may not be able to use the CCA deduction, or the full benefit of that deduction. Some examples of such a situation are:

- The owner is a non-profit organization, such as a school, hospital, or charity.
- The owner is a for-profit business, but either is losing money or is not earning enough to use the full amount of the available CCA.
- The owner is profitable, but pays taxes at a lower rate than potential lessors.

If any of these conditions exist, then the CCA is more valuable to a lessor than to the potential user of the asset. Lessors calculate their return on investment on an after-tax basis, and lease industry competition forces the lessor to pass the benefit of any tax reduction on to the lessee in the form of lower lease payments. Therefore, the asset can often be leased for a cash flow present value that is less than the amount the lessee would pay to buy the asset.

CONCEPT REVIEW

1. What is meant by off-balance-sheet financing?
2. Who holds legal title to a leased asset?
3. How can a lease be used to transfer CCA tax benefits from the lessee to the lessor?

AVOIDING LEASE CAPITALIZATION

At the beginning of this chapter, we stated that operating leases are relatively short-term leases that provide the lessee with temporary use of an asset. By assuming only temporary use of the asset, the lessee avoids many of the risks of ownership, including obsolescence. This relief from risk comes only at a price, however. Lessors will pass the cost of their ownership risk on to the lessee through a higher rental cost. In general, the shorter the lease for a particular asset, the higher the cost per period will be.

In accounting, operating leases are not defined directly and substantively, but rather are defined indirectly: *a lease is accounted for as an operating lease if it is not judged to be a finance lease.*

Operating lease treatment therefore is the "default" treatment for leases that fail to meet the basic criterion of conveying substantially all of the risks and benefits of ownership to the lessee, or for which there is no objectively determinable basis for arriving at a present value for the lease.

The problem with this approach is that it leads to an all-or-nothing approach to capitalization: if the guidelines are satisfied, the whole lease is capitalized, but if none of the guidelines are satisfied, then none of the lease is capitalized. This has led to a number of capitalization-avoidance techniques and to the development of a whole industry dedicated to devising ways of leasing assets to companies while avoiding the capitalization criteria. Three common methods of avoiding capitalization are to:

1. Base a large part of the lease payment on contingent rent;

2. Insert a third party between the lessee and the lessor; and

3. Shorten the lease term, but impose a substantial penalty for non-renewal.

Use Contingent Rent One of the guidelines for classification as a financial lease is that the present value of the lease payments amounts to substantially all of the lessor's investment in the leased asset. However, contingent rents are excluded from the definition of minimum net lease payments. When there are contingent rental payments, their probable future value is ignored when the lease is being evaluated as a possible finance lease. Therefore, the larger the amount of rental that can be made dependent on future events, the lower the minimum net lease payments will be.

Insert a Third Party This can occur in a number of ways. The most common is for the lessee to form a separate company, the purpose of which is to lease assets to the operating company. The separate company enters into the formal lease agreement with the lessor, obligating itself to pay for the full cost of the asset over the lease term, and then enters into a year-by-year lease with the operating lessee.

   This approach will not work under IFRS if the intermediate company is a subsidiary of the operating company because the operating company will be required to consolidate the leasing subsidiary. Instead, the intermediate company will be a company that has the same owners (e.g., shareholders or partners) as the operating company. Companies that have the same owners are known as *companies under common ownership*. The financial statements of companies under common ownership are not combined or consolidated, and therefore the operating company need not report the asset or the obligation on its balance sheet even though the lessor may clearly have entered into a finance lease.

Shorten the Lease Term The third approach is probably the most common. Corporations may lease major and crucial operating assets under lease agreements that provide for a year-by-year renewal (at the lessee's option) or for lease terms that are considerably shorter than the economic life of the asset. Operating leases can be the result of a well-thought-out strategic positioning, but quite often they are deliberate attempts to obtain assets through off-balance-sheet financing.

   For example, airlines commonly lease a significant part of their fleets through leases that run five to seven years. Since an airplane, properly maintained, can last for a very long time, there is no way that a seven-year lease will qualify as a finance lease. But without the aircraft, the airline cannot operate, and so at least a core of aircraft must be leased continuously. But by leasing everything in sight, the airline (or other such company) can avoid showing the lease obligations on the balance sheet. This practice is usually known as "cleaning up the balance sheet."

   Financial statement users need to be wary of such off-balance-sheet financing arrangements. A company that owns its essential assets, or leases them through finance leases, will show higher total assets (and thus a lower return on assets) and a higher debt-to-equity ratio than will a company that uses operating leases. But the user must not be misled into concluding that the company that owns its assets is the weaker performer. In fact, the company that owns its assets may be in a substantively stronger financial position. Short-term leases come at a higher price, so a "clean" balance sheet may hide a weak operating performance.

   There is widespread international dissatisfaction about perceived shortcomings in the reporting of operating leases among users and professional accountants alike. To consider alternatives and new approaches to lease accounting, the IASB and FASB have jointly established a new international working group to review lease accounting. We will discuss this initiative at the end of the chapter, in the Looking Ahead section.

LESSOR ACCOUNTING

Now that we've seen how lessees account for a finance lease, we can turn our attention to the other party in the transaction—the lessor.

Lessors: A Specialized Industry

Any company can be a lessee. In theory, any company could also be a lessor. In practice, however, lessors constitute a highly concentrated specialized industry. In accounting textbooks, we don't examine specialized industries. Banks, insurance companies, mutual funds, regulated public utilities, real estate development companies, and private investment companies are all examples of specialized industries. Lessors fit into that same general category.

Not just any company can be an effective lessor. The specialized nature of leasing is the result of the *Income Tax Act*. Only companies that derive at least 90% of their revenue from leasing are permitted to deduct CCA in excess of rental revenue—a crucial aspect of successful lessor activity. Lessors are financial intermediaries. Often, they are subsidiaries of broader financial institutions, such as chartered banks or asset-based lending institutions. There are no publicly listed lessors in Canada.

One example of a major lessor is International Lease Financing Corporation (ILFC), a U.S.–based company that leases aircraft and related equipment. In 2008, ILFC had 174 different airline companies as customers. The company is an indirect wholly-owned subsidiary of AIG. AIG is primarily an insurance company. IFLC operates mainly through operating leases, although the company does engage in some finance lease activity.

Another major international lessor is General Electric Capital Corporation (GECC). This company is an indirect wholly-owned subsidiary of the General Electric Company. GECC operates in four separate financial services businesses, one of which is GE Equipment and Other Services. The company engages in a very wide range of leasing through both finance and operating leases. You may often see the name, usually identified as "GE Capital," in the business news as providing financing solutions (including leases) to many companies. Air Canada is a customer of both IFLC and GECC.

Captive Finance Companies A finance company may also be a finance subsidiary of a manufacturer that was set up to facilitate sales of the manufacturer's products. These subsidiaries are known as **captive leasing companies**. For example, General Motors Acceptance Corporation of Canada is the sales-finance arm of General Motors (although it also offers other financial services such as insurance and home mortgages).

A manufacturing company also may carry out leasing services through a special-purpose entity (SPE) that is then consolidated into the parent company's financial statements if the parent company prepares consolidated statements. For example, Bombardier Inc. states in its financial statement notes that the company has created SPEs "to purchase regional aircraft from the Corporation and to lease these aircraft to airline companies."[7]

We will return to this topic of manufacturer's "sales-type leases" later in the chapter.

Differences between Lessee's and Lessor's Net Cash Flows

The lessor will work with the same basic set of lease terms, except that there is no prescribed interest rate. Instead, the lessor must use the rate of return that equates the PV of the lease payments to the cost of acquiring the asset, including any direct costs incurred in negotiations and any incidental costs to acquire the asset (e.g., transportation, commissions, and so forth). There are some aspects of the lease that do not apply to the lessee and that therefore differentiate the lessor's net cash flow from that of the lessee. The three most important differences are:

1. *The initial cost of the asset.* The lessor may obtain a more favourable price on the asset, often by bulk buying. For example, lessors that deal in aircraft leasing usually buy a large number of planes from the manufacturer and then lease them in smaller quantities to a several individual airlines. By bulk buying, the lessor can negotiate especially favourable

---

[7] From the Bombardier Inc. 2008 Annual Report, page 173; posted on SEDAR on 3 April 2009. Public companies are required to consolidate their subsidiaries and SPEs; private enterprises can choose whether to prepare consolidated statements or not—most don't.

prices that would not be available to individual airlines. Therefore, an asset's cost to the lessor may be significantly less than the asset's fair value as perceived by the lessee.

2. *Residual value.* The lessor may expect a significant residual value. An airplane can last a very long time if it is properly maintained. A major airline may lease new aircraft for only a limited number of years—its passengers want up-to-date planes, prompting competition between airlines for "the most modern fleet." However, the economic life of the aircraft will be longer than the useful life to a mainstream carrier. When an airplane's lease with a mainline carrier ends, the residual value of the plane may still be quite high because smaller carriers, charter airlines, and cargo lines can use older planes.

3. *Tax shield.* The lessor can gain a significant tax shield from the aircraft's depreciation. The early tax cash flow savings from deducting depreciation (CCA, in Canada) will increase the after-tax cash flow from the lease, especially in the early years, greatly affecting the IRR on the lease.

As we continue with our basic example, we will take the first two differences into account, but leave the third aside because it is a specialized topic that analysts must be aware of but need not be able to calculate.

Internal Rate of Return

The lessor accounts for the lease by the effective interest method. First, we must determine the interest rate implicit in the lease, which represents the internal rate of return (IRR) that Borat Corp. is earning (before tax) in this lease.

Our lessor, Borat Corp., will base its accounting on the lease cash flows (Exhibit 17-2) plus these additional factors:

- Borat Corp. negotiated a purchase price of $60,000 for the asset. Additional direct costs amounted to $1,500.
- The expected residual value at the end of the lease term (i.e., five years) is $4,300.

To find the internal rate of return, we find the value of *i* in the following equation:

$$\$60,000 + \$1,500 = \$20,000 \,(P/AD, i, 3) + \$5,000 \,(P/AD, i, 2) \,(P/F, i, 3) + \$4,300 (P/F, i, 5)$$

This equation can be solved by using a financial calculator or an Excel spreadsheet, or by trial-and-error using present value tables.

The value of *i* that satisfies this equation is 14%. The lessor's rate of return is significantly higher than the 8% cost to Lessee Limited. The higher rate is due to the lower purchase price that the lessor was able to negotiate, plus (to a lesser extent) the unguaranteed residual value. This phenomenon is what can make leasing quite attractive in the right circumstances.

Guaranteed versus Unguaranteed Residual Values It is important to understand the different roles of guaranteed and unguaranteed residual values in finance lease accounting:

- A *guaranteed* residual value is part of the definition of *net lease payments* for both the lessee and the lessor.
- The lessee uses the guaranteed residual value as part of its discounted cash flow because the lessee is committed to pay it if the lessor is not able to recover that amount by disposal of the asset at the end of the lease.
- The lessor, however, uses the lessor's estimate of residual value when determining the lease's implicit interest rate, regardless of whether it is guaranteed or unguaranteed by the lessee.

If the lessee *guarantees* a specified residual value, that guaranteed amount is the *minimum* residual value that the lessor would assume, but the lessor may well anticipate an even higher *unguaranteed* residual value, which is used in the lessor's analysis.

Lessor Accounting—Net Lease Basis

Initial Recording As we discussed previously, finance leasing companies almost always are financial institutions or financial intermediaries. Their business is to provide financing for an entity's asset acquisition, financing that is in the form of a lease rather than purchase financing such as a direct loan. The lessor doesn't want any physical assets lying around—the lessor's assets are *financial* assets. Thus, when a lessor acquires an asset on behalf of a lessee, the asset is delivered directly to the lessee.

Instead of recording the physical asset, the lessor records the *net lease receivable*. The **net lease receivable** is the amount that the lessor spent (or owes) for the asset and associated direct costs. The lessor negotiates a lease agreement with the lessee that will enable the lessor to recover the investment in the leased asset as well as earn interest. Thus, the net lease receivable is, by definition, equal to the costs incurred by the lessor. The entry for Borat would appear as follows:

Net lease receivable	61,500	
Cash (and/or accounts payable)		61,500

After initially recording the lease, Borat will account for each lease payment as a combination of (1) interest income and (2) principal payments to reduce the outstanding lease receivable. This is the reverse of the lessee's lease liability, but the amounts usually will be different because the lessor has a somewhat different cash flow. An amortization table can clarify the lessor's accounting.

Amortization Table The amortization table for Borat Corp. is shown in Exhibit 17-11. The first lease payment occurs at the commencement of the lease and immediately reduces the net lease receivable:

Cash	20,000	
Net lease receivable		20,000

This leaves $41,500 as the lease receivable throughout 20X2. At the end of 20X2, Borat must record the accrued interest, which is $41,500 \times 14\%$, or $5,810, as indicated in the amortization table. The remaining amount of the payment, $14,190, reduces the net lease receivable.

Recording by the Net Method The entire series of entries for Borat is shown in Exhibit 17-12. These entries are essentially the reverse of the lessee's entries, except that

---

EXHIBIT 17-11

LESSOR AMORTIZATION TABLE—BASIC EXAMPLE

1 January	Lease Receivable Before Payment	Interest @ 14%	Payment Received, 1 January	Lease Receivable Change	Lease Receivable After Payment
20X2	$61,500	$ —	$20,000	$(20,000)	$41,500
20X3	41,500	5,810	20,000	(14,190)	27,310
20X4	27,310	3,823	20,000	(16,177)	11,133
20X5	11,133	1,559	5,000	(3,441)	7,692
20X6	7,692	1,077	5,000	(3,923)	3,769
20X7	3,769	531*	4,300	(3,769)	0
Totals		$12,800	$74,300	$(61,500)	

*Rounded up by $3 to balance.

EXHIBIT 17-12

LESSOR RECORDING OF FINANCE LEASE—BASIC EXAMPLE

	Dr.	Cr.	Net Lease Receivable Balance—Dr.
31 December 20X1			
Lease receivable	61,500		
Cash, accounts payable		61,500	61,500
[Delivery of equipment and commencement of the lease]			
1 January 20X2			
Cash	20,000		
Lease receivable		20,000	**$41,500**
31 December 20X2			
Lease receivable	5,810		**$47,310**
Finance income—leases		5,810	
($41,500 × 14%)			
1 January 20X3			
Cash	20,000		
Lease receivable		20,000	**$27,310**
31 December 20X3			
Lease receivable	3,823		**$31,133**
Finance income—leases		3,823	
($27,310 × 14%)			
1 January 20X4			
Cash	20,000		
Lease receivable		20,000	**$11,133**
31 December 20X4			
Lease receivable	1,559		
Finance income—leases		1,559	
($11,133 × 14%)			**$12,692**
1 January 20X5			
Cash	5,000		
Lease receivable		5,000	**$ 7,692**
31 December 20X5			
Lease receivable	1,077		**$ 8,769**
Finance income—leases		1,077	
($7,692 × 14%)			
1 January 20X6			
Cash	5,000		
Lease receivable		5,000	**$ 3,769**
31 December 20X6			
Lease receivable	531		**$ 4,300**
Finance income—leases		531	
($3,769 × 14%)			
1 January 20X7			
Cash	4,300		
Lease receivable (to record the		4,300	**$ 0**
receipt of the residual value)*			

*The actual value received would be recorded, not the estimate. Any gain or loss is reported in earnings.

Borat makes no entries concerning the asset. The first two entries are to record the lease at its commencement and to record receipt of the first lease payment. At the end of 20X2, Borat must accrue the finance income earned on the principal balance of $41,500 that was outstanding throughout 20X2, computed by the implicit interest rate of 14%. The accrued income is debited to the lease receivable balance rather than being recorded as accrued finance income. Receipt of the 1 January 20X3 lease payment is then credited in its entirety to the lease receivable.

Current–non-current Distinction As we've discussed above, companies that negotiate leases are financial intermediaries. Financial institutions do not classify their assets on a current/non-current basis—the classification usually is in order of liquidity. Therefore, we don't need to determine how much of the receivable will be collected within the next year.

Lessor Accounting—Gross Lease Basis

It is easy to see that lessor accounting is essentially just the reverse of lessee accounting, *if* the net lease basis is used. However, lessors usually *record* their lease receivables on a **gross lease basis**. Under the gross lease basis, the lessor records not just the PV of the future cash flows. Instead, the lessor records the undiscounted cash flows offset by a contra-account for unearned finance income. At each reporting date, the lessor calculates the amount of finance income that has been earned for the reporting period. Instead of adding the accrued income to the lease receivable, it is deducted from the unearned finance income.

For *reporting*, the lessor will show only the net amount on the SFP. That is, the net asset is the remaining undiscounted lease payments minus the remaining unearned finance income.

Example Using the example above, the beginning net lease receivable consists of two amounts—(1) the total undiscounted cash flows that the lessor expects to receive, reduced by (2) the amount of interest that the lessor will recognize over the lease term:

Lease payments receivable	$70,000
Estimated residual value	4,300
Gross lease receivable (1)	74,300
Less unearned finance income (i.e., interest) (2)	12,800
Net lease receivable	$61,500

Using the basic example, the entry made at the commencement of the lease is as follows under each of the two different methods:

1. *Net lease method* (as in Exhibit 17-12):

31 December 20X1		
Lease receivable	61,500	
Cash, accounts payable		61,500

2. *Gross lease method*:

31 December 20X1		
Lease receivable	74,300	
Unrealized finance income		12,800
Cash, accounts payable		61,500

Under the gross method, the next three entries will be as follows (from Exhibit 17-12):

1 January 20X2		
Cash	20,000	
Lease receivable		20,000

31 December 20X2		
Unrealized finance income	5,810	
Finance income		5,810

1 January 20X3		
Cash	20,000	
Lease receivable		20,000

At the end of 20X2, the net balance of the lease receivable will be as follows:

Lease receivable ($74,300 − $20,000)	$54,300
Less unearned finance income ($12,800 − $5,810)	6,990
Net lease receivable	$47,310

This is the same amount shown in Exhibit 17-12 as the net lease receivable on 31 December 20X2. After the second $20,000 lease payment is made, the net balance drops to $27,310, which also can be verified by referring to Exhibit 17-12.

Why Use the Gross Method?

The gross and net methods yield the same results for the lessor's financial reporting. The net method is simpler and corresponds to the method normally used by lessees, and thus one might wonder why lessors use the gross method for recording.

Like almost all of the accounts shown on any company's balance sheet, the leases receivable account is a *control account*. The balance sheet amount is a total; underlying that total is a large number of individual leases. For good internal control, an important characteristic of a control account is that it can easily be reconciled to the underlying subsidiary records. For leases receivable, that means that the receivables for the individual leases can be added up to verify the balance in the control account. The gross method makes that reconciliation easier.

Lessors will have thousands, perhaps tens of thousands, of individual leases. Since the amounts in the lease payments receivable account are gross amounts, the balance can be verified by adding the remaining gross payments shown on all of the individual leases.

In contrast, under the net method it is necessary to compute the present value of each lease at a particular point of time in order to perform the reconciliation. Some of the leases may be in arrears, and the present values may not correspond with their planned amortization schedules. Reconciliation on the net method would be a major headache, even in computerized systems. Therefore, the gross method is used. The gross method has the additional advantage of separating the control account function (via the lease payments receivable) from the revenue recognition function (via the unearned finance revenue).

Lessees are likely to have only a few leases, and the leases are incidental to their principal operations. Therefore, maintaining balances by the net method is no great problem for most lessees. Every lease that is reported as a finance lease will have its own amortization table, and summing the present values is fairly straightforward.

Disclosure for Lessors

Lessors should disclose the following:

- A general description of the lessor's leasing arrangements;
- The aggregate future minimum lease payments receivable (that is, the gross amount) and the total amount of unearned finance income, reconciled to the present value of leases as shown on the SFP;
- The gross lease payments and PV of future minimum lease payments for each of the following periods:
  - Within the next year;
  - The total for years two through five; and
  - Later than the fifth year, in total
- Any contingent rentals that have been taken into income;
- The estimated amount of unguaranteed residual values; and
- The accumulated allowance for uncollectible lease payments.

CONCEPT REVIEW

1. Why do lessors usually use the gross method rather than the net method of accounting for capital leases?
2. Where does the *unearned finance revenue* account appear on the statement of financial position?

Leases by Manufacturers and Dealers

Basic Nature Manufacturers and dealers may use leasing as a way of making sales. We all are familiar with the automobile advertising that prominently features interest rates for leasing cars, sometimes as low as 0%. But automobiles are not the only product that is sold heavily via leases. Other examples include computer equipment, office equipment, many types of industrial equipment, and business jets. This type of lease is commonly known as a **sales-type lease** because the real point of it is to "move" the product. A sales-type lease is a finance lease that, from the lessor's point of view, represents the sale of an item of inventory.

Lessors in sales-type leases are manufacturers or dealers—they are not financial institutions and are not acting as financial intermediaries.

For the *lessee's* financial reporting, it doesn't matter whether the lessor is the producer of the product or is simply a financial intermediary. For the *lessor's* financial reporting, however, the distinction matters because a sales-type lease is viewed as two distinct (but linked) transactions:

1. The sale of the product, with recognition of a profit or loss on the sale; and
2. The financing of the sale through a finance lease, with finance income recognized over the lease term.

There is absolutely nothing new in recording or reporting a sales-type lease, once the transaction has been recognized as being two separate but related transactions. The sale is recorded at the fair value of the asset being sold, with the asset received in return being the present value of the lease payments. The lease is then accounted for as a **direct-financing lease**.

Example—Sales-type Lease Assume that on 31 December 20X1, Binary Corporation, a computer manufacturer, leases a large computer to a local university for five years at $200,000 per year, payable at the beginning of each lease year. The normal cash sales price of the computer is $820,000. The computer cost Binary Corporation (BC) $500,000 to build. The lease states that the computer will revert to BC at the end of the lease term, but a *side* *letter* from BC to the university states BC's intention not to actually reclaim the computer at the end of the lease.

The implicit interest rate that discounts the lease payments to the $820,000 fair value of the computer is 11.04%. Unless the cost of financing is well in excess of this rate, the lease can be assumed to be a finance lease. Because the lessor is the manufacturer of the product, and because the computer is carried on BC's books at a value that is less than fair value, the lease clearly is a sales-type lease.

The sale component of the transaction will be recorded as follows (using the net method):

31 December 20X1		
Lease payments receivable	820,000	
Sales revenue		820,000
Cost of goods sold	500,000	
Computer inventory		500,000

The first payment (at the inception of the lease) will be recorded as:

31 December 20X1		
Cash	200,000	
Lease payments receivable		200,000

The income statement for 20X1 will include a gross profit of $320,000 relating to the lease transaction, which is the profit on the sale. The statement of financial position on 31 December 20X1 will show a net lease receivable of $620,000: the gross lease payments of $1 million, minus the unearned finance revenue of $180,000, minus the first payment of $200,000.

In 20X2 and following years, the lease will be accounted for exactly as illustrated above for direct financing leases. Finance revenue (or interest income) will be accrued each reporting period at the rate of 11.04% on the net balance of the receivable and charged against the unearned finance revenue, while payments will be credited directly to the lease payments receivable account. The statement of financial position will include the *net* balance of the receivable.

Estimating the Selling Price In the example above, the implicit interest rate was obtained by finding the rate that discounted the lease payments to the cash selling price of $820,000. But, in practice, the fair value or "cash price" may not be so obvious. The problem arises because many products that are sold via sales-type leases are subject to discounts or special "deals" wherein the actual price is less than the stated list price. In theory, the lease payments should be discounted to equal the actual price rather than the list price. In practice, this is harder to do because the actual price is often hidden in the transaction.

Sometimes, the "true" selling price can be approximated by looking at the appropriateness of the implicit interest rate. For example, a common tactic in long-term automobile leasing is to advertise a very low rate of interest (e.g., 0.9%), a rate that clearly is below the market rate of interest. A super-low rate really represents a decrease in the price of the car. A potential lessee can see what price he or she is getting by discounting the lease payments at whatever rate the bank would be willing to finance the car (i.e., at the borrower's incremental borrowing rate).

This essentially is the solution offered by *IAS* 17— the sales revenue should be measured as the lower of:

- The selling price as recorded for outright sales; or
- The present value of the minimum lease payments accruing to the lessor, discounted at the market rate of interest.

The actual determination of the revenue split (and profit split) between the sale and the lease components of the transaction is a matter of considerable judgement. The split will affect (1) gross profit on the sale in the current period and (2) interest revenue in future periods. Management is likely to define the sales price in a way that best suits its reporting needs. If the statements are audited, the auditor must test the reasonableness of management's sales price definition.

Incidence of Sales-Type Leases Looking at Canadian financial statements, you will not see much, if any, evidence of sales-type leases. This is because the leases are negotiated through financing subsidiaries of the manufacturer or dealer. Those subsidiaries are then consolidated into the parent company's financial statements.

There are several reasons for using a subsidiary structure. A major reason is tax-motivated. A lessor will not be able to claim the full amount of CCA on leased assets if the CCA exceeds the lease payments received, *unless* the lessor qualifies as a lessor under the income tax regulations. To qualify, a lessor must obtain at least 90% of its revenue from leasing.

Therefore, in order for the lessor to receive full tax advantage from the lease, companies that use leasing as a sales technique will either (1) form a separate corporation to carry out the leasing activity or (2) arrange for a third-party lender to provide the lease arrangements.

Another important reason to form a separate finance subsidiary is that the subsidiary can then issue "commercial paper" in the form of debt certificates that can range in maturity from a few months to many years. For example, GE Capital recently issued over US$14 billion in notes with maturities ranging from 9 months to 60 years. The lease receivables held by the finance subsidiary are the security against which the notes are issued. If the parent company entered into sales-type leases directly, such secondary financing would not be possible because the lease receivables would be part of the general assets of the company.

CONCEPT REVIEW

1. What is the basic difference between a sales-type lease and a finance lease?
2. In a sales-type lease, why is it often difficult to determine objectively the sales price of the item being "sold"?

LEASES IN THE STATEMENT OF CASH FLOWS

Lease capitalization has an interesting impact on the statement of cash flows. If a lease is reported as an operating lease, the lease payments are deducted as an expense in determining net income. Since the expense does represent a cash flow, the impact of the lease payments stays in the cash flow from operations. The only exception arises when the cash flows are uneven or differ from the pattern of rent expense recognition. If lease payments in a year are different from the amount expensed, the difference will be an adjustment to cash flow from operations (if the indirect approach is used) or excluded from operating cash flows (if the direct approach is used).

If a lease is capitalized, on the other hand, the effects on the statement of cash flows are quite different:

- Although the initial lease agreement is viewed, in substance, as a purchase, the transaction is not shown on the statement of cash flows as an investing activity because it is a non-cash transaction—a lease obligation is exchanged for a leased asset.
- All expenses relating to the lease asset are removed from net income when determining cash flow from operations:
  - Depreciation expense relating to the leased asset is added back to net income; and
  - The implicit interest expense is segregated on the statement of cash flows as part of interest expense relating to long-term obligations.
- The principal repayment portion of the lease payments is shown as a financing activity (that is, as a reduction of a liability).

The overall effect of lease capitalization is to remove the lease payments from operating cash flow and reclassify them as financing activities. Over the life of the lease, the full amount of the net present value of the net lease payments is lifted out of operations (by adding back the depreciation) and instead is classified as a reduction of debt.

ETHICAL ISSUES

Leasing offers multiple opportunities for managers to commit actions that are explicitly intended to mislead financial statement users. The most obvious and widespread is the simple expedient of leasing long-term assets through relatively short-term leases. Accounting standards were not intended to make lease reporting an *option*. The intent was to *require* companies to report leases according to their substance.

In practice, though, managers often do choose the reporting method for long-term leased assets. By careful structuring of lease provisions, management (with the encouragement of the leasing industry) can obtain long-term use of assets while still reporting the leases as operating leases.

For managers who are trying to meet short-term profit goals, this practice has two primary advantages. When leases are classified as operating leases:

- Both the leased assets and the related liabilities are kept off the balance sheet; and
- The lease-related expenses flowing onto the income statement will be lower in the early years of the lease contracts.

This is a practice known as "window dressing"—making the financial position of the company look better than it really is. Since the intent is to mislead financial statement readers, it clearly is an unethical practice.

Leasing also provides an opportunity for unethical behaviour through the use of related parties. Leasing through a related third party, such as through a company controlled by an officer or shareholder of the lessee, provides an opportunity for the third party to skim off profits through inflated lease payments. The requirements for consolidating *special purpose entities* (called *variable interest entities* in the United States) are intended to keep a company from hiding leases off-balance-sheet, but this intent can be circumvented by unethical managers.

Finally, sale-and-leaseback arrangements provide an opportunity to manipulate earnings. This can be done by (1) either selling an entire asset and then leasing only part of it back, or (2) leasing it via a series of operating leases that permit the selling company to recognize gains from the transaction in net income.

Looking Ahead

The accounting profession's method of accounting for leases has always been unsatisfactory. The practice of financing assets through long-term leases has been an increasingly widespread practice (i.e., outside of the railroad industry) for at least 60 years. Although the finance industry always differentiated between a financial lease and an operating lease, the accounting practice had been to base accounting on where legal title rested. Since the lessor had title to the asset, all lease payments were reported as current expenses.

The traditional practice led to vast amounts of off-balance-sheet financing, and eventually the then-new FASB in the United States decided to issue a new accounting standard on the topic. As the result of its deliberations, the FASB issued the accounting standard that has, with little change, governed lease accounting for 40 years, classifying the continuum of leases into two categories—*operating* leases and *capital* leases (which are called *finance* leases in IFRS, and *financial* leases in the finance industry).

As a result of the new accounting standard, a whole new industry sprouted up, one that was dedicated to devising leases that were finance leases in substance but that avoided classification under the FASB guidelines.

Now, a widespread dissatisfaction with lease accounting has led accounting standard-setters to start over again and reconsider lease accounting.

In late 2006, the IASB and FASB jointly established the International Working Group on Lease Accounting. The working group began work in early 2007. The group consisted of 18 members from 10 countries. Most members are from either the leasing industry (e.g., Singapore Aircraft Leasing; GE Energy Financial Services) or major lessees (e.g., Canadian Pacific Railway; Walmart Stores Inc.; Qantas Airways).

In March 2009, the IASB and FASB jointly issued a 122-page document, *Discussion Paper—Leases, Preliminary Views*. After receiving and reviewing comment letters, the two boards have jointly been meeting to reach a consensus on how to improve lease accounting.

Since it is generally agreed that it is impossible to take a continuum and split it into two distinct categories, the general approach that the boards have agreed upon is quite simple, theoretically. Instead of fretting over classification, the boards decided tentatively that the approach would be to discount all future lease payment commitments, regardless of term, and report the present value as the lessee's *right-of-use asset*. The asset would be amortized by using the effective interest method. The amortization would be described in the financial statement as *amortization* rather than as *rent expense*.

There are many issues yet to be resolved, including definition of *lease term*, the treatment of renewals, and other implications that especially affect lessors.

At the time of writing this book, an exposure draft seems likely in 2011, with a final standard being issued a year or so later. Lease accounting will never be the same.

ACCOUNTING STANDARDS FOR PRIVATE ENTERPRISES

The leasing standards for private enterprises are, in substance, the same as for publicly-accountable enterprises. However, there are some differences in detail. One detail is that the *CICA Handbook,* Part II uses the term **capital lease** rather than the current IASB terminology of finance lease. This is not a substantive difference—capital lease, finance lease, and financial lease (the term used in the finance industry) all mean the same thing and are interchangeable. The standards do not require the use of only one term.

LESSEES

Criteria for Lease Capitalization

The basic guidelines (or criteria) for classifying a lease as a capital lease are essentially the same as in *IAS* 17, except:

- The *CICA Handbook* rejects the criterion of "specialized use" that is contained in *IAS* 17. The AcSB states that not only is "special purpose" difficult to define, but also "special purpose" does not, in itself, indicate that substantially all of the risks and rewards of ownership have been transferred to the lessee.
- The guidelines contain quantitative "bright lines" that have been carried over from earlier leasing standards in the United States and Canada:
  - For deciding whether the lease term is equal to a major portion of the asset's economic life, major portion is "usually 75% or more."
  - For comparing the present value of minimum lease payments to the fair value of the asset, the guideline is "usually 90% or more."

Although *IAS* 17 deliberately avoids specifying quantitative bright lines, those thresholds probably will continue to be used in practice in most entities, public and private, because they provide a target of "reasonableness" that tends to promote consistency. Nevertheless, the overall guiding principle for capital/finance leases continues to be whether the lease transfers substantially all of the risks and rewards of ownership to the lessee.

Interest Rate for Discounting

IAS 17 states that the interest rate should be the lessor's rate implicit in the lease, if known, and otherwise the lessee's IBR. In contrast, the *CICA Handbook* requires that the *lower* of the two rates be used. Since the lessor's implicit pre-tax rate of return is seldom known, the distinction may have little significance in general practice.

Leases of Land and Buildings

When a lease involves land *and* buildings, the lease payments are segregated between the land and buildings on the basis of the fair values of the underlying properties. This differs from *IAS* 17, in which the allocation is based on the *fair values of the leasehold rights*, not on the land and buildings themselves.

Disclosure

The disclosure requirements are relatively modest:

Operating Leases: For leases lasting more than one year, disclose the future minimum lease payments (1) for each of the next five years and (2) in total.

Capital Leases:

- The total amount of payments required for each of the next five years
- The interest rate, maturity date, and amount outstanding for capital leases
- The aggregate amount of interest expense, disclosed either separately or as part of interest on long-term debt
- Whether leases are secured (e.g., by other assets of the entity)
- For the leased asset(s), the cost (i.e., initial discounted present value), the depreciation method being used, and the amount of accumulated depreciation.

LESSORS

Classification

Whereas *IAS* 17 uses the same criteria for both lessees and lessors, the *CICA Handbook*, Part II, imposes additional requirements before the lessor can capitalize a lease:

- The lessor's credit risk relating to the lease and the lessee is normal, as compared to the collectibility of similar receivables; and
- The lessor's unreimbursable costs can be reasonably estimated.

Both of these additional requirements must be satisfied. If not, then the lease is reported as an operating lease rather than a capital lease.

An interesting result of this additional requirement is that the asset can end up being reported asymmetrically. If the lessee reports the lease as a finance lease while the lessor reports it as an operating lease, the asset will be reported on the SFP of *both* the lessee and the lessor.

If the criteria for capitalization are met, a lessor then must classify the lease as either a direct financing lease or as a sale-type lease. A direct financing lease is essentially the same as a finance lease under *IAS* 17.

Initial Direct Costs

Under *IAS* 17, the lessor's initial direct costs (e.g., commissions or legal fees) for finance leases are capitalized as part of the lessor's cash flow and amortized over the lease period. In contrast, the *CICA Handbook* says that the lessor's initial direct costs should be expensed, both for a direct financing lease and a sales-type lease. However, the *CICA Handbook*, Part II also requires that an equivalent amount of the unearned lease income be recognized. The net effect is that there is no difference in the impact on net income.

For operating leases, initial direct costs are deferred and amortized over the lease term.

Impairment

At the end of each reporting period, a private enterprise should assess the collectibility of the future cash flows from each lease. If future payments appear to be in doubt, such as by financial failure of the lessee, the lease should be written down to the highest estimated recoverable value, as either (1) the present value of the likely future cash flows or (2) the amount that can be realized by selling or re-leasing the asset.

Sale and Leaseback

The requirements for reporting sale-and-leaseback transactions are the same as IFRS except for some differences in accounting for a gain or loss from the sale:

- If the asset's fair value is less than its carrying value at the time of the sale, the loss should be recognized immediately because the asset was impaired at the date of sale.
- Otherwise, if the lease is a capital lease, any gain or loss from the sale transaction should be capitalized and amortized proportionate to the depreciation on the leased asset (i.e., *not* over the term of the lease as required by *IAS* 17).

RELEVANT STANDARDS

IASB:

- *IAS* 17, Leases

CICA Handbook, Part II
- Section 3065, Leases

SUMMARY OF KEY POINTS

1. A lease is an agreement that conveys from a lessor to a lessee the right to use real property, plant, or equipment for a contracted price per period.

2. The shorter the term of the lease, the higher the cost per period. As the lease term lengthens, the cost per period goes down because more of the risk of ownership (e.g., obsolescence) is borne by the lessee.

3. A lease for a relatively short period of an asset's useful life and that does not transfer substantially all of the asset's risks and benefits to the lessee is called an operating lease. Under an operating lease, rent payments are reported by the lessee as a current expense as the asset is used. For the lessor, the asset remains on the books and the rent payments are recorded as rent income.

4. A lease that transfers substantially all of the risks and benefits of ownership to the lessee is called a finance lease. There are four guidelines used to determine whether a lease is a finance lease: (1) does the lease terms make it highly likely that title to the asset will transfer to the lessee at the end of the lease term, (2) does the lessee enjoy the use of the asset over the major part of its economic life; (3) is the lessee committing to lease payments that will return substantially all of the lessor's investment in the leased asset plus a return on the investment, or (4) is the asset so special purpose for the lessee that it would have little benefit to others?

5. Finance leases are recorded by the lessee as though the asset had been purchased. For the lessee, the net lease payments over the lease term are discounted, usually at the lessee's incremental borrowing rate, and the present value is recorded as both an asset and a liability. Once recorded, the asset and the liability are accounted for independently.

6. The asset is depreciated in accordance with the lessee's policy for assets of that type, except that the depreciation period is limited to the minimum lease term (including

bargain renewal terms) unless there is a bargain purchase option or other transfer of title to the lessee at the end of the lease term.

7. The lessee's lease liability is accounted for as an instalment loan with blended payments. Interest expense is calculated at the same rate as was used for discounting the payments, and the excess of payments over interest expense reduces the outstanding liability balance.

8. The current portion of the lessee's lease liability consists of (1) accrued interest to the balance sheet date plus (2) the amount of principal that will be paid over the next year.

9. Finance leases are usually *taxed* as operating leases. As a result, temporary differences usually result in deferred income tax liabilities for the lessee.

10. One of the principal motivations for leasing is income taxation: if the lessor can receive greater benefits from the CCA tax shield than can the lessee, then the savings to the lessor are returned to the lessee through lower lease payments, thereby reducing the cost of the asset.

11. A sale and leaseback arrangement is an agreement in which the owner of an asset sells it to a lessor and simultaneously leases it back. The subsequent lease is accounted for as either finance or operating, as for other leases; any gain or loss on the sale is deferred and amortized over the lease term, except for a loss that reflects a decline in the fair value of the asset, in which case the loss is recognized immediately.

12. The amount of finance lease obligations and assets held under finance leases should be separately disclosed by both lessees and lessors. Lessees should also disclose their commitments under operating leases and under finance leases for the next year, for the next four years in total, and then the aggregate amount for all remaining years.

13. A sales-type lease has two profit components: (1) the profit or loss from the sale and (2) interest revenue from the lease financing.

14. The interest rate used in lessor accounting for a finance lease is the rate implicit in the lease. The net method and the gross method give the same results in the financial statements. Lessors normally use the gross method of recording finance leases to facilitate control.

15. A private enterprise lessor treats a lease as a finance lease if, in addition to transferring substantially all of the risks and rewards of ownership to the lessee, two other criteria are both met: (1) the credit risk is normal and (2) all executory and operating costs included in the lease payments can be reasonably estimated.

16. A private enterprise lessor must classify a finance lease as either a direct-financing lease or a sales-type lease. A direct financing lease arises when a lessor acts purely as a financial intermediary. A sales-type lease arises when a manufacturer or dealer uses leasing as a means of selling a product.

17. There is growing dissatisfaction about the all-or-nothing aspect of lease capitalization. International accounting standards almost certainly will be altered in the future to require capitalization of all leases of greater than one-year duration.

KEY TERMS

bargain purchase option, 979
bargain renewal terms, 979
capital lease, 1014
captive leasing companies, 1004
contingent lease payments, 979
contingent rent, 998
direct-financing lease, 1010

executory costs, 989
finance lease, 978
gross lease basis, 1008
guaranteed residual value, 979
implicit lease interest rate, 980
incremental borrowing rate (IBR), 980
initial direct costs, 980

REVIEW PROBLEM 1

Orion leased a computer to the Lenox Silver Company on 1 April 20X5. The terms of the lease are as follows:

• Lease term (fixed and non-cancellable)	3 years
• Estimated economic life of the computer	5 years
• Fair market value at lease inception	$5,000
• Bargain purchase offer	none
• Transfer of title	none
• Guaranteed residual value by lessee, 1 April 20X8	$1,000
• Lessee's normal depreciation method*	straight-line
• Lessee's incremental borrowing rate	11%
• Executory costs included in lease payments	none
• Initial direct costs	none
• Annual lease payment, beginning of each lease year	$1,620
• Lessor's implicit interest rate	10%
• Lessee's fiscal year-end	31 December

*Lenox Silver Company charges a half-year depreciation in the year of acquisition and a half-year in the year of disposition, regardless of the actual dates of acquisition and disposal.

Required:

1. Classify the lease from the perspective of the lessee.

2. Provide entries for the lease from 1 April 20X5 through 31 December 20X6.

3. Show how the leased asset and the lease obligation will be shown on the lessee's balance sheet at 31 December 20X6.

4. Suppose that at the end of the lease, the lessor tells the lessee to dispose of the asset, and to keep any proceeds in excess of the guaranteed residual value. Provide entries for the lessee on 1 April 20X8, assuming that the lessee sells the asset for $1,200 and remits the required $1,000 payment to the lessor.

REVIEW PROBLEM 1—SOLUTION

1. The lessor's implicit rate is known. Under *IAS* 17, the lessor's rate must be used if known. Under ASPE, the lessee uses the lower of the lessor's implicit rate or the lessee's incremental borrowing rate, IBR. Under either scenario, the discount rate will be 10%. Discounting the minimum lease payments, including the guaranteed residual value of $1,000, yields:

P = $1,620 (P/A due, 10%, 3) + $1,000(P/F, 10%, 3)
= $4,432 + $751 = $5,183

Clearly the lease is a finance lease because the present value of the minimum lease payments, $5,183, is greater than the $5,000 fair value of the leased property.

2. The asset and the offsetting liability must be capitalized. The capitalized value of the leased asset cannot be greater than the asset's fair value, and therefore the fair value of $5,000 must be used instead of the present value of $5,183. The entries at the inception of the lease will be:

1 April 20X5—commencement of the lease

Asset under finance lease	5,000	
Lease liability		5,000

1 April 20X5—first payment

Lease liability	1,620	
Cash		1,620

Since the lessee's IBR yields a present value that is higher than the fair value of the asset, it cannot be used for further accounting for the lease. Instead, the implicit rate *to the lessee* must be calculated by solving the following equation for *i*, the implicit interest rate:

$5,000 = $1,620 (P/A due, *i*, 3) + $1,000 (P/F, *i*, 3)

By using a computer spreadsheet, a financial calculator, or trial and error, we can find the implicit rate of 13.29%. This rate must then be used to accrue the interest and to record the components of the annual lease payments. The amortization table for the lease obligation is as follows:

Year	Beginning Balance	Interest Expense @ 13.29%	Cash Payment	Reduction of Principal	Ending Balance
20X5	$5,000	0	$1,620	$1,620	$3,380
20X6	3,380	$449	1,620	1,171	2,209
20X7	2,209	294	1,620	1,326	883
20X8	883	117	1,000	883	0

The entries to record the depreciation, interest accrual, and payments through 31 December 20X6 are shown below.

31 December 20X5—adjusting entries

Depreciation expense	667	
Accumulated depreciation		667
[($5,000 − $1000) ÷ 3 × 1/2 = $500]		

Interest expense	337	
Lease liability		337
[($5,000 − $1,620) × 13.29% = $449 × 9/12 = $337]		

1 April 20X6—interest accrual

Interest expense	112	
Lease liability		112
[($5,000 − $1,620) × 13.29% = $449 × 3/12 = $112]		

1 April 20X6—second payment

Lease liability	1,620	
Cash		1,620

31 December 20X6—adjusting entries

Depreciation expense	1,333	
Accumulated depreciation		1,333
[($5,000 − $1000) ÷ 3]		

Interest expense	221	
Lease liability		221
[$294 (from amortization table) × 9/12]		

3. The lessee's balance sheet at 31 December 20X6 will include the following amounts:

Capital assets

Asset under finance lease	$5,000
Less accumulated depreciation	(2,000)
	$3,000

Current liabilities

Current portion of finance lease liability	$1,547

[$221 accrued interest at 31 December 20X6, plus
$1,326 principal portion of the next payment
(from amortization table)]

Long-term liabilities

Obligation under finance lease (from amortization table)	$ 883

4. 1 April 20X8—sale of asset

Cash (received from sale)	1,200	
Lease liability	1,000	
Accumulated depreciation	4,000	
Asset under finance lease		5,000
Cash (paid to lessor)		1,000
Gain on disposal of leased asset		200

This entry assumes that adjustments have already been made to (1) accrue the last of the interest and (2) record depreciation for 20X8.

REVIEW PROBLEM 2

Orion leased a computer to the Lenox Silver Company on 1 January 20X5. The terms of the lease and other related information are as follows:

• Lease term (fixed and non-cancellable)	3 years
• Estimated economic life of the equipment	4 years
• Fair market value of the computer at lease inception	$5,000
• Lessor's cost of asset	$5,000
• Bargain purchase price	none
• Transfer of title	none
• Guaranteed residual value by lessee (excess to lessee)	
1 January 20X8	$1,000
• Collectibility of rental payments	assured
• Annual rental (1st payment 1 January 20X5)	$1,620

Required:

1. Provide entries for the lessor from 1 January 20X5 through 1 January 20X6, using the net method of recording.

2. Provide the lessor's journal entry at the termination of the lease on 1 January 20X8, assuming that the asset is sold by the lessee on that date for $1,200.

3. Prepare the entries at the commencement of the lease (i.e., 1 January 20X5) assuming that the gross method is used instead.

REVIEW PROBLEM 2—SOLUTION

The lease is a finance lease because the lease term (three years) is a major part of the economic life of the asset. The lessor must account for the lease by using the interest rate implicit in the lease. The interest rate that discounts the lease cash flows to $5,000 is 13.29% (before tax) (solved by spreadsheet).

1. Lease entries, net method:

   1 January 20X5—commencement of lease
Lease receivable	5,000	
Cash, Inventory, etc.		5,000

   1 January 20X5—first payment
Cash	1,620	
Lease receivable		1,620

   31 December 20X5—interest accrual
Lease receivable	449	
Finance income		449

         ($5,000 − $1,620) × 13.29% = $449

   1 January 20X6—second payment
Cash	1,620	
Lease receivable		1,620

2. Termination of lease

   1 January 20X8—receipt of guaranteed residual value from lessee
Cash	1,000	
Lease receivable		1,000

   The fact that the lessee was able to sell the asset for $1,200 is irrelevant. The lessee gets to keep the extra $200.

3. Lease commencement, gross method:

   1 January 20X5—commencement of lease
Lease receivable [($1,620 × 3) + $1,000]	5,860	
Unearned finance revenue		860
Cash, Inventory, etc.		5,000

   1 January 20X5—first payment
Cash	1,620	
Lease receivable		1,620

QUESTIONS

Q17-1 At the beginning of the fiscal year, a tenant signs a three-year lease to rent office space at the rate of $1,000 per month. The first six months are free. How much rent expense should be recognized in the first year of the lease?

Q17-2 Under what circumstances is a lease normally considered a finance lease? What role does judgement play?

Q17-3 Give three reasons that a company might enter into a long-term lease instead of buying an asset outright.

Q17-4 A car dealer advertises a new car lease with the following terms:
- $3,500 cash paid by the customer at the beginning of the lease;
- Monthly payments of $229 for 48 months; and
- The customer is required to pay $2,650 at the end of the lease, and then owns the vehicle.

What is the substance of the lease contract?

Q17-5 Under what circumstances would a deferred rent liability appear on the balance sheet of a company that is a lessee in an operating lease?

Q17-6 Define the following terms, as used in lease accounting standards:
- Bargain purchase option (BPO).
- Lease term.
- Minimum net lease payments.
- Contingent lease payments.
- Bargain renewal term.
- Guaranteed residual value.
- Incremental borrowing rate.
- Interest rate implicit in the lease.

Q17-7 Assume that a lessee signs a lease for a three-year term for $1,000 per year that has a renewal option at the lessee's option for a further three years for $1,000 per year. How long is the lease term, as defined by lease accounting standards?

Q17-8 How would your answer to Question 17-7 change if the renewal was at the lessor's option? If rental during the second term was $1 per year instead of $1,000?

Q17-9 A lessee signs a lease for a two-year term that requires a yearly payment of $14,000, which includes $2,500 for insurance and maintenance cost. At the end of the two-year term, there is a $1,000 BPO. How much are the minimum net lease payments?

Q17-10 Assume an asset has a fair market value of $48,500 and is leased for $10,000 per year for six years. Payments are made at the end of each year. Insurance costs included in this amount are $1,000, and there is a $6,000 guaranteed residual. What is the interest rate implicit in the lease for the lessee? Why is this not also the interest rate implicit in the lease for the lessor?

Q17-11 Assume a non-profit organization wishes to acquire a particular asset. Why might it be cheaper to lease rather than buy the asset?

Q17-12 Assume a lease involves payments of $20,000 per year, net of insurance costs, and is properly capitalized on the lessee's books at a 10% interest rate for $135,180. How much interest would be recognized in the first year of the lease if the payments were made at the beginning of the period? The second year?

Q17-13 A lessee enters into a five-year finance lease with a five-year bargain renewal option, and then the asset is returned to the lessor. How long would the depreciation period be for the asset? Assume that such an asset is expected to have a 12-year useful life.

Q17-14 How is the current portion of the lease liability determined if the lease payments are due and payable at the end of the fiscal year? How would your answer change if the payments were due at the beginning of the period?

Q17-15 What is a sale and leaseback? How are such transactions accounted for?

Q17-16 Suppose that a company owns a building. The company enters into a sale and leaseback arrangement to sell the building and then lease it back. The company makes a substantial profit on the sale. How should the gain from the sale be accounted for?

Q17-17 Suppose that a lessor is a private Canadian corporation. How does its status as a private corporation affect classification of a lease, as compared to a public corporation?

Q17-18 What interest rate does the lessor use for discounting calculations associated with a lease?

Q17-19 Describe the nature of a sales-type lease. What kinds of entities offer such leases?

Q17-20 In a sales-type lease, how does separation of the sale component from the lease component affect revenue recognition in the current and future years?

CASE 17-1

Warmth Home Comfort Limited (WHCL) is a Canadian manufacturer of furnaces and air-conditioning units. The company was acquired by a group of 15 investors eight years ago. Three of the investors are senior managers with the company, including Jacob Kovacs, who is president and chief executive officer.

Over the years WHCL had been quite successful, but it has struggled in the face of increased competition from overseas competitors. The owners believe that three years from now WHCL will be poised to be a major player in the Canadian and the U.S. heating and cooling markets and may consider going public. Summary financial statements are provided in Exhibit I. Kovacs points out that the company's financial performance seems to be improving, given the smaller loss in 20X7 and the increasing revenues after two years of falling sales.

Your firm has been auditor of WHCL since its first audit in 20X0. It is now January 20X8. This is the first year you are in charge of the audit. Yesterday, you visited WHCL and met with key personnel to discuss the forthcoming audit engagement. You obtained the following information.

1. In early fiscal 20X7, the company increased its debt load significantly by borrowing $300,000 from Colo Investors Ltd. Excerpts from the loan agreement are as follows:

   Warmth Home Comfort Limited (the borrower) covenants that:

   a. A current ratio of 1.2 or higher will be maintained; and
   b. The debt-to-equity ratio will not exceed 2:1. Debt is defined as all liabilities of the company.

2. In 20X1, WHCL introduced a new model of gas furnace that was popular with consumers because its reduced gas consumption resulted in lower heating bills. The furnace design has remained virtually unchanged since it was introduced. The furnaces are sold with 10-year warranties on parts and labour. Historically, claims have been minimal.

   In the summer of 20X7, several warranty claims were made against WHCL. Routine inspections by gas-company employees revealed cracked heat exchangers, which could leak gases that might cause health problems when mixed with warm air in a home. Thirty claims were made, and WHCL paid for repairs. The cost of repairing each furnace was $150, which was expensed by WHCL.

   Jacob Kovacs believes that the furnaces were damaged because of poor installation by contractors. He cannot see more than an additional 40 or 50 units being damaged. The 30 repaired furnaces were manufactured in 20X5 and 20X6. Over 10,000 units of this model have been sold over the past seven years.

   Later, in a discussion with the chief engineer, you learn that she had examined the heat exchanger used in the gas-furnace model in question and saw no evidence of a design flaw. However, she expressed concern that the problem might be due to heavy use of the furnace. She noted that the 30 reported problems were in northern locations where the demands on the equipment are considerable. Between 1,500 and 2,000 furnaces were installed in homes in those locations.

3. In January 20X7, WHCL bid on and won a $1.05 million contract to supply heating and air conditioning equipment for a large commercial and residential project. Construction on the project began in March 20X7.

   The fixed-price contract calls for WHCL to start delivering and installing the equipment in early September 20X7. In addition, WHCL has agreed to pay a penalty if the project is delayed because WHCL is unable to meet the agreed-to timetable. A brief strike by its factory employees has caused production and delivery to lag about two weeks behind schedule, so WHCL is shipping units as soon as they are produced. According to the agreement, half of the equipment has to be shipped and installed at the project site by the end of February 20X8. Jacob Kovacs is confident that WHCL will be able to catch up to the promised timetable.

   In 20X7, WHCL recognized $350,000 of revenue based on the number of units shipped to year-end. WHCL has received $50,000 for the units that have been installed by year-end.

4. Starting in February 20X8, WHCL will begin offering customers the option of paying a monthly fee for the use of a furnace. At the end of a certain number of years, the customer can purchase the unit for a nominal amount or ask for a replacement furnace and continue with the monthly payments. WHCL will do all maintenance at no cost until a customer purchases the unit. This scheme is intended to help WHCL remain competitive. The terms for such arrangements have not been finalized, but Jacob Kovacs is confident that they will increase sales revenue. Jacob has asked for advice on how to account for them.

Your partner asks you to prepare a memo for him outlining the accounting issues that came to your attention as a result of your visit, applying IFRS.

Required:
Prepare the memo.

Source: The Canadian Institute of Chartered Accountants, © 2010.

EXHIBIT I

WARMTH HOME COMFORT LIMITED

Extracts from the Draft Financial Statements
Balance Sheet

As at December 31
(in thousands of dollars)

	20X7 (Unaudited)	20X6 (Audited)
Assets		
Current:		
Cash	$ 15	$ 100
Accounts receivable	875	587
Inventory	500	540
Other current assets	56	120
	1,446	1,347
Capital assets	2,606	2,256
Accumulated depreciation	(1,071)	(926)
	1,535	1,330
Total assets	$2,981	$2,677

EXHIBIT I *(cont'd)*

	20X7 (Unaudited)	20X6 (Audited)
Liabilities		
Current:		
Bank indebtedness	$ 450	$ 400
Accounts payable	581	395
Other current liabilities	118	100
	1,149	895
Long-term debt	825	525
	1,974	1,420
Shareholders' equity:		
Share capital	100	100
Retained earnings	907	1,157
	1,007	1,257
Total liabilities and shareholders' equity	$2,981	$2,677

CASE 17-2

SANDSUPPORT CORPORATION

Sandsupport Corporation (SC) is a privately-owned company based in Alberta. The company provides support services for the oil and gas industry, especially for new exploration not only in Canada, but also in other countries such as Venezuela and Mexico.

Due to the ever-increasing worldwide demand for energy and the resultant increase in exploration activity, SC is planning a major expansion of its operational capacity. As part of this expansion, the company needs to acquire a significant amount of new equipment. In the past, the company has obtained external financing only through debt, mainly via private placements of secured first-mortgage debentures with pension funds and other institutional investors.

Additional financing will be needed to acquire the new equipment. However, management is hesitant about obtaining more straight debt financing due to restrictive covenants (e.g., on debt to equity ratio) that are in place for some of SC's existing debt. Therefore, management is considering three alternatives.

Leasing is the first possibility that management is considering. SC leases quite a lot of equipment to its clients on short-term leases for specific projects, and it seemed logical to look into leasing as way for SC to acquire the equipment. Management has been in contact with GWC Finance Corporation about negotiating a lease. Under the potential lease arrangements, GWC would purchase the equipment from its German manufacturer; the manufacturer would deliver the machinery directly to SC. SC would agree to a lease contract that would enable GWC to classify the lease as a finance lease, in accordance with its status as a tax-qualifying lessor. Since the equipment is quite specialized, the lease payments would be "front-loaded," with most of the total lease payments payable in the first five years. GWC has suggested that SC may be able to enter into an agreement with one of SC's major clients (e.g., Suncor or PetroCanada) for the client to guarantee a substantial residual value—enough to reduce the minimum lease payments to less than 90% of the equipment's fair value. SC would unofficially compensate the client through reduced fees for SC's services.

The second possibility would also involve leasing, but the lease would not be an obligation of SC. Instead, two SC shareholders would form a separate corporation and that corporation would enter into the lease with GWC. The new corporation would then lease the equipment to GWC with an initial lease term of five years. After the first five years, the lease would continue on a year-to-year basis automatically until the GWC lease expired. At that point, GWC would transfer title to the new corporation, which in turn would sell the equipment to SC for nominal consideration.

The third option involves the issuance of convertible preferred shares to the Alberta Teachers' Pension Plan (ATPP). The proceeds of the share issue would be used to buy the equipment. SC has never previously used outside equity financing, but preferred shares seems to be a logical answer to the financing problem faced by SC. SC would be obligated to pay dividends annually at 8% of the paid-in value of the shares. Anytime after five years, ATPP could convert to common shares (for whatever number of common shares will amount to a current market value equal to the preferred shares' original paid-in value). As well, SC would be able to call the shares for redemption at any time after five years.

Management is very experienced at being a lessor, but not at all experienced at being a lessee. Therefore, the CFO has come to you for advice on the best route to take for the new financing. In particular, the CFO is concerned about the financial statement impact of these three alternatives.

Required:

Analyze the consequences of each of the above alternatives in a memo to your superior. Explain which one you would recommend for SC.

CASE 17-3

BLISS AIR LINE LIMITED

Start-Up

Michael Bliss is the President, CEO, and controlling shareholder of Bliss Air Line Limited (BALL). He started the company four years ago to provide low-cost charter service to holiday destinations. Although the airline is low cost, it is not no-frills; the airline's motto is "Travel with Bliss and have a ball!"

To obtain initial working finance, Michael sold a long-distance trucking company that he owned, and he invested the proceeds in BALL. The new company acquired four old Boeing 737-100 aircraft that had been decommissioned by other airlines and were parked in the Arizona desert. The purchase price was $10 million each. Approximately $1 million per plane was needed to get the planes ready for recertification and to equip the interior to Michael's satisfaction. The money for acquisition and refurbishment was provided by a collateral loan from GE Capital.

The airline was successful from the beginning, and in the second year the company bought three slightly newer airplanes, Boeing 737-300s, for $25 million each. These newer planes had not been decommissioned, and therefore they were able to enter service quickly to provide much-needed capacity in BALL's second summer season.

In the third year, BALL was again short of capacity and had to rent two more 737s from a major competitor that was no longer using them. The cost is $115,000 per month to rent.

It became apparent to Michael that the company would need much more capacity. As well, the rapidly rising cost of fuel, terminal charges, and overhead all pointed to a need to reduce operating cost per seat mile. The old 737-100s were much less efficient than the latest models. As well, new anti-pollution standards were being phased in, which would require the 737-100s to be either retired or re-equipped with new engines in three years.

Capital Structure

Due to the need for new capital for expanded operations, Michael decided to make BALL a public company. The capital structure was altered to provide for four classes of shares.

1. An unlimited number of voting common shares;
2. An unlimited number of restricted common shares;
3. 70,000 non-voting retractable preferred shares; and
4. An unlimited number of non-voting, cumulative, non-participating preferred shares.

The voting common shares have 100 votes each. The restricted common shares have one vote each.

After approval by the securities commissions, the company issued the following:

- 150,000 voting common shares to Michael Bliss in exchange for his existing BALL shares;
- 17,000,000 restricted common shares issued at $20 per share in an initial public offering; and
- 11,000 retractable preferred shares to GE Capital to replace the $44,000,000 collateral loan (i.e., for the first group of aircraft).

The restricted voting shares were listed on the Toronto Stock Exchange.

The retractable preferred shares carry an annual cumulative preference dividend of $220 per share. The shares are not callable for the first four years. After that, BALL can call any or all of the shares for redemption at $4,100 per share. At any time, if BALL misses a dividend, GE Capital will have the right to demand redemption at $4,500 per share plus accrued dividends.

New Equipment

To provide additional capacity, the Board of Directors considered several possibilities. One was to buy new 737-700s outright. The planes cost $50 million each, and would be financed by secured long-term floating rate debt, privately negotiated with major U.S. and international lenders. Preliminary indications were that BALL could obtain the necessary financing at a current rate of 6.5%. Industry practice was to amortize that type of aircraft over 20 years, assuming a 10% residual value. Of course, the planes physically would last much longer if properly maintained, but obsolescence takes its toll.

A second alternative was to lease the new aircraft. A major leasing company indicated willingness to give BALL 14-year leases at $360,000 per month per plane. Of course, BALL could combine the two alternatives—buy some planes and lease others.

The new aircraft would be used not only for fleet expansion, but also to replace the old 737-100s, which soon would have to be retired. But to obtain more cash for operations (and new asset acquisition), the Board also was considering what to do with the three newer 737-300s. These planes had been purchased with instalment debt financing, and the Board thought it would be beneficial to "cash in" the ownership equity by entering into a sale-and-leaseback arrangement. Although the planes were becoming obsolete for top-tier airlines, they still were in demand by smaller airlines and by those in developing countries. Professional evaluations indicated that BALL could sell the planes for a profit of about $2 million each, and then lease them back for four years at $125,000 per month.

Recommendations Needed

The end of the first fiscal year of public ownership is rapidly approaching. Before making any decisions about leasing and/or buying new planes, and about sale-and-leaseback of the 737-300s, Michael and the Board need a professional opinion on the financial statement implications. The CFO, Michelle Bliss, has retained you, FCGA, for advice on these issues. The Board also wants advice on any other financial statement issues that you see.

Required:

Write the report.

ASSIGNMENTS

★ **A17-1 Operating Lease:** On 15 August 20X1, Argyle Ltd. signed a three-year lease to rent a computer system from Basil Ltd. for $10,000 per month. The lease will commence on 1 October 20X1. Three months' rent is payable at the lease inception; remaining rent is due at the beginning of each month. Basil will install the system and have it operational by 31 October 20X1.

The value of the computer equipment is $800,000. Basil is acquiring this equipment specifically for leasing to Argyle. Basil estimates that its installation cost will be $20,000. Basil uses 25% declining-balance depreciation for computer equipment, with no depreciation in the year of acquisition.

At the end of the lease, Argyle can either (1) terminate the lease and require Basil to remove the equipment, (2) renew the lease at the same monthly payment, or (3) negotiate a new lease with Basil for upgraded equipment.

Both companies have a 31 December fiscal year-end.

Required:

1. Prepare journal entries for Argyle for 20X1 and, in summary form, for 20X2.
2. Prepare journal entries for Basil for 20X1 and, in summary form, for 20X2.

★ **A17-2 Operating Lease—Lessee Inducement:** The Association of Western Agricultural Producers leases space in an office complex and has recently signed a new, five-year lease, at the rate of $4,000 per month. However, the lessor offered six months "free" rent at the beginning of the lease as an inducement for the Association to sign the lease agreement.

The lease agreement was signed on 1 October 20X1; the lease will commence on 1 November 20X1. The Association has a 31 December fiscal year-end. Rent is due on the first day of each month.

Required:

1. Prepare journal entries for the first, sixth, and seventh months of the lease. Assume that financial statements are prepared monthly.
2. What amounts would be shown on the association's income statement and statement of financial position for this lease as of 31 December 20X2?

★ **A17-3 Terminology, Classification, Entries:** Burrill Limited has an 7% incremental borrowing rate at the local bank. On 1 January 20X1, Burrill signed the following lease agreement for a piece of equipment. The equipment has a fair value of $170,000 and a 12-year economic life. Other information is as follows:

- The non-cancellable lease is for eight years.
- The lease payment is $24,000 annually, payable at the beginning of each lease year.
- Lease payments include $3,600 of maintenance expense annually.
- At the end of the lease term, the leased asset reverts back to the lessor.

OTHER INFORMATION:

- Burrill has a fiscal year that ends on 31 December.
- Burrill uses straight-line depreciation for similar capital assets.

Required:

1. For this lease, provide the:
    a. Lease term.
    b. Guaranteed residual value.
    c. Unguaranteed residual value.
    d. Bargain purchase option.

e. Minimum net lease payment.

f. Incremental borrowing rate.

If these amounts do not exist in the above lease, enter "none" as your response. State any assumptions.

2. Is this lease an operating lease or a finance lease for the lessee? Explain your reasoning.

3. Prepare the journal entries for the first year of the lease on Burrill's books.

4. Would your answer to requirement 2 change if the lease contained a guaranteed residual value of $50,000? Explain.

★ **A17-4 Finance Lease Fundamentals:** Niko Limited signed a lease for a five-year term that requires yearly, beginning-of-year payments of $104,000, including $9,600 of annual maintenance and property taxes. Niko guarantees a residual value of $26,500 at the end of the lease term, although both parties expect the asset to be sold as used equipment for approximately $35,000 at that time.

Required:

1. How much are Niko's minimum lease payments, as defined for lease accounting purposes?

2. If Niko's IBR is 10%, what amount will Niko record as an asset?

3. How much will Niko record as an asset if the residual value is *unguaranteed*?

4. Suppose that the fair value of the leased asset is $375,000 at the inception of the lease. How would this fact affect the amount recorded for the leased asset?

★★ **A17-5 Terminology, Classification, Entries:** Canadian Leasing Company leased a piece of machinery to Ornamental Concrete Limited, with the following terms:

- The lease is for five years; Ornamental cannot cancel the lease during this period.
- The lease payment is $79,600. Included in this is $7,900 in estimated insurance costs.
- At the end of the five-year initial lease term, Ornamental can elect to renew the lease for one additional five-year term at a price of $29,500, including $2,500 of estimated insurance costs. Market rentals are approximately twice as expensive.
- At the end of the first or second lease term, the leased asset reverts back to the lessor.
- Lease payments are due at the beginning of each lease year.

OTHER INFORMATION:

- Ornamental could borrow money to buy this asset at an interest rate of 8%.
- The equipment has a fair market value of $430,000 at the beginning of the lease term, and a useful life of approximately 12 years.
- The lease term corresponds to the fiscal year.
- Ornamental uses straight-line depreciation for all capital assets.

Required:

1. For this lease, provide the:
   a. Lease term.
   b. Guaranteed residual value.
   c. Unguaranteed residual value.
   d. Bargain purchase option.
   e. Bargain renewal terms.
   f. Minimum net lease payment.
   g. Incremental borrowing rate.

If these amounts do not exist in the above lease, enter "none" as your response. State any assumptions.

2. Is this lease an operating lease or a finance lease for the lessee? Why?

3. Prepare journal entries for the first year of the lease on Ornamental's books.

★★ **A17-6 Amortization Table; Entries:** Lu Limited is expanding and needs more manufacturing equipment. The company has been offered a lease contract for equipment with a fair value of $116,000. The lease has a five-year term, end of year payment renewable for a further two years at the option of the lessee. Annual rental for the first term is $28,600, for the second, $11,500. Payments are made each 31 December. The first term rental includes $2,600 for maintenance and insurance, the second, $1,500. Lease payments are close to market lease rates for both the first and second terms. At the end of the second term, Lu can buy the asset for $1. The machinery has an expected life of 10 years. Lu Limited has an incremental borrowing rate of 10%. Lu has been told that the interest rate implicit in Lease 1 is 8%.

Required:

1. Prepare an amortization table for the lease.

2. Assume that the lease was entered into on 1 January 20X2. Lu has a 31 December fiscal year-end. Prepare journal entries for the lease for 20X2, including any entries relating to the asset.

3. Prepare the entry to record exercise of the bargain purchase option.

★★ **A17-7 Amortization Table; Entries:** Hui Corporation has negotiated a lease for new machinery. The machinery has a fair value of $550,000 and an expected economic life of seven years. The lease has a five-year term. Annual rental is paid at the beginning of the lease year, in the amount of $104,300. Insurance and operating costs, approximately $16,500, are paid directly by Hui Corporation in addition to the lease payments. At the end of the lease term, the machinery will revert to the lessor, which will sell it for an expected $75,000. If the lessor does not realize $75,000 in the sale, then Hui has agreed to make up the difference. Hui does not know the lessor's implicit interest rate.

Required:

1. Prepare an amortization table for the lease. Hui's IBR is 10%.

2. Assume that the lease was entered into on 1 January 20X2. Hui Corporation has a 31 December fiscal year-end. Prepare journal entries for the lease for 20X2, including depreciation.

3. Prepare the entry to record the lease termination, assuming that the asset is sold by the lessor for $60,000 and that Hui Corporation makes up the $15,000 shortfall. Record interest to the date of the transaction first.

★★ **A17-8 Lease Motives:** Consider each of the following lease arrangements:

1. Abbaz Corporation signs a two-year lease for office space in a large, downtown office complex. Abbaz plans to have a permanent presence in the downtown area but has moved office premises several times in the past 10 years, motivated by factors such as convenience, quality of building, and price.

2. The Vital Organ Donation Society, a non-profit organization, must acquire a vehicle. It has the authority to borrow money for this purpose but is also considering a five-year lease arrangement, with a subsequent renewal option at a very favourable price, which appears to be much cheaper than the borrowing option.

3. Cahil Limited plans to acquire manufacturing equipment that it could buy outright. Since the company has no spare cash, all the money would have to be borrowed. However, existing loans required the company to maintain a debt-to-equity ratio of no more than 2 to 1, and the company's balance sheet reflects a ratio very close to this limit now. Cahil is considering a three-year lease with a low annual charge but material per-year contingent usage charges.

4. Bagg Limited has just completed the construction of a new warehouse facility. It is considering two financing options: a 25-year commercial mortgage or a 25-year lease. Under the mortgage agreement, interest rates would be fixed for five-year periods but would be renegotiated when each five-year period expired. Under the lease agreement, title would pass to Bagg Corporation at the end of the lease. The lease payments would be renegotiated every 10 years.

5. Dimmins College is considering an arrangement whereby it will sell all its rare book collection to a leasing company, and immediately lease back the collection on a 20-year lease, with fixed payments for each of the 20 years. At the end of the lease period, the collection will again belong to the College.

6. Elias Limited is attempting to acquire a $400,000 piece of manufacturing equipment for its plant operation, which it believes will significantly reduce its operating costs over the next four years. The equipment would likely be obsolete at that time. The company's friendly banker has offered a four-year loan, for up to $320,000, at prime interest rates. A friendly leasing company has offered a four-year lease covering all the equipment cost. The lease requires equal payments each year; payments are at the end of each year.

Required:
In each example, explain the company's motive for entering into the lease arrangement.

A17-9 Finance Lease—Lease year ≠ Fiscal Year: On 17 August 20X1, Renfrew Corporation negotiated a lease agreement with National Leasing Company (NLC) for computer equipment. The equipment has an expected economic life of 7 years and a fair market value of $36,000. The lease term is for 5 years, beginning on 1 October 20X1. Lease payments are $7,500 per year, payable at the beginning of each lease year. At the end of the lease term, Renfrew can negotiate a buyout price with NLC. If no buyout is negotiated, the equipment reverts to NCL.

Renfrew has an incremental borrowing rate of 8% and does not know NLC's interest rate implicit in the lease. Renfrew uses straight-line depreciation calculated on a monthly basis. Renfrew prepares financial statements only at the company's fiscal year-end of 31 December.

Required:
1. Is this a finance lease or an operating lease for Renfrew? Explain.
2. Prepare an amortization table.
3. Prepare Renfrew's journal entries for 20X1 and 20X2.
4. What is the balance of the lease liability account on 31 December 20X2? Reconcile this balance with your amortization schedule.
5. Renfrew uses current–non-current classification. How much of the year-end 20X2 lease liability will be shown as a current liability and how much as a long-term liability?

A17-10 Finance Lease; Quarterly Payments; Current/Non-Current Classification:
Packard Limited is planning on leasing 150 desktop computers from Hewlett Corporation. The list price for the computers is $2,000 each, or $300,000 in total. The lease will be for three years, starting on 1 October 20X4. The lease payments are $26,000 at the beginning of each quarter. Packard's incremental borrowing rate is 8% per annum. Packard's fiscal year ends on 31 December. The computers have an expected useful life of four years but will almost certainly have no market value at the end of the lease. Although it is not specified in the lease agreement, Packard's customary practice with such leases is to simply convey title to the computers at the end of the lease term, at a nominal payment by the lessee.

Required:
1. Prepare the journal entries to record the lease and lease payments for Packard's fiscal year ending 31 December 20X4.
2. What amounts relating to the lease liability will appear on Packard's 31 December 20X4 statement of financial position?

★★★ **A17-11 Finance Lease, Reporting:** Videos-to-Go signed a lease for a vehicle that had an expected economic life of eight years and a fair value of $18,000. The lessor is the leasing subsidiary of a national car manufacturer. The terms of the lease are as follows:

- The lease term begins on 1 January 20X2, and runs for five years.
- The lease requires payments of $5,800 each 1 January, including $1,700 for maintenance and insurance costs.
- At the end of the lease term, the lease is renewable for three one-year periods, for $2,600 per year, including $2,100 for maintenance and insurance. The normal rental costs for a similar used vehicle would be approximately double this amount.
- At the end of any lease term, if Videos-to-Go does not renew the contract, the vehicle reverts back to the lessor. The lessor may choose to leave the vehicle with Videos-to-Go if its value is low.

Videos-to-Go does not know the interest rate implicit in the lease from the lessor's perspective but has an incremental borrowing rate of 12%. Videos-to-Go has a 31 December year-end and uses straight-line depreciation for all assets.

Required:

1. Explain why this is a finance lease for the lessee.
2. Prepare a lease amortization schedule.
3. Prepare journal entries for 20X2 and 20X3.
4. Show how the lease would be reflected on the SFP, income statement, and CFS for 20X2 and 20X3. Segregate debt between its current and non-current components. Assume the indirect method for operating activities in the statement of cash flows.
5. How much interest expense would be reported on the income statement in each year from 20X2 to 20X10 if Videos-to-Go had a 31 May fiscal year-end?

★★ **A17-12 Finance Lease, Guaranteed Residual:** Access Limited has decided to lease office equipment with a fair market value of $580,000. The lease is with the Imperial Leasing Corporation, a U.S.–based subsidiary of a Japanese financial firm. The terms of the lease are as follows:

- The initial lease term is five years. The lease commences on 1 January 20X1.
- For the initial lease term, payments are $105,000 annually, made at the beginning of each lease year. Each payment includes an estimated $5,000 for insurance.
- There is a renewal term at the lessee's option for a further three years. Payments during the renewal term are $43,000, including $3,000 for insurance.
- Access Limited guarantees a residual value of $150,000 at the end of the first term if the renewal option is not exercised. If Access does renew, there will be no requirement to guarantee a residual value.
- If Access Limited did not lease the equipment from Imperial Leasing Corporation, the company would incur an incremental borrowing rate of 8%.

Required:

1. Is the lease a finance lease or an operating lease for Access Limited? Why?
2. Prepare a lease amortization schedule
3. Prepare entries for Access Limited for 20X1, assuming the company has a 31 December year-end and uses straight-line depreciation.
4. Prepare entries for Access Limited for the calendar year 20X1, assuming the company has a 31 March year-end instead.
5. Assuming that the company has a 31 March year-end, how would the lease liability appear in Access Limited's SFP at 31 March 20X1? Access Limited uses current–non-current classification.

★★★ **A17-13 Finance Lease, Guaranteed Residual:** Lessee Limited agreed to a non-cancellable lease for which the following information is available:

eXcel

a. The asset is new at the inception of the lease term and is worth $32,000.
b. Lease term is four years, starting 1 January 20X1.
c. Estimated useful life of the leased asset is six years.
d. The residual value of the leased asset will be $6,000 at the end of the lease term. The residual value is guaranteed by Lessee Limited.
e. The declining-balance depreciation method is used for the leased asset, at a rate of 30% per year.
f. Lessee's incremental borrowing rate is 10%.
g. Four annual lease payments will be made each 1 January during the lease term, and the first payment, due at inception of the lease term, is $8,626, including $1,100 of maintenance costs.
h. Lessee has a 31 December fiscal year-end.

Required:

1. Is this an operating lease or a finance lease? Explain.
2. Prepare a table showing how the lease liability reduces over the lease term. Record the entries for 20X1.
3. Prepare the financial statement presentation of all lease-related accounts as they would appear in the financial statements of the lessee at 31 December 20X1. Include note disclosure. Ignore income taxes.

★★ **A17-14 Finance Lease; Guaranteed Residual; Future Balance:** On 24 February 20X1, Ready Distributing Ltd., a public company, signed a lease for conveyor equipment. The equipment is intended to help Ready cope with an increased volume of business until the company is able to finance and build new facilities. The fair value of the leased equipment is $720,000.

The lease will commence on 1 October 20X1. The lease is for four years with lease payments of $30,000 per quarter (i.e., each three months), due at the beginning of each quarter. The lease is renewable for an additional four-year period at the same cost. If Ready does not renew after the initial lease term, the company must guarantee the lessor a residual value of $300,000. The lessor does not require a residual value guarantee at the end of the renewal period. The equipment's estimated economic life is 10 years.

Ready's incremental borrowing rate is a nominal 8% per annum, compounded quarterly.

Required:

1. Is this an operating lease or a finance lease? Explain.
2. Show the entry or entries that Ready should make for the fiscal year ending 31 December 20X1. The company uses straight-line depreciation for its equipment, with a full year's depreciation in the year of acquisition.
3. What amounts relating to the *lease liability* will appear on Ready's SFP for the year ending 31 December 20X3? Use the short-cut method, not an amortization table. [*Hint*: what is the PV of the future cash flows at that date? How does that compare to the PV of the future cash flows one year later?]

★★ **A17-15 Implicit Interest Rate; Future Balance:** Guido Limited is a retailer of home appliances. Guido leased a building for 25 years. The lease commenced on 1 January 20X1. The annual lease payment is $820,000, payable by the beginning of each lease year, and includes executory costs estimated at $80,000 per year. Guido is reporting the lease as a finance lease. Guido initially recorded the building at $10,027,266. The lease contains contingent rent payments that are based on (1) the amount by which real estate taxes exceed the estimated amount included in the lease payments plus (2) 2% of Guido's gross sales.

It is now 15 years later, 31 December 20X15. You are an auditor for Guido and you need to verify the amount that Guido is showing in the company's draft statement of financial position.

Required:

1. Find the interest rate that Guido Limited used for recording the lease.

2. What current and non-current amounts for the *lease liability* should appear on Guido's SFP for the year ending 31 December 20X15? Use the shortcut present value method, not an amortization table.

★★ **A17-16 Finance Lease; Quarterly Payments; Fair Value Cap:** Christal Corporation leased equipment from Henan Leasing Limited for three years at $30,000 per quarter. The lease begins on 1 May 20X5. Payments are due at the end of each lease quarter (that is, the first payment will be due on 31 July 20X5). The fair value of the equipment is $300,000. Christal Corporation's fiscal year-end is 31 December, and its incremental borrowing rate is 8% per annum. The equipment will be depreciated at a declining-balance rate of 30%. The first year's depreciation of the leased asset will be proportional.

Required:

1. In general journal form, prepare the appropriate entries at the inception of the lease.

2. Using a financial calculator or a computer spreadsheet, calculate the interest rate implicit in the lease for the *lessee*.

3. What will be the lease liability balance (including accrued interest, if any) on 31 December 20X5?

★★★ **A17-17 Finance Lease:** On 31 December 20X1, Lessee Limited entered into a lease agreement by which Lessee leased a jutling machine for six years. Annual lease payments are $20,000, payable at the beginning of each lease year (31 December). At the end of the lease, possession of the machine will revert to the lessor. The normal economic life for this type of machine is 8 to 10 years.

eXcel

At the time of the lease agreement, jutling machines could be purchased for approximately $90,000 cash. Equivalent financing for the machine could have been obtained from Lessee's bank at 14%.

Lessee's fiscal year coincides with the calendar year. Lessee uses straight-line depreciation for its jutling machines.

Required:

1. Prepare an amortization table for the lease, assuming that the lease will be capitalized by Lessee.

2. In general journal form, prepare all journal entries relating to the lease and the leased asset for 20X1, 20X2, and 20X3. Ignore income tax effects.

3. Repeat requirement (2) assuming that the fair market value of the equipment was $77,273 at the inception of the lease.

4. Return to the original facts of the situation. How would the amounts relating to the leased asset and lease liability be shown on Lessee's statement of financial position at 31 December 20X4?

★★★ **A17-18 Sale and Leaseback:** On 31 March 20X2, Supergrocery Inc., a private company, sold its major distribution facility, with a 30-year remaining life, to National Leasing Company for $9,000,000 cash. The facility had an original cost of $10,400,000 and accumulated depreciation of $3,600,000 on the date of sale.

Also on 31 March 20X2, Supergrocery signed a 20-year lease agreement with National Leasing Company, leasing the property back. At the end of the 20-year lease term, legal title to the facility will be transferred to Supergrocery. Annual payments, beginning on 31 March 20X2, are $875,000. Maintenance and repair costs are the responsibility of Supergrocery. Supergrocery has an incremental interest rate of 9%. The company uses straight-line depreciation and has a 31 December year-end. Supergrocery records a part-year's depreciation, based on the date of acquisition, whenever it buys finance assets.

Required:

1. Give the 20X2 entries that Supergrocery Incorporated would make to record the sale and the lease.

2. Give the entries Supergrocery would make in 20X3 and 20X4 in relation to this transaction.

3. Show how the statement of financial position and income statement would reflect the transactions at the end of 20X2, 20X3, and 20X4. Do not segregate SFP items between current and non-current items.

★★ **A17-19 Sale and Leaseback:** Central Purchasing Limited owns the building it uses; it had an original cost of $825,000 and a net book value of $450,000 as of 1 January 20X2. On this date, the building was sold to the Royal Leasing Company for $480,000, which also was the building's fair value, and simultaneously leased back to Central Purchasing Limited.

The lease has a guaranteed, 12-year term and required payments on 31 December of each year. The payments are $77,000, and the lease allows the property to revert to the lessee at the end of the lease. Central Purchasing could have mortgaged this property under similar terms at an interest rate of 10%. The Royal Leasing Company will pay property taxes estimated to be $6,000 per year. These costs are included in the lease payment. Central will pay maintenance and operating costs. The building is being depreciated straight-line, with an estimated remaining life of 16 years.

Required:

1. Prepare entries to record the sale and leaseback of the building.

2. Prepare year-end adjusting entries for 20X2.

3. Show how all amounts related to the sale and leaseback will be presented on the statement of financial position and income statement in 20X2.

★★ **A17-20 Sale and Leaseback:** Sportco Limited is suffering temporary cash flow difficulties due to poor economic conditions. To raise sufficient finance to allow operations to continue until economic conditions improve, Sportco entered into an agreement with a major lease corporation, Leaseco Limited. On 1 January 20X2, Sportco sold its largest manufacturing property to Leaseco at its fair market value, $1,750,000. The property had a net book value of $250,000 at the time of the sale.

Sportco, in turn, leased back the property from Leaseco for 15 years. The annual rent was $175,000, due each year starting on 1 January 20X2. Sportco can repurchase the property from Leaseco at the end of the lease term. The repurchase price (stated in the lease contract) is $2,500,000, based on projected fair values for the property. The land value is estimated to be 40% of the total fair market value of the property, while the building represents the other 60%. Sportco amortizes its buildings at a declining-balance rate of 10%.

Sportco's incremental borrowing rate is 7%. Its financial statements are prepared in accordance with generally accepted accounting standards.

Required:

How should Sportco account for this transaction in its financial statements for the year ending 31 December 20X2? Be specific, and explain the approach that you have chosen. Ignore any income tax issues and disclosure issues.

Source: The Canadian Institute of Chartered Accountants, © 2010.

★★ **A17-21 Classify Two Leases:** Belangier Corporation has signed two leases in the past year. One lease is for handling equipment, the other for a truck.

HANDLING EQUIPMENT:

The handling equipment has a fair market value of $274,000. Lease payments are made each 2 January, the date the lease was signed. The lease is for four years and requires payments of $55,000 per year on each 2 January, and can be renewed at the lessee's option for subsequent one-year terms up to three times, at a cost of $23,000 per year. At the end of any lease term, the equipment reverts back to the lessor if Belangier does not exercise its renewal option. Annual maintenance and insurance costs are paid by the lessor, and are estimated to be $5,000 per year for the first four years, and $3,000 per year thereafter. These costs are included in the lease payments. Belangier estimates that the equipment has an economic life of 8 to 10 years before it becomes obsolete.

TRUCK:

The truck has a list price of $135,000 but could be purchased by cash for 10% less. The truck lease runs for four years and has a quarterly lease payment of $5,000, due at the beginning of each quarter. The lease commences on 1 January. If the truck is used for more than 50,000 kilometres in any 12-month period, a payment of $0.25 per extra kilometre must be paid in addition to the annual rental. Belangier is responsible for all operating and maintenance costs.

At the end of the four-year lease agreement, Belangier may, at its option, renew the lease for an additional period; term and payments to be negotiated at that time.

Belangier has an 8% incremental borrowing rate. The company uses straight-line depreciation for all of its tangible capital assets, using the half-year convention (i.e., a half-year depreciation in the first and last years). The truck has an estimated useful life of 10 years.

Required:

Classify each lease as a finance or operating lease. Justify your response.

★★ **A17-22 Finance Lease—Lessor:** On 31 December 20X1, Lessor Limited leased a reaming machine to a client for six years at $48,000 per year. Lease payments are to be made at the beginning of each lease year. Lessor purchased the machine for $239,650. Lessor negotiated the lease so as to receive a 8% return (pre-tax) on the investment. Lessor anticipates no significant salvage value or removal costs at the end of the lease term.

Required:

1. Prepare an amortization schedule for the lease receivable, assuming that the lease is a finance lease.

2. Prepare journal entries to record the lease transactions for 20X1 through 20X2, assuming that the lease receivable is recorded by Lessor on the net method.

3. Repeat requirement (2) but assuming instead that the lease receivable is recorded on the gross method.

4. How would the amounts relating to the lease be shown on Lessor's balance sheet at 31 December 20X3? Assume that the lessor has an unclassified balance sheet.

★★ **A17-23 Finance Lease—Lessor:** On 2 January 20X2, the National Leasing Company, a leasing subsidiary of a major Canadian chartered bank, entered into a lease with Alphon Limited (the lessee) for computer equipment. Terms of the lease are as follows:

- The initial lease term is two years, with payments due each 31 December, at the end of each lease year.
- Payments are $16,000 per year, including $2,000 for maintenance costs.

- The lease is renewable for a further three years at the option of National Leasing Company, for $9,000 per year.
- At the end of the second lease term, the computer equipment will likely have a $1,000 value. National Leasing Company will resell the equipment at this time.
- National Leasing Company bought the equipment from Command Computers for $46,550 in order to lease it to Alphon.

Assume that the maintenance cost is paid by National Leasing Company to a third party every 31 December. Assume also that the National Leasing Company has a 31 December year-end.

Required:

1. What interest rate is implicit in the lease?
2. Prepare an amortization schedule that shows how the net lease receivable is reduced over the life of the lease.
3. Prepare journal entries to record the lease for 20X2 and 20X3 using the net method.
4. Prepare journal entries to record the lease for 20X2 and 20X3 using the gross method.

★★★ **A17-24 Finance Lease—Lessee and Lessor:** On 2 January 20X4, Yvan Limited entered into a five-year lease for office equipment from Jeffery Leasing Incorporation. The lease calls for annual lease payments of $100,000, payable at the beginning of each lease year. Yvan's incremental borrowing rate is 6%. The lessor's implicit rate in the lease is also 6%. The fair value of the equipment is $450,000. Yvan Limited amortizes office equipment on a straight-line basis.

Required:

1. Prepare the lease liability amortization schedule for Yvan Limited.
2. What amounts will appear on Yvan Limited's SFP, income statement, and statement of cash flows as of 31 December 20X4?
3. Prepare the journal entries relating to the leased asset and the lease liability for 20X5 for Yvan Limited. Use the net method of recording the liability.
4. Prepare the journal entries relating to the lease for Jeffrey Leasing Incorporated for 20X5. Use the gross method of recording the leased asset.

★★ **A17-25 Finance Lease—Lessee and Lessor:** Sondheim Limited entered into a direct financing lease with New Age Leasing Corporation. The lease is for new specialized factory equipment that has a fair value of $4,800,000. The expected useful life of the equipment is 15 years, although its physical life is far greater. The initial lease term begins on 1 April 20X2 and runs for 10 years. Annual lease payments are $600,000, payable at the beginning of each lease year. After the initial lease term, Sondheim has the option of renewing the lease on a year-by-year basis for as long as Sondheim wishes. Since the equipment will be obsolete by that time, the renewal is set at $15,000 per year, which is expected to be a fair rental value for equipment of that age. Other information is as follows:

- Sondheim's incremental borrowing rate is 6%.
- The implicit pre-tax interest rate in the lease is 7%, but this rate is not known to Sondheim.
- Sondheim will amortize the equipment on a straight-line basis, charging half-year depreciation in the first year.

Required:

1. Prepare the journal entries relating to the lease liability and the leased equipment for Sondheim for 20X2 including all appropriate adjusting entries. Use the net method of recording.

2. What amounts will appear on Sondheim's statement of financial position and statement of cash flows at 31 December 20X2? Assume that Sondheim uses the indirect approach to determining cash flow from operating activities.

3. Prepare the journal entries relating to the lease for New Age for 20X2. Use the gross method of recording. What is the net amount of lease receivable that will appear on New Age's statement of financial position on 31 December 20X2?

★★ **A17-26 Sales-type Lease:** Jordin Company is an equipment dealer that sometimes uses leasing as a means to sell its products. On 1 January 20X1, Jordin leased equipment to Easten Corporation. The lease term was four years with annual lease payments of $5,769 to be paid on each 31 December. The equipment has an estimated zero residual value at the end of the lease term. The equipment was carried in Jordin's accounts at a cost of $20,000. Jordin expects to collect all rentals from Easten, and there were no material cost uncertainties at the inception of the lease. The implicit interest rate in the lease was 11%.

Required:

1. Why is this a sales-type lease for Jordin?
2. How much is the gross profit or loss recognized by Jordin? The finance revenue recognized over the life of the lease?
3. Assume that the implicit interest rate is 4% (not 11%). How much is the gross profit or loss recognized by Jordin? The finance revenue recognized over the life of the lease?
4. Give the entries made by Jordan Company (based on the 11% rate) at the inception of the lease. Use the gross method.

★★ **A17-27 Finance Lease; Lessor, Lessee:** Parravano Incorporated has leased a serging machine from Xerox Leasing Corporation for annual beginning-of-year payments of $15,000 for 10 years. The lease term begins on 1 January 20X2. Parravano's fiscal year ends on 31 December. Parravano's incremental borrowing rate is 9% per annum. The fair value of a new serging machine is $105,000. The lease will be reported by both the lessee and the lessor as a finance lease. Parravano depreciates its separating machines on the straight-line basis, using the half-year convention.

Required:

1. Show all amounts relating to the lease and the leased asset that will appear on the statement of financial position and statement of comprehensive income of Parravano for the year ending 31 December 20X5.
2. Show all amounts relating to the lease that will appear on the SFP and statement of comprehensive income of Xerox Leasing Corporation at 31 December 20X5. The lessor uses the gross method of recording leases. The interest rate implicit in the lease is 9%.

★★★ **A17-28 Classification, Lessor and Lessee Financial Statements:** Lessor and lessee agreed to a non-cancellable lease for which the following information is available:

a. Lessor's cost of the asset leased is $40,308. The asset is new at the inception of the lease term.
b. Lease term is three years, starting 2 January 20X3.
c. Estimated useful life of the leased asset is six years.
d. On 2 January 20X3, the lessor estimated that the residual value of the leased asset would be $6,000 on the renewal option date (see (h) below) and zero at the end of its useful life. The residual value is not guaranteed.

e. The straight-line depreciation method is used for the leased asset.

f. Lessee's incremental borrowing rate is 7.5%. Lessee has an excellent credit rating.

g. Lessor's interest rate implicit in the lease is 8%. Lessee does not know this rate.

h. Renewal option, exercisable on 2 January 20X6, is for three years with an annual payment of $1,200 each 1 January. No insurance costs are included, as these will be the lessee's responsibility in the renewal period. This is a bargain renewal option.

i. Title to the leased asset is retained by the lessor.

j. Lessor has no unreimbursable cost uncertainties.

k. Annual lease payments will be made each 2 January during the lease term, which is three years. Payments will include $1,100 of estimated insurance costs for the first three years.

l. The lessor paid $2,200 in initial direct costs.

Required:

1. Calculate the annual payment that would be required for the first three years of the lease term.

2. Is this an operating lease or a finance lease to the lessee? Explain. Compute the lessee's capitalizable cost of the leased asset.

3. What type of lease is this to the lessor? Explain.

4. Prepare an amortization schedule showing how the lessor's net lease receivable would reduce over the life of the lease.

5. Show all lease-related accounts as they would appear in the statement of financial position and income statement of the lessee and the lessor at 31 December 20X3, for the year then ended. The lessor's statement of financial position is unclassified.

★★ **A17-29 Statement of Cash Flows Review:** Each of the following items must be considered in preparing a statement of cash flows for Phillie Fashions for the year ended 31 December 20X6:

1. Finance assets that had a cost of $10,000 6½ years before and were being depreciated straight-line on a 10-year basis, with no estimated scrap value, were sold for $3,125.

2. Phillie Company leased an asset to a customer, as a way of selling it, on 31 December 20X6. Phillie recognized a net receivable of $23,456, after the first payment of $8,700. The $8,700 payment was collected on 31 December. The gross profit on the sale was $5,670. There was unearned finance revenue of $6,200 over the lease term, which lasts four years.

3. During the year, goodwill of $5,000 was completely written off to expense.

4. During the year, 250 shares of common stock were issued for $32 per share.

5. Finance asset amortization amounted to $1,000, and patent amortization to $200.

6. Bonds payable with a par value of $12,000, on which there was an unamortized bond premium of $360, were redeemed at 103.

7. Phillie Company, as lessee, reported a net lease liability of $14,678 at the end of 20X6. In 20X5, the liability had been $15,766. The current portion of the liability was $2,410 each year.

Required:

For each item, state what would be included in the statement of cash flows, whether it is an inflow or outflow, and the amount(s). Assume that correct entries were made for all transactions as they took place and that the indirect method is to be used to disclose cash flow from operations. In your response, use a three-column format as follows:

Operating/Investing/Financing	Inflow/Outflow	Amount

★★★
eXcel

A17-30 Statement of Cash Flows Review: Laker Ltd., a public company, had the following information available at the end of 20X5:

Comparative balance sheets, as of 31 December

	20X5	20X4
Cash	$ 3,000	$ 800
Accounts receivable	3,500	2,590
Inventory	8,400	7,000
Prepaid rent	600	2,400
Prepaid insurance	420	180
Office supplies	200	150
Net lease receivable	25,000	35,000
Land and building	70,000	70,000
Accumulated depreciation	(21,000)	(17,500)
Equipment	105,000	80,000
Accumulated depreciation	(26,000)	(22,400)
Patent	9,000	10,000
Total assets	$178,120	$168,220
Accounts payable	$ 5,400	$ 6,400
Taxes payable	1,000	800
Wages payable	1,000	600
Short-term notes payable	2,000	2,000
Long-term notes payable	12,000	14,000
Bonds payable	80,000	80,000
Premium on bonds payable	4,060	5,170
Common shares	48,000	41,500
Retained earnings	24,660	17,750
Total liabilities and equity	$178,120	$168,220

*Not cash equivalents

Income statement information for year ended 31 December 20X5

	20X5	20X4
Sales revenue		$231,850
Cost of goods sold		149,583
Gross margin		82,267
Selling expenses	$ 15,840	
Administrative expenses	31,340	
Depreciation expense	8,100	55,280
Income from operations		26,987
Lease finance revenue	5,880	
Interest expense	(13,350)	(7,470)
Income before taxes		19,517
Income tax expense		7,807
Net income		$ 11,710
Dividends paid		4,800
Increase in retained earnings		$ 6,910

Required:

Prepare a statement of cash flows, using the indirect method to disclose operating activities.

CHAPTER 18

Post-employment Benefits

Many companies promise to provide their employees certain benefits after they retire. The most common form of *post-employment benefit* is a pension. However, a company may also provide other post-employment benefits such as life insurance or extended health care. These benefits are provided as compensation for employees' services during their working lives. Therefore, post-employment benefits are a form of deferred compensation, and the cost should be recognized in the periods during which the employee is working. However, the eventual cost is difficult to estimate. Some of the projections that have to be made are retention rates, mortality rates, retirement trends, future interest rates, and rates of return on fund assets.

To make matters more complicated, there are several different methods of measuring and allocating pension cost, known as *actuarial cost methods*. Every actuarial cost method allocates the future estimated cost of post-employment benefits to the years of an employee's service in an effort to determine appropriate funding. Each actuarial cost method provides a different funding pattern. For those who want a better understanding of actuarial methodology, a unit on Connect illustrates the three basic actuarial methods.

Pension plans are big business, and can affect an assessment of the solvency of the sponsoring company. For example, Air Canada reports total assets of $10.4 billion at the end of 2009, and shareholders' equity of $1.5 billion. The disclosure notes show that the pension plan, whose assets and liabilities are not separately recorded by Air Canada, has assets of $10.8 billion and obligations of $11.9 billion, making it pretty much just as large as the book value of the employer operation. The pension plan is underfunded by $1.2 billion, about 70% of the recorded equity of the employer company.

Pensions have been newsworthy over the last period because tumbling financial markets have caused significant declines in pension fund assets. Some sources estimate that major Canadian pension plans, those with more than $1 billion of assets, experienced asset declines of 18% in 2008.[1] The unfunded pension obligations of major car manufacturers in financial distress have been matters of public policy.

This chapter focuses primarily on accounting for pensions, but includes an example of other post-employment benefits. The general structure of pension calculations and assumptions are analyzed, various components of pension expense are explored, and a spreadsheet is introduced that helps to organize pension data. The extensive disclosure requirements for post-employment benefits are reviewed.

---

[1] As documented in Jacquie McNish, "Retirement Dreams Under Siege," *The Globe and Mail*, http://www.theglobeandmail.com/report-on-business/retirement/retirement-dreams-under-siege/article1327536/, accessed October 2009.

TYPES OF PENSION PLANS

There are two general types of pension plans:

1. Defined contribution plans, and

2. Defined benefit plans.

A **defined contribution plan** is one in which the employer makes agreed-upon (or *defined*) cash contributions to the plan each period, which are invested by a trustee on behalf of the employee. The employee may make contributions as well. For example, a plan might provide that the employer will contribute 6% of the employee's salary to the pension plan each year. The pension that the employee eventually receives as a result of those contributions is a function of the trustee's investment success; the pension annuity is determined by the amount of accumulated contributions plus earnings on those contributions at the time that the employee retires.

A **defined benefit plan** is one in which the eventual *benefits* to the employee are stated in the pension plan. The benefits are normally calculated on the basis of the employee's salary at or near retirement and the length of her employment with the company. It is the employer's responsibility to pay for this pension. For example, a company may provide that an employee will receive an annual pension that is equal to 2% of the employee's final year's salary for each year of service. If the employee is earning $100,000 in the year before retirement and has worked for the company for 35 years, the annual pension will be:

Annual pension annuity = $100,000 \times 2\% \times 35$ years = $70,000

The essential difference between the two types of plans can be summarized as follows:

Type of Plan	Contributions	Benefits	Risk
Defined contribution	Fixed	Variable	Employee has risk of low pension benefits
Defined benefit	Variable	Fixed	Employer has risk of high pension contributions

Classification of a plan as defined contribution or defined benefit rests on the *economic substance* of the plan, based on its terms and conditions. If the benefit formula is based on *more than* the contributions and the investment history to date, or if the employer guarantees some specific level of pension or plan earnings, then the plan is a defined benefit plan.

Since defined benefit plans entitle the employee to a specified (or *defined*) pension, the challenge for the employer is to make payments into the plan that will eventually provide enough money to pay the pension. If pension plan investments decline in value, then the company will have to provide more money to make up any deficiency. On the other hand, investment returns that are larger than expected will reduce the employer's necessary contributions to the plan.

The task of figuring out how much the employer should contribute to a defined benefit plan is the task of the **actuary**. An *actuary* is an expert who calculates statistical risks, life expectancy, payout probabilities, etc. Actuaries are typically employed by insurance agencies and other financial institutions. Actuarial science is a well-established and well-recognized profession, with a rigorous multi-stage qualification process.

PENSION VARIABLES

Contributory versus Non-Contributory

A **contributory pension plan** is one in which the *employee* makes contributions to the plan, in addition to those made by the employer. Defined contribution plans often are contributory, which acts to enforce some level of retirement savings. The other alternative is that the pension plan is **non-contributory**; the pension assets are contributed entirely by the employer, and the employee pays nothing.

Vesting

Pension plan benefits are said to be **vested** when the employee has the right to receive his pension entitlement even if he leaves the employer before retirement age. The pension is not actually paid until retirement, of course, but the funds in the pension plan are "earmarked" for that individual or rolled into the individual's RRSP. Some provinces require that benefits are immediately vested. Others require vesting after two years of service. Others apply the 10 + 45 rule; contributions become vested when the employee has worked for the same employer for 10 years *and* has reached age 45. Of course, employers may voluntarily commit themselves to faster vesting than provincial legislation requires. Note that any contributions to a pension plan made by an *employee* are automatically vested.

Trustee

Most pension plans are trusteed, which means that there is an independent **trustee** who receives the pension contributions from the employer (and, if appropriate, from the employee), invests the contributions in accordance with provincial regulations and agreed-upon guidelines, and pays out benefits to the pensioner. Trustees of pension funds are often financial institutions such as trust companies and banks; a pension trustee is not an individual person. Most plans are trusteed because:

- Trusteeship is required for a plan to be registered.
- From an accounting perspective, if a pension plan is not trusteed and instead is administered by the company, the company must report both the pension plan assets and the accrued pension liability on its SFP because the assets are under the control of the company. When a plan is administered by a trustee, however, the plan assets are beyond control of the company's managers and accounting recognition takes a different path.

Trusteeship does not absolve the employer of responsibility to ensure that a defined benefit pension plan is solvent and is able to pay out the benefits when they come due.

Registered

Pension plans normally are **registered** with the pension commissioner in the province of jurisdiction. The commissioner's office is responsible for seeing that the pension plan abides by pension legislation, including requirements for funding, reporting, trusteeship, actuarial valuation, and control over surpluses.

An important benefit of registration is that it also enables the company to deduct from taxable income amounts contributed to the plan. If the plan is not registered, the employer *cannot deduct the pension contributions;* tax deductions will come only when the pension is actually paid to the employee or when a pension annuity is purchased on behalf of the employee at the retirement date. Since pension contributions are material, this would delay the tax deduction for the company and would be highly undesirable!

CONCEPT REVIEW

1. Explain the difference between a defined contribution pension plan and a defined benefit pension plan.
2. Why is trusteeship critical when accounting for pensions?
3. What is the risk to an employee if pension rights are not vested?
4. Who makes contributions to the pension plan if it is non-contributory?

DEFINED CONTRIBUTION PLANS

The trend over the last 30 years, both in Canada and around the world, has been for private-sector companies that grant pensions to do so through a defined contribution plan. Over 80% of the private company pension plans in Canada are defined contribution plans. These plans have lower financial risk for the employer because the cost of the program is known with certainty.

Current Service Cost

Defined contribution pension plans are relatively easy to deal with for accounting purposes. Because the amount of the contribution is known, there is little uncertainty about either the cash flow or the accounting measurement. The contribution (i.e., the employer's annual cash outflow) is readily determinable from the terms of the pension plan. The accounting expense flows from the contribution; *the amount of the contribution defines the expense*. The employer's required contribution for services rendered during the period is known as the *current service cost* for the period.

Example Suppose that Enterprise Fourchu Limité (EFL) pays $60,000 into the pension plan at the end of 20X1 for 20X1 as required under its pension plan for services rendered. The entry is straightforward:

Pension expense	60,000	
Cash		60,000

Be careful to expense only amounts relating to the *current* year's service; there may well be an agreement covering 20X2, but it would not be recorded as a liability in 20X1.

Delayed Payment of Current Service Cost

Ordinarily, the employer pays the full amount of the current service cost into the pension plan in the current year. However, sometimes payments are made after the fiscal year-end. If some of the funding for current year service is to be paid into the plan in future years, the current service cost (the expense) is the amount of the current payments plus the *present value of future payments*. The difference between the expense and the amount actually paid is recognized as a liability. The discount rate is based on market interest rates for high-quality debt instruments of similar amount and timing. Payments to be made within the next year are not discounted.

Example Assume that EFL (above) has agreed to pay $60,000 at the end of 20X1 and *also* agrees to make another payment of $40,000 *relating to employees' 20X1 services* at the end of 20X4. Assuming an interest rate of 6%, the present value of the future payment is $40,000 × (P/F, 6%, 3) = $33,585. The entry to record 20X1 pension expense will be:

Pension expense	93,585	
Cash		60,000
Accrued pension liability		33,585

Interest Component When an entity has obligations that must be made in future periods as a result of employee services rendered during the current period or past periods, the entity must recognize interest on those accrued contributions. This is part of pension expense, not a separate interest expense. Interest is calculated by using the same rate that was used in discounting the obligation in the first place. Note the $33,585 pension liability recognized by EFL, above. In 20X2 EFL will record interest of $33,585 × 6% = $2,015 *as a part of pension expense*.

Other Aspects of a Defined Contribution Plan

There may be other aspects of pension plan accounting related to a defined benefit plan, although *these elements are rare.*

Vesting If the plan is not fully vested from the start of an individual's employment with the company, forfeitures *reverting back to the employer* are recognized as a *reduction of expense in the year of forfeit.* For example, assume that $155,000 would be paid to a pension plan for current service. However, an employee leaves the company, forfeiting $45,000 already in the pension plan from prior years but unvested. The employer would remit $110,000 to the plan, and $110,000 is the pension expense for the period. Forfeitures are not estimated in advance; they are considered in the year that the forfeiture occurs.

Prepaid Pension Amounts An employer may record a prepaid pension asset if there is a *prepayment that will lead to a reduction in a future payment or a cash refund.* For example, assume an employer contributes $200,000 to a plan, and then discovers that its payroll was less than expected for the year and the contribution should have been only $180,000. If the excess $20,000 can be obtained as a cash refund, or if the $20,000 can be used toward the next year's required payment, then a prepaid pension asset or account receivable is recorded and pension expense is $180,000. If no relief is offered for the overpayment, then pension expense is $200,000 and no asset exists.

Plan Earnings A defined contribution plan's assets, and the earnings on those assets, are normally entirely committed to paying pension benefits to employees, and thus no special accounting for the investment revenue is required, or allowed. In special circumstances, though, there may be *an unassigned surplus* of assets in the plan. This might happen if the $20,000 excess payment explained above is retained in the plan. Accordingly, *in rare circumstances* there would be assets in a contributory pension plan that would really accrue to the company, not the employees. If this were to happen, then investment earnings *on the unassigned assets* (not total assets) would be calculated, and reduce pension expense.

Reporting Example

Cameco Corporation is engaged in the exploration and development, mining, refining conversion, and fabrication of uranium for sale as fuel for generating electricity in nuclear power reactors. From Note 23 in the 2009 annual financial statements:

Cameco maintains both defined benefit and defined contribution plans providing pension and post-retirement benefits to substantially all of its employees.

...

Pension expense

...	2009	2008
Defined benefit pension expense	$ 2,485	$ 2,795
Defined contribution pension expense	13,506	13,005
Net pension expense	$15,991	$15,800

Source: www.sedar.com, Cameco Corporation, audited annual financial statements, accessed June 10, 2010.

Note that the defined contribution portion of pension expense represents over 80% of the total pension expense, implying that most employees are covered by defined contribution plans.

DEFINED BENEFIT PLANS—STRUCTURE

A defined benefit pension plan consists of the pension fund assets, placed with a trustee, and the post-employment obligation to employees. Accountants grapple with how to report this asset and liability in the financial statements of the sponsoring employer. While these issues are explored in depth as this chapter progresses, it helps at this point to have a clear view of the two "sides" to the pension fund itself.

Pension Plan Assets The assets of a pension fund increase when the employer or the employee makes contributions to the trustee, and when the assets generate return. The assets can decline if the plan generates a negative return, and assets also decline when benefits are paid to pensioners.

Defined Benefit Obligation The obligation of a pension plan to its members is measured as the *expected present value* of payments to be made to members when they retire. It is a cumulative amount that increases each year that the employee works, and earns a higher pension, and also increases annually for an interest component, because of the time value of money. It can increase or decrease when experience to date is different than the original estimate, and also increase or decrease when there are changed future estimates regarding mortality, future salary levels, and so on. The obligation will decrease when benefits are paid to retirees.

Basis for Pension Entitlements

In a defined benefit pension plan, the pension paid to a retiree must be based on some specific formula. Pensions that are based on some specific percentage of final year's salary are called **final pay pension plans**. Different formulas to determine the pension are possible. For example, the pension could be calculated on the basis of:

- **Flat benefit** per year of service, with no entitlement related to salary;
- Career average pay—that is, an average of the employee's earnings over the entire time spent with the employer;
- The best year's earnings (which permits employees to phase out toward the end of their careers); or
- An average of the last three (or five) years' earnings.

DEFINED BENEFIT PLANS—ACTUARIAL METHODS

Estimations

In a defined benefit plan, the future benefit is known, but estimates have to be made for the annual contributions that are necessary to provide that defined future benefit. Such estimates are made using complex mathematical models called **actuarial cost methods,** which link the terms of the pension plan to annual contributions. In these actuarial cost methods, many factors must be taken into account in order to estimate the current cost of the distant benefit. A few of the more important ones are as follows:

- *Investment earnings.* The lower the earnings on plan assets, the more that will have to be contributed to the plan to support benefits. Because of the long time period involved, even a small change in assumed earnings can have a significant impact on the current contributions and accounting expense.
- *Future salary increases.* Since pension benefits are often tied to the employee's future earnings, it is necessary to estimate (or *project*) the future salary increases. Salary increases are related, in part, to inflation rates. Therefore, it is necessary to estimate future inflation rates.
- *Employee turnover.* Vesting may not occur immediately in defined benefit plans. Therefore, it is usually necessary to estimate what proportion of employees will stay long enough for vesting to occur.

- *Mortality rates.* Mortality may be connected with vesting; if an employee dies before vesting occurs, then there may be no defined benefit obligation to the beneficiary. However, a pension plan may specify **death benefits** or **survivor benefits** that give lump-sum or continuing benefits to a surviving spouse, partner, and/or child. The mortality rate and the extent of any trailing entitlements must be estimated.
- *Life expectancy after retirement.* The longer a retired employee lives after retirement, the more must be paid out in pension. Most plans provide minimum guarantees; the pensioner's estate receives a lump-sum payment if the pension is not paid for a certain number of years. Some pension plans pass this risk on to insurance companies by purchasing a life annuity on behalf of the employee at retirement. Expected cash flows are affected by the terms of the plan and life expectancy.
- *Borrowing rates.* An interest rate must be chosen as a discount rate. This rate is established with reference to market yield on long-term debt in corporate bond markets.

It is the actuary's responsibility to make the estimates necessary for the measurement of pension funding amounts. However, an accountant should be particularly concerned about (1) investment earnings, (2) borrowing rates, and (3) future salary increases, because these components have a significant impact on accounting measurements.

Actuaries often are required to be quite conservative, and may estimate the return on plan assets on the low side and the projected rate of salary increases on the high side. The company need not use the same estimates for accounting purposes that are used by its actuaries for funding purposes.

ETHICAL ISSUES

The estimates used by management for pension measurements must represent *best estimates*. These metrics should be *unbiased* and must be internally consistent. For example, since the return on plan assets, inflation rates, and salary increases are related over the long run, it would make little sense to use a high estimated return on plan assets (which would include a high inflation allowance) while also assuming a very low rate of increase in salaries (which would imply a low future inflation rate). There is always room for bias in estimates, and there may be a corporate motive to minimize or maximize pension amounts. This objective can sometimes be met through manipulation of estimates, and care must be taken when looking at the quality of *best estimates*.

Funding versus Accounting

Accounting measurements must be separate from plan funding. **Funding** is the manner in which the actuary, on behalf of the employer, sets the necessary contributions to the plan. The accounting measurements determine pension expense, and do not have to be equal to funding. Similar factors and the same family of actuarial methods may be used for both—or not. Understanding pension accounting requires understanding pension funding, because they interact.

Funding Approaches There are several actuarial cost methods that actuaries can use to calculate the cash contributions that a company must make. It is important to emphasize that no one method is "better" than another; all methods provide full funding of benefits.

However, there is a significant difference between various actuarial cost methods in the *pattern* of payments made to the trustee over an employee's working life. If one particular actuarial cost method requires higher cash contributions in the early years of an employee's tenure with the company, it could be viewed as more fiscally conservative. Other actuarial cost methods require the bulk of funding to occur later in the employee's working life. All methods are acceptable for funding under pension legislation, and all are used in practice.

The three basic actuarial cost methods that can be used for funding can be described briefly as follows:

1. The **accumulated benefit method** calculates the contributions that an employer must make in order to fund the pension to which the employee currently is entitled, based on the *actual* years of service to date and on the *current* salary.

2. The **projected unit credit method** calculates the required funding based on the *actual* years of service to date but on a *projected* estimate of the employee's salary at the retirement date. (This method is also called the *accrued benefit method prorated on service*, and the *benefit/years of service method*.)

3. The **level contribution method** projects both the *final salary* and the *total* years of service, and then allocates the cost evenly over the years of service.

Clearly, the level contribution method involves *more projections*, and the accumulated benefit method involves *fewer projections*.

ACTUARIAL COST METHODS EXAMPLE

To illustrate the three actuarial cost methods, consider a basic illustration of a defined benefit pension. Assume that an employee named Chris begins working for Celebrities Limited at age 30. Assume the following:

- Chris's starting salary is $25,000 per year.
- The normal retirement age at Celebrities is 65.
- The pension plan provides that an employee will receive an annual pension of 2% of the final year's salary for each year of service.
- The pension is fully vested from the date of employment.

Some additional estimates are needed, which are provided by the actuary:

- The estimated life expectancy after retirement is 14 years.
- The expected return on the investment in pension plan assets will be 6%.
- Chris's salary will increase by a compound average annual rate of 3%.
- Chris will work for Celebrities for 35 years, until normal retirement age.

Comparison of Methods

The calculation details for each of the three methods are explained in a unit on Connect. Exhibit 18-1 summarizes the funding required under each of the actuarial cost methods at selected ages. Remember, a company may use any actuarial cost method to determine funding.

The allocation patterns are very different, and yet each method results in *full funding over the years of service*. The accumulated benefit method and the projected unit credit method both start with low payments and end with high payments. This pattern is most extreme with the accumulated benefit method. The level contribution method, as the name states, requires the same funding each year.

Bear in mind that the calculation is for just one employee, which is unrealistic. *A company's overall pension funding requirement is calculated for the employee group as a whole.* Employees just entering the workforce may have low pension amounts attributable to their service, which will offset the apparently dramatic increase in amounts for older employees. For an employee group as a whole, the relative difference in pension amounts between methods will level out *if the employee group is stable and has an even age composition*. However, the age and length-of-employment composition of employee groups are often unstable; there are usually more employees at the lower-experience levels of employment than at the senior levels. In practice, the differences between methods do not even out.

Sensitivity to Assumptions

The calculations are extremely sensitive to basic assumptions within methods. If the assumed rate of salary increase is changed from 3% to 4%, for example, all of the costs in

> **EXHIBIT 18-1**
>
> ## COMPARISON OF FUNDING REQUIREMENTS FOR CURRENT SERVICE USING DIFFERENT ACTUARIAL COST METHODS
>
> | | Allocated Funding under Each Method | | |
> |---|---|---|---|
> | Chris's Age | Accumulated Benefit | Projected Unit Credit | Level Contribution |
> | 30 | $ 679 | $ 1,856 | $4,227 |
> | 35 | 1,207 | 2,484 | 4,227 |
> | 40 | 2,111 | 3,324 | 4,227 |
> | 45 | 3,645 | 4,448 | 4,227 |
> | 50 | 6,228 | 5,953 | 4,227 |
> | 55 | 10,551 | 7,966 | 4,227 |
> | 60 | 17,748 | 10,660 | 4,227 |
> | 64 | 26,786 | 13,458 | 4,227 |

(IFRS suggests this method) [handwritten annotation above Projected Unit Credit column]

the table above would increase by almost 40%. The discount rate sensitivity is also great. If the assumed discount rate were increased from 6% to 8% in the preceding example, the required contributions at age 35 would change as shown below for the three methods:

Interest Rate Assumed	@ 6%	@ 8%
Accumulated benefit method	$1,207	$ 635
Projected unit credit method	2,484	1,305
Level contribution method	4,227	2,470

This highlights the need to use appropriate assumptions. As previously stated, the accounting standard requires use of "best estimate" assumptions that are internally consistent.

ACTUARIAL COST METHOD FOR ACCOUNTING PURPOSES

Accounting standards require the use of the *projected unit credit method* to calculate the annual **current service cost**. Current service cost is the actuarial present value of the pension entitlement earned by an employee group in a given year, and a major component of each year's pension expense. Companies are all required to use the same actuarial cost method to ensure that a common measurement tool is used, and thus comparability is preserved. Generally, this method is felt to best measure the cost of entitlements earned during the period, and standard-setters have been consistent in their preference for this method.

Differences between Funding and Accounting Amounts

Life is easy (relatively speaking) when the current service cost for accounting is the same as the current service contribution for funding. When that happens, the recorded pension expense directly offsets the expenditure of cash for funding. For example, assume that Celebrities uses the same method (projected unit credit method) and the same assumptions (best estimates) in its calculations for both accounting and funding. Refer to Exhibit 18-1. At the end of Chris's year 40, the entry to record the current service pension expense and the current service funding would appear as follows:

Pension expense	3,324	
Cash		3,324

Now suppose instead that Celebrities uses the accumulated benefit method for funding. The entry will no longer balance, because the amount recorded as expense ($3,324) is greater than the amount paid into the pension fund in that year ($2,111, from Exhibit 18-1). In order to balance the entry, the difference between these two amounts has to be credited to a liability account, often called an **accrued pension liability** (or accrued benefit liability):

Pension expense	3,324	
Cash		2,111
Accrued pension liability		1,213

If the accrued pension account has a debit balance, it is called an **accrued pension asset** (or accrued benefit asset).

Interpreting the Liability

If the accumulated amount is a credit (that is, the cost is being charged to expense faster than contributions are being made to the plan), it is tempting to say that the company "owes" the pension plan and the pension plan is underfunded. However, an accrued liability *caused by a different actuarial cost method used for funding and accounting* should *not* be interpreted in this way. The funding is *appropriate for the actuarial cost method being used.*

CONCEPT REVIEW

1. Name three actuarial cost methods and specify what projections, if any, are involved for each one.
2. Which actuarial method is required for accounting measurements for a defined benefit plan?
3. What is the significance of an accrued pension liability, caused by use of different actuarial cost methods?

DEFINED BENEFIT PLAN PENSION EXPENSE— LIST OF COMPONENTS

Pension expense for a defined benefit pension plan is the sum of *eight* components. That is, in order to calculate pension expense, it is necessary to gather these components together and add them up. For convenience, we will group these into *continuing components* and *special components.*

The following five components are continuing because they either will always exist or usually exist as part of pension expense. These five components are the main focus of the following sections.

Continuing components:

1. Current service cost;
2. *Plus:* Interest on the defined benefit obligation;
3. *Minus:* Expected earnings on plan assets;
4. *Plus:* Recognition of past service cost from plan initiation or amendment; and
5. *Plus (or minus)*: Recognition of actuarial loss (or gain).

Three special components arise only under certain circumstances. We will briefly explain each of these components later in the chapter.

Special components:

1. Plan settlement or curtailment;
2. Limit on accrued pension asset; and
3. Termination benefits.

CONTINUING COMPONENTS

Current Service Cost

The first and most significant element of pension cost is the *current service cost*. This is the annual measurement of the cost of the pension earned for work done during the year. Accounting standards require that current service cost be measured using the *projected unit credit method*. The actuary determines this figure and provides it in an actuarial report. It is an *expected present value* calculation based on numerous assumptions, as we have seen.

Interest on the Defined Benefit Obligation

The **defined benefit obligation** is the cumulative present value of post-employment benefits earned to date. It can also be pictured as the *cumulative current service cost* to date, plus interest, although it has other components, too. Since current service is a present value, interest on the cumulative balance accumulates as time passes.

Interest is calculated as the *discount rate multiplied by the defined benefit obligation throughout the period*. Interest is included as an element of pension expense. Since the reference is to the obligation *throughout the period*, a weighted average of the obligation over the year should be used. However, for computational simplicity, we will use *the opening obligation multiplied by the discount rate* to measure interest expense. There is little error involved in this simplification, given the magnitude of the many assumptions used in pension accounting. Alternatively, *interest may be calculated by the actuary* and provided in an actuarial report.

Discount Rate The rate used for measuring interest on the obligation must be consistent with the rate used to discount the obligation in the first place. Accounting standards require that this rate should be based on market interest rates for high-quality corporate bonds at the year-end date. Terms should match. For example, if the pensions will, on average, be paid out in 20 years' time, then a 20-year interest rate should be used.

Expected Earnings on Plan Assets

Expected earnings on plan assets *reduces* the amount of pension expense. Just as pension expense is increased for interest on the obligation, it is decreased by earnings on fund assets. The higher the earnings, the lower the overall pension expense to the company. Expected losses on fund assets increase pension expense.

Expected earnings are based on market expectations of the long-term rate of return at the start of the accounting period. Expected earnings are calculated as the *earnings rate multiplied by the plan assets throughout the period*. The value of the plan assets used in this calculation is the *fair value* of plan assets. A weighted average of the asset balance over the period should be used, but the *opening asset balance can be used* to approximate this value for simplicity. Alternatively, the actuary or plan trustee may provide this information.

Earnings Rate The earnings rate must be based on a coherent, defensible methodology. Factors to consider include asset allocation within the pension fund, volatility and duration of fund assets, historic rates of return, and market assessments by fund managers and other experts. The rate of return may be equal to the rate used by the actuary for funding calculations, but if the actuary's rate is conservative (i.e., low), then a more realistic rate should be used by the company to establish expected earnings for accounting purposes.

Offsetting Effects Interest cost and expected earnings tend to offset each other in the calculation of pension expense. However, the offset will be complete only *if*:

- The discount and earnings rates are identical;
- The same actuarial method is used for both accounting and funding;
- Assumptions underlying accounting measures are the same as those underlying the funding measures; and
- Pension amounts have been fully funded.

Very few companies will satisfy all four conditions, and therefore a complete offset of accrued interest and expected earnings is rare.

Actual versus Expected Return The expected return on plan assets is an estimate and will be incorrect, both over the long run and year-by-year. Some might suggest that *actual* earnings should be included in pension expense, rather than the *expected* earnings, since the real earnings are known and reflect "economic reality." However, actual earnings are volatile, and pensions are long-term arrangements, so use of expected return is felt to be preferable. It can be affected by reporting biases, though, and must be evaluated carefully.

Past Service Cost

When a pension plan is first started, employees *may* be given pension entitlements for their employment prior to the initiation of the plan. In other words, the pension plan may start out with a (potentially substantial) defined benefit obligation from past service rendered by current employees. This is known as **past service cost (PSC)**. From time to time, a company will amend its pension plan, often to increase benefits, but sometimes to decrease benefits. When an existing plan is amended to change benefits *based on years of service to date,* there is a change in the defined benefit obligation that relates to prior service. The change in liability that arises from a plan amendment is another source of PSC. It is calculated as the actuarial present value of pension benefits given in a newly introduced (or amended) pension plan for years of service already rendered by current employees.

Amortization Period Past service cost is included in pension cost, amortized on a straight-line basis over the *average period until the benefits vest.* If the benefits vest immediately, the cost is recognized immediately. If the employees have already retired, the benefits would be vested when they are granted, and again the cost is recognized immediately.

Funding As always, it is important to distinguish between *accounting* for past service costs and *funding* of past service costs. For *funding* purposes, pension legislation often gives an employer a specific period, often up to 15 years, to fund any pension liability from this source. Five years is often the limit for funding PSC from plan amendments. The funding period does not dictate the amortization period.

Recognition or Not? Past service cost is usually described as an incentive for existing workers in current and future periods. Therefore, restating past years for PSC is not appropriate, and the PSC is included in pension expense over current and future periods of service, over the vesting period. This means that it is recognized as a liability, but only over the vesting period. Some suggest that PSC should be a liability as soon as it is granted. Liabilities are present obligations that the company is responsible for settling. Since employers have the obligation to meet the funding requirements of the pension plan for past service then it seems that PSC is indeed a liability. The difficulty is what to debit. Is there an asset? A lump-sum current expense? A further alternative is to debit an equity account, a reserve. We will return to this discussion as part of the larger issue of recognition of the overall financial position of the fund.

Actuarial Gains and Losses

Previous sections of this chapter stressed that assumptions and estimates have a major impact on the measurement of pension amounts. An inevitable aspect of these estimates is that they will be wrong. Re-estimates will give rise to changes, which represent **actuarial gains and losses.** The two sources are:

1. *Experience gains and losses,* caused by actual experience that shows that *what has actually occurred* is different than the assumptions made, and

2. *Changes in assumptions,* increases or decreases to pension amounts caused by changes in the assumptions *about the future* that underlie calculation of the defined benefit obligation.

Pension legislation usually requires an employer to have an **actuarial revaluation** done at least once every three years. The actuary looks at the actual performance factors since the preceding revaluation (causing experience gains and losses) and at factors affecting future outlook (causing actuarial gains and losses), and restates the defined benefit obligation accordingly. If the defined benefit obligation increases as the result of a revaluation, a loss occurs; if the defined benefit obligation decreases, a gain occurs.

Experience Gains and Losses Experience gains and losses reflect the extent to which estimates made in previous years with respect to the time now passed have turned out to be incorrect. Experience gains and losses can relate to either the actuarial obligation or plan assets, or both. The most obvious example is the return on plan assets; calculations may have assumed a 4% average return, but the actual return this year might have been 13%, or −20%. This difference creates an experience gain or loss. Other factors that may turn out to have been different than expected include actual employee turnover, retirement rates, employee earnings growth, etc.

Changes in Assumptions Adjustments that arise from **changes in assumptions** are *forward looking*; they reflect changes in the defined benefit obligation that arise from altering one or more of the assumptions about the future. Changes could be made to the discount rate, salary levels, employee turnover, early retirements, and so forth. Some level of adjustment is expected every time there is a revaluation, because the estimates are so sensitive to estimated variables.

Actuarial Gains and Losses—Accounting Alternatives

The accounting standard allows four choices with respect to recognition of actuarial gains or losses:

1. Amortization through pension expense using the 10% corridor method; *(most commonly used)*
2. Amortization through pension expense using any systematic method that is faster than the corridor method;
3. Immediate recognition through pension expense; or
4. Immediate recognition through reserves, with the annual change excluded from pension expense. Instead, it is reported in comprehensive income (as an element of other comprehensive income).

Each of these alternatives will be explained in the sections that follow. Since there are alternatives, this is clearly an area where a company has to set (and disclose) its policy. Once adopted, a policy must be applied consistently year-by-year to both gains and losses.

#1 Amortization: The 10% Corridor Method The corridor method is based on the expectation that gains and losses will offset each other over time, as investment returns fluctuate and/or successive actuarial revaluations adjust the defined benefit obligation up or down. Therefore, a cushion should be provided to avoid having normal fluctuations affect earnings and net assets. Using this method, only actuarial gains and losses *in excess of the corridor* are amortized to pension expense. This is known as the **10% corridor method** for amortization, and allows that:

- Calculations *are based on balances as of the beginning of each year*. That is, gains and losses arising in any one year are not included in the test until the following year.
- *No amortization is needed* if the cumulative actuarial gains and losses are less than the 10% corridor.
- The 10% corridor is calculated as 10% of the *greater* of:
    1. The defined benefit obligation at the beginning of the year; or
    2. The fair value of plan assets at the beginning of the year.
- If the cumulative gains or losses are larger than the corridor, *only the excess is amortized.*
- Amortization is straight-line, over the expected **average remaining service period** (ARSP) of the employee group covered.

The ARSP is the length of time that, on average, the employee group is expected to stay on the job before retirement. It is a function of employee turnover, mortality rates, retirement age, average employee age, and employment expansion (or contraction) by the employer, among other things. ARSP is stable if the workforce is stable. However, when employees retire, new employees of various ages may be hired to replace them. *Therefore, the amortization period does not necessarily decline year by year.* ARSP is recalculated periodically, and may increase, decrease, or remain the same, depending on the changing composition of the workforce.

Example Assume that Maitland Packaging Limited has a pension plan that has been in effect for some time and is subject to an actuarial revaluation every two years. ARSP is 10 years in each year between 20X3 and 20X5; for Maitland, ARSP does not change because new hiring occurs each year. Other data relating to the plan at the beginning of 20X3 are as follows:

	Total	10%
Defined benefit obligation, beginning of 20X3	$100,000	$10,000
Fair value of plan assets, beginning of 20X3	120,000	12,000
Unamortized actuarial loss, beginning of 20X3		11,000

Since the $11,000 unamortized actuarial loss is less than 10% of the *greater* of the defined benefit obligation or pension plan assets ($12,000), no amortization is required for 20X3.

Now, assume that an actuarial revaluation occurs in 20X3. The result of the revaluation is that the pension plan has an additional actuarial loss of $7,000. This is not a factor in 20X3, because opening balances are used for the test. The relevant information for the beginning of 20X4 is:

	Total	10%
Defined benefit obligation, beginning of 20X4	$110,000	$11,000
Fair value of plan assets, beginning of 20X4	130,000	13,000
Unamortized actuarial loss, beginning of 20X4 ($11,000 + $7,000)		18,000

The $18,000 unamortized actuarial loss now exceeds the higher of the two 10% amounts ($13,000), and therefore the *excess* must be amortized. For 20X4, amortization of $500 will be added to pension expense:

($18,000 − $13,000) ÷ 10 years ARSP = $500

The *unamortized* amount at the beginning of 20X5 is $17,500.

This calculation does not imply an annual amortization of $500. Instead, amortization is *recalculated each year*. The amount of the excess will change every year because (1) the corridor will change because the amounts of the obligation and assets change and (2) there may be amortization and/or new actuarial gains or losses to change the balance in actuarial losses. For example, assume the following data for Maitland for 20X5:

	Total	10%
Defined benefit obligation, beginning 20X5	$125,000	$12,500
Fair value of plan assets, beginning of 20X5	150,000	15,000
Unamortized actuarial loss, beginning of 20X5 ($18,000 − $500)		17,500

Amortization for 20X5 will be $250:

$$(\$17,500 - \$15,000) \div 10 \text{ years ARSP} = \$250$$

The unamortized loss at the beginning of 20X6 is $17,250. If either the defined benefit obligation or the value of the plan assets increases to at least $172,500 by the beginning of 20X6, then no amortization will be required because the unamortized amount will not be in excess of the 10% corridor.

#2 Faster Amortization Alternative *The 10% corridor rule (as described above) sets the minimum amortization;* a company may amortize its actuarial gains and losses using a faster method if it wishes. *Any systematic method* that results in faster recognition of actuarial gains and losses is permitted, as long as the same basis is applied to both gains and losses, and the basis is used consistently from period to period. Alternatives are endless, but include:

- *Amortizing the excess above the corridor* using a more rapid amortization method, or simply recognizing the excess in full; and
- Amortizing the *full amount of the opening balance*, with no reference to a corridor, over ARSP or a shorter period.

For example, referring to the Maitland example above, if the company were to follow a practice of amortizing the entire opening balance of actuarial gains and losses over ARSP, with no reference to a corridor, then it would record, as part of pension expense:

- In 20X3, $1,100 ($11,000 ÷ 10)
- In 20X4, $1,690 ($11,000 − $1,100 + $7,000) = ($16,900 ÷ 10)
- In 20X5, $1,521 ($16,900 − $1,690) ÷ 10)

#3 Immediate Recognition through Earnings Alternative A company can elect to include the entire amount of actuarial gains and losses in pension expense immediately. Note that this has the potential to make pension expense quite volatile since gains and losses can swing significantly. It also has the end result of including *actual return on plan assets* in pension expense. For example, if expected return were $67,000, and actual return was $21,000, pension expense would include a *net* of ($21,000) if actuarial gains and losses are immediately recognized, because the expense would include:

- ($67,000) of expected return; and
- The $46,000 difference between actual and expected return.

This negates the smoothing advantage of using expected return rather than actual return. Note that if a company elects to use a policy of immediate recognition, the policy must be applied consistently to both gains and losses. This removes the temptation to recognize all gains immediately but defer and amortize losses to the extent possible.

#4 Immediate Recognition through Reserves/Other Comprehensive Income Alternative The final alternative is to recognize all the actuarial gains and losses as they arise, *but not in pension expense*. This allows actuarial gains and losses to *bypass pension expense and bypass earnings*. Instead, the charge or credit is recorded as an equity reserve and is included in other comprehensive income (OCI). If there was a $46,000 experience loss, as in the above example, the following entry would be made:

Reserve: actuarial loss	46,000	
Accrued pension liability		46,000

The debit creates a (negative) element of shareholders' equity on the SFP that accumulates over time. The change each year is included in OCI to arrive at comprehensive income. It is not part of earnings. For example, if earnings were $100,000, then comprehensive income would be $54,000 ($1200,000 − $46,000) and a debit reserve of $46,000 is reported on the SFP.

If chosen, this alternative must be applied to all pension plans, and *the amount cannot be recycled* out of the reserve and other comprehensive income (i.e., expensed) in a later period.

The recognition of actuarial gains and losses using this alternative has no impact on earnings, and effectively eliminates the continuing item of actuarial gains and losses from the calculation of pension expense. Removing an item that is clearly related to a cost of operating activities from earnings is curious, but standard-setters allowed this treatment on the basis that it might encourage a higher incidence of recording actuarial amounts.

When the amounts are recorded, the accrued pension liability on the SFP is closer to reflecting the net status of the plan, which seems to be a desirable reporting result. The challenge is that material unrecognized amounts can now accumulate within the (popular) corridor method, resulting in no accounting recognition. We will return to this discussion as part of the larger issue of recognition of the overall financial position of the fund.

Summary of Continuing Components

The continuing components of pension expense can be summarized as follows:

Pension Expense Continuing Components	Comment
Current service cost	Measure using projected unit credit method
Interest cost	Discount rate multiplied by defined benefit obligation Or, provided by actuary
Expected earnings	Earnings rate multiplied by plan assets
Past service cost	Amortize over period to vesting; immediate recognition if vesting immediate
Actuarial gains and losses	Choice of policy: 1. Minimum is excess over 10% corridor calculated annually; amortized over average remaining service period (ARSP); or 2. Other systematic amortization, faster than corridor result; or 3. Immediate recognition in pension expense; or 4. Immediate recognition in reserves and report in other comprehensive income (i.e., exclude from pension expense).

Pension Asset/Liability Reconciliation

Pension expense is not the same as the cash paid to the pension trustee; this gives rise to an accrued pension liability or asset, as we have seen. While the change in this account is the residual amount in the pension journal entry, the resulting cumulative pension account can be proven through a reconciliation. The asset or liability pension account on the SFP is the sum of:

1. The defined benefit obligation of the pension plan;

2. Less, pension plan assets;

3. Less, any unrecognized past service cost; and

4. Less, any unrecognized actuarial losses (plus gains).

This reconciliation will be demonstrated in the example that follows.

PAYMENT OF BENEFITS

In the preceding discussion, there has been little mention of actual pension benefits paid to retired ex-employees. The reason is that the benefits payments are the responsibility of the pension plan itself (under control of the trustee), rather than of the employer. The payment of benefits *reduces both the plan assets and the accrued obligation,* but it does not affect pension expense.

In the long term, the employer must make up any deficiency in the pension plan due to higher average payouts than originally estimated, through the periodic actuarial revaluations (i.e., experience gains and losses), but these are the result of probabilistic outcomes rather than of specific payments to specific retirees.

CONCEPT REVIEW

1. List the five components that are the continuing elements of pension expense.
2. What two situations give rise to past service cost?
3. What are the alternatives for recognition of actuarial gains and losses?
4. If the 10% corridor rule is used, what is the amortization period?
5. What accounts, when combined, will equal the recorded accrued pension asset or liability?

PENSION EXPENSE EXAMPLE

Refer to Exhibit 18-2 for data for Gertron Corporation.

EXHIBIT 18-2

PENSION EXAMPLE DATA

Gertron Corporation has a defined benefit pension plan.
The following data applies to the plan:

Current service cost for 20X5, measured using the projected unit credit method	$ 556,700
Benefit payments to retired employees	134,800
Funding contributions made to the pension trustee in 20X5	1,030,000
Actual return on plan assets in 20X5	157,900

Expected return on plan assets, 5%
Interest rate related to long-term debt, 6%
Employee average remaining service life, 12 years

Balances, end of 20X4:

Defined benefit obligation, end of 20X4	$13,675,000
Pension plan assets, market value, end of 20X4	8,010,000
Unrecognized past service cost (Originally $810,000; being amortized over 2-year vesting period)	405,000
Unrecognized actuarial losses	2,260,000
Accrued pension liability in the financial statements	3,000,000

Gertron uses the 10% corridor method for amortization of unrecognized actuarial gains and losses.

To calculate 20X5 pension expense, it is necessary to gather together the five components discussed:

1. Current service cost, measured using the projected unit credit method (given)	$ 556,700
2. Interest on defined benefit obligation ($13,675,000 × 6%)	820,500
3. Expected return on plan assets ($8,010,000 × 5%)	(400,500)
4. Past service cost (remainder)	405,000
5. Actuarial gains and losses ($2,260,000 − (10% of $13,675,000)) = $892,500; $892,500/12	74,375
	$1,456,075

Highlights of the calculations:

- Interest and expected return are calculated on the opening balances. These figures may be provided by the actuary or trustee but often have to be calculated based on the information given.
- Amortization of the accumulated actuarial losses is subject to the 10% corridor. This is 10% of the defined benefit obligation (10% of $13,675,000), because the obligation is larger than pension assets. Note also that this calculation is done with *opening* balances, and *only* the portion of the unrecognized loss that is *over the corridor* is amortized.
- The amortization period is ARSP for actuarial gains and losses.
- Past service cost was originally $810,000, amortized over two years to vesting. This is the second year and the remaining $405,000 is included in pension expense.
- Benefits paid to pensioners are not a component of pension expense because these amounts are accrued over the pensioner's working life; payment is not the event that triggers an expense.

Since the funding amount is $1,030,000, the company would make an entry as follows:

Pension expense	1,456,075	
Cash		1,030,000
Accrued pension liability		426,075

The ending balance of the accrued pension liability, which appears on the SFP, is therefore $3,426,075, which is the $3,000,000 opening balance plus $426,075 from the entry above.

Reconciliation It is possible to derive the closing balances in the major pension fund elements, and use these numbers to prove the $3,426,075 accrued pension liability account.

Defined benefit obligation		
Opening balance—(credit)		$(13,675,000)
Increase due to current service cost		(556,700)
Increase due to interest accrued		(820,500)
Decrease due to pension benefits paid to pensioners		134,800
Closing balance		$(14,917,400)
Pension fund assets		
Opening balance—debit		$ 8,010,000
Increase due to actual investment income earned		157,900
Decrease due to pension benefits paid to pensioners		(134,800)
Increase due to contributions during the year		1,030,000
Closing balance		$ 9,063,100
Unamortized past service cost		
Opening balance—debit		$ 405,000
Decrease due to current year amortization		(405,000)
Closing balance		$ 0
Unrecognized actuarial losses		
Opening balance—debit		$ 2,260,000
Loss due to earnings results in the current year		
Expected earnings	$400,500	
Actual earnings	(157,900)	242,600
Decrease due to amortization		(74,375)
Closing balance		$ 2,428,225

The net amount of these accounts will be equal to the company's reported accrued pension liability:

Defined benefit obligation	$(14,917,400) credit
Pension fund assets	9,063,100 debit
Unamortized past service cost	0
Unrecognized actuarial losses	2,428,225 debit
Accrued pension liability	$ (3,426,075) credit

Notice that this liability account is the $5,854,300 net underfunded status of the plan (calculated as the defined benefit obligation of $14,917,400 less plan assets of $9,063,100) *less the unrecognized past service cost and unrecognized actuarial losses.* Since the unrecognized losses total about $2.5 million, the net status of the fund is "scaled back" on the SFP from $5.8 million and is shown as a liability of $3.4 million.

SPREADSHEET ILLUSTRATION

One of the practical problems in pension accounting is simply keeping track of all of the different amounts that are involved, and a spreadsheet helps.

First Year To begin the spreadsheet illustration, we will assume that the company, St. Mark Spas Limited (SMS) establishes a pension plan at the end of year 20X0, effective 1 January 20X1. The employees will receive pension entitlements for past years' service. The plan will be accounted for by the projected unit credit method, using "best estimate" assumptions. Additional information is obtained from the pension plan trustee and the actuary.

- The assumed earnings on plan assets and the interest rate for the defined benefit obligation is 8%.
- At 31 December 20X0, the present value of the defined benefit obligation for past service is $100,000 (at the 8% rate).
- The period to vesting of the past service costs is 10 years.
- Current service cost for the year 20X1 is $30,000, using the projected unit credit method.
- To adequately *fund* the current service cost and part of the past service cost, the company is required to make a cash contribution of $65,000 to the plan at the end of 20X1.
- Since there are no fund assets or actuarial gains or losses at the beginning of the year, expected return on fund assets is zero and there is no amortization of unrecognized actuarial amounts.

Pension expense for 20X1 is the sum of:

Current service cost (given)	$30,000
PSC amortization (straight-line over 10 years) ($100,000 ÷ 10)	10,000
Interest on the beginning-of-year defined benefit obligation ($100,000 × 8%)	8,000
Pension expense, 20X1	$48,000

Since $65,000 was paid, there will be a $17,000 ($65,000 − $48,000) accrued pension asset reported as a long-term asset.

Spreadsheet Exhibit 18-3 shows a pension plan spreadsheet. Refer to this exhibit as the explanation proceeds, below. The columnar arrangement is as follows:

- The first two numerical columns keep track of the amount of the defined benefit obligation (credit) and the pension assets (debit).

- The next two columns keep track of the unamortized pension costs. In this example, there is a separate column for past service cost and actuarial gains, because they each have a different amortization scheme.
- The next column is used for summarizing pension expense. The entries in this column will come from several of the preceding columns.
- Finally, there is a column for the recorded accrued pension asset or liability. Pension expense will be a *credit* to this account, and pension funding will be a *debit*.

As an opening 20X1 position, the $100,000 defined benefit obligation (credit, in brackets) and unrecognized past service cost (debit) are entered. They offset, and there is no opening asset or liability account on the company's books. That is, *the first four columns cross-add to equal the sixth column.*

First Year Current service cost of $30,000 increases the liability (first column) and pension expense (fifth column), as does the $8,000 interest on the opening liability. PSC amortization of $10,000 decreases the unrecognized PSC (fourth column), and increases pension expense. The $65,000 funding contribution increases fund assets (second column) and the pension asset account; pension expense, once complete, is transferred to the pension asset account. The columns are then added. Note that the first four columns again add to equal the final column. This is the reconciliation of the pension asset account, and proves that the spreadsheet is complete.

The entries for amounts are as follows:

Pension expense	48,000	
Accrued pension asset/liability		48,000
Accrued pension asset/liability	65,000	
Cash		65,000

Second Year For 20X2, there will be another calculation of current service cost. There now will be some earnings on the plan assets. SMS will receive a report from the pension plan trustee shortly after the end of the year that explains the investment activity and investment results. Assume the following:

- Current service cost is $35,000.
- The *actual* return on the plan assets was $7,200 (a return of approximately 11% on the $65,000 in the plan at the *beginning* of 20X2).
- SMS contributes $68,000 cash to the plan at the end of 20X2, in accordance with the actuary's calculations for funding.
- The value of the plan assets at the end of 20X2 is $140,200.

The *expected* return on the plan assets for 20X2 was 8% of the beginning-of-year plan assets of $65,000, or $5,200. The actual return was $7,200. The extra return of $2,000 above the expected return is an *experience gain*, which is one type of actuarial gain.

Actuarial gains/losses are not included directly in the calculation of pension expense. Instead, they are tracked in a separate schedule off the financial statements, and the accumulated actuarial gain/loss is subject to the 10% corridor test in the subsequent year. At the *beginning* of 20X2, there were no accumulated actuarial gains or losses, and therefore the corridor test is not necessary for 20X2.

The calculation of 20X2 pension expense is as follows:

Current service cost	$35,000
Past service cost amortization	10,000
Interest on defined benefit obligation, based on beginning-of-year balance ($138,000 × 8%)	11,040
Expected earnings on plan assets ($65,000 × 8%)	(5,200)
	$50,840

EXHIBIT 18-3

PENSION PLAN SPREADSHEET

| | Memorandum Accounts | | | | Statement Accounts | |
| | Values | | Unrecognized Pension Costs | | | |
	Defined Benefit Obligation dr./(cr.)	Plan Assets dr./(cr.)	Unamortized Actuarial Loss (Gain)	Past Service Cost	Pension Expense	Accrued Pension Asset (Liability)
20X1						
Beginning balances	$(100,000)			$100,000		0
Current service cost	(30,000)				$30,000 dr.	
Interest on obligation	(8,000)				8,000 dr.	
PSC amortization				(10,000)	10,000 dr.	
					$48,000 dr.	$(48,000) cr.
Funding contribution		$ 65,000				65,000 dr.
Ending balance	**$(138,000)**	**$ 65,000**	**—**	**$ 90,000**		**$ 17,000 dr.**
20X2						
Current service cost	(35,000)				35,000 dr.	
Interest on obligation	(11,040)				11,040 dr.	
Actual return on assets		7,200	$ (7,200)			
Expected return on assets			5,200		(5,200) cr.	
PSC amortization				(10,000)	10,000 dr.	
					$50,840 dr.	(50,840) cr.
Funding contribution		68,000				68,000 dr.
Ending balance	**$(184,040)**	**$140,200**	**$ (2,000)**	**$ 80,000**		**$ 34,160 dr.**
20X3						
Current service cost	(32,000)				32,000 dr.	
Interest on obligation	(14,723)				14,723 dr.	
Actual return on assets		14,000	(14,000)			
Expected return on assets			11,216		(11,216) cr.	
Actuarial revaluation	22,000		(22,000)			
PSC amortization				(10,000)	10,000 dr.	
					$45,507 dr.	(45,507) cr.
Funding contribution		37,000				37,000 dr.
Ending balance	**$(208,763)**	**$191,200**	**$(26,784)**	**$ 70,000**		**$ 25,653 dr.**
20X4						
Current service cost	(43,000)				43,000 dr.	
Interest on obligation	(16,701)				16,701 dr.	
Actual return on assets		10,000	(10,000)			
Expected return on assets			15,296		(15,296) cr.	
Benefit payments	18,000	(18,000)				
PSC amortization				(10,000)	10,000 dr.	
Excess actuarial gain amortization			591		(591) cr.*	
					$53,814 dr.	(53,814) cr.
Funding contribution		68,000				68,000 dr.
Ending balance	**$(250,464)**	**$251,200**	**$(20,897)**	**$ 60,000**		**$ 39,839 dr.**

*[$26,784 − (208,763 × 10%)] ÷ 10 years = $591 amortization of excess.

The entries for the 20X2 expense and funding payment are as follows:

Pension expense	50,840	
Accrued pension asset/liability		50,840
Accrued pension asset/liability	68,000	
Cash		68,000

Refer again to the spreadsheet in Exhibit 18-3. Find the following items:

- Current service cost of $35,000 increases the defined benefit obligation and pension expense.
- Interest on the defined benefit obligation of $11,040 also increases the defined benefit obligation and pension expense.
- The actual return in plan assets of $7,200 increases fund assets *but is then entered as a credit in the unamortized gains and losses column*, column 3. Actual return is *not* part of pension expense.
- Expected return of $5,200 is also entered in column 3, as a debit, and is recorded as a reduction to pension expense. In column 3, this leaves the difference between actual and expected return. This is an experience gain (credit) of $2,000.
- As in 20X1, past service cost is amortized by $10,000, increasing pension expense and reducing the unamortized amount.
- Funding contributions of $68,000 increase fund assets and are entered as a debit in the final column.
- To complete the spreadsheet, pension expense is totalled and entered as a credit in the final column. The columns are totalled and cross-added. Again, the total of the first four columns equals the final column, the pension asset account.

Third Year Assume the following additional facts for 20X3:

- Current service cost is $32,000, as calculated by the actuary.
- Actual return on the plan assets is $14,000.
- The first biennial actuarial revaluation occurs. Due to changes in assumptions, the defined benefit obligation is decreased by $22,000.
- SMS contributes $37,000 cash to the plan at the end of 20X3.

At the beginning of 20X3, there was an unamortized actuarial gain (i.e., an experience gain) of $2,000. A corridor test must be applied to this amount to see whether any amortization is needed in 20X3. Amortization is not necessary if the unamortized actuarial gain is less than 10% of the *higher* of the beginning-of-year accrued obligation and the beginning-of-year pension plan assets:

	Total	10%
Defined benefit obligation	$184,040	$18,404
Pension plan assets	140,200	14,020

The unamortized actuarial gain of $2,000 is well below the 10% limit of $18,404, and therefore no amortization is necessary. Bear in mind, however, that the company can establish another policy regarding recognition of this amount as long as it results in faster, or complete, recognition. The company may also record this amount in OCI. Amortization using the 10% corridor method is only one alternative policy choice.

The calculation of pension expense is as follows:

Current service cost	$32,000
Past service cost amortization	10,000
Interest on defined benefit obligation, beginning-of-year balance ($184,040 × 8%)	14,723
Expected earnings on plan assets ($140,200 × 8%)	(11,216)
	$45,507

The entries for these amounts are as follows:

Pension expense	45,507	
Accrued pension asset/liability		45,507
Accrued pension asset/liability	37,000	
Cash		37,000

Spreadsheet Refer to Exhibit 18-3. The following items are entered on the spreadsheet:

- The current service cost of $32,000 and the interest on the defined benefit obligation of $14,723 are added to the obligation and to pension expense.
- *Actual* earnings on the plan assets of $14,000 are entered in column 2 (as an increase in the value of the plan assets) and in column 3 (unamortized actuarial gain).
- The *expected* earnings on plan assets of $11,216 partially offsets the actual actuarial gain in column 3, leaving only the difference between expected and actual in the unamortized column. Expected earnings are also entered in column 5, pension expense.
- The $22,000 gain from the actuarial revaluation *reduces* the defined benefit obligation, and it also is entered in column 3 as a credit (gain) in the unamortized actuarial gain column.
- The past service cost amortization of $10,000 reduces the unamortized amount and is a component of pension expense.
- Total pension expense is credited to the accrued pension asset/liability, in the last column.
- The funding contribution is added to the pension plan assets and is debited to the accrued pension asset/liability.

In 20X3, the expense is higher than the funding, and therefore the debit balance of the accrued pension asset is reduced by $8,507, to a debit balance of $25,653 ($34,160 − $8,507).

Fourth Year During the fourth year, the SMS pension plan pays benefits to retired employees. Assume the following facts for 20X4:

- Current service cost is $43,000;
- Actual return on plan assets is $10,000;
- SMS contributes $68,000 to the plan;
- Benefits of $18,000 are paid to retirees by the trustee; and
- ARSP is 10 years.

The first four lines of the 20X4 section at the bottom of Exhibit 18-3 are essentially the same as has been described above for 20X3—amounts are for current service cost, interest, actual return on assets, and expected return on assets.

The fifth line introduces something new to our example—the payment of benefits. Benefits are paid by the trustee out of plan assets, and therefore they represent a decrease in the value of the plan assets. As well, part of the defined benefit obligation to these employees has been fulfilled, and benefit payments reduce the defined benefit obligation as well. Benefit payments have no impact on pension *expense*.

The next line shows the amortization of past service cost; there is no change in this item from previous years.

At the beginning of 20X4, there is an accumulated actuarial gain of $26,784. This amount comprises experience gains arising from strong earnings on the plan assets, plus the $22,000 actuarial revaluation in 20X3. The corridor test must be applied to see whether we should amortize any of this gain.

The higher of the obligation and the assets *at the beginning of the year* is the $208,763 defined benefit obligation. Ten percent of that amount is $20,876. The accumulated actuarial gain is greater than that amount, and therefore amortization of the excess is necessary in 20X4. The amortization is $591:

$$[\$26,784 - (\$208,763 \times 10\%)] \div 10 \text{ years ARSP} = \$591$$

This amortization reduces the unamortized amount and is *credited* to pension expense (it is a gain) in Exhibit 18-3 in the seventh line for 20X4.

Summary of Spreadsheet Adjustments

Refer to the following table for a summary of spreadsheet items caused by continuing elements of pension expense.

Column	Normal Balance	Increase	Decrease	Either Increase or Decrease
Defined benefit obligation	Credit	• Current service cost • Interest on obligation • New past service cost	• Benefit payments to retirees	• Actuarial revaluation (credit this column if liability increases and debit this column if liability decreases)
Pension plan assets	Debit	• Annual funding contribution • Actual earnings	• Benefit payments to retirees • Actual losses	
Unamortized actuarial gains or losses	Debit if loss Credit if gain		• Amortization of opening balance, if any	• New actuarial revaluations (debit this column if liability increases and credit this column if liability decreases) • Difference between actual fund earnings (credit this column) and expected earnings (debit this column)
Unamortized PSC	Debit	• Past service cost from plan initiation or amendment	• Amortization of opening balance	
Pension expense	Debit	• Current service cost • Interest on obligation • Amortization of PSC	• Expected earnings on plan assets	• Amortization of experience gains (decrease expense) or losses (increase expense)
Accrued pension asset/liability	Debit if an asset Credit if a liability			• Credit for the expense amount • Debit for the funding amount

1. How does expected return affect pension expense?

2. How is the corridor calculated with reference to unamortized actuarial gains and losses?

3. What two spreadsheet accounts are changed by benefits paid to employees?

4. What two spreadsheet accounts are changed by newly arising actuarial losses?

SPECIAL COMPONENTS OF PENSION EXPENSE

Plan Settlements and Curtailments

On occasion, an employer may end its legal liability under an existing defined benefit pension plan, or end a portion of the benefits under a plan. This is called a **pension plan settlement**; the obligation to the pensionable group is settled by transferring assets to a trustee, purchasing specified annuities for employees, or otherwise terminating the financial commitments of the employer.

A pension plan curtailment takes place when there is a significant reduction in the number of employees covered by a plan, or some significant element of future service will no longer qualify for benefits. This may happen when a company closes down a division or otherwise significantly restructures or downsizes operations. It may also happen when workers agree to a major change in benefits, perhaps to preserve competitiveness.

In these circumstances, there is likely to be a substantial gain. Normally, the pension is closed out at the entitlement *earned by the employees to date* rather than at the entitlement projected in the actuarial estimates. That is, the accounting numbers are based on the projected unit credit method but the legal obligation on settlement is based on the benefits accumulated to date. Sometimes, a curtailment or settlement agreement may include special pension benefits that will increase the company's obligation and thereby result in a loss. It depends on the situational variables. *The gain or loss is the sum of the change in the defined benefit obligation, the change in pension assets, and the write-off of related, unrecognized amounts.*

Gains and losses that arise from settlements or curtailments *are recognized immediately* in the period when the company has a demonstrable commitment. The gains and losses are not subject to amortization. Settlements often relate to employees who are no longer with the company, and therefore the ARSP related to these employees is zero.

Classification Classification of a gain or loss on settlement or curtailment will depend on circumstances. The gain or loss would be included in pension expense if a plan settlement arises in the continuing segments of the business. Often, though, plan settlements and curtailments arise when a company restructures or discontinues some aspect(s) of its operations. When this happens, the costs associated with this business reorganization are presented separately in earnings, as *discontinued operations*. Separate line item disclosure also is usually given to the costs of *restructuring*, typically as an unusual item. Therefore, settlement/curtailment gains and losses arising from discontinued operations or from major restructuring will be included with that item, wherever it is classified.

Limit on Accrued Pension Asset

We observed earlier in this chapter that a company may fund its pension plan faster than it records pension expense, resulting in an asset that is akin to a "prepaid pension." This might happen if (1) the plan is funded by the level contribution method, while accounting uses the projected unit credit method, or (2) the assumptions used by the actuary for funding are more conservative than the "best estimate" assumptions used for accounting.

Another set of circumstances that will result in an accrued pension asset is when unrecognized past service costs plus unrecognized actuarial losses are significant in relation to the defined benefit obligation and plan assets. This was demonstrated in the spreadsheet example, above, where, in 20X1, the defined benefit obligation was $138,000 and pension assets were $65,000. This plan is therefore underfunded by accounting measures in the amount of ($73,000). However, because of the $90,000 unamortized PSC, there was an *accrued pension asset* of $17,000.

Whatever the cause, pension assets result. Every asset must be subject to a validity check to *ensure that the asset is not overvalued and that the enterprise will obtain value from that asset in the future.* This applies to pension assets as well. Therefore, standards require that an enterprise limit any pension asset to the amount that can be *recovered in the future.* Sometimes such future recoveries are realized through a **pension holiday,** whereby the employer in an overfunded plan is permitted to temporarily reduce or eliminate payments for the current service funding requirements. In other cases, recoveries are through use: simply through amortization of PSC and actuarial losses. There are complex rules and definitions in this area to establish the recoverable amount, which is called the *asset ceiling.* In general, if a company has a pension asset, and if it is limited by the asset ceiling, *additional pension expense is recorded in the period.* Valuations are done yearly.

Termination Benefits

An employer sometimes offers special incentives to induce employees to retire, or to take early retirement. Enhanced retirement offers are called **termination benefits,** and may include lump-sum payments, continuation of salary, and enhanced pension benefits. With respect to enhanced pension benefits, these special termination benefits are in addition to the benefits normally offered to employees. Therefore, the cost of providing these special benefits has not been included in the actuarial calculations for the employee group, either for funding or for accounting purposes. Consequently, special termination benefits require recognition of extra cost.

The costs of special termination benefits are accrued in the financial statements as an expense and a liability, once a company is demonstrably committed to the termination. This commitment must take the form of a formal and detailed plan. The cost is recognized as a lump sum. Since the employees are leaving the company, amortization of the cost over future periods is not appropriate.

The cost of pension benefits included in termination benefits may be part of pension expense, if they are in the ordinary course of business. Alternatively, they may be part of discontinued operations or restructuring, as described for settlements and curtailments.

Transitional Amortization

Historically, Canadian companies have been permitted to avoid complete retrospective application of changes in pension accounting standards, because of the complexity of estimates. Companies were permitted to establish an unrecognized *transitional amount* for the difference between measurements under old and new standards. This transitional amount was amortized over the ARSP. Under IFRS, the pension standard must be applied **retrospectively**, with all prior years restated, and thus transitional amounts cease to exist.

CONCEPT REVIEW

1. Sometimes losses or gains from plan settlements, plan curtailments, and termination benefits are not included as part of *pension expense* in earnings but are reported elsewhere. When (and where) would such losses or gains be reported separately from pension expense?

2. Under what circumstances will a company have to place a limit on an accrued pension asset? How will this affect pension expense?

RECORDING THE NET PENSION PLAN STATUS

This chapter has shown that the net pension asset or liability consists of the following elements:

1. Defined benefit obligation (credit)
2. Pension fund assets (debit),
3. All unrecognized amounts, such as PSC (debit), or actuarial losses (debit) or actuarial gains (credit)

= Accrued pension asset/liability (debit or credit)

Companies with underfunded plans *and large unrecognized amounts* might actually show *pension assets*. The following might be typical early in the life of a pension plan, or after plan amendment:

Defined benefit obligation	$(675,000)
Pension fund assets	100,000
Unrecognized PSC	600,000
Accrued pension asset	$ 25,000

That is, there are significant obligations, minimal assets, and major unamortized past service costs. The result is a pension asset, which seems counter-intuitive: the pension plan is *underfunded*, but the financial statements show a pension fund *asset?*

The same result could occur if there were actuarial losses that were not yet recognized in pension expense because of the corridor rule. That is, there is an underfunded plan, but an asset is recognized because the unrecognized losses are large. This may well happen after large losses on the investment portfolio. *A reported asset seems to misstate the economic substance of the pension plan.*

Now, it may well be that the underfunded position of the plan is no cause for concern among pensioners. If the underfunded position is caused by past service from plan initiation or amendment, there is likely a 5, 10, or 15-year plan to address the underfunded position. Alternatively, the underfunded portion of the pension plan can be a cause of financial instability for the company and a significant cause for concern for employees and retirees.

Recording Alternative A pension represents an obligation of the company that will use future resources. Its net status is not necessarily recorded in the statement of financial position. There are those who feel strongly that the net underfunded position of the plan, which is $575,000 in the above example, should be recorded as a liability.[2] The suggestion is that the offsetting debit would be reflected in reserves, and recognized in comprehensive income as an element of other comprehensive income. The adjustment would not change earnings. Some of the arguments in favour of recording the net pension amount are:

1. The net position of the plan appears to meet the definition of a liability, since it is a present economic obligation for which the company is responsible. Since the company is a going concern, it is obliged to meet pension obligations.

---

[2] Another alternative is that the entire defined benefit obligation should be recorded as a liability, and pension fund assets reported as a separate long-term asset. This is an issue of reporting entity and will not be pursued in this discussion.

2. Pension amounts are subject to certain estimates, but these estimates can be made sufficiently reliable such that recognition is appropriate.

3. Some research indicates that analysts and other users react differently to the underfunded status of the plan if it were recorded in the SFP, versus if it were simply disclosed in the notes. If this is true, then disclosure is not a good substitute for recognition.[3]

The amounts involved are material, and widespread. One estimate is that the average Canadian corporate plan is underfunded by approximately 20%, a total of about $50 billion for the economy as a whole.[4] The autoparts, forestry, and manufacturing sectors, which are labour intensive, are particularly affected.[5]

Accounting standards in the United States now require recognition of the net status of the plan. As we have seen, the IASB allows recognition of actuarial amounts through reserves, reported as an element of other comprehensive income. This is less than complete recognition, but it is an attempt to *increase the portion of the plan status that is recognized versus unrecognized.* The IASB has a pension accounting project underway, which may result in required recognition of the net status of the plan in a manner similar to the U.S. approach. In the meantime, note disclosure for pension plan information is critical in understanding the financial commitments of the company.

OTHER POST-EMPLOYMENT BENEFITS

Post-employment benefits typically involve more than pensions. Employers may include supplementary health care, prescription drug plans, dental benefits, and various insurance plans for retirees. Because of universal health care in Canada, the cost of these benefits is less than in the United States. However, the cost of **other post-employment benefits** (OPEBs) can still be substantial.

There are some practical differences between pensions and other post-employment benefits, summarized as follows:

	Pensions	Other Post-employment Benefits
Use	Regular monthly payments with predictable or estimable increases until entitlements cease	Sporadic use from employee to employee and unpredictable cost increases
Beneficiary	Retired employee usually with some survivor rights	Retired employee and family members, as specified in the plan
Funding	Plans are typically registered; likely to be fully or mostly funded during the working life of the employee	Plans are typically unregistered. Likely to be substantially unfunded because contributions to unregistered plans are not tax deductible for the employer
Revaluations	Periodic as required by legislation	Likely frequent, to reflect changed cost estimates

The differences in usage of the plans, in particular, make cost estimation even more uncertain than the already-uncertain pension estimates. Nonetheless, the relevance of the information dictates that reliability be sacrificed, with appropriate disclosure of variables used.

---

[3] Refer to the discussion in Marc Picconi, "The Perils of Pensions: Does Pension Accounting Lead Investors and Analysts Astray?" *The Accounting Review*, 81, No. 4 (July 2006), pages 925–955.

[4] Jacquie McNish, "Retirement Dreams Under Siege."

[5] See Allan Robinson, "U.S. Accounting Changes May Affect Canadian Firms," *The Globe and Mail*, September 29, 2006, n.p.

For many years, the cost of OPEBs was accounted for on a *pay-as-you-go* basis. That is, when the benefits were actually paid out, or health care premiums paid for employees after retirement, the amount would be expensed at that time. This method was obviously flawed, because the benefit was earned by the employee during employment, and *the company had an obligation prior to the retirement period.* Therefore, accounting standards now require that OPEBs be accounted for in a similar manner as pensions. That is, the annual expense is:

1. Current service cost;

2. *Plus* interest on the OPEB obligation;

3. *Minus* expected earnings on segregated fund assets, if any;

4. *Plus* recognition of past service costs;

5. *Plus or minus* recognition of actuarial gains or losses (alternative policies permitted).

From an accounting perspective, the most significant difference between OPEB and pension situations is that there are unlikely to be much, if any, in segregated asset balances for OPEBs (see chart, above).

Example Review the spreadsheet in Exhibit 18-4, which reflects the following data for 20X8:

Opening OPEB liability	$175,000	Interest rate for assets	4%
Opening plan assets	10,000	Contribution paid to other post-employment health care fund	$22,000
Opening unamortized PSC	$15,000	Benefits paid by other post-employment health care fund to retirees during the period	$24,000
Opening unamortized actuarial loss; corridor method is used	$18,700	ARSP	12 years
Current service cost	$34,000	Vesting period remaining	5 years
Interest rate for obligation	6%	Actual return on plan assets	$250

This spreadsheet follows the now-familiar pattern. Current service cost of $34,000 increases the obligation and the expense, as does the $10,500 interest calculated on the opening obligation balance. Expected earnings of $400 reduce the expense, and actual earnings increase the fund balance, while the difference between actual ($250) and expected ($400) earnings is part of the unrecognized amount. Past service cost is amortized over the five-year vesting period, reducing the unrecognized amount and increasing expense. The excess unamortized actuarial amount, based on the corridor method and opening balances, is amortized to the expense. Finally, cash paid to the fund increases the asset balance and affects the asset or liability account, and benefits paid reduce assets and the obligation.

CASH FLOW STATEMENT

The cash flows relating to pensions are almost certainly different from the accounting expense. On the cash flow statement, the difference between pension expense and pension cash flow is an adjustment for "non-cash items." Cash paid to the pension fund during the year is required disclosure in the pension note.

EXHIBIT 18-4

OPEB SPREADSHEET

20X8	OPEB Obligation	Plan Assets	Actuarial G/L	PSC	OPEB Expense	Accrued Asset(Liab)
			Memorandum Accounts		**Statement Accounts**	
			Unrecognized			
Opening	$(175,000)	$10,000	$18,700	$15,000		$(131,300)*
Current service cost	(34,000)				$34,000	
Interest expense (6%)	(10,500)				10,500	
Expected earnings (4%)			400		(400)	
Actual return		250	(250)			
Amortization of PSC (5 years)				(3,000)	3,000	
Amortization of actuarial gain outside corridor**			(100)		100	
Contribution		22,000				22,000
Benefits paid	24,000	(24,000)			$47,200	(47,200)
Totals	$(195,500)	$ 8,250	$18,750	$12,000		$(156,500)*

*Sum of first four columns
**($18,700 − $17,500)/12

DISCLOSURE RECOMMENDATIONS

The disclosure recommendations for post-employment benefits are unusually extensive. The financial statements themselves include only two elements relating to pensions and other post-employment benefits:

1. On the statement of comprehensive income, the amount of expense relating to providing post-employment benefits; and

2. On the statement of financial position, the net *accrued pension asset or liability* that reflects the difference between the accumulated accounting expense and the accumulated funding. This represents the net position of the pension fund *after unrecognized amounts are netted out.*

These amounts provide little direct information about the nature of post-employment benefits and the manner in which they are being recognized. Therefore, disclosure is the only viable way to assist users.

Basic Disclosures

Companies must disclose adequate information to allow readers to evaluate the nature of the defined benefit plans and the financial effects of changes in those plans during the period. A description of the plan is required. Disclosure includes important accounting policy choices (particularly the method chosen for recognition of actuarial gains and losses) and information about measurements used for pension accounting. Measurement disclosures are extensive. All calculations and assumptions must be disclosed. *Some* major items:

1. A reconciliation of relevant pension amounts to the asset or liability account (that is, the first four spreadsheet columns, to equal the asset or liability account);

2. Amount of expense recognized for the period, and the components of the expense;

3. Changes in reserves and other comprehensive income related to the pension, if any;

4. A reconciliation of the defined benefit obligation, from the beginning to the end of the year, labelling each major element of change;

5. A reconciliation of pension plan assets, from the beginning to the end of the year, labeling each major element of change;

6. Description of the basis used to determine expected return on plan assets;

7. Actual return on assets during the year;

8. Amount of funding contributions made by the company expected for the next period;

9. Major actuarial assumptions—the interest rate used for the defined benefit obligation, expected long-term rate on plan assets, the projected rate of salary increase, and the assumed health care cost trend rate; and

10. The effect of a 1% change, both up and down, in medical costs.

The daunting list of disclosures represents an attempt to converge the disclosures required in many jurisdictions.

Disclosure Example

Daimler AG provides an example of post-employment benefit disclosure. The accounting policy note states:

Pension benefits

Pensions and similar obligations. The measurement of defined benefit plans for pensions and other post-employment benefits (e.g. medical care) in accordance with *IAS 19 Employee Benefits* is based on the projected unit credit method. For the valuation of defined post-employment benefit plans, differences between actuarial assumptions used and actual results and changes in actuarial assumptions result in actuarial gains and losses, which have to be amortized in future periods. Amortization of unrecognized actuarial gains and losses. ... is recorded in accordance with the "corridor approach." This approach requires partial amortization of actuarial gains and losses in the following year with an effect on earnings if the unrecognized gains and losses exceed 10 percent of the greater of (1) the defined postemployment benefit obligation or (2) the fair value of the plan assets. In such cases, the amount of amortization recognized by the Group is the resulting excess divided by the average remaining service period of active employees expected to receive benefits under the plan. When the benefits of a plan are changed, the portion of the change in benefit relating to past service by employees is recognized in profit or loss on a straight-line basis over the average period until the benefits become vested. To the extent that the benefits vest immediately, the impact is recognized directly in profit or loss. ...

Source: http://www.daimler.com/Projects/c2c/channel/documents/1813321_DAI_2009_Annual_Report.pdf accessed June 2010.

Exhibit 18-5 shows *a portion* of the company's note relating to post-employment benefits. Read it carefully. Note:

• The plans are underfunded by €5,905 million at the end of 2009 but Daimler records less than this (€3,109 million) as a pension liability on the SFP because of unrecognized actuarial losses.

• There are €2,795 million of unrecognized actuarial losses, but only €27 million of actuarial losses are included in pension expense because the corridor method is used.

• The largest single component of pension expense is interest, at €847 million. Expected return is €660 million, and current service cost is €295 million.

• Information regarding the change in the defined benefit obligation and plan assets is provided.

• Key assumptions are provided, and explained in a portion of the pension note that is not repeated. These assumptions include interest and asset return rates, and also wage increase assumptions.

EXHIBIT 18-5

DAIMLER AG—PENSION DISCLOSURES

The Group provides pension benefits with defined entitlements to almost all of its employees, which have to be accounted for as defined benefit plans and are funded in large part with assets. Starting in 2008, the majority of the active employees are entitled to pay-related defined pension benefits. Under these plans, employees earn benefits for each year of service. The benefits earned per year of service are based on the salary level and age of the respective employee.

The following information with respect to the Group's pension plans is presented separately for German plans and non-German plans. . . .

As at December 31, 2009
[Comparative data omitted]

In millions of €	Total	German plans	Non-German plans
Present value of defined pension obligations	16,529	14,183	2,346
Less fair value of plan assets	(10,624)	(9,197)	(1,427)
Funded status deficit (surplus)	5,905	4,986	919
A reconciliation of the funded status to the net amounts recognized in the consolidated statement of financial position is as follows:			
Funded status	5,905	4,986	919
Unrecognized actuarial net losses	(2,795)	(2,465)	(330)
Unrecognized past service cost	(1)		(1)
Net amounts recognized	3,109	2,521	588
...			
The development of the present value of the defined benefit obligations and the fair value of plan assets is as follows:			
Present value of the defined benefit obligation as of January 1	15,044	12,780	2,264
Current service cost	295	226	69
Interest cost	847	734	113
Contributions by plan participants	57	54	3
Actuarial (gains) losses	1,134	1,015	119
Past service cost (income)	4	—	4
Curtailments	—	—	—
Settlements	(101)	—	(101)
Pension benefits paid	(733)	(626)	(107)
Currency exchange-rate and other changes	(18)	—	(18)
Present value of the defined benefit obligation as of December 31	16,529	14,183	2,346
...			

continued on next page

EXHIBIT 18-5 (cont'd)

In millions of €	Total	German plans	Non-German plans
Fair value of plan assets as January 1 ...	10,110	8,796	1,314
Actual return on plan assets	628	452	176
Contributions by the employer	602	500	102
Contributions by plan participants	3	—	3
Settlements	(89)	—	(89)
Benefits paid	(645)	(551)	(94)
Currency exchange-rate and other changes	15	—	15
Fair value of plan assets as of December 31	10,624	9,197	1,427

...

The components of net pension cost ...

	Total	German plans	Non-German plans
Current service cost	295	226	69
Interest cost	847	734	113
Expected return on plan assets	(660)	(568)	(92)
Amortization of net actuarial (gains)/losses	27	14	13
Past service cost/(income)	5	—	5
Net periodic pension cost (income)...	514	406	108
Curtailments and settlements	17	—	17
Net pension cost (income)...	531	406	125

Source: © Daimler AG.

CONCEPT REVIEW

1. What are the arguments in favour of recording the net status of a pension plan, without netting unrecognized amounts?
2. Name the five continuing components of the expense for a post-employment benefit such as extended medical care.
3. What is the likely intent of requiring extensive disclosures for pension assumptions?

PROPOSALS FOR CHANGE

The IASB is considering an exposure draft that would make some significant changes to pension accounting. As an overview, the changes suggest that the cost of long-term employee benefits should be segmented; the elements would be classified and measured as follows:

Element	Measurement	Recognized in
Service cost	Current service cost, plus past service cost granted in the period	Earnings
Net interest	(Defined benefit obligation, less pension fund assets) × Interest rate based on corporate bond yield	Earnings, as a finance revenue or expense
Remeasurement	Actuarial and experience gains and losses	Reserves and other comprehensive income

Of note:

- Service cost would include only current service cost and past service cost; past service cost would not be amortized. This expense would be reported with operating expenses.
- The *interest component* is treated quite differently than under current standards. Interest expense and interest revenue would no longer be separately measured for the defined benefit obligations and the fund assets, using different interest rates. Instead, the *net position* of the fund would be used to base a single interest calculation. This interest element would not be reported as part of pension expense, but rather as a separate finance revenue or expense.
- All remeasurements (actuarial and experience gains and losses) would be recorded immediately, but not to earnings. Instead, an equity reserve account would be used to permanently reflect these amounts.
- The exposure draft also includes suggested for revised disclosure.

Pension standards are overdue for revisions, but changes are complex because the underlying economics and legalities of pensions are so complicated. Since the size of pension plans is material, changes can result in significant differences in financial reporting metrics. Standard-setters must proceed with caution. If adopted, these changes would likely be implemented in 2013 or beyond.

ACCOUNTING STANDARDS FOR PRIVATE ENTERPRISES

Defined Contribution Plans Private enterprises with defined contribution plans follow the approach described in the chapter material. There are no differences between ASPE and IFRS standards in this category.

Defined Benefit Plans—Simplified Approach Private companies with defined benefit plans are granted a simplified accounting approach under ASPE *if the company chooses.* This simplified accounting works as follows:

- The actuarial cost method used for accounting must be the same as that adopted for funding.
- Pension expense includes current service cost, interest on the defined benefit obligation, the *actual return on fund assets, ALL PSC, and ALL actuarial gains and losses.* There are no amortizations.

Defined Benefit Plans—Standard Approach Under ASPE, pension expense for defined benefit plans can be determined using the approach used in Canadian standards pre-2011. This method must be used if the simplified approach is not adopted. The continuing elements of pension expense:

Pension Expense Continuing Components	Comment
Current service cost	Measure using projected benefit method (identical to projected unit credit method)
Interest cost	Appropriate borrowing rate multiplied by the defined benefit obligation
Expected return	Expected long-term earnings rate multiplied by plan assets; plan assets valued at fair value, or on a *market-related fair value* that approaches fair value over an averaging period
Past service cost	Amortize over employee group *expected period to full eligibility (EPFE)* for pension benefits
Actuarial gains and losses	Minimum is excess over 10% corridor calculated annually; amortized to pension expense over average remaining service period (ARSP), or *any other recognition or amortization method* to pension expense that is faster than corridor result

Note that, under ASPE, PSC is amortized over a long-term period, the **expected period to full eligibility (EPFE),** while IASB standards use the *vesting period.* The EPFE is the length of time that, on average, the current employee group must work to be entitled to full pension. EPFE may be compared to the average remaining service period (ARSP) of the employee group. For example, say that an employee is entitled to 2% of her final pay for each year worked, to a maximum of 60% of final pay. This takes 30 years. Assume that the employee is hired at age 25, and will likely work until she is 65. Her ARSP is her 40-year working life, but her EPFE is 30 years, because she has "maxed out" her pension entitlements at that point.

As compared to IFRS, the ASPE approach has differences related to asset valuation and rates of return to be used. In addition, under ASPE, actuarial gains and losses cannot be recognized in reserves and other comprehensive income. The corridor method may be used, but all amortization or recognition *must be included in pension expense.*

An example is included with the review question at the end of the chapter.

There are many other differences between ASPE requirements and IFRS, related to plan curtailment and settlement, multi-employer plans, measurement dates, and the like.

RELEVANT STANDARDS

IASB:

• *IAS* 19, Employee Benefits

CICA Handbook Part II:

• Section 3461, Employee Future Benefits

SUMMARY OF KEY POINTS

1. In a defined contribution pension plan, the amounts to be paid into the pension plan fund are determined, and the eventual pension is a function of the amounts paid in plus the earnings accumulated in the pension fund. The annual expense is normally equal to the contribution made to the plan.

2. In a defined benefit pension plan, the retirement benefits are defined as a function of either years of service or employee earnings, or both. The employer is responsible for contributing enough into the fund that, combined with investment earnings, will pay the pension to which the employee is entitled.

3. Pension plans are contributory when the employee pays into the plan. An employee has ownership of pension assets when rights have vested. Vesting is governed by pension legislation and pension contracts.

4. An employer's annual contribution to a defined benefit pension plan is calculated with use of actuarial cost methods. Alternatives exist with respect to the variables that are projected, and the funding patterns.

5. Because of the long time span involved in pension estimates, current service and past service costs are sensitive to the underlying assumptions used, including the interest rate assumption. Best estimates must be used for accounting purposes.

6. For a defined benefit pension plan, pension expense for a year is a combination of (1) current service cost measured using the projected unit credit actuarial cost method, (2) plus interest on the defined benefit obligation, (3) minus expected earnings on the plan assets, (4) plus recognition of past service cost, (5) plus or minus recognition of actuarial gains or losses. Other special components of pension expense may arise from time to time.

7. Current service cost is an estimate of the cost of providing the pension entitlement that the employee has earned in the current year of employment. Past service cost is an estimate of the expected present value of retrospective pension entitlements relating to previous years' service when a new pension plan is instituted or when an existing plan is amended. Past service costs are included in pension expense over the vesting period.

8. Actuarial gains and losses arise either because actual experience is different from expectations or because assumptions about the future are changed, or both. The 10% corridor method establishes the minimum amount to include in pension expense, but a faster amortization method may be used. Another alternative is immediate recognition in pension expense. Immediate recognition in reserves, reported as an element of other comprehensive income, is also allowed.

9. Benefits paid to retirees reduce the value of the plan assets and reduce the defined benefit obligation. Benefits paid do not enter directly into the calculation of pension expense.

10. The difference between the recognized pension expense and cash paid to the pension trustee is accumulated in an asset or liability account called an accrued pension asset/ liability. This account is equal to the *defined benefit obligation, netted with fund assets and all unrecognized amounts.*

11. A spreadsheet is a useful way to organize data needed for pension plan accounting. The spreadsheet tracks the defined benefit obligation, pension plan assets, unrecognized amounts, pension expense, and the asset or liability pension account.

12. Special components of pension expense include gains and losses on plan settlement or curtailment (unless part of a discontinued operation or unusual item), recognition of termination benefits, and any adjustment to the expense needed to avoid overvaluation of a net pension asset.

13. Some suggest that the pension plan obligation, net of plan assets (but not net of unrecorded amounts) should be recorded as an asset or liability element. This is justified based on the definition of a liability, the ability to measure the amounts reliably, and the improved usefulness of the financial statements for users.

14. Other post-employment benefits include supplementary medical and dental plans for retirees. These benefits are accounted for in a similar fashion as pensions, with the cost accrued over the working life of the employee.

15. Companies must provide extensive pensions disclosures with respect to accounting policies and measurement of estimates. Disclosures include plan assets, the defined benefit obligation, and all unrecognized amounts, reconciled to the recorded pension asset or liability.

16. Private Canadian companies with defined benefit pension plans may opt to use a simplified version of pension accounting, where the funding method is used for accounting measurements and there are no amortizations. Otherwise, the measurement of pension expense follows pre-2011 Canadian GAAP standards, with PSC amortized over EPFE and fewer options available for actuarial gains and losses.

KEY TERMS

10% corridor method, 1053
accrued pension liability/asset, 1050
accumulated benefit method, 1048
actuarial cost methods, 1046
actuarial gains and losses, 1052
actuarial revaluations, 1053
actuary, 1042
average remaining service period
   (ARSP), 1053
changes in assumptions, 1053
contributory pension plan, 1042
current service cost, 1049
death benefits, 1046
defined benefit obligation, 1051
defined benefit plan, 1042
defined contribution plan, 1042
expected period to full eligibility
   (EPFE), 1075

final pay pension plan, 1046
flat benefit pension plan, 1046
funding, 1046
level contribution method, 1048
non-contributory pension plan, 1043
other post-employment benefits, 1068
past service cost (PSC), 1052
pension holiday, 1066
pension plan curtailment, 1065
pension plan settlement, 1065
projected unit credit method, 1048
recycling, 1056
registered pension plan, 1043
survivor benefits, 1046
termination benefits, 1067
trustee, 1043
vested benefits, 1043

REVIEW PROBLEM

The following data relate to a defined benefit pension plan:

Defined benefit obligation, 1 January 20X6	$25,000
Long-term interest rate on debt	10%
Unrecognized past service cost from amendment dated 31 December 20X5 (not amortized in 20X5)	$10,000
Unrecognized PSC from plan initiation: $10,000 at the initiation date of 1 January 20X0; unrecognized amount at 1 January 20X6. Original vesting period was 10 years	$4,000
Unrecognized actuarial gain, 1 January 20X6	$4,700
Actual return on plan assets for 20X6	$2,000
Fair value of plan assets, 1 January 20X6	$16,000
Long-run expected rate of return on plan assets	10%
Average remaining service life of the employee group	14 years
Vesting period re: PSC from plan amendment	5 years
Funding payment at year-end 20X6	$4,000
Benefits paid to retirees in 20X6	$5,000
Current service cost for 20X6	$9,000

Required:

1. Compute pension expense for 20X6.
2. Compute the defined benefit obligation at 1 January 20X7.
3. Compute the fair value of plan assets at 1 January 20X7.
4. Compute the unrecognized actuarial gain at 1 January 20X7. Also compute the 20X7 amortization.
5. Assume instead that this pension plan is sponsored by a private company, and ASPE applies. The standard accounting approach is adopted, and the corridor approach is used. Compute pension expense for 20X6. EPFE for the PSC caused by plan amendment in 20X5 was 20 years and the original EPFE for the PSC related to plan adoption was 25 years; the unamortized amount is $7,600 at 1 January 20X6.
6. Assume instead that this pension plan is sponsored by a private company, and ASPE applies. The simplified accounting approach is adopted. Compute pension expense for 20X6. There are no carry-forward unamortized amounts because all past service cost and actuarial and experience gains and losses were recognized immediately.

REVIEW PROBLEM—SOLUTION

1. Pension expense, 20X6

Current service cost (given)		$ 9,000
Interest ($25,000 × 10%)		2,500
Expected return on plan assets ($16,000 × 10%)		(1,600)
Amortizations:		
Past service cost from amendment: $10,000 ÷ 5 years	$2,000	
Past service cost from initiation: $10,000 ÷ 10 years	1,000	
Excess actuarial gain:		
[$4,700 − ($25,000 × 10%)] = $2,200 ÷ 14 =	(157)	2,843
		$12,743

2. Defined benefit obligation, 1 January 20X7

Obligation, 1 January 20X6	$25,000
Current service cost, 20X6	9,000
Interest	2,500
Benefits paid	(5,000)
	$31,500

3. Fair value of plan assets, 1 January 20X7

Value at 1 January 20X6	$16,000
Actual earnings on plan assets	2,000
Funding contributions	4,000
Benefits paid	(5,000)
	$17,000

4. Unrecognized actuarial gain at 1 January 20X7

Unrecognized gain, 1 January 20X6	$ 4,700
Extra earnings on plan assets, 20X6:	
$2,000 actual − $1,600 estimated	400
Amortization, 20X6	(157)
	$ 4,943

Amortization, 20X7
Excess over corridor:
Higher of accrued obligation or plan assets,
1 January 20X7 = $31,500
10% × $31,500 = $3,150 corridor limit
Amortization: ($4,943 − $3,150) = $1,793 ÷ 14 = $ 128

Note: ARSP is assumed to continue to be 14 years. If the employee group is stable, with new employees entering the workforce to replace retiring employees, ARSP will also be stable. ARSP will decline only if retiring workers are not being replaced by younger employees.

Pension Plan Spreadsheet (optional)

	Memorandum Accounts				Statement Accounts	
			Unrecognized			
20X6	**Defined Benefit Obligation**	**Plan Assets**	**Actuarial G/L**	**PSC**	**Pension Expense**	**Accrued Asset (Liab)**
Opening	$(25,000)	$16,000	$(4,700) (gain)	$10,000 4,000		$ 300*
				$14,000		
Current service cost	(9,000)				$ 9,000	
Interest (10%)	(2,500)				2,500	
Actual return		2,000	(2,000)			
Expected return (10%)			1,600		(1,600)	
Amortization of PSC— amendment				(2,000)	2,000	
Amortization of PSC— initiation				(1,000)	1,000	
Amortization of actuarial gain outside corridor			157		(157)	
Benefits paid	5,000	(5,000)			$12,743	(12,743)
Funding		4,000				4,000
Totals	$(31,500)	$17,000	$(4,943)	8,000 3,000		$(8,443)
				$11,000		

*Sum of first four columns

5. Pension expense, 20X6, under ASPE standard rules

Current service cost (no change)		$ 9,000
Interest ($25,000 × 10%) (no change)		2,500
Expected return on plan assets ($16,000 × 10%) (no change)		(1,600)
Amortizations:		
Past service cost from amendment:		
$10,000 ÷ 20 year EPFE	$500	
Past service cost from initiation: $10,000 ÷ 25 years	400	
Excess actuarial gain: (no change)		
[$4,700 − ($25,000 × 10%)] = $2,200 ÷ 14 =	(157)	743
		$10,643

6. Pension expense, 20X6, under ASPE simplified approach

Current service cost (no change)	$ 9,000
Interest ($25,000 × 10%) (no change)	2,500
Actual return on plan assets	(2,000)
Amortizations	none
	$ 9,500

QUESTIONS

Q18-1 Distinguish between a defined contribution pension plan and a defined benefit pension plan. Why are defined contribution plans attractive to employers?

Q18-2 Distinguish between a contributory pension plan and a non-contributory pension plan.

Q18-3 Why is it logical that contributions made by an employee to a pension plan vest immediately, while an employer's contributions may vest only after a certain period of time?

Q18-4 What is the incentive to the company for registering a pension plan?

Q18-5 Explain the impact each of the following variables would have on the yearly expense associated with a defined benefit pension plan:
   a. An increased rate of return on investments held by the pension plan
   b. Lower than expected employee mortality rates
   c. Higher than expected employee turnover
   d. A rollback of wages by 3%

Q18-6 Assume that a pension plan must accumulate $700,000 by an employee's retirement age in order to fund a pension. Three different funding models have been used to project funding requirements for the first year. The estimates are $2,600, $6,300, and $1,100. Identify three different funding methods and the funding level most likely associated with each.

Q18-7 In each of the following circumstances, identify the funding method that an employer would likely find most appealing:
   a. Conserve current cash balances.
   b. Have equal cash requirements each year.
   c. Use a funding pattern that could also be used to measure the pension expense.

Q18-8   List and define the five continuing components of pension expense.

Q18-9   How is interest on the defined benefit obligation measured?

Q18-10 What is a past service cost? How is it accounted for as part of pension expense?

Q18-11 Define the ARSP and explain when it is used as an amortization period.

Q18-12 What is the difference between an experience gain or loss and a gain or loss caused by a change in assumptions? How are the two accounted for in the calculation of net pension expense? What alternatives exist?

Q18-13 A company follows the practice of amortizing actuarial gains and losses to pension expense when the amount is outside the 10% corridor. At the beginning of 20X4, the balance of unamortized actuarial gains was $27,000. If the opening values of pension assets and obligations were both $230,000 and the ARSP was 10 years, how much amortization would be recognized in 20X4?

Q18-14 What limit is placed on pension fund assets?

Q18-15 When are gains and losses related to pension plan settlements and curtailments recognized?

Q18-16 When are the costs of enhanced pension entitlements associated with termination packages included in income?

Q18-17 If a pension has a benefit obligation of $400,000, pension fund assets of $250,000, and unrecognized losses of $175,000, what will be the resulting recognized accrued asset or liability pension account?

Q18-18 What justification is there for recording the net position of the pension plan, rather than the net position of the plan less unrecognized amounts?

Q18-19 Why are post-employment benefits other than pensions less likely to be fully funded? What difference will this make in financial statement treatment?

Q18-20 How would a private company account for a defined benefit pension plan if the simplified approach is used?

CASE 18-1

DELIVERIES-R-US

Deliveries-R-Us is a public company offering express freight transportation, small package ground delivery services, and other freight services. Capital assets include a broad range of assets, including a large fleet of aircraft and vehicles.

The liability and equity portion of the SFP is shown in Exhibit 1, and demonstrates a 20X2 debt-to-equity ratio of 0.65 (($4,524 + $1,930 + $2,342) ÷ $13,630). You are a market analyst assigned to evaluate this company. Looking at the note disclosures in Exhibits 2, 3, and 4, you are concerned that the liabilities are significantly understated.

Required:

Analyze the information provided and prepare an analysis, both qualitative and quantitative, that explores the liability issues presented.

> ◤ **EXHIBIT 1** ◥

Deliveries-R-Us

LIABILITIES AND SHAREHOLDERS' EQUITY

As of 31 December 20X2

LIABILITIES AND SHAREHOLDERS' EQUITY (in millions)	20X2
Current Liabilities	
Current portion of long-term debt	$ 653
Accrued salaries and employee benefits	861
Accounts payable	1,372
Accrued expenses	1,638
Total current liabilities	**4,524**
Long-term Debt, less current portion, interest rates 4%–6%	**1,930**
Other Long-term Liabilities	
Future income tax	1,071
Pension and post-retirement health care benefit obligations	813
Lease obligations	294
Other liabilities	164
Total other long-term liabilities	**2,342**
Commitments and Contingencies	—
Common Shareholders' Equity	
Common shares; 800 million shares authorized;	
312 million shares issued	2,084
Retained earnings	12,919
Reserve	(1,373)
Total common shareholders' equity	**13,630**
	$22,426

> ◤ **EXHIBIT 2** ◥

Deliveries-R-Us

NOTE DISCLOSURE: LEASES

As of 31 December 20X2

We utilize certain aircraft, land, facilities, retail locations, and equipment under capital and operating leases that expire at various dates through 20X12. Some aircraft are leased by us under agreements that provide for cancellation upon 30 days' notice. Our leased facilities include national and regional sorting facilities, retail facilities, and administrative buildings.

A summary follows of future minimum lease payments under capital leases and operating leases with an initial or remaining normal term in excess of one year at the end of 20X2 (in millions):

continued on next page

> **EXHIBIT 2** *(cont'd)*

| | Capital Leases | Operating Leases | | Total Operating Leases |
		Aircraft and Related Equipment	Facilities and Other	
20X3	$164	$ 512	$1,247	$ 1,759
20X4	20	526	1,086	1,612
20X5	8	504	947	1,451
20X6	119	499	817	1,316
20X7	2	472	694	1,166
Thereafter	15	2,458	4,894	7,352
Total	328	$4,971	$9,685	$14,656
Less amount representing interest	34			
Present value of net minimum lease payments	$294			

The weighted-average remaining lease term of all operating leases outstanding at the end of 20X2 was approximately six years.

> **EXHIBIT 3**

Deliveries-R-Us

NOTE DISCLOSURE: CONTINGENCIES

As of 31 December 20X2

We are a defendant in a number of lawsuits containing various class-action allegations of wage-and-hour violations. The plaintiffs in these lawsuits allege, among other things, that they were forced to work "off the clock," were not paid overtime, or were not provided work breaks or other benefits. The complaints generally seek unspecified monetary damages, injunctive relief, or both.

In March 20X2, the court granted class certification in 19 cases, and denied class certification in nine cases. The court has not yet ruled on class certification in the 16 remaining cases that are pending in the multidistrict litigation.

Given the nature and status of these lawsuits, we cannot yet determine the amount or a reasonable range of potential loss, if any, but it is reasonably possible that such potential loss could be material. However, we do not believe that a material loss is probable in any of these matters.

EXHIBIT 4

Deliveries-R-Us

NOTE DISCLOSURE: PENSIONS AND OTHER POST-RETIREMENT HEALTH CARE

As of 31 December 20X2

We sponsor programs that provide retirement benefits to most of our employees. These programs include defined benefit pension plans, defined contribution plans and post-employment health care plans. The accounting for pension and post-employment health care plans includes numerous assumptions, such as discount rates, expected long-term investment returns on plan assets, future salary increases, employee turnover, mortality, and retirement ages.

Financial information:

	Pension Plans 20X2	Post-employment Health Care Plans 20X2
Defined Benefit Obligation		
Balance at the beginning of year	$11,617	$ 492
Service cost	499	31
Interest cost	798	33
Actuarial loss (gain)	1,420	(94)
Benefits paid	(351)	(42)
Amendments	(1)	—
Other	(16)	21
Balance at the end of year	$13,966	$ 441
Plan Assets		
Fair value of plan assets at beginning of year	$11,879	$ —
Actual return on plan assets	(2,306)	—
Company contributions	1,146	21
Benefits paid	(351)	(42)
Other	(2)	21
Fair value of plan assets at end of year	$10,366	$ —
Amount recognized in the SFP:		
Funded status of the plan	$ (3,600)	$ (441)
Unrecognized PSC	417	—
Unrecognized actuarial losses	2,611	200
Net amount recognized	$ (572)	$ (241)

CASE 18-2

RECOGNITION ISSUES

For organizations with defined benefit pension plans, the actuary's estimate of the organization's obligation for pension benefits must be disclosed. The market value of pension plan assets available to satisfy that obligation is also disclosed in the notes to the financial statements. Within accounting circles, there has been considerable debate as to whether it would be more appropriate to recognize the net status of the plan (pension assets less pension liabilities) of the plan as an asset or obligation on the face of the SFP instead of relying on disclosure. Consider, for example, the following conversation, between the chief financial officer (CFO) of a large corporation and a financial analyst (FA) from a brokerage firm:

FA: "I'm sick and tired of having to adjust liabilities on the statement of financial position for footnote liabilities, such as the net pension obligation! The projected benefit obligation is that of the organization, not the pension fund, and it belongs, net of related plan assets, on the organization's statement of financial position."

CFO: "I was under the impression that it was the extent of disclosure, not the form, that mattered to you analysts."

FA: "That's not the point. A statement of financial position must be complete to be useful. It seems to me that the defined benefit obligation meets any reasonable definition of a liability, and it belongs with other liabilities. Besides, some users might be misled because they expect the SFP to contain all liabilities."

CFO: "I have some concerns about putting the pension obligation on the statement of financial position. For one thing, the pension fund is a separate legal entity. Take my organization for example. We have agreed with our union to work toward a goal of having the plan, which is currently underfunded, fully funded by 20X20. Our only obligation is to make contributions to the pension fund as suggested by the actuary in order to achieve our funding objective.

"Also, the benefit obligation is based on the *projected salaries* of our employees. If we used *current salaries*, with an actuarial method such as the accumulated benefit method, our defined benefit obligation would reflect our current obligations and be much lower. This is what we'd have to pay if we terminated the plan at any point, and it makes more sense as a SFP position.

"I further have concerns that the obligation is too soft a number to warrant recognition along with other liabilities. For example, consider our plan formula, which provides for an annual post-employment pension benefit of 2% of the employee's career average earnings for each year of service, to be paid each year beyond retirement until death. All payments are fully indexed to cost-of-living increases after retirement. There are many uncertainties related to measurement.

"And one more thing. How is our auditor supposed to be able to express an opinion as to whether the obligation is fairly presented? That means a lot of hours spent with the actuary, hours that our organization will have to pay for! Things are much simpler for the auditor when the obligation appears in a disclosure note only."

FA: "The need to make estimates about the future is not unique to pensions. I wonder whether the claim about uncertainties related to measurement is just an excuse you use to conceal your real concerns."

CFO: "Well, to be honest, our organization does have concerns about the economic consequences resulting from putting the net pension liability on the statement of financial position. Our stock price could be adversely affected, not to mention our credit rating, borrowing capacity, and management compensation contracts."

FA: "It seems that the controversy regarding pension accounting continues!"

Required:
Discuss the issues raised.

Source: The Canadian Institute of Chartered Accountants, © 2010.

CASE 18-3

CANDIDA LIMITED

Candida Limited is a Canadian public company in the business of exploration, production, and marketing of natural gas. It also has power generation operations. Earnings in 20X5 were $2.4 billion, and total assets were $24.1 billion.

You have recently begun work in the finance and accounting department. Your immediate task is to analyze and report on the pension information (see Exhibit 1) included in the last annual report. Your supervisor provided this information with a request:

> We have to prepare for an upcoming meeting of the audit committee. We have several new members of the committee, and the chairperson has suggested that we provide a brief report on Candida's pension issues to get everyone up to speed. It's been several years since we've discussed this issue in depth; this is the opportunity.
>
> Your report should include an explanation of defined benefit versus contribution plans (we have both but are curtailing the former), and the financial statement elements that relate to each plan. It will be necessary to explain the nature of the defined benefit obligation for the defined benefit plans, and the pension plan asset balances, and relate these amounts to the $45 million pension asset we disclose on the statement of financial position.
>
> We're particularly concerned about our potential pension position for 20X6, the coming year. We'll see an increase in compensation cost of about 5%, which will accordingly increase pension cost. On top of the large investment losses we experienced last year, this may mean serious increases in pension amounts. Your report should review the accounting treatment of the loss but also project our 20X6 pension expense. Finally, since our pension expense is likely going to be problematic next year, you should identify some key assumptions that Candida can consider to help reduce pension expense.

Required:
Prepare the report.

EXHIBIT 1

CANDIDA LIMITED

Selected Pension Information (in Millions)

Statement of Comprehensive Income	20X5	20X4	20X3
Total expense for defined contribution plans	$12	$9	$ 6
Total expense for defined benefit plans	$12	$6	$10
Statement of Financial Position			
Accrued pension asset	$45	$7	$16

Disclosure Notes

For Defined Benefit Plans	20X5
Defined benefit obligation	$228
Fair value of plan assets	113
Unamortized net actuarial loss	147
Unamortized past service cost	13

Current service cost was $7 in 20X5, and $3 in 20X4.
The company contributed $50 to all pension plans in total during 20X5.
The company uses the 10% corridor method for net actuarial losses.

Included in the above defined benefit obligation of $228 is $14 of unfunded benefit obligation related to the Company's other post-employment benefits.

Assumptions are as follows:	20X5	20X4
Discount rate	6.0%	6.5%
Rate of compensation increase	4.75%	3.0%
Expected rate of return on plan assets	6.2%	6.6%
Average remaining service life	12 years	
Average period to vesting	4 years	
Health care costs trend rate for next year	+10%	

ASSIGNMENTS

★ **A18-1 Pension Terms:** Complete the sentences below:

1. The actuarial cost method that must be used to determine current service cost is the _____.

2. Actuarial gains and losses have two causes: _____ and _____.

3. The 10% corridor method uses 10% of the greater of two amounts as a corridor. These are the _____ and the _____.

4. The statement of financial position will include one of two accounts when there is a defined benefit pension plan; either an _____ or an _____.

5. If actuarial gains and losses are to be recognized all in one year, they can be recognized in _____ or in _____.

6. The ARSP is defined as _____.

7. Past service cost will be included in pension expense in the year it is granted if _____ _____.

8. An experience gain or loss related to annual return on plan assets is the difference between _____ and _____.

9. The costs of pension benefit changes caused by _____ and _____ are often included in discontinued operations rather than pension expense.

10. The expected present value of future pension benefits, evaluated using present value and actuarial expectations, including mortality, turnover, and the effects of current and future compensation levels, is called _____.

11. _____ will decrease pension expense.

★ **A18-2 Amortization Periods:** Carson Industries Limited (CIL) has a defined benefit pension plan covering all employees. The defined benefit obligation was $7,004,000 at the beginning of the current year, which is $1,675,000 higher than fund assets. Plan revaluation is done every three years, and plan improvements are expected approximately every six years.

Required:

1. CIL has an ARSP of 14 years, and benefits in the pension plan *vest* after a total of 10 years. Explain the meaning of each of these terms.

2. CIL reports unamortized past service cost of $880,000; the PSC has already been amortized for four years. CIL has unamortized actuarial losses of $224,000 at the beginning of the current year. Explain how each of these amounts arose.

3. CIL has four alternatives for recognition of the actuarial losses. Calculate the amount in pension expense, if any, under each alternative.

4. Calculate the PSC to be included in pension expense.

★ **A18-3 Defined Contribution Plan:** TGY Limited has a defined contribution plan for its 160 employees. The plan is trusteed, and each year the company makes an annual contribution, matching employee contributions to the plan to a certain maximum. The funds are invested for the employees by the pension fund trustee using pre-determined parameters.

The pension plan was established to target roughly 60% of final pay to employees as a pension, with survivor benefits or a minimum 10-year payout. None of these targets are guaranteed. Calculations were done based on mortality assumptions, and an expected 5% fund earnings rate. Contributions are re-evaluated every three years. Based on these assumptions, TGY paid $234,000 to the fund in 20X7. At the end of 20X7, plan assets total $2,890,000.

Required:

1. What are the employees of TGY entitled to as a result of this pension? How is this different than a defined benefit plan?
2. What difference would it make if the targets established above were guaranteed by the company?
3. What amount of pension expense would TGY report in 20X7?
4. If fund earnings were to be 8% in 20X8, instead of the 5% predicted, who would benefit? Explain.

★ **A18-4 Defined Contribution Plan:** A market analyst was quoted as saying:

Defined benefit pension plans are really dead. Within 20 years, no companies in the private sector will be offering these plans —and the public sector is just daft if they don't follow suit. Why, in the first four months of this year, I know of dozens of companies that have frozen or closed their defined benefit plans. They allow new employees access to only defined contribution plans. Many of these companies just make end-of-year grants to employees directly into their personal RRSP accounts, and allow—force—the employees to make their own investment decisions. Of course, with employees more mobile between companies, and less likely to stay with one employer all their lives, it can be attractive. Some people just like to get their hands on the money!

Required:

1. What factors associated with defined benefit plans have led to the trend toward defined contribution plans?
2. Evaluate the attractiveness of defined contribution plans for employees.

★ **A18-5 Defined Contribution Plan:** Zio Ltd. established a defined contribution pension plan at the beginning of 20X9. The company will contribute 3% of each employee's salary annually. Total salaries in 20X9 were expected to be $7.3 million. Accordingly, Zio paid $219,000 into the fund. After the year-end, it was determined that actual salaries were $6.5 million. Interest rates are in the range of 6%.

Required:

1. Is pension expense $219,000, or a lesser number? Explain.
2. Assume instead that Zio has agreed to pay $165,000 into the fund in 20X9. During the year an employee left the company, forfeiting $35,000 of unvested pension benefits earmarked in the pension fund. Calculate the payment to the fund, and the pension expense.
3. Assume instead that Zio agreed to pay $150,000 to the pension trustee in 20X9 but, because of cash flow issues, paid only $100,000. Zio agrees to pay the shortfall at the end of 20X11. In 20X10, the company makes a scheduled $150,000 payment to the pension fund for normal 20X10 pension entitlements. The same annual scheduled payment is made in 2011, plus the $50,000 arrears from 20X9. How much is pension expense and cash paid in each of 20X9, 20X10, and 20X11?

★ **A18-6 Accrued Pension Asset:** Morocco Corporation initiated a defined benefit pension plan on 1 January 20X5. The plan does not provide any past service benefits for existing employees. The pension funding payment is made to the trustee on 31 December of each year. The following information is available for 20X5 and 20X6:

	20X5	20X6
Current service cost	$150,000	$165,000
Funding payment	170,000	185,000
Interest on defined benefit obligation	10,000	15,000
Expected return on plan assets	10,000	18,000

Required:

1. Prepare the journal entry to record pension expense for 20X6.

2. What amount appears on the 31 December 20X6 statement of financial position related to the pension?

3. What limits are there on the accrued pension asset on the statement of financial position?

★ **A18-7 Defined Benefit Obligation and Pension Fund Assets:** Belfiori Limited reports the following data for 20X8:

Plan assets (at fair value)	
Balance, 1 January	$342,800
Balance, 31 December	344,100
Defined benefit obligation	
Balance, 1 January	$599,690
Balance, 31 December	704,200

The company has a contributory, defined benefit pension plan covering all employees over the age of 30.

Required:

1. How much did the pension plan assets change during the year? Name three items that would cause plan assets to change.

2. How much did the defined benefit obligation increase during the year? Name five items that would cause this amount to change.

3. Compute the amount of the underfunded (overfunded) net position of the pension plan for accounting purposes at the beginning and the end of the year. Explain what these amounts mean.

★★ **A18-8 Pension Expense:** The following information relates to a defined benefit pension plan:

Defined benefit obligation, 1 January 20X5	$60,000
Initial past service cost awarded, 1 January 20X3	
(this amount will vest over 10 years)	20,000 4th item
Reduction in pension liability from curtailing pension plan in 20X5, measured at 31 December 20X5	18,000
Interest rate	8%
Unrecognized actuarial gains and losses, net gain, 1 January 20X5	10,000 5th item
Current service cost, 20X5	14,000
Contributions, 20X5	16,000
Expected earnings, 20X5 (opening assets, $50,000)	4,000
Actual return, 20X5	6,000
ARSP in 20X5	15 years

Not dealing (handwritten annotation)

Required:

1. Provide the entries to record pension expense and cash paid to the trustee for 20X5. The company follows the practice of amortizing actuarial gains and losses to pension expense when the 1 January amount is outside the 10% corridor. The curtailment involves benefits to employees' activities in the normal course of business.

2. Repeat requirement (1) assuming that the company includes all actuarial gains and losses in pension expense in the year that they arise. For this part, the unrecognized actuarial gains and losses at 1 January 20X5 are zero.

3. Calculate pension expense for 20X5 assuming this is a private company that has elected to use the simplified approach to pension accounting. Assume that there was no curtailment in this requirement, and no carryforwards of actuarial gains.

★★   **A18-9 Pension Expense:** From Limited has a non-contributory, defined benefit pension plan. Pension plan data to be used for accounting purposes for the 20X9 year are as follows (in $ thousands):

a. *Pension plan assets*

Balance, 1 January, at market value	$560,000
Actual return; (expected return, 4%)	2,000
Contribution to the pension fund by From	103,200
Benefits paid to retirees	(16,400)
Balance, 31 December	$648,800

b. *Projected benefit obligation*

Balance, 1 January	$720,000
Current service cost	97,100
Interest cost	39,700
Loss due to change in actuarial assumptions, as of 31 December, 20X9	10,000
Increase caused by termination benefits; part of restructuring program	8,000
Pension benefits paid	(16,400)
Balance, 31 December	$858,400

Average remaining service period, 14 years
Vesting period, 2 years

c. *Company records*

1 January 20X9 unamortized amounts:

Unamortized past service cost (1 year amortized, 1 year remaining)	$18,000
Unamortized actuarial gain/loss	$(95,400)
	(gain)

Required:

1. Calculate pension expense for 20X9. The company follows the practice of amortizing actuarial gains and losses to pension expense when the 1 January amount is outside the 10% corridor.

2. Calculate the amortization of relevant amounts for 20X9, and the unamortized amounts for carryforward.

3. Give the 31 December 20X9 entries to record pension expense and funding for From.

4. Recalculate your response to requirement 1 assuming that this is a private company that has elected to use the simplified approach to pension accounting. Assume that there are no carryforwards of past service cost or actuarial gains in this requirement.

★★   **A18-10 Pension Expense:** HTR Resources Ltd. has a non-contributory defined benefit pension plan for its employees. At the beginning of 20X8, there is unrecognized past service

eXcel

cost of $4,380 and unrecognized actuarial losses of $5,460 (all amounts in thousands). The data for 20X8 is as follows:

Plan assets at fair market value, 1 January	$32,520
Actual return	2,760
Contributions made by employer	9,600
Pension benefits paid	(5,100)
Plan assets at fair market value, 31 December	$39,780
Projected benefit obligation, 1 January	$52,560
Current service cost	7,140
Interest cost	4,200
Loss from actuarial assumption changes, 31 December	570
Increase from improved pension benefits granted in a restructuring	4,000
Pension benefits paid	(5,100)
Projected benefit obligation, 31 December	$63,370

HTR amortizes gains or losses based on opening balances using the corridor method. The vesting period is 12 years and ARSP is 18 years. The expected rate of return on fund assets is 7%.

Required:

1. Compute the accrued pension liability/asset on the statement of financial position at 1 January 20X8.
2. Prepare the 20X8 journal entry to record pension expense.
3. Compute the accrued pension liability/asset on the statement of financial position at 31 December 20X8.

Source: Reproduced with permission from CGA-Canada.

★ **A18-11 Pension Expense:** The 20X5 records of Jax Company provided the following data related to its non-contributory, defined benefit pension plan (in $ thousands):

a. Defined benefit obligation (report of actuary)

Balance, 1 January 20X5	$23,000
Current service cost	1,200
Interest cost	1,840
Pension benefits paid, 20X5	(400)
Balance, 31 December 20X5	$25,640

b. Plan assets at fair value (report of trustee)

Balance, 1 January 20X5	$ 2,408
Actual return on plan assets	190
Contributions, 20X5	3,214
Pension benefits paid, 20X5	(400)
Balance, 31 December 20X5	$ 5,412

Expected long-term rate of return on plan assets, 7%

c. 1 January 20X5, balance of unamortized past service cost, $10,000. Amortization period remaining, 6 years.

d. There are no unamortized experience gains or losses at 1 January 20X5.

Required:

1. Compute 20X5 pension expense.
2. Give the 20X5 entry(ies) for Jax Company to record pension expense and funding.
3. Past service cost is being amortized over six years. What term is this? If this were a private company, what term would be used?

4. Prepare the required note disclosure of the amounts of pension fund assets and defined benefit obligations. This schedule should include unrecognized amounts and sum to the recorded pension liability. Is the pension fund overfunded or underfunded from an accounting perspective?

★★ **A18-12 Recognition Alternatives: Actuarial Gains and Losses:** The following information relates to the pension plan of CCL Corporation, which has a contributory defined benefit pension plan:

Current service cost for 20X2	280,000
Interest on defined benefit obligation	107,000
Defined benefit obligation at the beginning of 20X2	2,100,000
Increase to defined benefit obligation caused by change in mortality rates; valuation performed in 20X2	105,000
Past service cost to include in 20X2 expense	15,000
Benefit payments to retired employees in 20X2	86,000
ARSP	20 years
Payment to pension trustee in 20X2	280,000
Pension assets at the beginning of 20X2	600,000
Actual fund earnings (loss)	(18,000)

The following cases are independent.

Case A
CCL includes expected earnings at a rate of 4% in the calculation of pension expense. Opening unrecognized actuarial losses were $340,000 and the company uses the 10% corridor method based on opening balances.

Case B
CCL includes expected earnings at a rate of 4% in the calculation of pension expense. Opening unrecognized actuarial losses were $340,000 and the company is amortizing the full opening balance of actuarial gains or losses to pension expense over the ARSP, with no reference to a corridor.

Case C
CCL includes expected earnings at a rate of 4% in the calculation of pension expense. Opening unrecognized actuarial losses were $340,000 and the company is using a 10% corridor approach, with any excess actuarial gains or losses amortized to earnings over five years.

Case D
CCL includes expected earnings at a rate of 4% in the calculation of pension expense. Actuarial gains and losses are included in pension expense in the year they arise. There was no opening balance of unrecognized actuarial gains or losses.

Case E
CCL includes expected earnings at a rate of 4% in the calculation of pension expense. Actuarial gains and losses are recorded as an adjustment to reserves and included as an element of other comprehensive income in the year they arise. There was no opening balance of unrecognized actuarial gains or losses.

Required:
For each case,

1. Compute 20X2 pension expense.
2. Give the 20X2 entry(ies) for CCL Company to record pension expense (and other adjustments in Case E) and funding.

★ **A18-13 Recognition Alternatives: Actuarial Gains and Losses:** The following information relates to the pension plan of Butler Machinery Corporation, which has a contributory defined benefit pension plan:

Current service cost for 20X2	67,000
Interest on defined benefit obligation	32,000
Defined benefit obligation at the beginning of 20X2	910,000
Increase to defined benefit obligation caused by change in mortality rates; valuation performed in 20X2	54,000
Past service cost to include in 20X2 expense	20,000
Benefit payments to retired employees in 20X2	104,000
ARSP	10 years
Payment to pension trustee in 20X2	80,000
Pension assets at the beginning of 20X2	505,000
Actual fund earnings	3,000

The following cases are independent.

Case A
Butler includes expected earnings at a rate of 5% in the calculation of pension expense. Opening unrecognized actuarial losses were $87,000 and the company uses the 10% corridor method based on opening balances.

Case B
Butler includes expected earnings at a rate of 5% in the calculation of pension expense. Opening unrecognized actuarial losses were $87,000 and the company is amortizing the full opening balance of actuarial gains or losses to pension expense over the ARSP, with no reference to a corridor.

Case C
Butler includes expected earnings at a rate of 5% in the calculation of pension expense. Actuarial gains and losses are included in pension expense in the year they arise. There was no opening balance of unrecognized actuarial gains or losses.

Case D
Butler includes expected earnings at a rate of 5% in the calculation of pension expense. Actuarial gains and losses are recorded as an adjustment to reserves and included as an element of other comprehensive income in the year they arise. There was no opening balance of unrecognized actuarial gains or losses.

Required:
For each case,

1. Compute 20X2 pension expense.
2. Give the 20X2 entry(ies) for Butler Company to record pension expense (and other adjustments in Case D) and funding.
3. In which case is the recorded pension asset or liability account likely to be more consistent with the net unfunded position of the plan? Explain; do not calculate.

★ **A18-14 Corridor Rule:** Lowen Limited has a defined benefit pension plan. Data with respect to the plan, which was initiated in 20X0 (in thousands) is as follows:

	20X0	20X1	20X2	20X3	20X4
Plan assets (31 December)	$ 845	$1,210	$1,890	$2,005	$2,475
Defined benefit obligation (31 December)	1,050	1,450	1,620	2,345	2,810
New actuarial (gains)/losses arising during year	100	200	(175)	(316)	(60)
ARSP (years)	18	20	19	21	20

Required:

1. Using the 10% corridor rule, determine the actuarial gain or loss to be included in pension expense in each year from 20X0 to 20X4. Round any amortization to the nearest thousand.

2. Prepare a schedule of unamortized actuarial gains and losses carryforward, assuming use of the corridor rule, for each year from 20X0 to 20X4.

★ **A18-15 Corridor Rule:** Fenerty Fabrics has a defined benefit pension plan that arose in 20X3. The following information relates to the plan:

(in $ thousands)	20X3	20X4	20X5	20X6	20X7
Plan assets (31 December)	$500	$260	$320	$350	$200
Defined benefit obligation (31 December)	450	410	360	330	356
New actuarial (gains)/losses arising in year	(46)	16	(45)	21	(4)
ARSP (years)	15	9	11	12	10

Required:

1. What alternatives does Fenerty have to account for its actuarial gains and losses? Explain.
2. For each year, what amount would be included in pension expense if actuarial gains and losses were recognized in the year that they arose?
3. Calculate the amount of actuarial gain and loss that should be included in pension expense each year, assuming that the company follows the practice of amortizing actuarial gains and losses to pension expense when the amount is outside the 10% corridor. Note that the amortization is based on opening cumulative balances.
4. Prepare a schedule of unamortized actuarial gains and losses for carryforward, assuming that the company follows the accounting policy in requirement (3).

★★ **A18-16 Pension Spreadsheet:** Okamura Construction Corp. has a defined benefit pension plan. Information concerning the 20X7 and 20X8 fiscal years are presented below:

From the Plan Actuary:

- Current service cost in 20X7 is $430,000 and in 20X8 is $488,000.
- Defined benefit obligation is $4,975,000 at the beginning of 20X7.
- Unamortized past service cost at the beginning of 20X7 was $180,000.
- ARSP is 24 years at the beginning of 20X7; 23 years, at the beginning of 20X8. The vesting period is five years, of which there are three years remaining at the beginning of 20X7 for the past service cost amounts.
- Unrecognized actuarial loss at the beginning of 20X7 was $987,000.
- Benefits paid to retirees, $235,000 in 20X7 and $295,000 in 20X8.
- Actuarial revaluation at the end of 20X7 showed a $406,000 increase in the obligation. Revaluations take place every four years.

From the Plan Trustee:

- Plan assets at market value at the beginning of 20X7 were $3,705,000.
- 20X7 contributions were $510,000 and in 20X8, $525,000.
- Actual earnings were $276,000 in 20X7 and $80,000 in 20X8.

Other Information:

- Interest rate on long-term debt, stable in 20X7 and 20X8, 6%.
- Expected rate of return on asset, stable at 4% in 20X7 and 20X8.
- The company uses the corridor method for actuarial losses, and amortizes excess amounts over the maximum period.

Required:

Prepare a spreadsheet for 20X7 and 20X8 that determines pension expense, and also the closing accrued pension asset or liability account. Round amounts to the nearest $100.

★★ **A18-17 Pension Expense; Spreadsheet:** Fox Company has a non-contributory, defined benefit pension plan adopted on 1 January 20X5. On 31 December 20X5, the following information is available:

For accounting purposes

- Interest rate used for discounting and asset return, 5%.
- Past service cost, granted as of 1 January, $200,000. This is also the defined benefit obligation on 1 January. These benefits vest over 10 years.
- ARSP is 14 years.
- Current service cost for 20X5, appropriately measured for accounting purposes, $67,000.

For funding purposes

- Funding was $99,500 for all pension amounts. The payment was made on 31 December.
- Actual earnings on fund assets, zero.

Required:

1. Compute pension expense for 20X5, and indicate the closing pension asset or liability account as of 31 December 20X5. The company follows the practice of amortizing actuarial gains and losses to pension expense when the 1 January amount is outside the 10% corridor.

2. Prepare a pension spreadsheet that summarizes relevant pension data for 20X5.

3. Prepare a pension spreadsheet that summarizes relevant pension data for 20X6. The following facts relate to 20X6:

   - Current service cost for accounting was $96,000. Interest on the defined benefit obligation was $13,850.
   - A plan amendment resulted in a past service cost of $40,000 being granted as of 1 January 20X6 (31 December 20X5). This amount vests immediately.
   - Total funding of the pension plan was $118,000, on 31 December 20X6.
   - Actual return on fund assets was $8,900.
   - An actuarial revaluation was done to reflect new information about expected turnover rates in the employee population. This resulted in a $35,000 increase in the defined benefit obligation, as of 31 December 20X6.

★★ **A18-18 Pension Expense; Spreadsheet:** Super Sport Limited sponsors a defined benefit pension plan for its employees. At the beginning of 20X3, there is a pension asset of $139,200, as follows:

Defined benefit obligation	$(509,100)
Plan assets (fair value)	356,300
Unamortized past service cost (vesting over five years; two years remaining at the beginning of 20X3)	158,400
Unamortized actuarial losses	133,600
Accrued pension asset	$139,200

The following data relate to the operation of the plan for the years 20X3 and 20X4:

	20X3	20X4
Current service cost	49,000	$42,000
Expected rate of return	5%	5.5%
Actual return on plan assets	(17,000)	21,000
Annual funding contributions, at year-end	65,000	82,000
Benefits paid to retirees	45,500	106,000
Increase in defined benefit obligation due to changes in actuarial assumptions as of 31 December each year	86,000	34,000
Interest on defined benefit obligation	33,200	41,700
ARSP	20 years	17 years

Required:

1. Calculate the corridor test to establish required amortization of actuarial gains and losses in 20X3 and 20X4, as needed. The company follows the practice of amortizing actuarial gains and losses to pension expense when the 1 January amount is outside the 10% corridor.

2. Prepare a spreadsheet that summarizes relevant pension data for 20X3 and 20X4. As part of the spreadsheet, calculate pension expense and the related pension accrued benefit asset/liability for 20X3 and 20X4.

★★ **A18-19 Other Post-employment Benefits:** Hruska Corp. provides post-employment benefits to its retirees for dental and supplementary health care. The following information relates to these benefits:

eXcel

Benefit obligation, 1 January 20X6	$56,000
Current service cost for 20X6	16,000
Unamortized actuarial loss, 1 January 20X6	42,200
Fund assets, 1 January 20X6	7,000
Contributions to the benefit fund for 20X6	9,000
Benefit payments to retired employees for 20X6	12,000
Expected return on plan assets	6%
Actual return on fund assets	350
Discount rate for obligation	7%
ARSP, 1 January 20X6	20 years

Required:

1. Calculate the accrued asset or liability position as of 1 January 20X6.

2. Compute the benefit obligation for post-employment benefits at 31 December 20X6, and plan assets at 31 December 20X6.

3. Compute the appropriate expense for post-employment benefits for the year ended 31 December 20X6. Hruska uses the corridor method with excess amounts amortized over the ARSP.

4. Prepare a reconciliation of the accrued asset or liability position at 31 December 20X6.

Note: The solution to this question is based on a spreadsheet.

★★ **A18-20 Other Post-employment Benefits; Spreadsheet:** Lin Developments Ltd. provides post-employment benefits to its retirees for supplementary health care, including prescription medication. Lin had an unamortized past service cost of $176,400; the remaining amortization period is eight years. Also unamortized is an experience loss of $78,500, related primarily to unexpected cost increases in prescription medication.

Lin does not fund these health care benefits to any great extent. As a result, there is only $21,500 in the fund asset account at the beginning of the year, while the estimated obligation for supplementary health care benefits is $566,300. Actual earnings of the fund this year were $600. Contributions of $46,400 were made to the fund and benefits paid out were $43,900. In the current year, actuarial estimates indicate that current service cost is $67,800.

Required:

Prepare a spreadsheet for the current year that determines the expense for post-employment benefits, and also the closing accrued asset or liability with respect to the benefits. Note that the long-term interest rate is 5%, assets are expected to earn 2% on average, and Lin uses the corridor method with amortization over the ARSP, which is 18 years.

★★ **A18-21 Pension Information, Interpretation:** The following information relates to the contributory defined benefit pension plan of Daniels Corporation:

Financial Accounting Information, 20X5

Statement of Comprehensive Income		Items Not Yet Recognized in Earnings	
Pension expense:			
Current service cost	$200	Unamortized past service cost	$950
Interest cost	120	Unamortized net loss	$226
Return on plan assets	(176)		
Net amortization	163		
	$307		

Statement of Financial Position		Pension Fund Status 31 December 20X5	
Accrued pension asset	$373		
		Defined benefit obligation	$(1,820)
		Plan assets at fair value	1,017
		Funded status	$ (803)

The information was prepared for the 20X5 annual financial statements and is accurate; the pension plan terms granted PSC entitlements in 20X2 when the plan was amended. The president of Daniels Corporation has asked for clarification of the following:

a. What likely caused the unrecognized net loss ($226) and why is it not recognized immediately?

b. What is the nature of the net amortization in the calculation of pension expense and why does it increase pension expense?

c. If the plan is underfunded by $803, why does the company show an accrued pension asset of $373 (i.e., what does this $373 represent?)

d. Which of the above measurements are dependent on estimates? Explain.

e. In general, how long is the amortization period for past service cost?

Required:

Respond to the requests of the company president.

★★ **A18-22 Pension Information, Interpretation:** Extracts from the pension disclosures of Blue Pony Limited are shown below.

Pension Benefits

The estimated present value of accrued plan benefits and the estimated market value of the net assets available to provide for these benefits are as follows:

	20X2	20X1
Plan assets, at fair value	$545	$484
Defined benefit obligation	612	575
Deficiency	(67)	(91)
Unamortized past service cost	7	10
Unamortized net actuarial loss	94	113
Accrued pension asset	$ 34	$ 32

Actuarial assumptions:

	20X2	20X1
Weighted average discount rate for defined benefit obligations	5.25%	5.3%
Weighted average rate of compensation increase for defined benefit obligation	3.50%	4.00%
Weighted average expected long-term rate of return on plan assets	4.75%	6.25%

Required:

1. With respect to the assumptions listed, explain how each actuarial assumption would be developed. Indicate whether the trend in each assumption would lead to higher or lower pension expense.

2. Explain the funded status of the plan in comparison to the recorded pension asset account.

3. Assume that the company adopted a policy of recognizing all actuarial gains and losses immediately in reserves, with the annual change included as an element of other comprehensive income. How would the recorded asset amount change? Indicate accounts and amounts.

★★ **A18-23 Pension Expense:** In late 20X0, Winnipeg Valves Limited established a defined benefit pension plan for its employees. At the inception of the plan, the actuary determined the present value of the defined benefit obligation relating to employees' past services to be $1 million, as of the end of 20X0. This amount vests over 10 years.

In each year following inception of the plan, the actuary measured the defined benefit obligation arising from employees' services in that year. These current service costs amounted to $80,000 in 20X1, $82,000 in 20X2, and $85,000 in 20X3. The costs were determined by using an actuarial cost method based on employees' projected earnings.

All actuarial obligations and funding payments were determined by assuming an interest rate of 6%, which was the long-term borrowing rate. This rate is also management's best estimate of the long-term rate of return on plan assets for the asset mix of the plan. In accordance with provincial legislation, the past service cost was to be funded over 15 years, the maximum period allowed. Current service costs were to be fully funded at the end of each year.

In 20X4 the actuary conducted the mandatory triennial revaluation. The revaluation revealed that the plan assets at the end of 20X3 were $611,471. At this point, the average remaining service period of employees covered by the plan was 21 years. In conjunction with the actuary, management decided not to make any changes in assumptions, including the assumption that the long-term rate of return would be 6%. The actuary also determined that the current service cost for 20X4 was $87,500. There was an experience gain of $21,870 on the pension plan obligation, arising in 20X4. The actual plan earnings for 20X4 were $55,055.

Required:

1. Determine the amount of pension expense for 20X4. The company follows the policy of including all actuarial gains and losses in income in the year in which they arise.

2. Determine the amount of pension expense for 20X4. The company follows the policy of including all actuarial gains and losses in reserves and as an element of other comprehensive income in the year in which they arise.

3. Determine the amount of pension expense for 20X4. Assume that the company is a private company and the company elects to use the simplified approach.

Source: The Canadian Institute of Chartered Accountants, © 2010.

★★★ **A18-24 Pension Expense; Spreadsheet:** Markon Consultants Limited began a pension fund in the year 20X3, effective 1 January 20X4. Terms of the pension plan follow:

- The expected earnings rate on plan assets is 6%.

- Employees will receive partial credit for past service. The past service obligation, valued using the projected benefit actuarial cost method and a discount rate of 6%, is $216,000 as of 1 January 20X4.

- Past service cost will be funded over 15 years. The initial payment, on 1 January 20X4, is $20,000. After that, another $20,000 will be added to the 31 December current service funding amount, including the 31 December 20X4 payment. The amount of past service funding will be reviewed every five years to ensure its adequacy.

- The past service cost vests over five years.

- Current service cost will be fully funded each 31 December, plus or minus any actuarial or experience gains related to the pension liability. Experience gains and losses related to the difference between actual and expected earnings on fund assets will not affect plan funding in the short run, as they are expected to offset over time.

Data for 20X4 and 20X5

	20X4	20X5
Current service cost	$51,000	$57,000
Funding amount, 1 January 20X4	20,000	
Funding amount, 31 December	??	??
Actual return on fund assets	1,000	6,800
Increase in actuarial liability at year-end due to change in assumptions	—	16,000
ARSP for all employees	26 years	25 years

Required:

1. Prepare a spreadsheet containing all relevant pension information. The company follows the practice of amortizing actuarial gains and losses to pension expense when the amount at the beginning of the year is outside the 10% corridor.

2. Complete a spreadsheet for 20X6 and 20X7. Further data for Markon Consultants related to 20X6 and 20X7 is as follows:

	20X6	20X7
Current service cost	$65,000	$72,000
Actual return on fund assets	12,610	11,440
Increase (decrease) in actuarial liability at year-end		
due to change in assumption	(5,000)	—
Pension benefits paid, at end of the year	12,000	23,000
ARSP for all employees	24 years	27 years

3. Prepare journal entries to record pension expense and funding for 20X4 through 20X7.

★★★ **A18-25 Pension Issues, Comprehensive:** Power Ltd. has a defined benefit pension plan. At the end of 20X0, the financial statements showed the following:

Long-term liabilities	
Accrued pension liability	$ (450,000)

The notes to the financial statements disclose:

Defined benefit obligation	$2,567,000
Pension fund assets	2,117,000
Accrued pension liability	$ (450,000)

Actuarial assumptions:	
Long-term borrowing rate for defined benefit obligation	5%
Weighted average long-term earnings rate for pension assets	3%

Assumptions and policies have not changed in 20X1. Actual fund earnings in 20X1 were a loss of $156,000. Current service cost was $246,000 in 20X1, and benefits paid to pensioners were $219,000. In 20X1, there was an actuarial review that showed that the corrected value for the opening defined benefit obligation was $2,899,000, not $2,567,000 (a $332,000 increase). The estimate was changed because of longer expected lives of employees. This amount has already vested. In addition, Power granted past service cost benefits to employees with an effect of increasing the accrued benefit obligation by $675,000 (effective 1 January). Amortization of this amount will commence in 20X1, over the five-year vesting period. As a result of these two adjustments, the defined benefit obligation was $3,574,000 ($2,567,000 + $332,000 + $675,000) on 1 January 20X1. The average remaining service period and the expected period to full eligibility of the employee group is 18 years. At the end of the year, Power funded current service cost plus $40,000 for partial payment of past service cost, plus another $100,000 in part payment for the change in actuarial liability. Power uses the corridor method for changes in the defined benefit obligation caused by changes in estimates; the 20X1 change was effective 1 January and should be evaluated for amortization in 20X1.

Required:

1. What actuarial cost method would have been used to calculate current service cost? What is/are the major forecasted variable(s) in this actuarial cost model that is/are different than those of the other actuarial cost models?
2. Calculate pension expense for 20X1, and the closing balance of the recorded accrued pension liability. Also calculate the closing balance of the defined benefit obligation and the fund assets held by the trustee.
3. Explain how (or if) the economic status (funded status) of the pension plan differs from the recorded pension asset or liability position at the end of 20X0 and then at the end of 20X1 if Power used the accounting policies as in requirement 2.
4. Calculate pension expense for 20X1, assuming that the company includes all actuarial gains and losses in earnings as they occur.
5. Calculate pension expense, and prepare the pension entry(ies), assuming that the company includes all actuarial gains and losses as a reserve as they occur, with the annual actuarial gains and losses reported as an element of other comprehensive income.

6. Comment on the differences in requirements 2, 4, and 5.
7. Calculate pension expense for 20X1 if Power were a private corporation that has elected to use the simplified approach to pension accounting.
8. Calculate pension expense for 20X1 if Power were a private company and the pre-2011 Canadian GAAP approach to pension accounting is used. Use the 10% corridor rule for actuarial gains and losses.

★★ **A18-26 Pension Spreadsheet:** The following partial spreadsheet has been prepared:

eXcel

20X3	Pension Obligation	Plan Assets	Actuarial G/L	PSC	Pension Expense	Accrued Asset (Liab)
Opening balance	(476,100)	272,300	3,400 dr	158,400		??
Current service	(78,000)					
Interest						
Actual return		36,000				
Change in assumptions	(79,800)					
Funding		95,000				
Benefits paid	31,500					
Closing balances						
20X4						
Current service	(48,000)					
Interest						
Actual return		66,000				
Change in assumptions	(56,200)					
Funding		81,000				
Benefits paid	194,000					
Closing balances						

Memorandum Accounts: Pension Obligation, Plan Assets, Unrecognized (Actuarial G/L, PSC). Statement Accounts: Pension Expense, Accrued Asset (Liab).

Required:
Complete the spreadsheet. Label any lines added. The interest rate and earnings rate, as needed, is 6% Assume that the amortization period for all amounts is 15 years. The company uses the 10% corridor rule for actuarial gains and losses.

★★★ **A18-27 Pension Issues, Comprehensive:** Scharf Limited has a defined benefit pension plan. The following information relates to this plan:

Accrued pension asset, 1 January	$ 52,500
Defined benefit pension obligation, 1 January	??
Actuarial loss on change in assumptions, arising during 20X1	16,000
Actual return on plan assets for 20X1—loss	2,000
Unrecognized actuarial loss, 1 January	117,900
Increase in defined benefit pension obligation due to new past service cost, new on 1 January (begin amortization in 20X1)	25,000
Fair value of plan assets, 1 January	244,000
Current service cost for 20X1	19,200
Plan contribution for 20X1	24,000
Benefits paid in 20X1	7,000
Expected rate of return on plan assets	4%
Interest rate on long-term debt	4.5%
Average remaining service period	16 years
Vesting period for past service cost	5 years

Required:

1. Calculate pension expense for 20X1, and the closing balance of the recorded accrued pension asset. Reconcile the recorded pension asset balance to the assets and defined benefit obligation of the pension plan. The company uses the 10% corridor method for actuarial gains and losses.

2. Does the statement of financial position reflect the economic position of the plan? Comment.

3. Describe the note disclosures that the company is required to include with respect to this plan.

4. Calculate pension expense assuming that the company recognizes all the actuarial gains and losses in reserves, with the annual change included as an element of other comprehensive income. There are no opening unrecognized amounts in this case, and, at the beginning of 20X1, there is a $65,400 accrued pension liability. Cumulative reserves have a debit balance of $117,900 with respect to the pension. What are the closing SFP balances? Does the SFP reflect the economic position of the plan? Comment.

★★ **A18-28 Pension Expense, Explanation, Calculation:** Neotech Industries (NI) was created in 20X0. The company is in the optical equipment industry. Its made-to-order scientific and medical equipment requires large investments in research and development. To fund these needs, Neotech completed a public stock offering, in 20X4. Although the offering was reasonably successful, NI's ambitious management is convinced that the company must report a good profit this year (20X5) to maintain the current market price of its stock. NI's president recently stressed this point when he told his controller, "We need to report at least $1.1 million in pre-tax profit or our stock price will plummet!" NI's pre-tax profit was $1.1 million, before adjustments. However, appropriate pension accounting has yet to be resolved.

As of the beginning of fiscal year 20X5, NI instituted an employee pension plan with defined benefits. The plan is operated by a trustee. At the inception of the plan, the unfunded past service cost was $3,000,000. NI agreed to fund this amount through equal payments over 20 years, and made the first payment on 1 January 20X5. A 7% interest rate is appropriate and the funding is calculated as an annuity due. The payments were blended payments, including both principal and interest. For 20X5, current service cost was $650,000, funded at year-end. The average vesting period of employees covered by the plan is 24 years. No payments were made to pensioners during the year. NI has expensed all payments made to the trustee. Expected earnings are 7%.

The president has also asked what estimates could be revised to minimize pension expense.

Required:

Respond to the issues raised and make appropriate recommendations. Your answer should include a recalculation of pre-tax income.

★★ **A18-29 Pension Expense:** Computer Imaging Ltd. (CIL) established a formal pension plan 10 years ago to provide retirement benefits for all employees. The plan is non-contributory and is funded through a trustee, which invests all funds and pays all benefits as they become due. Vesting occurs when the employee reaches age 45 and has been employed by CIL 10 years.

At the inception of the plan, past service cost (PSC) amounted to $300,000. For accounting purposes, PSC is being amortized over 15 years (average period to vesting) on a straight-line basis. The past service cost is being funded over 10 years by level annual end-of-year payments calculated at 5%, which is a reasonable approximation of long-term borrowing rates (see actuarial report for the funding amount, following). Each year, the company also funds an amount equal to current service cost less actuarial gains or plus actuarial losses on the pension obligation. The assumed average annual return on plan assets is projected at 6%.

At the beginning of 20X8, the defined benefit obligation was $1,296,330. Opening unrecognized actuarial gains were $154,250. In 20X8, the average remaining service period of the whole employee group was estimated to be 20 years.

The independent actuary's biennial revaluation report follows.

Computer Imaging Limited
Non-contributory Defined Benefit Pension Plan
Actuarial Report, 31 December 20X8

Current Service Cost
Computed by the projected unit credit method $ 85,375

Actuarial revaluation
Experience gains for
  Mortality $ 7,875
  Employee turnover   12,625
Reduction in defined benefit obligation due to
  layoffs; part of restructuring program   20,000
Decrease in defined benefit obligation
  due to increase in discount rate   29,500
Net actuarial gains $ 70,000

20X8 funding
Current service cost $85,375
Past service cost   38,853
Less revaluation gains of 20X8   (70,000)
Total cash contribution to plan $ 54,228

Pension plan asset portfolio
Market value, 31 December 20X7 $1,375,790
Portfolio performance, 20X8
  Interest, dividends, and capital gains   151,685
Market value, 31 December 20X8 $1,527,475
Investment performance for 20X8   11.025%

Required:
Calculate pension expense for 20X8, and the year-end balance of the defined benefit obligation. Also provide a calculation of the unrecognized actuarial gains and losses at the end of 20X8. The company follows the practice of amortizing actuarial gains and losses to pension expense when the 1 January amount is outside the 10% corridor.

★★★ **A18-30 Comprehensive; Chapters 12, 13, 14, 17, 18:** Oilfield Multiservices Ltd. (OML) offers oilfield operation services to the oil and gas industry in Alberta and Texas. OML owns no natural resource properties itself, but assists in exploration activities through cementing and stimulation services. OML complies with ASPE. The company has prepared draft financial statements (Exhibit 1). However, some transactions during the year have not been properly reflected in the financial statements (Exhibit 2). Additional information on financial statement elements are provided in Exhibit 3. OML is required, as part of its bond agreement, to maintain a minimum level of retained earnings of $30 million, and a maximum debt-to-equity ratio of 1.5. In the debt-to-equity ratio, the numerator is "total liabilities." Since a number of the transactions that have not been processed affect debt and/or equity, the CFO is concerned that these key financial targets continue to be met.

Required:
1. Provide journal entries to account for the information provided in Exhibits 2 and 3. None of the adjustments mentioned alter income tax expense, income tax payable, or future income tax. Round all adjustments to the nearest thousand. All amounts are given in thousands, except share volumes and per share amounts.

2. Prepare a revised statement of financial position, statement of comprehensive income, and statement of retained earnings.
3. Evaluate the key financial targets and suggest action for the coming year if there are concerns.

EXHIBIT 1

OILFIELD MULTISERVICES LTD.—DRAFT FINANCIAL STATEMENTS FOR THE YEAR ENDED 31 DECEMBER 20X7 (IN THOUSANDS)

STATEMENT OF FINANCIAL POSITION

Assets

Cash		$ 14,960
Accounts receivable		30,497
Inventory		1,958
Prepaid expenses and deposits		930
Current assets		48,345
Capital assets, net		78,441
Intangible assets		890
Suspense		8,338
Total assets		**$136,014**

Liabilities

Accounts payable and accrued liabilities		$ 19,511
Income tax payable		1,600
Current bank loan		12,100
Current liabilities		33,211
Lease liability		3,985
Long-term debt	30,000	
Premium	1,210	31,210
Future income tax		6,900
Defined benefit obligation		620
Total liabilities		75,926

Shareholders' equity

Preferred shares		5,100
Common shares		11,050
Contributed capital on common stock retirement		788
Stock options outstanding		450
Retained earnings		42,700
Total shareholders' equity		60,088
Total liabilities and shareholders' equity		**$136,014**

STATEMENT OF EARNINGS; YEAR ENDED 31 DECEMBER 20X7

Sales	$146,560

Expenses

Operating	103,490
Selling, general, and administration	8,385
Interest	2,355
Amortization	8,420
	122,650
Income before tax	23,910
Income tax	5,950
Net income	**$ 17,960**

STATEMENT OF RETAINED EARNINGS; YEAR ENDED 31 DECEMBER 20X7

Retained earnings, beginning of year	$ 27,965
Common share retirement	0
Dividends:	
Preferred dividends	0
Common share dividends	(3,225)
Stock dividends	0
Net income	17,960
Retained earnings, end of year	$ 42,700

EXHIBIT 2

OILFIELD MULTISERVICES LTD.—OUTSTANDING TRANSACTIONS

Note: Amounts are in thousands, except share volumes and per share amounts

1. Preferred dividends were declared but not paid. They have not yet been recorded. They should be included in "Accounts payable and accrued liabilities."

2. On 1 October 20X7, 865,000 common shares were re-acquired from a shareholder and retired. The $6,240 payment was debited to the "suspense" account, which now appears as an asset.

3. No premium amortization on the bond has been recorded for 20X7.

4. No adjustment has been made for compensation expense inherent in stock option plans.

5. The $2,098 payment made to the pension trustee was debited to the "suspense" account. No pension expense has been recorded in the 20X7 financial statements. The pension plan covers operating employees (85%) and administrative staff (15%).

6. A stock dividend of 10% was declared and distributed on 31 December on common shares. The Board of Directors agreed that this was to be capitalized at a value of $8 per share. The stock dividend has not yet been recorded.

7. The lease liability must be adjusted for interest and the current portion, which will be classified as part of the current liability "Current bank loan."

EXHIBIT 3

OILFIELD MULTISERVICES LTD.—ADDITIONAL INFORMATION

Note: Amounts are in thousands, except share volumes and per share amounts

1. *Lease obligation*

   The lease obligation is the remaining portion of a 20-year capital lease with annual payments each 1 January of $612. The 1 January 20X7 payment was properly recorded. The interest rate used for lease capitalization was 7%. No interest has been recorded in 20X7, nor has the current portion of the lease liability been recorded.

2. *Share information*

   Preferred shares—$6 cumulative no-par preferred shares outstanding, 51,000 shares outstanding during the entire year in 20X7.

   Common shares—No-par common shares outstanding at the beginning of 20X7, 6,210,000 shares. During the year, 865,000 shares were retired on 1 October and a 10% stock dividend was declared and distributed on 31 December.

3. *Bonds payable*

Long-term debt consists of:
Bonds payable, 6 1/4%, due 30 June 20X21 $30,000
Premium amortization of $83 has yet to be recorded for the year.

4. *Outstanding stock options*

Stock options have been outstanding during 20X7 for 265,000 shares. These options are held by senior administrative employees. They may be exercised for the first time on 1 January 20X9, and the related cost is being amortized over four years. The options were originally valued at $900 using the binomial option pricing model.

5. *Pension information*

According to a recent actuarial evaluation, the defined benefit pension plan had $8,475 in assets and $9,716 of defined benefit obligation at the beginning of 20X7. The actual return on assets was $680, while $495 was expected. Current service cost in 20X7 was $1,700 using the projected unit credit actuarial cost method. A long-term interest rate of 6% was considered appropriate to measure interest cost. The company uses the corridor method to evaluate the need to amortize actuarial gains and losses, and no amortization was needed in 20X7. Benefits paid to pensioners were $500. The unamortized balance of past service cost from plan adoption and amendment was $600 at the beginning of 20X7. The amortization period relating to this amount was 10 years at the beginning of 20X7.

Source: Reproduced with permission from CGA-Canada.

CHAPTER 19

Earnings per Share

References to earnings data expressed as earnings per share (EPS) are common in the financial press. Public companies report their EPS numbers quarterly, and use the statistic to benchmark results and communicate targets. For example, Tim Horton's reported 2009 EPS of $1.64, in line with analysts' estimates, and simultaneously issued a press release outlining its growth strategy for 2010, complete with estimates of 2010 EPS in the $1.95 to $2.05 range.

Earnings per share is calculated in order to indicate the *proportionate* per share interest in the company's earnings. An *absolute* increase in earnings is not, in itself, an adequate indicator because earnings may go up as a result of increased investment. For example, a company may issue more shares for cash. The increased investment would be expected to generate additional earnings for the company. For an individual shareholder, the real question is whether profit increased *enough* to compensate for the increased number of shares outstanding. If the proportionate increase in earnings is higher than the proportionate increase in outstanding shares, then earnings attributable to each share will increase.

In this chapter, we demonstrate how to calculate basic EPS, which is defined as the profit or loss attributable to ordinary equity holders, divided by the weighted-average number of ordinary shares outstanding. The chapter also addresses the intricacies of diluted EPS, a "what-if" statistic presented to give investors information about the potential decline in EPS if outstanding options, convertible securities, and contingently issuable ordinary shares were to result in the issuance of shares. Finally, the uses and limitations of earnings per share data are explored.

EPS FIGURES

Companies must report basic and diluted EPS on the statement of comprehensive income. Basic EPS is useful for comparing a company's current performance with its past record. **Basic earnings per share** is calculated based on:

1. Profit or loss from continuing operations, if presented; and then

2. Profit or loss.

Basic EPS is calculated as profit or loss attributable to common shareholders (profit or loss less preferred share claims and other prior claims) divided by the weighted-average ordinary (common) shares outstanding. The per-share amount of discontinued operations on their own may be disclosed with EPS or in a disclosure note. If there are no discontinued operations, then only EPS based on profit and loss is reported.

Some companies have significant potential share commitments in their capital structure. That is, there may be convertible securities and/or stock options outstanding, and/or contingent commitments to issue ordinary (common) shares. These commitments raise the possibility of substantial change in the corporation's capital structure. Therefore, in order to provide a basis for useful forward predictions, diluted EPS must also be disclosed. **Diluted earnings per share** shows the maximum dilution to EPS that could occur if all dilutive potential ordinary shares were issued—that is, if all dilutive stock options were exercised, all dilutive convertible debt and convertible preferred shares were converted to common shares, and all contingently issuable shares were issued.

Diluted EPS must also be calculated both on (1) profit or loss from continuing operations, if presented, and then (2) profit or loss.

INTERPRETING EPS

EPS numbers can be used as follows:

- *Basic EPS.* This is an historical amount. It can be compared with basic EPS numbers from past years to see whether the company is earning more or less for its common shareholders. It is a common way to communicate earnings information to shareholders. Basic EPS may indicate a trend to assist in forecasting.

- *Diluted EPS.* Companies usually issue convertible securities with the hope and expectation that they will convert to common shares and become part of the permanent capital of the company. That is, if the company is successful in its financing strategy, the convertible senior securities will be converted rather than repaid. Therefore, diluted EPS gives an indication of the long-run impact that conversions (and options) will have on the earnings attributable to common shares.

One important aspect of EPS numbers is that they mean nothing by themselves. Like all economic indices, they are meaningful only as part of a series. Trend over time is important. The EPS trend may be easier to interpret than the trend in earnings because EPS is adjusted for changes in capital structure. This removes the normal earnings expansion effect that arises through additional share capital.

By definition, discontinued operations will wind down and cease to be a factor in operating results, although this may take several years. EPS numbers based on earnings from continuing operations are likely more relevant when contemplating projections.

The absolute level of EPS is relatively meaningless. The fact that one company has EPS of $4 per share while another has EPS of $28 per share does not demonstrate that the company with the higher number is more profitable. It all depends on the number of shares outstanding. Therefore, one company's EPS cannot be compared to another's. EPS numbers are meaningful only as part of the statistical series of the reporting company's historical and projected earnings per share.

Because it encapsulates a company's entire reported results for the year in a single number, EPS hides much more than it shows. Placing strong reliance on EPS as an indicator of a company's performance is accepting on faith the message put forth by management in its selection of accounting policies, accounting estimates, and measurement and reporting of unusual items. A knowledgeable user will use EPS only as a rough guide; it is no substitute for an informed analysis of the company's reporting practices.

ETHICAL ISSUES

EPS calculations are complex, and their meaning is sufficiently uncertain that many accountants believe the level of reliance on them is unwarranted. Using EPS as an important element in a company's goal structure can contribute to a short-term management attitude. This can lead to decisions that are detrimental to the long-term productivity and financial health of the company. For example, rather than investing cash in productive activities that enhance the company's earnings, management may engage in share buybacks in order to decrease the denominator of the EPS calculation.

Nevertheless, EPS computations continue to be reported by companies and anticipated by shareholders, analysts, and management. Knowledge of how EPS amounts are calculated is essential if intelligent use is to be made of the resulting figures.

BASIC EARNINGS PER SHARE

The basic earnings per share calculation for the year is as follows:

$$\frac{\text{Net profit or loss available to ordinary shareholders}}{\text{Weighted-average number of ordinary shares outstanding}}$$

The following sections explain more fully both the numerator and denominator of the basic EPS calculation.

Ordinary Shares

EPS is calculated with reference to **ordinary shares**, defined as equity instruments that are subordinate to all other classes of equity instruments. There may also be **senior shares**, which are any shares that have claims with higher priority than ordinary shares. Typically, common shares are ordinary shares and preferred shares are senior shares. It is possible for an entity to have more than one class of ordinary share. For example, if there are preferred shares that participate fully in dividends with common shares, then they are not considered to be senior shares for the purpose of EPS calculation, regardless of whether they are called "preferred shares" or "senior shares" in the corporate charter. See the section on multiple classes of shares, following.

Net Profit or Loss Available to Ordinary Shareholders

The numerator, *net profit or loss available to ordinary shareholders*, is net earnings of the company, less claims to earnings that take precedence over the ordinary share claim. The most usual prior claim to earnings is the dividend entitlement of senior (preferred) shares. The preferential dividend rights of senior shares are deducted from earnings when calculating EPS as follows:

- For *cumulative* senior shares, the annual dividend is subtracted from earnings regardless of whether it has been declared for the year; any future dividend distributions to ordinary shareholders can be made only after senior shares' dividends in arrears have been paid.
- For *non-cumulative* senior shares, only those dividends actually declared during the period are subtracted in determining the EPS numerator.

What happens if cumulative preferred share dividends go in arrears, and, say, three years' dividends are paid in year 3 to clear up the arrears and bring the shares up to date? In years 1 and 2, when no dividends were paid, the annual dividend entitlement would have been deducted from earnings in order to calculate basic EPS. In the third year, three years' dividends are paid, but *only the current year dividend is deducted* when calculating basic EPS. It would be double counting (or double deducting!) to take year 1 and year 2 dividends off *again*. So, for cumulative shares, the maximum deduction is one year's dividend. If shares are non-cumulative, a deduction is made for any and all dividends declared in the period. This represents their maximum claim to earnings.

Some preferred shares are classified as debt because they have fixed repayment terms, or other characteristics that, in substance, render the shares debt rather than equity. Dividends on these preferred shares are deducted to arrive at earnings, like interest, rather than classified as a deduction from retained earnings. *As a result, earnings will already be net of these preferred dividends.* Be sure to understand the starting point; preferred dividends are deducted only once!

Other Adjustments While dividends on preferred shares are the most frequent adjustment to the earnings line in basic EPS, more adjustments may be needed. For example:

- If preferred shares are retired during the period, a "loss" will be recorded directly in shareholders' equity, if the price paid is higher than the average issuance price to date. This was described in Chapter 13. This loss is not included in net earnings, but is included (subtracted) in the numerator of basic EPS.

- If there is a *capital charge* on a convertible bond that is recorded as a direct deduction from retained earnings, this amount is also subtracted in the numerator of basic EPS.

The important question is always *what are the earnings available to ordinary shareholders?* Increases or decreases to all equity accounts should be carefully reviewed before EPS is calculated.

Weighted Average Number of Shares

The denominator of the EPS calculation reflects the number of ordinary shares, on average, that were outstanding during the year. Usually, ordinary shares are *common shares.* However, the denominator will include all classes of shares that have residual claim (last call) on dividends, regardless of the name given to them in the corporate charter or in the accounting records. The denominator is weighted by the proportion of the year that shares are outstanding. The result is **weighted average ordinary shares (WAOS)** outstanding.

In this calculation, shares are weighted by the length of time they are outstanding during the period. If a corporation issues additional shares during the year, additional capital invested in the business should increase earnings. Similarly, if the number of shares outstanding during the year is reduced through a share buy-back program, withdrawal of capital from the business can be expected to reduce earnings. The intent of the EPS calculation is to reflect the relative effect on earnings after including the change in shares outstanding.

Daily averaging is the most accurate, and is technically required. However, *calculations done by full month are permitted* (8/12, 4/12, etc.), as an expedient and reasonable way to approximate the result that a more detailed daily analysis would provide. Calculations may have to be done more precisely if the approximation is not adequate in the circumstances. For instance, if outstanding shares fluctuated heavily during a month, full-month weighting would be inappropriate.

Example Assume that a company has 9,000,000 common shares outstanding at the beginning of the year. The fiscal year for this company is the calendar year. An additional 3,000,000 shares are issued on 1 September. There will have been 9,000,000 shares outstanding for the first eight months of the year, followed by 12,000,000 for the last four months. The weighted-average number of shares outstanding is 10,000,000. This can be calculated using a number of approaches. For example,

Method 1

9,000,000 shares outstanding for eight months: 9,000,000 × 8/12	=	6,000,000
12,000,000 shares outstanding for four months: 12,000,000 × 4/12	=	4,000,000
WAOS	=	10,000,000

Method 2	Number of Shares	×	Months Outstanding	=	Weighted No. of Shares
	9,000,000		8		72,000,000
	12,000,000		4		48,000,000
	Total				120,000,000

WAOS = 120,000,000 ÷ 12 months = 10,000,000

Method 3

9,000,000 shares outstanding for the full year: 9,000,000 × 12/12	=	9,000,000
3,000,000 shares outstanding for four months: 3,000,000 × 4/12	–	1,000,000
WAOS	=	10,000,000

easy to use in exam (handwritten note)

Each of these methods generates the same, correct answer and all are acceptable approaches. Illustrations in this chapter will use the first method.

Contingently Issuable Shares

Contingently issuable ordinary shares are ordinary shares that are issuable for little or no cash, upon the satisfaction of specific conditions in a contingent share agreement. For example, a company may agree to issue common shares to a stakeholder if a licence for a new product is granted, or issue shares to the former shareholders of an acquisition target company if the acquired operation achieves a certain level of post-acquisition profit. Contingently issuable shares are included as outstanding in WAOS *from the date that the necessary conditions have been met*. This applies even if the shares are not issued until a later date.

For example, assume that Chairot Limited signed an agreement as part of a business acquisition that committed Chairot to issue 10,000 common shares for no cash consideration if the target company produced 500,000 units of a sub-assembly in the first quarter after acquisition. This target was met at the end of March 20X0 and the shares were issued in July 20X0. For the purposes of WAOS calculation, the shares would be treated as though they were issued when the contingency was met, at the end of March 20X0.

Stock Splits and Stock Dividends

An entity may issue or reduce shares outstanding without a corresponding change in resources: that is, for no consideration. If shares are issued under such circumstances, they are sometimes called **bonus shares**. Two common examples of this situation are in the case of a **stock dividend** or a **stock split**. A stock dividend is a dividend payable by issue of shares of the company's own common stock. Such shares *are not weight-averaged*. Instead, the stock dividend or stock split is treated as though it had been in effect for the whole period. It is also *adjusted through all prior years* disclosed as comparative data. That is, dividend shares and split shares are treated as though they have always been outstanding.

Remember, when a share dividend or split occurs, common share equity is not changed, nor is the composition of the broader capital structure affected (i.e., no change to long-term debt or other elements). There is no substantive change to the corporation's net asset structure. Splits and dividends do not bring new assets into the corporation and therefore cannot be expected to generate additional earnings. Earnings are simply split up into pieces of different size.

In order to assure comparability of EPS, *all* reported prior years' EPS numbers are restated to reflect splits and dividends. In the case of a 2-for-1 split, all prior EPS figures will be divided by two because one share outstanding in previous years is equivalent to two shares outstanding after the split. The denominator of the fraction doubles, so the product is halved.

Example   The following example illustrates the calculation of WAOS when there are bonus shares.

- A corporation has 5,000 common shares outstanding on 1 January, the beginning of the fiscal year.
- On 31 March, the conversion privilege on convertible bonds is exercised by the bondholders, resulting in an additional 2,400 shares being issued.
- On 1 September, the shares are split 2-for-1.
- On 1 October, an additional 3,000 shares are issued for cash.

In this example, each share outstanding prior to 1 September is equivalent to two shares outstanding after that date. The denominator of the EPS calculation must be adjusted to reflect the shares outstanding at the end of the year, after the stock split. The discontinuity that occurs as the result of the stock split must be adjusted by multiplying the pre-September outstanding shares by the split factor (in this example, $\times$ **2**) as follows:

WAOS calculation:		
1 January–31 March (pre-split)	5,000 $\times$ **2** $\times$ 3/12	2,500
1 April–31 August (pre-split)	7,400 $\times$ **2** $\times$ 5/12	6,167
1 September–30 September	14,800 $\times$ 1/12	1,233
1 October–31 December	17,800 $\times$ 3/12	4,450
WAOS		14,350

The 5,000 shares outstanding for the first three months are equivalent to 10,000 (5,000 $\times$ 2) shares after the split. Similarly, the 7,400 shares are multiplied by two to arrive at 14,800 post-split shares. Shares from the date of the split are *not* multiplied by two, because they are stated in post-split shares.

Post Year-end Split or Dividend   If there is a stock dividend or stock split *after the end of the year* (in the next fiscal period), it is factored into the weighted-average calculation of the *current year*. This applies to stock dividends and splits that take place before the audit report is signed. Assume a company's fiscal year ends on 31 December 20X5. Thirty thousand common shares have been outstanding for the entire period. On 15 January 20X6, before the audit is complete, there is a reverse stock split, 1-for-3. The 30,000 shares become 10,000 shares. This 10,000 figure will be used for EPS calculations even though the reverse split happened after the end of the year. After all, by the time the financial statements are released, the shareholders will be holding their new, smaller shares, and all data should be applicable to this new capital arrangement.

Other Effects of a Split or Dividend   A split or dividend will change the terms of all outstanding share commitment contracts. That is, when there is a stock split or stock dividend, the number of shares into which each senior security is convertible is adjusted accordingly. For example, if a $1,000 bond was convertible into four common shares prior to a 2-for-1 split (i.e., a conversion price of $250), then it will automatically be convertible into eight shares (a conversion price of $125) after the split. There is *always* an anti-dilution provision to protect the holders of convertible securities and options. Option contracts will also be changed, increasing the number of shares offered and decreasing the option price.

Example: Basic EPS

Exhibit 19-1 shows the computation of basic EPS in a situation involving a simple capital structure that has non-convertible preferred shares. It is based on the following facts:

1. Capital structure:

Common shares, no-par, outstanding on 1 January	90,000 shares
Common shares, issued 1 May for cash	6,000 shares
Preferred shares, no-par, $1.20 (cumulative, nonconvertible) outstanding on 1 January	5,000 shares

2. Earnings data for the year ending 31 December:

Net earnings from continuing operations	$147,000
Discontinued operations, net of tax	30,000
Net earnings and comprehensive income	$177,000

Exhibit 19-1 presents the computation of the weighted-average number of common shares outstanding during the year. The numerator for basic EPS is adjusted for preferred dividends. Remember that earnings is *before* these dividends, and an adjustment is needed.

The two EPS figures of $1.50 and $1.82 must be reported on the face of the statement of comprehensive income. The $0.32 EPS figure for discontinued operations may be reported either on the statement of comprehensive income or in the disclosure notes.

Multiple Classes of Common Shares

As we saw in Chapter 13, Canadian corporations may have multiple classes of common, or ordinary, shares outstanding. These share classes *participate* in dividends. A primary reason for having two or more classes of common shares is to vary the voting rights between

---

EXHIBIT 19-1

BASIC EPS CALCULATION

	Earnings Available to Common Shares	Weighted- Average Number of Shares	Earnings per Share
Earnings:			
Net earnings from continuing operations	$147,000		
Less preferred dividend entitlement:			
5,000 shares × $1.20	(6,000)		
Earnings available to common, continuing operations	$141,000		
Net earnings	$177,000		
Less preferred dividend entitlement:			
5,000 shares × $1.20	(6,000)		
Earnings available to common, net earnings	$171,000		
Shares outstanding:			
90,000 × 4/12		30,000	
96,000 × 8/12		64,000	
Weighted average		94,000	
Basic EPS:			
Earnings from continuing operations	$141,000	94,000	$1.50
Discontinued operations*	30,000	94,000	0.32
Net earnings	$171,000	94,000	$1.82

*Per share amount may be included in the disclosure notes

the different classes, normally in order to prevent the controlling shareholders from losing control to hostile investors. So-called "preferred shares" may also be *ordinary shares* if they participate fully in dividends.

When evaluating a company with multiple classes of shares, it is important to evaluate their dividend privileges. If the dividend privileges are *different*, then EPS calculations must be done for each class. *If two or more classes share dividends equally, share for share, then they are all ordinary shares and are lumped together in the denominator of the EPS calculation.* For example, assume that a corporation has two classes of ordinary voting shares, Class 1 and Class 2. The shares have equal dividend rights. If there were 100,000 Class 1 shares and 400,000 Class 2 shares outstanding throughout the year, then 500,000 shares would be used for WAOS.

Unequal Dividend Entitlements If the sharing of dividends is *unequal*, more than one basic EPS statistic will be calculated. For example, assume that a corporation has two classes of ordinary voting shares, Class A and Class B. Class A shares receive three times the dividend declared on Class B shares. If there were 20,000 Class A shares and 80,000 Class B shares outstanding throughout the year, then 140,000 shares ((20,000 Class A shares × 3) plus 80,000 Class B shares) would be used for WAOS. If the result was $1 per share, basic EPS would be reported as $1 per share for Class B and $3 for Class A.

Complex/Unequal Dividend Entitlements Dividend arrangements often provide a base dividend, followed by participation in any remaining dividends declared. For example, assume now that both Class A and Class B ordinary shares are entitled to receive a $1 per share dividend. After this amount, Class A shares are entitled to receive $2 per share in dividends for every $1 per share paid to Class B. Profit for the year was $220,000. There were 20,000 Class A shares and 80,000 Class B shares outstanding throughout the year.

To keep it simple, also assume that there are no preferred shares, no shares issued or retired during the year, and no discontinued operations included in earnings.

To calculate basic EPS when the two share classes participate differently in dividend declarations, profit is assigned to the classes according to the base dividend, then *all* of the remaining profit is allocated according to the sharing arrangement. This allocation is based on a ratio, which is a combination of the number of shares outstanding in each class and their relative dividend entitlement. The result is two earnings pools, which are then divided by the number of shares for each respective pool. Finally, EPS for each pool is the additive sum of the base dividend and the entitlement to undistributed earnings. The calculations:

Step 1—Calculate earnings minus the base dividend

Profit is $220,000, and the base dividend is $100,000
  ($1 × (20,000 Class A shares plus 80,000 Class B shares))
Unallocated profit is $120,000

Step 2—Allocate undistributed earnings to the share classes

Class A receives $120,000 × 1/3* = $40,000
Class B receives $120,000 × 2/3* = $80,000

*A shares, in equivalent Class B shares = 40,000 (20,000 × 2)**

There are 80,000 Class B shares outstanding = 80,000
Fractions: A: 40 ÷ (40 + 80) = 1/3; B: 80 ÷ (40 + 80) = 2/3

**There are 20,000 Class A shares outstanding, entitled to two times the Class B dividend.

Step 3—Determine per share amounts (from Step 2)

Class A: $40,000 ÷ 20,000 shares = $2
Class B: $80,000 ÷ 80,000 shares = $1

Step 4—Add base dividend to the Step 3 amounts

Class A: $1 + $2 = $3
Class B: $1 + $1 = $2

Basic EPS for each class reflects both the base dividend plus the dividend that would be received if *all earnings* were declared as dividends. The denominator would be a weighted average for each class if shares outstanding had changed during the period.

Declared or Not? This example assumes that the base dividend was declared. If the dividend is not declared, but is *cumulative*, then nothing changes. However, if the base dividend is *not cumulative*, then it is lost if it is not declared, and excess dividends over the base in future years would follow the (step 2) residual allocation. Therefore, if the base is not cumulative and is not declared, step 1 would not be required in the EPS calculation. In the vast majority of cases, the base dividend is cumulative, so all steps are needed.

CONCEPT REVIEW

1. What type of corporation is required to disclose earnings per share amounts?
2. What is the formula for basic earnings per share?
3. How does earnings available to ordinary shares differ from net earnings?
4. Asquith Corporation has 2,000 common shares outstanding on 1 January 20X0, issues another 400 shares on 1 July 20X0, and declares a 2-for-1 stock split on 31 December 20X0. What is the weighted-average number of shares outstanding for the year? What is the impact of the stock split on prior years' EPS amounts?
5. List the steps in calculating basic EPS when there are multiple common share classes.

DILUTED EARNINGS PER SHARE

Earnings dilution occurs when additional shares are issued without a sufficient proportionate increase in the level of earnings. EPS will decline, or is diluted. Diluted EPS is meant to reflect any potential for earnings dilution because of *dilutive potential ordinary shares* from existing share contracts. It is based on the *hypothetical situation* of complete share issuance for any contract that may entitle its holder to ordinary shares in the future. Diluted EPS is hypothetical in that it reflects the results of share transactions that have not taken place but could take place in the future. It's often called a "what if" number—that is, what happens *if potential ordinary shares were all issued?*

Elements to Include Diluted EPS reflects the *hypothetical* earnings dilution resulting from potential share transactions in the following circumstances:

- Dilutive options to purchase shares are exercised, *and*
- Dilutive convertible senior securities outstanding are converted to common shares, *and*
- Dilutive *contingently issuable ordinary shares* are issued, *and*
- Any shares actually issued *during the year* because of (dilutive) convertible senior securities, share option contracts, or contingently issuable ordinary shares are issued a*t the beginning* of the fiscal year.

Convertible senior securities include debt and preferred shares, senior to common shares in their entitlement to interest or dividends. If these are convertible to common shares at some point in the future, or have been converted to common shares during the period, they will enter into the calculation of diluted EPS.

A **stock option** gives the holder the right to acquire a share at a stated price. Options sometimes are issued as a part of a package offering of securities (i.e., as a sweetener to attract buyers to a bond issue) and also are widely used as a form of executive compensation. There are various types of options, including stock rights, warrants, and employee stock options. In this chapter, the word "options" will be used to encompass all alternatives.

If options were exercised and/or are outstanding, they will be considered when calculating diluted EPS.

As previously discussed, *contingently issuable ordinary shares* are ordinary shares that are issuable for little or no cash, upon the satisfaction of specific conditions in a contingent share agreement. If these agreements are in place, or such shares have been issued during the year, they will be a factor in diluted EPS.

Dilutive versus Anti-Dilutive Diluted EPS is meant to be a worst-case scenario. **Dilutive** elements are those that, when included in EPS calculations, cause a decrease in earnings per share (or an increase in a loss per share). **Anti-dilutive** elements are those that cause earnings per share to increase (or a loss per share to decrease). If share agreements are anti-dilutive contracts, they are *excluded* from the calculation of diluted EPS. It is assumed that the investors holding anti-dilutive elements would not convert to ordinary shares in these circumstances.

Diluted EPS Calculation

To calculate diluted EPS, adjustments are made to basic EPS for dilutive potential ordinary shares.

Adjustment for Dilutive Options Options are dilutive when they are in-the-money. Options are said to be **in-the-money** *if the exercise price is lower than the market value of common shares.* For example, if an option contract specifies a share price of $34.50, and the share price is $50, then the options are in-the-money. If the share price is $20, the options are not in-the-money. *Options are included in diluted EPS calculations when dilutive; that is, only when they are in-the-money.*

Treasury Stock Method Option adjustments are based on the **treasury stock method**—proceeds are assumed to be used to reacquire and retire common shares at the average market price during the period. Assume that 1,000 options are outstanding with an exercise price of $10. The average price of common shares during the year was $40, so these options are in-the-money. If the options were exercised, another 1,000 shares would be outstanding for the period, and the company would receive $10,000 ($10 × 1,000). In diluted EPS calculations, it is assumed that this $10,000 is used to repurchase and retire other common shares, also at the beginning of the year. Ten thousand dollars would buy 250 shares ($10,000 ÷ $40). The *denominator* of diluted EPS would be increased by 1,000 shares issued and decreased by 250 shares retired. The net adjustment is an increase of 750 shares. These 750 shares are sometimes referred to as "bonus shares." This is based on the reasoning that the whole transaction can be viewed as $10,000 ($10 × 1,000) raised for 250 shares at full price ($10,000 total proceeds ÷ $40) and 750 shares issued for no consideration. The 750 bonus shares can be directly calculated as 1,000 × ($40 − $10) ÷ $40.

Note that options are dilutive when the number of shares issued is greater than the shares retired; this occurs *only when options are in-the-money.*

Adjustment for Contingently Issuable Shares As previously described, contingently issuable shares involve little or no cash consideration, and must be issued on the resolution of a specified contingency. If the contingency is resolved during the period, and the shares become issuable, the shares are included in WAOS for basic EPS as of the date that the contingency was resolved. If all the necessary conditions have not been satisfied, *the shares might have to be included when calculating diluted EPS.* Shares are included if the only unmet condition is that the date of the contingency period has not yet expired. That is, shares are included *based on the shares issuable if the end of the reporting period were the end of the contingency period.* The shares are included in the denominator as of the beginning of the reporting period, or the date of the contingent share agreement, if later. Contingently issuable shares have no impact on earnings, and thus there is *no change to the numerator* of diluted EPS.

For example, assume that HyperForce Ltd. acquired GH Resources for $15 million early in 20X1. The purchase and sale agreement specified that if GH's core operations earned at least $4,000,000 per year for three years, the former shareholders of GH would be entitled to

100,000 ordinary shares in HyperForce. The GH operation earned $5,800,000 during 20X1. If the contingency, earnings performance, were to have concluded at the end of 20X1 (i.e., been for one year only), the shares would be issuable. Therefore, the 100,000 common shares are included in the denominator of diluted EPS calculation for 20X1, at least backdated to the date in early 20X1 when the acquisition became effective. These shares are included even though the agreement states that *three years* of earnings must be earned to satisfy the contingency. All that is required for inclusion in diluted EPS is that the necessary conditions are met *if the contingency period ended at the end of 20X1*. If, on the other hand, the agreement were written to require *cumulative earnings of $12 million* before the shares were issuable, then the shares would not have been included in diluted EPS at the end of 20X1 because the condition was not met.

Adjustment for Dilutive Senior Securities Bond and preferred share adjustments are based on the **if-converted method**—that is, the numerator and denominator are adjusted to reflect what would have been *if the securities were converted at the beginning of the period (or the date of issue, if later)*. The numerator of the EPS fraction is adjusted for dividends or after-tax interest that would be saved if the bonds or preferred shares were converted. In other words, how would the numerator be different if the convertible bonds didn't exist? Interest expense would be eliminated. What if the preferred shares didn't exist? There would be no dividends. The effect to the denominator is straightforward in both cases. More shares would be outstanding!

Technicalities to note:

1. If there are a variety of conversion terms, perhaps depending on when the conversion were to take place, *the most dilutive alternative must be used.*

2. If the securities were issued during the year, the assumed conversion goes *back only to the date of issue*, not the beginning of the year.

3. If the conversion option lapsed during the year, or if the security was redeemed or settled during the year, the conversion is still included (if dilutive) *for the period of time it was outstanding.*

Calculation Rules To summarize the potential adjustments:

Element	Change to Numerator	Change to Denominator
Options—treasury stock method	None	1. Increase by shares issued 2. Decrease by shares retired (Proceeds ÷ market value)
Contingently issuable shares	None	Increase by shares issued
Convertible bonds—if-converted method	Increase by after-tax interest avoided	Increase by shares issued
Convertible preferred shares—if-converted method	Increase by dividend claim avoided*	Increase by shares issued

*If there were any other items recorded in the financial statements, such as gains or losses on preferred share retirement, these items would have been adjusted when calculating the basic EPS numerator and also included in the numerator adjustment here.

Individual Effect Notice that convertible bonds and convertible preferred shares involve a change to the numerator *and* a change to the denominator. The **individual effect** of each convertible item is represented by this ratio. For instance, if there was $10,000 of after-tax interest on a bond that was convertible into 40,000 common shares, the individual effect would be $0.25 ($10,000 ÷ 40,000). The *individual effect* must be calculated separately for each potentially dilutive element. It is the change to earnings entitlement divided by additional shares that would have to be issued, and it is used to establish dilution or anti-dilution and sequence for convertible senior securities.

Steps in Calculating Diluted EPS

The steps in calculating diluted EPS are listed in Exhibit 19-2. A flow chart of the process is shown in Exhibit 19-3. We will explain these steps in the example that follows; refer to the list as the example progresses.

EXHIBIT 19-2

STEPS IN CALCULATING DILUTED EPS

To Calculate Diluted EPS:

1. **Begin with the basic EPS numbers**, based on *earnings from continuing operations*. If there were no discontinued operations, begin with the only basic EPS number available, basic EPS based on net earnings.

2. If any options were **exercised** during the period, **determine if the options exercised were in-the-money**, and thus dilutive. **Adjust the denominator** as though these shares were issued at the beginning of the period, using the **treasury stock method**.

3. **Identify options outstanding during the year**, the option price, and the average share price for the period. Determine if the options are in-the-money, and thus dilutive. **Adjust the denominator** as though these shares were issued at the beginning of the period, using the **treasury stock method**. Calculate a subtotal at this point.

4. If any contingently issuable shares were **issued** during the period, **adjust the denominator** as though these shares were issued at the beginning of the period. This moves the share issuance back to the beginning of the year.

5. **Identify contingently issuable shares outstanding at the end of the year**. Calculate the number of shares, if any, that would be issued if the contingency period were to end at the end of the current fiscal year. **Adjust the denominator** as though these shares were issued at the beginning of the period. Calculate a subtotal at this point.

6. **Identify any convertible senior debt or shares that actually converted** during the period. **Calculate the individual effect** of the converted securities, using the **if-converted method**. This adjustment moves the conversion back to the beginning of the year. The individual effect is after-tax interest or dividends divided by shares issued. Both the numerator and denominator reflect the number of months **before conversion** in the fiscal year.

7. **Identify the terms and conditions of convertible senior shares and debt outstanding during the year.** If there are various conversion alternatives at different dates, use the most dilutive alternative. **Calculate the individual effect** of the converted securities, using the if-converted method.

8. Compare the individual effects of the items identified in Steps 6 and 7. **Rank the items,** from most dilutive (lowest) to least dilutive (highest).

9. Return to the subtotal taken in Step 5. **Include the effects of actual and potential conversions** in cascading order, from most dilutive to least dilutive. Use the ranking from Step 8. **Calculate a subtotal** after each item is added. Exclude anti-dilutive items.

10. Use the **lowest calculation** as diluted EPS.

11. **Repeat the process,** beginning with *basic EPS for net earnings*. Use exactly the same adjustments to the numerator and the denominator as in the first calculation. (No second test for anti-dilution is allowed.)

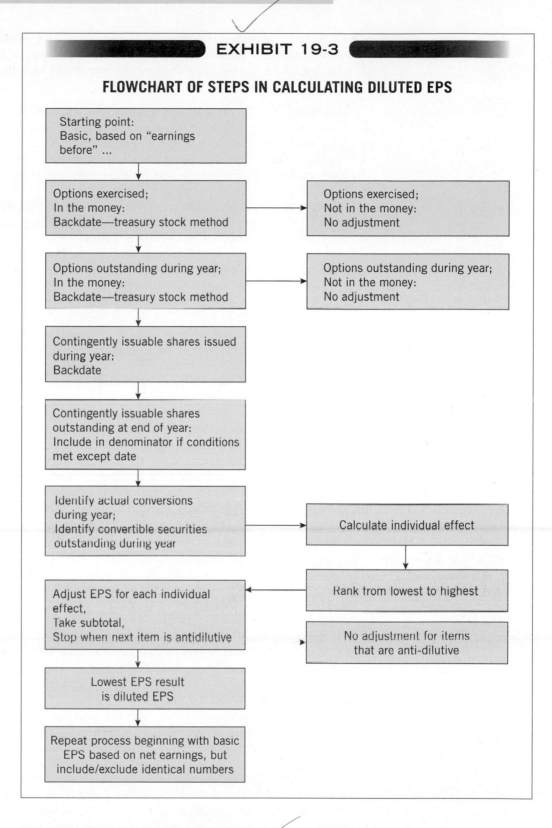

EXHIBIT 19-3

FLOWCHART OF STEPS IN CALCULATING DILUTED EPS

Starting point:
Basic, based on "earnings before" ...

↓

Options exercised;
In the money:
Backdate—treasury stock method

→ Options exercised;
Not in the money:
No adjustment

↓

Options outstanding during year;
In the money:
Backdate—treasury stock method

→ Options outstanding during year;
Not in the money:
No adjustment

↓

Contingently issuable shares issued during year:
Backdate

↓

Contingently issuable shares outstanding at end of year:
Include in denominator if conditions met except date

↓

Identify actual conversions during year;
Identify convertible securities outstanding during year

→ Calculate individual effect

↓

Rank from lowest to highest

↓

Adjust EPS for each individual effect,
Take subtotal,
Stop when next item is antidilutive

No adjustment for items that are anti-dilutive

↓

Lowest EPS result is diluted EPS

↓

Repeat process beginning with basic EPS based on net earnings, but include/exclude identical numbers

Diluted EPS Calculation: Example

Assume that a corporation has the following capital structure for all of 20X1:

- Convertible debentures: $1,000,000 maturity value, issued at 110; $100,000 of proceeds were attributable to the conversion option (and classified as shareholders' equity); 12% interest per annum, paid quarterly; convertible into 10 common shares for each $1,000 of bond maturity value at the option of the investor.

3 adjustments (2, 6, 8) have been identified based on Prof's notes

- Convertible preferred shares: 1,000 shares issued and outstanding; $150 annual per share dividend, cumulative; callable at $1,200 per share; convertible into common shares on a 5:1 basis until 20X5; convertible on a 10:1 basis thereafter.
- Common shares: 20,000 shares issued and outstanding all year.

Net earnings for 20X1 is $600,000. There are no discontinued operations. The corporation's income tax rate is 40%. There are no contingently issuable common shares. There are executive stock options outstanding all year, allowing purchase of 4,000 common shares at an option price of $50. The average market value of common shares during the period was $125. Interest expense for the year for the convertible bond was $120,000 ($1,000,000 × 12%).

Basic EPS for 20X1 is calculated at the top of Exhibit 19-4. Preferred dividends are deducted from net earnings to find the earnings available to common shares, and this amount is divided by 20,000 common shares outstanding.

In the first step in diluted EPS calculation (refer to Exhibit 19-2 for the list of steps), the basic EPS numbers are carried forward. There are no discontinued operations, no shares were issued under option contracts during the year, and there were no contingently issuable common shares. There were no actual conversions of senior securities during the period. Steps 2, 4, 5, 6, and 11 can be skipped. Later examples deal with these situations.

Outstanding options are the next thing to consider, in Step 3. There are options outstanding at the end of the year to issue 4,000 common shares at $50. These options are *in-the-money*, and therefore dilutive, because the $50 option price is less than the $125 average market price of shares during the period. They must be included when calculating diluted EPS.

If these shares had been issued at the beginning of the period, another 4,000 shares would have been outstanding for the whole period, and the denominator would be increased by 4,000 shares. A total of $200,000 (4,000 × $50) would have been raised by the company.

In the diluted EPS calculation, using the treasury stock method, the assumption is that the proceeds would have been used to retire other common shares at the market price: 1,600 shares ($200,000 ÷ $125). The denominator increases by 2,400 shares (4,000 − 1,600) and the numerator doesn't change. It is also possible to make this 2,400 share calculation directly, as ((4,000 × ($125 − $50) ÷ $125). A subtotal shows that the EPS amount has declined to $20.09.

In Step 7, the individual effects of assumed conversion of the two convertible securities are calculated. The numerator of the EPS fraction is adjusted by adjusting for dividends or after-tax interest that will be saved if the senior securities are converted. The effect to the denominator is the additional shares promised.

Note that the bond interest is deductible for income tax purposes, and since net earnings is an after-tax amount, the interest saved must be calculated on an after-tax basis. Assuming a tax rate of 40%, the interest saving is multiplied by the 60% after-tax equivalent: $120,000 × (1.0 − 0.4) = $72,000. Shares issued would be 10,000, and the individual effect of this convertible security is $7.20 ($72,000 ÷ 10,000). This is dilutive in relation to basic EPS of $22.50 (that is, $7.20 is lower than $22.50).

For preferred shares, $150,000 of dividends would be avoided if the preferred shares had been converted to common shares at the beginning of the period. Dividends are not tax deductible, and there is no need to adjust for tax. The shares may be converted at the rate of 5:1 until the end of 20X5, and then the conversion ratio changes to 10:1. *The worst-case scenario, or more dilutive alternative, must be used in these calculations.* This is the 10:1 ratio. Thus, another 10,000 shares would be issued. There is an individual effect of $15, dilutive in relation to basic EPS, but less dilutive than the $7.20 bonds. This comparison is the Step 8 ranking.

Now for Step 9. The bonds are adjusted first, because they are more dilutive than the preferred shares. The subtotal is taken. Inclusion of the bonds reduces diluted EPS to $16.11, and the preferred shares, with an individual affect of $15, are still dilutive. They are then added in. Step 10 is the final determination of diluted EPS—$15.85.

> **EXHIBIT 19-4**

BASIC AND DILUTED EPS CALCULATIONS

	Earnings Available to Common Shares	Weighted-Average Number of Shares	Earnings per Share
Basic EPS:			
Earnings:			
Net earnings and comprehensive income	$600,000		
Less preferred dividends:			
1,000 shares × $150	(150,000)		
Net earnings available to common	450,000		
Shares outstanding		20,000	
Basic EPS	**$450,000**	**20,000**	**$22.50**
Diluted EPS:			
Data from basic EPS, above	$450,000	20,000	$22.50
Adjustments for assumed options exercise:			
Shares issued		4,000	
Shares retired		(1,600)	
Subtotal	$450,000	22,400	$20.09
Adjustments for debenture conversion:			
Interest avoided (after-tax equivalent)	72,000		
Additional common shares issued		10,000	
Subtotal	$522,000	32,400	$16.11
Adjustments for preferred share conversion:			
Dividends avoided	150,000		
Additional common shares issued		10,000	
Diluted EPS	**$672,000**	**42,400**	**$15.85**

(handwritten annotations: $= (20,000 \times \frac{12}{12})$; $\frac{450,000}{20,000}$; $\frac{4000 \times 50\$}{\$125}$)

Reporting Diluted EPS

Diluted EPS is reported on the face of the statement of comprehensive income, given equal prominence with basic EPS. Even if the two numbers are identical, they must both be disclosed. In the above example, the company would report:

Basic EPS	$22.50
Diluted EPS	$15.85

Diluted EPS Cascade

In Exhibit 19-4, we illustrated the diluted EPS calculation as a **cascade** of adjustments, going from the most dilutive to the least dilutive. Note that options that are in-the-money (and any contingently issuable ordinary shares) are always dilutive, because they involve no increase to the numerator. That's why they're *always done first* in diluted EPS calculations.

After options, the convertible securities with the *lowest individual EPS effect* are the most dilutive, and are entered first. If inclusion of a later item causes EPS to *increase*, it is *anti-dilutive and excluded*. For instance, assume that basic EPS is $1, the result of dividing $100,000 earnings available to common shareholders by 100,000 weighted-average ordinary shares. Two potentially dilutive securities are outstanding: preferred shares, with a $45,000 dividend, and a 100,000 share entitlement ($0.45 individual effect), and bonds, with after-tax interest of $68,000, and a share entitlement of 75,000 shares ($0.91 individual effect). Preferred shares are the more dilutive but both elements look dilutive when compared to basic EPS of $1.

After the more dilutive element is included, diluted EPS is $0.73 ($100,000 + $45,000) ÷ (100,000 + 100,000). The second item, with an individual effect of $0.91, is *no longer dilutive*. If it were included, the EPS would *increase* to $0.77 ($100,000 + $45,000 + $68,000) ÷ (100,000 + 100,000 + 75,000).

Diluted EPS is reported as $0.73, and the second security is omitted from the calculation. This is the cascade approach to diluted EPS calculations, and it results in diluted EPS being reported as the lowest possible number.

Actual Conversions During the Period

So far, we've illustrated diluted EPS giving effect to the year-end obligations to issue shares. Diluted EPS must also include calculations that reflect actual conversions, actual contingently issuable shares issued, and actual options exercised during the period. This adjustment is often called **backdating**: *adjusting the actual issuance to pretend it took place at the beginning of the period*. Backdating is done only if the result is dilutive. Backdating puts actual conversions on the same footing as potential conversions, which are effectively backdated to the beginning of the fiscal period. Steps 2, 4 and 6 in Exhibit 19-2 deal with backdating.

The examples that follow demonstrate actual conversions of preferred shares, actual conversion of debt, and shares issued on the exercise of options.

Example 1—Converted Preferred Shares Assume that a corporation has two classes of shares outstanding:

- Class A preferred shares, 600 shares issued and outstanding at the beginning of the year; annual dividend rate of $1,000 per share, cumulative, dividend paid at the end of each quarter; each share is convertible into 50 shares of Class B common.

- Class B common shares, 50,000 shares issued and outstanding at the beginning of the year.

Also assume that:

- There are no other senior securities. [handwritten: means no convertible debt or convertible shares]

- Net earnings for 20X1, the year of the conversion, is $2,175,000; there are no discontinued operations.

- All 600 shares of Class A are converted into 30,000 Class B shares on 1 October 20X1; dividends for the first three quarters of the year were fully paid.

- Options are outstanding to issue 10,000 common shares to senior executives for $1 per share; the average share price during the year was $8. No options were exercised during the period. These options were outstanding during the whole year. [handwritten: Treasury Stock method]

Basic earnings per share for 20X1 is $30, as calculated at the top of Exhibit 19-5. Diluted EPS begins with this figure, and then includes the effect of options. (Step 3 as listed in Exhibit 19-2). This reduces EPS to $26.04. Note that the options effect could be directly calculated as a reduction to the denominator of 8,750 shares ((10,000 × ($8 − $1) ÷ $8). The result is the same.

In the year of conversion, 7,500 shares (600 shares × 50 common shares = 30,000, multiplied by the three months they were outstanding, or 3/12) were added to the *weighted-average* number of shares used in basic EPS. In future years, there will be 30,000 additional Class B shares outstanding *all year*. Diluted EPS backdates the conversion (Step 6). This is demonstrated in the highlighted section of Exhibit 19-5. The essence of backdating is twofold:

- Profit available to common shareholders, the numerator, is adjusted for the dividends on the converted Class A shares that would not have been paid if the shares had converted at the beginning of the period. This is $450,000 ($250 per quarter × 600 shares × 3 quarters).
- The weighted-average number of shares is adjusted to reflect the full volume of additional Class B shares issued for the conversion. That is, 30,000 shares × 9/12, or 22,500 shares.

The individual effect of this conversion is $20 ($450,000 ÷ 22,500), which is dilutive in relation to the diluted EPS subtotal of $26.04. The result of the calculation is diluted EPS of $24.51.

EXHIBIT 19-5

BASIC AND DILUTED EPS CALCULATIONS

Actual Conversion of Preferred Shares

	Earnings Available to Common Shares	Weighted- Average Number of Shares	Earnings per Share
Basic EPS:			
Earnings:			
Net earnings	$2,175,000		
Less preferred dividends:			
600 shares × $250 per quarter × three quarters	(450,000)		
Earnings available to common	$1,725,000		
Shares outstanding			
50,000 × 9/12		37,500	
[50,000 + (600 Class A × 50 Class B)] × 3/12		20,000	
Basic EPS	**$1,725,000**	**57,500**	**$30.00**
Diluted EPS			
Data from basic EPS, above	$1,725,000	57,500	
Adjustments for assumed options exercise:			
Shares issued		10,000	
Shares retired (10,000 × $1) ÷ $8		(1,250)	
Subtotal	$1,725,000	66,250	$26.04
Adjustments for converted shares:			
Dividends on converted shares:			
600 shares × $250 × three quarters	450,000		
Adjust shares for preceding three quarters:			
(600 Class A × 50 Class B) × 9/12		22,500	
Diluted EPS	**$2,175,000**	**88,750**	**$24.51**

Handwritten annotations: "{3 quarters, cumulative, removed}" next to the (450,000) preferred dividends line.

*means
No pref. share*

Example 2—Converted Debt Assume that a corporation has one class of shares outstanding but also has convertible bonds that partially converted during the period:

- There are 50,000 common shares outstanding at the beginning of 20X1.
- Reported profit for 20X1, the year of the conversion, is $3,000,000; there are no discontinued operations.
- The corporation has $40 million principal amount of 10-year, 9%, convertible debentures that were issued five years previously. The bonds are convertible at the investor's option. The full amount is outstanding at the beginning of 20X1. Interest is paid semiannually on 1 March and 1 September.
- The net proceeds from the bond issue amounted to $42 million. The present value of the liability cash flow at the date of issue was $40 million; the remaining $2 million was allocated to the conversion option. At the date of issuance, the market rate of interest for non-convertible bonds of similar risk was 9%. Each $1,000 face value of bonds is convertible into two shares of common stock.
- On 30 June 20X1, one-quarter of the bonds are converted.
- The corporation's income tax rate is 40%.

The conversion of $10,000,000 principal amount of bonds results in an additional 20,000 shares issued. In the basic EPS calculation, the additional shares are outstanding for the second half of the year and are weighted proportionately in the denominator. The EPS numerator already includes, in earnings, a deduction for interest expense on the $40,000,000 liability for the first half of the year and for the $30,000,000 liability for the second half of the year, following conversion. The calculation of basic EPS is shown at the top of Exhibit 19-6.

To calculate diluted EPS, the actual conversion must be backdated to the beginning of the year (Step 6). The effect of the remaining unconverted bonds must be included (Step 9). Both of these adjustments are made *only if dilutive.*

The interest that must be adjusted in backdating is six months' interest on the $10,000,000 principal amount of converted bonds. (The bonds were outstanding for six months.) At 9% per annum and with a 40% income tax rate, the impact of interest on the converted bonds is:

*one quarter of
40,000,000*

Interest expense = $10,000,000 × 9% × (1.0 − 0.4) × 6/12 = $270,000

In general, the formula for computing the interest savings from conversion is:

Principal amount converted × interest rate × (1 − tax rate) × fraction of year
before conversion.

For example, if the bonds had been retired after four months of the fiscal year, four months of interest would be added back.

The highlighted section of Exhibit 19-6 shows the add-back of $270,000 after-tax interest expense, and the weighted-average number of shares is increased to reflect the full amount of shares issued on conversion. Shares are calculated as 20,000 shares × 6/12. The individual EPS effect is $27 ($270,000 ÷ 10,000), which is dilutive to basic EPS of $50. Next, the assumed conversion of the remaining dilutive convertible bonds, still outstanding at the end of the year, is considered. The impact of interest is:

Interest expense = $30,000,000 × 9% × (1.0 − 0.4) = $1,620,000

Shares to be issued would be 60,000 [($30,000,000 ÷ $1,000) × 2], and the individual effect of the bonds is $27 ($1,620,000 ÷ 60,000). These bonds are dilutive. The adjustment is included in Exhibit 19-6, resulting in diluted EPS of $37.62. Note that the individual effect of the converted bonds and the unconverted bonds is identical; it does not matter which is done first in the cascade.

Example 3—Exercised Options If options were exercised during the period, an adjustment would be made to backdate these shares to the beginning of the period *if they were dilutive*. Again, the treasury stock method would be applied and other common shares assumed retired for that portion of the year.

For example, assume that as a result of an options exercise, 10,000 shares were issued on 1 November for $50,000. The average share price for the first 10 months of the year was $18. These shares would have been weight-averaged for two months when calculating *basic EPS*. For diluted EPS, in Step (2), the shares are backdated. The denominator would be increased by 8,333 (10,000 × 10/12) for shares issued, and shares assumed retired for the 10 months, 2,315 (($50,000 ÷ $18) × 10/12), would be deducted. The adjustment is made only if dilutive. Note that the $18 average market price used was the average for the first 10 months of the year, which is more applicable to this calculation than the average for the entire year.

EXHIBIT 19-6

BASIC AND DILUTED EPS CALCULATIONS
Partial Actual Conversion Of Debt

	Earnings Available to Common Shares	Weighted-average Number of Shares	Earnings per Share
Basic EPS:			
Earnings:			
Net earnings	$3,000,000		
Earnings available to common	$3,000,000		
Shares outstanding:	*no prefs.*		
50,000 shares × 6/12		25,000	
70,000 shares × 6/12		35,000	
Basic EPS	**$3,000,000**	**60,000**	**$50.00**
Diluted EPS:			
Data from basic EPS, above	$3,000,000	60,000 *Refer notes*	
Adjustments for converted debt:			
Remove after-tax interest on converted debt: $10,000,000 × 9% × (1.0 − 0.4) × 6/12	270,000		
Adjust shares for first six months: 20,000 shares × 6/12		10,000	
Subtotal	$3,270,000	70,000	$46.71
Adjustment for remaining convertible debt:			
Removed after-tax interest on remaining debt: $30,000,000 × 9% × (1.0 − 0.4)	1,620,000		
Shares ($30,000,000 ÷ $1,000) × 2 shares per bond		60,000	
Diluted EPS	**$4,890,000**	**130,000**	**$37.62**

1. What is the purpose of calculating diluted EPS?

2. Explain the difference between dilutive and anti-dilutive.

3. What is added to the numerator of diluted EPS for convertible bonds? Pre-ferred shares?

4. Assume basic EPS is $5. Two potentially dilutive elements exist, with an individual effect of $1 and $4.50, respectively. Under what circumstances would the $4.50 item be considered anti-dilutive?

5. How do actual conversions of senior securities affect the calculation of diluted EPS?

6. What assumption is made regarding the proceeds of option contracts when calculating diluted EPS? When are options dilutive?

COMPLICATING FACTORS

Convertible Securities and Options Issued During the Year

If convertible securities are issued during the year, the effect of a hypothetical conversion is backdated in the calculation of diluted EPS *only to the date of issue*. For example, suppose that DRV Corporation issued 8% convertible bonds payable on 1 November. When measuring interest expense, of course, only two months' interest would have been recorded. In calculating diluted EPS, two months' interest (not 12 months'!) is added to the numerator and two months of shares (not 12 months'!) are added to the denominator. That is, the bond is assumed to be converted on the date of issuance *if it was issued during the period*. Next year, when the bonds have been outstanding for a full year, the adjustments revert to normal: a full year.

Similarly, if options are issued during the year, they are backdated *only to the date of issuance* in diluted EPS calculations. *Employee stock options are often issued at the end of a fiscal period, which means that they do not affect diluted EPS in their first year.*

An illustration of this situation is included in the final example in the chapter.

Convertible Securities and Options Extinguished During the Year

What happens if a company has convertible securities or options during the year that are redeemed or settled in cash, or expire during the year? Potential common shares, *if dilutive,* are included in the calculation of diluted EPS up to the date of redemption, settlement, or expiry.

For example, assume that a convertible bond was repaid on 1 March, in cash. That is, the bond was extinguished for cash and the conversion option was not exercised. If the conversion terms were dilutive, interest and shares would be included in diluted EPS calculations for the two months that the bond was outstanding.

Alternatively, assume that options were outstanding until 30 September, when they expired. The fact that they expired unexercised means that they were not in-the-money in the period leading up to the expiry date, but they may well have been in-the-money earlier in the fiscal year. The options would be factored into diluted EPS for any period before 30 September during which they were in-the-money.

Reference Point for Diluted EPS

Assume that basic EPS based on net earnings (e.g., $2.00) is lower than EPS based on earnings from continuing operations (e.g., $2.50), because of a loss from discontinued operations. Assume that a potentially dilutive security has an individual effect (e.g., $2.25) that is anti-dilutive to EPS based on net earnings, but dilutive to EPS based on earnings before the discontinued operation. Should it be included or not? Accounting standards require that the only yardstick used be *EPS based on earnings from continuing operations.* All decisions are made with this as the starting point. So, if an item is included for earnings from continuing operations, it is *also always included* for EPS based on net earnings.

For example, assume that earnings from continuing operations is $450,000, and there is an after-tax loss from discontinued operations of $200,000, so net earnings are $250,000. There are 10,000 common shares outstanding all year, and no preferred shares. Basic EPS is $45 based on earnings before the discontinued operation, and $25 based on net earnings. Convertible debt, with after-tax interest of $70,000 and a share entitlement of 2,500 shares, is outstanding.

The individual dilutive effect of the convertible debt is $28 ($70,000 ÷ 2,500). This is dilutive to EPS calculated on earnings from continuing operations, but anti-dilutive to EPS calculated on net earnings. The item is included in diluted EPS for *both measures of diluted EPS.* Diluted EPS for earnings from continuing operations is reported as $41.60 ($450,000 + $70,000) ÷ (10,000 + 2,500). Diluted EPS for the discontinued operation is ($16) ($200,000 loss ÷ 12,500), and diluted EPS for net earnings is $25.60 (($250,000 + $70,000) ÷ 12,500). Diluted EPS for net earnings, at $25.60, is higher than basic EPS of $25! But the bonds have to be included for both diluted EPS measures, since they were definitely dilutive for earnings before the discontinued operation.

Measuring Interest Expense

In the example shown in Exhibit 19-4, the bond was issued at 110, and the premium on issuance was entirely attributable to the conversion option. Thus, the convertible bonds' nominal interest rate could be used to measure interest expense. In this example, interest expense was measured (appropriately) at 12%.

There are many situations in which a bond is offered at a discount or premium. When that happens, interest *expense* will include discount or premium amortization and will not coincide with interest *paid.* In diluted EPS calculations, the adjustment to the numerator (i.e., earnings available to common shareholders) must be for interest *expense.* A simple adjustment based on the nominal rate of interest will not work—discount or premium amortization must also be taken into account.

For example, suppose that convertible, 10-year bonds with a stated interest rate of 9% payable semi-annually were issued for $40 million. The bonds have a par value of $40 million and are convertible at the investor's option. Some of the proceeds must be allocated to the conversion option, and therefore a discount on the bonds will arise. If the market rate of interest for non-convertible bonds of similar risk and maturity was 10% at the time of issuance, the allocation of $40 million proceeds would have been as follows:

Present value of liability:	
Interest = [($40,000,000 × 4.5%) × (P/A, 5%, 20)] =	$22,431,979
Principal = $40,000,000 × (P/F, 5%, 20) =	15,075,579
	$37,507,558
Common share conversion option (the residual)	2,492,442
Net proceeds	$40,000,000

The bond issuance would have been recorded as follows:

Cash	40,000,000	
Discount on bonds payable	2,492,442	
Bonds payable		40,000,000
Common share conversion rights		2,492,442

Each year, interest expense is recorded using the effective interest method. In the first period, interest expense is \$1,875,378 (\$37,507,558 × 5%); the discount is amortized, and the net carrying value of the bond is adjusted. This is not interest paid, which is \$1,800,000 (\$40,000,000 × 4.5%).

When making the adjustment to earnings available to common shareholders in EPS calculations, the adjustment must be for interest expense, not interest paid. In the examples and problems in this chapter, it is often assumed that the nominal interest rate is the same as the market rate to simplify calculations. But be aware that if this simplifying assumption is not in place, the required adjustment is for interest expense, not interest paid.

Measuring Share Price

Average share price is used to determine whether options are in-the-money, and to calculate the share adjustment for the denominator of diluted EPS. The accounting standards state that a simple average of weekly or monthly prices is usually appropriate. If prices fluctuate widely over the period being used, an average of the high and low point for the period will usually be a more representative value than the closing price. If shares are thinly traded, an average of bid and asked price may be appropriate.

Use of average share price is justified because profit (the numerator for EPS) is generated *over the period,* and the denominator should also reflect the entire year. However, use of averages can be problematic. Assume that share price on average was \$40 for the period, but falls to \$25 at the end of the fiscal year. Options are outstanding with a per-share price of \$30. These options are in-the-money with respect to average share price, but not in relation to the closing price. If the closing market price is a good predictor of share price through the coming year, diluted EPS will imply an option exercise that would not be economically logical. Several exposure drafts in this area have suggested the use of closing market values, but standard-setters have not yet made any change. Average share price is used.

Diluted EPS in a Loss Year

When a company has reported a loss, adding *anything* positive to the numerator, and/or increasing the number of common shares outstanding, will *reduce the loss per share* and be anti-dilutive. Thus, diluted EPS is generally equal to basic EPS in a loss year because all potentially dilutive items are classified as anti-dilutive.

For example, assume a company reports a \$100,000 loss. It has 40,000 weighted-average ordinary shares outstanding, and 10,000 cumulative preferred shares outstanding, with a total dividend entitlement of \$5,000, convertible into 20,000 common shares. Basic *loss* per share is (\$2.63) [(\$100,000 + \$5,000) ÷ 40,000]. The preferred dividend *increases* the loss per share. If the preferred shares were assumed converted, diluted EPS would be (\$1.67) (\$105,000 − \$5,000) ÷ (40,000 + 20,000). A smaller loss per share—*a better number*—results and demonstrates that the preferred shares are anti-dilutive. Diluted EPS would be reported as (\$2.63).

What if this company reported a loss of \$100,000 from continuing operations, and a \$500,000 gain from discontinued operations? Net earnings would be positive, at \$400,000. The preferred shares *are still classified as anti-dilutive*, because the dilution test is performed with reference to earnings from continuing operations. If it is dilutive—or anti-dilutive—to the top line, it must be classified consistently thereafter.

Another twist relates to options. Are out-of-the-money options dilutive in a loss year? Use of the formula for shares issued and retired results in a *reduction of shares*, and thus a (dilutive; bad news) increase in the loss per share. Despite this dilutive mathematical result, it makes no economic sense to suggest that option holders would buy shares if the exercise price were higher than market value. Accordingly, the accounting standard clearly states that only in-the-money options can be considered for diluted EPS calculations. These are anti-dilutive in a loss year.

Bonds Convertible at the Issuer's Option

Convertible bonds may be convertible at either the option of the investor or the issuer. The examples shown above have dealt with convertible bonds that are convertible at the option of the investor. *If it is the company's option to issue shares or cash on the maturity date, the bonds still must be considered for diluted EPS calculations.* The company cannot avoid inclusion by claiming that it intends to repay the bond with cash rather than shares. If the result is dilutive, the bond is included in diluted EPS calculations.

FVTPL Liabilities

Most liabilities are carried at amortized cost. Some, however, are classified as fair value through profit and loss (FVTPL) financial instruments. A company may designate a liability as FVTPL on initial recognition for a variety of reasons, including the need to avoid a mismatch if a related, hedged asset must be valued at fair value, if the liabilities are managed with reference to their fair value, or to simplify valuation if there is an embedded derivative in the liability. FVTPL liabilities are valued at fair value, and changes in fair value are recorded as a component of earnings. If these liabilities are convertible bonds, then in the calculation of diluted EPS, their effect on net earnings includes fair value changes. Any gain or loss on the change in fair value that is included in net earnings must be adjusted on the numerator, after tax, and considered when evaluating whether the liability is dilutive or anti-dilutive.

CONCEPT REVIEW

1. What is the reference point for the dilution test?
2. When there is a difference between interest expense and interest paid, which number is used for convertible bonds in diluted EPS?
3. Why is diluted EPS generally equal to basic EPS in a loss year?

COMPREHENSIVE ILLUSTRATION

Having discussed all of the pieces of basic and diluted EPS, we'll now turn to a comprehensive illustration. Exhibit 19-7 contains the information for this example, and Exhibit 19-8 works through the EPS calculations.

This example uses data from FRM Corporation, a public corporation. The company has a complex capital structure that includes bonds and three classes of shares. At the beginning of the year, one class of convertible bond was outstanding, and a second class of convertible bonds was issued during the year. The Class A shares are publicly-traded and are listed on the TSX. Each Class A share has one vote. The Class B common shares have 20 votes each. Class B shares are closely held by the company's founding family, as are the preferred shares. Although Class A and Class B have different voting rights, in all other respects the two classes of common shares are equal, including the rights to dividends and to assets upon dissolution.

As can be seen in Exhibit 19-7, two of the bond issues are convertible (into Class A), as are the preferred shares (into Class B). In addition, there are contingently issuable Class A shares and employee stock options outstanding that give the holder the right to acquire one Class A share for each option held.

Before beginning the calculations, it is important to take notice of any changes in the capital structure that occurred during the year. Exhibit 19-7 shows the capital structure at the *end* of the fiscal year, but the *additional information* states that there was a partial conversion of the 10% debentures on 1 October. That piece of information is important for two reasons:

1. Shares were outstanding for only *part* of the year, which means that the weighted-average number of shares outstanding must be calculated for basic EPS, *and*

2. If dilutive, the conversion must be backdated when calculating diluted EPS.

▬▬▬▬▬▬ EXHIBIT 19-7 ▬▬▬▬▬▬

FRM CORPORATION

Data for Comprehensive EPS Illustration

Year Ended 31 December 20X1

Capital structure, 31 December 20X1:

Long-term debt:

12% first mortgage bonds, due 1 July 20X9	$1,300,000
10% unsecured debentures, due 31 July 20X7, convertible into Class A common shares at $50 at any time prior to maturity	$ 960,000
8% unsecured debentures, due 15 April 20X20, convertible into 10,300 Class A common shares on or after 31 December 20X12	$1,500,000

Share capital:

Preferred shares, dividend rate of $20 per share, cumulative and non-participating, convertible to Class B common shares at the rate of two shares of Class B for each share of preferred	5,000 shares
Class A common shares, one vote per share	104,800 shares
Class B common shares, 20 votes per share, sharing dividends equally with Class A common shares	10,000 shares

Options:

3,000 employee stock options issued on 31 December 20X0, each exchangeable for one Class A share as follows:

> $30 per share prior to 1 January 20X4
> $40 per share between 1 January 20X4 and 31 December 20X7
> $55 per share between 1 January 20X8 and 31 December 20X10
> The options expire at the close of business on 31 December 20X10

5,000 employee stock options, issued on 31 December 20X1, each exchangeable for one Class A share at a price of $25 per share prior to 31 December 20X11. The options expire at the close of business on 31 December 20X11.

Contingent shares:

FRM entered into a contingent share agreement in 20X0 when it acquired another company. FRM must issue 9,000 Class A shares in March of 20X4 if the acquired company's core operations earn $400,000 before tax each year from the acquisition date through 20X3. To date, earnings have surpassed this level.

Additional Information:

- After-tax earnings for the year ended 31 December 20X1 were $1,200,000; this was after a $200,000 after-tax gain from discontinued operations.
- The income tax rate was 40%.
- The average market value of common shares during the period was $45.
- Dividends were paid quarterly on the preferred shares; there are no dividends in arrears.
- Dividends of $1 per quarter were declared on both Class A and Class B shares; the dividends were payable to shareholders of record at the end of each calendar quarter, and were paid five business days thereafter.
- On 1 October 20X1, 10% debentures with a principal amount of $240,000 were converted into 4,800 Class A shares (included in the outstanding shares listed above). At the beginning of the year, the total principal amount of the 10% debentures was $1,200,000.
- On 1 May 20X1, FRM issued $ 1,500,000 face value of 8% unsecured debentures, due 15 April 20X20, convertible into 10,300 Class A common shares on or after 31 December 20X12. The bonds were issued for $1,650,000, and $150,000 of the proceeds was classified in equity as the value of the conversion option.

In addition, the 8% convertible bonds were issued on 1 May. This is important because when the bonds are considered for diluted EPS calculation, they will be backdated only to the date of issue, or 8/12 of the year. Also note that the second set of options was issued on 31 December 20X1, at the end of the fiscal year. When backdating, these options are also backdated to the day of issue, giving them a weight of 0/12.

Basic EPS The top section of Exhibit 19-8 presents the calculation of basic EPS. The starting point is earnings from continuing operations, which is then reduced by the preferred dividends. Class A and Class B share *equally* in dividends, and therefore they are added together for the denominator without adjustment. The weighted-average number of shares reflects the new shares issued on 1 October. Basic EPS is $8.09 for earnings from continuing operations. The EPS effect of the discontinued operation is $1.80 ($200,000 ÷ 111,200) and EPS for net earnings is $9.89 [($1,200,000 − $100,000) ÷ 111,200].

Diluted EPS Diluted EPS must be calculated. The first item to evaluate is options, dilutive when the option price is less than market value. Refer back to the steps needed to calculate diluted EPS (see Exhibit 19-2). This is Step 3; Step 2 is not needed. Only the first group of options, for 3,000 shares, must be evaluated. The second set was issued on 31 December 20X1, and has no EPS effect because it is backdated only to the day of issue (0/12). Returning to the first set of options, the lowest option price, $30, is used because it will be the most dilutive and is in-the-money. The options allow the purchase of 3,000 shares. This will raise capital of $90,000 (3,000 × $30). Retirement is calculated as $90,000/$45, or 2,000 shares. The net increase to the denominator is 1,000 shares (3,000 − 2,000). This can be directly calculated as (3,000 × ($45 − $30))/$45.

Contingently issuable shares are evaluated as Step 5; Step 4 is not needed because no such shares were issued during the period. The 9,000 shares must be included in the denominator of diluted EPS because if the contingency period were to have ended at the end of 20X1, the shares would have to be issued because earnings targets have been met to date. There is no adjustment to the numerator for contingently issuable shares. These numbers are included in the calculation of diluted EPS, reducing the subtotal to $7.43.

We now proceed to Steps 6, 7, and 8 (See Exhibit 19-2.). The highlighted section of Exhibit 19-8 shows the calculation of individual effects for the preferred shares and convertible debt:

- *Preferred shares.* Each share of the convertible preferred has a dividend of $20. Each is convertible into two shares of Class B common. The individual effect is $20 ÷ 2 = $10. This is clearly anti-dilutive to basic EPS of $8.09. Preferred shares will be excluded from the diluted EPS calculation. (Note that the individual effect calculation can be based on the outstanding preferred share issue as a whole or on a per-share basis; the result is the same.)

- *10% debenture, actual conversion.* The conversion has to be backdated for 9/12 of the year, back from 1 October to 1 January. Both after-tax interest and shares are adjusted. Interest would be $24,000 ($240,000 × 10%) for a year, but is $10,800 after multiplied by (1 − tax rate) and 9/12 of the year. Shares issued were 4,800, as used in the basic calculation, but are backdated by multiplying by 9/12 of the year. The individual effect is $3.00.

- *10% debentures.* Interest on the $960,000 principal amount is $96,000. Since the interest is deductible for income tax purposes, the effect of the interest on net earnings is $57,600 ($96,000 × (1 − 0.4)). At a conversion price of $50, the $960,000 bonds can be converted into 19,200 ($960,000 ÷ $50) Class A common shares. The individual effect is $3.00.

- *8% debentures.* These debentures involve after-tax interest of $72,000 and are convertible into 10,300 Class A common shares. Both the interest and shares to be issued are backdated from 31 December to the date of issuance, 1 May of the current year. This is a factor of 8/12 for both the numerator and the denominator. The individual effect is $6.99.

In Steps 9 and 10 (see Exhibit 19-2) the securities are included in diluted EPS *in order of their dilutive effects:* first the 10% debentures, both the actual conversion and the assumed conversion. Their order doesn't matter since their individual effects are the same. The subtotal is now $6.73. The 8% debentures, which looked dilutive with respect to basic EPS of

EXHIBIT 19-8

FRM CORPORATION

Comprehensive EPS Illustration

(Based on Data in Exhibit 19-7)

	Earnings Available to Common Shares	Weighted-average Number of Shares	Earnings per Share
Basic EPS:			
Earnings from continuing operations	$1,000,000		
Less preferred dividends: 5,000 shares × $20	(100,000)		
Shares outstanding:			
Class A			
100,000 × 9/12		75,000	
104,800 × 3/12		26,200	
Class B 10,000 × 12/12		10,000	
Basic EPS	**$ 900,000**	**111,200**	**$ 8.09**
Individual effect ratios:			
Preferred shares (per share)	$ 20	2	$10.00
Actual conversion of 10% debenture			
Interest saved: ($240,000 × 10%) × (1 − 0.4) × 9/12	10,800		
Additional shares: 4,800 × 9/12		3,600	3.00
10% debentures (remainder)			
Interest saved: ($960,000 × 10%) × (1 − 0.4)	57,600		
Additional shares: $960,000 ÷ $50		19,200	3.00
8% debentures			
Interest saved: ($1,500,000 × 8%) × (1 − 0.4) × 8/12	48,000		
Additional shares: given 10,300 × 8/12		6,867	6.99
Diluted EPS:			
Data from basic	$ 900,000	111,200	
Adjustment for assumed options exercise:			
Shares issued		3,000	
Shares retired		(2,000)	
Subtotal	900,000	112,200	$ 8.02
Adjustment for contingently issuable shares:		9,000	
Subtotal	900,000	121,200	$ 7.43
Actual conversion of 10% debenture:			
Interest saved	10,800		
Additional shares		3,600	
Subtotal	910,800	124,800	7.30
Adjustments for potential conversions:			
10% debenture:			
Interest avoided (after-tax equivalent)	57,600		
Additional shares		19,200	
Subtotal	968,400	144,000	6.73
8% debenture:			
Anti-dilutive since $6.99 is higher than $6.73	—		
Adjustment for preferred shares:			
Anti-dilutive since $10.00 is higher than $6.73		—	
Diluted EPS	**$ 968,400**	**144,000**	**$ 6.73**

$8.09, are anti-dilutive to the subtotal of $6.73. They are excluded. The preferred shares, with an individual effect of $10, are also anti-dilutive and excluded. The result is diluted EPS of $6.73 for earnings from continuing operations.

Finally, the process is repeated because of the discontinued operations; this is Step 11 (see Exhibit 19-2). Diluted EPS for net earnings is $8.11 (($1,200,000 − $100,000 + $10,800 + $57,600) ÷ 144,000). Note that the same adjustments are made to the numerator with no dilution testing. EPS for discontinued operations is disclosed as $1.80 ($200,000 ÷ 111,200 shares) for basic and $1.38 ($200,000 ÷ 144,000 shares) for diluted.

EPS disclosure on the statement of comprehensive income would be as follows:

Earnings per share:	Basic	Diluted
Earnings from continuing operations	$8.09	$6.73
Discontinued operations	1.80	1.38
Net earnings	$9.89	$8.11

The individual effect of the discontinued operations may, alternatively, be included in the disclosure notes.

RESTATEMENT OF EARNINGS PER SHARE INFORMATION

Once earnings are reported, they are restated (changed) only in limited circumstances. We'll take a close look at this in Chapter 20. Changes in estimates, the most common classification of accounting change, affect only the current year and future years. Past earnings are changed only to correct an error, and to reflect the retrospective effect of a change in accounting policy. These retrospective changes are allowed to improve the integrity and the comparability of the financial statements. Reported EPS is also not often revised. EPS will be recalculated if:

- There has been a retrospective change in accounting policy or an error correction. Prior earnings will change and prior EPS also has to be revised.
- There has been a stock dividend or stock split during the fiscal year (or after the fiscal year but before the financial statements are issued). EPS data is retrospectively restated to reflect the different size of shares that are now outstanding—EPS numbers would halve after a 2-for-1 stock split, for instance.

Needless to say, the discontinuity is accompanied by extensive disclosure to ensure that financial statement users are adequately informed.

SUBSEQUENT CHANGES IN SHARE CAPITAL

Companies have special disclosures required for *subsequent events*—transactions or events that take place in the period between the end of the fiscal period and the date that financial statements are released. If there have been common share transactions in this period, then the effects of these share transactions must be disclosed. That is, if a subsequent event would significantly change the number of common shares or the potential common shares used in basic or diluted EPS, the transaction must be disclosed and described. Companies have a relatively short period after their fiscal year in which to report; they obviously have added incentive to report quickly, to reduce the reporting burden by keeping this time period short.

Examples of transactions that would have to be disclosed include issuing common shares for cash, on the exercise of options, or for cash with the proceeds used to pay out other sources of financing. For example, if common shares were issued after the end of the fiscal year and the proceeds were used to retire preferred shares or debt, disclosure would be required. Issuance of new options or convertible securities would introduce a new element into diluted EPS (potential shares) and also qualify for disclosure.

REQUIRED DISCLOSURE

Accounting standards recommend that financial statements include the following:

1. Basic and diluted EPS must be disclosed on the face of the statement of comprehensive income for net earnings from continuing operations, and for net earnings. Basic and diluted EPS must both be disclosed, regardless of the magnitude of the difference between the two. Materiality cannot be invoked to avoid disclosing diluted EPS! The EPS effect of the discontinued operation must also be disclosed, either on the statement of comprehensive income or in a disclosure note.

2. A disclosure note must include:
   • The amounts used as the numerator and denominator for basic and diluted EPS.
   • A reconciliation of the numerators of basic and diluted EPS to the profit or loss numbers reported. This includes an explanation of adjustments to the numerator of diluted EPS for each individual effect by class of instrument.
   • A reconciliation of the denominators of basic and diluted EPS to the number of common shares outstanding.
   • Details of securities excluded from the calculation of diluted EPS because they were anti-dilutive.
   • Details of share transactions, in the period after the end of the fiscal year but before the financial statements are issued, including stock dividends or splits.
   • Details of convertible securities, options, and any other share contracts issued in the period after the end of the fiscal year but before the financial statements are issued.

Reporting Example The Koninklijke Philips Electronics discloses 2008 basic and diluted EPS of ($0.09). This company has no preferred shares, but does have options and convertible debentures that would reduce EPS if exercised. Since 2008 was a loss year, all potentially dilutive elements are anti-dilutive and have been excluded. Details of the excluded anti-dilutive securities have been provided. There is a large discontinued operation element in 2006, largely wound down by 2008.

Note disclosure is as follows:

NOTE 1
SIGNIFICANT ACCOUNTING POLICIES

Earnings per Share

The Company presents basic and diluted earnings per share (EPS) data for its common shares. Basic EPS is calculated by dividing the net earnings attributable to shareholders of the Company by the weighted average number of common shares outstanding during the period. Diluted EPS is determined by adjusting the profit or loss attributable to shareholders and the weighted average number of common shares outstanding for the effects of all dilutive potential common shares, which comprise convertible personnel debentures, restricted shares and share options granted to employees.

continued on next page

Note 44
Earnings per Share

	2006		2007		2008
Income (loss) from continuing operations		€ 999		€5,011	€(94)
Income (loss) from discontinued operations		4,154		(138)	3
Net income (loss) attributable to holders of common shares		€5,153		€4,873	€(91)
Weighted average number of common shares		1,174,924,579		1,086,128,418	991,420,017
Plus incremental shares from assumed conversion of:					
Options and restricted shares	7,531,636		11,669,275		5,191,635
Convertible debentures	1,174,299		1,127,690		102,249
Dilutive potential common shares		8,705,935		12,796,965	5,293,884
Adjusted weighted average number of common shares		1,183,630,514		1,098,925,383	996,713,901
Basic earnings per share in euros					
Income (loss) from continuing operations		0.85		4.61	(0.09)
Income (loss) from discontinued operations		3.54		(0.12)	—
Net income (loss) attributable to stockholders		4.39		4.49	(0.09)
Diluted earnings per share in euros					
Income (loss) from continuing operations		0.84		4.56	(0.09) (1)
Income (loss) from discontinued operations		3.51		(0.13)	—
Net income (loss) attributable to stockholders		4.35		4.43	(0.09) (1)

In 2008, 2007 and 2006, respectively, 48 million, 27 million and 19 million securities that could potentially dilute basic EPS were not included in the computation of dilutive EPS because the effect would have been anti-dilutive for the periods presented. In 2008, the incremental shares from assumed conversion are not taken into account as the effect would be anti-dilutive.

Source: http://www.philips.com/about/investor/financialresults/annualreports, accessed June 2010.

OTHER PER SHARE AMOUNTS

EPS is not the only per share statistic that may be presented in the audited financial statements. Companies are permitted to disclose per share numbers other than basic and diluted figures, preferably in the disclosure notes. For example, a reported component of earnings may be reported on a per-share basis. The denominator must be calculated using WAOS as per basic and diluted requirements, and the company must disclose the basis on which the numerator is determined, including whether it is before or after tax.

Some companies publish a statistic called **cash flow per share**, based on some SCF subtotal. Some companies use cash flow from operating activities as the basis for this calculation, and some have used an intermediate subtotal, such as earnings adjusted for non-cash items such as depreciation and gains and losses. Inclusion of cash flow per share is permitted under international standards, subject to the calculation and disclosure requirements described above. However, securities regulators in Canada generally look for such disclosures to be presented less prominently than the GAAP EPS requirement. Presentation in the disclosure notes would be more appropriate than on the statement of cash flows or the statement of comprehensive income.

ACCOUNTING STANDARDS FOR PRIVATE ENTERPRISES

Private companies may voluntarily decide to present EPS data, if they believe that it would useful to their financial statement users. Private companies with a larger shareholder group, such as co-operatives and employee-owned companies, might present EPS as a standard part of financial reporting. There is no private company Canadian GAAP with respect to EPS; private companies might also look to *IAS* 33 for guidance, or may design a statistic that meets their users' requirements. Disclosure of the calculation approach used is obviously important to improve understanding.

RELEVANT STANDARDS

IASB:

- *IAS* 33, Earnings per Share

CICA Handbook, Part II:
- None

SUMMARY OF KEY POINTS

1. Earnings per share is intended to provide information about earnings in comparison to the common share base. Basic EPS is the basis for comparing the current period's earnings with that of prior periods, while diluted EPS gives an indication of the long-run impact that conversions and options could have on common earnings. Because it is computed on a *per share* basis, EPS removes the effect of increases in net earnings due to larger invested capital obtained through new share issues.

2. EPS figures are computed for earnings from continuing operations and for net earnings.

3. Basic EPS is calculated by dividing earnings available to common shareholders (e.g., earnings less preferred dividend claim) by the weighted-average number of shares outstanding.

4. Weighted-average ordinary shares (WAOS), used in the denominator of basic EPS, is calculated by weighting shares for the number of months they are outstanding. However, if there was a stock dividend or stock split during the reporting period, these additional ordinary shares are not weight-averaged, but treated as though they have always been outstanding.

5. If there are multiple classes of common shares with different dividend entitlements, separate basic EPS statistics must be calculated to reflect their claims.

6. When a company has dilutive senior securities, contingently issuable shares or options, diluted EPS must be calculated. The steps to calculate diluted EPS are shown in Exhibit 19-2. For the purposes of calculating diluted EPS, elements are included at their most unfavourable (lowest) price. Potentially dilutive items are included in diluted EPS calculations in a cascade, beginning with the most dilutive.

7. Diluted EPS excludes the effects of any convertible securities or options contracts that are anti-dilutive. Anti-dilutive items have the effect of *increasing* EPS in relation to EPS from continuing operations.

8. When calculating diluted EPS, in-the-money options are assumed to be issued at the beginning of the fiscal period and proceeds used to retire shares at average market values. This is called the treasury stock method.

9. Contingently issuable shares are included in diluted EPS if the shares would be issuable if the contingency period were to end at the end of the current fiscal year.

10. Convertible bonds and preferred shares are included in diluted EPS calculations using the if-converted method, whereby after-tax interest and preferred dividends are adjusted on the numerator, and common shares issued for the denominator. This reflects a hypothetical conversion to common shares at the beginning of the year.

11. Diluted EPS includes an adjustment that backdates actual conversions of senior securities (convertible debt and preferred shares) and shares issued under option contracts to the beginning of the fiscal period, if dilutive.

12. Securities and options issued during the period are backdated only to the date of issue. Dilutive conversion privileges and options that expired or were extinguished during the period are included for the period during which they were outstanding.

13. All potentially dilutive elements are anti-dilutive in a loss year because they would *decrease* a loss per share; this means that diluted EPS is equal to basic EPS in a loss year.

14. EPS is reported on the statement of comprehensive income. A disclosure note must include calculation details, including reconciliation of earnings and WAOS data, and details of excluded anti-dilutive elements.

KEY TERMS

anti-dilutive element, 1116
backdating, 1122
bonus shares, 1111
basic earnings per share, 1108
cascade, 1121
cash flow per share, 1135
contingently issuable ordinary shares 1111
convertible senior securities, 1115
diluted earnings per share, 1108
dilutive, 1116
earnings dilution, 1115

if-converted method, 1117
in-the-money, 1116
individual effect, 1117
ordinary shares, 1109
senior shares, 1109
stock dividend, 1111
stock option, 1115
stock split, 1111
treasury stock method, 1116
weighted average ordinary shares
    outstanding (WAOS), 1110

REVIEW PROBLEM

Ice King Products Incorporated reported after-tax profit of $6.5 million in 20X5. Its capital structure included the following as of 31 December 20X5, the *end* of the company's fiscal year:

Long-term debt:
    Bonds payable, due 20X11, 12% $ 5,000,000
    Bonds payable, due 20X15, 9%, convertible into common
        shares at the rate of two shares per $100 $10,000,000
Shareholders' equity:
    Preferred shares, $4.50, no-par, cumulative, convertible into
        common shares at the rate of two common shares for each
        preferred share, shares outstanding, 150,000
    Preferred shares, $2.50, no-par, cumulative, convertible into
        common shares at the rate of one common share for each
        preferred share, shares outstanding, 400,000
    Common shares, shares outstanding, 1,500,000

Options to purchase common shares (options have been outstanding all year):
    Purchase price, $20; expire 20X11, 100,000 options
    Purchase price, $52; expire 20X14, 200,000 options
Each option allows the purchase of one share.

Transactions during 20X5:
    On 1 July, 400,000 common shares were issued on the
        conversion of 200,000 of the $4.50 preferred shares.
    On 1 December, 100,000 common shares were issued
        for cash.

Other information:
    Average common share price, stable during the year, $40
    Tax rate, 25%
    Quarterly dividends were declared on 31 March, 30 June,
        30 September, and 31 December

Required:
Calculate basic and diluted earnings per share.

REVIEW PROBLEM—SOLUTION

	Earnings Available to Common Shares	Weighted-average Number of Shares	Earnings per Share
Basic EPS:			
Net profit	$6,500,000		
Less dividends on $4.50 preferred:			
($4.50 ÷ 4) × 350,000 shares × 2 quarters	(787,500)		
($4.50 ÷ 4) × 150,000 shares × 2 quarters	(337,500)		
Less dividends on $2.50 preferred:			
400,000 shares × $2.50	(1,000,000)		
WAOS:			
1,000,000 shares × 6/12		500,000	
1,400,000 shares × 5/12		583,333	
1,500,000 shares × 1/12		125,000	
Basic EPS	**$4,375,000**	**1,208,333**	**$3.62**

Individual effect; dilution test

9% Bonds:			
Interest, ($10,000,000 × 9%) × (1.00 − .25)	$ 675,000		
Shares, ($10,000,000 ÷ $100) × 2		200,000	$3.38
$4.50 preferred actual conversion:			
Dividend adjustment:			
(4.50 ÷ 4) × 200,000 shares × 2 quarters	$ 450,000		
Add'l weighted-average shares: 400,000 × 6/12		200,000	$2.25
$4.50 preferred			
Dividends, $4.50 × 150,000 shares	$ 675,000		
Shares, 150,000 × 2 common shares		300,000	$2.25
$2.50 preferred			
Dividends, $2.50 × 400,000	$1,000,000		
Shares, 400,000 × 1 share		400,000	$2.50

Diluted EPS

Basic EPS	$4,375,000	1,208,333	$3.62
$20 options—shares issued		100,000	
—shares retired (100,000 × $20) ÷ $40		(50,000)	
$52 options—excluded, $52 > $40			
Subtotal	$4,375,000	1,258,333	$3.48
$4.50 preferred actual conversion:			
Dividend adjustment:			
(4.50 ÷ 4) × 200,000 shares × 2 quarters	450,000		
Add'l weighted average shares 400,000 × 6/12		200,000	
$4.50 preferred:			
Dividends, $4.50 × 150,000 shares	675,000		
Shares, 150,000 preferred × 2 common shares		300,000	
Subtotal	5,500,000	1,758,333	3.13
$2.50 preferred shares: dividends, $2.50 × 400,000	1,000,000	400,000	
Subtotal	$6,500,000	2,158,333	3.01
9% Bonds			
Bonds, with an individual effect of $3.38, are anti-dilutive as their inclusion would increase diluted EPS above $3.01.	—	—	
Diluted EPS	**$6,500,000**	**2,158,333**	**$3.01**

QUESTIONS

Q19-1 What is the formula for basic EPS? Describe the numerator and the denominator.

Q19-2 Explain why and when dividends on non-cumulative preferred shares must be subtracted from earnings to compute basic EPS.

Q19-3 What adjustments, in addition to preferred dividends, may be made to the numerator of basic EPS?

Q19-4 Why are weighted-average ordinary shares used in EPS calculations?

Q19-5 If common shares are issued during the year under a contract that involved meeting a contingent requirement, as of what date are the shares included in the weighted average ordinary share calculation?

Q19-6   A company split its common shares 2-for-1 on 30 June of its fiscal year, which ends on 31 December. Before the split, 4,000 common shares were outstanding. How many weighted-average ordinary shares should be used in computing EPS? How many shares should be used in computing a comparative EPS amount for the preceding year?

Q19-7   What is the required EPS disclosure if discontinued operations are reported?

Q19-8   Assume that a company has two classes of shares that both have voting rights and are entitled to the proceeds of net assets on dissolution. One class is entitled to receive 10 times the dividends of the other class. How would the two classes be treated in calculating basic EPS?

Q19-9   What is the purpose of diluted EPS?

Q19-10 A company has basic EPS based on earnings from continuing operations of $4.50 and on net earnings, $3.50. A potentially dilutive element has an individual effect of $4.00. Is the element dilutive or anti-dilutive?

Q19-11 Specify the numerator and/or denominator item(s) that would be used when calculating diluted EPS for dilutive (a) convertible preferred shares, (b) convertible debt, (c) contingently issuable shares, and (d) options.

Q19-12 Options are outstanding for 100,000 shares at $10. The average market price during the period is $25. What adjustment would be made to the denominator of diluted EPS?

Q19-13 What is the difference between a dilutive security and an anti-dilutive security? Why is the distinction important in EPS considerations?

Q19-14 What does it mean if options are said to be in-the-money? Are options dilutive when they are in-the-money? Explain.

Q19-15 A company has an agreement outstanding at the end of the fiscal year that requires it to issue common shares in the future for no additional cash consideration if certain conditions are met. How does the company decide whether to include the shares in diluted EPS or exclude them?

Q19-16 CH Holdings has basic EPS of $14. The individual effect of convertible preferred shares is $12, and the individual effect of convertible bonds is $6. In which order should the convertible elements be included in diluted calculations? In what circumstances would the convertible preferred shares be anti-dilutive in sequence?

Q19-17 ABC Company has a $14 million convertible bond outstanding that requires payment of $1.2 million in interest annually. Interest expense is $1.35 million. Why is interest expense different than the interest paid? For the purposes of diluted EPS, which interest figure is relevant?

Q19-18 Wilcorp Limited reported basic EPS of ($1.11), a loss of $1.11 per common share, calculated as ($610,500) ÷ 550,000. The company has stock options outstanding for 100,000 common shares at $10 per share. The average common share price was $25 during the period. Calculate diluted EPS.

Q19-19 Under what circumstances are the EPS of prior years to be restated?

Q19-20 A company with a 31 December year-end issues shares for cash and retires nonconvertible bonds with the proceeds on 10 January of the next fiscal year. What disclosure is required in the 31 December financial statements? Why?

Q19-21 Barbaro Ltd. plans to disclose a calculation of per share cash flow from operating activities in addition to EPS. What conditions must the company meet?

CASE 19-1

DRUGSTORE DEPOT LIMITED

Drugstore Depot Limited (DDL) is a diversified Canadian company whose key businesses include retailing of drug store and food products, and real estate interests. Real estate is primarily held for DDL occupancy, although where DDL retail operations are an anchor tenant in a smaller mall, DDL prefers to own the commercial real estate property and act as landlord to other tenants. The company is public, with both debt and shares traded on public markets. Common shares traded in the $8–$14 range in 20X2.

Extracts from the financial statements are included in Exhibit 1, and information on share capital is included in Exhibit 2.

DDL labels gains on sale of real estate as "capital gains" on the statement of comprehensive income. The term is not used in its income tax context; it is just a term assigned to a "gain on sale." The company regularly calculates and disseminates information on basic and diluted EPS numbers, before and after capital gains and income tax. Company management prefers to focus on results before capital gains and income tax when communicating to shareholders, because gains from sale of real estate are sporadic, and business units have operating targets on a pre-tax basis. In 20X1, the company recorded earnings before capital gains and income tax of $5.60 per share, and diluted EPS before capital gains and income tax of $5.56. After capital gains and income tax, the numbers were $5.03 and $4.99.

You are an accountant in the corporate reporting department of DDL. Financial statements are in the process of being finalized for the 20X2 fiscal year, which ended on 31 December 20X2. The audit committee will meet next week, with several accounting policy issues left to resolve. EPS calculations must also be completed.

Effective 31 December 20X2, DDL sold certain real estate properties to Dixon Real Estate Investment Trust (Dixon REIT). The properties had a book value of $239 million, and were sold for $374 million gross cash proceeds. In addition, DDL received units in Dixon REIT estimated to be worth $50 million. There were brokerage and legal costs of $7 million associated with the sale. Income tax triggered by the sale amounted to $27 million in current taxes payable, and another $4 million in deferred income tax. The transfer has yet to be reflected in the 20X2 financial statements. As part of the transaction, DDL entered into new lease agreements with respect to its occupancy in a portion of the real estate properties now owned by Dixon REIT. The leases have an expected total term of between 17 and 23 years; initial lease arrangements are established for five years, followed by renewal periods to the end of the term. Minimum rents range from $8 to $14 per square foot, plus a percentage of gross revenue, and there are planned base rental increases every five years.

In the late fall of 20X2, one major real estate property owned by DDL burned to the ground. DDL was the sole occupant of this building, which had a book value of $17 million. Inventory with a book value of $7.2 million was destroyed in the fire. Investigation into the cause of the fire, thought to be electrical in nature, is under way. DDL carries property and casualty insurance, and has filed a claim for $32.2 million, allocated $25 million to the building, and $7.2 million for inventory. Income tax triggered by the insurance proceeds has been estimated to be $1.4 million in current taxes payable, and another $0.7 million in deferred income tax. Lawyers for DDL believe that DDL is entitled to insurance recovery for the fair value of the property and inventory destroyed, in excess of the $1 million deductible under the policy. Accordingly, the expected payout is $31.2 million. A team of insurance adjustors is assessing the situation. The fire investigators and the insurance adjustors have yet to file their reports. The property and inventory remain on DDL's books in the meantime.

DDL entered into a five-year referral contract during the year. Physiotherapy and chiropractic services represent a large and growing market in Canada, and pharmacists in DDL stores are often consulted by customers about appropriate action. Any retail customer who requests physiotherapy and chiropractic advice or services in a DDL store will be referred to Nature Force Limited, a national chain that is the Canadian leader in such services. The agreement specifies that DDL will be paid $1 million minimum the first year of the agreement, or 30% of client billings resulting from referrals, whichever is higher. Revenues in the second year are 30% of billings, with no minimum, and then the percentage reduces from 30% to 25%, then 20% and 15% over the remaining three years of the contact. After the first year, either side can end the agreement with 60 days' notice. An appropriate information system has been established to ascertain the extent of billings Nature Force realizes from the referrals, subject to external verification.

To date, Nature Force has not made any payment to DDL for Year 1 minimum payment, because the amount is not due until the 12-month anniversary of the agreement, which occurs in October 20X3. No revenue has been recorded by DDL in the 20X2 financial statements. The pharmacists report that referrals have been "quite strong," although there are regional differences.

Required:

In preparation for the coming audit committee meeting, prepare a report that includes analysis of the accounting issues inherent in the transactions above, and any other reporting issues. Recalculate net earnings, if appropriate, and prepare EPS calculations for 20X2.

EXHIBIT 1

DRUGSTORE DEPOT LIMITED

Extracts from Financial Statements

31 December 20X2

(in millions)	20X2 Draft	20X1
Statement of comprehensive income		
Revenue	$15,015	$14,065
Operating earnings	$ 468	$ 473
Earnings before capital gains	$ 388	$ 368
Capital gains	—	89
Income tax	116	126
Net earnings and comprehensive income	$ 272	$ 331
Statement of financial position		
Capital stock	$ 365.7	$ 257.7
Contributed surplus	2	0.1
Retained earnings	2,405	2,207

EXHIBIT 2

DRUGSTORE DEPOT LIMITED
Share Capital Information
31 December 20X2

(in millions)	20X2 Draft	20X1
Preferred shares, par value $25 each, Series 2 cumulative, redeemable at the company's option, dividend 3%, convertible 2-for-1 into Class A shares, unlimited shares authorized, 1,680,000 shares outstanding (20X1, 2,600,000 shares)	$ 42	$ 65
Class A shares, with no par value, entitled to dividends on an equal per share basis with Class B shares, voting, one vote per share, unlimited shares authorized, 34,000,000 shares outstanding (20X1, 31,300,000 shares)	316.1	185.1
Class B shares, voting, three votes per share, unlimited shares authorized, 34,000,000 shares outstanding	7.6	7.6

In January 20X2, 190,000 options were issued. Options allow the holders to purchase 190,000 Class A shares at nil cost beginning in 20X11 and expiring in 20X15 and 20X16.

In late March 20X2, 1,200,000 Class A shares were purchased for cancellation at a cost of $60 million. Other shares were issued for cash in July 20X2. In December 20X2, 920,000 Series 2 preferred shares were purchased for cancellation at a cost of $25 million.

CASE 19-2

G SHOES LTD.

G Shoes Ltd. (GSL) is an integrated manufacturer and retailer of moderately priced high-fashion footwear, leather goods, and accessories. GSL is a public company listed on the Toronto Stock Exchange. GSL has stores in over 180 major Canadian shopping malls, and operates over 50 "boutiques" in larger retail stores. Until the current year, GSL had three retail stores in the United States. In general, operating results in 20X9 have been disappointing, with lower same-store sales trends and higher costs across the board.

Preliminary operating results for 20X9 are shown in Exhibit 1. Details of accounting issues that must be resolved before the financial statements can be finalized are in Exhibit 2. In particular, the company is discussing with the auditor whether the closure of the three U.S. retail stores, which occurred in March 20X9, can be accounted for as a discontinued operation. Company management has asked that any quantitative analysis reflect two alternatives—treating the closure as an unusual item, and then as a discontinued operation. Draft financial statements reflect the unusual item treatment. In addition, no accounting recognition has been given to stock options outstanding or granted during the year, as valuation estimates were not complete when the draft financial statements were prepared. This information has recently been provided. Finally, EPS calculations for 20X9 have not yet been made.

Required:

Analyze the accounting issues as identified, and prepare revised draft statement of comprehensive income, and EPS calculations.

EXHIBIT 1

G SHOES LIMITED

Draft Statement of Comprehensive Income

(in $ thousands)

For year ended 31 December	20X9
Revenue	
Sales	$166,200
Investment and other revenue	4,320
	170,520
Expenses	
Cost of sales, selling, and administrative	142,860
Amortization	10,700
Closure costs, U.S. operations	1,450
Interest, net	2,230
	157,240
Operating earnings, before tax	13,280
Income tax	5,180
Net earnings and comprehensive income	$ 8,100

EXHIBIT 2

G SHOES LIMITED

Additional Information

1. Outstanding share information:

	Number	Consideration (in thousands)
A. Multiple voting shares,		
31 December 20X8 and 20X9	1,580,000	Nominal
B. Subordinate voting shares		
Balance, 31 December 20X8	5,225,000	$23,890
Shares repurchased 20 March 20X9	(816,000)	(3,730)
Shares issued on exercise of stock options		
31 August 20X9	78,000	728
Balance, 31 December 20X9	4,487,000	$20,888

The multiple voting shares and subordinate voting shares have identical attributes except that the multiple voting shares entitle the holder to four votes per share and are entitled to four times the dividend, if declared, on the subordinate voting shares. The multiple voting shares are held by the company founder and his family. Only the subordinated voting shares are publicly-traded.

> ### EXHIBIT 2 *(cont'd)*

2. On 2 March 20X9, the company received permission from the Ontario Securities Commission for a Normal Course Issuer Bid that allows the company to repurchase up to 20% of its outstanding shares, or approximately 1,045,000 shares during the period from March 2, 20X9 to March 2, 20X10. The share transaction in March 20X9 was made pursuant to this Bid agreement. Consideration of $6,840 (thousand) was paid for the shares, with the excess over average paid-in capital to date charged to retained earnings.

3. On 24 February 20X6, GSL issued $40 million of convertible senior subordinated notes payable. The net proceeds after deducting offering expenses and underwriter's commissions were $37 million. The convertible debt was allocated between debt and equity elements, which are classified separately on the statement of financial position. The value of the debt element was based on the present value of the interest stream over the life of the note using an interest rate for a similar liability that did not have an associated conversion feature. The balance was recorded as equity.

   The notes are convertible at GSL's option at various dates between 20X14 and the maturity date of the note, 24 February 20X17. The conversion price is set at $15.00 per share until 20X15 and then changes to $10.00 per share. In 20X9, there is a charge for interest expense amounting to $1,780 and a $590 after-tax reduction to retained earnings, representing accretion on the equity amount. When calculating basic EPS, the $590 must be deducted from the numerator.

4. GSL maintains a stock option plan for the benefit of directors, officers, and senior management. The granting of options and the related vesting period are at the discretion of the Board of Directors. The option price is set as the five-day average of the trading price of the subordinated voting shares prior to the effective date of the grant. Options granted vest 36 months after the date of issuance, and can be exercised from the vesting date until 10 years after the date of grant. Options are granted on 31 December in the year of grant.

   Using the Black-Scholes option pricing model, the fair value of options granted was as follows:

Year of Grant	Per Share Value	Share Entitlements Originally Granted
Prior to 20X6	$4.785	404,000
20X6	4.270	210,000
20X7	6.473	176,000
20X8	5.540	206,000
20X9	7.180	25,000

A summary of the status of outstanding options:

	Shares under Option	Weighted Average Exercise Price
Outstanding at the beginning of the year	695,000	$11.21
Granted, 31 December, 20X9	25,000	10.53
Exercised	(78,000)	6.62
Outstanding at the end of the year	642,000	11.10
Options exercisable at the end of the year	405,800	10.90

At the end of the year, the market price of subordinated voting shares was $11.25, and had been stable for most of the year. Any recorded compensation cost is a permanent difference for tax purposes and will not change recorded tax amounts.

5. In March 20X9, GSL announced that it would close its U.S. retail operation, consisting of three retail stores. The stores had been a separate division of the

EXHIBIT 2 *(cont'd)*

company, reported separately with a dedicated retail manager. The stores were run using normal retail protocols established for other stores, and relied on GSL infrastructure. However, fashion trends appeared to be unique in these locations, and GSL did not have adequate brand recognition to reach required sales targets. Two retail stores were closed at the end of March, with the third one closed at the end of April. Pre-tax information (in thousands) concerning these locations:

	20X9
Sales	$ 532
Operating loss	(467)
Writedown of capital assets	(1,045)
Lease and employee termination costs	(405)
Current assets	$ 23
Capital assets	—
Current liabilities	—

CASE 19-3

THURTECH LIMITED

ThurTech Limited (TTL) is a Canadian public company involved in network technology for mobility telecommunications. This network technology allows additional data services to be offered through a mobile platform, as a strategy to increase average revenue per user for the carriers. TTL's customers are mobility carriers throughout North America and internationally.

Through the first three quarters of 20X3, revenues were relatively flat, and profit forecasts, which promised growth of approximately 12% in EPS, were not achieved. An earnings growth rate of 8% was reported, largely generated through cost reduction. Internal projections indicated that this 8% growth in EPS would be reported for the annual results. At the beginning of the fourth quarter, senior management began to discuss ways to "close the gap" between the 12% target and the 8% actual EPS growth. (Projected annual 20X3 EPS figures, reflecting the 8% results from operations, are shown in Exhibit 1.) Mindful of the sluggish stock market share price, and with an eye on its own compensation and stock option packages, management has expressed interest in changes before the end of the 20X3 fiscal year.

TTL has 1.2 million common shares promised for future distribution under option contracts granted to senior management. Stock options are a material element of compensation. Additional options will be granted at the end of 20X3. The options granted will be at a price equal to the current share price and will vest immediately. They may be exercised in four years' time, as long as the manager is still with TTL. The quantity to be granted depends on corporate performance but could range from zero to 400,000 shares under option.

A number of situations and/or opportunities that would potentially affect EPS for the year have been discussed internally. For example, management has proposed that 850,000 common shares be repurchased and retired in the fourth quarter. The required funding for this, $16,150,000, would have to be borrowed. Management is permitted to borrow up to $2 billion without further Board of Directors' approval; at the end of the third quarter, outstanding debt amounted to $1.8 billion.

TTL has idle land on the books at an historical cost of $695,000. The market value of this land is $1,180,000; sale would therefore generate a before-tax profit of $485,000. The land is adjacent to one of the five current manufacturing facilities of TTL and has been held for future expansion. Management is confident that, when future expansion is necessary, land can be obtained at one or another of the existing locations for a reasonable sum. Therefore, sale of this idle land has been proposed in the fourth quarter of 20X3.

TTL reports one particular bond payable of $500 million on the books, at a fixed interest rate of 6%. Since market interest rates are now in the range of 8%, the present value of this debt is $470 million. Management has suggested that this debt be recorded at its present value, recognizing the reduction in debt as a financing gain on the statement of comprehensive income.

TTL has several major orders for product that will be delivered in the first quarter of 20X4. Management is considering ways to expedite these orders to ensure that delivery is completed in the fourth quarter of 20X3. Management is confident that the company can complete production, although not installation at the customer site. In fact, one customer has indicated that installation will not be possible in 20X3, because of operational and technological issues. However, the customer is willing to accept delivery of the product on the condition that payment not be expected any earlier than if the regular delivery schedule were in force. TTL is willing to accept this condition and indeed will offer it to all customers with orders in 20X4 that will accept delivery in 20X3. If these orders are booked in 20X3, gross profit will increase in the range of $800,000 to $1.2 million.

TTL expects to conclude a transaction with a company located in India, Bombay Telecom Limited (BTL), in the fourth quarter of 20X3. In this transaction, TTL network technology will be exchanged for manufacturing equipment procured by BTL. This equipment will be used to produce a particular component for TTL that will help establish TTL's leading-edge product. Valuation of the transaction is problematic, however. TTL knows that the technology it is shipping to BTL would sell in the range of $1.5 million, but sales of this line are not common and the product was specifically produced for BTL at a cost of $600,000. The equipment acquired does not have a readily established market value, because it is unique. The product line that the equipment supports is projected to have a 10-year life, producing gross margins of 60%, but the eventual volume is highly speculative.

Required:

Analyze, for management, the EPS effect of the situations described above. Include a discussion of any concerns for management to consider. TTL has a 40% marginal tax rate.

EXHIBIT 1

PROJECTED EPS—20X3

Basic EPS: $\dfrac{\text{Net income} - \text{Preferred dividends}}{\text{Weighted-average ordinary shares}} = \dfrac{\$50,621,900 - \$2,000,000}{19,765,500}$

$= \dfrac{\$48,621,900}{19,765,500}$

$= \underline{\$2.46}$ ($2.27 in 20X2)

Diluted EPS:

$\dfrac{\text{Basic} + \text{preferred dividends}}{\text{Basic} + \text{common shares for preferred}} = \dfrac{(\$48,621,900 + \$2,000,000)}{(19,765,500 + 1,600,000)}$

$\dfrac{+ \text{ shares under stock options}}{- \text{ shares retired with option proceeds}} \qquad +1,200,000 - 160,000$

$= \dfrac{\$50,621,900}{22,405,500}$

$= \underline{\$2.26}$ ($2.10 in 20X2)

ASSIGNMENTS

★★ **A19-1 Basic EPS:** The Duckworth Ltd. 20X5 financial statements include the following:

eXcel

Statement of comprehensive income
Year ended 31 December 20X5

Earnings from continuing operations	$ 3,336,000
Discontinued operations (net of tax)	432,000
Net earnings and comprehensive income	$ 3,768,000

Statement of financial position
31 December 20X5

Bonds payable, 5%, non-convertible		$10,000,000
Preferred shares, no-par value, $0.90, non-convertible, non-cumulative, outstanding during year, 500,000 shares		10,000,000
Common shares, no-par value:		
Outstanding 1 Jan., 34,000,000 shares	$7,360,000	
Sold and issued 1 April, 3,240,000 shares	1,400,000	
Issued 10% stock dividend, 30 Sept., 3,724,000 shares	1,490,000	10,250,000
Retained earnings		7,910,000

The company declared and paid preferred dividends of $20,000 during the year, and had an effective tax rate of 40%.

Required:

1. Compute basic EPS.
2. Repeat requirement (1), assuming that the preferred shares are cumulative.

★★ **A19-2 EPS Interpretation:** EPS information from the 20X3 Foran Resources Corp. financial statements is as follows:

	20X3	20X2
Basic		
Earnings from continuing operations	$3.38	$2.98
Discontinued operations	(.27)	.13
Net earnings	$3.11	$3.11
Diluted		
Earnings from continuing operations	$2.62	$2.75
Discontinued operations	(.22)	.11
Net earnings	$2.40	$2.86

Required:

1. Explain how basic EPS is calculated.
2. Suggest a predicted target for basic EPS for 20X4, based on trends. Justify your choice.
3. Explain the meaning of diluted EPS. What elements must Foran have in its capital structure?
4. Interpret the trend in diluted EPS.

★★ **A19-3 Basic EPS, Interpretation:** Huron Resources is a public oil field services company. Selected information follows:

	20X4	20X3
Bonds payable, 7%, due 20X16	$ 6,000,000	$ 6,000,000
Preferred shares, $3 dividend, non-cumulative, 100,000 shares outstanding	$ 1,600,000	$ 1,600,000
Preferred shares, $2 dividend, cumulative, 50,000 shares outstanding. Redemption price $20 per share plus dividends in arrears, if any	$ 2,100,000	$ 2,100,000
Common shares, 900,000 shares outstanding at the end of 20X4 after 300,000 shares were issued for cash on 31 October 20X4; no share transactions in 20X3	$16,200,000	$10,700,000
Dividends declared during the year	$ 540,000	0
Net earnings and comprehensive income	$ 700,000	$ 400,000

Required:

1. Calculate basic EPS for 20X4 and 20X3.
2. Interpret the trend in basic EPS.
3. Repeat requirement (1) assuming that the shares issued in 20X4 were issued as a result of a stock dividend.

★★ **A19-4 Basic EPS, Interpretation:** Gannon Ltd. reported earnings as follows:

Year ended 31 December	20X2	20X1
Earnings from continuing operations	$993,000	1,019,000
Discontinued operations (net of tax)	(116,000)	77,000
Net earnings and comprehensive income	$877,000	$1,096,000

The capital structure of Gannon Ltd included the following :

31 December	20X2	20X1
Bonds payable, 5%, due 20X15	$5,000,000	$5,000,000
Class B Preferred shares, $0.70, cumulative, non participating; shares issued and outstanding, 120,000 shares, issued 1 January 20X2	3,000,000	—
Class A Preferred shares, $1, non-cumulative, non-participating; shares issued and outstanding, 50,000 shares	1,250,000	1,250,000
Common shares, no-par, authorized unlimited shares; issued and outstanding on January 1, 20X1, 150,000 shares. Retired for cash, on 1 November 20X1, 50,000 shares. Shares were split 3-for-1 on 30 November 20X2. Outstanding 31 December 20X2, 300,000 shares.	3,500,000	3,500,000
Retained earnings; no dividends declared in 20X2 or 20X1	2,570,000	1,693,000

Required:

1. Calculate 20X2 basic EPS, including the comparative 20X1 calculation.
2. Interpret the trend in basic EPS.

★ **A19-5 Weighted Average Ordinary Shares:** The following cases are independent.

Case A   Reclamation Resources Limited had 2,860,000 common shares outstanding on 1 January 20X8. On 1 March, 286,000 common shares were issued as a 10% stock dividend. On 1 June, 200,000 common shares were repurchased and retired. On 1 November, 400,000 shares were issued as part of a contingent share agreement. The contingency had been met on 1 August, but the shares were not issued until 1 November.

Case B   Canadian Ore Corp. had 3,000,000 common shares outstanding on 1 January 20X8. On 1 March, 400,000 common shares were issued for cash. On 1 July, 200,000 common shares were repurchased and retired. On 1 November, 640,000 common shares were issued as a stock dividend.

Case C   Minerals Limited had 6,950,000 common shares outstanding on 1 January 20X8. No shares were issued or retired during 20X8, which has a 31 December year-end. On 15 January 20X9, before the audit report was issued, a one-for-four reverse stock split was effective.

Required:
For each case, calculate the weighted-average number of common shares to use in the calculation of basic EPS in 20X8.

★ **A19-6 Weighted Average Ordinary Shares:** The following cases are independent.

Case A   Knowledge Kingdom Corporation had 500,000 Series A shares and 250,000 Series B shares outstanding on January 1. Each non-voting Series A share has a $2 per share cumulative dividend paid quarterly and is convertible into four Series B shares. Series B shares are voting shares with the residual interest in net assets. During the year, 40,000 Series A shares converted to B shares on 1 October. On 1 December, 100,000 Series B shares were retired for cash.

Case B   Kotlier Company began the year with 40,000 Class A shares and 100,000 class B shares. Class A shares are convertible 1-for-1 to Class B shares and have identical rights except Class A shares have 10 votes each and Class B shares have 1 vote each. An additional 100,000 Class B were issued for cash on April 30.

Case C   Jasper Limited has 1,000,000 common shares outstanding on 1 January. On 27 February 200,000 shares were issued for land and buildings, and another 300,000 shares were issued under a contingent share agreement on 1 August. The contingency has been cleared in late March, but there was a delay in issuing shares. A 2-for-1 stock split was distributed on 30 August.

Required:
For each case, calculate the number of weighted-average ordinary shares to use in the calculation of basic EPS.

★ **A19-7 Basic EPS for Three Years:** Ramca Corporation's accounting year ends on 31 December. During the three most recent years, its common shares outstanding changed as follows:

	20X7	20X6	20X5
Shares outstanding, 1 January	150,000	120,000	100,000
Shares sold, 1 April 20X5			20,000
25% stock dividend, 1 July 20X6		30,000	
2-for-1 stock split, 1 July 20X7	150,000		
Shares sold, 1 October 20X7	50,000		
Shares outstanding, 31 December	350,000	150,000	120,000
Net earnings and comprehensive income	$375,000	$330,000	$299,000

Required:

1. For purposes of calculating EPS at the end of each year, for each year independently, determine the weighted-average number of shares outstanding.

2. For purposes of calculating EPS at the end of 20X7, when comparative statements are being prepared on a three-year basis, determine the weighted-average number of shares outstanding for each year.

3. Compute EPS for each year based on computations in requirement (2). There were no preferred shares outstanding.

★ **A19-8 Basic EPS:** At the end of 20X6, the records of Security Systems Corporation showed the following:

*e*X*cel*

Bonds payable, 7%, non-convertible	$ 320,000
Preferred shares:	
Class A, no-par, $0.60, non-convertible, non-cumulative, outstanding 60,000 shares	300,000
Class B, no-par, $0.70, non-convertible, cumulative, outstanding 30,000 shares	600,000
Common shares, no-par, authorized unlimited shares:	
Outstanding 1 January, 186,000 shares $1,785,000	
Retired shares 1 May, 36,000 shares (345,483)	
Issued a 300% stock dividend on 1 November, on outstanding shares (450,000 additional shares)	1,439,517
Retained earnings (no dividends declared)	1,710,000
Earnings from continuing operations	$ 160,500
Discontinued operations, net of tax	10,000
Net earnings	$ 170,500

Required:
Compute basic EPS. Show computations.

★ **A19-9 Multiple Common Share Classes:** In 20X2, McCullough Limited earned $8,040,000, and dividends of $2,250,000 were declared and paid. The company has two classes of voting shares. Class A shares have eight votes per share, while Class B shares have one vote per share. Both participate in the distribution of net assets in the event of dissolution. There were 500,000 Class A shares outstanding all during 20X2, and 1,500,000 Class B shares.

Class A shares are entitled to dividends as declared, in the amount of $0.90 per share, before the Class B shares receive any dividends. After the Class A dividend, Class B shares will receive dividends as declared up to $1.20 per share. If any dividends are declared above this amount, both classes are to be allocated an identical per share dividend.

Required:

1. Determine basic EPS for each share class for 20X2.

2. Repeat requirement (1) assuming that there is no base dividend and dividends are split on a per-share basis between the two classes such that Class A shares receive 10 times the Class B entitlement per share.

★ **A19-10 Multiple Common Share Classes:** Home Lake Mines Limited reported earnings of $984,000 in 20X8 and declared no dividends. At the end of 20X8, Home Lake Mines reported the following in the disclosure notes:

Share Capital

> Multiple Voting Shares: 400,000 shares are authorized but 60,000 shares were issued and outstanding all year. Multiple voting shares are voting shares with a residual interest in assets. Multiple voting shares are entitled to a base dividend of $3 per share. Dividends declared above the base level (the total of $3 for multiple voting shares plus $0.60 for subordinated voting shares), are distributed between the two share classes. Multiple voting shares receive "extra" dividends at the rate of 15 times the "extra" dividend on subordinated voting shares. Multiple voting shares have six votes per share.

> Subordinated Voting Shares: unlimited shares are authorized but 750,000 shares were issued and outstanding all year. Subordinated voting shares are voting shares with one vote each and a residual interest in assets. Subordinated voting shares are entitled to a base dividend of $0.60 per share. Dividends declared above the base level (the total of $3 for multiple voting shares plus $0.60 for subordinated voting shares) are distributed between the two share classes as described above.

Required:

1. Calculate basic EPS for 20X8.
2. Repeat requirement (1) assuming that multiple voting shares are entitled to five times the dividend of subordinated shares, as declared, with no minimum.

★ **A19-11 Contingently Issuable Shares:** On 1 January 20X1, Barnhill Information Technologies reported 3,650,000 common shares outstanding, with a reported dollar balance of $9,933,000. During the prior year, 20X0, the company had acquired Semere Systems, a supplier company, in a cash and share transaction. Part of the purchase agreement stated that:

1. Barnhill agreed to issue an additional 2,500,000 common shares to the prior shareholders of Semere if the operating profit of the Semere business unit, as defined by agreement, was in excess of $1,000,000 for each of 20X0, 20X1 and 20X2;
2. Barnhill agreed to issue an additional 200,000 shares to the prior shareholders of Semere if a lawsuit outstanding in 20X0 against Semere were resolved for a net cost, including legal fees, of less than $150,000; and
3. Barnhill agreed to issue to issue an additional 1,000,000 shares to the prior shareholders of Semere if a new product under development by Semere were to be patented before 20X4.

In 20X1, Barnhill reported earnings of $3,741,000. The lawsuit against Semere was dismissed in court action in late March 20X1, with costs recorded of $92,000. Accordingly, 200,000 common shares were issued to the prior shareholders of Semere, on 31 October 20X1. The Semere business unit turned in strong operating results, with $1,500,000 profit earned, similar to their results in 20X0. However, the product under development had not advanced to the patent stage by the end of 20X1. Barnhill had no other share transactions in 20X1.

Required:
Calculate basic and diluted earnings per share figures for 20X1.

★ **A19-12 Contingently Issuable Shares:** On 1 January 20X1, Aker Aviation Services Ltd. entered into an agreement to purchase Moore Fuels Limited. The agreement included the following terms:

1. Aker agreed to issue an additional 2,000,000 shares to the prior shareholders of Moore if Aker retained 80% of the customers of Moore at the end of 20X3.

future condition

2. Aker agreed to issue 1,300,000 common shares to the prior shareholders of Moore if five key employees remained with Aker through the end of 20X5. *future cond.*

3. Aker agreed to issue an additional 500,000 shares to the prior shareholders of Moore if five new retail fuel units were opened before the end of 20X4. *present or future cond.*

Aker had 11,500,000 common shares outstanding at the beginning of 20X2. Net earnings were $1,445,000 in 20X2. To date, customer retention was in the range of 75%, and the key employees have remained in Aker's employment. Four new retail outlets were opened in 20X1, and one in early February 20X2. Accordingly, 500,000 common shares were issued to the prior shareholders of Moore, but not until 31 August 20X2. Aker had no other share transactions in 20X2.

Required:
Calculate basic and diluted earnings per share figures for 20X2.

★★ **A19-13 Basic and Diluted EPS:** Wilcox Enterprises, a public company, is required to disclose earnings per share information in its financial statements for the year ended 31 December 20X6. The facts about Wilcox's situation:

a. At the beginning of the year, 450,000 common shares, issued for $5.75 million, were outstanding. The authorized number of common shares is 1 million. On 1 January, 50,000, $5 cumulative preferred shares were also outstanding. They had been issued for $500,000.

b. On 30 September 20X6, Wilcox issued 100,000 common shares for $1.5 million cash.

c. Wilcox reported earnings of $2.5 million for the year ended 31 December 20X6.

d. At 1 January 20X6, Wilcox had outstanding $1 million (par value) of 8% convertible bonds ($1,000 face value), with interest payable on 30 June and 31 December of each year. Each $1,000 bond is convertible into 65 common shares, at the option of the holder, at any time before 31 December 20X11.

c. Wilcox has options outstanding for 50,000 common shares at a price of $5 per share. The average market value of common shares during the period was $20.

f. Wilcox Enterprises has an effective tax rate of 40%.

Required:
Calculate the basic and diluted earnings per share figures for 20X6.

★★ **A19-14 Diluted EPS, Actual Conversions:** Waves Sound Solutions (WSS) reports the following calculations for basic EPS, for the year ended 31 December 20X4:

Numerator:	Net earnings, $18,600,000, less preferred dividends of $1,500,000
Denominator:	Weighted-average ordinary shares outstanding, 6,240,000
Basic EPS:	$2.74 ($17,100,000 ÷ 6,240,000)

Case A and Case B are independent.

Case A Assume that WSS had 800,000 convertible preferred shares outstanding at the beginning of the year. Each share was entitled to a dividend of $2.00 per year, payable $.50 each quarter. Each share is convertible into three common shares. After the third-quarter dividend was paid, 200,000 preferred shares converted to 600,000 common shares. The information above regarding dividends paid and the weighted-average ordinary shares outstanding properly reflects the conversion for the purposes of calculating basic EPS.

Case B Assume instead that WSS had non-convertible preferred shares outstanding in 20X4, on which dividends of $1,500,000 were paid. Also assume that WSS had convertible bonds outstanding at the beginning of 20X4. On 1 November, the entire bond issue was converted to 2,400,000 common shares, per the bond agreement. The information above regarding earnings properly reflects interest expense of $291,667 to 1 November. The weighted-average ordinary share figure also reflects the appropriate common shares for the conversion. The tax rate is 30%.

WSS also had options outstanding at the end of the fiscal year, for 500,000 common shares at an option price of $15. The average common share price was $28 during the period.

Required:
Calculate diluted EPS for Case A and Case B, independently.

★★   **A19-15 Basic and Diluted EPS, Actual Conversions:** Information regarding Zhi Ltd:

- Common shares outstanding on December 31, 20X1: 100,000. The company had issued 40,000 shares under a contingent share agreement on 1 December 20X2. It had also issued 50,000 common shares when preferred shares converted on 30 September 20X2.
- The average price of common shares was $14.
- The 40,000 shares issued under a contingent share agreement were issued under an agreement with a previously acquired company. The agreement stated that if a lawsuit that had been filed against this acquired company (before it was acquired by Zhi) were to be dismissed in court action, then 40,000 shares would be issued. The court dismissed the lawsuit in late November, and shares were issued on 1 December.
- A second contingent share agreement related to profit levels of a target company. This contingent share agreement calls for an additional 50,000 common shares to be issued in 20X5 if 20X2, 20X3, and 20X4 earnings from the target company each reach a certain level. This level was attained in 20X2.
- Preferred shares, $3, cumulative: these shares were convertible 5-for-1. At the beginning of the year, 30,000 shares were outstanding and 10,000 shares converted on September 30, 20X2. The dividend is paid quarterly.
- Zhi Ltd. has $3,000,000 par value convertible bonds outstanding. There is $104,000 in a common stock conversion rights account with respect to the bonds. The bonds are convertible into 50,000 common shares. Interest paid on the bond was $180,000, and there was discount amortization of $17,000. The bonds are convertible at any time before their maturity date in 20X20.
- Net earnings in 20X2, $602,000.
- The tax rate was 40%.

Required:
Calculate basic and diluted EPS for 20X2.

★   **A19-16 Basic and Diluted EPS:** The following data relates to Gertron Ltd, a public company. Shares were outstanding for the entire year.

Case	Common Shares Outstanding	Preferred Shares Outstanding	Net Earnings	Pref. Share Dividend	Pref. Shares Convertible (2)	Pref. Shares Cumulative
A	350,000	50,000	$680,000 (1)	$2 per share; not declared	No	Yes
B	350,000	40,000	$750,000	$4 per share; declared	Yes	Yes
C	400,000	50,000	$675,000	$7 per share; declared	Yes	No
D	400,000	75,000	$540,000	$3 per share; not declared	Yes	No

(1) Includes $135,000 loss on discontinued operations in case A only.
(2) If preferred shares are convertible, each preferred share is entitled to five common shares.

Required:
For each case, calculate basic and diluted EPS, as appropriate.

★ ★ **A19-17 Basic and Diluted EPS:** The shareholders' equity of Cameron Corporation as of 31 December 20X6, the *end* of the current fiscal year, is as follows:

$1 cumulative preferred shares, no-par, convertible at the rate of 4-for-1; 350,000 shares outstanding	$ 9,150,000
Common shares, no-par; 3,500,000 shares outstanding	15,000,000
Common stock conversion rights	231,000
Retained earnings	30,600,000

Other information:

- On 1 July 20X6, 150,000 preferred shares were converted to common shares at the rate of 4-for-1.
- During 20X6, Cameron had convertible subordinated debentures outstanding with a face value of $4,000,000. The debentures are due in 20X12, at which time they may be converted to common shares or repaid at the option of the holder. The conversion rate is 12 common shares for each $100 debenture. Interest expense of $175,000 was recorded in 20X6.
- The convertible preferred shares had been issued in 20X0. Quarterly dividends, on 31 March, 30 June, 30 September, and 31 December, have been regularly declared.
- The company's 20X6 net earnings were $2,289,000, after tax at 48%. Common shares traded for an average price of $18, stable in each quarter of the year.
- Cameron had certain employee stock options outstanding all year. The options were to purchase 600,000 common shares at a price of $14 per share. The options become exercisable in 20X13.
- Cameron had another 100,000 employee stock options outstanding on 1 January 20X6, at an exercise price of $22. They expired on 30 June 20X6.

Required:
Show the EPS presentation that Cameron would include on its 20X6 statement of comprehensive income.

★ ★ **A19-18 Basic and Diluted EPS:** At the end of 20X7, the records of Info Solutions Limited reflected the following:

Statement of financial position	
Bonds payable, 10%, $600,000 par value, issued 1 January 20X0; entirely converted to common shares on 1 December 20X7; each $1,000 bond was convertible to 110 common shares	$ 0
Preferred shares, $0.50, convertible 2-for-1 into common shares, cumulative, non-participating; shares issued and outstanding during year, 30,000 shares	390,000
Common shares, no-par value, authorized unlimited shares; issued and outstanding throughout the period to 1 July 20X7, 150,000 shares. 300,000 shares were sold for cash on 1 July 20X7, additional shares were also issued on 1 December when bondholders converted	2,820,000
Common stock conversion rights, related to 10% bonds payable, above	0
Retained earnings (no dividends declared during year)	1,710,000
Statement of comprehensive income	
Net earnings (after $47,250 of interest expense to 1 December on convertible bonds, above)	366,000

Average tax rate, 30%.

Required:
Compute the required EPS amounts. Show computations and round to two decimal places.

★★ **A19-19 Basic and Diluted EPS:** MacDonald Company has reported basic earnings per Class A common share of $2.61. MacDonald has a tax rate of 40%. The average share price during the year was $42. Review each of the following items:

A. Class B non-voting cumulative $1 shares, 75,000 shares outstanding all year, convertible into Class A shares at the rate of four Class B shares for one Class A share. Dividends of $0.50 were declared this year and basic EPS properly reflects the dividend entitlement of these preferred shares.

B. Class A common stock options outstanding all year for 30,000 shares at a price of $65.

C. Class A common stock options outstanding all year for 30,000 shares at a price of $35.

D. Class A common stock options granted at the end of the fiscal year for 10,000 shares at $32 per share.

E. 12%, eight-year $5,000,000 convertible bonds outstanding all year, convertible into 18 Class A common shares for every $1,000 bond. A bond discount was recorded when the bond was originally issued and amortization of $43,750 was recorded on the discount this year. On issuance, $420,000 of common stock conversion rights were recorded in shareholders' equity.

F. 8%, 15-year, $9,000,000 convertible bonds outstanding all year, convertible into 24 Class A common shares for every $1,000 bond. A bond discount was recorded on issuance, and amortization of $19,200 was recorded on the discount this year. On issuance, $145,000 of common stock conversion rights were recorded in shareholders' equity.

G. 6%, 15-year, $9,000,000 convertible bonds outstanding at the beginning of the year, convertible into 20 Class A common shares for every $1,000 bond. A bond discount was recorded when the bond was originally issued, and amortization of $2,500 was recorded on the discount this year. On issuance, $145,000 of common stock conversion rights were recorded in shareholders' equity. The bonds converted into common stock on 1 April of the current year, and basic EPS properly reflects the common shares outstanding since 1 April.

Required:

Indicate whether each of the above times would be included or excluded in a calculation of diluted EPS, and why. The solution should include the individual effect of each item, as applicable. If the item is included, indicate the change to the numerator and denominator of diluted EPS.

★★ **A19-20 Basic and Diluted EPS; Split:** Accounting staff at Linfei Corporation have gathered the following information:

- Common shares outstanding on 31 December 20X4, 300,000.
- A 3-for-1 stock split was distributed on 1 February 20X4.
- 280,000 common shares were sold for cash of $50 per share on 1 March 20X4.
- Linfei purchased and retired 40,000 common shares on 1 June 20X4.
- 50,000 Series II options were issued in 20X1, originally allowing the holder to buy one share at $25 for every option held beginning in 20X8. Terms of the options were adjusted for the split in February. (The shares were tripled and the price reduced to one-third.)
- Linfei has $4,000,000 par-value convertible bonds outstanding. There is $692,000 in a common stock conversion rights account with respect to the bonds. Each $1,000 bond was originally convertible into 30 common shares. Terms were adjusted for the split in February. Interest expense on the bond, including discount amortization of $48,000, was $420,000 in 20X4. The bonds are convertible at any time before their maturity date in 20X18.
- Net profit in 20X4 was $860,000.
- The tax rate was 40% and the average common share price in 20X4, after being adjusted for the split, was $20.

Required:

Calculate all EPS disclosures for 20X4. Note that there were 300,000 common shares outstanding at the *end* of the fiscal period and calculations must work backward from this date.

★★ **A19-21 EPS Computation:** Sea Products Corporation (SPC) reported $6,080,000 of earnings from continuing operations for the 20X4 fiscal year, and an after-tax loss from discontinued operations of $760,000. Net earnings were $5,320,000. Earnings amounts are reported before preferred dividends. Preferred dividends and a common dividend of $1 per share were declared in 20X4. The average common share price was $7 during the period (adjusted for the split; see below), and the tax rate was 35%.

SPC reported the following financial instruments as part of its capital structure at the end of 20X4:

1. 4,900,000 common shares outstanding. Of these, 2,450,000 had been issued as a 2-for-1 stock split on 1 October 20X4. The terms of all share contracts were adjusted to reflect the split, and adjusted values are given in the information that follows.

2. $5,000,000 of bonds payable, convertible into 120,000 common shares beginning in 20X12 at the option of the investor. The bonds are reported as a liability, with a discount, and as an element of equity. Interest paid this year was $240,000, and there was $50,600 of discount amortization recorded.

2. 600,000 preferred shares, with a $2 per share cumulative dividend. There had been 700,000 shares outstanding at the beginning of 20X3. In January, 100,000 shares, with an average issuance price of $625,000, were retired for $699,000.

4. Options outstanding: 150,000 shares at an option price of $10, exercisable beginning in 20X7; 500,000 shares at an option price of $5, exercisable beginning in 20X12; 200,000 shares at an option price of $4, exercisable beginning in 20X13.

Required:
Calculate required EPS disclosures.

★★ **A19-22 EPS Computations, Financial Instruments:** On 31 December 20X3, the capital structure of Victor Varieties Limited was as follows:

- $4,500,000 face value of 12% debentures, due 1 April 20X10, convertible into eight common shares per $1,000. Interest on the 12% debentures is paid on 1 April and 1 October of each year. On 2 April 20X3, 12% debentures with a face value of $1,500,000 had been converted. Interest expense on these bonds was $48,000 in 20X3. Interest expense on all the 12% bonds amounted to $624,000, including the $48,000.

- $3,000,000 face value of 12.4% debentures, due 30 June 20X15, convertible into eight common shares per $1,000 after 30 June 20X7. Interest expense related to these bonds was $450,000 in 20X3. Interest is paid on 30 June and 31 December of each year.

- 30,000 cumulative preferred shares issued and outstanding, $8 per share dividend, redeemable at the shareholder's option at $100 per share. These preferred shares are classified as debt. Dividends are reported as a financing expense in earnings.

- 100,000 options outstanding to senior management, exerciseable in 20X14. The options allow purchase of 100,000 at $25 per share. Average market price in 20X3 was $14.

- 60,000 common shares issued and outstanding.

Victor Varieties reported net earnings after tax of $600,000 for 20X3. The tax rate was 40%.

Required:
Compute EPS for 20X3.

★ **A19-23 Diluted EPS, Cascade:** The Birch Corporation has the following items in its capital structure at 31 December 20X7, the end of the fiscal year:

a. Options to purchase 400,000 common shares were outstanding for the entire period. The exercise price is $17.50 per share. The average common share price during the period was $40.

b. Preferred shares, $2, cumulative, no-par, convertible into common shares at the rate of five shares of common for each preferred share. Dividends were declared quarterly. Seven thousand shares were outstanding for the whole year.

c. $3 million par value of 9% debentures, outstanding for the entire year. Debentures are convertible into five common shares for each $100 bond. Interest expense of $285,000 was recognized during the year.

d. Preferred shares, $5, cumulative, no-par, convertible into common shares at the rate of three shares of common for each one preferred share. Four thousand shares were outstanding for the entire year. No dividends were declared in 20X7 on these shares.

e. $8 million par value of 11.5% debentures, outstanding for the entire year. Debentures are convertible into a total of 520,000 common shares. Interest expense of $660,000 was recognized during the year.

Required:

1. Calculate the individual effect for diluted EPS for each of the above items. The tax rate is 35%. For options, calculate shares issued and shares retired.

2. Assume Birch reported basic EPS from continuing operations items of $1.29 (($1,000,000 − $14,000 − $20,000) ÷ 750,000), discontinued operations gain of $1.00 ($750,000 ÷ 750,000) and EPS for net earnings of $2.29 (($1,750,000 − $14,000 − $20,000) ÷ 750,000). Calculate diluted EPS, and show how it would be presented on the statement of comprehensive income.

★★ **A19-24 Diluted EPS, Cascade:** Bytol Corp had the following common share transactions and balances during 20X8:

  1 January—140,000 shares outstanding
  30 April—55,000 shares issued on conversion of $5,000,000 bonds payable
  30 September—25,000 shares issued on conversion of preferred shares
  1 December—3-for-1 stock dividend

Bytol reported net earnings of $920,000 in the year. The bond that converted on 30 April had been a 6%, five-year $5,000,000 convertible bond. It converted at maturity. There had originally been a bond discount recorded, with a remaining balance of $8,333 at the beginning of the year. There was also a $216,000 common stock conversion option recorded in equity with respect to this bond. This was transferred to the common share account on bond conversion. There were preferred shares outstanding, $2.00 cumulative shares, convertible 5-for-1 prior to the split and 15-for-1 after the split. The preferred dividend was payable quarterly (that is, $0.50 per quarter) and 5,000 of the total 20,000 outstanding preferred shares converted after the dividend paid on 30 September. The tax rate was 40%.

Required:
Calculate basic and diluted EPS for 20X8.

★★ **A19-25 Diluted EPS, Cascade:** Ashante Sports Collections Limited (ASCL) ended 20X5 with 700,000 common shares outstanding, after issuing 200,000 common shares for cash on 31 December. The tax rate is 40%. There were no other common share transactions during the period. Net earnings were $1,300,000. The following elements are part of ASCL's capital structure:

a. ASCL had $5,000,000 (par value) of 8% bonds payable outstanding during the year. The bonds are convertible into 80 common shares for each $1,000 bond. Bond interest expense was $403,000 for the year.

b. ASCL had 40,000 options outstanding throughout 20X5 to purchase 120,000 common shares for $3 per share. The average share price during the year was $15. The options were not exercisable until 20X10.

c. ASCL had 70,000, $1.25 preferred shares outstanding. The shares were cumulative. No dividends were declared in 20X6. The shares were convertible into 50,000 common shares.

d. ASCL had a contingent share agreement outstanding to issue 50,000 common shares to the prior shareholders of a company that ASCL had acquired in 20X2. The shares become issuable if the acquired company's operations accumulate $5,000,000 of post-acquisition earnings before the end of 20X8. Earnings have been $3,500,000 to date, and the target is expected to be met in 20X7.

e. ASCL had $8,000,000 (par value) of 6% bonds payable, issued on 31 March 20X5. The bonds are convertible into 40 common shares for each $1,000 bond. Bond interest expense was $285,750 for the nine months of the year that the bond was outstanding.

Required:
Compute basic and diluted EPS for 20X5.

★ **A19-26 Loss per Share:** Brandon Limited's statement of financial position at 31 December 20X2 reported the following:

Long-term notes payable, 6%, due in 20X9	4,000,000
Bonds payable, par value $10,000,000, 6.5%, each $1,000 of face value is convertible into 70 Class B shares; bonds mature in 20X13, net of discount	8,200,000
Common stock conversion rights	590,000
Class A shares, no-par, $5, non-convertible, cumulative, non-voting (45,000 shares outstanding at year-end)	3,500,000
Class B shares, voting, 950,000 shares outstanding	26,000,000

Additional data:

a. During 20X2, 30,000 Class A shares were issued at $50 on 1 July. Dividends were declared and paid semi-annually, on 31 May and 30 November.

b. Common share options are outstanding, entitling holders to acquire 700,000 Class B shares at $9 per share.

c. Interest expense on the convertible bonds was $525,000 in 20X2.

d. Income tax rate is 40%.

e. Class B share price average for the year was $11.

f. The net loss, after tax, for 20X2 was $350,000.

Required:
Compute the EPS amount(s) that Brandon should report for 20X2.

★★ **A19-27 Basic and Diluted EPS:** MacDonald Corporation had the following securities outstanding at its fiscal year-end 31 December 20X7:

eXcel

Long-term debt:	
Notes payable, 14%	$4,500,000
8% convertible debentures, par value $2,500,000, net of discount	2,410,000
9.5% convertible debentures, par value $2,500,000, net of discount	2,452,000
Equity:	
Preferred shares, $5 dividend, payable as $1.25 per quarter, no-par, cumulative convertible shares; authorized, 100,000 shares; issued, 30,000 shares	4,700,000
Common shares, no-par; authorized, 5,000,000 shares; issued, 600,000 shares	2,000,000
Common share conversion rights	189,000

Other information:

a. No dividends were declared in 20X7.

b. 20X7 net earnings were $790,000. Interest expense was $216,000 on the 8% debentures, and $250,000 on the 9.5% debentures.

c. Options were outstanding all year to purchase 200,000 common shares at $11 per share beginning in 20X15.

d. Options were issued on 1 May 20X7 to purchase 50,000 common shares at $27 per share in 20X9. The price per share becomes $25 in 20X10, and $20 in 20X11. The options expire at the end of 20X11.

e. The preferred shares are convertible into common shares at a rate of 9-for-1. They were issued on 1 October 20X7.

f. The 8% convertible debentures are convertible at the rate of seven shares for each $100 bond. The 9.5% convertible debentures are convertible at the rate of six shares for each $100 bond.

g. The tax rate is 40%; common shares traded for an average of $40 during the year.

h. No common shares were issued or retired during the year.

Required:
Calculate all EPS disclosures.

★★★ **A19-28 Complex EPS; Interpretation:** Marcella Corporation reported net earnings in 20X6 of $1,345,000, after an after-tax loss from discontinued operations of $677,800. Earnings from continuing operations was $2,022,800. The tax rate was 30%.

Marcella reports the following information regarding its securities:

a. 400,000 $2 no-par cumulative preferred shares, issued 1 July 20X6. The shares are convertible into Class A common shares 6-for-1 at the option of the investor. The dividend was paid on a quarterly basis.

b. There are 175,000 $1.20 no-par cumulative preferred shares outstanding during 20X6. These shares were convertible into Class A common shares 4-for-1 at the option of the investor. All preferred shares converted to Class A common shares on 31 December 20X6 after the preferred dividend was paid.

c. There are $3,000,000 of convertible bonds payable outstanding during 20X6, convertible into Class A shares at the rate of 30 shares per $1,000 bond, at the option of the investor. This bond was recorded as a hybrid financial instrument. During the year, interest expense of $281,000 was recorded.

d. Marcella had 2,300,000 Class A common shares outstanding at the beginning of the year. On 1 February, the company repurchased and retired 750,000 Class A common shares on the open market for $18 per share. Marcella issued 50,000 common shares for $22 per share on 1 December.

At the beginning of the year, 200,000 options were outstanding, allowing senior management to purchase 200,000 Class A shares for $5 per share. On 1 September, 60,000 of these options were exercised, when the market value of the common shares was $19 per share. The average market value for the first eight months of the year was $15 per share. The remaining options are still outstanding and will expire in 20X10.

All preferred dividends, plus common dividends of $1 per share, were paid on schedule in 20X6.

At the end of 20X6, another 400,000 options, for 400,000 Class A shares at a price of $24, were issued to management. These options have an expiry date of 20X15. The average common share price for the entire year was $22 per share.

Required:

1. Calculate required EPS disclosures.
2. Interpret the EPS results

★★★

eXcel

A19-29 Basic and Diluted EPS; Split: At 31 December 20X1, Regina Realty Limited had the following items on the statement of financial position:

Preferred shares, Class A, non-voting, cumulative, par $10, $0.50 dividend per share, redeemable at the investor's option at par in 20X11; 200,000 authorized, 30,000 issued	$ 300,000
Preferred shares, Class B, voting, cumulative, par $15, $0.90 dividend per share, redeemable at the company's option at par plus 20%; convertible at the rate of one preferred share to two Class A common shares; 200,000 authorized, 90,000 issued	$1,350,000
Common shares, Class A, voting with one vote per share; unlimited shares authorized, 500,000 shares issued	$5,357,000
Common shares, Class B, voting with ten votes per share; entitled to two times the dividends of a Class A common share, unlimited shares authorized, 50,000 shares issued	587,000
Retained earnings	$2,966,000

The Class A preferred shares are redeemable in 20X11 at the investors' option and are classified as a liability. Dividends on these shares are reported as interest expense and have been deducted from earnings.

At 31 December 20X1, there were two common share Class A stock options outstanding:

a. $10 per share exercise price and 60,000 shares, able to be exercised after 1 July 20X1 and expiring on 1 July 20X3.
b. $9 per share exercise price and 88,000 shares, able to be exercised after 1 July 20X18 and expiring on 1 July 20X20.

During 20X2, the following occurred:

a. Net earnings was $1,140,000, correctly calculated.
b. Class A common shares were issued on 1 March 20X2 when the $10 options described above were fully exercised.
c. The tax rate was 40%.
d. The average Class A common share price during the period was $12, after giving effect to the stock split described in (f). The adjusted average for January and February was $14.
e. No dividends were declared or paid to any of the shareholders.
f. There was a 3-for-1 stock split of the Class A and Class B common shares on 1 November. All outstanding shares, option contracts, and conversion terms were adjusted accordingly. (That is, the number of shares increased and the price per share decreased.)

Required:

Prepare the earnings per share disclosure for the year ended 31 December 20X2 in good form.

Source: The Canadian Institute of Chartered Accountants, © 2010.

★★★   **A19-30 Complex EPS:** The following data relate to Freeman Incorporation:

Year Ended 31 December 20X6

From the statement of comprehensive income	
Net earnings and comprehensive income	$18,000,000
From the statement of financial position	
Long-term debt:	
10% convertible debentures, due 1 October 20X13	$ 9,000,000
Shareholders' equity	
Convertible, callable, voting preferred shares of	
no-par value, 20-cent cumulative dividend; authorized	
600,000 shares; issued and outstanding 600,000 shares	10,600,000
Common shares, voting, no-par, authorized 5,000,000	
shares; issued and outstanding, 3,320,000 shares	13,700,000
Common stock conversion rights	375,000

FROM THE DISCLOSURE NOTES

- The 20-cent convertible preferred shares are callable by the company after 31 March 20X14, at $60 per share. Each share is convertible into one common share.
- Options to acquire 500,000 common shares at $53 per share were outstanding during 20X6.

Other information:

a. Cash dividends of 12.5 cents per common share were declared and paid each quarter.
b. The 10% convertible debentures with a principal amount of $10,000,000 due 1 October 20X13, were issued 1 October 20X3. A discount was originally recorded, and discount amortization was $20,000 in the current year. Each $100 debenture is convertible into two common shares. On 31 December 20X6, ten thousand $100 debentures with a total face value of $1,000,000 were converted to common shares. Interest was paid to the date of conversion, but the newly issued common shares did not qualify for the 31 December common dividend.
c. The 600,000 convertible preferred shares were issued for assets in a purchase transaction in 20X4. The dividend was declared and paid on 15 December 20X6. Each share is convertible into one common share.
d. Options to buy 500,000 common shares at $53 per share for a period of five years were issued along with the convertible preferred shares mentioned in (c).
e. At the end of 20X5, 3,300,000 common shares were outstanding. On 31 December 20X6, 20,000 shares were issued on the conversion of bonds.
f. A tax rate of 40% is assumed.
g. Common shares traded at an average market price of $75 during the year.

Required:
Calculate all EPS disclosures.

CHAPTER 20

Accounting Changes

INTRODUCTION

In fiscal year 2009, Bombardier Inc. changed four of its accounting policies. The changes were required by new or revised accounting standards. Some of the changes were for fair value measurement, and were applied in the current year "without restatement of prior years." The company also changed several aspects of its inventory policy, including the company's cost allocation method (from average cost to the unit cost method) and the overhead allocation policy. In the previous year, 2008, the company adopted three new accounting standards, while in fiscal 2007 the company "early adopted" two other new standards. Over those three years, the company implemented nine accounting policy changes.

Looking ahead, Commercial Bank International PSC alerted its 2009 financial statement readers to the forthcoming implementation of 10 new IFRS standards in 2010 and 2011. Already, as this book is being written in 2010, other new standards are being issued that will become effective in 2012 and 2013. Change has been constant and pervasive. The financial statements of 2013 will have little resemblance to financial statements of 2003, let alone of 1993! Financial analysts often use 10-year analyses of earnings trends and returns on equity, but those measures are moving targets—the measurement rules have varied substantially over the past 10 years, and will continue to change in the foreseeable future.

Accounting attempts to deal with these policy changes by requiring retrospective application of accounting policy changes. That means that prior comparative financial statements and historical data series (e.g., earnings per share) should be restated as though the new policies have always been in effect.

While restatement is the ideal, it often is not possible. The detailed data upon which earlier measures of earnings, EPS, and net assets were made are simply not available. As accounting has moved to encompass more fair value reporting, the only information available from the past is historical cost information. Thus, most policy changes actually are not fully reflected in restated statements and statistics. This fact is reflected in Bombardier's disclosures, which repeatedly state that prior years' statements have *not* been restated.

This chapter will explore the ways that accounting policy changes can be reported and the circumstances that govern each approach. As well, we will look at changes in estimates and corrections of errors, which are other types of accounting changes.

TYPES OF ACCOUNTING CHANGES

There are three types of accounting changes:

1. Change in accounting estimate;

2. Change in accounting policy; and

3. Correction of an *error* in prior years' financial statements.

We'll discuss the nature of each of these types of changes in the following sections. Some changes require adjustment to prior years' financial statements, known as **restatement**, but other changes do not. It is important to understand the differences between the different types of changes and the impact of each type on the financial statements of prior, current, and future years.

CHANGES IN ACCOUNTING ESTIMATES

Changes in accounting estimates are fairly common. Many financial statement elements require estimates of future values or events, and estimates are frequently changed. Examples of significant accounting estimates include the following:

- Uncollectible accounts receivable;
- Inventory obsolescence;
- Fair values of financial assets; and
- Judgement concerning one or more of the criteria for capitalizing development costs.

A **change in accounting estimate** occurs when management decides that assumptions used for accounting measurements in the past should be revised in light of new information or new circumstances. Changes can occur for several reasons:

- New, reliable information is available.
- Experience has provided insights into operating factors such as usage patterns or benefits.
- The company's economic environment has changed, requiring a re-evaluation of the assumptions underlying management's accounting estimates.
- Probabilities underlying accounting estimates have changed.
- There has been a shift in the nature of the company's business operations, so that past estimates may need adjustment to fit current business strategies.

Accounting for Changes in Estimates

Changes in accounting estimates are part of the accounting routine. They reflect the environmental changes that affect an organization on a continuing basis rather than reflecting substantive changes in the *way* that accounting is being done. Therefore, changes in accounting estimates are accounted for *prospectively*, by applying them only in the current and future periods.

Prospective application means that the new or revised estimate is used in the current and future periods, until new evidence or circumstances indicate that the estimate needs to be changed again.

One example is depreciation policy. The estimates underlying depreciation are (1) useful life, (2) residual value, (3) depreciation method, and (4) pattern of asset usage. Any or all of these estimates may change over time as a company gains more experience with various types of assets, or as changes in technology may alter the estimates. When the underlying estimates are changed, the new estimates are used for current and future depreciation calculations—that is, they are applied *prospectively*. Prior years' financial statements are not restated.

Disclosure Requirements

Disclosure requirements for changes in estimates are minimal. *IAS* 8 states that a company should disclose "the nature and amount of a change in an accounting estimate that has an effect in the current period or is expected to have an effect in future periods . . ." On the surface, this seems to say that companies should disclose *any* change in estimate.

However, it really has an impact only for estimates that are "fixed," such as the useful life estimates used for depreciation and amortization. Most estimates are "flexible" in the sense that they fluctuate over time, sometimes year-to-year, depending on the company's business environment. The estimate of uncollectible accounts receivable, for example, is subject to adjustment with the rise and fall of the economy (or of the company's customers).

For an example that requires *multiple* estimates, consider the estimates underlying the revenue recognition policy for CAE Inc. CAE's revenue recognition policy is stated as follows:

> Revenue for long-term contracts for the design, engineering and manufacturing of flight simulators is recognized using the percentage of completion method when there is persuasive evidence of an arrangement, when the fee is fixed or determinable and when collection is reasonably certain.[1]

This is a typical disclosure for any company that produces under long-term contracts. Remember from Chapter 6 that recognition under percentage of completion always requires many estimates. These estimates are applied on a contract-by-contract basis, and may change even for an individual contract from year to year. We saw in Chapter 6 that even the amount of supposedly fixed-fee contract revenue is actually an estimate because the final revenue can change due to contract "change orders" and/or changes in specifications.

Similarly, estimates for items such as uncollectible accounts receivable and warranty expense depend on year-by-year estimates. Therefore, disclosure of changes in estimates is rare—changes in estimates happen every year for at least some of the financial statement elements in every company.

Disclosure Examples

In its 2008 financial statements, confectionary company Nestlé S.A. reported that the company had increased the useful lives of many of its long-lived assets, as shown in Exhibit 20-1. All of these changes have a forward effect on Nestlé's financial statements.

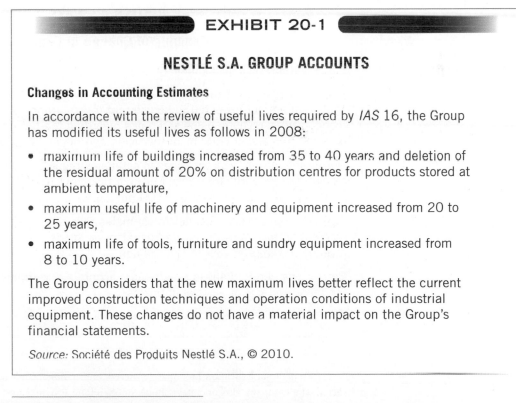

EXHIBIT 20-1

NESTLÉ S.A. GROUP ACCOUNTS

Changes in Accounting Estimates

In accordance with the review of useful lives required by *IAS* 16, the Group has modified its useful lives as follows in 2008:

- maximum life of buildings increased from 35 to 40 years and deletion of the residual amount of 20% on distribution centres for products stored at ambient temperature,
- maximum useful life of machinery and equipment increased from 20 to 25 years,
- maximum life of tools, furniture and sundry equipment increased from 8 to 10 years.

The Group considers that the new maximum lives better reflect the current improved construction techniques and operation conditions of industrial equipment. These changes do not have a material impact on the Group's financial statements.

Source: Société des Produits Nestlé S.A., © 2010.

---

[1] The CAE Inc. 2009 Annual Report, Note 2, page 78.

Although changes in estimates are accounted for prospectively, they still may have an impact on the comparative prior year financial statements. For example, Access International Education Ltd.[2] reported in Note 2 of its 2009 financial statements that:

> The Company changed its estimate on the collection of Goods and Services Tax receivable [by] which all related input tax credit receivables in the amount of $5,410 (2008 − $35,735) have been expensed as the collection is uncertain."

The change in estimate occurred in 2009, but it affects the opening balance sheet because the comparative opening balance of the receivable must be restated. This, in turn, means that the receivable balance on the 2008 balance sheet has to be adjusted to reflect the revised estimate.

A final example is British Airways' changes in revenue estimates, shown in Exhibit 20-2. This note describes two somewhat different changes in estimate—(1) a change in 2008 relating to *restricted* tickets and (2) a change in 2009 relating to *flexible* tickets. The effect was to increase revenues in each year that a change was made.

Although each change increased revenue in the short run, it may not affect long-term revenues since the effect may be simply to recognize revenues earlier than by using the old estimation techniques. That is, the entire revenue stream may be moved earlier, which should not change the overall level but will give more timely information both to the company and to its financial statement readers.

Change in Policy or Estimate?

Accounting estimates are changed very often, sometimes annually, as a company accumulates new information and gains more experience. Normally, the financial statement effect is less dramatic with a change in estimate rather than a change in policy.

Also, the application method is usually different—policy changes are applied retrospectively while estimate changes are applied prospectively. Therefore, it is important to

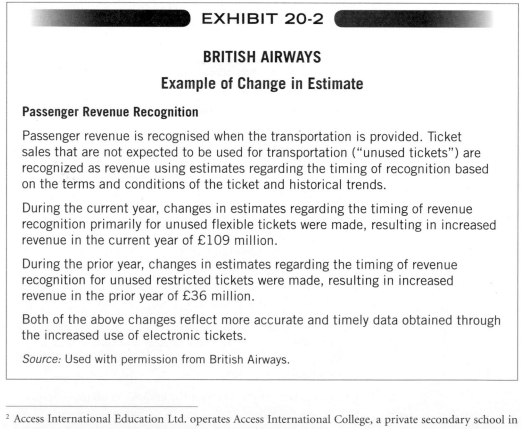

EXHIBIT 20-2

BRITISH AIRWAYS

Example of Change in Estimate

Passenger Revenue Recognition

Passenger revenue is recognised when the transportation is provided. Ticket sales that are not expected to be used for transportation ("unused tickets") are recognized as revenue using estimates regarding the timing of recognition based on the terms and conditions of the ticket and historical trends.

During the current year, changes in estimates regarding the timing of revenue recognition primarily for unused flexible tickets were made, resulting in increased revenue in the current year of £109 million.

During the prior year, changes in estimates regarding the timing of revenue recognition for unused restricted tickets were made, resulting in increased revenue in the prior year of £36 million.

Both of the above changes reflect more accurate and timely data obtained through the increased use of electronic tickets.

Source: Used with permission from British Airways.

---

[2] Access International Education Ltd. operates Access International College, a private secondary school in Calgary. The company also operates schools in Shandong Province and in Guanzhou, China, through joint ventures.

distinguish between estimates and policies. When it is difficult to decide whether a change is a change in policy or estimate, *the change should be treated as a change in estimate.*

Example—Changes in Depreciation Method Companies occasionally change the depreciation methods for tangible capital assets. Since this is an easy change to make, and the allocation of the cost of capital assets between periods is so arbitrary, there is often a hint that the primary reason for the change is to alter reported results—for example, to improve net income and net assets.

A change in estimated residual value or in the estimated useful life of a tangible capital asset can easily be seen as a change in estimate. On the other hand, a change from declining-balance to straight-line may appear to be a change in policy because the depreciation *method* has changed, not just the estimates underlying application of the method. However, the choice of depreciation method reflects management's estimate of the expected pattern of use. If the pattern of use is different than expected, then the change in method is a change of estimate, not policy.

CONCEPT REVIEW

1. A company has accounts receivable of $200,000 and an allowance for doubtful accounts of $40,000. Bad debts have been estimated in the past at 25% of accounts receivable but now are estimated to be 15%. How much is bad debt expense (recovery) this year?

2. Capital assets with a cost of $500,000 have been depreciated for three years assuming a useful life of five years and no residual value. This year, revised estimates are a total of eight years of useful life with no residual value. What is the amount of depreciation expense for this year?

ETHICAL ISSUES

Most changes in accounting estimates are not disclosed. This is one of the "unknowns" that make financial statement analysis a bit of a challenge. Is the company using essentially the same estimates this year as it did in prior years? There is no way of knowing without inside information.

This lack of transparency leads to a potential ethical concern. Since estimates underlie virtually every amount in the balance sheet, fairly subtle simultaneous changes in many estimates can have a significant impact on reported earnings. Individual changes may be immaterial, but the cumulative effect of many changes can be quite material.

For example, if a company's senior management wants to increase reported earnings, they may decrease the estimate of uncollectible receivables, prolong depreciation and amortization, take "the benefit of the doubt" about inventory items of dubious salability, use relatively lower estimates of accrued liabilities, and so forth.

The changes wrought by each individual change in estimate may be relatively minor, but if the changes increase EPS by a few cents to meet the company's earnings projections, it's a successful management strategy (although deficient in ethics). Remember that net income is a residual number; if net income is 10% of revenue, then changing estimates to reduce total reported expense by 1% will increase net income by almost 10% as those expense reductions flow through to earnings. Variation in estimates is not trivial.

By definition, all estimates are just that—*estimates*, not known or verifiable amounts. There always is a feasible range of estimates. Managers and accountants should strive to base their judgements on reasonable estimates that don't push at the limits, high or low, of the feasible range.

CHANGES IN ACCOUNTING POLICIES

A **change in accounting policy** is a change in the way that a company accounts for a particular type of transaction or event, or for the resulting asset or liability. Accounting policy changes can be mandatory or voluntary:

- A change is **mandatory** when the IASB issues a new accounting standard or revises an existing standard. There have been many changes in standards over the past decade, and all indications are that more changes are on their way. GAAP-constrained companies must alter their policies to conform to the new recommendations.
- A change is **voluntary** when management changes from one acceptable method of accounting to another acceptable method in order to provide more reliable and relevant information to users.

Notice that both types of *changes are from one policy to another*. That is what differentiates a *change* in accounting policy from adopting a *new* policy. We'll talk about adopting new accounting policies a little later in the chapter.

Mandatory Changes Mandatory changes in accounting policy have been pervasive in recent years as new accounting standards have been introduced and existing standards altered. *Financial Reporting in Canada 2008* found that 187 of the 200 sample companies reported a change in accounting policy in the most recent survey year. Eleven new or revised standards became effective in 2007, four more in 2008, six in 2009 (including a revised standard on financial statement presentation), and four in 2010.

With full adoption of IFRS in Canada, 2011 was the year of the "big bang." Adopting IFRS affects virtually every Canadian public company. Further, several additional new or revised IFRS standards are expected to become effective in 2013 or 2014. Thus, it will be the rare company that experiences no mandatory changes in accounting policies.

Voluntary Changes Voluntary accounting policy changes are allowed only if the new policy results in information that is both (1) reliable and (2) more relevant for financial statement users.

Clearly, information has to be *reliable* in order to be included in the financial statements. However, the new policy has to be *more relevant* than the old policy in order to be adopted. IFRS does not provide guidance for judging the relevance of resulting information. Relevancy is subjective, so this will be a difficult judgement in some circumstances.

Management may make a voluntary change in accounting policy in response to changes in the reporting enterprise's reporting circumstances, such as:

- A change in reporting objectives;
- A change in the way of doing business—for example, a shift to higher-risk business strategies that make the prediction of future outcomes more difficult and less reliable; or
- A desire to conform to industry practice.

One of the most common reasons for changing one or more accounting policies is a change in reporting objectives. For example, when the ownership of a company changes, the priority of objectives often changes or new objectives that previously did not exist suddenly become important. Examples of changes in ownership include the following:

- A company that previously was privately-held may decide to issue shares on the public market and will discontinue use of private enterprise reporting standards and adopt IFRS instead.
- Control of the reporting enterprise may be acquired by another corporation in a business combination, and the acquired company may need to change its accounting policies to be consistent with those used by its new parent company.
- A new investor may purchase shares in a private company and have the power to specify that certain reporting objectives, such as cash flow prediction, are adopted.

> ### ETHICAL ISSUES
>
> Although information should be more relevant to the users, an underlying motive for accounting changes may be management's desire to manage earnings. Management may wish to change accounting policies:
>
> - To satisfy ratios specified in lending covenants;
> - To meet the published expectations of financial analysts, feeding stock prices; or
> - To maximize the value of stock options granted to management.
>
> While these objectives may seem highly desirable to managers, they do not satisfy the IFRS requirement that new policies must be *more relevant* to financial statement users. Senior accountants and auditors must be alert to such "window dressing," which is exactly what the requirement for increased relevance is intended to discourage. All changes in accounting policy must be evaluated in an objective fashion before being approved by senior financial officers and/or auditors.

REPORTING ACCOUNTING CHANGES

General Methodology

Retrospective Application with Full Restatement The basic approach to accounting for changes in policy is **retrospective restatement**.[3] The process is as follows:

- The new accounting policy is applied to events and transactions from the date of origin of each event or transaction.
- The financial statements for each prior period that are presented for comparative purposes are restated to reflect the new policy.
- Opening retained earnings (or other component of share equity, as appropriate) for each comparative period is adjusted for the cumulative prior income effect.
- All summary financial information for earlier periods, such as net income, total assets, earnings per share, etc., is restated as well. All reported financial results after the change look as though the new policy had always been in effect.

Retrospective application of an accounting policy change is intended to make *current and future* financial information comparable with reported results for comparative prior periods. Earnings trends and other analytical data that are based on historical comparisons are not valid unless the same accounting policies are used throughout the time series. The qualitative criteria of *consistency* and *comparability* are enhanced by restatement, at least in the short run.

Retrospective Application with Partial Restatement Often, it is impracticable to apply full retrospective restatement. Retrospective restatement is *impracticable* if:

- It is not possible or feasible to determine the effects of the new policy on previous period(s);
- Application would require assumptions about management's intent in prior period(s); or
- It is impossible to reliably know what the appropriate measurements and valuations would have been in the prior period(s).

If full restatement is impracticable, the next best approach is to restate as far back as possible with the data available. Sometimes, this is possible for the past five years (the normal

---

[3] The word "retrospective" is used in *IAS* 8. Previously, Canadian standards and companies used "retroactive." "Retrospective" and "retroactive" mean the same thing when used in accounting. Many companies continue to use "retroactive."

period that companies publish comparative series of financial performance indicators). To go back further often is impossible.

In practice, *partial restatement* usually means restating the opening balances of the prior and current years. The new policy is applied in full for both the current and prior years. Thus, both the financial position and the earnings are based on the new standard, thereby facilitating comparison.

All retrospective application requires the company to restate balances as far back as possible. That means that at the date that the new policy is applied, the opening SFP balances should incorporate the effect of the new policy as though it had been applied throughout the life of the enterprise.

Prospective Application Even partial restatement is not always feasible. A company may not be able to measure the cumulative effect on opening SFP balances. If so, then prospective application may be used. Under *prospective application*, adjustments are made from the start of the current period. Indeed, it might be impracticable to measure the effect of an accounting policy change to *any* prior period, including the immediately preceding year. In that case, the policy is applied from the date of adoption forward, with no adjustment to restate opening SFP balances.

Comparability of Statistical Series—A Caution The objective of retrospective restatement is, as explained above, to promote inter-year comparability. However, this works only in the short run. Long-run comparative series such as net earnings, EPS, operating margin, and return on investment are all compromised by frequent changes in accounting policies. It is impossible for a company to go back 10 or often even 5 years and restate those statistics in any meaningful way. The data simply isn't there, and even if it were, it would be both a monumental task and very costly for a company to attempt full restatement of 10 prior years' results.

Such an extensive restatement of statistics (e.g., EPS) may have been feasible in years past when accounting standards were changed infrequently. However, the flurry of new and revised standards in recent years renders the task virtually impossible. Many analysts work with 10- and 20-year series of earnings and returns, but the ground has rapidly been shifting under those measurements.

More than 20 new or revised standards became effective between 2006 and 2010. Sometimes standards even affect the way an enterprise arranges its business affairs. We cannot be too confident that prior years' comparative data has been fully adjusted for all of the effects of those many changes. Normally, data going back more than five years will not be fully adjusted. Almost certainly, any statistical series that have been compiled by analysts will not have been adjusted because the analysts don't have access to the internal company data that is required to make the adjustments.

One might argue that the nature of a business's operations has also been changing and thus the ingredients of earnings are ever-changing. While that may well be true, applying changing measurement to changing conditions just makes the statistical series even less meaningful. It's like constructing a price index that prices a different set of goods each year—it will yield a statistical series of prices, but comparisons won't have much meaning because the measurement method is not consistent—garbage in, garbage out.

RETROSPECTIVE APPLICATION

The basic rule in adjusting for changes in accounting policy is really quite simple:

> *Restate prior period reported amounts as far back as practicable; if you don't have the information to enable restatement, then apply the new policy in the current and future years.*

This is not official terminology, but it is the essence. Now, let's go on to the application of this simple rule.

Guidelines The following guidelines apply to accounting policy changes that are applied by restating prior years. The same approach is used for correction of prior years' accounting errors, which we will discuss in more detail in the last major section of this chapter.

In the following list, notice that the first guideline refers to *recording* the change in the company's books, while the next four guidelines refer to *reporting* in the financial statements and disclosure notes.

For *recording* in the entity's accounts:

1. The *cumulative* impact of the change on the *beginning* balances of the current year must be calculated. These changes are *recorded* in the accounts by means of a general journal entry. The cumulative impact of the accounting policy change on prior year's net income is recorded as an adjustment to the beginning balance of retained earnings.

For financial statement *presentation*:

2. The information necessary to make the change *in the current and prior periods* must be obtained from the underlying accounting records.

3. Account balances that affect the prior years' comparative financial statements must be recalculated using the new policy, including all affected balance sheet and income statement accounts. The comparative statements must be restated to reflect the changed amounts in the full financial statements.

4. Summary comparative information (e.g., earnings per share, total assets, shareholders' equity) that are presented publicly, such as in the annual report, must be recalculated using the new policy.

5. Opening retained earnings is restated to remove the effect of the accounting change from prior earnings. Opening retained earnings *as restated* is shown as a subtotal. This is done for all comparative years. The amount of the adjustment will change as the *number of prior years* declines.

Under retrospective restatement, all prior-period data are restated for financial reporting purposes. However, the entry to record the cumulative effect of the change is made only in the current year. Prior years' books have been closed—the cumulative adjustment must be made to opening retained earnings of the current year.

Illustration

Exhibit 20-3 presents the data for an illustration of the retrospective approach with restatement. In this example, we assume that Sunset Corporation has decided to change its method of accounting for inventories from average cost (AC) to first-in, first-out (FIFO), in the fiscal year ending 31 December 20X5. To make the change, Sunset must recalculate its inventory balances for the end of 20X4 in order to determine net income for 20X5, but also must recalculate its inventory balances for the beginning of 20X4 in order to restate the comparative results for 20X4.

The first step in restatement is to determine which balances will be affected by the change. For a change in inventory method, the following balances will be affected:

- Beginning inventory;
- Ending inventory;
- Cost of goods sold;
- Income tax expense;
- Deferred income tax (on the SFP); and
- Retained earnings.

The statement of comprehensive income, statement of financial position, and the retained earnings section of the statement of changes in equity will all require restatement for 20X4. A change in accounting policy does not affect cash flows, but a change in inventory method will affect the amounts reported in the operations section of the cash flow statement if the company uses the indirect method of presenting cash from operations, because:

- The policy change will alter both cost of goods sold and income tax expense, which affects net income, the starting point for determining cash flow from operations (using the indirect presentation approach); and
- The change in inventory and the change in deferred income tax are adjustments to convert net income to cash flow.

These two adjustments will net out, causing no change in the total reported cash from operations. Nevertheless, the changes must be made to maintain the articulation between the cash flow statement and the other two statements.

In our inventory example, the following impacts of the accounting change must be calculated:

1. The cumulative effect on balances up to 1 January 20X5 (the year of the change);

2. The cumulative effect on balances up to 1 January 20X4; and

3. The specific impact on the accounts for the year 20X4, for comparative restatement purposes.

The new basis of accounting must then be used for the current year, 20X5. The calculations for Sunset Corporation are as follows, using the amounts presented in Exhibit 20-3.

EXHIBIT 20-3

SUNSET CORPORATION DATA FOR CHANGE IN ACCOUNTING POLICY

Change from Average Cost (AC) to FIFO for Inventory

1. During 20X5, Sunset Corporation decides to change its inventory cost method from average cost (AC) to first-in, first-out (FIFO) for accounting purposes, effective for fiscal year 20X5. The change will also be made for tax purposes. The reporting year ends on 31 December, and the company's income tax rate is 30%.
2. From its records, the company determines the following information relating to the change:

	20X5 FIFO	20X5 AC	20X4 FIFO	20X4 AC
Statement of Financial Position				
a. Beginning inventory	$ 60,000	$ 50,000	$ 47,000	$ 45,000
b. Ending inventory	80,000	65,000	60,000	50,000
Statement of Changes in Equity				
d. Retained earnings, beginning balance	$201,000			$ 92,000
e. Net income (see below)	210,000			189,000
f. Dividends declared and paid	88,000			80,000
g. Retained earnings, ending balance	$323,000			$201,000
Statement of Comprehensive Income				
h. Income before income tax	300,000*			270,000
i. Income tax expense	90,000			81,000
j. Net income	$210,000			$189,000

*Reflects FIFO policy.

Recording—Impact to 1 January 20X5

The journal entry to record the effects of the change in policy must be based on the cumulative effect at the *beginning* of 20X5. Opening inventory was $50,000 under AC and is $60,000 under FIFO, an increase of $10,000. The $10,000 increase in 20X5 opening inventory means that prior years' restated cumulative earnings was $10,000 higher than previously reported—an increase in 20X5 beginning inventory means an increase in 20X4 ending inventory, which means lower cost of goods sold. This retrospective additional earnings flows to retained earnings, not to 20X5 earnings.

For reporting purposes, the cumulative increase belongs to earnings retained from prior years. In contrast, the full impact of the restatement will flow through to taxable earnings in 20X5 because prior years' income tax returns cannot be changed retroactively. Therefore, the adjustment to retained earnings must take into account the additional taxes that will be due for 20X5. After tax (at 30%), the net increase in retained earnings is $7,000. The entry to restate prior years' earnings is:

Inventory	10,000	
Current income tax payable (30% tax rate)		3,000
Retained earnings		7,000
[cumulative effect of policy change prior to 20X5]		

This entry establishes the new accounting policy in the accounts as of the *beginning* of 20X5; all future entries will be made on the basis of the new accounting policy. No additional entries are recorded in the accounts.

Reporting—Impact to 1 January 20X4

The change in beginning inventory for 20X4 reflects the cumulative impact of the change in policy on the cost of goods sold for all years prior to 20X4. The change in cost of goods sold flows through to net income and thus to the 20X4 opening retained earnings. The cost of goods adjustment is:

$47,000 (FIFO) − $45,000 (Average Cost) = $2,000; income is higher.

After income tax, assuming a 30% tax rate, the impact on accumulated earnings is:

$2,000 × (1 − 30%) = $1,400; income is higher.

This adjustment for pre-20X4 is not recorded in the books. The effect has already been captured in the retained earnings adjusting entry made in 20X5, as described just above.

Reporting—Effect on the Financial Statements of 20X4

Restatement of the 20X4 financial statements requires changing the beginning and ending inventory balance on the SFP and the cost of goods sold on the statement of comprehensive income. Changing the cost of goods sold has an impact on income tax expense, net income, and income tax. The change in net income flows through to retained earnings and therefore to total shareholders' equity.

The ending 20X4 inventory under FIFO is $60,000, compared to the $50,000 originally reported in the 20X4 financial statements, as shown in Exhibit 20-3. Opening inventory is now $47,000, instead of $45,000. The effect on 20X4 net income is as follows:

- FIFO has a higher beginning inventory, increasing cost of goods sold and lowering pretax net income by $2,000.

- FIFO also has a higher ending inventory, lowering cost of the goods sold and increasing pre-tax net income by $10,000.
- The net effect of the changes in the beginning and ending inventories is to increase 20X4 income before tax by $8,000—the $10,000 increase due to the impact on ending inventory minus the $2,000 decrease caused by the change in beginning inventory.
- The income tax rate is 30%; the increase in income tax expense from the change in policy is $2,400: $8,000 × 30%.

The changes to the 20X4 statements can be summarized as follows:

Statement of Comprehensive Income
Cost of goods sold decreases by $8,000 (credit).
Income tax expense increases by $2,400 (debit).
Net income increases by $5,600 (credit).

Statement of Financial Position
Inventory (ending) increases by $10,000 (debit).
Current income tax payable changes by $3,000 (credit).
Retained earnings increases by $7,000 (credit).

Notice that the changes in the statement of comprehensive income reflect the impact of the accounting policy change *only* for 20X4. The change in the SFP, however, reflects the *cumulative* impact of the changes up to the end of 20X4. The difference between the total adjustment of $7,000 and the 20X4-related adjustment is the amount related to periods *prior* to 20X4:

Total change in retained earnings	$7,000 credit
Less impact on the net income and retained earnings for 20X4, as calculated above	5,600 credit
Impact on retained earnings prior to the beginning of 20X4	$1,400 credit

Restated Financial Statements Exhibit 20-4 shows the relevant amounts from the 20X5 and restated 20X4 comparative statements. The figures in the statements are based on the amounts shown in Exhibit 20-3, except that the 20X4 statement amounts have been restated for the change to FIFO, based on the analysis above. The comparative 20X4 SFP includes inventory at FIFO instead of average cost. The deferred income tax amounts are also restated.

The retained earnings statement shows an adjustment for *both* years, instead of just the single adjustment of $7,000 that was recorded. The adjustment is based on the amount of adjustment for *prior* years. Remember that it's the *beginning* balances that are being adjusted. The pre-20X4 adjustment is effective at the beginning of 20X4; the restatement adjustment relating to 20X4 affects the beginning balance for 20X5.

Observe that the restated beginning balance for 20X5 agrees with the restated ending balance for 20X4, as it should. These amounts are highlighted in Exhibit 20-4.

The note discloses the impact of the change on each of 20X4 and 20X5. The 20X4 impact is apparent from the adjustments. The 20X5 impact, however, is derived from Exhibit 20-3. Under average cost, the increase in inventory for 20X5 would have been $15,000. Under FIFO, the increase is $20,000. FIFO causes an additional $5,000 of cost to flow into inventory rather than into cost of goods sold; the after-tax impact is $3,500 (i.e., $5,000 × 70%).

Restating Statistical Series Assume that Sunset Corporation issues a five-year summary of prior years' results, such as total revenue, cost of goods sold, net earnings, and EPS. To apply full restatement, Sunset must restate that comparative information as well as restating the 20X4 financial statements. Revenue will not be affected by the change in inventory method, but CGS, net earnings, and EPS will be affected (although perhaps not by much).

EXHIBIT 20-4

SUNSET CORPORATION

Selected Amounts from Comparative Financial Statements
Change from Average Cost to FIFO for Inventory—Retrospective Application

	20X5 (FIFO Basis)	(Restated) 20X4 (FIFO Basis)
Statement of Financial Position		
Ending inventory (FIFO)	$ 80,000	$ 60,000
Statement of Comprehensive Income—		
Earnings Section		
Income before income tax	$300,000	$278,000[1]
Income tax expense	90,000	83,400[2]
Net income	$210,000	$194,600
Earnings per share (100,000 shares assumed)	$ 2.10	$ 1.95
Statement of Changes in Equity—Retained		
Earnings Section		
Beginning balance, as previously reported	$201,000	$ 92,000

Add: Cumulative effect of inventory accounting
    policy change, net of tax of $2,400 in 20X5
    (20X4—$600)
	7,000	1,400

Beginning balance, restated	**208,000**	93,400
Add: Net income (from above)	210,000	194,600
Deduct: Dividends declared	(88,000)	(80,000)
Ending balance	$330,000	**$208,000**

(1) $278,000 − $270,000 + $8,000 (decrease in 20X4 CGS due to accounting change)

(2) $83,400 = $81,000 + $2,400 (income tax expense for 20X4 due to accounting change)

Note to Financial Statements
During 20X5, the Corporation changed its accounting policy for inventory from average cost to first in, first out. As a result, restated 20X4 net income was increased by $5,600 (5.6¢ per share). The change increased 20X5 net income by $3,500 (3.5¢ per share). The 20X4 statements have been restated to reflect the change in accounting policy.

To restate the years prior to 20X4 (i.e., 20X0 through 20X3), Sunset must have the prior years' inventory data in its computer archives. These data can be retrieved to make the restatement. The adjustment to restate will be quite straight-forward as long as the inventory data are in sufficient detail to convert from average cost to FIFO.

There is no need to go through a full CGS analysis. The impact on those statistical series can be measured by calculating the effect of the change in policy on opening and ending inventories for each of the preceding five years:

- An increase in *opening* inventory will increase the year's CGS and decrease net earnings and EPS; a decrease in opening inventory will have the opposite effects.
- An increase in *ending* inventory will decrease that year's CGS and increase net earnings and EPS; a decrease in ending inventory will have the opposite effects.

Remember that *full restatement* requires all historical series to be restated, not simply the prior year's financial statements.

Disclosure Requirements

When a company changes an accounting policy, the company should explain in the company's disclosure notes:

- The nature of the change;
- The amount of the adjustment for the current and prior period for each financial line item that is affected by the change;
- The amount of adjustments for periods prior to those presented in the comparative statements, to the extent practicable; and
- If retrospective restatement is not applied or applied fully, the reason(s) that retrospective application is wholly or partially impracticable should be explained.

If the change is due to a new or revised accounting standard, the company should also disclose the title of the standard and its transition provisions.

If the change is *voluntary*, the company should explain why the new policy provides better and more useful (i.e., "reliable and more relevant") information for financial statement users.

Reporting Example

Montreal-based Metro Inc. operates over 800 food stores and drug stores in Quebec and Ontario. In its 2009 financial statements, Metro reports four changes in accounting standards:

- Amended disclosure requirements regarding fair value measurement of interest rate swaps and forward exchange contracts;
- A new requirement for determining the fair value of financial assets and financial liabilities;
- New criteria for recognizing goodwill and intangible assets; and
- A change in the method of determining the cost of inventories.

In the disclosure note, the company states that the first of these four changes "had no effect on the Company's results, financial position, or cash flows." The second and third changes "did not have any material effect on the Company's results, financial position, or cash flows" for 2008 and 2009.

However, the revised inventory standard did have an effect on earnings and financial position that required restatement. The revised standard requires that inventory cost include "all costs incurred in bringing the inventories to their present location and condition." Metro had not previously included this type of cost, such as receiving and shelving costs, in inventory as well as costs for products transformed in store. The company's policy had been to treat these costs as current expenses.

Exhibit 20-5 shows the adjustments that the company made for the prior year's statements, the year ending 27 September 2008, including both the inventory adjustments and the reclassification of goodwill.

- The last column (2008) shows the adjustment that was *recorded* in Metro's accounts.
- The other column (2007) shows the adjustment made to the *presentation* of 2008 in the 2009 financial statements.

These adjustments for the 2008 financial statements were made in the first quarter of fiscal year 2009. Exhibit 20-6 shows Metro's retained earnings statement for 2009, which discloses the adjustments. In the company's 2009 statements, the 2008 comparative column is headed "2008 (Restated—Note 3)." Exhibit 20-7 summarizes the differences between the original 2008 statements and the restated amounts, showing the adjustments for inventory and goodwill.

EXHIBIT 20-5

METRO INC.

Adjustments for Change in Inventory Accounting Policy

(millions of dollars, except per share amounts)

BALANCE SHEET COMPONENTS

Increase or (Decrease)	Beginning balance September 30, 2007	Ending balance September 27, 2008
Inventories	$ 26.8	$ 26.0
Goodwill	(11.5)	(11.5)
Long-term future income tax liabilities	7.6	7.3
Retained earnings	7.7	7.2

EARNINGS COMPONENTS

Increase or (Decrease)	2008
Cost of sales and operating expenses	$ 0.8
Income taxes	(0.3)
Net earnings	(0.5)
Basic net earnings per share (Dollars)	—
Fully diluted net earnings per share (Dollars)	—

Source: http://www.sedar.com, Metro Inc., Audited Annual Financial Statements, 26 September 2009, Note 3.

EXHIBIT 20-6

METRO INC.

Consolidated Statements of Retained Earnings
Years ended September 26, 2009 and September 27, 2008

(Millions of dollars)	2009	2008 (Restated–note 3)
Balance, beginning of year	$1,359.6	$1,214.3
Adjustment due to a new accounting policy related to inventories (note 3)	7.2	7.7
Restated balance	1,366.8	1,222.0
Net earnings	354.4	292.2
Dividends	(59.3)	(55.3)
Share redemption premium	(116.2)	(92.1)
Balance, end of year	$1,545.7	$1,366.8

Source: http://www.sedar.com, Metro Inc., Audited Annual Financial Statements, 26 September 2009.

EXHIBIT 20-7

METRO INC.

Restated 2008 Financial Statement Amounts

(Millions of dollars)	2008 Original	2008 Restated	Change Dr./(Cr.)
Balance sheet			
Assets:			
Inventories	615.6	641.6	$ 26.0
Goodwill	1,490.1	1,478.6	(11.5)
			$ 14.5
Liabilities and shareholders' equity:			
Future income taxes	133.5	140.8	$ (7.3)
Retained earnings	1,359.6	1,366.8	(7.2)
			$(14.5)

Source: http://www.sedar.com, Metro Inc., Audited Annual Financial Statements, 26 September 2009.

Example of Restating Series

Potash Corporation of Saskatchewan Inc. includes an 11-year summary of Financial Performance Indicators as part of its annual financial statements. There have been many changes in accounting standards over the time frame of this summary. One change was applied at the beginning of 2009. The company summarizes the impact of this change as follows:

> Prior year figures have been restated to reflect the impact of new accounting standards on goodwill and intangible assets, including the withdrawal and amendment of certain standards which the Canadian accounting standards setters concluded permitted deferral of costs (such as pre-production costs) that did not meet the definition of an asset. The standards were effective for the company on January 1, 2009, and resulted in it reclassifying costs that were deferred as pre-production costs in 1999 through 2001, amortized in 2002 and written off as impaired in 2003 to instead impact net income in each year incurred. The impact of these adjustments changed net income in 2003, 2002, 2001, 2000 and 1999 by 42.3, 1.6, (26.6), (14.1) and (3.2), respectively. The change also impacted potash sales, potash gross margin, operating income (loss), net income (loss) working capital, total assets and shareholders' equity.
>
> *Source:* Potash Corporation of Saskatchewan Inc. 2009 Financial Review Annual Report, "11 Year Report," page 75, footnote 3; posted on SEDAR 26 February 2010.

A full restatement means going back all those years and restating any figures that are used for comparison, such as the 11-year financial summary that Potash Corporation provides in each set of annual financial statements.

CONCEPT REVIEW

1. A company changes from declining-balance to straight-line depreciation, resulting in a decrease to the accumulated depreciation account. Will the deferred income tax account be debited or credited as a result? Explain.

2. A company changes from FIFO to weighted-average cost flow assumptions regarding inventory. At the beginning of the year, the FIFO inventory was $120,000, while weighted average was $105,000. If the tax rate is 30%, what is the amount of the cumulative adjustment to opening retained earnings?

3. Refer to the data in question 2. Does retained earnings increase or decrease?

PROSPECTIVE APPLICATION

If a company cannot restate its prior year's financial results due to a lack of sufficiently detailed information, the company can use prospective application. In this situation, the effect of the change is reported as far back as possible. Usually, this means that the company makes a single catch-up adjustment in the year of the change, but prior years' comparative statements and summary information are not restated.

The prospective approach also is used for a change in accounting policy if it's permitted by a new accounting standard. The transition provisions in any new or revised accounting standard will say whether the prospective approach is permitted.

Guidelines The following guidelines apply to accounting policy changes that are reported by using the prospective approach:

1. The cumulative impact of the change on all of the relevant beginning balances for the current year is computed and *recorded*, including the change in retained earnings.

2. The cumulative impact of the change is reported in the financial statements as an adjustment to opening retained earnings for the current year.

3. Prior years' financial statements included for comparative purposes remain unchanged. All summary information reported for earlier years also remains unchanged.

Comparative Illustration To illustrate the difference between retrospective and prospective application, assume the same facts as in the previous example for retrospective application (Exhibit 20-3), *except* that Sunset Corporation does not have adequate information to determine the 20X4 beginning inventory on the FIFO basis. If the opening 20X4 inventory at FIFO is not available, then it is not possible to restate the 20X4 financial statements; we can restate only the ending balance of 20X4 (which is the beginning balance of 20X5). The adjustment for 20X5 is exactly as illustrated above:

Inventory	10,000	
Current income tax payable (30% tax rate)		3,000
Retained earnings,		7,000
[cumulative effect of policy change prior to 20X5]		

Under prospective application, the $7,000 adjustment cannot be allocated between 20X4 and 20X5; the entire adjustment must be both *recorded* and *reported* in 20X5.

However, this does not mean that 20X4 escapes adjustment entirely. 20X4 had a beginning inventory of $45,000 at average cost. The ending inventory was $60,000 at FIFO. The original 20X4 statements were prepared using AC for both ending and beginning inventories. The difference can be illustrated as follows:

Selected comparative statement amounts are shown in Exhibit 20-8. Note that there are no adjustments to the original 20X4 amounts. Nevertheless, the year-end 20X5 amounts are identical to those in Exhibit 20-3 under retrospective application.

Use of Prospective Application Prospective application of accounting policy changes is quite restricted. If a company does not have the information necessary to restate at least the prior year's results, the change normally should be delayed for one year so that the necessary information can be accumulated to make a smooth transition. That is the reason that most new or revised accounting standards become effective more than one year after they've been issued—the delay gives companies time to adjust their information collection process. Sometimes, however, standard-setters believe that it is more important to make significant and meaningful changes quickly than to delay implementation until sufficient comparative information can be accumulated.

The change in inventory method that we illustrated above is really a *voluntary* change because both inventory methods are acceptable under GAAP. Voluntary changes always

---

EXHIBIT 20-8

SUNSET CORPORATION

Selected Amounts from Comparative Financial Statements
Change from Average Cost to FIFO for Inventory—Prospective Application

	20X5 (FIFO Basis)	20X4 (AC Basis)
Statement of Financial Position		
Ending inventory (FIFO)	$ 80,000	$ 50,000
Statement of Comprehensive Income— Earnings Section		
Income before income tax	$300,000	$270,000
Income tax expense	90,000	81,000
Net income	$210,000	$189,000
Earnings per share (100,000 shares assumed)	$ 2.10	$ 1.89
Statement of Changes in Equity—Retained Earnings Section		
Beginning balance, as previously reported	**$201,000**	$ 92,000
Add: Cumulative effect of inventory accounting policy change, net of tax of $3,000	7,000	—
Beginning balance, restated	206,600	
Add: Net income (from above)	210,000	189,000
Deduct: Dividends declared	(88,000)	(80,000)
Ending balance	$330,600	**$201,000**

Note to Financial Statements
During 20X5, the Corporation changed its accounting policy for inventory from average cost to first in, first out. Insufficient information was available to adjust 20X4 opening inventories to FIFO. As a result, 20X4 financial statements have not been restated. All relevant adjustments have been recorded in 20X5.

should be made only after sufficient information has been obtained to restate comparative numbers. Otherwise, users may suspect that the company is trying to hide something during a changeover without restatement. We used this inventory example only in order to emphasize the difference between retrospective and prospective application. In the following section, we will look at two examples of prospective restatement in practice.

Disclosures When prospective application is used for changes in accounting policy, reporting requirements are reduced to the following disclosures:

1. The fact that the change has not been applied retrospectively;

2. The effect of the change on current and future financial statements; and

3. The reasons that retrospective application cannot be done.

Reporting Examples

Inventory Hart Stores Inc. is a Quebec-based company that operates a network of 89 mid-sized department stores in secondary and tertiary markets throughout Eastern Canada. In its 2009 financial statements, the company reported a change in its method of accounting for inventories. The change was due to a standards revision that brought Canadian practice into line with international practice (*IAS* 2). The company chose to implement the change prospectively, as permitted by the new standard. Hart Stores' disclosure of this change is as follows, in part:

> … The impact of re-measuring our inventory at cost net of all trade discounts or at net realizable value was recognized in opening retained earnings. The impact of adoption of this new Standard on the consolidated financial statements reduced opening inventory by $1.2 million, opening retained earnings by approximately $0.8 million (net of income taxes recovery of $0.4 million). The adjustment relates to overhead costs that are excluded from the cost of inventory under the new Section. The new Section allows the application to be either retro-actively adjusted or prospectively with an adjustment made to retained earnings. The Company decided to apply this new Section prospectively with fiscal year starting February 3, 2008 and update the opening retained earnings without any prior year restatement.[4]

The company's consolidated statement of shareholders' equity showed the following amounts relating to retained earnings:

(in thousands of dollars)	
Balance, as of February 3, 2007	$20,973
Net earnings and comprehensive income	3,472
Dividends	(1,358)
Balance, as of February 2, 2008	$23,087
Transitional adjustment on adoption of new accounting policies—Inventories (note 2)	(821)
Net earnings and comprehensive income	1,196
Dividends	(1,365)
Balance, as of January 31, 2009	$22,097

---

[4] Hart Stores Inc. consolidated financial statements for the years ended January 31, 2009 and February 2, 2008; Note 2.

Notice the types of adjustments that Hart Stores Inc. made to its inventory carrying value:

- Adjust inventory to a *net* basis, with trade discounts subtracted from the inventory cost;
- Value at net realizable value (instead of at the earlier version of LCM, which was based on replacement cost); and
- Remove overhead costs.

These adjustments are relatively easy to make for the current period, including the opening inventory, but would be very difficult to extract from the accounting records for prior periods. This is probably the reason that Hart Stores chose to apply the change prospectively—and why the revised standard permitted prospective application.

Reclassification In its fiscal year 2009, Vancouver-based Absolute Software Corporation adopted a newly revised standard on intangible assets. The company has contracts for delivery of software in future periods. Associated with those contracts are warranty costs. The company defers costs incurred to date on contracts, in accordance with standards on long-term service contracts. In previous years, the company included future warranty costs in deferred contact costs, but the new standard does not permit such treatment. Therefore, Absolute Software changed its accounting policy. The change in policy affected amounts only on the balance sheet—a reclassification effect, in this example. The full note describing the change is shown in Exhibit 20-9.

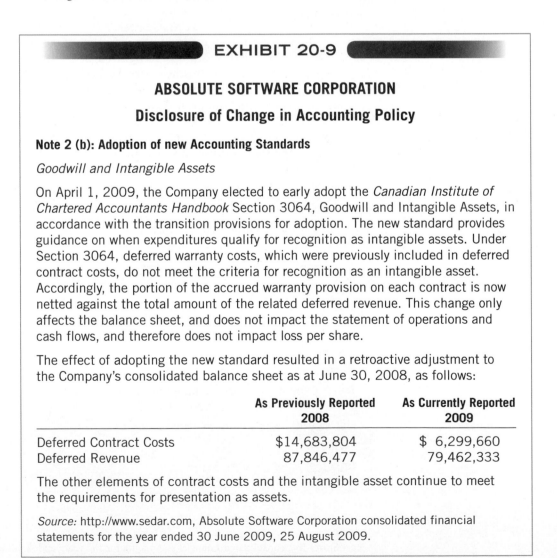

EXHIBIT 20-9

ABSOLUTE SOFTWARE CORPORATION

Disclosure of Change in Accounting Policy

Note 2 (b): Adoption of new Accounting Standards

Goodwill and Intangible Assets

On April 1, 2009, the Company elected to early adopt the *Canadian Institute of Chartered Accountants Handbook* Section 3064, Goodwill and Intangible Assets, in accordance with the transition provisions for adoption. The new standard provides guidance on when expenditures qualify for recognition as intangible assets. Under Section 3064, deferred warranty costs, which were previously included in deferred contract costs, do not meet the criteria for recognition as an intangible asset. Accordingly, the portion of the accrued warranty provision on each contract is now netted against the total amount of the related deferred revenue. This change only affects the balance sheet, and does not impact the statement of operations and cash flows, and therefore does not impact loss per share.

The effect of adopting the new standard resulted in a retroactive adjustment to the Company's consolidated balance sheet as at June 30, 2008, as follows:

	As Previously Reported 2008	As Currently Reported 2009
Deferred Contract Costs	$14,683,804	$ 6,299,660
Deferred Revenue	87,846,477	79,462,333

The other elements of contract costs and the intangible asset continue to meet the requirements for presentation as assets.

Source: http://www.sedar.com, Absolute Software Corporation consolidated financial statements for the year ended 30 June 2009, 25 August 2009.

The last column of the small table, "As Currently Reported, 2009," is the amount for 2008 as restated for the 2009 comparative statements. The net amount (deferred revenue minus deferred contract costs) is the same in both columns—$73,162,673. The difference is that deferred warranty costs of $8,384,111 were moved from deferred costs to deferred revenue. Sometimes it takes a little effort to figure out just what happens when policies are changed.

Early Adoption   One thing to observe about the preceding example is that Absolute Software "early adopted" this revised standard. **Early adoption** means that a company applies a new or revised standard prior to the mandatory effective date. Some new and revised standards permit early adoption—others prohibit it. There are two main reasons for prohibiting early adoption:

- To promote comparability. If the change is substantial and may significantly affect users' inter-company comparisons, it is best if all companies make the change in the same year.
- To give time to collect data. Early adoption usually means that a company will not restate (or not be able to restate) its prior-period data. By prohibiting early adoption, standard-setters remove any excuse for not restating at least the most recent one or two prior years.

IFRS 9 (Financial Instruments) is an example of a new standard that permits early adoption and prospective application. The mandatory effective date is for fiscal periods beginning on or after 1 January 2013. In addition, though, the standard explicitly states that if the new standard is applied prior to 1 January 2012, the company "need not restate prior periods," which of course indicates that prospective application is permitted within a restricted period of time but not by companies that apply the standard on the mandatory adoption date.

When "New" Is Not a "Change"

Throughout our discussion of accounting policy changes, we have repeatedly referred to (1) mandatory implementation of new or revised standards and (2) voluntary changes in policy. However, there is one other instance in which a company adopts a "new" (to it) accounting policy. Adopting a *new accounting policy* must not be confused with a *change* in accounting policy. The following are not *changes* in accounting policy.

1. *Adopting an accounting policy for transactions or other events that differ in substance from those previously occurring.* An example would be a change in the method of generating revenue, such as by introducing instalment sales in addition to sales that require full payment. There is a substantive difference in the way that revenue will be realized, and this change may call for applying a different accounting policy than the one previously used.

2. *Adopting a new accounting policy for transactions or other events that did not occur previously or were immaterial.* For example, a company may have been expensing all product development costs without applying the criteria for capitalization because such costs were immaterial. If development costs become significant, the company then will begin applying deferral criteria. This is adoption of an accounting policy and is new to the company, but is not a *change* of accounting policy because a material amount of development costs had not previously been incurred.

When a company adopts an accounting policy for the first time due to new types of contracts, transactions or events, the new policy must be added to the company's accounting policy disclosure note with an explanation of why a new policy has been adopted. Obviously, there would be no question of restatement, either because (1) that type of transaction or event has not arisen in prior periods or (2) the transaction or event has not been materially significant in prior years—any adjustment would also be immaterial.

CORRECTION OF A PRIOR-PERIOD ERROR

Prior-period errors are omissions or mistakes that were made in the application of accounting principles in one or more earlier periods. Mistakes can be mathematical errors, oversights, misinterpretations of fact, or intentional fraud. Errors relate to information that:

1. Was available when the prior-period's financial statements were prepared; and

2. Could reasonably be expected to have been obtained and taken into account in the preparation and presentation of those financial statements.

An error correction is *not* an adjustment of an accounting estimate of a prior period. For example, suppose that, in 20X1, a company uses past experience with existing products to estimate a warranty liability for a new product. In 20X2, that estimate turns out to be seriously inadequate. In 20X2, the company will adjust its warranty liability and the related expense to recognize the new reality—a *change in accounting estimate*. However, if it turns out that the company's managers overlooked clear evidence that the liability would be significantly higher, and the evidence was available in 20X1, then the misstatement calls for an error correction.

Again, hindsight is not permitted to dictate error classification, but hindsight can be very illuminating when evaluating facts. Sometimes errors are quite clear cut:

- Management discovers that a portion of inventory at the beginning of the year was overlooked when the physical count was taken.
- The company sells through agents; the company failed to accrue commission liabilities that had not been paid at the end of the fiscal year.
- Routine repairs to equipment were capitalized instead of expensed.

However, errors are not always simple. In particular, revenue recognition errors can be a nightmare to correct because so many different accounts are affected by erroneous revenue recognition practices—i.e., inventories, accounts receivable, doubtful accounts, commissions, warranty liabilities, and so forth.

Events Not Reportable as Errors A vital aspect of errors is that they do not arise from a change in estimate or a change in policy. They are mistakes, whether accidental or intentional. Any item that is in error should have been recorded differently in the previous period given the accounting policies and accounting estimates at the time.

For example, a company may have followed a practice of capitalizing and amortizing development costs in earlier periods, only to discover later that the company would receive no future benefit from the expenditures. The policy to capitalize and amortize may have been completely rational and justifiable on the evidence at the time, but later evidence alters the situation. The company would write off the development costs when it became clear that no future benefit would be derived, but that is a *change in estimate*, not an error.

Another example of an event that is *not* accounted for as an error correction is an income tax audit. The income tax reported for a year is considered to be an estimate until confirmed by a CRA audit. If, in 20X5, an audit results in $100,000 of extra tax paid, specifically relating to 20X2 and 20X3, restatement is not appropriate. Instead, 20X5 income tax expense is increased by $100,000. This is prospective treatment.

Error Correction

The correction of an accounting error is accounted for retrospectively, with restatement. The error should not have happened, which means that the statements for one or more past periods were simply wrong. In many cases, the error will have reversed itself by the current period, requiring no adjustment to the current period's statements. In other cases, reversal is not complete and correction is needed.

For example, suppose that the inventory stored in a Cuban warehouse was accidentally not included in the ending inventory count for 20X1. The oversight will have understated ending inventory for 20X1, overstated cost of goods sold, and thereby understated net income for that year. The resulting understatement of beginning inventory in 20X2 will cause an understatement of cost of goods sold and an overstatement of net income for 20X2. If the ending inventory for 20X2 is correctly stated (that is, including the Cuban inventory), the cumulative error will wash out because the overstatement of 20X2 net income will offset the understatement of 20X1 net income; retained earnings at the end of 20X2 will be correct.

If the error is discovered in 20X3, no adjustment needs to be made *on the books* because there are no misstated accounts (either SFP or income statement) for 20X3. But an error that self-corrects over time still causes misstatements for the earlier periods that were affected. The comparative statements must be changed.

Counterbalancing Errors

Most changes flow through retained earnings at some point in time. If and when the impact of the change has "washed through," no entry for the change is needed. For example, assume that an amortizable asset with a cost of $15,000 and a useful life of three years was expensed when it was purchased in early 20X1 instead of being capitalized and amortized over its three-year life. If the error is discovered in late 20X2, the following adjustment must be made, assuming there is no income tax:

Amortization expense [20X2 ($15,000 ÷ 3)]	5,000	
Capital assets	15,000	
Accumulated amortization		10,000
Retained earnings ($15,000 − $5,000		
20X1 amortization)		10,000

However, if this error is discovered in 20X4, no entry is needed. The asset would have been fully amortized by the end of 20X3 and removed from the books. The $15,000 amortization that should have been recorded in 20X1, 20X2, and 20X3 is fully offset by the $15,000 expense erroneously recorded in 20X1. Both retained earnings and net assets are correct without any entries. The comparative figures must be adjusted for *reporting,* but such a restatement does not require a book entry for *recording.*

Example: Inventory Errors Counterbalancing takes place in the course of one year for errors that are made in valuing inventory, since closing inventory for one year is opening inventory for the next year. Consider the data in Exhibit 20-10. Look first at the original data.

What will change if the 20X5 closing inventory is found to be overstated by $25,000? That is, assume that the correct closing inventory for 20X5 is $425,000, not $450,000. Refer to the corrected numbers in **boldface** in Exhibit 20-10. The error has made 20X5 income, assets, and retained earnings too high by $25,000, and they are corrected downward. However, 20X6 income was too low by $25,000, and it is corrected upward. By the end of 20X6, retained earnings and inventory are correctly stated. No entry is needed in 20X6 for this correction, although *comparative financial results must be changed.*

EXHIBIT 20-10

COUNTERBALANCING INVENTORY ERRORS

Income Statement:	20X6—Original	20X6—Restated	20X5—Original	20X5—Restated
Sales	$6,000,000	$6,000,000	$5,500,000	$5,500,000
Opening inventory	450,000	**425,000**	325,000	325,000
Purchases	3,520,000	3,520,000	3,400,000	3,400,000
Closing inventory	(345,000)	(345,000)	(450,000)	**(425,000)**
Cost of goods sold	3,625,000	**3,600,000**	3,275,000	**3,300,000**
Gross profit	$2,375,000	**$2,400,000**	$2,225,000	**$2,200,000**
Statement of Financial Position:				
Closing inventory	$ 345,000	$ 345,000	$ 450,000	**$ 425,000**
Retained earnings	$1,345,000	$1,345,000	$1,240,000	**$1,215,000**

Impractibility On rare occasion, restatement may be **impracticable**. This situation arises when the company does not have sufficient detail available in prior years to enable the company to restate prior years with sufficient accuracy. This may happen, for example, if fair values were incorrectly assigned to inventories (e.g., biological assets) or to investment properties over several years.

It may not always be feasible to determine the correct values in retrospect. When remeasuring the effect of the error in *all* prior years is impracticable, the error should be reported prospectively from the earliest date practicable, which usually will be the beginning of the year in which the error was discovered. If the error cannot be corrected even at the beginning of the current year, then no restatement of balances can be made and the correct accounting method and/or measurements must be applied completely prospectively.

CONCEPT REVIEW

1. A company has begun offering new products to its customers that provides the basic product, a right to upgrades at nominal cost, and a built-in service contract. The company has begun to use a new revenue recognition policy. Should this new policy be accounted for as a *change* in accounting policy? Explain.

2. An internal auditor has discovered that, in the previous year, her company accidentally applied the estimation technique for doubtful accounts "upside-down," assigning the greatest risk of default to the newest accounts receivable and the lowest risk of default to the oldest accounts. This resulted in a very large charge of $5 million for doubtful accounts in that year instead of the $1.5 million that a proper estimate would have yielded. In the current year, the technique was applied correctly and the appropriate adjustment was made to the allowance account. What action should the company take, if any, to correct this estimation error?

SUMMARY OF APPROACHES FOR ACCOUNTING CHANGES

Exhibit 20-11 shows the decision process for applying the three kinds of accounting changes. Exhibit 20-14 summarizes the treatment of cumulative effects and prior-period restatements. These two exhibits may be helpful when trying to conceptualize and remember the different approaches to accounting changes.

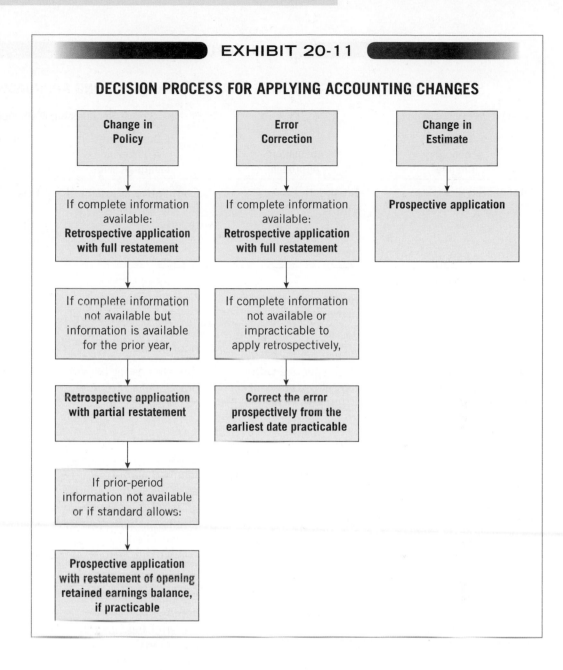

EXHIBIT 20-11

DECISION PROCESS FOR APPLYING ACCOUNTING CHANGES

CASH FLOW STATEMENT

Previous sections have shown that accounting changes affect the balance sheet, the retained earnings statement, and sometimes the income statement. It is not so obvious, however, that a new accounting policy may also affect the cash flow statement. A change in accounting policy will not usually affect the net change in cash—the "bottom line" of the cash flow statement. However, a new accounting policy may affect the classification of amounts in the cash flow statement.

For example, a change from capitalizing to expensing of start-up costs will move the annual start-up cost from the investing section to the operations section. Cash flow from operations will decrease because the expense is no longer included, while the cash outflow for investment in long-term assets (i.e., capitalized start-up costs) will also decrease. The long-term effect on the cash flow statement, therefore, will be to shift the start-up costs from the *investment activities* section to the *operating activities* section of the cash flow statement. The shift will decrease the apparent cash flow from operations, even though the overall cash flow is not affected.

EXHIBIT 20-12

SUMMARY OF ACCOUNTING CHANGES AND REPORTING APPROACHES

Type of Accounting Change	Accounting Approach	Restatement Methodology	
		Cumulative Adjustment Identified With	Comparative Statements and Results of Prior Years
Accounting Estimate	Prospective	Cumulative adjustment not computed or reported	Prior years' results remain unchanged. New estimates applied only to accounting for current and future periods.
Accounting Policy			
a. Complete information about impact in prior years is available	Retrospective with full restatement	Opening retained earnings retrospectively restated in all affected prior periods	Comparative prior years' results and statistical series restated to new policy
b. Not feasible to restate all prior years— sufficiently detailed information not available	Retrospective with partial restatement	Restated as far back as practicable, often only the previous year	One or more recent years restated; earlier years and statistical summaries unchanged
c. If (1) impracticable to determine cumulative effect at beginning of current period or (2) specifically permitted by a new accounting standard	Prospective without restatement	Current year's opening retained earnings adjusted for cumulative effect of the change, if known; if effect not known, then no adjustment	Prior years' results remain unchanged; new policy applied only to current and future events and transactions
Accounting Error			
a. Complete information about impact in prior years is available	Retrospective with full restatement	Opening retained earnings restated (if the error has not self-corrected)	Prior years' results restated to correct the error
b. Not feasible to restate all prior years— sufficiently detailed information not available	Retrospective with partial restatement	Restated as far back as practicable, usually only the previous year	One or more recent years restated; earlier years and statistical summaries unchanged

Similarly, the *correction of prior-period errors* may affect the amounts shown in prior-periods' cash flow statements if the error affects the amounts previously reported.

Changes in accounting estimates will not affect the classification of cash flows because such changes are applied prospectively. Changes in accounting estimates do not affect the method of reporting individual types of cash flows.

ETHICAL ISSUES

Accounting changes present something of an ethical minefield for the unwary professional accountant. Management is, quite properly, always concerned about the perceptions of outsiders who use the financial statements. Managers can often feel tempted to alter accounting policies to mollify the concerns of statement users. However, the current standards on policy changes do make it rather difficult for a company to make voluntary accounting policy changes, especially in a public company. Very few voluntary changes are observable in public companies. Private companies, however, have more opportunities to make policy changes because they are subject to less scrutiny and because they are less tightly constrained by a requirement for GAAP compliance.

Sometimes, an accounting policy is changed effectively, though not technically, by a change in assumptions and estimates. For example, Canadian software companies usually followed the IFRS (and ASPE) requirement that companies capitalize and amortize development costs if certain criteria are satisfied. In doing so, however, the companies found themselves penalized in the U.S. stock market because they did not treat all development costs as expense, as required by U.S. GAAP. To make themselves more comparable to their U.S. competitors, many companies simply decided that the criteria for deferral were no longer being met, and therefore that the costs should be expensed immediately. This was not a change in accounting policy *per se*, but it had the same effect by means of a declared change in assumptions.

That particular example is fairly innocent in that the change had the effect of lowering reported earnings but improved investor perception of the transparency of financial reporting. The change did seem to provide more relevant information for the U.S. users, who felt that non-American standards were substandard and therefore discounted the companies' share value.

In other instances, however, voluntary policy changes may be driven primarily by management's desire to maximize earnings or to maximize their own compensation rather than by any really demonstrable benefit to users. These changes lay a trap for the accountant who goes along with management's desires to manipulate earnings, and severe penalties may lie down the road.

Of course, we all are well aware of the subjectivity of accounting estimates. This subjectivity is unavoidable—it is the nature of estimates. But there is a fine line between reasonable estimates on one hand and earnings manipulation on the other hand. Manipulation leads to misstatement, and where the misstatement is deliberate, the accountant is guilty of fraud, even if the accountant is following instructions of his or her employer.

ACCOUNTING STANDARDS FOR PRIVATE ENTERPRISES

The requirements for all types of accounting changes are essentially the same in Section 1506 as in *IAS* 8. Section 1506 has been harmonized with *IAS* 8.

RELEVANT STANDARDS

IASB:
- *IAS* 8, Accounting Policies, Changes in Accounting Estimates, and Errors

CICA Handbook, Part II:
- Section 1506, Accounting Changes

SUMMARY OF KEY POINTS

1. Changes in accounting *estimates* may be caused by new information or by recent experience that changes previous predictions or perceptions. Changes in accounting estimates must always be applied prospectively.

2. If there is doubt as to whether a change is a change in estimate or a change in policy, it should be assumed to be a change in estimate.

3. Changes in accounting policy may be *mandatory*, caused by a new or revised accounting standard.

4. Changes in accounting policy may be *voluntary*, but only if the change results in information that is both reliable and more relevant.

5. Changes in accounting policy must be accounted for *retrospectively* (also known as *retroactively*), with restatement of prior periods if practicable. Statistical series such as earnings and return on equity should also be restated to reflect the new policy.

6. If full restatement of prior periods is not practicable, then application should be retrospective as far back as possible, with an adjustment to retained earnings for any earlier cumulative effect of the change.

7. If restatement is impracticable, opening retained earnings for the current period should be adjusted for the cumulative effect of the policy change, and the effect of the change should be accounted for *prospectively* in the current period and future periods.

8. If it is not feasible to measure the cumulative effect of a policy change, the change can be applied prospectively in the current period without adjusting retained earnings.

9. In the event that cumulative effect is not measureable, it is desirable to delay implementation until sufficient information has been accumulated to permit restatement of opening balances.

10. Some new or revised accounting standards permit early adoption. When early adoption is permitted, prospective application may be permitted.

11. Information must be disclosed to allow users to understand (1) why an accounting change has been made and (2) the effect of the accounting change.

12. On occasion, a company (or its auditors) discovers that there was an accounting error in a prior period. If the error was material, the error must be corrected in the comparative figures even if it has self-corrected over the long run. If it is impracticable to restate, the error must be corrected prospectively.

13. Accounting changes do not typically affect underlying cash flows, but they can affect the amounts presented on prior years' cash flow statements by changing the section in which the cash flows are reported.

KEY TERMS

change in accounting estimate, 1164
change in accounting policy, 1168
early adoption, 1183
impracticable, 1186
mandatory changes in accounting
   policy, 1168
prior-period errors, 1184

prospective application, 1164
restatement, 1164
retrospective restatement, 1169
retrospective application, 1169
voluntary changes in accounting
   policy, 1168

REVIEW PROBLEM

Each of the following situations is independent:

1. *Change in estimated useful life and residual value.* Phelps Company purchases equipment on 1 January 20X6 for $36,000. The company uses the straight-line method of depreciation, taking a full year's depreciation in the year of acquisition. The equipment has an estimated residual value of $6,000 and an estimated useful life of three years. In 20X7, Phelps decides that the machine really has an original total life of four years and a residual value of $5,000.

Required:
What is the depreciation expense for 20X7?

2. *Retrospective change in accounting policy.* Rhein Inc. (a private enterprise) changes its method of accounting for long-term construction contracts from the percentage of completion method (PC) to the completed-contract method (CC) in 20X7. The years affected by the change, and incomes under both methods, appear below (ignore income tax):

Year	PC	CC
20X5	$400	$200
20X6	300	150
20X7	500	800

Required:
If the financial statements for 20X6 and 20X7 are shown comparatively, what is the amount of the accounting policy adjustment to the 1 January balance of retained earnings for 20X6 and 20X7?

3. *Error correction and retrospective adjustment.* Helms Limited purchases a delivery truck for $14,000 on 1 January 20X6. Helms expects to use the truck for only two years and then sell it for $4,000. The accountant is instructed to use straight-line depreciation but neglects to record any depreciation in 20X6. Rather, the accountant charges the entire cost to delivery expense in 20X6. The company's controller discovers the error late in 20X7.

Required:
Provide the 20X7 entries to record depreciation and the error correction, and indicate the amounts of the cumulative retrospective adjustment to opening retained earnings appearing in the 20X6 and 20X7 comparative retained earnings statements. Ignore income tax.

4. *Error correction, retrospective adjustment, and comparative statements.* On 1 July 20X7, a full year's insurance of $2,400, covering the period from 1 July 20X7 through 30 June 20X8, was paid and debited to insurance expense. Assume:

- The company uses a calendar fiscal year.
- Retained earnings at 1 January 20X7 is $20,000.
- No adjusting entry for insurance is made on 31 December 20X7.
- Reported net income for 20X7 (in error) is $22,800.
- Net income for 20X8 is $30,000 (assuming that the error has not been discovered).
- Net income for 20X9 is $40,000.
- There is no income tax.

Required:
a. List the effect of the error on relevant accounts, and net income, in 20X7 and 20X8.
b. Prepare the entry to record the error if it was discovered in 20X7.

    c. Prepare the entry to record the error if it was discovered in 20X8, and prepare the 20X7 and 20X8 comparative retained earnings statements. The amount is deemed material.

    d. Prepare the entry (if needed) to record the error if discovered in 20X9.

REVIEW PROBLEM—SOLUTION

1. Book value, 1 January 20X7 = $36,000 − [($36,000 − $6,000) × 1/3] = $26,000

    Depreciation for 20X7 = ($26,000 − $5,000) × 1/(4 − 1) = $7,000

2. The impact on the opening retained earnings is the cumulative difference in prior years' net income under the two methods:

    At 1 January 20X6: $200 dr. This is the $200 decline in 20X5 income from $400 under PC to $200 under CC.

    At 1 January 20X7: $350 dr. Also a decline in income, for 20X5 and 20X6: ($400 + $300) − ($200 + $150).

3. The purchase should have been debited to equipment, but instead was debited to delivery expense, which has since been closed to retained earnings. Therefore, retained earnings must be reduced (credited) by the difference between the (correct) depreciation expense and the (incorrect) recorded delivery expense. The 20X7 entry to record the error correction is:

Equipment	14,000	
Retained earnings, error correction		9,000
Accumulated depreciation—equipment		5,000

[20X6 depreciation = ($14,000 − $4,000) × 1/2 = $5,000]

In 20X7, depreciation expense is recorded for that year:

Depreciation expense	5,000	
Accumulated depreciation—equipment		5,000

The opening retained earnings adjustment would be $9,000 for 20X7. There is none in 20X6, since the equipment did not exist prior to 20X6.

4. a. *Effect of error if not discovered* (− means understated; + means overstated)

Item	20X7	20X8
Insurance expense	+$1,200	−$1,200
Ending prepaid insurance	− 1,200	No effect
Net income	− 1,200	+ 1,200
Ending retained earnings	− 1,200	now correct

    b. *If error discovered in 20X7*

Prepaid insurance	1,200	
Insurance expense		1,200

    c. *If error discovered in 20X8*

Prepaid insurance	1,200	
Retained earnings, error correction		1,200

A second entry would be made to record 20X8 insurance expenses:

Insurance expense	1,200	
Prepaid insurance		1,200

Comparative retained earnings statement:

	20X8	20X7
Retained earnings, 1 January, as previously reported	$42,800*	$20,000
Error correction	1,200	0†
Retained earnings, 1 January, restated	44,000	20,000
Net income	28,800‡	24,000§
Retained earnings, 31 December	$72,800	$44,000

* This balance reflects erroneous 20X7 income: $42,800 = $20,000 + $22,800.
† No year prior to 20X7 was affected by the error.
‡ $30,000 erroneous income − $1,200 (20X8 income was overstated).
§ $22,800 + $1,200.

d. *If error discovered in 20X9*

No entry is needed because the error has counterbalanced.

QUESTIONS

Q20-1 A company has always used the allowance method to value accounts receivable and establish a bad debt expense on the income statement. In the current year, it changed from using the aging method to the percentage of sales method to determine the extent of the required allowance. How would you classify the change?

Q20-2 Why are changes in estimates so prevalent?

Q20-3 How is a change in accounting estimate accounted for?

Q20-4 A $100,000 asset is depreciated for six years on a straight-line basis using a 10-year life and a $10,000 residual value. In year 7, the remaining life is changed to five years, with a $2,000 residual value. How much depreciation expense should be recorded in year 7?

Q20-5 If there is doubt about whether a change is a change in policy or a change in estimate, how should it be treated? Why do you think accounting standards have this requirement?

Q20-6 Explain the difference between a voluntary and mandatory change in accounting policy.

Q20-7 What criteria must be met for a voluntary accounting policy change to be allowed? What difficulty is there in justifying a voluntary change?

Q20-8 What role do a company's reporting objectives play in changes in accounting policy?

Q20-9 Explain the difference between a change in estimate and an error correction.

Q20-10 Accounting changes involve (a) policies and (b) estimates. Using these letters and the letter (c) for error corrections, identify each of the following types of change:

a. A lessor discovers, while a long-term capital lease term is in progress, that an estimated material unguaranteed residual value of the leased property has probably become zero.

b. After five years of use, an asset originally estimated to have a 15-year total life is now to be depreciated on the basis of a 22-year total life.

c. Because of inability to estimate reliably, a contractor began business using the completed-contract method. Now that reliable estimates can be made, the percentage of completion method is adopted.

d. Office equipment purchased last year is discovered to have been debited to office expense when acquired. Appropriate accounting is to be applied at the discovery date.

e. A company that used 1% of sales to predict its bad debt expense discovers losses are running higher than expected and changes to 2%.

Q20-11 How is an accounting error accounted for?

Q20-12 What are the advantages of retrospective restatement for a change in accounting policy? Why is it not required for *all* changes in accounting policy?

Q20-13 Assume that a company had traditionally expensed development costs but now satisfies capitalization criteria and thus has changed its policy. Explain how the change in development cost accounting will affect the cash flow statement.

CASE 20-1

MOUNTAIN MINES LUBRICATION LTD.

Mountain Mines Lubrication Ltd. (MML), a Canadian private company, supplies lubricant to mining operations in northern British Columbia and the Northwest Territories. MML commenced operations four years ago and is based in Prince George, B.C. MML has two lubricant products: "Slip Coat" and "Maximum Guard." MML's lubricants are used in large, expensive mining machines and are crucial to the operation of the machines. Without good lubrication, the machines will overheat and break down.

The mining industry has not performed well in recent years, but over the last summer the economy has picked up and, according to MML's owner, Max Mulholland, the B.C. mines are running at peak capacity. Customer service is key to the business. Max says that MML has been able to survive the hard times because it is more flexible and its products cost less than those of its competitors.

MML is a new client of your firm. You, CA, have been assigned to conduct the review engagement. You have met with Max and with Nina Verhan, the bookkeeper. Your notes are in Exhibits I and II. You have been working at the client's office for two days. The partner would like a memo analyzing the issues you have identified in the review.

Required:
Prepare the memo.

EXHIBIT I

Excerpts from Your Discussion with Max Mulholland

"I do everything I can to keep costs down. Take the bank, for example. It had wanted audited financial statements, prepared in accordance with IFRS, before it would approve my new line of credit, but I know how much you guys charge for an audit. I've got product at remote locations, and it would cost a fortune just to fly you out there to look at my inventory. So I talked the bank down to accept a report based on a review engagement, for now.

"Minimizing costs is vital in our business. Take shipping costs. Some of my clients are in pretty remote areas, and it costs a lot to ship lubricant up there. So I send enough lubricant up there in one shipment to last them for a year. They put the stuff in their machines as they need it, and report to me how much they've used. When my salesman makes the annual delivery, he confirms the information they have provided. That way they are happy because they don't have to wait for lubricant to be delivered, and I keep my costs and my prices low.

"Of course, there are always problems. On August 30, the supervisor at Scorched Earth called to warn me they were really low on lubricant. That was a bit of a surprise to me, because we shipped a lot up there in the spring, but I know they've been working hard in August and those older machines really go through the stuff.

"Flexibility is another strong point. You know things have been bad in the mining industry, but they have picked up this year, which means that our business has picked up as well. Some mines were experiencing cash flow problems and, even though lubricant is not their biggest expense, every little bit helps. So instead of charging them for product as they put it into their machines, I've arranged to have meters installed to read the number of hours a machine is in use and they are charged based on hours of usage. It takes about four weeks before a machine needs to have its lubricant tanks refilled, if it is running at peak capacity."

EXHIBIT II

Excerpts from Your Discussion with Nina Verhan, Bookkeeper

"Max is excited about this year. A lot of orders have come in since the mines started picking up. We were concerned about cash flows, but Max thinks they are going to be okay. Big Scar Mine, a new diamond mine in the Northwest Territories, has started operations, and we are its supplier.

"Max told you about our new charging plan, based on hourly usage. When the mine workers pour lubricant into the tank on one of their machines, they let me know by fax. I send them a "no charge" invoice, and at the same time I charge the cost of lubricant to cost of sales. Max thinks that it is a good reminder of the special deal we are giving them. Then, each week, they fax in their meter readings, and I charge them based on the hours of operation of the machine and I record the revenue at that time. We just started doing it this way this year, for three of our four customers. Here is our inventory list for all our mines (see Exhibit III).

"I've also prepared draft financial statements for you. Here are some excerpts (see Exhibit IV).

"Our three BC mine customers have really picked up over the summer. For July, August, and September they have been running at full capacity. The Scorched Earth Mine is the only one in BC not owned by Broken Wing Properties, and it has really been financially squeezed lately. Scorched Earth was pretty eager to switch to our new hourly usage billing, because its cash flow was tight.

"Based on our average selling prices and costs, you will see that our percentage gross margins have increased over last year, and our volume of sales has also increased nicely. I would say we have had a pretty good year.

"The Big Scar Mine has a large amount of our inventory on site. That mine is owned and operated by North Canadian Developments Ltd., a subsidiary of Broken Wing Properties.

"We have received all the meter readings from our hourly usage customers, up to August 31. I noticed that the Scorched Earth Mine meter reading is low, so I will ask our salesman to recheck the meter when he makes another delivery this week. I have billed Scorched Earth for August on the hours that the mine has provided."

◀ EXHIBIT III ▶

MOUNTAIN MINES LUBRICATION LTD.

Current Inventory List (Note 1)

as at 31 August, 20X9

	Slip Coat	Maximum Guard
Average sales price per kg		
20X9	$16.00	$22.50
20X8	15.00	21.00
Average cost per kg		
20X9	$13.50	$18.25
20X8	13.00	17.25
Prince George warehouse	3,000 kg	1,000 kg
Scorched Earth Mine (BC)		
On-site (Note 2)	0 kg	20 kg
Mining machine capacity	50 kg	50 kg
Date of last top-up	25 August	25 August
Moon Crater Mine (BC)		
On-site (Note 2)	300 kg	300 kg
Mining machine capacity	50 kg	50 kg
Date of last top-up	13 August	13 August
Dead Fish Mine (BC)		
On-site (Note 2)	800 kg	900 kg
Mining machine capacity	20 kg	20 kg
Date of last top-up	n/a	n/a
Big Scar Mine (NWT)		
On-site (Note 2)	3,500 kg	5,000 kg
Mining machine capacity	200 kg	300 kg
Date of last top-up	28 August	28 August

Notes:

1. Scorched Earth Mine, Moon Crater Mine, and Big Scar Mine are billed by hourly machine usage. Dead Fish Mine is billed for product when it is poured into the tanks.
2. On-site does not include lubricant contained in the machines.

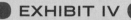

EXHIBIT IV

MOUNTAIN MINES LUBRICATION LTD.

Excerpts from Draft Financial Statements

Income Statement

For the years ended 31 August

	20X9	20X8
Sales	$336,250	$276,390
Cost of sales	286,291	232,090
Gross margin	49,959	44,300
Other expenses	37,309	36,150
Income before taxes	12,650	8,150
Income tax expense	3,500	2,490
Net income	9,150	5,660
Retained earnings—opening	37,750	32,090
Retained earnings—closing	$ 46,900	$ 37,750

Balance Sheet

As at 31 August

	20X9	20X8
Cash	$ —	$ 8,790
Accounts receivable	67,540	57,423
Inventory	234,365	156,837
Property, plant, and equipment	146,600	113,600
	$448,505	$336,650
Bank overdraft	$ 37,929	$ —
Accounts payable	143,476	63,700
Current portion, long-term debt	60,000	20,000
Long-term debt	115,000	175,000
Common stock	45,200	40,200
Retained earnings	46,900	37,750
	$448,505	$336,650

Gross Margin per Product:

	Slip Coat	Maximum Guard	Total
20X9			
Sales	$136,000	$200,250	$336,250
Cost of sales	117,933	168,358	286,291
Gross margin	$ 18,067	$ 31,892	$ 49,959
Number of kg sold	8,500	8,900	17,400
20X8			
Sales	$111,750	$164,640	$276,390
Cost of sales	96,850	135,240	232,090
Gross margin	$ 14,900	$ 29,400	$ 44,300
Number of kg sold	7,450	7,840	15,290

(CICA)

REGIONAL AIRLINES

Regional Airlines (RA) is a wholly owned subsidiary of National Commercial Airlines (NCA). Both companies prepare financial statements in accordance with International Financial Reporting Standards (IFRS). RA is reviewing the basis upon which it records depreciation on the fuselage of certain aircraft. There will be no change to the depreciation of all other aircraft components.

Up until the current year, RA had always depreciated aircraft fuselage on a 4% declining-balance basis. This was based on the belief that RA would use the aircraft for 12 years, at which time the residual value was estimated to be 52% of the original cost. RA now recognizes that the aircraft will be used in operations for more than 12 years. Accordingly, the company will change the way it records depreciation in the current year.

The proposal is to depreciate aircraft fuselage on a straight-line basis over 20 years, with a 20% residual value. The controller, Daniel Davison, asserted:

> I know this still works out to depreciation of 4% per year. However, we are not just changing two estimates: useful life and residual value. We are also changing the method of depreciating the fuselage. We agree with NCA's Board of Directors that the straight-line method is more relevant and reliable than declining-balance. And it makes sense for RA to use the same depreciation method as our parent company. This change in an accounting policy should be accounted for retrospectively by adjusting opening retained earnings. However, NCA's auditors are arguing that all changes should be accounted for prospectively. How can that be?

According to one international survey:

> Depreciation is a prominent feature of the financial reporting in an industry that is as capital intensive as the airline industry. Estimated useful lives and residual values are subjective, and management scrutiny is essential due to the potential for technological change and development changes in the market for used aircraft and various fleet planning considerations.

This study established that the most common method of depreciation used for aircraft fuselage was straight-line. For a given aircraft classification, the estimates of useful lives ranged from 10 to 25 years and residual values ranged from zero to 40% of cost. Airlines typically review estimated useful life annually, and 10 of 24 airlines in the survey changed their estimates within the last three years. Finally, the survey noted that material profits were reported on a number of aircraft sales by airlines included in the survey. This implied that depreciation rates generally were conservative and that book values were low when compared to market values.

Davison felt that the survey supported RA's position to depreciate more of the cost of the aircraft fuselage. Some of RA's aircraft are now in their 11th year of use by the company. A 12-year life did not seem realistic, since the aircraft would not be retired or sold in the next (12th) fiscal year. A change in estimated useful life was deemed necessary.

Furthermore, RA's aircraft are declining in value at a very low and somewhat steady rate. Market information suggests that these aircraft have held their market value extremely well. In addition, the standard industry price reference book, *Airline Pricing Guide,* included data that supported a 4% annual decline in market value and a residual value of 20%.

Davison acknowledged that changes to estimates must be accounted for on a prospective basis, from the day of the change forward. However, he feels that this is, in essence, a change in depreciation policy and that the new method has different variables than the old method. According to Davison's calculations, a retrospective adjustment would increase depreciation in prior years by about $1,800,000. Net income and retained earnings would decrease. Depreciation expense for the current year will increase by $0.2 million.

The auditors, who issued unqualified audit reports in all prior years, argue that all depreciation changes should be dealt with on a prospective basis. Accordingly, all of the $2.0 million charge should appear on this year's income statement.

Davison is furious. "Our management incentives are based on income before interest and taxes. We're fine with using the same accounting method as NCA, but not if it means that we will not receive a full bonus!"

Davison would like you to provide him with a report to help him deal with the issues discussed and the arguments put forward by the auditors.

Required:
Prepare the report.

(Professor Judy Cumby, adapted)

CASE 20-3

LALANI COUTURE

Lalani Couture Limited (LCL) is a privately held company headquartered in Montreal. The company operates a chain of retail clothing stores in major cities across Canada, although the bulk of the company stores are in Ontario and Quebec. LCL manufactures most of its apparel in its facility in Montreal, although some manufacture is also contracted out to other manufacturers, principally in Quebec. The company prides itself on getting the latest fashions to its stores in a very short time, usually within a couple of weeks after a particular fashion trend has been detected. Because of the chain's quick response to the market, the company has been able to serve the youth market quite well despite offering no major "name brand" clothing. The primary emphasis is on clothing and fashion for young women, but about 20% of sales are of young men's clothing such as trendy jeans and pullovers.

Historically, the company has been quite successful. This success is largely due to employing a small group of young adults whose job it is to detect fashion trends among young people well before the major fashion houses do—finding out what's "cool" among youth. The local manufacturing then makes it relatively easy for LCL to quickly design and manufacture new styles of clothing, and to deliver the merchandise to the stores.

No merchandise stays in the stores very long. The store managers are told that as soon as sales of a product begin to decline, the product should go on sale at increasing discounts until it is all sold.

The founder-owners of the company no longer take an active part in running the day-to-day business. Operational activity is the responsibility of the professional managers. Financing has come mainly from retained earnings, although the balance sheet does show a moderate amount of long-term debt. That debt is in the form of debentures held by a municipal employees' pension fund investment trust, secured by LCL's tangible capital assets. Short-term financing is provided by a bank line of credit. The line of credit is secured by a proportion of accounts receivable and inventory. However, the accounts receivable are minimal, since the company's sales are mainly by cash and general credit card (i.e., Visa, MasterCard, and American Express). Therefore, inventory is the primary security. The balance sheet also shows a small amount of capital lease liability.

Recently, LCL has begun to have difficulty in achieving the profit levels to which the owners have been accustomed, although the company certainly is not in any financial distress. It now is nearing the end of 20X9 and LCL's financial group is prepared for the year-end closing. LCL managers have decided to look more closely at certain aspects of the way LCL does business, as well as how the company reports the results of operations.

1. In 20X7, LCL purchased 100% of the shares of a small clothing manufacturer in Montreal, which then became a subsidiary of LCL. LCL was one of its customers, as were several other retailers. LCL paid $5,000,000 for that company, of which $2,000,000 was allocated to goodwill. Within a year of the purchase, many of the subsidiary's other customers left because they were concerned that LCL might steal their clothing designs. LCL managers had not expected those defections since LCL's designs were generally

ahead of their competitors. As a result, the subsidiary has not been able to stay profit-able. LCL has been in talks to possibly sell the subsidiary to a U.S.–based clothing chain.

2. LCL owns none of its stores because they are all located in shopping malls. LCL has preferred to use short-term leases (e.g., five years) in order to maintain flexibility. The company is now planning to renegotiate the leases for longer terms in order to spread the cost of store design (furniture and fixtures) over a longer time span.

3. The company has followed a practice of deferring and amortizing the start-up costs for new stores. However, a recent change in accounting standards has decreed that start-up costs cannot be deferred and amortized. LCL must present audited statements both to the provider of long-term debt and to many of the major shopping mall landlords. LCL reports on the basis of Canadian ASPE.

4. LCL has large electronic billboards mounted on the fronts and roofs of some buildings, space that is leased from the building owners. The lease contracts require LCL to restore the facades and roofs to the owner's satisfaction at expiry. The LCL financial man-ager has discovered that LCL completely overlooked one significant lease and has not accounted for that restoration cost. As well, due to a decline in interest rates in 20X9, the auditor recommends that LCL remeasure all of LCL's asset retirement obligations.

5. The company has been following income tax allocation procedures. LCL's financial manager is concerned that deferred income tax expense unrealistically depresses LCL's earnings. Therefore, he has proposed that the company change to the taxes payable method beginning in the current year. The auditor does not object to the change.

6. In 20X8, the company's designers had made a rare error in anticipating a fashion trend that failed to develop. As a result, the company ended the previous year with a severe overstock of that line of clothing. In retrospect, the company should have written down that portion of the inventory. Instead, the merchandise was sold for about 20% of its manufacturing cost to a clearance house in San Francisco. The merchandise manager has recommended that the opening inventory for 20X9 be restated to recognize the loss in value of those items.

Required:

Assume that you are Christopher Robins, an independent accounting consultant. The CFO of LCL has asked for a memo on the reporting implications for each of these issues. Write the memo.

CASE 20-4

MTC

Philip Roth is just finishing his first week as chief financial officer of MTC. He was recruited from Atkins Consulting to replace the former CFO who had been relieved of his duties when major errors and shortfalls in certain inventory and trading accounts were discovered.

MTC is the current corporate name of an enterprise once known as Midlands Tele-phone Corporation. Midlands had been providing landline telephone service to several midcountry provinces for most of the 20th century and into the 21st century. The company had been reorganized in the early 1980s to separate its regulated telephone service from its more adventurous, non-regulated endeavours. The company had grown to a billion-dollar enterprise with investments in several fields, acquired largely through purchases of other going concerns. The core of MTC's earnings, however, remained in the telephone business.

Early this year, the company lost an appeal to the regulatory agency to protect its base market. The agency had ruled that MTC would no longer have a protected monopoly for landline telephone service in its service region, but that other companies (including TV cable companies and wireless companies) could compete for local telephone service. MTC had an enormous asset base, built up over the years in order to generate the highest possible earnings. As is typical in regulated industries, the company had been permitted to set rates that would enable it to earn a set rate of return on its asset base—the larger the asset base, the higher the earnings. The company capitalized all betterments and replacements, and used the longest possible depreciation periods for its capital assets. With the advent of deregulation, the company would no longer be able to generate such an attractive rate of return on its assets, which raised questions in the financial press about the "overvaluation" of its capital asset base.

This regulatory ruling was only one of several blows that the company had suffered in recent months. A previous loss of protection in the long-distance telephone market had caused MTC's earnings to drop sharply, with the result that MTC had the first loss of its history in its telephone business last year. The loss was expected to be even larger in the current year.

To make matters worse, rumours began to circulate in the financial community that MTC was covering up huge losses in one of its non-telephone divisions, one that manufactured copper wire and electrical switching devices. Copper is a world-traded commodity that has a very volatile price, and most companies that use copper are engaged in hedging operations to protect themselves. MTC's Board of Directors hired Atkins Consulting to find out if there was any truth to the rumours, and, unfortunately, there was. Managers and traders in the division had been speculating heavily in copper, and had covered up massive trading losses over the past three years, some of which were hidden in fictitious inventory records. MTC's copper inventory (and other accounts) turned out to be overstated by over $100 million.

The company's employees were also becoming restive. In its latest labour negotiations, just completed last month for the telephone operations, the company had to promise redundancy protection for employees if the company was required to downsize its telephone operations. The company agreed not to lay off any employees with more than 15 years of service, although the company would have the right to place them in a "redundancy pool" to be redeployed anywhere else in the company that they might be useful. Employees who are laid off will be given a severance package amounting to two months' salary plus one month's additional salary for each year of service. The severance would not be given as a lump sum but would be paid to the individual over a one-year period following the departure. Furthermore, the new labour agreement provided that pension benefits for any laid-off employee would automatically vest, even if the employee hadn't reached the point at which the benefits would normally become vested. The remaining employees would benefit from a significant enhancement of their defined benefit pension plan; employees' benefits would increase by between 10% and 20%, depending on the length of service.

The company had just served notice to the first 1,200 of its employees that they would be laid off, but the Board of Directors expected that at least 5,000 employees would be laid off over the next two years.

Philip Roth was one of the consultants who uncovered the rogue copper trading. He had been hired as CFO of MTC to "clean up the mess" in the financial reporting and control areas. One of his first responsibilities was to recommend to the audit committee of the Board of Directors how the company should report the impacts of its recent changes in fortune in its financial statements for the current year. Although the company was only midway through the fiscal year, the Board and CEO would have to discuss financial projections in a public forum, and particularly with the investment analysts who closely followed the company's performance.

Required:
Assume that you are Philip Roth. Prepare a report to the audit committee.

ASSIGNMENTS

★ **A20-1 Overview—Types of Accounting Changes:** Analyze each case and choose a letter code under each category (type and approach) to indicate the preferable accounting for each case.

Type of Change	Accounting Treatment
P = Policy	RFR = Retrospective with Full Restatement
E = Estimate	RPR = Retrospective with Partial Restatement
AE = Accounting error	PNR = Prospective with No Restatement

a. Changed depreciation method from declining-balance to straight-line because of information about how the assets were really used over the past three years.

b. Changed from cost method to revaluation method for capital assets; prior years' valuations are not obtainable.

c. Changed useful life of a machine based on evidence of wear and tear over time.

d. Changed from FIFO to average cost for inventory to conform to reduce accounting costs. Only the opening balance can be reconstructed.

e. Changed residual value of an intangible capital asset to zero based on new economic circumstances.

f. Recorded expense, $17,200; should be $71,200.

g. A private company changed from the percentage of completion method to completed-contract method for all contracts currently in process and for all new contracts. All prior balances can be reconstructed.

h. Discovered that a $400,000 acquisition of machinery two years ago was debited to the land account.

i. Changed from historical cost to net realizable value for inventory valuation to comply with new accounting standards. The opening balance cannot be reconstructed.

j. Changed measurement method for asset retirement obligations to present value basis instead of undiscounted estimated costs.

★ **A20-2 Overview—Types of Accounting Changes:** Analyze each case and choose a letter code under each category (type and approach) to indicate the preferable accounting for each case.

Type	Approach
P = Policy	RWR = Retrospective with restatement
E = Estimate	RNR = Retrospective, no restatement
AE = Accounting error	P = Prospective

a. Changed the expected useful lives of depreciable assets from 15 years to 10 years to conform with industry practice.

b. Discovered that a capital asset with a 10-year life had been expensed when acquired 5 years ago.

c. Began calculating EPS in a different manner because of a change in accounting standards.

d. Changed from straight-line to accelerated depreciation to reflect the company's changing technological environment.

e. Changed the percentage of bad debts accrued from 1% of credit sales to 3% of credit sales.

f. Recognized an impairment of $1.5 million in a capital asset group. An impairment of $1.0 million became apparent two years previously, but had not been recorded until this year.

g. Switched from FIFO to average cost to conform to parent company preferences. Only opening balances for the current year can be reconstructed.

h. Used the instalment sales method in the past five years; an internal audit revealed that use of this method was intended to delay revenue recognition even though the customers were highly credit-worthy.

i. Began capitalizing development costs because criteria for deferral were met this year for the first time; in the past, future markets had been too uncertain to justify capitalization.

j. Changed inventory cost method to exclude warehousing costs, as required by IFRS.

★★ **A20-3 Overview—Types of Accounting Changes:** The following 10 situations all involve a change in accounting. For each situation, assume the company is public unless specified otherwise.

a. Straight-line depreciation for the past three years has been calculated with no deduction for residual value because none was expected; management now believes a residual value of 10% of original cost is appropriate.

b. Straight-line depreciation for the past three years has been calculated with no deduction for residual value because of an oversight.

c. A private company had been using full allocation for income taxes; the company changes to the taxes payable method for the current year.

d. Arithmetic error was made in calculating the closing inventory for 20X1; it now is 20X3.

e. A tree farm changed its inventory valuation method from historical cost to net realizable value to comply with the requirements of *IAS* 41. Past NRVs cannot be determined.

f. Investment property was reported at fair value in prior years but the measurement method was discovered to be flawed. A more accurate method has been adopted for the current year.

g. Changed from straight line depreciation to units-of-production depreciation to conform to industry practice.

h. The unamortized balance of capitalized development costs is deemed worthless as the result of technological changes; all further development costs will be expensed.

i. A private company adopted percentage of completion for long-term construction contract; all prior contracts were short term and used completed-contract.

j. Changed from revenue recognition at cash collection to revenue recognition at point of delivery because of a marked improvement in the creditworthiness of the customer.

Required:

For each of these situations, briefly explain:

1. The type of accounting change.

2. The appropriate method for reporting the change, including a discussion of how amounts, if any, are determined.

3. The effect of the change on the financial statements, if any.

★ **A20-4 Rationale for Accounting Changes:** Arctic Charm Manufacturing Corporation is a privately-owned Canadian company. The company experienced poor operating results in the years 20X0 to 20X3, and, in 20X3, it reorganized and refinanced its operations. Creditors were asked to accept partial payment; shareholders invested additional capital. As part of the restructuring, Arctic Charm accepted covenants imposed by Spenser Venture Capital Corporation. Violation of these debt covenants would trigger a demand for immediate repayment of long-term debt and almost certainly mean that the company would be placed in receivership or bankruptcy. The covenants included minimum working capital requirements, and an upper limit on the overall debt-to-equity ratio.

The 20X4 pre-tax operating results were acceptable. The company wishes to make the following two accounting changes before issuing its financial statements for 20X4:

a. Change from comprehensive tax allocation to the taxes payable method.

b. Change depreciation policies from declining-balance to straight-line. Capital assets are fairly new but have been depreciated for three to five years under declining-balance rates. The company would adjust all capital asset balances to the amounts that would have existed had straight-line depreciation always been used. The company believes that straight-line depreciation is more indicative of the equipment's actual usage. The equipment is not subject to rapid technological obsolescence.

Artic Charm's CFO met with officials from Spenser to obtain their consent to these changes. The officials accepted Artic Charm's proposed changes as being in compliance with ASPE as required by the loan agreement.

Required:
Describe the impact of these changes on the financial statements and debt covenants. Consider the appropriateness of these changes in your response.

★★ **A20-5 Accounting Changes:** Mohammed Motors Limited made the following changes to its accounting in 20X5:

a. Increased the interest rate used to discount its pension obligations from 6.0% to 6.5%.
b. Renewed a lease on a roof that the company has been using for a microwave transmission tower. The original lease had four years yet to run; the renewal is for an additional five years. The company is obligated to remove the tower and completely restore the roof when the lease expires.
c. Decided that it is more likely than not that the future benefits of tax loss carryforwards of $3.0 million will be realized. The company's tax rate is 30%.
d. Realized that a $10.0 million improvement in an automated production line had been charged as an expense in 20X3, rather than being recorded as a betterment of a capital asset. The production line should be depreciated at 20% per year, declining-balance, with a full-year depreciation in the year of acquisition.

Required:
Describe the impact of these changes on the financial statements. Whenever possible, determine the amount of financial statement impacts.

★★ **A20-6 Accounting Changes:** Ng Holdings Limited had its first audit in 20X4. Its preliminary income figure, before tax, was $786,000. The following items were discovered:

a. Ng issued a bond payable at the beginning of 20X1 and received par value for its $1,000,000 convertible bond. The bond is convertible at the option of the investor. A value of $84,000 should have been assigned to the conversion option and classified in shareholders' equity. Any discount on the bond should be amortized over its 15-year life, straight-line.
b. The company uses the aging method of estimating the required allowance for doubtful accounts. However, the method had been incorrectly applied in 20X4, with the result that the allowance was understated by $26,000 at the end of 20X4.
c. In April 20X4, a building site was swapped for another, similar property. No cash changed hands. The land had a book value of $233,000; the transaction was recorded at the appraised value of the property being given up, which was $325,000.
d. The company had accumulated tax loss carryforwards amounting to $400,000 at the end of 20X4. None of the deferred tax benefit of these carryforwards had previously been recognized. In January 20X5, however, company managers decided that, for preparing the 20X4 financial statements, it now was probable that the benefits will be realized within the carryforward period.

Required:
1. Classify each of the changes described above and identify the correct accounting treatment.
2. Calculate revised 20X4 net income. The tax rate is 25%.
3. If a retrospective adjustment to retained earnings is needed, calculate the retrospective adjustment. The tax rate is 25%.

★ **A20-7 Change in Estimated Useful Life—Entries and Reporting:** Stacey Corporation has been depreciating equipment over a 10-year life on a straight-line basis. The equipment, which cost $24,000, was purchased on 1 January 20X1. It has an estimated residual value of $6,000. On the basis of experience since acquisition, management has decided in 20X5 to depreciate it over a total life of 14 years instead of 10 years, with no change in the estimated residual value. The change is to be effective on 1 January 20X5. The 20X5 financial statements are prepared on a comparative basis; 20X4 and 20X5 incomes before depreciation were $49,800 and $52,800, respectively. Disregard income tax considerations.

Required:

1. Identify the type of accounting change involved and analyze the effects of the change. Which approach should be used—prospective without restatement, retrospective with partial restatement, or retrospective with full restatement? Explain.
2. Prepare the entry, or entries, to appropriately reflect the change (if any) and 20X5 depreciation in the accounts for 20X5, the year of the change.
3. Illustrate how the change, the equipment, and the related depreciation should be reported on the 20X5 financial statements, including comparative 20X4 results.

★ **A20-8 Change in Estimate:** Barker Company, which has a calendar fiscal year, purchased its only depreciable capital asset on 1 January 20X3. Information related to the asset:

Original cost	$560,000
Estimated residual value	48,000
Depreciation method	Declining-balance
Depreciation rate	20%

In 20X5, Barker decreased the estimated residual value to $16,000, and increased the depreciation rate to 30%. Both changes are the result of experience with the asset and revised expectations about the pattern of usage.

Additional information:

	20X5	20X4
Revenue	$2,800,000	$2,240,000
Expenses other than depreciation and tax	1,680,000	1,534,400
Gain (loss) from discontinued operations, before tax	(40,000)	—
Tax rate	25%	25%

Required:

1. Calculate the ending 20X5 balance of accumulated depreciation, and show the 20X5 entry/entries for depreciation.
2. Provide the condensed comparative statement of comprehensive income for 20X5, including disclosures related to the accounting change.

★★ **A20-9 Accounting Changes—Inventory and Revenue:** Late in 20X6, the management of Richter Minerals Inc., a Canadian private company, decided to change the company's inventory valuation method and, concurrently, its revenue recognition method. Historically, the company had used an average cost basis for all inventories and had recognized revenue when minerals were shipped to customers. Now, effective with the year beginning 1 January 20X7, Richter will recognize revenue when the minerals have been refined and are ready for sale, at which point the inventory will be adjusted to net realizable value at the end of each reporting period. Richter's minerals are easily sold at any time on the world market via electronic trading. Richter's shareholders and principal lenders have approved the change in policy.

At the end of 20X6, Richter had inventory (at cost of production) totalling $70 million. Of that total, $20 million was of unrefined ore and $50 million was refined minerals. At NRV, Richter's refined minerals inventory was $72 million. The 20X6 opening inventory contained refined minerals of $44 million at cost; using market price indices, Richter's management was able to determine that the 20X6 opening inventory was worth $60 million at NRV. Richter's 20X6 sales revenue was $250 million.

During 20X7, Richter recognized revenue of $360 million, on the new reporting basis. Ending inventory of refined minerals amounted to $82 million; production cost was $55 million.

The income tax rate was 25% in both years.

Required:

1. How much will this change affect the previously reported net income for 20X6?

2. Can this change be applied retrospectively with restatement? Explain the difficulties that management might encounter when restating years prior to 20X6.

3. Prepare any journal entries that are necessary to record the change in accounting policies.

★★ **A20-10 Accounting Changes—Depreciable Assets:** Tech Manufacturing Corporation reports the following situations in 20X6 with respect to its high-tech manufacturing equipment:

a. Machine 1 was acquired at a cost of $872,000 in 20X3. The machine was depreciated on a straight-line basis over its expected six-year life. At the end of 20X6, management decided that this machine should have been depreciated over a total useful life of eight years. Salvage value, expected to be negligible, has not changed.

b. Machine 2 was acquired at a cost of $448,500 in 20X5. It was being depreciated on a declining-balance method using a rate of 40%. Salvage values were expected to be minimal. In 20X6, management decided that, based on the usage patterns seen to date, units-of-production would be a more appropriate method of depreciation. The machine is used sporadically and suffers from wear and tear only as used (that is, obsolescence is not much of a factor in the loss of utility). Estimated units-of-production total 350,000, of which 75,000 units were produced in 20X5 and 30,000 units in 20X6.

c. Machine 3 was acquired in 20X3 at a cost of $325,000. Management discovered in 20X6 that the machine was expensed in 20X3, despite the fact that it had a useful life of 10 years, with a 10% salvage value. Straight-line depreciation should have been used for this asset.

For all depreciation methods, the company follows a policy of recording a full year of depreciation charged in the first year, but no depreciation is charged in the year of disposal.

Required:

1. Classify each of the changes described above and identify the correct accounting treatment.

2. For each machine, calculate 20X6 depreciation.

3. If a retrospective adjustment is needed, calculate the retrospective adjustment in 20X6. The tax rate is 25%.

★★ **A20-11 Change in Resource Exploration Costs—Entries and Reporting:** Gunnard Company (a public company) was formed in 20X4 and has a 31 December year-end. Gunnard Company changed from successful efforts (SE) to full costing (FC) for its resource exploration costs in 20X5. SE is still used for tax purposes. The change was made to reflect changed corporate reporting objectives; more stable net income was deemed desirable to support a more stable stock market share price. Under FC, all exploration costs are deferred; under SE, only a portion are deferred. Under both approaches, the deferred cost balance is amortized yearly.

Had FC been used in 20X4, a total of $3,200,000 of costs originally written off under SE would have been capitalized. A total of $4,700,000 of such costs were incurred in 20X5. Gunnard discloses 20X4 and 20X5 results comparatively in its annual financial statements. The tax rate is 30% in both years.

	SE	FC
Amortization of resource development costs:		
20X4	$ 40,000	$ 240,000
20X5	200,000	850,000
Resource development costs expensed:		
20X4	$3,200,000	—
20X5	4,700,000	—

Additional information for Gunnard:

	20X5	20X4
Revenues	$7,100,000	$4,400,000
Expenses other than resource development costs, amortization, and income tax	2,050,000	720,000

Required:

1. Prepare a 20X5 comparative statement of comprehensive income using the old policy, successful efforts.

2. Prepare the 20X5 entry/entries for FC amortization, and the accounting change. Assume that no amortization has been recorded by Gunnard to date in 20X5.

3. Prepare the comparative statements of comprehensive income under FC, and include disclosures related to the accounting change.

4. Prepare the comparative retained earnings section of the statement of changes in shareholders' equity for 20X5, reflecting the change.

5. How will the classification of development costs on the CFS change as a result of the new policy?

★ **A20-12 Error Correction:** Shariff Ltd. signed an operating lease on 1 January 20X0. The lease was a 40-year term on a piece of land. The land reverts to the lessor at the end of the lease term. The lease requires annual payments, on each 1 January, of $45,000 for the first 10 years. Annual 1 January payments of $20,000 were required for the second 10 years, 1 January payments of $10,000 for the third 10 years, and 1 January payments of $2,000 for the final 10 years. The lease payments have all been made on schedule, but have all been expensed as paid. (That is, it is now the end of 20X4 and the 20X3 rent has been paid and expensed, but the 20X4 books are still open.) The lease should have been expensed evenly over the lease term, regardless of the payment scheme.

Required:

1. Provide the entry to correct the error.

2. Determine the amount by which pre-tax earnings must be adjusted for each prior year when Shariff prepares a five-year summary of financial results.

★ **A20-13 Error Correction:** In 20X6, Cathode Company, a calendar fiscal-year company, discovered that depreciation expense was erroneously overstated $40,000 in both 20X4 and 20X5 for financial reporting purposes. Net income in 20X6 is correct. The tax rate is 30%. The error was made only for financial reporting, affecting depreciation and deferred income tax accounts., CCA had been recorded correctly, and thus there will be no change in taxes payable.

Additional Information:

	20X6	20X5
Beginning retained earnings	$265,000	$180,000
Net income (includes error in 20X5)	125,000	145,000
Dividends declared	80,000	60,000

Required:

1. Record the entry in 20X6 to correct the error.
2. Provide the comparative retained earnings statement for 20X6, including any required note disclosure.

★★ **A20-14 Error Correction:** Excerpts from the 31 December financial statements of Simpson Limited, before any corrections.

	20X7	20X6	20X5
Income statement			
Cost of goods sold	$790,000	$705,200	$676,800
Balance sheet			
Inventory	$ 34,500	$ 30,900	$ 16,100
Retained earnings statement			
Opening retained earnings	$331,000	$260,800	$211,500
Net income	104,700	91,200	70,300
Dividends	(21,000)	(21,000)	(21,000)
Closing retained earnings	$414,700	$331,000	$260,800

After these financial statements were prepared, but before they were issued for 20X7, a routine review revealed a major mathematical error in calculating 20X5 closing inventory. Instead of $19,700, closing inventory should have been $16,100.

There is no income tax.

Required:

1. What entry is needed to correct the error in 20X7? Explain.
2. Restate all the above information, as appropriate, to retrospectively correct the error.
3. What disclosure of the error is needed?

★★ **A20-15 Error Correction:** Trelarkin Forpas Limited (TFL) reported the following in its 31 December financial statements:

	20X9	20X8	20X7
Income statement			
Depreciation expense (all assets)	$ 100,400	$ 91,600	$ 92,400
Balance sheet			
Capital assets (net)	$1,216,200	$1,147,600	$1,005,400
Retained earnings statement			
Opening retained earnings	$ 879,200	$ 905,800	$ 655,800
Net income (loss)	(135,700)	41,200	317,800
Dividends	(67,800)	(67,800)	(67,800)
Closing retained earnings	$ 675,700	$ 879,200	$ 905,800

After the draft 20X9 financial statements were prepared but before they were issued, TFL discovered that a capital asset was incorrectly accounted for in 20X5. A $200,000 capital asset was purchased early in 20X5, and it should have been depreciated straight-line over eight years with a $40,000 residual value. Instead, it was written off to expense.

The error was made on the books, but the capital asset was accounted for correctly for tax purposes. The tax rate was 25%.

Required:

1. What entry is needed to correct the error in 20X9?
2. Restate all the above information, as appropriate, to retrospectively correct the error.
3. What disclosure of the error is needed?

★★   **A20-16 Accounting Change—Bad Debts:** Betteroff Company was incorporated on 1 January 20X3. In the past, it has not provided an allowance for doubtful accounts. Instead, uncollectible accounts were expensed when written off and recoveries were credited to bad debt expense when collected. Accounts were written off if they were outstanding for more than four months.

In December 20X5, the company decided to change its accounting policy to account for bad debts as a percentage of credit sales, in compliance with GAAP and with industry practice. Statistics for the past three years are summarized as follows:

		Accounts Written off and Year of Sale			Recoveries and Year of Sale	
Year	Credit Sales	20X3	20X4	20X5	20X3	20X4
20X3	$100,000	$550	—	—	$10	—
20X4	150,000	650	$750	—	30	$20
20X5	225,000	—	900	$950	—	40

Accounts receivable at 31 December 20X5 were $50,000 after write-offs but before any allowance for doubtful accounts.

Required:

1. How should the change in accounting policy be accounted for?
2. Prepare the journal entry to reflect the change in accounting policy and to adjust 20X5 bad debt expense. State your assumptions and show your supporting calculations, in arriving at a percentage rate for bad debts. Disregard income tax.

Source: Reproduced with permission from CGA-Canada.

★★   **A20-17 Change from AC to FIFO—Entries and Reporting:** On 1 January 20X5, Baker Company decided to change the inventory costing method used from average cost (AC) to FIFO to conform to industry practice. The annual reporting period ends on 31 December. The average income tax rate is 30%. The following related data were developed:

	AC Basis	FIFO Basis
Beginning inventory, 20X4	$ 30,000	$30,000
Ending inventory		
20X4	40,000	70,000
20X5	44,000	76,000
Net income		
20X4: AC basis	80,000	
20X5: FIFO basis		82,000
Retained earnings		
20X4 beginning balance	120,000	
Dividends declared and paid		
20X4	64,000	
20X5		70,000
Common shares outstanding, 10,000		

Required:

1. Identify the type of accounting change involved. Which approach should be used—prospective, retrospective without restatement, or retrospective with restatement? Explain.
2. Give the entry to record the effect of the change, assuming the change was made only for accounting purposes, not for income tax purposes.
3. Complete the following schedule:

	FIFO Basis	
	20X5	**20X4**
Statement of financial position		
Inventory	$	$
Retained earnings		
Statement of comprehensive income		
Net income and comprehensive income		
Earnings per share		
Statement of changes in equity—retained earnings section		
Beginning balance, as previously reported		
Cumulative effect of accounting change		
Beginning balance restated		
Net income		
Dividends declared and paid		
Ending balance		

★★★ **A20-18 Retrospective Policy Changes:** Linfei Limited has a 31 December year-end, and a tax rate of 25%. Management has asked you to respond to the following situations:

1. The company has always used the FIFO method of determining inventory costs; starting in 20X7, it will now use weighted-average cost. Opening and closing inventories for 20X7 under FIFO are $2,655,000 and $3,300,000, respectively. Opening and closing inventories under weighted average are $2,100,000 and $2,600,000, respectively. Provide the journal entry to record the change.

2. Return to requirement (1). Additional information is as follows:
   - In 20X7, opening retained earnings was $4,365,000. Net income, before any adjustment due to the change in inventory method, was $1,600,000. Dividends were $235,000.
   - In 20X6, opening retained earnings was $4,010,000, net income was $565,000, and dividends were $210,000.
   - For 20X6, opening inventory was 2,400,000 under FIFO and $2,000,000 under weighted average.

   Prepare a comparative retained earnings section of the statement of changes in equity, giving retrospective effect to the change in accounting policy.

3. Return to your retained earnings statement in requirement (2). Prepare a comparative retained earnings statement assuming that comparative balances could not be restated; that is, the only information you have to work with, in addition to the income, retained earnings, and dividend information, is that provided about opening and closing inventory balances in requirement (1).

4. An asset was acquired in 20X4 at a cost of $400,000. The salvage value of $40,000 was estimated. The asset has been depreciated on the declining-balance method at a rate of 20% in each of 20X4, 20X5, and 20X6. On 1 October of this year, 20X7, management decided to change depreciation methods and will now use the straight-line method. This change is made on the basis of usage information that indicates that the asset is used about the same amount in each year of life. The new estimates are a *total* life of 12 years

and a salvage value of $25,000. Depreciation expense has not yet been recorded for 20X7. Provide the appropriate journal entry/entries.

★★ **A20-19 Policy Changes:** Kate Limited has asked you to prepare appropriate journal entries for the following unrelated situations. There is no income tax.

Case A   An investment with an original cost of $400,000 was accounted for using the cost method in 20X0, 20X1, and 20X2. This year, 20X3, the company must conform to new accounting standards and report the investment at fair value. Fair values were $390,000, $410,000, and $450,000 at the end of 20X0, 20X1, and 20X2, respectively. The investment had a fair value of $466,000 at the end of 20X3. The change is to be accounted for retrospectively with restatement of the prior year's statements. The company wishes to record the change in 20X3, and to adjust the investment account to fair value at the end of 20X3. *Note*: The change affects the shareholders' equity account, *unrealized holding gains* (a separate component of other comprehensive income), instead of retained earnings.

Case B   The company has always recognized revenue on delivery but, because of a change in reporting objectives, will now recognize revenue according to the industry norm, which is on cash collection. Opening and closing accounts receivable are $1,600,000 and $2,355,000, respectively. The gross profit margin is 60%. (*Note*: Accounts receivable are recorded but no unearned revenue is on the books.)

Required:
Prepare appropriate journal entries for these two situations. Ignore income tax considerations.

★★ **A20-20 Retrospective Policy Change:** Armstrong Limited has used the average cost (AC) method to determine inventory values since first formed in 20X3. In 20X7, the company decided to switch to the FIFO method, to conform to industry practice. Armstrong will still use average cost for tax purposes. The tax rate is 30%. The following data has been assembled:

	20X3	20X4	20X5	20X6	20X7
Net income, as reported, after tax	$56,000*	$65,000*	$216,000*	$255,000*	$125,000**
Closing inventory, AC	35,000	45,000	56,000	91,000	116,000
Closing inventory, FIFO	41,000	57,000	52,000	84,000	130,000
Dividends	5,000	7,000	7,000	10,000	14,000

*Using the old policy, average cost
**Using the new policy, FIFO.

Required:
Present the comparative retained earnings statement for 20X7, giving effect to the change in accounting policy.

★★ **A20-21 Change Regarding Construction Contracts:** KLB Corporation, a private company, has used the completed-contract method to account for its long-term construction contracts since its inception in 20X3. On 1 January 20X7, management decided to change to the percentage of completion method to better reflect operating activities and conform to industry norms. Completed-contract was used for income tax purposes and will continue to be used for income tax purposes in the future. The income tax rate is 40%. The following information has been assembled:

Year ended 31 December	20X3	20X4	20X5	20X6	20X7
Net income, as reported	$100,000	$120,000	$150,000	$140,000	160,000*
CC income, included in above	0	60,000	0	120,000	0
PC income, as calculated	40,000	65,000	50,000	40,000	75,000
Opening retained earnings	0	90,000	190,000	320,000	440,000
Dividends	10,000	20,000	20,000	20,000	20,000
Closing retained earnings	90,000	190,000	320,000	440,000	580,000

*Includes PC income, not CC income, in earnings.

Required:

1. Identify the type of accounting change involved. Which approach should be used—retrospective with full restatement, or retrospective with limited restatement, or prospective without restatement? Explain.

2. Give the entry to appropriately reflect the accounting change in 20X7, the year of the change.

3. Restate the 20X7 retained earnings section of the statement of changes in equity, including the 20X6 comparative figures.

4. Assume that only the opening balance in 20X7 can be restated and that the cumulative effect cannot be allocated to individual years. Recast the 20X7 comparative retained earnings section of the CSE accordingly.

5. Assume that no balances can be restated. Can the change be made in 20X7? Explain.

★★ **A20-22 Change in Policy, Error:** TXL Corporation (a public company) has tentatively computed income before tax as $660,000 for 20X4. Retained earnings at the beginning of 20X4 had a balance of $3,600,000. Dividends of $270,000 were paid during 20X4. There were dividends payable of $60,000 at the end of 20X3 and $90,000 at the end of 20X4. The following information has been provided:

1. The company used FIFO for costing inventory in deriving net income of $660,000. It wishes to change to average cost to be comparable with other companies in the industry. Accordingly, the change in policy should be applied retrospectively. The comparable figures for ending inventory under the two methods are as follows:

December 31	FIFO	Average
20X1	$408,000	$420,000
20X2	450,000	435,000
20X3	480,000	462,000
20X4	486,000	510,000

2. In January 20X3, the company acquired some equipment for $3,000,000. At that time, it estimated the equipment would have an estimated useful life of 12 years and a salvage value of $360,000. In 20X3, the company received a government grant of $480,000, which assisted in purchasing the equipment. The grant was credited to income in error. The company has been depreciating the equipment on the straight-line basis and has already provided for depreciation for 20X4 without considering the government grant. Management realizes that the company must account for the government grant by crediting it directly to the equipment account.

The income tax rate for the company is 30%. Assume that all of the stated items are fully taxable or deductible for income tax purposes.

Required:

1. Prepare a schedule to show the calculation of the correct net income for 20X4 in accordance with generally accepted accounting principles.

2. Prepare, in good form, the retained earnings section of TXL's statement of comprehensive income for the year ended 31 December 20X4. Comparative figures need not be provided.

Source: Reproduced with permission from CGA-Canada.

★★ **A20-23 Change in Accounting for Natural Resources:** In 20X6, Black Oil Company changed its method of accounting for oil exploration costs from the successful efforts method (SE) to full costing (FC) for financial reporting because of a change in corporate reporting objectives. Black Oil has been in the oil exploration business since January 20X3; prior to that, the company was active in oil transportation.

	SE	FC
20X3	$ 15,000	$ 45,000
20X4	66,000	75,000
20X5	75,000	105,000
20X6	120,000	180,000

Black Oil reports the result of years 20X4 through 20X6 in its 20X6 annual report and has a calendar fiscal year. The tax rate is 30%. The change is made for accounting purposes but not for tax purposes. Thus, the deferred income tax account is changed.

Additional Information:

	20X3	20X4	20X5	20X6
Ending retained earnings (SE basis)	$54,000	$69,000	$93,000	n/a
Dividends declared	27,000	31,200	28,500	$36,000

Required:

1. Prepare the entry in 20X6 to record the accounting change. Use "natural resources" as the depletable asset account.

2. Prepare the retained earnings section of the comparative SCE. Include three years: 20X6, 20X5, and 20X4.

3. Describe how the accounting policy change would affect the cash flow statement.

★★ **A20-24 Accounting Changes, Comprehensive:** EC Construction Limited (EC) has 100,000 common shares outstanding in public hands. The balance of retained earnings at the beginning of 20X7 was $2,400,000. On 15 December 20X7 EC declared dividends of $3 per share payable on 5 January 20X8. Income before income tax was $600,000 based on the records of the company's accountant.

Additional information on selected transactions/events is provided below:

a. At the beginning of 20X6, EC purchased some equipment for $230,000 (salvage value of $30,000) that had a useful life of five years. The accountant used a 40% declining-balance method of depreciation, but mistakenly deducted the salvage value in calculating depreciation expense in 20X6 and 20X7.

b. As a result of an income tax audit of 20X5 taxable income, $74,000 of expenses claimed as deductible expenses for tax purposes was disallowed by the CRA. This error cost the company $29,600 in additional tax. This amount was paid in 20X7 but has been debited to a prepaid expense account.

c. EC contracted to build an office building for RD Corporation. The construction began in 20X6 and will be completed in 20X8. The contract has a price of $30 million. The following data (in millions of dollars) relates to the construction period to date:

	20X6	20X7
Costs incurred to date	$ 8	$13
Estimated costs to complete	12	7
Progress billings during the year	6	10
Cash collected on billings during the year	5	8

The accountant used the completed-contract method in accounting for this contract, which is not permitted for a public company.

d. On 1 January 20X7, EC purchased, as a long-term investment, 19% of the common shares of One Limited for $50,000. On that date, the fair value of identifiable assets of One Limited was $220,000 and was equal to the book value of identifiable assets. Goodwill has not been impaired. No investment income has been recorded. One paid no dividends, but reported income of $25,000 in the year. EC has significant influence over One.

e. EC has an effective tax rate of 40%.

Required:

1. Calculate 20X7 net income for EC.

2. Prepare the 20X7 retained earnings statement in good form. Comparative numbers need not be shown.

★★★   **A20-25 Multiple Accounting Changes:** Zealand Company made several financial accounting changes in 20X6:

First, the company changed the total useful life from 20 years to 14 years on a $350,000 asset purchased 1 January 20X2. The asset was originally expected to be sold for $50,000 at the end of its useful life, but that amount was also changed in 20X6, to $200,000. Zealand applies the straight-line method of depreciation to this asset. Depreciation has not yet been recorded in 20X6.

Second, the company decided to change inventory costing from FIFO to weighted average (WA) but is unable to accurately determine WA inventory in prior year-ends. The FIFO 20X6 beginning and ending inventories are $30,000 and $45,000. Under WA, the 20X6 ending inventory is $35,000. The company expects WA to render income numbers more useful for prediction, given inflation.

Third, the company changed its policy for accounting for certain staff training costs. Previously, the costs were capitalized and amortized straight-line over three years, starting with the year of the expenditure. The new policy is to expense training costs as incurred, in compliance with revised accounting standards for intangible assets. A total of $100,000 was expended in 20X3, $0 in 20X4, $60,000 in 20X5, and $45,000 in 20X6.

Fourth, an error in amortizing patents was discovered in 20X6. Patents costing $510,000 on 1 January 20X4 have been amortized over their legal life (20 years). The accountant neglected to obtain an estimate of the patents' economic life, which totalled only five years.

Zealand is a calendar fiscal-year company and is subject to a 30% tax rate.

Other information:

	20X6	20X5
Beginning retained earnings	$489,000	$319,000
Net income, after tax	335,000*	220,000
Dividends declared	70,000	50,000

*This is the correct reported amount and includes the appropriate amounts related to all the expenses affected by the accounting changes except for the full impact of the change from FIFO to WA.

Required:

1. Record the 20X6 entries necessary to make the accounting changes. If the change cannot be made, explain why.

2. Prepare the 20X5 and 20X6 retained earnings section of the comparative statement of changes in equity, with note disclosures for the accounting changes.

CHAPTER 21

Financial Statement Analysis

Between 2004 and 2007, WestJet Airlines Ltd. increased revenue by 54% and net earnings by over 700%. That sounds really impressive, but the percentages depend partially on the starting point—the denominator. Between 2007 and 2009, revenue increased by 30% while net earnings declined by 15%. What happened? Well, we can make some guesses—the company's revenues are mainly in Canadian dollars while its aircraft purchases, aircraft lease payments, and fuel costs are all in U.S. dollars. Rising fuel prices and changing exchange rates are always a worry. On the financing side, WestJet's long-term debt load has been declining as a proportion of total assets, but still amounts to almost $1.4 billion.

If you were a major lender to WestJet, or an investor, how would you go about analyzing the company's asset and liability structure, its earnings performance, its return on assets and equity, and its ability to service its large debt load? If you were an employee representative, how would you appraise a company's ability to increase wages or to meet pension funding obligations?

Financial statement analysis is a broad and complex field. Entire books (and whole university courses) are devoted to financial statement analysis. In this chapter, we can touch only on the major aspects of financial analysis. Nevertheless, any aspiring accountant should be familiar with the basic analytical techniques and processes. After all, if we as accountants are putting together the numbers in the financial statements, we also should know how to take them apart and analyze their significance.

The emphasis in the main part of the chapter is on basic analytical techniques. However, it often is necessary to recast a company's financial statements in order to make them more useful for the analyst's specific needs. The appendix to this chapter contains an example of recasting. The example is a real company (although disguised), not fictional.

OVERVIEW OF STATEMENT ANALYSIS

Company analysis must always be a forward-looking process. In this chapter, the focus will be on analysis of the statements themselves. But the statements of individual companies must be interpreted within a broader context of:

- The general economic environment;
- The economic and competitive climate of the country or region in which the company operates; and
- The structure and outlook of the industry in which the company competes.

For investors, the company's financial outlook must be evaluated in relationship to the market price of its shares. For lenders, the company's future must be evaluated as its ability to service its debt without binding its current operations and its competitiveness.

This chapter describes several different techniques for analysis, but most space is devoted to traditional ratio analysis. It is possible to compute dozens of financial statement ratios, but an analyst should decide first what he or she needs to find out and then select just a few ratios to look at.

Ratios are useless unless they can be compared to something else, such as historical trends or "average" ratios of other companies or benchmark ratios of companies in the same industry. To be comparable, the companies used for comparison must have similar accounting policies (and estimates). Ratio analysis can be useful, but can also be very misleading if inappropriate comparisons are made.

Clarify the Decision Focus

The starting point is to be clear about what decision is to be made as a result of the financial statement analysis. A sample of possible decisions is:

1. Equity investment decision;
2. Lending decision;
3. Contractual decision, such as accepting employment, negotiating collective agreements, or entering into a joint venture; and
4. Regulatory decision, including the need for rate or price increases, or the impact of past regulatory decisions.

Each of these decisions will require a somewhat different approach to the analysis and a different set of priorities. For example, a prospective investor in common shares will be concerned primarily with the long-term profitability of the company while a trade creditor will be primarily interested in short-run liquidity. This difference in emphasis is illustrated by the fact that many creditors will continue to extend credit to a company with declining profitability in which no rational investor would buy shares.

There also is a difference between looking at a company (1) as a new, prospective stakeholder and (2) as an existing stakeholder who needs to decide whether to continue the relationship or to bail out. A new stakeholder (e.g., an investor, creditor, or contractor) is concerned about the future safety and profitability of a contemplated investment or contract. In contrast, an existing stakeholder will be concerned about the financial and/or operational ramifications of terminating an existing investment or contract.

Therefore, it is crucial to know the nature of the decision in question.

Examine the Auditor's Report

A public company must have an unqualified audit opinion in order to be traded on major stock exchanges, but a private company may use one or more non-GAAP accounting policies. In such cases, the auditor will qualify the opinion. A qualification in an **auditor's report** should not *necessarily* be cause for concern. A company may choose to use accounting policies that are more in accordance with the interests of the primary stakeholders than GAAP would be. A privately held company, for example, may:

- Report its pension expense on the basis of its funding in order to achieve closer correspondence between reported earnings and cash flow from operations, or

- Report its capital assets at a restated value that reflects the value against which its lenders have extended loans.

Normally, an auditor will attempt to quantify the impact (i.e., on net income) of a deviation from GAAP and will either report the impact in the auditor's report or refer the reader to a financial statement note that discusses the deviation.

If a private company does not have an audit, a public accountant may nevertheless be retained for a **review engagement**, in which a full audit is not performed but the auditor does review the financial statements for general consistency with GAAP (or with a disclosed basis of accounting) and for reasonableness of presentation. Banks often rely on auditors' statements in review engagements as assurance that the company's accounting practices are reasonable and that the financial statements are plausible.

However, a review engagement provides no assurance that the company's internal control policies and procedures are operating properly, or that there is external evidence to support the amounts presented on the financial statements. Investors and lenders use unaudited statements at their own risk!

Examine Accounting Policies

We have stressed throughout this book that managers' accounting policy choices are governed by the objectives of financial reporting in the particular circumstance.

The financial reporting objectives adopted by a company may not correspond with a specific user's preferred objectives. Therefore, the first task of an analyst is to determine the reporting objectives that are implicit in the financial statements. If the implicit objectives do not correspond to the user's objectives, then adjustments to the financial statements will probably be needed before they are of maximum use. Discerning the implicit objectives often is easier said than done.

Notes to Financial Statements To the extent that they exist, most of the clues to the implicit reporting objectives can be found in the notes to the financial statements. The first note to financial statements is the accounting policy note, in which the company describes its accounting policy choices. In practice, the information revealed is often not very helpful. Three problems arise:

1. The disclosure is too vague to be useful without additional inside information.

2. The disclosure is specific, but the numerical data needed to make sense of possible alternatives is not disclosed.

3. There is no disclosure at all of crucial policies, such as revenue recognition.

Often, the accounting policy note gives only the broadest possible explanation of an accounting policy, but more information can be found in the other notes. For example, details on depreciation methods may be more complete in the plant and equipment note than in the policy note, and the policy on financial instruments may be more fully explained in the long-term debt note.

Lack of detail is also a problem. The note on inventories may say simply that "some of the inventory has been valued on a lower-of-cost-or-fair value" basis, or "inventories are valued on a variety of bases, predominantly at average cost" without being more specific about which types of inventories are valued on which bases, or how much of the inventory has been reported at fair value rather than at cost.

Focus of the Analyst An analyst looks in the notes mainly for revenue and expense recognition policies. For example:

- If a company is using policies that tend to recognize revenue early in the earnings cycle but that defer many costs to later periods (i.e., capitalize and amortize), then the company seems to be applying a profit maximization strategy.

- If both revenue and expense tend to be deferred and amortized, then a smoothing strategy may be paramount.

- If revenue recognition is deferred but all operating costs are expensed as incurred, income minimization may be the objective for income tax or political reasons.

Other accounting (and operating) policies relate to the statement of financial position, and the analyst must examine those as well. Is the company keeping its capital assets at a minimum by using operating leases to acquire the use of assets that are crucial to its operations? Such a practice suggests that the company has both off-balance-sheet assets and liabilities. Off-balance-sheet assets will increase the apparent return on assets, while off-balance-sheet financing will improve the apparent debt-to-equity ratio. But the use of operating leases may be significantly more expensive than simply buying assets or entering into long-term capital leases, as we discussed in Chapter 17.

A further clue may be gleaned from the cash flow statement. If earnings (with amortization added back) are significantly and repeatedly larger than cash flow from operations, the company may be maximizing net income. If cash flow is significantly larger than earnings, the company may be very conservative in its accounting practices, reporting minimum net earnings (for example, by anticipating future expenditures through current provisions), or may be trying to minimize its current tax bill.

As well, the analyst will look at the cash flow statement to see if cash flow from operations excludes important operating expenses (such as development costs) that management has capitalized and thereby shifted from the operating section to the investing section. Many analysts reclassify such expenses for cash flow analysis purposes (and sometimes for recomputing net income), and may also reclassify to operations the necessary continuing reinvestment in equipment.

For example, a computer training company must continually upgrade its computers in order to be able to provide currently relevant courses to its clients. Since the computers are amortized over three to five years, they are reported as an investing activity. However, the expenditure is crucial to the successful operation of the company, and therefore some analysts (including some bankers) will reclassify the purchase of new computers as part of operating (or "free") cash flow. In such a situation, it is important to try to distinguish between replacements needed to maintain current operations and those that represent expansion of operations.

For a public company, the MD&A (Management's Discussion and Analysis) may help distinguish between replacements and new investment. For a private company, the analyst usually has no choice but to ask management. Management makes itself open to questions from major external users such as bankers, but may not respond to information requests from relatively minor users.

Finally, the income statement must be examined for non-recurring items. Companies have a tendency to include non-recurring gains along with operating revenues while showing non-recurring losses as unusual items. Of course, given the extreme brevity of most published income statements, significant non-recurring gains and losses may easily be included with operating items and not be separately disclosed.

Recast the Financial Statements

An analyst may need to recast the financial statements to suit her or his needs before applying analytical approaches. The restatement is an approximation because the analyst never has full information. Situations that suggest a needed restatement include the following examples:

- The earnings statement is revised to remove non-recurring gains and losses.
- The earnings statement and SFP are revised to remove the effects of deferred income tax liabilities and assets.
- The earnings statement and SFP are revised to reflect a different policy on capitalization of certain costs:
  - capitalized costs are shifted to the earnings statement in the year they occurred, and amortization is removed; or
  - expenditures charged directly to the earnings statement are removed, capitalized, and amortization is added.
- Necessary recurring reinvestments are reclassified on the statement of cash flow from investing activities to operating activities.
- Loans to and from shareholders are reclassified as owners' equity.

- Retractable preferred shares are reclassified as long-term debt.
- The estimated present value of assets under operating leases is added to capital assets and to liabilities.

In recasting the statement to reflect different accounting policies, it is important to remember to adjust for both sides of transactions. For example, deleting deferred income tax expense must be accompanied by adding the balance of the deferred income tax liability to retained earnings and not by simply *ignoring* the balance.

An illustration of recasting financial statements is presented in the Appendix to this chapter.

Seek Comparative Information

Data are useless unless there is some basis for comparison. Sometimes the comparison is with a mental database accumulated by the analyst over years of experience in analyzing similar companies. For less experienced analysts, empirical comparisons are necessary. There are two bases for comparison: (1) cross-sectional and (2) longitudinal.

Cross-sectional comparison analyzes a company in relation to other companies in the same year. Comparisons of this type frequently appear in the business press in articles that compare the recent performance of one company with its competitors. Cross-sectional comparison is very useful, but caution must be exercised that similar measurements are being used. If the comparison companies used significantly different accounting policies, then no comparison can be valid unless the companies have all been adjusted to reflect similar accounting policies. Comparison of the return on assets for a company that owns all of its capital assets with one that uses operating leases for its capital assets will be invalid.

Longitudinal comparisons look at a company over time, comparing this year's performance with earlier years. A comparison is often made to other companies or to general economic returns during the same time span.

Some databases facilitate both types of comparison on an industry basis. These industry comparisons can be helpful but must be used with a great deal of caution. Industry statistics are constructed without attention to underlying reporting differences or accounting policy differences, and therefore it seldom is clear whether the comparisons are truly valid. In addition, it is tempting to decide that one company is a good investment (for example) because its profitability ratios are better than its competitors. It may well be, however, that the entire industry is sick, and that the company being analyzed is perhaps less sick.

Apply Analytical Techniques

Once the statements have been adjusted to suit the needs of the analyst (that is, to facilitate making the decision at hand), the statements may be subject to numerical analysis or "number crunching." The basic tool of numerical analysis is ratios. A ratio is simply one number divided by another. Given the number of numbers in a set of financial statements, especially over a series of years, an incredible number of ratios could be computed. The trick to avoiding overwork (and total confusion) is to identify which ratios have meaning for the analyst's purpose, and then focus just on those few instead of computing every possible ratio.

Certain types of ratios have been given generic names. Two commonly cited types of ratio are:

1. *Vertical analysis* or *common-size analysis*, in which the components of one year's individual financial statements are computed as a percentage of a base amount, using (for example) total assets as the base (= 100) for the SFP and net sales as the base for the income statement.

2. *Horizontal analysis* or *trend analysis*, in which longitudinal ratios for a single financial statement component (e.g., sales) are computed with a base year's amount set at 100 and other years' amounts recomputed relative to the base amount.

Both vertical analysis and horizontal analysis are really just the construction of index numbers within a year (vertical) or between years (horizontal). All index numbers must have a *base*, and the base amount is set at 100%.

Vertical Analysis **Vertical analysis** is useful for seeing the relative composition of the balance sheet or income statement. Analysts sometimes use these numbers for comparisons with industry norms. For example, an analyst may want to compare the *gross margin* of one company with another by comparing the relative proportion of sales that is consumed by cost of goods sold (when cost of goods sold is disclosed). Similarly, an analyst may look at common-size numbers to see if a company's inventory is too large, relative to others in the industry. Vertical analysis is the simplest of a broader set of techniques known as *decomposition analysis*; the more complex approaches to decomposition analysis will not be discussed in this text.

Managers sometimes are sensitive to the uses that analysts make of vertical analysis and adopt accounting policies accordingly. For example, managers who are aware that analysts look closely at the relative proportion of cost of goods sold may elect accounting policies that treat most overhead costs as period costs rather than as inventory costs. By reducing inventory costs, the gross margin percentage appears to be higher (i.e., cost of goods sold is lower relative to sales because fewer costs are inventoried), and the relative proportion of inventory in the total asset mix is also reduced.

Horizontal Analysis **Horizontal analysis** is used to determine the relative change in amounts between years. Obvious calculations include the trend of sales over time and the trend of net income over time. Analysts may construct special measures, such as EBIT (earnings before interest and taxes) or EBITDA (earnings before interest, taxes, depreciation, and amortization), and perform trend analysis on those measures. If the trend of sales is stronger than the trend of earnings, then the company is experiencing declining earnings relative to sales, even though earnings are increasing in absolute terms. That may be either good or bad (as will be explained in the following section), depending on other factors in the analysis.

Illustration

The basic data for the illustration is drawn from the SEDAR filings of a major Canadian company. Exhibit 21-1 shows the company's SFP for two years and the earnings section of the income statement for three years. These data are in the format and level of detail shown by the company in its annual financial statements and annual report. Notice that no individual expenses are disclosed, other than those required by accounting standards.

The vertical analysis is shown in Exhibit 21-2. On the balance sheet, total assets is set equal to 100%, and all other numbers are computed as a percentage of total assets.[1] For example, property, plant, and equipment was 49.0% of assets in 20X2 but is 52.9% of assets in 20X3.

In the income statement, the base (= 100%) is sales revenue. All other amounts are calculated as a proportion of sales. In Exhibit 21-2, we can see that cost of sales declined slightly from 20X1 to 20X2, then rose significantly to 64.3% of revenue) in 20X3. The increase in cost of sales largely accounted for the dip in net earnings in 20X3 (10.5%) from 20X2 (13.3%).

The horizontal analysis is presented in Exhibit 21-3. In this example, the earliest year (20X1 or 20X2) is set as the base year (that is, equal to 100%) and all other years' amounts are calculated as a percentage of the base year. The base year doesn't have to be the earliest year—it could just as well be the most recent year.

Horizontal analysis is best used when the nature of the company's operations is relatively stable, with few changes in lines of business and without significant business combinations. Otherwise, it is difficult, if not impossible, to discern whether significant changes in SFP and P&L amounts are the result of continuing business or of entering and leaving new lines of business. This is particularly a problem with conglomerate companies that buy many other companies during a year.

---

[1] The calculations for vertical and horizontal analysis are easy to do in a computer spreadsheet, since in each case the process is simply one of dividing all cells by a constant. The tedious part is entering the data in the worksheet in the first place.

EXHIBIT 21-1

DATA FOR VERTICAL AND HORIZONTAL ANALYSIS

Consolidated Statements of Financial Position
31 December

(in millions of Canadian dollars)	20X3	20X2
Assets		
Current assets:		
Cash and cash equivalents	$ 17.1	$ 88.8
Short-term investments	45.8	75.9
Accounts receivable	373.1	378.2
Inventories	136.3	130.9
	572.3	673.8
Property, plant, and equipment	1,245.7	1,165.7
Intangible assets	171.7	163.4
Goodwill	366.8	375.5
Total assets	$2,356.5	$2,378.4
Liabilities and shareholders' equity		
Current liabilities:		
Accounts payable and accrued liabilities	$ 514.5	$ 609.6
Long-term debt due within one year	55.8	87.9
	570.3	697.5
Long-term debt	937.6	962.7
Deferred income taxes	98.4	106.1
	1,606.3	1,766.3
Shareholders' equity		
Capital stock	190.5	186.8
Retained earnings	559.7	425.3
	750.2	612.1
Total liabilities and shareholders' equity	$2,356.5	$2,378.4

Consolidated Statements of Income—Earnings Section
Years ended 31 December

(in millions of Canadian dollars)	20X3	20X2	20X1
Revenue	$1,116.7	$1,127.6	$893.8
Cost of sales	718.0	690.7	556.3
Other operating expenses	190.9	194.8	185.5
	908.9	885.5	741.8
Earnings from continuing operations	207.8	242.1	152.0
Interest expense (recovery)	30.4	22.7	(6.3)
Income tax	60.2	69.9	52.2
Net earnings	$ 117.2	$ 149.5	$106.1

For this example, horizontal analysis emphasizes the decrease in cash and short-term investments (19% and 60% of the base year), and the 7% increase in property, plant, and equipment. There has been a significant decrease (to 82%) in current liabilities and retained earnings has grown to 132% of the base.

EXHIBIT 21-2

VERTICAL ANALYSIS*

Consolidated Statements of Financial Position
31 December

	20X3	20X2
Assets		
Current assets:		
Cash and cash equivalents	0.7	3.7
Short-term investments	1.9	3.2
Accounts receivable	15.8	15.9
Inventories	5.8	5.5
	24.2	28.3
Property, plant, and equipment	52.9	49.0
Intangible assets	7.3	6.9
Goodwill	15.6	15.8
	100.0%	100.0%
Liabilities and shareholders' equity		
Current liabilities:		
Accounts payable and accrued liabilities	21.8	25.6
Long-term debt due within one year	2.4	3.7
	24.2	29.3
Long-term debt	39.8	40.5
Deferred income taxes	4.2	4.5
	68.2	74.3
Shareholders' equity		
Capital stock	8.1	7.8
Retained earnings	23.8	17.9
	31.8	25.7
	100.0%	100.0%

Consolidated Income Statements of Comprehensive Income—Earnings Section
Year Ended 31 December

	20X3	20X2	20X1
Revenue	100.0%	100.0%	100.0%
Cost of sales	64.3	61.3	62.2
Other operating expenses	17.1	17.3	20.8
Total operating expenses	81.4	78.5	83.0
Earnings from continuing operations	18.6	21.5	17.0
Interest expense	2.7	2.0	(0.7)
Income tax	5.4	6.2	5.8
Net earnings	10.5%	13.3%	11.9%

On the income statement, revenue grew 25% since 20X1, while profit jumped by 41% in 20X2, only to drop back to an overall increase of only 11% over the two years. Obviously, revenue is growing faster than profit. What about interest expense—did it really go down by almost 500%? Well, hardly! The percentages not only were on a small base, but also the base

EXHIBIT 21-3

HORIZONTAL ANALYSIS

Consolidated Statements of Financial Position
31 December

	20X3	20X2
Assets		
Current assets:		
Cash and cash equivalents	19%	100%
Short-term investments	60	100
Accounts receivable	99	100
Inventories	104	100
	85	100
Property, plant, and equipment	107	100
Intangible assets	105	100
Goodwill	98	100
	99%	100%
Liabilities and shareholders' equity		
Current liabilities:		
Accounts payable and accrued liabilities	84%	100%
Long-term debt due within one year	63	100
	82	100
Long-term debt	97	100
Deferred income taxes	93	100
	91	100
Shareholders' equity		
Capital stock	102	100
Retained earnings	132	100
	123	100
	99%	100%

Consolidated Statements of Comprehensive Income—Earnings Section
Years ended 31 December

	20X3	20X2	20X1
Revenue	125%	126%	100%
Cost of sales	129	124	100
Other operating expenses	103	105	100
Total operating expenses	123	119	100
Earnings from continuing operations	137	159	100
Interest expense	(483)	(360)	100
Income tax	115	134	100
Net earnings	111%	141%	100%

was a negative expense. One must be very wary of large percentage changes like this. They almost always are the result of small base numbers and the percentages usually have little significance.

One thing to notice about horizontal analysis—you cannot add up the percentages in a given year to derive any totals. That is why there are no underscores in Exhibit 21-3.

1. Why is it crucial to approach financial statement analysis with a clear understanding of the decision focus?

2. How can an analyst find out what accounting policies a company is using?

3. Why would a financial analyst want to recast a company's financial statements before performing ratio analysis or other analytical techniques?

4. What is the difference between *vertical* analysis and *horizontal* analysis of financial statement components?

RATIO ANALYSIS

Common-size (vertical) and trend (horizontal) analysis are systematic computations of index ratios, but the term **ratio analysis** is most commonly applied to a large family of ratios that compare the proportional *relationship* between two different accounts amounts in a single year's financial statements. Common-size ratios are strictly within single financial statements, but other ratio analyses can be either between amounts within a single statement or between amounts in two statements. However, there are some potential drawbacks to using ratios:

- Ratios are meaningful only if there is a clear understanding of the purpose of each relationship.
- Ratios are only as valid as the data from which they are derived.
- Ratios require a basis for comparison.
- Ratios are a clue to areas needing investigation—they rarely, if ever, supply answers.

Throughout this book, we have emphasized that different accounting policy decisions and different accounting estimates can yield dramatically different reported results. If the basic financial data are subject to variability, then ratios calculated from that data are unreliable.

Indeed, managers may deliberately select accounting policies and estimates with the intent of affecting certain ratios; we have repeatedly referred to this motivation throughout the book. For example, the decision to lease major operating assets through an operating lease rather than a capital lease often is motivated by management's desire to keep the implicit debt off the balance sheet. In using ratios, therefore, the rule most certainly must be: *analyst be wary!*

There are literally dozens of ratios that can be computed from a single year's financial statements. The important task for an analyst is to focus on the ratios that have primary meaning for the decision at hand. There are many ways of grouping ratios, but those that will be discussed in the following pages are grouped as follows:

- Profitability ratios;
- Efficiency ratios;
- Solvency ratios; and
- Liquidity ratios.

Profitability Ratios

It is common for the press and individual investors to talk about the return on sales that a company is earning, such as "Canadian Tire had 2008 earnings of $374 million on revenues of $9,121 million, a return of only 4%."

Statements like this suggest that the most important profit relationship is between profit and revenue. However, the driving force in capitalistic enterprise is to earn a return *on invested capital*. If you are going to put money into a savings account, you normally will want to put it in the bank or trust company that will give you the largest interest rate. You want to know how much you will make on your investment, *in percentage terms*. You will compare *rates* of interest, not absolute amounts, because the quantity of dollars or euros or yuan that you have in your savings account probably will vary over time.

The same principle is true for all investments. An enterprise's profitability is measured by the rate of return that it can earn on its invested capital, and not by the absolute dollar profit that it generates. It is common in the newspapers and other popular press to cite huge profit figures, such as the multi-billion dollar profits for the large Canadian banks. There is always a strong undertow of suspicion that these amounts are "excessive" because they are so large.

A billion dollars in profit is high if it was earned on an investment of only $2 or $3 billion. But if it was the return on a $50 billion investment, then the investment is yielding very poor returns indeed.

Similarly, companies may proudly cite sharply increased profit figures, perhaps up 40% or 50% over the preceding year or maybe even doubled, as evidence of the managers' fiscal and business acumen. But if a 50% increase in profit was accompanied by a 100% increase in invested capital, then the return on investment has gone down, not up.

Sometimes an increase in absolute profit is due to a takeover of another company; the current year's earnings are a reflection of *both* companies' performance, whereas the previous year's results included only the parent company. The return on the current combined company has to be compared to the return on the sum of both companies in the previous year in order to get any meaningful comparison.

The basic point is that *profitability must always be assessed as some form of return on investment*. By its very nature, a return on investment figure will consist of a numerator from the income statement and a denominator from the SFP. Therefore, **profitability ratios** always cross statements. Assessments of profitability that focus only on the income statement will always be inadequate. The ratio of net income to sales is of limited use because it says nothing about the amount of investment that was employed to generate that level of sales and net income.

A return on investment figure will always reflect the impact of the accounting policy choices made by the company (as will all ratios), and often it is necessary to recast the statements before computing the ratios. There is no truer context for the old GIGO adage (garbage in, garbage out); ratios are only as useful as the measurements underlying the numerator and denominator.

Types of Profitability Ratios When profitability is assessed, the analyst has to view investment from the appropriate standpoint for the decision at hand. A common shareholder will be interested primarily in **return on common share equity**; a preferred shareholder will be interested in the return on total shareholders' equity; and a bond holder will be interested in the return on long term capital (i.e., shareholders' equity plus long-term debt, often called **total capitalization**). All analysts will be interested in the underlying **return on total assets**. These are some of the possible denominators for a profitability ratio.

The numerator of any profitability ratio will reflect a return *over time* because it is derived from the earnings statement. In contrast, the denominator will reflect SFP values at a *point in time*. In order to make the numerator and denominator consistent, the denominator should be calculated as the *average* over the year. Ideally, the denominator should be based on an average of monthly or quarterly investment, but a simpler and more common approach is to average the SFP numbers at the beginning and end of the year being analyzed. However, if there were major changes in investment during the year (such as the acquisition of another company in the first quarter of the year), then a weighted average should be estimated.

The numerator of any ratio must be consistent with its denominator in substance as well as on the time dimension. The return to common shareholders is measured not by net earnings, but by *earnings available to common shareholders* (which basically is net earnings less preferred share dividends, as explained in Chapter 19).

Similarly, the **return on long-term capital** must be calculated by dividing total capitalization into a profit measure that removes the effects of financing. Since interest expense is included in net income, and since interest also affects income tax, the numerator must have the effects of interest on long-term debt removed and must adjust income tax, either (1) by removing tax completely (to get EBIT, a pre-tax return on investment) or (2) by adding back the after-tax interest expense by multiplying interest by $1 - t$, where $t =$ average tax rate for the corporation.

Return ratios are as follows:

Return on long-term capital, before tax:

$$\frac{\text{Net income} + \text{Interest on long-term debt} + \text{Income tax expense (i.e., EBIT)}}{\text{Average long-term debt} + \text{Average total owner's equity}}$$

Return on long-term capital, after tax:

$$\frac{\text{Net income} + [\text{Interest on long-term debt} \times (1 - t)]}{\text{Average long-term debt} + \text{Average total owner's equity}}$$

Return on *total assets* can be measured by dividing total assets into EBIT, where the interest addback is for total interest, on both long-term and short-term debt. This will yield a pre-tax return:

Return on total assets, before tax:

$$\frac{\text{Net income} + \text{Total interest expense} + \text{Income tax expense}}{\text{Average total assets}}$$

Return on total assets, after tax:

$$\frac{\text{Net income} + [\text{Total interest expense} \times (1 - t)]}{\text{Average total assets}}$$

Whatever profitability ratio(s) is (are) used, the effects of accounting policies (and of operating policies, where these create off-balance-sheet assets and liabilities) must be considered. Even when assets are reflected on the SFP, their values are hard to assess. Asset carrying values are normally at historical cost, which means that the equity values also implicitly reflect historical costs. If the assets are old and the profitability is compared to a company that has newer assets, the company with the older assets should appear to be more profitable because its asset base reflects pre-inflationary dollars and is more fully depreciated. The net income figure will reflect lower relative depreciation expenses, due to the relatively lower cost of older assets. The apparent profitability in such a company can be quite misleading; if new investment were made, the same return would probably not be earned.

Some analysts attempt to adjust for differing relative accumulated depreciation by basing the measurement on EBITDA, earnings before interest, taxes, depreciation, and amortization.[2]

---

[2] In the airline industry, aircraft rental payments usually are also added back, so the measure becomes EBITADAR: earnings before interest, tax, amortization, depreciation, and aircraft rental.

Return on gross assets, before tax:

$$\frac{\text{Net income + Depreciation and amortization expense + Total interest expense + Income tax expense}}{\text{Average total assets + Average accumulated depreciation and amortization}}$$

Return on common shareholders' equity:

$$\frac{\text{Net income − Preferred dividends}}{\text{Average shareholders' equity}}$$

This ratio measures the return that the company has been able to earn on the shareholders' equity after all other prior claims on the company's earnings have been subtracted. Net income already includes interest expense (and its tax benefit), and thus it is necessary only to deduct the dividends on any preferred shares that are outstanding. The preferred dividends are deducted *whether or not they have been paid*, as long as they are cumulative.

It is very useful to compare this ratio with the return on assets. If financial leverage is positive, the return on shareholder's equity will be higher than the return on assets. However, if after-tax interest on debt is higher than the return on assets, this ratio will be lower than the return on assets and may be negative.

Operating margin:

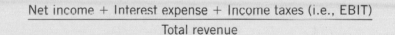

$$\frac{\text{Net income + Interest expense + Income taxes (i.e., EBIT)}}{\text{Total revenue}}$$

In the financial press, this is the most commonly-used ratio. It tells us how much the company earns on each dollar (or euro, yuan, yen, peso, etc.) of revenue. Since the numerator is EBIT, it removes the effect of financing and makes it easier to compare profitability between companies that use different proportions of debt versus equity.

However, this is an incomplete ratio. It gives no indication of the return on *investment* that the company is achieving. Operating margin must be used in conjunction with asset turnover, a ratio that we discuss in the next section (and is illustrated in Exhibit 21-5).

Lessons to Remember When Evaluating Profitability The moral of this tale is:

- Profitability ratios must have a measure of investment in the denominator (based on the statement of financial position) and a measure of profitability in the numerator (based on the income statement, excluding other comprehensive income).
- The denominator and the numerator must be logically consistent.
- Both the denominator and the numerator are the product of many accounting policy choices and even more accounting estimates by management.
- Both components of the ratio may need adjustment both for accounting policies and for off-balance-sheet financing and investment.

Profitability ratios are summarized in Exhibit 21-4.

EXHIBIT 21-4

SUMMARY OF PROFITABILITY RATIOS

Ratio Name	Computation	Significance and Difficulties
Return on long-term capital, before tax	$$\frac{\text{Net income} + \text{Interest expense on long-term debt} + \text{Income tax}}{\text{Average long-term debt} + \text{Average owners' equity}}$$	Indicates the return on invested capital, before considering the form of financing. Useful for comparing to interest rates to test for leverage effect.
Return on long-term capital, after tax	$$\frac{\text{Net income} + [\text{Interest expense on long-term debt} \times (1 - t)]}{\text{Average long-term debt} + \text{Average owners' equity}}$$	Measures the return on long-term capital investment, excluding current liabilities.
Return on total assets, before tax	$$\frac{\text{Net income} + \text{Total interest expense} + \text{Income tax expense*}}{\text{Average total assets}}$$	Indicates the overall return that the company is earning on its asset investment. Old, depreciated assets will tend to increase the apparent rate of return.
Return on total assets, after tax	$$\frac{\text{Net income} + [\text{Total interest expense} \times (1 - t)]}{\text{Average total assets}}$$	Similar to the above, but after taxes.
Return on common shareholders' equity	$$\frac{\text{Net income} - \text{Preferred dividends}}{\text{Average total shareholders' equity} - \text{Average preferred share equity}}$$	Shows the historical after-tax return to shareholders for the period. Uses *earnings available to common shareholders*, which is after interest and dividends for all senior securities.
Return on gross assets, before tax	$$\frac{\text{EBIT} + \text{Depr./Amortization**}}{\text{Average total assets} + \text{Average accum. depr./amortization}}$$	Indicates the return on invested capital before deducting depreciation or amortization.
Operating margin	$$\frac{\text{Net income} + \text{Interest expense} + \text{Income taxes}}{\text{Total revenue}}$$	Indicates the profit margin (before taxes) earned on each dollar of sales. Should be used in conjunction with *asset turnover*.

*usually called EBIT: **E**arnings **B**efore **I**nterest and **T**axes
called EBITDA: **Earnings **B**efore **I**nterest, **T**axes, **D**epreciation and **A**mortization

Profitability ratios do have one clear advantage over other measures of profitability (such as earnings per share or total net income). The advantage is that since profitability is expressed as a *percentage of investment* (except for operating margin), it is possible to separate true increased profitability from normal growth. Most profitable companies pay out only a portion of their earnings as dividends. Some companies pay no dividends at all. The earnings retained by the company are reinvested in operations; since shareholders' equity increases, so must the net assets of the company. Since there is more invested capital, the company will have to generate a larger net income in order to maintain the same return on invested capital. This is normal growth.

The proper test of managerial competence is not whether management has been able to increase EPS or net income; in a profitable industry and good economic times, managers have to be truly incompetent *not* to enjoy increased profits. The proper test is whether management has been able to maintain or, preferably, increase the rate of return on the increasing investment base.

Components of Profitability Ratios The previous section discussed several overall measures of profitability. A key to profitability analysis, however, involves breaking profitability down to its basic components. For example, any company's return on total assets can be dissected into two components: asset turnover and operating margin. Recall that return on assets is calculated as follows:

Earnings before interest and taxes (EBIT) ÷ Average total assets = *Return on assets*

This can be disaggregated into two other ratios:

1. EBIT ÷ Total revenue = *Operating margin*
2. Total revenue ÷ Average total assets = *Asset turnover*

Operating margin multiplied by asset turnover equals return on assets:

$$\frac{EBIT}{Revenue} \times \frac{Revenue}{Assets} = \frac{EBIT}{Assets}$$

Earlier, we pointed out that earnings as a proportion of revenues (i.e., **operating margin**), by itself, is not a useful measure of profitability because it ignores the amount of investment that was employed to generate that level of sales and income. A valid and often successful strategy for a company is to increase its sales volume (i.e., its *asset turnover*) by cutting its profit margin. Although the profit margin goes down, the return on assets will rise if the increase in sales volume is enough to make up for the reduced profit margin.

Other companies may use a strategy of increasing the operating margin, even at the risk of a possible loss of sales volume. If the operating margin is very small, such as 4%, only a 2% increase in price will increase the operating margin by 50% (that is, from 4% of sales to 6% of sales). The company will be better off unless sales volume drops by 33%; that will depend on the price elasticity of demand. In a highly competitive market, a small increase in price could easily cost the company more through a drop in sales volume than it gains in margin.

The point is that *judging profitability by using only the operating margin is always wrong*. Operating margin does not reflect the level of investment, and profitability can be judged only in relation to investment.

Efficiency Ratios

The objective of **efficiency ratios** is to analyze certain aspects of operational efficiency. Efficiency ratios are also known as **turnover ratios** because the two most commonly cited efficiency ratios are *accounts receivable turnover* and *inventory turnover*.

Accounts Receivable Turnover This ratio is intended to measure the average length of time that it takes to collect accounts receivable. The turnover ratio is determined by dividing sales revenue by average accounts receivable.

Accounts receivable turnover = Sales revenue ÷ Average accounts receivable

If the ratio is 4:1, for example, it supposedly indicates that, on average, the accounts receivable "turns over" four times a year, which implies that the average collection period is one fourth of a year, or three months.

This ratio is translated into a parallel ratio called the **average collection period of accounts receivable** by dividing the accounts receivable turnover into 365 days; a turnover of four yields an apparent collection period of 91 days.

The numerator should include only sales on account, but an external analyst of a retail enterprise will have no way of knowing how much of the sales revenue was on account. In some industries, however, it is rare to have cash sales and therefore the total sales can safely be assumed to be sales on account.

The **accounts receivable turnover ratio** is difficult to interpret. Presumably, a short period is better than a long one because it indicates that the company is able to realize cash from its sales in a shorter period of time. It also implies that there are very few long-outstanding accounts that may prove to be uncollectible. This might be true for companies in industries where there is a widespread customer base and essentially equal terms given by each company to its customers.

However, one is quite likely to encounter companies that have special relationships with major customers. The major customers may effectively dictate payment terms. For example, a company that derives most of its revenue from government contracts may show a very slow turnover, and yet the collectibility of the accounts is assured despite the "age" of the accounts.

Another problem for an external analyst is that the accounts receivable shown on the balance sheet may not be typical throughout the year. The fiscal year of a business may be established on the basis of the *natural business year* and the balance sheet date may be the lowest period of activity in a seasonal business. The accounts receivable may be at their lowest level of the whole year. Bankers and other analysts who use the turnover ratio may insist on monthly data. However, an even more likely scenario for such analysts is to request an **accounts receivable aging schedule**, in which the receivables are categorized by the length of time they have been outstanding (e.g., less than 30 days, 31–60 days, 61–90 days, and more than 90 days). Any special payment terms (such as extra-long payments for related companies) are specifically indicated.[3]

In summary, the accounts receivable turnover ratio can be used by an external analyst only as a very rough indication of collection period. It is difficult to interpret, but it can be used as the basis of inquiries to the company's management. Because of the problems cited above, an analyst may be more interested in the *trend* of the ratio, as an indicator of whether the collection period is stable or is getting longer or shorter. If the ratio is changing, it will not be easy for an external analyst to determine the cause of the change and whether the change is good or bad.

For detailed analysis of the creditworthiness of the accounts receivable, an aging schedule is much more useful but is unavailable to most external analysts.

Inventory Turnover The **inventory turnover ratio** indicates the relationship between the cost of goods sold and the average inventory balance:

Inventory turnover = Cost of goods sold ÷ Average inventory

A high turnover ratio is often presumed to be better than a low ratio because a high ratio suggests that less investment in inventory is needed to generate sales. A low ratio, on the other hand, suggests that there may be excessive quantities of inventory on hand or that there are a lot of slow-moving or unsaleable items in inventory.

The objective of inventory management is to maintain *optimum* inventory levels rather than *minimum* inventory levels. Maintaining too low an inventory may result in items not being available for sale when the customer requests them, and therefore sales are less than they should be. Furthermore, with the advent of just-in-time inventory systems in many

---

[3] Some companies give different payment terms to different customers. In that case, aging schedules are usually based on the due date of payment and reflect the number of days past due.

businesses, suppliers are sometimes left with the burden of maintaining inventories. This means that a supplier's finished goods inventory may be higher than in former years, and yet the sale ability of that inventory may be virtually guaranteed through the supplier arrangements. Therefore, a low inventory turnover may not necessarily be bad, and a high turnover may not necessarily be ideal.

Asset Turnover As we have seen, **asset turnover** is a major component of return on assets. It measures the sales dollars generated by assets. The higher this ratio, the more efficient the company is at using its assets in its sales effort.

The principal efficiency ratios are summarized in Exhibit 21-5.

Solvency Ratios

The basic objective of **solvency ratios** is to assess the ability of the company to make both the interest and principal payments on its long-term obligations. These ratios stress the long-term financial and operating structure of the company. They can be further classified as follows:

- **Leverage ratios**, which measure the relative amount of the company's financing that was obtained through debt; and
- **Debt service ratios**, which test the ability of the company to generate sufficient cash flow from operations to pay the debt interest or the debt interest plus principal payments.

EXHIBIT 21-5

SUMMARY OF EFFICIENCY RATIOS

Ratio Name	Computation	Significance and Difficulties
Accounts receivable turnover	$\dfrac{\text{Sales revenue (on account)}}{\text{Average trade accounts receivable}}$	Indicates efficiency of trade accounts receivable collection but is difficult to interpret without knowledge of the customer base. Average year-end accounts receivable balances may not be representative of seasonal variation.
Average collection period of accounts receivable	$\dfrac{365 \text{ (days)}}{\text{Accounts receivable turnover}}$	Converts the accounts receivable turnover into the average collection period, in days. Has the same measurement problems as does the turnover ratio.
Inventory turnover	$\dfrac{\text{Cost of goods sold}}{\text{Average inventory}}$	Yields the number of times that the inventory "turns over" during a year. A low ratio may indicate possible overstocking, if valid comparative information is available. Year-end average inventory balances may not be representative of seasonal variation.
Asset turnover	$\dfrac{\text{Total revenue}}{\text{Average total assets}}$	Shows the level of sales that are being generated per dollar of investment in assets. This is one component of return on assets, and should be used in conjunction with *operating margin* (see Exhibit 21-4).

Solvency ratios interact with profitability ratios, because a company's long-run solvency is in doubt if the company cannot generate enough profit not only to service the debt but also to earn an adequate return for shareholders.

Leverage Ratios Leverage is the extent to which a company uses fixed-term obligations to finance its assets. In public companies, the focus is on long-term debt (plus retractable preferred shares, if any). For analysis of a private company, the focus is on interest-bearing debt, primarily bank debt, both short term and long term; loans from shareholders are not included but are reclassified as owners' equity.[4]

The concept of **leverage** is that if a company can earn a rate of return on its assets that is higher than the rate it has to pay on debt, the shareholders will benefit because the surplus return (i.e., above the rate of interest) will flow through to benefit the shareholders in the form of higher earnings per share. Of course, if a company earns *less* on its investment than the rate of interest, the shareholders' interests will suffer; this is known as **negative leverage**. Therefore, leverage plays an important role in the assessment of profitability because it affects the distribution of the earnings to the different providers of capital. Leverage also is a measure of solvency, because it is one measure of risk.

If a company has a large amount of debt relative to its owners' equity, the company is said to be *highly levered* (or *highly leveraged*). Leverage increases the volatility of the residual earnings to the shareholders, because fluctuations in earnings will be amplified when the constant of interest expense is deducted.

Some companies try to lessen this risk by entering into variable-rate loans instead of fixed-rate loans. If the company's earnings are responsive to the general economy, and if interest rates tend to decrease when the economy slows, then a decrease in earnings might be at least partially matched by a decrease in interest rates. Some companies that have substantial fixed-rate obligations effectively convert these to variable-rate obligations by entering into interest rate swaps.

The most basic measure of leverage is the **debt-to-equity ratio**. The denominator is the total owners' equity (excluding retractable preferred shares, which should be classified as debt, but including shareholders' loans). The numerator of the ratio can be defined in a number of ways, depending on the nature of the company and the objectives of the analyst. At a minimum, the numerator would include all long-term fixed-term obligations and any retractable preferred shares that may exist. Many analysts reclassify the deferred income tax liability as equity. Included in the numerator can be the following:

- Retractable preferred shares;
- Capital lease obligations shown on the SFP;
- Estimated present value of operating lease obligations on assets essential to operations;
- Current portion of long-term debt;
- Short-term bank loans; and
- All other monetary obligations, including trade accounts payable.

When the ratio is computed for assessing solvency (and risk of insolvency), all monetary obligations are normally included (excluding deferred income taxes, unearned revenues, and other miscellaneous deferred credits). The return on total assets (EBIT ÷ total assets) can be directly compared to the average interest rate on debt to see if leverage is positive or negative. The margin by which the return on assets exceeds the average interest rate is the **margin of safety**; the closer they get, the greater the risk of negative leverage.

---

[4] The concept of leverage is discussed more extensively in financial management texts. For example, see *Fundamentals of Corporate Finance, 4th Canadian Edition* by Richard Brealey, Elizabeth Maynes, et al. (McGraw-Hill Ryerson, 2009).

Variants to the basic debt-to-equity ratio use some measure of *invested capital* as the denominator, which includes both debt and equity. These can be defined as follows:

Debt-to-total capitalization = Long-term debt
$$\div \text{ (Long-term debt + Owners' equity)}$$

Debt-to-capital employed = (Long-term debt + Current liabilities)
$$\div \text{ (Long-term debt + Current liabilities − Current}$$
$$\text{assets (or liquid current assets) + Owners' equity)}$$

Debt-to-total assets = (Long-term debt + Current liabilities)
$$\div \text{ Total assets}$$

Instead of computing debt relative to owners' equity, these variants calculate debt as a portion of a broader definition of investment.

As is the case with the basic debt-to-equity ratio, the numerator and denominator may vary somewhat depending on the point of view of the analyst. These ratios answer the question: *how much of the company's invested capital has been obtained through debt?* The components of these alternative ratios are the same as for the basic debt-to-equity ratio, except that the numerator is also included in the denominator. Therefore, the value for a debt-to-equity ratio will be higher than for a debt-to-total-assets ratio. A debt-to-equity ratio of 1:1 will be a debt-to-total capitalization ratio of 1:2. This arithmetic may seem obvious, but since all of these types of ratios are commonly referred to as debt-to-equity ratios, it is important to be clear when discussing a debt-to-equity ratio that all parties to the discussion are in agreement on the definition of the ratio.

The debt-to-equity ratio (and its variants) is a measure of **financial risk**. Because leverage increases the volatility of earnings, the increase in return to shareholders is offset by an increase in risk. A high debt-to-equity ratio is safest when a company has a high and steady level of earnings, particularly when the company can control its return on assets. High levels of financial risk can be most safely used in companies that have low levels of *operating risk*. **Operating risk** is the responsiveness of a company's earnings to fluctuations in its level of revenue. The more volatile operating earnings are, the less a company should rely on financial leverage.

For example, leverage is high in the financial services sector and in regulated public utilities. In financial institutions, the interest being paid on debt and the interest charged to borrowers are both responsive to money market conditions. As long as the debt portfolio is matched (in maturities) to the asset portfolio, net earnings can be relatively stable. In public utilities, rates are set in order to achieve a rate of return on assets that has been approved by the regulators; the permitted rate of return on assets is too low to attract share equity, but by levering up the earnings through lower-rate debt, utilities can provide an adequate return to attract share capital.

Debt-service Ratios A traditional ratio used in solvency analysis is the **times-interest-earned ratio**, which is the ratio of interest expense to earnings before interest and taxes (EBIT). This is believed to indicate the relative amount by which earnings can decrease before there is not enough net income to pay the interest. In reality, the interest would be paid, since failure to do so would risk throwing the company into receivership and possibly bankruptcy.

Since interest expense is tax deductible, the numerator of the ratio normally is EBIT. Again, it may be appropriate to use earnings adjusted for accounting policies, as described in earlier sections. Also, the numerator should include interest on all indebtedness, long term and short term, plus interest on capital leases. Default on any component of interest can have dire consequences.

If a times-interest-earned ratio is approaching 1:1, the company already is suffering negative financial leverage. It is possible to estimate the number of times by which EBIT must exceed interest expense in order to avoid negative leverage. To avoid negative leverage, a company must earn an overall rate on its total capitalization that is at least equal to the interest being charged on the debt. Therefore, if the amount of owners' equity is three times the amount of debt, EBIT should be at least four times the total interest expense (that is, the earnings on one part debt *plus* three parts owners' equity).

A broader debt-service ratio is **times debt service earned**. This ratio goes well beyond the times-interest-earned ratio to look not only at the amount of interest that must be paid, but also at the amount of principal payments that must be made. The times-interest-earned ratio implicitly assumes that debt can be refinanced, which may be a valid assumption in prosperous times. But if the company's fortunes decline, the financial markets freeze up, or interest rates soar, it may be difficult to obtain new financing to "roll over" the debt. The debt-service ratio therefore attempts to look at the ability of a company to *service* its overall debt load.

The numerator of this ratio is *cash*, not earnings. The starting point is the cash flow from operations as reported on the cash flow statement. This amount should be adjusted by adding back interest paid. Interest is tax deductible, and therefore the current income tax paid should also be added back to the cash flow from operations—$C_{op}BIT$ instead of EBIT.

The denominator should include not only interest paid, but also the cash outflows for principal repayments and capital lease payments. Of interest are not only the flows in the current period but also the flows disclosed for future periods. The numerator is not always easy to measure and requires a careful reading of the notes. The cash flows relating to debt and capital leases for the next five years should be disclosed in the notes to the financial statements.

Taxes raise a particular problem, because interest is deductible for tax purposes while principal payments are not. Since principal payments have to be paid in after-tax dollars, it takes a higher pre-tax cash flow from operations to generate enough cash to repay principal. On the other hand, capital lease payments usually are deductible in full, including both the capital portion and the implicit interest expense, thereby adding an additional complication. The easiest way around this problem is to divide the non-tax-deductible cash flows by 1 minus the company's average tax rate: $1 - t$. This converts the principal payments to pre-tax equivalents and then all amounts in the ratio are comparable.

Major solvency ratios are summarized in Exhibit 21-6.

Liquidity Ratios

The general objective of **liquidity ratios** is to test the company's ability to meet its short-term financial obligations. Therefore, the focus is on the composition of current assets and current liabilities.

Current Ratio   The grandparent of all ratios is the **current ratio**. Use of this ratio has been traced back almost 100 years. It is a simple ratio to calculate:

$$\text{Current ratio} = \text{Current assets} \div \text{Current liabilities}$$

The current assets are the "reservoir" of assets from which the current liabilities will be paid. Therefore, this ratio suggests the margin of safety for creditors. A common rule of thumb is that current assets should be twice the current liabilities; the ratio should be 2:1. But like all rules of thumb, a ratio of 2:1 may not be appropriate for a particular company. If cash flows are steady and reliable, then there is no need for such a high ratio. On the other hand, a volatile cash inflow may require a higher average ratio in order to provide a margin of safety so that the company can continue to pay its payroll and other immediate cash expenses.

If the current ratio is used as a measure of liquidity, then the components of current assets must be "liquid" or realizable in the short run. Current assets include inventory and prepaid expenses. Prepaid expenses obviously are not convertible into cash, but they do indicate expenses that have already been paid and that therefore will not require an additional cash outflow in the next period.

EXHIBIT 21-6

SUMMARY OF SOLVENCY RATIOS

Ratio Name	Computation	Significance and Difficulties
Debt-to-equity	$$\frac{\text{Total long-term debt}}{\text{Total owners' equity}}$$	Indicates the relative proportions by which "permanent" investment is financed through debt versus owners' equity. Retractable preferred shares and loans from shareholders should be classified in accordance with their substance.
	or	Some analysts also reclassify the deferred income tax liability as equity.
	$$\frac{\text{Total liabilities, current + long-term}}{\text{Total owners' equity}}$$	Similar indication as above, but includes *all* liabilities. May vary if the level of current liabilities changes year by year.
		Reclassifications may be necessary, as indicated above.
Debt-to-total-capitalization	$$\frac{\text{Long-term debt}}{\text{Long-term debt + Owners' equity}}$$	Indicates the proportion of long-term capital that is financed through debt.
Debt to capital employed	$$\frac{\text{Long-term debt + Current liabilities}}{\begin{array}{c}\text{Long-term debt + Current liabilities}\\ - \text{Current assets + Owners' equity}\end{array}}$$	Shows the total debt burden of the company when current assets are netted out. Deferred income tax is often excluded, and only liquid current assets may be netted against current liabilities.
Debt to total assets	$$\frac{\text{Long-term + Current liabilities}}{\text{Total assets}}$$	Indicates the proportion by which assets are financed through debt.
Times interest-earned	$$\frac{\text{Net income +}}{\begin{array}{c}\text{Interest expense + Tax}\\ \hline \text{Interest expense}\end{array}}$$	Indicates the ability of the company to withstand a downturn in earnings and still be able to earn enough to pay interest (and avoid default). Reflects accounting earnings rather than cash flow.
Times debt service earned	$$\frac{\begin{array}{c}\text{Cash flow from operations}\\ + \text{Interest + Tax}\end{array}}{\begin{array}{c}\text{Interest + [(Projected}\\ \text{annual principal payments and}\\ \text{capital lease payments)} \div (1 - t)]\end{array}}$$	Indicates the ability of the company to service its debt, including leases, from its pre-tax operating cash flow. Operating cash flow must include changes in current monetary items.

Inventories are a bigger problem. If the inventories are readily saleable, then it is appropriate to include them as a liquid asset. But there is no way for an external analyst to tell whether the inventories are saleable or not; there is no disclosure that can help. In fact, inventories that are not very saleable will accumulate, increasing the current assets and improving the current ratio. If inventories are an important component of current assets, increasing inventory levels can be a danger sign.

Current liabilities may include unearned revenue. As with prepaid expenses, unearned revenue represents past cash flow. It does not represent a cash obligation of the company in the same way that accounts and notes payable do.

Quick Ratio   The **quick ratio** is also called the **acid-test ratio.** It is intended to overcome the deficiencies of the current ratio by excluding inventories and other non-monetary current assets. To be consistent, non-monetary current liabilities (e.g., unearned revenue and other deferred credits) should also be excluded. Therefore, the ratio is determined as follows:

Quick ratio = Monetary current assets ÷ Monetary current liabilities

A ratio of less than 1:1 is generally undesirable. However, a low ratio is no cause for concern if the company's operating cash flow is steady and reliable. As with solvency ratios, liquidity ratios can be effectively interpreted only in reference to the *operating risk* and *financial risk* of the company. If cash inflows are stable, a low liquidity ratio should not be cause for concern. But if cash flows are very volatile, even a high liquidity ratio should not make the analyst complacent. Cash can vanish from a high-risk operation very quickly.

Defensive-interval Ratio   The current ratio and the quick ratio are static ratios, in that they look only at the ability of the company to pay its short-term obligations with the short-term assets that exist at the balance sheet date. Both ratios are flawed because they do not consider the rate at which expenditures are incurred. An alternative ratio is one that tests the number of days that the company could operate if the cash inflow were cut off, such as by a strike or by an emergency shutdown. While many expenses are eliminated in a shutdown, others continue. In order for a company to survive a shutdown, it has to be able to pay its continuing operating costs. The intent of the **defensive-interval ratio** is to see how many days the company could pay its continuing expenses in the absence of an inflow of cash from operating revenue. The basic form of the ratio is as follows:

$$\frac{\text{Monetary current assets}}{\text{Annual operating expenditures} \div 365}$$

The difficulty with this ratio is in deciding what should be in the numerator and what should be in the denominator. The numerator clearly should be restricted to monetary assets (e.g., cash, accounts receivable, and temporary investments).

The denominator would include only those cash expenses that will continue in the event of a shutdown. Many labour costs would be eliminated in a shutdown, as would acquisitions of new inventories and supplies. The problem for the external analyst, however, is that the financial statements seldom give enough detail to permit this analysis. Therefore, external analysts usually use short-term monetary assets (without deduction for monetary liabilities) as the numerator and operating expenses less non-cash charges (e.g., depreciation and amortization) in the denominator. The name of the ratio, by the way, comes from the concept of the short-term monetary assets as being *defensive assets*.

The major liquidity ratios are summarized in Exhibit 21-7.

Consolidated Statements

Most Canadian corporations, whether incorporated federally or provincially, operate through a series of subsidiaries. This is true even of some quite small companies. One small chain of three restaurants, for example, has each restaurant set up as a separate corporation. A company that operates in more than one province almost certainly will have at least one

EXHIBIT 21-7

SUMMARY OF LIQUIDITY RATIOS

Ratio Name	Computation	Significance and Difficulties
Current	$\dfrac{\text{Current assets}}{\text{Current liabilities}}$	Indicates ability to pay liabilities with current assets; but includes inventories, deferred charges, and deferred credits.
Quick (acid-test)	$\dfrac{\text{Monetary current assets}}{\text{Monetary current liabilities}}$	A more refined test than the current ratio because it excludes non-monetary assets and liabilities.
Defensive interval	$\dfrac{\text{Monetary current assets}}{\text{Projected daily operating expenditures}}$	Indicates the approximate number of days that the company can continue to operate with the currently available liquid assets. Denominator is very difficult to estimate by an external analyst.

subsidiary in each province. Therefore, the analyst must be aware of just what he or she is analyzing: an individual corporation or a corporate group?

IFRS requires that the primary set of statements for a public company with subsidiaries is the *consolidated* financial statements, wherein all of the assets, liabilities, revenues, and expenses of all of the companies in the group are combined. The statements will give no clue as to which items belong to which legal corporate entity within the corporate group. But if the company is a private corporation, there may be no consolidated statements because under ASPE, consolidation is an *option*, not a requirement.

An investor who is considering purchasing the shares of a corporation usually will want to see statements that show the full resources under control of the corporation, including those held by subsidiaries. The prospective investor is investing in the *economic entity*, and the consolidated statements are the appropriate basis of analysis.

A creditor or lender is in a different position, however. A creditor or lender holds an obligation only of the *separate legal entity*, not of the corporate group. Therefore, creditors or lenders must be careful to analyze the separate entity statements of the specific corporation to which they are extending credit or granting loans.

The consolidated statements can give a very misleading view; lenders have been burnt in the past by lending money to a parent company on the basis of consolidated statements only to discover later that all of the cash flow is in the operating subsidiaries. Lenders may demand cross-company guarantees of debt, but trade creditors usually cannot demand such a guarantee. Cross-company guarantees may not be very effective anyway, since they are usually subordinated and there may be legal impediments to their enforcement when they cross borders, especially national borders.

Therefore, financial statement analysis must be performed on the statements that are appropriate for the decision being made. Generally speaking, equity investors will use consolidated statements while creditors and lenders should use unconsolidated statements for their primary analysis.

Multi-industry Corporations

Many corporations engage in several lines of business. These corporations may be either publicly or privately owned. Because they have a broad spectrum of activities, they cannot be classified as being in a specific industry. Since industry comparisons are a common aspect of financial statement analysis (and particularly of ratio analysis), the inability to slot many corporations into a specific industry classification may appear to create a problem for the analyst. However, the inability to classify a corporation by industry should not, in itself, be of concern.

At the level of profitability analysis, the rate of return *on investment* should not vary by industry. The competition for capital is economy-wide and worldwide, so an investor should expect the same return on investment *at a given level of risk* no matter what industry or industries a company is in.

Risk Assessment is also a function of risk and return—while companies in a certain industry often have similar capital structures because of an underlying commonality of operating risk, there also are significant differences between companies in an industry. Industry classification is not an adequate definition of risk. For example, there is a relatively low risk level inherent in the operations of established mobile phone companies as contrasted to the high risk borne by new entrants to the market.

The key is *risk*; the analyst must be able to evaluate the risks to the company and its ability to survive downturns and benefit from upturns in its fortunes. Industry analysis is useful because the general *market risk* is broadly similar to all of the players in that market. When a company's participation in several different markets is summarized in annual financial statements, it is impossible to tell just what the company's exposure to different risks is in different markets. Therefore, public companies are required to provide **segment reporting** as supplementary information in their annual financial statements. The volume of activity is reported both by industry and by geographic region.

Segment reporting gives the analyst a better idea of the exposure of the company to the risks inherent in different industries and in different parts of the world. However, it is not feasible to perform ratio analysis at the same level of detail as for the company as a whole, because the numbers included in the segment data are distinctly "fuzzy"; the revenues include revenues between segments at transfer prices, the costs include allocated amounts with no useful disclosure of the nature of the allocations, and the operating profits therefore are the net result of two approximations. Segment disclosures certainly are better than no disclosures at all, but they do need to be taken with a grain of salt.

Conclusion

The following are some concluding observations on ratio analysis:

- The apparent simplicity of ratio analysis is deceptive; ratios are only as good as the underlying data.
- The analyst must take care to analyze the correct set of financial statements: consolidated or separate legal entity.
- Financial statements often have to be adjusted to suit the analyst's needs before meaningful ratio analysis can be performed.
- Industry comparisons can be helpful, but there is no assurance that the industry averages (or quartiles) are "right" or are based on similar accounting policies and measurements.
- Assessments of profitability, solvency, and liquidity are not really industry-dependent, but they do depend to some extent on an analysis of risk for each line of business.
- There is no point in computing masses of ratios; it is more important to identify one or two key ratios in each category that are relevant to the analyst's decision needs and concentrate on those.
- Given the many estimates and approximations underlying both the numerator and denominator of *all* ratios, it is absurd to calculate them to more than two significant digits; computing to three or more digits gives ratios an appearance of precision that is completely unwarranted.

CONCEPT REVIEW

1. What is the essential relationship between the numerator and denominator of any effective profitability ratio?

2. Is it necessarily a good thing for efficiency ratios to be very high?

3. Why do some analysts prefer to use debt-service ratios such as times debt service earned rather than the more common times interest earned?

4. Why should creditors and lenders be wary of basing their analyses on consolidated financial statements?

OTHER ANALYTICAL TECHNIQUES

In addition to basic ratio analysis, other more sophisticated analytical techniques can be applied to the amounts in the financial statements or to the ratios themselves. These techniques include the following:

- *Time-series analysis.* The purpose of time-series analysis is to predict the future values of the ratios. Time-series analysis can be applied to cross-sectional ratios themselves or to the underlying financial data. The data can be used "raw," or can be subjected to transformations such as logarithmic transformation.

- *Residual analysis.* This is a time-series analysis based on the differences between computed ratios and industry (or economy) averages. The intent is to identify the extent to which changes in a company's ratios are common to the industry (or economy) as a whole. Such an analysis may help to discover when a company is performing better or worse than other companies over a period of time.

- *Statistical multivariate ratio analysis.* In this approach, ratios are not analyzed one by one but fitted into a statistical model in an attempt to predict some type of outcome, such as impending bankruptcy.

An implicit assumption of these approaches is that the underlying *economic processes* that generate the numbers and ratios are stable. Furthermore, there is an implicit assumption that the underlying *measurement methods* (i.e., accounting policies and accounting estimates) also are stable and remain unchanged over the period of analysis and into the period being predicted. Neither assumption should automatically be taken as correct in a rapidly changing economic environment, especially in light of the dozens of changes in accounting standards over the past decade. This book will not delve further into these sophisticated statistical approaches.

SUMMARY OF KEY POINTS

1. Before analyzing the financial statements of a company, it is essential to clearly understand the objective of the analysis.

2. The auditor's report (if any) should be reviewed with an eye to qualifications and to comments regarding accounting policies, if any. The auditor's report serves only as an assurance that accounting policies meet current accounting standards.

3. The essential first step in statement analysis is to fully understand the financial statements. The statements cannot be meaningfully analyzed unless they are viewed within the framework of management's reporting objectives and accounting policies.

4. Clues to the accounting policies being used by management may be found in the notes to the financial statements. The policy note may give only sketchy information, but the notes relating to individual financial statement components may provide more useful information.

5. The accounting policies used by management may not be the most suitable for the purpose of the analyst's decision needs. The analyst may find it useful to recast the financial statements using different policies, such as by removing the effects of nonrecurring gains and losses from net income, or by treating as expense certain expenditures that the company has capitalized.

6. When the analyst recasts a company's financial statements, there may not be adequate information provided in the notes for an accurate restatement. Approximations often are necessary.

7. *Vertical analysis* (or *common-size analysis*) involves calculating financial statement components as a percentage of the total, such as balance sheet amounts as a percentage of total assets.

8. Vertical analysis is useful for removing the effects of absolute changes in amounts; changes in the relative composition of SFP and income statement components may become more readily apparent.

9. *Horizontal analysis* (or *trend analysis*) involves calculating individual financial statement components over several years as an index number, with a base year set at 100. Horizontal analysis is used to determine the relative change in amounts between years.

10. *Ratio analysis* compares the proportional relationship between different items within a single year's financial statements. Often, it is necessary to adjust the numerator and denominator of a ratio by excluding or reclassifying certain components.

11. *Profitability ratios* are those that compare a measure of earnings (the numerator) to a measure of investment (the denominator). It is essential that the numerator and denominator be logically consistent.

12. *Efficiency ratios* attempt to measure selected aspects of the company's operations, such as inventory turnover or the accounts receivable collection period. Efficiency ratios must be used with great caution by an external analyst because the balance sheet amounts may not be typical of the balances throughout the period.

13. *Solvency ratios* reflect the ability of the company to meet its long-term obligations. Static solvency ratios include various forms of the debt-to-equity ratio; flow ratios examine the ability of the company to meet its debt financing obligations through its cash flows from operations.

14. *Liquidity ratios* test the company's ability to cover its short-term obligations with its existing monetary assets.

15. All ratios are based on accounting numbers that are the result of the company's accounting policies and that include the effects of many estimates made by management. Despite the fact that ratios can be computed to many decimals, they really are very approximate measures that must be interpreted with extreme caution.

KEY TERMS

accounts receivable aging schedule, 1230
accounts receivable turnover ratio, 1230
acid-test ratio, 1236
asset turnover ratio, 1231
auditor's report, 1216
average collection period of accounts
    receivable, 1230
cross-sectional comparison, 1219
current ratio, 1234
debt service ratios, 1231
debt-to-capital employed ratio, 1233
debt-to-equity ratio, 1232
debt-to-total assets ratio, 1233
debt-to-total-capitalization ratio, 1233
defensive-interval ratio, 1236
efficiency ratios, 1229
financial risk, 1233
horizontal (trend) analysis, 1220
inventory turnover ratio, 1230
leverage, 1232
leverage ratios, 1231

liquidity ratios, 1234
longitudinal comparisons, 1219
margin of safety, 1232
negative leverage, 1232
operating margin, 1229
operating risk, 1233
profitability ratios, 1225
quick ratio, 1236
ratio analysis, 1224
return on common share equity ratio, 1225
return on long-term capital ratio, 1225
return on total assets ratio, 1225
review engagement, 1217
segment reporting, 1238
solvency ratios, 1231
times-debt-service-earned ratio, 1234
times-interest-earned ratio, 1233
total capitalization, 1225
turnover ratios, 1229
vertical (common size) analysis, 1220

APPENDIX

RECASTING FINANCIAL STATEMENTS— DEMONSTRATION CASE

Introduction

This chapter has emphasized that it may be necessary for an analyst to recast a company's financial statements before any ratio analysis is undertaken. To illustrate the task of restatement, we have chosen the financial statements of a Canadian company, QDO Limited (not the real name). We will restate these financial statements to reflect different accounting policy choices. After the restatement, we will compare the results of ratio analysis before and after restatement.

The Company

QDO is a privately-owned software development company. Its primary line of business is the design and development of large-scale custom software for specific large clients. Clients include several of the provinces, one Canadian bank, and two international insurance companies. Between 20X5 and 20X8, gross revenue tripled and net income increased from $262,725 to over $2 million. Operating margin, based on the published (and audited)

EXHIBIT 21A-1

QDO LIMITED

Consolidated Statements of Income and Retained Earnings

Years ended 31 December

(thousands of Canadian dollars)	20X8	20X7	20X6	20X5
Gross revenue	$29,276	$19,305	$14,317	$10,231
Investment income (interest on cash deposits)	1,265	—	—	—
	30,541	19,305	14,317	10,231
Less cost of hardware sold	4,497	2,519	1,519	1,407
Operating revenue	26,044	16,786	12,798	8,824
Expenses				
Operating and administrative*	22,762	15,108	11,718	8,323
Depreciation and amortization				
Fixed assets	203	49	22	6
Capital leases	143	85	23	1
Software development costs	141	67	—	—
Interest	164	224	238	95
	23,413	15,533	12,001	8,425
Income before income tax	2,631	1,253	797	399
Income tax expense (recovery)	569	(199)	(3)	137
Net income	$ 2,062	$ 1,452	$ 800	$ 262
Retained earnings, beginning of year	1,952	1,056	475	252
Dividends declared	(14)	(295)	(176)	(33)
Cost of share issue net of income tax	(1,185)	(202)		
Premium on shares purchased for cancellation		(59)	(43)	(6)
Loss on sale of repurchased common shares	(46)			
Retained earnings, end of year	$ 2,769	$ 1,952	$ 1,056	$ 475
Net income per common share	$ 0.19	$ 0.16	$ 0.09	$ 0.03

*Includes $372 of amortization of other development costs in 20X8

financial statements, increased from 0.26% in 20X5 to 7% in 20X8. The company's statements of operations for the most recent four years are shown in Exhibit 21A-1; the balance sheets are shown in Exhibit 21A-2; the statement of cash flows are shown in Exhibit 21A-3. The terminology used in these exhibits is that used by the company.

EXHIBIT 21A-2

QDO LIMITED

Consolidated Balance Sheets

Years ended 31 December

(thousands of Canadian dollars)	20X8	20X7	20X6	20X5
ASSETS				
Current assets				
Short-term deposits	$ 8,716	$ —	$ —	$ —
Accounts receivable	6,459	4,658	5,112	2,370
Work in progress	7,451	2,780	—	—
Hardware inventory	569	—	—	—
Prepaid expenses and supplies inventory	1,151	470	126	123
	24,346	7,908	5,238	2,493
Fixed assets				
Leasehold improvements	852	317	278	16
Furniture, fixtures and computer equipment	624	121	138	16
Assets under capital lease	1,374	817	359	156
	2,850	1,255	775	188
Less accumulated amortization	(293)	(90)	(38)	(11)
	2,557	1,165	737	177
Other assets				
Software development costs	13,037	5,157	1,580	112
Leasehold improvements	2,196	—	—	—
Deferred income tax	—	355	409	409
	15,233	5,512	1,989	521
Total assets	$42,136	$14,585	$7,964	$3,191
LIABILITIES AND SHAREHOLDERS' EQUITY				
Current liabilities				
Bank and other loans	$ 2,806	$ 3,371	$2,653	$ 900
Accounts payable and accrued liabilities	7,054	3,550	2,131	918
Current portion of non-current liabilities	281	161	85	23
Deferred revenue	530	461	183	140
	10,671	7,543	5,052	1,981
Non-current liabilities				
Capital lease obligations	1,488	1,101	662	134
Deferred income tax	214	—	104	104
Total liabilities	12,373	8,644	5,818	2,219
Shareholders' equity				
Share capital	29,892	3,989	1,090	497
Retained earnings	2,769	1,952	1,056	475
Less: treasury shares	(2,898)	—	—	—
	29,763	5,941	2,146	972
	$42,136	$14,585	$7,964	$3,191

EXHIBIT 21A-3

QDO LIMITED

Consolidated Statements of Cash Flows

Years ended 31 December

(thousands of Canadian dollars)	20X8	20X7	20X6	20X5
Operations				
Net income for the year	$ 2,062	$ 1,452	$ 800	$ 262
Add non-cash items				
Future (deferred) income tax	569	(50)	—	50
Depreciation and amortization	859	200	45	7
Deferred lease rent credits	—	82	142	—
	3,490	1,684	987	319
Net change in working capital items	(3,846)	(724)	(1,427)	(294)
Cash provided by (used for) operating activities	(356)	960	(440)	25
Investment				
Investment in software products	(8,020)	(3,645)	(1,469)	(110)
Other development costs	(2,568)	—	—	—
Purchase of fixed assets	(1,034)	(36)	(162)	(89)
Proceeds from disposal of fixed assets	—	—	—	160
Cash provided by (used for) investment activities	(11,622)	(3,681)	(1,631)	(39)
Financing				
Current maturities of lease obligations	(325)	(161)	(55)	(24)
Issue of shares	21,858	2,525	2,138	244
Loss on sale of repurchased shares	(46)	—	—	—
Dividends declared	(14)	(295)	(176)	(33)
Shares purchased and cancelled	(214)	(66)	(1,588)	(9)
Cash provided by (used for) financing activities	21,259	2,003	319	178
Increase (decrease) in cash during year	$ 9,281	$ (718)	$ (1,753)	$ 164
Cash and short-term investments, beginning of year, net of current borrowings	(3,371)	(2,653)	(901)	(1,065)
Cash and short-term investments, end of year, net of current borrowings	$ 5,910	$ (3,371)	$ (2,653)	$ (901)
Changes in cash and cash equivalents				
Increase (decrease) in cash and short-term investments	$ 8,716	—	—	—
Decrease (increase) in current borrowings	565	$ (718)	$ (1,753)	$ 165
Net change in cash and cash equivalents	$ 9,281	$ (718)	$ (1,753)	$ 165

In 20X7, the company's managers decided to develop some of its large-scale custom software designs into off-the-shelf turn-key proprietary products that would be adaptable to any prospective user. In addition, the company launched an ambitious sales expansion plan, establishing 11 offices in Canadian cities and 10 in U.S. cities, plus one in Singapore. To help finance the expansion, the company raised approximately $22 million through a public issue of common shares early in 20X8. The company also increased its line of credit with Royal Dominion Bank to $5 million.

The product development expenditures for the proprietary products were accounted for in accordance with accounting standards. Since, in management's judgement, all of the criteria for capitalization were satisfied, it was acceptable to capitalize the development expenditures. Also, the costs of establishing the international sales offices were deferred as "leasehold improvements" on the balance sheet.

It is now 20X9. Over the first three months of the year, the company has completely used the cash and short-term deposits that are shown on the year-end 20X8 balance sheet, and is near the limit of its line of credit. The company's CEO has approached the Royal Dominion Bank with a proposal to further extend the company's line of credit to enable the company to continue development of its proprietary software and to support the costs of the new sales offices until the offices become self-supporting.

Task

You are an analyst for the Royal Dominion Bank. The bank's Credit Committee is interested in the sustainable operating cash flow of QDO. Investment in software development is considered by the bank to be an ongoing operating activity, crucial to the success of the company. Therefore, the chair of the credit committee has asked you to recast QDO's 20X7 and 20X8 financial statements as follows:

- Development costs incurred in each year should be shown as a current expense.
- All deferred income tax amounts should be reversed out of the statements.

Once the statements have been restated, the Credit Committee would like you to calculate a few ratios that relate to the company's ability to sustain increased borrowing. Specifically, the requested ratios are:

1. Return on total assets, before tax;
2. Total liabilities to shareholders' equity; and
3. Times interest earned.

Non-recurring items of revenue or expense should be eliminated before calculating any ratios based on net income. The ratios should be calculated both on the original financial statements and on the restated amounts.

Additional Information

The following information is extracted from QDO's disclosure notes:

1. **Summary of significant accounting policies**

   (c) *Software product costs*
   Costs, including an allocation of interest and overhead, which relate to the development and acquisition of computer-based systems, where the systems are expected to be sold in substantially the same form in the future, are capitalized. It is the Company's policy to charge these costs to income, commencing in the year of development completion, based on projected unit sales over a period of not longer than three years or when it is determined that the costs will not be recovered from related future revenues.

   (d) *Leasehold improvements*
   During 20X7 the Company established 22 branch sales offices in Canada, USA, and Singapore. The costs of setting up these branch sales offices have been capitalized. These capitalized costs are being charged to earnings over the subsequent four quarters.

5. **Software product costs**
   The following is an analysis of software product costs:

	20X8	20X7
Balance, beginning of year	$ 5,157,271	$1,579,174
Additions during the year	8,020,181	3,644,763
	13,177,452	5,223,937
Less: amortization	(140,753)	(66,666)
Balance, end of year	$13,036,699	$5,157,271

6. Leasehold improvements

Other development costs at 31 December 20X8 include:

Sales network development costs	$ 842,531
Software implementation costs—branch sales offices	1,725,506
	2,568,037
Less amounts charged to income in 20X8	(371,958)
	$2,196,079

Demonstration Case—Solution

Approach

The assignment from the Credit Committee is to recast the statements by making two changes:

- The accounting policy for development costs should be changed from capitalization to immediate expensing.
- The effects of income tax allocation are to be removed, so that the statements reflect only the current income tax due.

To make these changes, we need to take the following steps:

1. *Income statement*

- Add expenditures on development costs to expenses.
- Remove amortization expense relating to development costs and leasehold improvements from expenses (to avoid double-counting).
- Remove deferred income tax, if any.
- Adjust retained earnings balances for the restated net income.

2. *Statement of financial position*

- Remove development costs from assets.
- Reclassify deferred income tax balances—move from other assets and non-current liabilities to retained earnings.
- Restate retained earnings.

3. *Statement of cash flow*

- Reclassify development expenditures—move from investing activities to operations.
- Remove development cost amortization addbacks.
- Remove deferred income tax addbacks.

Income Statement

The income statement shows "software development costs" of $141 for 20X8 and $67 for 20X7. These numbers tie in to Note 5, which shows the same amounts as amortization. Therefore, these amounts must be removed from the income statement. As well, Note 6 shows amortization of leasehold improvements of $372, which must be removed from operating and administrative expenses. Expenditures on development costs are shown in Notes 5 and 6. These must be added to expenses in the recast income statements.

Since the bank wants to see the effects of using a "flow-through" approach for income tax, the deferred income tax expense must be removed. The 20X7 balance sheet shows a debit balance for deferred income taxes of $355. In 20X8, the balance is a credit of $214. The net change, therefore, is a credit of $569 on the balance sheet. To balance, the company must have charged $569 in deferred income tax to the income statement. This amount can be verified by referring to the statement of cash flow, which shows a non-cash addback of $569 for deferred income taxes. This is also the total amount of income tax expense shown in the income statement. The company had no current taxes due in 20X8.

For 20X7, the statement of cash flow shows a *negative* addback for deferred income tax of $50. This indicates that the amount was a *credit* to income. This can be verified by looking at the change in the net balance of deferred income taxes on the balance sheet. At the end of 20X6, there were two deferred income tax balances, a credit for $104 and a non-current debit of $409, for a net debit balance of $305. In 20X7, the company recorded a net deferred income tax credit to income of $50. The net change can be reconciled in the form of a general journal entry:

Change in Deferred Tax Amounts, Year-end 20X6 to Year-End 20X7

Deferred income tax liability ($104 − $0)	104	
Deferred income tax asset ($409 − $355)		54
Income tax expense, deferred		50

The balance sheet effect of this change is to eliminate the liability balance of $104 and reduce the asset balance from $409 to $355.

In summary, the adjustments to net income for 20X8 and 20X7 are as follows:

	20X8	20X7
Net income, as reported	$ 2,062	$ 1,452
Plus amortization of software development costs	141	67
Plus amortization of leasehold improvements	372	—
Less expenditures on software development costs	(8,020)	(3,645)
Less expenditures on other development costs	(2,568)	—
Plus (less) deferred income tax expense (credit)	569	(50)
Restated net income (loss)	$(7,444)	$(2,176)

These adjustments obviously will change retained earnings for both year-ends. However, there are two other adjustments that must be made to the 20X7 *beginning* balance of retained earnings:

1. The balance sheet at year-end 20X6 shows software development costs as an asset of $1,580. Using the bank's preferred policy of expensing development costs, these costs would have been charged to operations when incurred. Reclassifying this amount means removing it as an asset and charging it against year-end 20X6 retained earnings.

2. The change to flow-through reporting of income tax expense requires that the balances of both the current and non-current future tax balances at the beginning of 20X7 (i.e., at year-end 20X6) be eliminated. The net balance at the end of 20X6 is $409 asset minus $104 liability, for a further net reduction in retained earnings of $305.

Therefore, the 20X7 beginning retained earnings on the statement of income and retained earnings must be restated to a deficit of $829:

	20X6
Ending retained earnings, as reported	$1,056
Adjustment to reclassify capitalized software development costs	(1,580)
Adjustment to eliminate deferred tax balances	(305)
Restated retained earnings (deficit), 31 December 20X6	$ (829)

The adjustments shown above for 20X6 retained earnings and for 20X7 and 20X8 net income can be used to restate the statements of income and retained earnings for the two years. The restated income statements are shown in Exhibit 21A-4.

Statement of Financial Position

The restated retained earnings amounts that are shown in Exhibit 21A-4 are used in the restated SFP (balance sheet). Other adjustments are:

- The asset amounts shown for software development costs and leasehold improvements in the original SFPs are both removed.
- The deferred income tax balances are removed.
- The restated balance sheets are shown in Exhibit 21A-5.

EXHIBIT 21A-4

QDO LIMITED

Consolidated Statements of Income and Retained Earnings

Years ended 31 December

(thousands of Canadian dollars)	As Reported		Restated	
	20X8	20X7	20X8	20X7
Gross revenue	$29,276	$19,305	$ 29,276	$19,305
Investment income	1,265	—	1,265	—
	30,541	19,305	30,541	19,305
Less cost of hardware sold	4,497	2,519	4,497	2,519
Operating revenue	26,044	16,786	26,044	16,786
Expenses				
Operating and administrative	22,762	15,108	22,390	15,108
Depreciation and amortization				
Fixed assets	203	49	203	49
Capital leases	143	85	143	85
Software development costs	141	67	8,020	3,645
Leasehold improvements			2,568	
Interest	164	224	164	224
	23,413	15,533	33,488	19,111
Income before income tax	2,631	1,253	(7,444)	(2,325)
Income tax	569	(199)	—	(149)
Net income	$ 2,062	$ 1,452	$ (7,444)	$ (2,176)
Retained earnings, beginning of year	1,952	1,056	(3,561)	(829)
Dividends declared	(14)	(295)	(14)	(295)
Cost of share issue net of income taxes	(1,185)	(202)	(1,185)	(202)
Premium on shares purchased for cancellation		(59)		(59)
Loss on sale of repurchased common shares	(46)		(46)	
Retained earnings, end of year	$ 2,769	$ 1,952	$(12,250)	$ (3,561)

Cash Flow Statement

On the cash flow statement, the operations section begins with the restated net income for each year. The two amounts of amortization must be adjusted by the amounts of amortization included in the original statements but now eliminated in the restatement. Also, the addback for deferred income taxes is eliminated.

In the investment section, investment in software products and leasehold improvements must be eliminated. The total cash flows for each year do not change, of course, but the subtotals for operating and investment change considerably. The restated cash flow statements are shown in Exhibit 21A-6.

Ratios

It is obvious that changing the development cost accounting has a major impact on QDO's financial statements. Instead of showing a profit, the restated amounts indicate a substantial loss. Assets are significantly reduced and retained earnings goes into a deficit position.

The operating loss situation in 20X8 is actually even worse than stated, when nonrecurring items are considered, as requested. Net income for the most recent year includes

EXHIBIT 21A-5

QDO LIMITED

Consolidated Balance Sheets

Years ended 31 December

	As Reported		Restated	
(thousands of Canadian dollars)	20X8	20X7	20X8	20X7
ASSETS				
Current assets				
Short-term deposits	$ 8,716	$ —	$ 8,716	$ —
Accounts receivable	6,459	4,658	6,459	4,658
Work in progress	7,451	2,780	7,451	2,780
Hardware inventory	569	—	569	—
Prepaid expenses and supplies inventory	1,151	470	1,151	470
	24,346	7,908	24,346	7,908
Fixed assets				
Leasehold improvements	852	317	852	317
Furniture, fixtures and computer equipment	624	121	624	121
Assets under capital lease	1,374	817	1,374	817
	2,850	1,255	2,850	1,255
Less accumulated amortization	(293)	(90)	(293)	(90)
	2,557	1,165	2,557	1,165
Other assets				
Software development costs	13,037	5,157		
Leasehold improvements	2,196			
Deferred income tax	—	355		
	15,233	5,512		
Total assets	$42,136	$14,585	$26,903	$9,073
LIABILITIES AND SHAREHOLDERS' EQUITY				
Current liabilities				
Bank and other loans	$ 2,806	$ 3,371	$ 2,806	$3,371
Accounts payable and accrued liabilities	7,054	3,550	7,054	3,550
Current portion of non-current liabilities	281	161	281	161
Deferred revenue	530	461	530	461
	10,671	7,543	10,671	7,543
Non-current liabilities				
Capital lease obligations	1,488	1,101	1,488	1,101
Deferred income tax	214	—	—	—
Total liabilities	12,373	8,644	12,159	8,644
Shareholders' equity				
Share capital	29,892	3,989	29,892	3,989
Retained earnings	2,769	1,952	(12,250)	(3,561)
Less treasury shares	(2,898)	—	(2,898)	—
	29,763	5,941	14,744	428
	$42,136	$14,585	$26,903	$9,073

EXHIBIT 21A-6

CONSOLIDATED STATEMENTS OF CASH FLOWS—RESTATED [in $ Thousands]

Years ended 31 December	As Reported 20X8	As Reported 20X7	Restated 20X8	Restated 20X7
Operations				
Net income for the year	$ 2,062	$ 1,452	$ (7,444)	$(2,176)
Add items not involving working capital				
Deferred income tax	569	(50)	—	—
Depreciation and amortization	859	200	346	133
Deferred lease rent credits	—	82	—	82
	3,490	1,684	(7,098)	(1,961)
Net change in working capital items	(3,846)	(724)	(3,846)	(724)
	(356)	960	(10,944)	(2,685)
Investment				
Investment in software products	(8,020)	(3,645)		
Leasehold improvements	(2,568)	—		
Purchase of fixed assets	(1,034)	(36)	(1,034)	(36)
Proceeds from disposal of fixed assets	—	—	—	—
	(11,622)	(3,681)	(1,034)	(36)
Financing				
Current maturities of lease obligations	(325)	(161)	(325)	(161)
Issue of shares	21,858	2,525	21,858	2,525
Loss on sale of repurchased shares	(46)	—	(46)	—
Dividends declared	(14)	(295)	(14)	(295)
Shares purchased and cancelled	(214)	(66)	(214)	(66)
	21,259	2,003	21,259	2,003
Increase (decrease) in cash during year	$ 9,281	$ (718)	$ 9,281	$ (718)
Cash and short-term investments, beginning of year, net of current borrowings	(3,371)	(2,653)	(3,371)	(2,653)
Cash and short-term investments, end of year, net of current borrowings	$ 5,910	$(3,371)	$ 5,910	$(3,371)
Changes in cash and cash equivalents				
Increase (decrease) in cash and short-term investments	$ 8,716	—	$ 8,716	—
Decrease (increase) in current borrowings	565	$ (718)	565	$ (718)
Net change in cash and cash equivalents	$ 9,281	$ (718)	$ 9,281	$ (718)

investment income of $1,265,000. This investment income is the result of temporary investment of the proceeds of the common share issue. The case states that all of the cash and short-term investments were used in operations (and development) early in 20X9. Since there are no investments, there will be no investment income in 20X9. Removing the non-recurring income increases the 20X8 loss:

	As Reported	Restated
Net income (loss)	$2,062	$(7,444)
Less: non-recurring investment income	(1,265)	(1,265)
Income (loss) on continuing operations	$ 797	$(8,709)

The ratios requested, before and after restatement, are as follows:

1. Return on total assets, before tax, 20X8

$$\frac{\text{Net income} + \text{Interest expense} + \text{Income tax expense}}{\text{Total assets (average)}}$$

Before restatement:
($2,062 + $164 + $569) ÷ [($14,585 + $42,136) ÷ 2] = $2,795 ÷
$28,361 = **9.9%**

After restatement:
(−$8,709 + $164) + [($9,073 + $26,903) ÷ 2] = − $8,545 ÷ $17,988
= **−47.5%**

2. Total liabilities to shareholders' equity

$$\frac{\text{Total liabilities}}{\text{Shareholders' equity}}$$

Before restatement: $12,373 ÷ $29,763 = **42%**
After restatement: $12,159 ÷ $14,744 = **82%**

Times interest earned

$$\frac{\text{Net income} + \text{Interest expense} + \text{Income tax expense}}{\text{Interest expense}}$$

Before restatement: ($2,062 + $164 + $569) ÷ $164 = $2,795 ÷ $164
= **17.0**
After restatement: (−$8,709 + $164) ÷ $164 = −$8,545 ÷ $164 = **−52.1**

Conclusion

This case demonstrates not only the process that must be followed for restatements, but also the importance of ensuring that the financial statements reflect accounting policies that are consistent with the decision to be made. If the bank looked at the financial condition of the company only as shown in the published statements, it would receive a much different picture of the financial health and profitability of the company than is presented in the recast statements. Changing the underlying reporting objective to cash flow prediction results in using accounting policies that give a much more negative view of the company.

The moral of this story? It is foolish to undertake any ratio analysis without first examining the appropriateness of the underlying financial accounting policies of the company!

QUESTIONS

Q21-1 List three financial statement users and a decision for each that may rest on financial statement analysis.

Q21-2 Why is a potential investor's perspective different than an existing investor's perspective?

Q21-3 Explain why financial analysts and others, in analyzing financial statements, examine the summary of accounting policies.

Q21-4 Explain why the actual disclosure of accounting policies in financial statements might not be as helpful as analysts and other financial statement users might wish.

Q21-5 What does it mean to "recast" the financial statements? Why are financial statements recast?

Q21-6 Distinguish between vertical and horizontal analysis. Briefly explain the use of each.

Q21-7 Explain the two ratios that combine to form return on assets. What strategies can a company use to maximize return on assets?

Q21-8 Explain the return-on-assets ratio. Why is it a fundamental measure of profitability?

Q21-9 Moller Company's average collection period for accounts receivable is 24 days. Interpret this figure. What is the accounts receivable turnover ratio? What does it reveal?

Q21-10 Maddox Steel Company has an inventory turnover of 9; interpret this figure.

Q21-11 Explain the circumstances where a company has debt financing and the leverage factor is (a) positive, (b) negative, and (c) zero.

Q21-12 Current assets and current liabilities for two companies with the same amount of working capital are summarized below. Evaluate their relative liquidity positions.

	Co. X	Co. Y
Current assets	$300,000	$900,000
Current liabilities	100,000	700,000
Working capital	$200,000	$200,000

CASE 21-1

PETERSON PRODUCTS LIMITED

You have just returned from a meeting with a friend who is considering an opportunity to invest in non-voting shares in Peterson Products Limited (PPL). PPL is a private company that is offering to issue this new class of shares to a select group of private investors. Your classmate was very enthusiastic about the company, pointing out the company's unusually high return on assets, its low debt-to-equity ratio, and its high operating margin, as compared to other companies of a similar nature. Your classmate is also impressed with the company's high positive cash flow, which has exceeded $1 million in each of the past two years.

PPL is a product development company. It contracts with other companies to develop product ideas to a state where they can be readily produced and marketed. The services offered by PPL range from lining up suppliers to provide the raw product, to packaging and distribution of a rather simple product at the most modest level of service, to full development and design work, manufacturing design, pilot plant construction, and product testing for complex industrial products.

The development of specific products is done under contract. The standard contract provides for PPL to be reimbursed for all direct costs plus a fixed percentage of direct costs to cover overhead and provide a profit. Most contracts contain an upper limit on costs that PPL cannot exceed without approval of the contracting party.

Some of the work on contracts is carried out directly by engineering and other product staff who are employed directly by PPL. Frequently, however, segments of contracts are subcontracted to specialist companies. The subcontracts usually are fixed-fee contracts, and since any cost overruns will have to be absorbed by the subcontractor, it is the practice of PPL to recognize all of PPL's profit on the subcontracted portion of the contract as soon as the subcontract is signed. About 60% of PPL's contracts have been fulfilled by subcontractors in the past two years, and the new president intends to increase that proportion in order to "reduce the overhead" of PPL.

Although specific product development is done under contract, PPL also engages in development work of its own in order to have a storehouse of development knowledge and expertise that it can apply to future contracts. The amortization of these development costs is included in the overhead component of contracts.

While the company has been in existence for over 25 years, it has become much more aggressive in the last two years since Dale Peterson assumed the positions of president and CEO. Dale is the daughter of Ian Peterson, the founder of the company. She completed an MBA at Concordia University and took over management of the company when her father decided to retire to Australia.

The new president and CEO has altered the way in which PPL acquires its equipment. In previous years, PPL purchased the equipment and other fixed assets that it needed. Now the company owns only minor furniture, etc. The bulk of assets are leased on a month-to-month basis from IRS Ltd. IRS purchased $1,433 million of equipment for PPL in 20X7 ($1,385 million in 20X6). IRS rents the equipment to PPL for $29,500 per month. Ninety percent of the equipment that PPL owned three years ago has since been sold, much of it to IRS, at fair market values. IRS finances purchase of the assets through bank loans. IRS is owned by Dale Peterson. Dale and other shareholders have personally guaranteed the IRS bank loans, but PPL is not a guarantor.

PPL's shares at present are owned equally by Ian, Dale, and Christopher, Dale's brother. Christopher does not participate in the management of the company or take any active interest in its affairs aside from welcoming the dividends that he receives.

Dale has proposed issuing 100 shares of a new class of non-voting shares to a limited number of new investors for $10,000 per share. The new shares would receive dividends equally with the voting common shares and would have the same rights as voting shares if the company is liquidated. The non-voting shareholders would be able to sell their shares back to the company at any year-end at the net book value per share.

Your friend has left with you, for your perusal, the audited financial statements that follow. He also left some information that shows the following comparative ratios for product development companies:

Debt-to-equity	0.67
Operating margin	6%
Return on assets, after tax	10%

Required:

Analyze the financial statements of Peterson Products Limited and advise your friend as to the wisdom of investing in PPL non-voting shares.

PETERSON PRODUCTS LIMITED
STATEMENT OF FINANCIAL POSITION
Years ending 31 March

(all amounts in millions of Canadian dollars)	20X7	20X6
Current assets		
Cash	$ 75	$ 58
Contract billings receivable	520	413
Unbilled contract receivables	417	110
Work in progress	541	736
	1,553	1,317
Equipment, furniture, and fixtures—net	350	1,750
Patents	1,512	917
Total assets	$3,415	$3,984
Current liabilities		
Accounts payable and accrued expenses	$ 487	$ 441
Bank overdraft	—	1,000
	487	1,441
Deferred income tax	915	615
	1,402	2,056
Shareholders' equity		
Common shares	600	600
Retained earnings	1,413	1,328
	2,013	1,928
Total liabilities and shareholders' equity	$3,415	$3,984

PETERSON PRODUCTS LIMITED

STATEMENT OF INCOME AND RETAINED EARNINGS
Years ending 31 March

(all amounts in millions of Canadian dollars)	20X7	20X6
Revenue		
Contract revenue	$5,250	$4,640
Gain on disposal of fixed assets	340	104
	5,590	4,744
Expenses		
Contract costs	3,870	3,169
General selling and administrative expenses	805	670
Interest expense	70	175
Income tax expense	410	355
	5,155	4,369
Net income	$ 435	$ 375
Retained earnings, 1 April 20X6	1,328	1,403
Dividends	(350)	(450)
Balance, 31 March 20X7	$1,413	$1,328

PETERSON PRODUCTS LIMITED

STATEMENT OF CASH FLOWS
Years ended 31 March

(all amounts in millions of Canadian dollars)	20X7	20X6
Operating activities:		
Net income	$ 435	$ 375
Depreciation	123	263
Patent amortization	183	121
Deferred income tax	300	230
Gain on sale of fixed assets	(340)	(104)
	701	885
Decrease (increase) in working capital balances	(173)	(244)
Cash provided by operations	528	641
Financing activities:		
Dividends paid	(350)	(450)
Investing activities:		
Patents	(778)	(432)
Proceeds from disposal of fixed assets	1,617	1,472
Increase (decrease) in cash and cash equivalents	$1,017	$1,231

CASE 21-2

FOREST INDUSTRY

You are evaluating two public companies in the forest industry. Both companies are public, and are integrated companies that own or lease timber properties, harvest trees, and make building supplies and paper products. This industry is very volatile. The profiles are as follows:

Canamora Forest Products Inc.

The company is a leading Canadian integrated forest products company. The company employs approximately 6,800 people. The company has extensive production facilities in British Columbia and Alberta, and a lumber remanufacturing plant in the United States. The company is a major producer and supplier of lumber and bleached kraft pulp. It also produces semi-bleached and unbleached kraft pulp, bleached and unbleached kraft paper, plywood, remanufactured lumber products, hardboard panelling and a range of specialized wood products, including baled fibre and fibremat. Products are sold in global markets.

Fallsview Building Materials Ltd.

Fallsview is a North American–based producer of building materials including oriented strand board, medium-density fibreboard, hardwood plywood, lumber, I-joists, specialty papers, and pulp. The company is also the United Kingdom's largest producer of wood-based panels, including particleboard and value-added products. The company employs over 2,600 people in North America and 1,000 in the United Kingdom.

You have obtained some limited industry norms that relate to years prior to those presented for the two companies; industry norms are difficult to establish for the current years.

Selected ratios for the forest industry in Canada

	20X5	20X4	20X3
Debt to equity (%)	81	68	72
Operating profit margin	15.8	13.4	7.7
Return on assets	7.6	6	0.7
Return on equity	17.4	12.5	1.5
Current ratio	2.1	2.1	1.9

Summarized financial data for each company is shown in Exhibit 1. A standard financial statement analysis form is included.

The companies both have unqualified audit reports and have similar accounting policies except for the following:

1. Fallsview uses FIFO while Canamora uses weighted-average cost for inventory.
2. Both companies use a combination of straight-line and units-of-production amortization methods for capital assets, but Fallsview uses useful lives that are approximately 25% longer than those used by Canamora.

Required:

Provide an analysis that compares Fallsview and Canamora from the perspective of:

1. A potential short-term creditor.
2. A potential common stock investor.

Assume a tax rate of 30% for both companies.

EXHIBIT 1

COMPARATIVE FINANCIAL STATEMENTS (IN MILLIONS)

Statements of Financial Position

	Fallsview		Canamora	
	20X6	20X5	20X6	20X5
Assets				
Cash and cash equivalents	$ 208	$ 17	$ 20	$ 67
Temporary investments	24	—	—	—
Accounts receivable	304	321	267	242
Inventory	325	381	515	530
Total current assets	861	719	802	839
Property, plant, and equipment	1,469	1,518	1,984	1,903
Other assets	230	190	27	22
Total assets	$2,560	$2,427	$2,813	$2,764
Liabilities				
Current liabilities:				
Accounts payable	$ 480	$ 364	$ 323	$ 316
Current portion of long-term debt	53	49	4	15
Total current liabilities	533	413	327	331
Long-term debt	556	384	1,077	921
Other liabilities	170	65	96	97
Deferred income tax	147	363	38	112
	873	812	1,211	1,130
Total liabilities	1,406	1,225	1,538	1,461
Shareholders' equity				
Preferred shares	—	—	60	60
Common shares	657	657	889	880
Retained earnings	497	545	326	363
	1,154	1,202	1,275	1,303
Total liabilities and equity	$2,560	$2,427	$2,813	$2,764

	Fallsview		Canamora	
	20X6	20X5	20X6	20X5
Net sales	$1,986	$2,265	$2,066	$2,134
Costs and expenses				
Manufacturing/product costs	1,759	1,622	1,793	1,722
Amortization and depletion	106	113	148	144
Selling and administration	58	67	90	90
	1,923	1,802	2,031	1,956
Operating income	**63**	**463**	**35**	**178**
Interest expense	64	60	52	40
Other (income) expense	(9)	(6)	(62)	25
Income before income tax	8	409	45	113
Income tax expense (recovery)	(18)	84	26	(34)
Net income	$ 26	$ 325	$ 19	$ 147
Dividends				
Preferred	—	—	$ 2	$ 2
Common	$ 74	$ 25	$ 54	$ 50

Source: Reproduced with permission from CGA-Canada.

ASSIGNMENTS

A21-1 Horizontal and Vertical Analysis—Income Statement: Simard Trading Company's income statements (condensed) for two years are shown below:

31 December	20X4	20X5
Gross sales	$550,000	$606,000
Sales returns	(10,000)	(6,000)
	540,000	600,000
Cost of goods sold	(270,000)	(360,000)
Gross margin	270,000	240,000
Expenses		
Selling expenses	120,600	130,700
Administrative expenses	75,600	66,000
Restructuring	10,800	8,000
Interest	5,400	6,000
Income tax expense	14,400	7,300
	226,800	218,000
Net income and comprehensive income	$ 43,200	$ 22,000

Required:

1. Prepare vertical percentage analysis of the income statement. Round to the nearest percent. Comment on any particularly notable changes from 20X4 to 20X5.

2. Prepare a horizontal percentage analysis of the income statement. Use a single-step format. Round to the nearest percent. Comment on any significant changes from 20X4 to 20X5.

A21-2 Horizontal and Vertical Analysis—SFP: Bryant Company's statement of financial position (condensed and unclassified) for two years is shown below:

31 December	20X4	20X5
Cash	$ 60,000	$ 80,000
Accounts receivable (net)	120,000	116,000
Inventory (FIFO, LCM)	144,000	192,000
Prepaid expenses	8,000	4,000
Funds and investments (at cost)	60,000	88,000
Tangible capital assets	560,000	664,000
Accumulated depreciation	(104,000)	(196,000)
Intangible assets	12,000	60,000
Total	$860,000	$1,008,000
Accounts payable	$160,000	$100,000
Other current liabilities	40,000	40,000
Long-term mortgage payable	200,000	172,000
Common shares, no par	340,000	520,000
Retained earnings	120,000	176,000
Total	$860,000	$1,008,000

Required:

1. Prepare a comparative balance sheet in good form, including vertical percentage analysis. Round to the nearest percent.

2. Prepare a horizontal percentage analysis of the comparative balance sheet. Round to the nearest percent.

★★   **A21-3 Vertical and Horizontal Analysis:** The SFP for Heresy Limited is as follows:

| | 31 December | | |
Statement of Financial Position	20X5	20X4	20X3
Cash	$ 516,000	$ 330,000	$ 295,000
Marketable securities	420,000	570,000	630,000
Receivables, net	450,000	510,000	550,000
Inventory	1,725,000	1,494,000	934,000
Tangible capital assets	7,644,000	5,439,000	4,039,000
Less accumulated depreciation	(1,951,200)	(1,461,000)	(976,000)
Intangible capital assets	378,000	405,000	350,000
	$9,181,800	$7,287,000	$5,822,000
Current liabilities	$ 279,000	$ 258,000	$ 579,000
Debentures payable	1,978,500	2,022,000	800,000
Common shares	3,450,000	2,100,000	2,100,000
Retained earnings	3,474,300	2,907,000	2,343,000
	$9,181,800	$7,287,000	$5,822,000

Required:

1. Prepare a comparative vertical percentage analysis. Round to the nearest percent.
2. Prepare a horizontal percentage analysis of the comparative balance sheet. Round to the nearest percent.
3. What conclusions can you reach about the changes in the company's asset and liability structure between 20X3 and 20X5?

★★   **A21-4 Ratio Interpretation:** Wilcox Limited has total assets of $35,000,000, and manufactures fine hand tools. Selected financial ratios for Wilcox and industry averages are as follows:

| | Wilcox | | | Industry |
	20X5	20X4	20X3	Average
Current ratio	2.41	2.12	2.04	2.28
Quick ratio	1.11	1.10	1.05	1.22
Inventory turnover	2.62	2.78	2.90	3.50
Return on equity	0.16	0.14	0.15	0.11
Debt-to-equity ratio	1.44	1.37	1.41	0.95
Return on assets	.12	.11	.11	.10
Asset turnover	3.14	3.01	3.00	3.70
Operating margin	.06	.05	.05	.05
Basic EPS	.48	.45	.43	1.43
Diluted EPS	.31	.30	.29	1.41

Required:

Referring to the information presented above:

1. Identify two financial ratios of particular interest to:
   a. A financial institution that provides an operating line of credit for daily cash management needs. The line of credit is secured with a charge on inventory.
   b. A supplier, about to decide whether to sell to Wilcox on credit.
   c. An investment banker, consulting with Wilcox on a potential public offering of common shares.
2. Explain why diluted EPS is lower than EPS.
3. Discuss what these financial ratios reveal about Wilcox.

★★ **A21-5 Vertical and Horizontal Analysis:** Four-year comparative income statements and SFPs for Firenza Products Inc. (FPI) are shown below. FPI has been undergoing an extensive restructuring in which the company has discontinued or sold several divisions in order to concentrate on its core business. As a result, the size of the company has decreased considerably.

Statement of Comprehensive Income

Years ended 31 December	20X8	20X7	20X6	20X5
Net sales	$284.1	$949.6	$1,388.8	$2,153.9
Cost of products sold	369.2	793.5	1,045.9	1,649.0
Depreciation, depletion, and amortization	38.4	94.8	88.7	146.9
Selling and administrative	46.4	49.0	53.4	82.7
Operating earnings (loss)	(169.9)	12.3	200.8	275.3
Interest expense	(1.7)	(14.8)	(16.2)	(40.5)
Other income (expense)	32.6	(0.5)	(5.3)	34.8
Earnings (loss) from continuing operations before income tax	(139.0)	(3.0)	179.3	269.6
Income tax (recovery)	(46.9)	(2.6)	79.7	115.4
Earnings (loss) from continuing operations	(92.1)	(0.4)	99.6	154.2
Earnings (loss) from discontinued operations	390.7	119.9	54.8	—
Net earnings and comprehensive income	$298.6	$119.5	$ 154.4	$ 154.2

Condensed Statements of Financial Position

31 December	20X8	20X7	20X6	20X5
Assets				
Current assets	$ 957.7	$ 407.6	$ 126.2	$ 197.7
Investments and other	90.6	36.3	65.8	97.8
Fixed assets	1,289.2	1,286.5	1,318.2	2,200.3
Assets of discontinued operations	—	647.4	1,262.9	—
Net assets	$2,337.5	$2,377.8	$2,773.1	$2,495.8
Liabilities and shareholders' equity				
Current liabilities	$ 736.5	$ 329.0	$ 157.3	$ 131.3
Long-term debt	—		75.0	227.6
Deferred income taxes	161.8	202.8	136.7	190.0
Liabilities of discontinued operations	—	174.5	438.3	—
Preferred shares issued by subsidiaries	—	—	—	34.3
Non-controlling interest	—	—	176.2	174.5
Shareholders' equity	1,439.2	1,671.5	1,789.6	1,738.1
Total liabilities and shareholders' equity	$2,337.5	$2,377.8	$2,773.1	$2,495.8

Required:

1. Prepare a vertical analysis of both the income statement and the SFP.
2. Prepare a horizontal analysis of the income statement and SFP. Use 20X5 as the base year.
3. What conclusions about the company and its financial practices can you discern from your analysis?

★ **A21-6 Ratio Interpretation:** The following ratios are available for a three-year period for Woolfrey Limited.

	20X6	20X7	20X8
Current ratio	1.7	1.8	1.9
Quick ratio	1.1	0.9	1.0
Average collection period of accounts receivable	51 days	57 days	66 days
Inventory turnover	4.5	4.0	3.3
Debt to total assets	51%	46%	41%
Long-term debt to shareholders' equity	52%	57%	62%
Sales as a percentage of 20X6 sales	100%	103%	107%
Gross profit percentage	36%	35%	35%
Operating margin	7%	7%	7%
Return on total assets	8%	8%	8%
Return on shareholders' equity	14%	13%	13%

Required:

1. Explain why the current ratio is increasing while the quick ratio is decreasing.
2. Comment on the company's use of financial leverage.

★★ **A21-7 Compute and Explain Profitability Ratios:** The 20X5 comparative financial statements for Thompson Corporation reported the following information:

	20X3	20X4	20X5
Sales revenue	$18,000,000	$19,500,000	$20,250,000
Net income	150,000	180,000	142,500
Interest expense, long-term debt	15,000	18,000	27,000
Income tax expense	60,000	90,000	90,000
Long-term debt	1,200,000	1,500,000	1,650,000
Shareholders' equity, common and preferred*	2,100,000	2,175,000	2,190,000
Total assets	5,250,000	5,250,000	5,700,000
Preferred share dividends	9,000	15,000	18,000
Income tax rate	30%	35%	40%

*Preferred shares, $150,000 in all years.

Required:

1. Based on the above financial data, compute the following ratios for 20X4 and 20X5:
   a. Return on total assets, before tax.
   b. Return on total assets, after tax.
   c. Return on long-term capital, before tax.
   d. Return on long-term capital, after tax.
   e. Return on common shareholders' equity.
   f. Operating margin.
   g. Asset turnover.
2. As an investor in the common shares of Thompson, which ratio would you prefer as a primary measure of profitability? Why?
3. Explain any significant trends that appear to be developing.

★★ **A21-8 Ratio Analysis:** The table below shows selected information reported by Canadian Tire Corporation for five years, 2005 through 2009:

(millions of dollars, except EPS)	2009	2008	2007	2006	2005
Gross operating revenue	$ 8,687	$ 9,121	$ 8,606	$ 8,253	$ 7,714
Operating expenses	7,788	8,200	7,694	7,416	6,896
Depreciation and amortization	248	226	207	192	185
Interest expense	147	123	63	76	84
Income taxes	144	168	200	201	190
Net earnings	335	375	412	355	330
Current assets	5,113	3,979	3,138	2,541	2,973
Inventories	934	917	779	667	675
Property and equipment (net)	3,180	3,199	3,284	2,881	2,744
Total assets	8,790	7,784	6,765	5,805	5,956
Current liabilities	2,564	2,000	2,114	1,664	1,821
Long-term debt (excl. current)	1,102	1,374	1,342	1,168	1,171
Shareholders' equity	3,687	3,565	3,108	2,785	2,511
Basic EPS	$ 4.10	$ 4.60	$ 5.05	$ 4.35	$ 4.04
No. of common shares at year-end (000s)	78,178	78,178	78,048	78,047	78,033
No. of Canadian Tire stores	479	475	473	468	462
No. of PartSource stores	87	86	71	63	57
No. of Mark's Work Wearhouse stores	378	372	358	339	334
No. of gas bars	272	273	266	260	259

Required:
Based on the data above, analyze the changes that have occurred over this five-year period in terms of profitability and solvency.

★ **A21-9 Ratio Analysis; Liquidity and Efficiency:** The condensed financial information given below was taken from the annual financial statements of Conter Corporation:

	20X3	20X4	20X5
Current assets (including inventory)	$ 840,000	$1,008,000	$1,176,000
Current liabilities	630,000	672,000	588,000
Cash sales	3,360,000	3,276,000	3,444,000
Credit sales	840,000	1,176,000	1,050,000
Cost of goods sold	2,352,000	2,457,000	2,520,000
Inventory (ending)	504,000	588,000	420,000
Accounts receivable	252,000	268,800	256,200
Total assets (net)	4,200,000	5,040,000	5,880,000
Projected daily operating expenditures	12,600	13,020	12,180

Required:
1. Based on the above data, calculate the following ratios for 20X4 and 20X5. Briefly explain the significance of each ratio listed. Use the following format:

Ratio	20X4	20X5	Significance
Current			
Quick			
Defensive interval			
Asset turnover			
Accounts receivable turnover			
Average collection period of accounts receivable			
Inventory turnover			

2. Evaluate the overall results of the ratios, including trends.

A21-10 Compute and Summarize Significance of Ratios: Fader Corporation's 20X4 and 20X5 SFPs and 20X5 income statement are as follows (in $ millions, except per share amounts):

Statements of Financial Position

31 December	20X4		20X5	
Cash	$ 11		$ 20	
Investments (short-term)	3		4	
Accounts receivable (net of allowance)	23		19	
Inventory (FIFO, LCM)	31		37	
Prepaid expenses	4		3	
Funds and investments, long-term	31		31	
Capital assets (net of accumulated depreciation of $29 (20X4), $37 (20X5)	81		72	
Accounts payable		$ 22		$ 10
Accrued liabilities		2		2
Notes payable, long-term		41		45
Common shares, no par (60,000 shares outstanding)		76		76
Retained earnings (including 20X4 and 20X5 income)		43		53
Totals	$184	$184	$186	$186

Statement of Comprehensive Income, 20X5

Sales revenue (1/3 were credit sales)	$153
Investment revenue	4
Cost of goods sold	(70)
Distribution expense	(20)
Administrative expense (includes $8 of depreciation)	(15)
Interest expense	(4)
Income tax expense (the tax rate is 40%)	(20)
Net income and comprehensive income	$ 28

Other information
Cash flow from operations	$ 22

Required:

Compute the 20X5 ratios that measure:

a. Profitability (after tax only)
b. Efficiency
c. Solvency
d. Liquidity

For each category, use a format similar to the following (example given):

Ratio	Formula	Computation	Significance
Current ratio	Current assets / Current liabilities	$83 ÷ $12 = 6.9	Short-term liquidity; adequacy of working capital

A21-11 Selected Ratios: The 20X9 condensed income statement and the 20X9 and 20X8 condensed SFPs for Farrokh Limited are shown below. All sales are on credit.

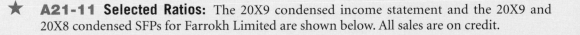

Condensed Statement of Comprehensive Income

Year ended 31 December 20X9

Sales revenue (all on credit)	$40,000
Cost of goods sold	22,500
Gross profit	17,500
Operating expenses	12,100
Operating income	5,400
Interest expense	1,500
Income before income taxes	3,900
Income tax expense	1,100
Net income and comprehensive income	$ 2,800

Condensed Statement of Financial Position

31 December	20X9	20X8
Cash	$ 5,500	$ 7,500
Accounts receivable (net)	13,500	14,500
Inventory	8,000	6,000
Plant and equipment	40,000	38,000
Accumulated depreciation	(18,000)	(22,500)
Land	35,000	30,500
Total	$84,000	$74,000
Accounts payable	$ 5,800	$ 6,000
Long-term notes payable	13,700	10,000
Common shares	20,000	15,000
Retained earnings	44,500	43,000
Total	$84,000	$74,000

Required:

Compute the following ratios for 20X9:

a. Return on assets before taxes.
b. Asset turnover.
c. Operating margin.
d. Return on shareholders' equity.
e. Inventory turnover.
f. Average collection period of accounts receivable.

Source: Reproduced with permission from CGA-Canada.

★ **A21-12 Profitability and Solvency Ratios, Competing Companies:** Abacus Limited and Zandi Corporation are competing businesses. Abacus owns all of its operating assets, financed largely by secured loans. Zandi rents its operating assets from a major industrial leasing company. The 20X2 income statements and SFPs for the two companies are shown below.

Statements of Comprehensive Income

Year ended 31 December 20X2	Abacus	Zandi
Sales revenue	$ 540,000	$270,000
Direct costs of providing services	300,000	150,000
Depreciation	100,000	10,000
Other expenses	60,000	87,000
Total operating expenses	460,000	247,000
Net operating earnings	80,000	23,000
Interest expense	24,000	—
Earnings before income taxes	56,000	23,000
Provision for income taxes	17,000	7,000
Net earnings and comprehensive income	$ 39,000	$ 16,000

Statements of Financial Position

31 December 20X2	Abacus	Zandi
Current assets	$ 260,000	$130,000
Tangible capital assets	1,000,000	50,000
Accumulated depreciation	(600,000)	(30,000)
Total assets	660,000	$150,000
Current liabilities	$ 120,000	$ 60,000
Long-term liabilities	360,000	—
Common shares	100,000	50,000
Retained earnings	80,000	40,000
Total liabilities and shareholders' equity	$ 660,000	$150,000

Required:

1. Compute the following ratios for both companies (for convenience, use 20X2 year-end balance sheet amounts instead of averages):
   a. Operating margin.
   b. Asset turnover.
   c. Return on assets.
   d. Return on share equity.
   e. Total debt-to-shareholder's equity.
2. Evaluate the two companies, based on the ratios you have calculated. Which company do you think is more profitable?

★ **A21-13 Competing Companies, Continuation:** Refer to the information in A21-12; Zandi's financial statements contain the following note disclosure:

Commitments:
The Company has commitments for operating lease payments for the next five years as follows:

20X3	$53,000
20X4	49,000
20X5	45,000
20X6	40,000
20X7	35,000

Required:
Determine how this additional information would affect the ratios for Zandi that are required in A21-12. Assume that the disclosed lease payments are due at the end of each year and that Zandi's incremental borrowing rate is 8%. Ignore any income tax impact.

★★ **A21-14 Leverage—Sell Share Capital versus Debt, Analysis:** Bui Limited is considering building a second plant at a cost of $7,600,000. Management has two alternatives to obtain the funds: (a) sell additional common shares or (b) issue $7,600,000, five-year bonds payable at 10% interest. Management believes that the bonds can be sold at par for $7,600,000 and the shares at $80 per share. The statement of financial position (before the new financing) shows the following:

Average income for past several years (net of tax)	400,000
Long-term liabilities	$1,600,000
Common shares, no par (40,000 shares)	3,200,000
Retained earnings	1,300,000

The average income tax rate is 30%. Dividends per share have been $6.00 per share per year. Expected increase in pre-tax income (excluding interest expense) from the new plant is $1,500,000 per year.

Required:

1. Prepare an analysis to show, for each financing alternative,
   a. Expected total net income after the addition;
   b. After-tax cash flows from the company to prospective owners of the new capital; and
   c. The (leverage) advantage or disadvantage to the present shareholders of issuing the bonds to obtain the financing, as represented by comparing return on assets to return on equity.

2. What are the principal arguments for and against issuing the bonds, as opposed to selling the common shares?

★★ **A21-15 Comparative Analysis:** Frank Smythe, the owner of Cuppola Limited, has asked you to compare the operations and financial position of his company with those of Ling Limited, a large company in the same business and a company that Frank Smythe considers representative of the industry.

	Cuppola Limited		Ling Limited	
	20X1	**20X0**	**20X1**	**20X0**
Statement of Financial Position				
Assets				
Cash	$ 100,000	$ 20,000	$ 100,000	$ 125,000
Accounts receivable	70,000	60,000	800,000	750,000
Inventories	230,000	190,000	2,400,000	1,825,000
	400,000	270,000	3,300,000	2,700,000
Capital assets	500,000	500,000	5,300,000	5,000,000
Accumulated depreciation	(300,000)	(270,000)	(2,600,000)	(2,300,000)
Goodwill	—	—	500,000	500,000
	200,000	230,000	3,200,000	3,200,000
	$ 600,000	$ 500,000	$6,500,000	$5,900,000
Liabilities and shareholders' equity				
Bank indebtedness	$ 40,000	$ 30,000	$ 500,000	$ 300,000
Trade accounts payable	135,000	100,000	1,300,000	650,000
Current portion of long-term debt	20,000	20,000	300,000	300,000
	195,000	150,000	2,100,000	1,250,000
Long-term debt	30,000	50,000	1,400,000	1,700,000
	225,000	200,000	3,500,000	2,950,000
Shares issued and outstanding				
— preferred	—	—	500,000	500,000
— common	50,000	50,000	1,500,000	1,500,000
Retained earnings	325,000	250,000	1,000,000	950,000
	375,000	300,000	3,000,000	2,950,000
	$ 600,000	$ 500,000	$6,500,000	$5,900,000
Statement of Comprehensive Income				
Sales	$1,300,000	$1,000,000	$9,000,000	$7,500,000
Cost of sales	(936,000)	(700,000)	(6,120,000)	(5,250,000)
Expenses, including income tax	(266,500)	(250,000)	(2,100,000)	(1,800,000)
Net income and comprehensive income	$ 97,500	$ 50,000	$ 780,000	$ 450,000

Required:

Compare the operations and financial positions of the two companies, supporting your comments with useful ratios and percentages.

★★ **A21-16 Investment Analysis:** Sandy Panchaud has come to you for some independent financial advice. He is considering investing some of his money in an operating company and he wants to know which of the two alternatives he has identified is the better investment. They are both in the same industry, and Mr. Panchaud feels he could buy either for book value.

Required:
Prepare a response to Mr. Panchaud. Your response should include an appropriate selection of ratios and a common-size (vertical analysis) income statement.

	Company A	Company B
Statement of Comprehensive Income		
Sales	$2,797,000	$2,454,000
Cost of goods sold	1,790,000	1,594,000
Gross margin	1,007,000	860,000
Operating expenses	807,000	663,000
Operating income	200,000	197,000
Interest expense	70,000	43,000
Income before income tax	130,000	154,000
Income tax expense	52,000	62,000
Net income and comprehensive income	$ 78,000	$ 92,000

	Company A	Company B
Statement of Financial Position		
Cash	$ 66,000	$ 27,000
Accounts receivable (net)	241,000	262,000
Merchandise inventory	87,000	110,000
Prepaid expenses	12,000	7,000
Plant and equipment (net)	792,000	704,000
	$1,198,000	$1,110,000
Accounts payable and accrued liabilities	$ 191,000	$ 173,000
Long-term debt	635,000	310,000
Common shares	50,000	200,000
Retained earnings	322,000	427,000
	$1,198,000	$1,110,000

★★ **A21-17 Recasting, Selected Ratios (Appendix):** A loan officer for the Dominion Bank of Alberta wishes to recast her client's financial statements so that they reflect income tax expense on a taxes payable basis. The tax rate is 30%. One of her clients is Frobisher Bay Corporation (FBC). FBC's condensed year-end 20X4 statements are shown in Exhibit 1.

Required:
1. Recast FBC's statements.
2. Compute the following ratios, both before and after recasting the statements:
   a. Operating margin.
   b. Return on total assets (after tax).
   c. Total liabilities to shareholders' equity.

Statement of Comprehensive Income

Year ended 31 December 20X4

Sales revenue	$660,000
Cost of goods sold	360,000
Depreciation expense	72,000
Interest expense	12,000

Other expenses	96,000
	540,000
Earnings before income tax	120,000
Income tax:	
—current	14,400
—deferred	21,600
	36,000
Net earnings and comprehensive income	$ 84,000

Statement of Financial Position

31 December 20X4

Current assets	$144,000
Capital assets:	
—Tangible (net)	624,000
—Identifiable intangible	168,000
Total assets	$936,000
Current liabilities:	
Accounts payable	96,000
Accrued liabilities	24,000
	120,000
Long-term debt	384,000
Deferred income tax	192,000
Total liabilities	696,000
Common shares	60,000
Retained earnings	180,000
Total shareholders' equity	240,000
Total liabilities and shareholders' equity	$936,000

★★ **A21-18 Integrative Problem:** The following information is available for Davison Limited, a private company, for the year ended 31 December 20X6:

Statement of Financial Position
31 December

	($ thousands)	
	20X6	**20X5**
Cash	$ 1,720	$1,110
Receivables, net	1,150	1,170
Marketable securities	450	550
Inventory	2,575	2,110
Tangible capital assets	3,984	3,396
Less: accumulated depreciation	(1,650)	(1,487)
Intangible assets	555	417
Goodwill	135	135
	$ 8,919	$7,401
Current liabilities	$ 2,190	$1,900
Convertible bond payable	833	834
Deferred income tax	619	585
Preferred shares	500	500
Common stock conversion rights	166	166
Common shares	2,150	1,700
Retained earnings	2,461	1,716
	$ 8,919	$7,401

Statement of Comprehensive Income

for the year ended 31 December	20X6
Sales (on account)	$10,450
Cost of goods sold	7,619
	2,831
Operating expenses	1,548
	1,283
Income tax	385
Net income and comprehensive income	$ 898

Other information:

- The company has a $1,000,000, 10% bond outstanding. Each $1,000 bond is convertible into 50 common shares at the investor's option. The bond proceeds were split between the debt and equity when the bond was issued. In 20X6, interest expense of $98 per bond was recognized.
- The tax rate is 30%.
- In 20X6, stock options were outstanding to key employees allowing them to buy 40,000 common shares for $16 per share at any time after 1 January 20X18. The average common share price during the year was $20.
- 420,000 common shares were outstanding on 31 December 20X6; 40,000 of those shares had been issued for cash on 1 February 20X6.
- Preferred shares are cumulative, and have a dividend of $4 per share; 10,000 shares are outstanding. Each share can be converted into four common shares at any time.
- Davidson Limited declared and paid dividends totalling $25,000 in 20X6.

Required:
Calculate the following ratios for 20X6 based on the financial statements above.

a. Basic EPS.
b. Diluted EPS.
c. Debt-to-equity (total debt).
d. Inventory turnover.
e. Quick ratio.
f. Return on assets (after tax).
g. Return on common shareholders' equity.
h. Accounts receivable turnover (all sales are on account).
i. Asset turnover.
j. Return on long-term capital, after tax.
k. Operating margin.

TABLE I-1: Present value of 1: (P/F, i, n)

$$P/F = \frac{1}{(1 + i)^n}$$

n	2%	2.5%	3%	4%	5%	6%	7%	8%	9%	10%	11%	12%	14%	15%
1	0.98039	0.97561	0.97087	0.96154	0.95238	0.94340	0.93458	0.92593	0.91743	0.90909	0.90090	0.89286	0.87719	0.86957
2	0.96117	0.95181	0.94260	0.92456	0.90703	0.89000	0.87344	0.85734	0.84168	0.82645	0.81162	0.79719	0.76947	0.75614
3	0.94232	0.92860	0.91514	0.88900	0.86384	0.83962	0.81630	0.79383	0.77218	0.75131	0.73119	0.71178	0.67497	0.65752
4	0.92385	0.90595	0.88849	0.85480	0.82270	0.79209	0.76290	0.73503	0.70843	0.68301	0.65873	0.63552	0.59208	0.57175
5	0.90573	0.88385	0.86261	0.82193	0.78353	0.74726	0.71299	0.68058	0.64993	0.62092	0.59345	0.56743	0.51937	0.49718
6	0.88797	0.86230	0.83748	0.79031	0.74622	0.70496	0.66634	0.63017	0.59627	0.56447	0.53464	0.50663	0.45559	0.43233
7	0.87056	0.84127	0.81309	0.75992	0.71068	0.66506	0.62275	0.58349	0.54703	0.51316	0.48166	0.45235	0.39964	0.37594
8	0.85349	0.82075	0.78941	0.73069	0.67684	0.62741	0.58201	0.54027	0.50187	0.46651	0.43393	0.40388	0.35056	0.32690
9	0.83676	0.80073	0.76642	0.70259	0.64461	0.59190	0.54393	0.50025	0.46043	0.42410	0.39092	0.36061	0.30751	0.28426
10	0.82035	0.78120	0.74409	0.67556	0.61391	0.55839	0.50835	0.46319	0.42241	0.38554	0.35218	0.32197	0.26974	0.24718
11	0.80426	0.76214	0.72242	0.64958	0.58468	0.52679	0.47509	0.42888	0.38753	0.35049	0.31728	0.28748	0.23662	0.21494
12	0.78849	0.74356	0.70138	0.62460	0.55684	0.49697	0.44401	0.39711	0.35553	0.31863	0.28584	0.25668	0.20756	0.18691
13	0.77303	0.72542	0.68095	0.60057	0.53032	0.46884	0.41496	0.36770	0.32618	0.28966	0.25751	0.22917	0.18207	0.16253
14	0.75788	0.70773	0.66112	0.57748	0.50507	0.44230	0.38782	0.34046	0.29925	0.26333	0.23199	0.20462	0.15971	0.14133
15	0.74301	0.69047	0.64186	0.55526	0.48102	0.41727	0.36245	0.31524	0.27454	0.23939	0.20900	0.18270	0.14010	0.12289
16	0.72845	0.67362	0.62317	0.53391	0.45811	0.39365	0.33873	0.29189	0.25187	0.21763	0.18829	0.16312	0.12289	0.10686
17	0.71416	0.65720	0.60502	0.51337	0.43630	0.37136	0.31657	0.27027	0.23107	0.19784	0.16963	0.14564	0.10780	0.09293
18	0.70016	0.64117	0.58739	0.49363	0.41552	0.35034	0.29586	0.25025	0.21199	0.17986	0.15282	0.13004	0.09456	0.08081
19	0.68643	0.62553	0.57029	0.47464	0.39573	0.33051	0.27651	0.23171	0.19449	0.16351	0.13768	0.11611	0.08295	0.07027
20	0.67297	0.61027	0.55368	0.45639	0.37689	0.31180	0.25842	0.21455	0.17843	0.14864	0.12403	0.10367	0.07276	0.06110
21	0.65978	0.59539	0.53755	0.43883	0.35894	0.29416	0.24151	0.19866	0.16370	0.13513	0.11174	0.09256	0.06383	0.05313
22	0.64684	0.58086	0.52189	0.42196	0.34185	0.27751	0.22571	0.18394	0.15018	0.12285	0.10067	0.08264	0.05599	0.04620
23	0.63416	0.56670	0.50669	0.40573	0.32557	0.26180	0.21095	0.17032	0.13778	0.11168	0.09069	0.07379	0.04911	0.04017
24	0.62172	0.55288	0.49193	0.39012	0.31007	0.24698	0.19715	0.15770	0.12640	0.10153	0.08170	0.06588	0.04308	0.03493
25	0.60953	0.53939	0.47761	0.37512	0.29530	0.23300	0.18425	0.14602	0.11597	0.09230	0.07361	0.05882	0.03779	0.03038
26	0.59758	0.52623	0.46369	0.36069	0.28124	0.21981	0.17220	0.13520	0.10639	0.08391	0.06631	0.05252	0.03315	0.02642
27	0.58586	0.51340	0.45019	0.34682	0.26785	0.20737	0.16093	0.12519	0.09761	0.07628	0.05974	0.04689	0.02908	0.02297
28	0.57437	0.50088	0.43708	0.33348	0.25509	0.19563	0.15040	0.11591	0.08955	0.06934	0.05382	0.04187	0.02551	0.01997
29	0.56311	0.48866	0.42435	0.32065	0.24295	0.18456	0.14056	0.10733	0.08215	0.06304	0.04849	0.03738	0.02237	0.01737
30	0.55207	0.47674	0.41199	0.30832	0.23138	0.17411	0.13137	0.09938	0.07537	0.05731	0.04368	0.03338	0.01963	0.01510
31	0.54125	0.46511	0.39999	0.29646	0.22036	0.16425	0.12277	0.09202	0.06915	0.05210	0.03935	0.02980	0.01722	0.01313
32	0.53063	0.45377	0.38834	0.28506	0.20987	0.15496	0.11474	0.08520	0.06344	0.04736	0.03545	0.02661	0.01510	0.01142
33	0.52023	0.44270	0.37703	0.27409	0.19987	0.14619	0.10723	0.07889	0.05820	0.04306	0.03194	0.02376	0.01325	0.00993
34	0.51003	0.43191	0.36604	0.26355	0.19035	0.13791	0.10022	0.07305	0.05339	0.03914	0.02878	0.02121	0.01162	0.00864
35	0.50003	0.42137	0.35538	0.25342	0.18129	0.13011	0.09366	0.06763	0.04899	0.03558	0.02592	0.01894	0.01019	0.00751
36	0.49022	0.41109	0.34503	0.24367	0.17266	0.12274	0.08754	0.06262	0.04494	0.03235	0.02335	0.01691	0.00894	0.00653
37	0.48061	0.40107	0.33498	0.23430	0.16444	0.11579	0.08181	0.05799	0.04123	0.02941	0.02104	0.01510	0.00784	0.00568
38	0.47119	0.39128	0.32523	0.22529	0.15661	0.10924	0.07646	0.05369	0.03783	0.02673	0.01896	0.01348	0.00688	0.00494
39	0.46195	0.38174	0.31575	0.21662	0.14915	0.10306	0.07146	0.04971	0.03470	0.02430	0.01708	0.01204	0.00604	0.00429
40	0.45289	0.37243	0.30656	0.20829	0.14205	0.09722	0.06678	0.04603	0.03184	0.02209	0.01538	0.01075	0.00529	0.00373
45	0.41020	0.32917	0.26444	0.17120	0.11130	0.07265	0.04761	0.03133	0.02069	0.01372	0.00913	0.00610	0.00275	0.00186
50	0.37153	0.29094	0.22811	0.14071	0.08720	0.05429	0.03395	0.02132	0.01345	0.00852	0.00542	0.00346	0.00143	0.00092

TABLE I-2: Present value of an ordinary annuity of n payments of 1: (P/A, i, n)

$$P/A = \frac{1 - \dfrac{1}{(1 + i)^n}}{i}$$

n	2%	2.5%	3%	4%	5%	6%	7%	8%	9%	10%	11%	12%	14%	15%
1	0.98039	0.97561	0.97087	0.96154	0.95238	0.94340	0.93458	0.92593	0.91743	0.90909	0.90090	0.89286	0.87719	0.86957
2	1.94156	1.92742	1.91347	1.88609	1.85941	1.83339	1.80802	1.78326	1.75911	1.73554	1.71252	1.69005	1.64666	1.62571
3	2.88388	2.85602	2.82861	2.77509	2.72325	2.67301	2.62432	2.57710	2.53129	2.48685	2.44371	2.40183	2.32163	2.28323
4	3.80773	3.76197	3.71710	3.62990	3.54595	3.46511	3.38721	3.31213	3.23972	3.16987	3.10245	3.03735	2.91371	2.85498
5	4.71346	4.64583	4.57971	4.45182	4.32948	4.21236	4.10020	3.99271	3.88965	3.79079	3.69590	3.60478	3.43308	3.35216
6	5.60143	5.50813	5.41719	5.24214	5.07569	4.91732	4.76654	4.62288	4.48592	4.35526	4.23054	4.11141	3.88867	3.78448
7	6.47199	6.34939	6.23028	6.00205	5.78637	5.58238	5.38929	5.20637	5.03295	4.86842	4.71220	4.56376	4.28830	4.16042
8	7.32548	7.17014	7.01969	6.73274	6.46321	6.20979	5.97130	5.74664	5.53482	5.33493	5.14612	4.96764	4.63886	4.48732
9	8.16224	7.97087	7.78611	7.43533	7.10782	6.80169	6.51523	6.24689	5.99525	5.75902	5.53705	5.32825	4.94637	4.77158
10	8.98259	8.75206	8.53020	8.11090	7.72173	7.36009	7.02358	6.71008	6.41766	6.14457	5.88923	5.65022	5.21612	5.01877
11	9.78685	9.51421	9.25262	8.76048	8.30641	7.88687	7.49867	7.13896	6.80519	6.49506	6.20652	5.93770	5.45273	5.23371
12	10.57534	10.25776	9.95400	9.38507	8.86325	8.38384	7.94269	7.53608	7.16073	6.81369	6.49236	6.19437	5.66029	5.42062
13	11.34837	10.98318	10.63496	9.98565	9.39357	8.85268	8.35765	7.90378	7.48690	7.10336	6.74987	6.42355	5.84236	5.58315
14	12.10625	11.69091	11.29607	10.56312	9.89864	9.29498	8.74547	8.24424	7.78615	7.36669	6.98187	6.62817	6.00207	5.72448
15	12.84926	12.38138	11.93794	11.11839	10.37966	9.71225	9.10791	8.55948	8.06069	7.60608	7.19087	6.81086	6.14217	5.84737
16	13.57771	13.05500	12.56110	11.65230	10.83777	10.10590	9.44665	8.85137	8.31256	7.82371	7.37916	6.97399	6.26506	5.95423
17	14.29187	13.71220	13.16612	12.16567	11.27407	10.47726	9.76322	9.12164	8.54363	8.02155	7.54879	7.11963	6.37286	6.04716
18	14.99203	14.35336	13.75351	12.65930	11.68959	10.82760	10.05909	9.37189	8.75563	8.20141	7.70162	7.24967	6.46742	6.12797
19	15.67846	14.97889	14.32380	13.13394	12.08532	11.15812	10.33560	9.60360	8.95011	8.36492	7.83929	7.36578	6.55037	6.19823
20	16.35143	15.58916	14.87747	13.59033	12.46221	11.46992	10.59401	9.81815	9.12855	8.51356	7.96333	7.46944	6.62313	6.25933
21	17.01121	16.18455	15.41502	14.02916	12.82115	11.76408	10.83553	10.01680	9.29224	8.64869	8.07507	7.56200	6.68696	6.31246
22	17.65805	16.76541	15.93692	14.45112	13.16300	12.04158	11.06124	10.20074	9.44243	8.77154	8.17574	7.64465	6.74294	6.35866
23	18.29220	17.33211	16.44361	14.85684	13.48857	12.30338	11.27219	10.37106	9.58021	8.88322	8.26643	7.71843	6.79206	6.39884
24	18.91393	17.88499	16.93554	15.24696	13.79864	12.55036	11.46933	10.52876	9.70661	8.98474	8.34814	7.78432	6.83514	6.43377
25	19.52346	18.42438	17.41315	15.62208	14.09394	12.78336	11.65358	10.67478	9.82258	9.07704	8.42174	7.84314	6.87293	6.46415
26	20.12104	18.95061	17.87684	15.98277	14.37519	13.00317	11.82578	10.80998	9.92897	9.16095	8.48806	7.89566	6.90608	6.49056
27	20.70690	19.46401	18.32703	16.32959	14.64303	13.21053	11.98671	10.93516	10.02658	9.23722	8.54780	7.94255	6.93515	6.51353
28	21.28127	19.96489	18.76411	16.66306	14.89813	13.40616	12.13711	11.05108	10.11613	9.30657	8.60162	7.98442	6.96066	6.53351
29	21.84438	20.45355	19.18845	16.98371	15.14107	13.59072	12.27767	11.15841	10.19828	9.36961	8.65011	8.02181	6.98304	6.55088
30	22.39646	20.93029	19.60044	17.29203	15.37245	13.76483	12.40904	11.25778	10.27365	9.42691	8.69379	8.05518	7.00266	6.56598
31	22.93770	21.39541	20.00043	17.58849	15.59281	13.92909	12.53181	11.34980	10.34280	9.47901	8.73315	8.08499	7.01988	6.57911
32	23.46833	21.84918	20.38877	17.87355	15.80268	14.08404	12.64656	11.43500	10.40624	9.52638	8.76860	8.11159	7.03498	6.59053
33	23.98856	22.29188	20.76579	18.14765	16.00255	14.23023	12.75379	11.51389	10.46444	9.56943	8.80054	8.13535	7.04823	6.60046
34	24.49859	22.72379	21.13184	18.41120	16.19290	14.36814	12.85401	11.58693	10.51784	9.60857	8.82932	8.15656	7.05985	6.60910
35	24.99862	23.14516	21.48722	18.66461	16.37419	14.49825	12.94767	11.65457	10.56682	9.64416	8.85524	8.17550	7.07005	6.61661
36	25.48884	23.55625	21.83225	18.90828	16.54685	14.62099	13.03521	11.71719	10.61176	9.67651	8.87859	8.19241	7.07899	6.62314
37	25.96945	23.95732	22.16724	19.14258	16.71129	14.73678	13.11702	11.77518	10.65299	9.70592	8.89963	8.20751	7.08683	6.62881
38	26.44064	24.34860	22.49246	19.36786	16.86789	14.84602	13.19347	11.82887	10.69082	9.73265	8.91859	8.22099	7.09371	6.63375
39	26.90259	24.73034	22.80822	19.58448	17.01704	14.94907	13.26493	11.87858	10.72552	9.75696	8.93567	8.23303	7.09975	6.63805
40	27.35548	25.10278	23.11477	19.79277	17.15909	15.04630	13.33171	11.92461	10.75736	9.77905	8.95105	8.24378	7.10504	6.64178
45	29.49016	26.83302	24.51871	20.72004	17.77407	15.45583	13.60552	12.10840	10.88120	9.86281	9.00791	8.28252	7.12322	6.65429
50	31.42361	28.36231	25.72976	21.48218	18.25593	15.76186	13.80075	12.23348	10.96168	9.91481	9.04165	8.30450	7.13266	6.66051

TABLE I-3: Present value of an annuity due of n payments of 1: (P/AD, i, n)

$$P/AD = \left[\frac{1 - \dfrac{1}{(1+i)^n}}{i} \right] \times (1+i)$$

n	2%	2.5%	3%	4%	5%	6%	7%	8%	9%	10%	11%	12%	14%	15%
1	1.00000	1.00000	1.00000	1.00000	1.00000	1.00000	1.00000	1.00000	1.00000	1.00000	1.00000	1.00000	1.00000	1.00000
2	1.98039	1.97561	1.97087	1.96154	1.95238	1.94340	1.93458	1.92593	1.91743	1.90909	1.90090	1.89286	1.87719	1.86957
3	2.94156	2.92742	2.91347	2.88609	2.85941	2.83339	2.80802	2.78326	2.75911	2.73554	2.71252	2.69005	2.64666	2.62571
4	3.88388	3.85602	3.82861	3.77509	3.72325	3.67301	3.62432	3.57710	3.53129	3.48685	3.44371	3.40183	3.32163	3.28323
5	4.80773	4.76197	4.71710	4.62990	4.54595	4.46511	4.38721	4.31213	4.23972	4.16987	4.10245	4.03735	3.91371	3.85498
6	5.71346	5.64583	5.57971	5.45182	5.32948	5.21236	5.10020	4.99271	4.88965	4.79079	4.69590	4.60478	4.43308	4.35216
7	6.60143	6.50813	6.41719	6.24214	6.07569	5.91732	5.76654	5.62288	5.48592	5.35526	5.23054	5.11141	4.88867	4.78448
8	7.47199	7.34939	7.23028	7.00205	6.78637	6.58238	6.38929	6.20637	6.03295	5.86842	5.71220	5.56376	5.28830	5.16042
9	8.32548	8.17014	8.01969	7.73274	7.46321	7.20979	6.97130	6.74664	6.53482	6.33493	6.14612	5.96764	5.63886	5.48732
10	9.16224	8.97087	8.78611	8.43533	8.10782	7.80169	7.51523	7.24689	6.99525	6.75902	6.53705	6.32825	5.94637	5.77158
11	9.98259	9.75206	9.53020	9.11090	8.72173	8.36009	8.02358	7.71008	7.41766	7.14457	6.88923	6.65022	6.21612	6.01877
12	10.78685	10.51421	10.25262	9.76048	9.30641	8.88687	8.49867	8.13896	7.80519	7.49506	7.20652	6.93770	6.45273	6.23371
13	11.57534	11.25776	10.95400	10.38507	9.86325	9.38384	8.94269	8.53608	8.16073	7.81369	7.49236	7.19437	6.66029	6.42062
14	12.34837	11.98318	11.63496	10.98565	10.39357	9.85268	9.35765	8.90378	8.48690	8.10336	7.74987	7.42355	6.84236	6.58315
15	13.10625	12.69091	12.29607	11.56312	10.89864	10.29498	9.74547	9.24424	8.78615	8.36669	7.98187	7.62817	7.00207	6.72448
16	13.84926	13.38138	12.93794	12.11839	11.37966	10.71225	10.10791	9.55948	9.06069	8.60608	8.19087	7.81086	7.14217	6.84737
17	14.57771	14.05500	13.56110	12.65230	11.83777	11.10590	10.44665	9.85137	9.31256	8.82371	8.37916	7.97399	7.26506	6.95423
18	15.29187	14.71220	14.16612	13.16567	12.27407	11.47726	10.76322	10.12164	9.54363	9.02155	8.54879	8.11963	7.37286	7.04716
19	15.99203	15.35336	14.75351	13.65930	12.68959	11.82760	11.05909	10.37189	9.75563	9.20141	8.70162	8.24967	7.46742	7.12797
20	16.67846	15.97889	15.32380	14.13394	13.08532	12.15812	11.33560	10.60360	9.95011	9.36492	8.83929	8.36578	7.55037	7.19823
21	17.35143	16.58916	15.87747	14.59033	13.46221	12.46992	11.59401	10.81815	10.12855	9.51356	8.96333	8.46944	7.62313	7.25933
22	18.01121	17.18455	16.41502	15.02916	13.82115	12.76408	11.83553	11.01680	10.29224	9.64869	9.07507	8.56200	7.68696	7.31246
23	18.65805	17.76541	16.93692	15.45112	14.16300	13.04158	12.06124	11.20074	10.44243	9.77154	9.17574	8.64465	7.74294	7.35866
24	19.29220	18.33211	17.44361	15.85684	14.48857	13.30338	12.27219	11.37106	10.58021	9.88322	9.26643	8.71843	7.79206	7.39884
25	19.91393	18.88499	17.93554	16.24696	14.79864	13.55036	12.46933	11.52876	10.70661	9.98474	9.34814	8.78432	7.83514	7.43377
26	20.52346	19.42438	18.41315	16.62208	15.09394	13.78336	12.65358	11.67478	10.82258	10.07704	9.42174	8.84314	7.87293	7.46415
27	21.12104	19.95061	18.87684	16.98277	15.37519	14.00317	12.82578	11.80998	10.92897	10.16095	9.48806	8.89566	7.90608	7.49056
28	21.70690	20.46401	19.32703	17.32959	15.64303	14.21053	12.98671	11.93516	11.02658	10.23722	9.54780	8.94255	7.93515	7.51353
29	22.28127	20.96489	19.76411	17.66306	15.89813	14.40616	13.13711	12.05108	11.11613	10.30657	9.60162	8.98442	7.96066	7.53351
30	22.84438	21.45355	20.18845	17.98371	16.14107	14.59072	13.27767	12.15841	11.19828	10.36961	9.65011	9.02181	7.98304	7.55088
31	23.39646	21.93029	20.60044	18.29203	16.37245	14.76483	13.40904	12.25778	11.27365	10.42691	9.69379	9.05518	8.00266	7.56598
32	23.93770	22.39541	21.00043	18.58849	16.59281	14.92909	13.53181	12.34980	11.34280	10.47901	9.73315	9.08499	8.01988	7.57911
33	24.46833	22.84918	21.38877	18.87355	16.80268	15.08404	13.64656	12.43500	11.40624	10.52638	9.76860	9.11159	8.03498	7.59053
34	24.98856	23.29188	21.76579	19.14765	17.00255	15.23023	13.75379	12.51389	11.46444	10.56943	9.80054	9.13535	8.04823	7.60046
35	25.49859	23.72379	22.13184	19.41120	17.19290	15.36814	13.85401	12.58693	11.51784	10.60857	9.82932	9.15656	8.05985	7.60910
36	25.99862	24.14516	22.48722	19.66461	17.37419	15.49825	13.94767	12.65457	11.56682	10.64416	9.85524	9.17550	8.07005	7.61661
37	26.48884	24.55625	22.83225	19.90828	17.54685	15.62099	14.03521	12.71719	11.61176	10.67651	9.87859	9.19241	8.07899	7.62314
38	26.96945	24.95732	23.16724	20.14258	17.71129	15.73678	14.11702	12.77518	11.65299	10.70592	9.89963	9.20751	8.08683	7.62881
39	27.44064	25.34860	23.49246	20.36786	17.86789	15.84602	14.19347	12.82887	11.69082	10.73265	9.91859	9.22099	8.09371	7.63375
40	27.90259	25.73034	23.80822	20.58448	18.01704	15.94907	14.26493	12.87858	11.72552	10.75696	9.93567	9.23303	8.09975	7.63805
45	30.07996	27.50385	25.25427	21.54884	18.66277	16.38318	14.55791	13.07707	11.86051	10.84909	9.99878	9.27642	8.12047	7.65244
50	32.05208	29.07137	26.50166	22.34147	19.16872	16.70757	14.76680	13.21216	11.94823	10.90630	10.03624	9.30104	8.13123	7.65959

Index